T0312174

THE ROUTLEDGE COMPANION TO MARKETING RESEARCH

This single-volume reference provides an alternative to traditional marketing research methods handbooks, focusing entirely on the new and innovative methods and technologies that are transforming marketing research and practice.

Including original contributions and case studies from leading global specialists, this handbook covers many pioneering methods, such as:

- Methods for the analysis of user- and customer-generated data, including opinion mining and sentiment analysis
- Big data
- Neuroscientific techniques and physiological measures
- Voice prints
- Human–computer interaction
- Emerging approaches such as shadowing, netnographies and ethnographies

Transcending the old divisions between qualitative and quantitative research methods, this book is an essential tool for market researchers in academia and practice.

Len Tiu Wright is Editor-in-Chief of *Cogent Business and Management* and Emeritus Professor of Marketing at De Montfort University, UK.

Luiz Moutinho is Visiting Professor of Marketing at University of Suffolk Business School, UK, and Adjunct Professor at the Graduate School of Business at University of the South Pacific, Fiji.

Merlin Stone is Visiting Professor at the University of Portsmouth and St. Mary's University, UK.

Richard P. Bagozzi is Dwight F. Benton Professor of Behavioral Science in Management at Ross School of Business at the University of Michigan, USA.

THE ROUTLEDGE COMPANION TO MARKETING RESEARCH

Edited by Len Tiu Wright, Luiz Moutinho, Merlin Stone and Richard P. Bagozzi

LONDON AND NEW YORK

First published 2021
by Routledge
2 Park Square, Milton Park, Abingdon, Oxon OX14 4RN

and by Routledge
605 Third Avenue, New York, NY 10158

Routledge is an imprint of the Taylor & Francis Group, an informa business

British Library Cataloguing-in-Publication Data
A catalogue record for this book is available from the British Library

Library of Congress Cataloging-in-Publication Data
Names: Wright, Len Tiu, editor. | Moutinho, Luiz, editor. |
Stone, Merlin, 1948– editor.
Title: The Routledge companion to marketing research / edited by Len Tiu Wright, Luiz Moutinho, Merlin Stone and Richard P. Bagozzi.
Description: New York : Routledge, 2021. | Series: Routledge companions in business, management and accounting | Includes bibliographical references and index.
Subjects: LCSH: Marketing research.
Classification: LCC HF5415.2 .R68 2021 (print) | LCC HF5415.2 (ebook) | DDC 658.8/3—dc23
LC record available at https://lccn.loc.gov/2020054947
LC ebook record available at https://lccn.loc.gov/2020054948

ISBN: 978-1-138-68278-8 (hbk)
ISBN: 978-0-367-69431-9 (pbk)
ISBN: 978-1-315-54489-2 (ebk)

Typeset in Bembo
by Apex CoVantage, LLC

CONTENTS

Contents

CONTRIBUTORS

Esra AlDhaen is Executive Director of Quality Assurance and Assistant Professor at Ahlia University, Bahrain. She is an expert in strategic planning, measurement and evaluation for higher education. She has published articles in the area of strategy and quality management and in higher education management, including quality assurance, strategic decision-making and teaching practices. She is an expert in curriculum review, design and mapping to the National Qualification Framework.

Leonids Aleksandrovs obtained his PhD in applied economics at the Faculty of Business and Economics (University of Antwerp) and was thereafter a freelance researcher at the same university. His research interests are data analytics, management and economics. He has published in the *Journal of Advertising Research*, *International Journal of Market Research* and *Applied Stochastic Models in Business and Industry*. He has worked for UCB Pharma, Becton Dickinson and the United Nations, and he is currently Head of Data Intelligence at Napoleon Sports and Casinos.

Eleni Aravopoulou is Senior Lecturer in Business (MBA Programme) at the University of Sunderland. She is on two journal editorial boards and is an active member of professional bodies, including a member of the Chartered Institute of Personnel and Development, Chartered Management Institute and the British Academy of Management (BAM). She has undertaken several roles as an independent business consultant, project manager, business researcher and business analyst.

Richard P. Bagozzi is the Dwight F. Benton Professor of Behavioral Science in Management at the Ross School of Business, University of Michigan. His research interests span attitude theory, emotions, theory and philosophy of mind, social identity, neuroscience, psychological underpinnings of brands, ethical and moral behaviour, foundations of marketing thought and structural equation models.

Pekka Berg has a PhD from Tampere University of Technology in innovation management. He is a partner and consultant to Innoman, Ltd. He works with public policy makers and companies like Toyota, Volkswagen, Nokia, Panasonic, Mitsubishi, Rolls-Royce, UNICEF, World Bank and Red Cross. He is also a visiting fellow at Aalto University School of Science,

Finland, working on the Aalto Ventures Program, the International Design Business Management Program and the Aalto Executive Education MBA Program. He also works with St. Gallen University, Aalborg University and Stanford University. His current is on strategic innovation management and collaboration in innovation ecosystems.

Robin Birn is Senior Lecturer in Marketing at St Mary's University, Twickenham. He is also a fellow of the Chartered Institute of Marketing and The Market Research Society. He has served as Vice Chairman of the Market Research Society and Chairman of MRS Membership. He has been a marketing consultant for over 40 years, specialising in market research and the development of customer insight. He is author of over ten books, including *The Effective Use of Market Research*, which has been published in five languages.

Sérgio Brodsky is the Founder of SURGE Advisory, Executive Producer and Co-Host of Futurecast, Columnist and Editorial Board Advisor at *Marketing Mag* and the Inaugural Chair of The Marketing Academy Australia Alumni. He is one of the few rare formally trained brand and foresight strategists in Australia and the creator of the radically innovative to-brand communications model "Urban Brand-Utility", through which a brand's touchpoints become the deliverers of public utility services, underpinned by a circular revenue model.

Raymond R. Burke is a pioneer in the field of shopper marketing, with a research program that extends over 30 years. He is the Founding Director of the Customer Interface Laboratory and has served on the faculties of Indiana University's Kelley School of Business, the Harvard Business School and the University of Pennsylvania's Wharton School. His articles have appeared in the *Harvard Business Review, Journal of Consumer Research, Journal of Marketing, International Journal of Research in Marketing* and *Marketing Science*, among other. He has received four patents for innovations in marketing research methodology and digitally enhanced shopping experiences.

Helen Huifen Cai is a senior lecturer in international management and innovation at the Business School, Middlesex University. She worked in banking before her university career. Her research focuses on firm innovation and R&D, multinational enterprises and foreign direct investment, international marketing, corporate governance and firm-level industry dynamics in emerging markets. She is on the editorial board of the *Journal of World Business*, and her work has been published in journals such as the *Journal of Business Research, Technological Forecasting and Social Change, Journal of Accounting and Finance, European Business Review* and the *Journal of Business and Industrial Marketing*.

Ala' Omar Dandis is an assistant professor at the Department of Marketing, Applied Science Private University, Jordan, and an editor of the journal *Cogent Business & Management*. He obtained his PhD from the University of Huddersfield, UK, in 2016. His research interests include consumer behaviour and service marketing. He has presented at conferences and published internationally.

Nathalie Dens is a professor of marketing at the Faculty of Business and Economics (Antwerp University). Her research focuses on advertising effectiveness, contemporary communication formats, advertising on social media and electronic word-of-mouth, health communications and co-creation innovation networks. She has published in journals such as *Computers in Human Behavior, Health Communication, Journal of Advertising, Journal of Advertising Research, Journal of*

Business Research, International Journal of Advertising, Journal of Interactive Marketing and *Marketing Letters*. She serves on the editorial board of the *Journal of Business Research* and the *International Journal of Advertising* and reviews ad hoc for different other journals.

Patrick De Pelsmacker is a professor of marketing at the Faculty of Business and Economics (Antwerp University). His research focuses on advertising effectiveness, contemporary communication formats, advertising on social media and electronic word-of-mouth and sustainable consumer behaviour. He has published in journals such as *Computers in Human Behavior, Journal of Advertising, Journal of Advertising Research, Journal of Business Research, International Journal of Advertising, Journal of Interactive Marketing, Journal of Environmental Psychology, Ecological Economics* and *Journal of Cleaner Production*. He serves on the editorial board of, amongst others, *International Journal of Advertising, Journal of Advertising* and *Journal of Interactive Marketing*.

Yuksel Ekinci is Professor of Marketing at the University of Portsmouth, teaching global marketing and research methods to postgraduates. His research focuses on consumer behaviour, business research methods and service brand management. His articles have been published in the *European Journal of Marketing, Journal of Business Research, Journal of Travel Research, Annals of Tourism Research,* the *International Journal of Human Resources Management* and others. He is an associate editor of the *International Journal of Market Research* and an editorial board member of five marketing/tourism journals. He is interested in the practical side of marketing and passionate about solving marketing problems.

Geraint Evans has delivered award-winning marketing and digital innovation for major brands such as ODEON Cinemas Group & Virgin Media, as well as supporting growth for several start-ups. A published writer and award-winning academic researcher, Geraint is a visiting research fellow at St Marys University, London, and The University of South Wales and is also a member of the editorial board of *The Bottom Line*. His research focuses of AI, smart cities, digital consumer behaviour and global marketing have seen him regularly keynote various global conferences and contribute to online press, for example, *Forbes* and *Entrepreneur*.

Pantea Foroudi is Business Manager and Solution Architect at Foroudi Consultancy as well as a member of the Marketing, Branding, and Tourism department, Middlesex University, London. She earned her PhD from Brunel University, London. Her research interests include marketing, branding, communications, visual identity/design, stakeholders, social media and e-marketing from a multi-disciplinary approach. Pantea has published widely in international academic journals such as the *International Journal of Hospitality Management, Journal of Business Research* and the *European Journal of Marketing*.

Hazem Gaber is a lecturer in Marketing at the Arab Academy for Science, Technology and Maritime Transport in Egypt. Much of his research focuses on branding, social media marketing, consumer behaviour and corporate social responsibility. He has published several academic articles in the area of digital marketing, branding and corporate social responsibility.

Peter Goos is Professor of Statistics at the Faculty of Bio-Science Engineering (University of Leuven) and at the Faculty of Business and Economics (University of Antwerp). His main research area is the statistical design and analysis of experiments. Besides numerous journal articles, he has published several books on experimental design and statistics. He has received various awards from the American Society for Quality, the American Statistical Association and the European Network for Business and Industrial Statistics. He serves on the editorial board of the *Journal of Quality Technology*.

Suraksha Gupta is a professor of marketing at Newcastle University, London, and head of the marketing department there. Her research interests include the international marketing of multinational firms (MNEs) in emerging markets. She focuses on the market penetration strategies of MNEs using effectuation and causation theory of knowledge exchange. She worked for many years in industry in sectors as varied as foods and systems and has extensive experience of business consulting and industrial and consumer marketing research.

Matt Hobbs is Accenture's Managing Director, Financial Services, Europe. His career includes a period marketing Internet services for Demon Internet, leading IBM's EMEA CRM outsourcing practice and then IBM's global multi-channel transformation practice. He spent several years as a partner at PwC, focusing on customer management and CRM systems, especially Salesforce.com. He is now responsible for Accenture's Salesforce.com practice in financial services across Europe and a member of Accenture's Customer Insight & Growth leadership team for Financial Services, driving change for Accenture's clients with customer transformation and cost effective revenue growth.

Abraham Joseph is a doctoral researcher at Newcastle University London and a lecturer at Coventry University, London. His research and teaching interests include corporate brands, corporate rebranding, strategic management and research methods. Abraham qualified as a computer science engineer and then spent eight years in the IT industry. After a successful period in various customer-facing and managerial roles, he moved to academia.

Jonathan Knapper is a CEO and founder of Handl, a venture backed by the founders of Brewdog, Skyscanner and working in partnership with organisations such as Jaguar Land Rover. He is dedicated to finding solutions which deliver value and convenience to Handl's users. Jonathan worked as a product manager at inMotion Ventures, the investment and innovation arm of Jaguar Land Rover, and as a business development manager for self-driving shuttle automaker NAVYA. He is focused on connected and autonomous vehicle solutions and has taken part in a number of Scottish government roundtables discussing mobility in Scotland.

Kaouther Kooli is a principal academic in marketing in the Department of Marketing, Strategy and Innovation in the Faculty of Management, Bournemouth University. She has over 18 years of higher education teaching experience in Tunisia, the United Kingdom and France. Her research interests are B2B marketing, consumer behaviour and digital marketing. She is the Associate Editor of the *Journal of Customer Behaviour* and Chair of the Academy of Marketing B2B Special Interest Group. She is on the editorial board of the *Journal of Business to Business Marketing* and has a strong interest in technological innovation in marketing.

Emmanuel Kosack is a strategist to the Director of the Institute of Business, Law and Society and Lecturer at St Mary's University, Twickenham, London. He graduated in health management and worked as a marketing intern, leading five successful marketing projects. He took the MSc International Business Management at St Mary's with distinction. He is module convenor of Digital Business, the most popular postgraduate course in the Business School. His research interests include in e-marketing, market research, e-commerce, digital finance and digital supply chain management. He is a non-executive member of St Mary's University's Advisory Board.

Ashraf Labib is Professor at University of Portsmouth, UK. His main research interests are in operational research and decision analysis in applications such as reliability, risk, security and healthcare. He is a fellow of the Operational Research Society and the Institute of Engineering and Technology, a senior fellow of the Higher Education Academy and a chartered engineer. He received five Highly Commended awards for published papers from the Literati Club, MCB Press. He receives research funding from the UK's Engineering and Physical Sciences Research Council and the Economic and Social Research Council, from EU sources and from industry.

Paul Laughlin is the founder of Laughlin Consultancy and the host of the Customer Insight Leader podcast. He has worked as a data and analytics leader for over 20 years, creating and developing teams for leading businesses. He now mentors leaders and trains their teams. His areas of expertise include customer insight, commercial awareness, customer analytics, data visualisation, stakeholder management, leadership development and softer skills for analysts. He is also an active blogger, trainer, mentor, professional speaker and qualified executive coach.

Alex Leykin is a researcher into applying computer vision and machine learning techniques to consumer behaviour, including store traffic and activity analysis, eye tracking and visual attention. The aim of this research is to develop non-intrusive methods of visual surveillance that allow researchers to analyse the behaviour of shoppers as they navigate through stores and make their purchase decisions. He works at the Customer Interface Laboratory at Indiana University's Kelley School of Business and has published in the *Journal of Marketing* and *Journal of Vision* and presented at several computer vision conferences.

Jon Machtynger is a visiting research fellow in ethics and artificial intelligence at the University of Surrey. Currently a lead solution architect for the public sector with Microsoft specialising in data and artificial intelligence, he has worked for 30 years in many industries at different levels defining enterprise systems. He has been an independent industry advisor with many organisations and is on the editorial board of *The Bottom Line*, an information management journal.

Liz Machtynger is a leading expert in the area of customer management strategy evaluation and development, organisational development for customer management, customer proposition development, key account management, customer knowledge strategies and customer management programme design. She is also a senior lecturer in strategy, marketing and innovation at Kingston University. Her career includes long periods working in business-to-business marketing, initially at BP and then at IBM, and also running her own consultancy business, Customer Essential Ltd., for 17 years.

Reem Refai A. Mahmoud is a visiting postdoctoral scholar at the University of Basel, Faculty of Business and Economics, Switzerland and Assistant Professor of Business Administration, School of Business, Suez Canal University, Egypt. Her research interests include consumer neuroscience, moral and self-conscious emotions, consumers choices, co-creation of value, ethical consumerism and evaluative conditioning.

Tony Mooney has built and directed a number of world-leading data and insight organisations for major corporations over the past 25 years, including Sky, Orange and Centrica. In each case, he designed, created and deployed advanced consumer data and insight capabilities to deliver growth and competitive advantage and help achieve business objectives. He has specialised in ensuring that investment in data, analytics and insight truly drives business performance. He has also led B2B service businesses for Experian and Sky, providing data and insight services to large consumer brands across the world, including Lloyds Bank, Barclays, RBS, Orange, Vodafone, Zurich, Prudential and Microsoft.

Luiz Moutinho is Visiting Professor of Marketing at the University of Suffolk Business School, England, and Adjunct Professor at the Graduate School of Business, University of the South Pacific, Fiji. He has held many other professorial posts and is the Founding Editor-in-Chief of the *Journal of Modelling in Management* and Co-Editor-in-Chief of the *Innovative Marketing Journal*. He has another four associate editorships and is on another 47 journal editorial boards. He has nearly 200 publications in marketing. His areas of research interest encompass marketing technology, big data, biometrics, artificial intelligence, neuroscience in marketing, futures research and future-casting.

Maria Palazzo is a research fellow at the Department of Political and Communication Studies, University of Salerno, Italy, and a member of its Sustainability Communication Centre. She has held posts are universities in the United Kingdom, Spain and Colombia. She is also an academic tutor and lecturer at the Universitas Mercatorum, Rome, Italy. Her articles have been published in *The TQM Journal, Qualitative Market Research: An International Journal, Journal of Business-to-Business Marketing, Journal of Communication Management, Journal of Brand Management* and other academic journals.

Brett Parnell is a principal consultant with one of the world's largest project and programme management consultancies, MI-GSO | PCUBED. He has led and delivered many engagements, driving transformation and change across both private and public sectors, focusing on securing target outcomes to enable enduring value through assured delivery. Brett has also developed and implemented project portfolio prioritisation methods, helping distil business strategy to achieve clarity of intent. Brett is trained and certified in project, programme and risk management, has a range of computing skills and achieved his MSc in leadership and management (focusing on business models) at Portsmouth University.

Maria Helena Pestana is Professor of Statistics, Data Analysis and Marketing Research at Lisbon University and also works at the Universidade Europeia-Laureate International University in Lisbon and the Research and Education Unit on Ageing at Porto University. Helena's current research interests are consumer behaviour, advertising, tourism by seniors, online customer and hotel reviews in tourism, Alzheimer's disease, analysis of big data, Python, bibliometrics and applications of multivariate data in social sciences and health.

Robin Robin is Lecturer in Marketing at Oxford Brookes Business School. His interests and recent work are on consumer behaviour and digital marketing, particularly in the relationship of digital marketing practice with privacy issues. He has presented his works in international marketing conferences and published in conference proceedings and international journals. Before coming to academia, he worked in banking and manufacturing in Southeast Asia for seven years.

Qianhui Shen is a member of Credit Operation Centre at Bank of Ningbo Co., Ltd. Jiaxing Branch, China. She works for the Global Alliance of Marketing & Management Associations (GAMMA) as an assistant to the newsletter editor. Her current research focuses on the factors influencing consumer purchase intentions.

Merlin Stone is Visiting Professor at the University of Portsmouth and St Mary's University. He has worked as a consultant and manager on hundreds of commercial projects in marketing, strategy and information technology His research covers business information management, customer relationship management and the relevance of academic research to commercial practice. He is on the editorial boards of several academic journals.

Ryan Stott is a consulting manager at International Data Corporation (IDC), advising the world's largest technology companies on market opportunities and trends related to the digitization of business models, cloud technologies and the role of external ecosystems in delivering ecosystem-enabled business models. He is the founder of several small UK start-ups in the renewable energy and property sector. He regularly co-authors academic articles on the practical application of business model theories to industry.

Rui Su is a senior lecturer in tourism at the Business School, Middlesex University. Her research interests are mainly in cultural tourism, heritage interpretations, cultural political economy and urban tourism. Rui has been involved in several research projects, such as Church Action on Poverty, Poverty Reduction and Inter-Sectoral Linkage in Lao PDR and the Storytelling Festival in the United Kingdom. Her work has been published in journals such as *Annals of Tourism Research, Journal of Heritage Tourism* and *Journal of Tourism and Cultural Change.*

Samina Sumrin is a PhD student at the Newcastle University London. Her doctoral research covers green marketing, eco-innovation, waste management and packaging for the environment. Her research articles have covered the importance of managerial decisions, eco-capabilities, eco-innovation, environmental concerns and green marketing/branding.

Yang Sun is Associate Professor in the Department of Marketing at the School of Business Administration, Northeastern University, China. He is a guest editor for the *Asia Pacific Journal of Marketing and Logistics* and an editorial board member for the *Journal of Global Scholars of Marketing Science.* He also works for the Global Alliance of Marketing and Management Associations (GAMMA), serving as track chair and newsletter editor. His research focuses on consumer resistance to innovation, customer equity and fashion marketing.

Jyrki Suomala is a principal lecturer at the Laurea University of Applied Sciences and an adjunct professor at the University of Oulu. His research covers human decision-making within innovation management, purchasing and marketing from a neuroscientific perspective. He has also worked at Innoman, Ltd. as an expert in several commercial projects in which he has helped companies to solve their problems based on neuroscientific knowledge about human behaviour. He has published over 100 articles and book chapters both in scientific journals and popular media.

Nektarios Tzempelikos is Principal Lecturer in Marketing and Research Lead for the School of Management of Faculty of Business and Law, Anglia Ruskin University. His research interests include key account management, relationship marketing, relevance of marketing research and business-to-business marketing. His research has been published in *Industrial Marketing Management,* the *Journal of Business & Industrial Marketing,* the *Journal of Business-to-Business Marketing,* the *Journal of Strategic Marketing,* the *IMP Journal* and the *Journal of Relationship Marketing,* among others. He is on the editorial board of *Industrial Marketing Management,* the *Journal of Business & Industrial Marketing* and the *Journal of Business-to-Business Marketing.*

Wan-Chen Wang is an associate professor in the Department of Marketing, Feng Chia University, Taiwan. She teaches consumer behaviour, advertising and marketing, and her research interests include consumer behaviour, particularly in relation to voice and gender and older adult/senior tourism; modelling consumer response to advertising using neural networks; the impact of brand slogans; and, in more general terms, the impact of emption on consumer behaviour.

Neil Woodcock is Global President of Transformation at Dentsu Media and Professor of Customer Engagement and Insight at De Montfort University. He is an expert in customer strategy and organisational transformation, having worked as a consultant in almost every business sector on every continent. Before becoming a consultant, he worked in business-to-business sales, marketing and systems. He was the lead innovator behind the development of SCHEMA®, The Customer Framework's agile transformation methodology, which is used to benchmark the effectiveness of customer management and accelerate the transformation of large organisations.

James Woudhuysen is a physics graduate and professor of forecasting and innovation in the School of Engineering at London South Bank University, as well as a writer, speaker, broadcaster and activist. He covers the economics, technology and sociology of construction, energy, IT, leisure, manufacturing, healthcare, retailing and transport. He was editor of *Design* magazine, a director at designers Fitch and forecasters the Henley Centre and head of market intelligence at Philips Consumer electronics, Eindhoven, the Netherlands. He does not forecast the stock market, horse races or the weather.

Len Tiu Wright is Editor-in-Chief of the open-access journal *Cogent Open Access Business & Management*, Founding Editor of *Qualitative Market Research* and Emeritus Professor of Marketing at De Montfort University, UK. She has held professorships at several UK universities. She worked in industry prior to working at universities. Her research interests include qualitative dimensions in marketing research and marketing. She has chaired and co-organised conferences in the United Kingdom and overseas. Her writings have appeared in books, in American and European academic journals and at major conferences, where some gained best paper awards.

FOREWORD

The Market Research Society is the world's oldest professional association for marketing research and has long been a world leader in qualification and training for research professionals. Since 1946, we have been encouraging the development of the sector, celebrating success and amplifying the voices of academics and leading practitioners. This book is an important contribution to professional learning. In bringing together academics and practitioners, it very usefully combines several thought-provoking case studies.

Intelligence capital – the development of customer insight, organisational learning and a corporate-wide ability to act on that insight and learning – is a critical competitive asset. For that reason, the sector may seem short of detailed evidenced case studies. This book helps address this gap, and the studies included help illustrate why intelligence capital should be treated as an investment in organisational success alongside other assets such as human capital.

The book is not a manual for how to do research, but in illustrating some of the best of recent thinking, it should certainly be on the reading list for serious research professionals to consult.

Jane Frost CBE
Chief Executive Officer
The Market Research Society
United Kingdom

EDITORS' INTRODUCTION

The landscape for marketing research is dynamic and full of potential. It is demonstrated in this book through the rich contributions of authors showcasing their ideas and techniques or analysing and evaluating marketing or business activities and the impact of changes in lifestyles, demography, technology and product use. Propelled by the growth of the Internet and social media, with new technologies harnessing the power of computing, robotics and artificial intelligence, marketing research must be at the forefront to keep pace with business developments.

Marketing researchers in public, private and voluntary sectors must be up to date with the many ways information is generated, searched for, collected, analysed and distributed. They must lead discussions on or at least be fully conversant with present and future trends concerning people's attitudes, behaviour and activities; how (big) data is stored and retrieved; and the implications of what these might mean for people in their personal leisure, social and work situations.

We acknowledge that academics and practitioners face different goals in the generation of knowledge, theory development and empirical research. So, each chapter represents the views and work of its authors and not of the editors. The book is aimed at practitioners, researchers and academics in marketing research and related disciplines. It is aimed at research students, lecturers and professors and at senior managers and practitioners of marketing research. While the book is not a basic do-it-step-by-step textbook, undergraduates will also find this book of value because it demonstrates how marketing research can take the lead in exploring the world of consumers, business and organisational customers. Those who are new to the subject and want to explore marketing research more broadly and deeply will also find the book of value.

The *Routledge Companion to Marketing Research* brings together in one volume a wealth of writings from authors all over the globe who have offered their expertise and perspectives on a wide range of topics. This book would not be possible without them. Our journey in producing this book has been greatly enriched by the knowledge and creativity of the community of scholars and practitioners that produced it.

Organisation of the book

This book explores the frontiers of marketing research for academic researchers and for practitioners.

The first section is conceptual. It explores the evolution of marketing research, taking into account developments in areas such as big data, interactive marketing and business models.

The second section on methods includes setting up research projects and the methods that can be used to gather and analyse marketing research data and with the use of secondary data. It also outlines a view of how marketing research should be managed.

The third section gives details on a range of different and new techniques for gathering data from respondents.

The fourth section delves into areas such as retailing, marketing to older adults, smart cities and design and Islamic banking.

The final section focuses on futures, reflections from practitioners and strategy.

Len Tiu Wright
Luiz Moutinho
Merlin Stone
Richard P. Bagozzi

PART I

Conceptual

1

THE EVOLUTION OF MARKETING RESEARCH

Merlin Stone, Len Tiu Wright and Luiz Moutinho

Summary

This chapter develops hypotheses and scenarios about the evolution of marketing research. It considers the impact on marketing research of the appearance and development of new digital data sources and of the rise and rapid rise to market dominance of new companies that create and then exploit this data. It investigates the role of academic research versus that of grey literature and how the relative roles of these two ways of publishing research may change. It also considers how digital developments may affect decisions about whether to use primary or secondary research approaches. It investigates the rise of the discipline of customer or consumer insight and how this affects the world of marketing research. We then consider how these developments might change what clients need and how marketing researchers might respond to their new and ever-changing needs, using several scenarios whose characteristics and probabilities are discussed.

Introduction

What is the future of marketing research as an industry? What is the future of marketing researchers? These are big questions, which we answer in this book in many ways by giving examples of good academic marketing research but digging into the future of big data, platforms, smart cities or technologies designed to relate what goes on in your brain to what you think about products and services and what you buy.

However, our overall conclusion is clear. If you are a marketing researcher, or want to be one, and are worried about the future of the industry or about whether the skills that you are acquiring as a student will be useful, our advice to you is that you should only be worried if you see your core skills as devising ways to collect yet more data in ways that comply with archaic self-imposed regulations and practices relating to anonymity of respondents and avoidance of bias in sampling. For you, the future is pretty bleak, because you are not providing what the market wants, because you are surrounded by organisations which are making powerful use of data about named customers and by customers whose view is that so long as the data is being used to help meet their needs, and being handled responsibility, anonymity is not an issue for them.

On the other hand, if you see yourself as expert in making sense of what the new types of data say, of exploring it, of channelling it into decision-making or even encouraging new types of decisions, then your time has come – but it may not be in a conventional marketing research company. If you take the latter view, then your aim is to help organisations by improving the breadth, depth, quality and timeliness of insight and foresight. Your aim is not necessarily to worry too much about the quality of an individual finding or piece of research but rather to help organisations make sense of multiple sources, using them to triangulate the sources and view data from different angles. Your aim is also to inspire creativity and innovation in your clients, not just to help them achieve what they have told you they want to achieve. In other words, one of your aims is to identify new things that they can aspire to achieve.

Definitions – what do marketing researchers do?

The traditional concepts of marketing research have been completely overtaken by the consequences of changes in the social, economic, technological, business and marketing environments. A traditional academic way of proceeding by reading about concepts, developing further concepts and seeing how they apply in the field has been challenged and perhaps even overtaken by empirical evidence and shaken to the core by global events, such as the Covid-19 pandemic and impact of global warming on business and consumer demand. Pandemic lockdown measures coupled with government rules on social distancing based on fears of the spread of the coronavirus have affected businesses, communities and organisations, including universities world-wide, with GDP growth in countries taking a severe hit (The Economist 2020). For example, in the many countries whose economies depend on manufacturing products and on providing face-to-face consumer services, demand for these decreased during government lockdown restrictions as stores, restaurants, hotels and leisure facilities were closed. Redundancies increased; workers were furloughed; and the aviation, hospitality, tourism and leisure industries suffered as consumers were restricted to being allowed out for exercise and to shop only for necessities. Universities sent students home and went online to teach and examine during the pandemic.

Such changes affected data provision, with shortages of consumer and business information occurring where this information was provided face to face, while the boom in online shopping home delivery and home entertainment led to a surge in new customers for companies such as Amazon and Netflix and home delivery networks. As noted by *The Economist* (2020, p. 69), "sectors of the economy most affected by lockdowns. . . . often have the longest lags in reporting, making early estimates especially unreliable . . . in some cases, collecting data is impossible." Suppliers of credit cards and contactless payments benefited and will continue doing so, as many companies refused cash payments for health reasons, so the shift to online shopping and entertainment and the resulting surge in credit card usage and contactless payments (Financial Times 2020a) gives meaning to the cashless society, thus also making digital data collection easier. In such conditions, senior executives in organisations in these sectors who are responsible for strategic decision-making should not assume a continuous stream of data and analytical conclusions. Marketing researchers have needed to adapt to environmental uncertainties in data provision, often reflecting radical changes in behaviour and switches between brands.

For this and other reasons identified throughout this book, the role of marketing research has certainly changed in the last few decades, mostly under pressure from new data. Individual research projects to quantify product usage and attitudes, identify optimum channels of distribution and work out which advertisements are more effective – these have been or are being swept away because the answer to these questions is increasingly provided automatically as part of the data that flows between customers and companies in marketing and sales operations or from social media where customers reveal and discuss their usage, perceptions and attitudes. In other words, the sources of data have changed. However, the old questions that marketing researchers have conventionally answered remain, though they are not posed in the same way.

For example, it is conventional to say that marketing researchers are now less involved in quantitative studies of what customers do, how often and how much, and more focused on understanding why. However, we must be careful about this assumption. Why do clients need to know why? In some cases, the reason they want to know why people like or do not like a product or service is so that they can plan the next one better. However, if social media gives them some guidance as to the question why, and new product ideas can be tested much more easily, quickly and at low cost, then improving, say, product design using marketing research information may not be such a good strategy when different designs can be tested quickly using digital interaction with clients and the best product identified.

This example demonstrates that we should pose the question about the future of market research differently, not in terms of what we do know, for example, qualitative vs quantitative, survey vs ethnography, but in terms of what insight and foresight users need. Yes, we may need to translate these into categories with which we are familiar, but we need to start with the future of clients' needs, not the future of the techniques that we use and with which we are familiar.

So, the purpose of this chapter is to visualise the future needs of clients relating to insight and foresight and then translate them into how marketing researchers can meet them. In this, we try to avoid seeing marketing research as an industry but rather as a set of capabilities which may or may not be collected into a company that calls itself a marketing research company.

Data, data everywhere – data collection and making sense of information overload

Information overload, a term attributed to a US social scientist, Bertram Gross (1964), and popularised from the mid-1960s, is predicated upon human dependence on technology. An array of modern products combining the power of computers and the Internet, increasingly accessed by mobile devices that give information on the location of the customer, has long transformed the old-fashioned image of a marketing researcher with a clipboard asking questions of selected passers-by or conducting group discussions. Modern marketing research takes place in a world of what would once have been called technophiles, saturated by emails in inboxes and using LinkedIn, Twitter, Facebook, Snapchat or whatever new social medium comes down the track; blogging to transmit information to countless more people; or responding to or commenting on any of these. Digital intrusion is normal, whether through the impossibility of gaining the attention of respondents talking into or tapping smartphones or through unwanted messages appearing when a respondent is trying to concentrate on answering an online questionnaire. However, one strong point of marketing researchers is (or should be) coping with the reality of data collection, whether in designing research strategies, sampling, collecting the data and designing questionnaires and whether using qualitative, quantitative or mixed methodologies or deriving and validating results to support marketing decision-making,

Primary or secondary research?

In today's fast-moving data situation, due to a range of pressures, such as the academic requirement for early posting of research or the increasing use of marketing research as published thought leadership, resulting in widespread publicity being given to research studies, much research that would once have been regarded as primary becomes secondary data very rapidly. So it is not surprising the authors have been asked by students new to marketing research about what the definition of secondary data is. The traditional definition of secondary data is previously published and accessible works, such as government and industry publications, bibliographic databases and syndicated services that have been collected for purposes other than for the research problem immediate to the researcher (Wright and Crimp 2000). In contrast, primary or field and in-laboratory research is devised by a researcher with the intention of solving a problem at hand. As we shall see throughout this book, this simple distinction may not work in many situations.

Search behaviour

In understanding users' search behaviour, our students generally use Google and Google Scholar and their university's own library search engine (which indexes not only the titles and summaries but also the full content of articles). A common practice among marketing and marketing research students and – increasingly – marketing consultants is to start their searches using Google and Google Scholar, and, where these searches yield results which are not publicly available (e.g. via Research Gate, Academia.eu or other posting sites through university open access archives), to search their own university or corporate library to see if the library's subscription includes the required article.

Academic journals

Journal publishers perform a range of valuable functions, which have been enumerated in many publications and blogs, such as that of Anderson (2018). They include the soliciting, assessing, aggregating and integration of content, as well as its production, distribution, marketing and hosting. Authoring and review management are very labour intensive but increasingly automated. Workflow analytics have become very important for checking the performance of journals and authors. There has also been a rise in the sales of individual articles from journals and individual chapters from books, although sales of whole journal subscriptions still dominate (Johnson *et al.* 2018).

Data on the number of reputable management journals seems to be harder to find, but the Scimago (2019) ranking gives nearly 178 marketing journals (although many of these are not pure marketing). The globalisation of enterprise and the rise of the digital economy have posed particular challenges to academic communities, encouraging them to update their research and make it more relevant internationally, but, according to McDonald (2003, 2009), Hughes *et al.* (2018), Stone (2013) and others, this has not led to the production of research that is more relevant to industry needs.

Given the increasing drive towards open access and the enormous volume of research which is published as grey literature, we expect this kind of open browsing to be used with increasing frequency, whether by students or professionals. There are few general questions about the behaviour of customers that no one has researched, so increasingly marketing research focuses on specific applications, for example, not whether travellers like to use smart-cards for ticketing (researchers only need to look at the great transport authorities such as Singapore or London to find the answer to that) but whether the same will be true for their particular country or for the market segment they are interested in. The same would be true of older adults' attitudes to the use of robots to provide services to them. Both these are issues discussed in this book.

Grey literature is more likely to be found via a Google search than by searching more academically focused indices, for example, Web of Science, Scopus. The suppliers of many types of grey literature are keen to have it accessed free and so focus strongly on making their content likely to be listed in the first or early pages of any search. Some researchers are wise to this and may first use Google Scholar to identify "respectable" research and then move to Google with more specific search terms to find other works published by the same researcher or supplier or a public version of an article (e.g. an earlier draft) that is not available publicly in its final form. Google Scholar will also give an indication of the usefulness and academic respectability of the work through its citation analysis.

However, there is one serious problem with using grey literature, and that is that often the producers of thought leadership research or of analysis (e.g. in the information technology or financial services industries) take down their research from the Internet after a couple of years, so that researchers trying to build a picture of the evolution of thinking about a particular topic may find gaps, often in the form of cited URLs that do not work anymore.

Insight versus foresight

Insight is rapidly becoming the term used by clients to describe how they bring together marketing research and analysis of data about customers and other entities. Many companies now have customer insight functions. Foresight is a term which used to be used to refer to forecasting but is attracting a wider interpretation relating to preparing a client for the future not just by forecasting and competitive intelligence but also by learning how to handle data about the future. This is a critical area where marketing researchers have been less active but where there is an opportunity for them to bring together the different business and social science disciplines to help clients manage their futures.

Key hypothesis

At the centre of our thinking, as can be seen previously, is our hypothesis that the focus of marketing research will shift completely away from the collection of data and the validity of the collection and sampling process to the interpretation of data from a variety of digital sources and the generation of foresight and insight to increasingly support strategic decisions of all kinds, as operational marketing and related decisions become much more testable using digital techniques. This shift will take the industry into severe competition with firms from closely related sectors, such as marketing services, consultancy and analysis, as well as from clients themselves. Netflix demonstrates clearly how companies can create their own approach to understanding their markets but also that the kind of capabilities and skills that they build are almost identical to those that would once have been considered the domain of marketing researchers. The digital world poses another threat, too, which is that it is much easier for new players, including clients themselves, to enter into new businesses, which include the business of insight and foresight. One of the best examples of this is Accenture, formerly a management consultancy and now the world's largest digital marketing agency. The extent to which co-creation and user innovation can take over some or all the role of suppliers has been noted in software markets as well.

The response to this is not to retreat into a shell but to innovate in return, to come up with new ways of developing insight and foresight to meet the needs that are articulated in this chapter. This includes the development of new attitudes and skills, not just advanced statistical skills, or not even these skills, as artificial intelligence and related techniques including creative visualisation software may prove much better than humans in interpreting the data. We believe it is more likely that the key contribution made by marketing researchers will be to help clients think about how they use insight and foresight as a competitive weapon and to create new combinations of sources and interpretation to help them do it.

Scenarios

We are not "all-seeing." Forecasting is not easy and is beset with all the problems of information and disinformation. One way of dealing with this is to develop scenarios that reflect different possible futures, together with reasons which might lead to one or the other scenario turning out to be the one that actually happens. Here, we identify the scenarios and keep them in our sights as we go through the chapter, ending with our views on which scenarios seem most likely to turn out to be the case.

The scenarios we are using are as follows:

- Business as usual
- Gradual shifting and absorbing
- The industry wakes up

Business as usual

The industry will continue playing its current roles in different industries and situations and gradually shrink as foresight and insight activities become dominated by other players as described in the hypothesis section previously.

Gradual shifting and absorbing

The industry will shift gradually from its current position, adapting gradually to changing needs, merging with the other players mentioned previously, so that it is no longer identifiable as an industry.

The industry wakes up

The industry will wake up and redefine foresight and insight, owning the territory and becoming a much more important part of the marketing services ecosystem, whether as individual firms or merged into other firms.

Some big issues

What are the main issues which will influence the development of the marketing research industry and those who work in research, insight and foresight? Here we identify the questions that marketing researchers should ask and the approaches that marketing researchers might take to help clients make sense of the evolving world and their markets and to take advantage of this evolution.

We see seven areas where developments are taking place rapidly and will continue to do so as areas which provide opportunity for marketing researchers.

- Digital technology and its exploitation
- Big data
- Trust, accuracy, ethics and faith
- User experience
- Lifelogging
- Artificial intelligence and machine learning
- Economy, society and demography

The evolution of digital technology and the responses of individuals

The evolution of digital technology has progressed so fast and is so all embracing that some companies have banned the use of the word "digital" as applied to marketing, because they consider all marketing at least partly if not fully digital. In the digital world, companies can listen to, see and respond to (by immediate optimisation and by planning their marketing mix) what customers, prospects and influencers (other companies, bloggers, the media etc.) are searching for, recommending, liking, forwarding, sharing, discussing and buying (own and competitive products, products in parallel markets). New types of intermediaries and platforms – sometimes on a global stage – have sprung up to connect and optimise relationships between buyers and sellers. If anything, this trend is accelerating as new forms of business or business behaviour (business models) are developed, while different types of buyer behaviour emerge (e.g. the sharing economy, online buying for same-day delivery) in response to these new forms of business. Here, we see the role of the marketing researcher as embracing this change and accelerating it by helping companies identify gaps which can be met by even more innovation. Examples which we have been involved in include:

- Helping older adults and their suppliers and carers use robots to optimise care and well-being;
- Assisting in informing consumers about innovative products via activity trackers and monitors of general health;
- Identifying what aspects of real branding and presence can be translated into the digital world;
- Helping different suppliers in an ecosystem make sense of how the ecosystem's different aspects affect users.

The volume of big data streaming out of digital interactions with customers

As suggested previously, this changes dramatically our view of what insight and foresight are. Without the capability to handle the very high volumes of data coming from digital interactions, companies would drown in the data, which in principle allows clients to do a wide range of different things, from interpreting their reality across many different markets, to improving grouping and segmentation, through to handling individual customers differently. In the latter case, there may be issues with data protection relating to identification of customers who believed that they were unidentifiable (the problem of combining apparently unrelated data). Marketing researchers obviously have a role to play in identifying the risks in this area but more importantly have the opportunity to help companies identify ways to exploit the opportunities presented, moving from "if only we knew" to "if only we can find a way to make money/help" by using the data we have or data that we can obtain.

Trust, accuracy, ethics and faith

These deeply human aspects of research are much more important in an age of digital technology and big data, not helped by the rise of digital fraud (Financial Times 2020b) and of companies that aim to exploit data illegally or inappropriately. Further problems are posed by regulators and industry bodies operating with outdated regulations and codes of practices designed to restrain what was seen as bad behaviour without focusing on the positive side, despite improved provisions in national and regional regulation (European Commission 2018). The net result of this is that companies that can happily operate outside these codes of practice and pay the occasional fine imposed by regulators tend to thrive, while those that try to behave, reach trust and meet the needs of customers end up being very restricted and losing market share to the new players. Commentators often express shock about "how much they – Netflix, Amazon, Uber etc. – know about us", but of course consumers of these services are now much better served than in the days when their data was not used to optimise service to them. Nonetheless, marketing researchers can do a lot to help ensure that what clients do does not breach trust or belief and is as accurate as it can be. Commercial banks and various associations for marketing researchers, for example, the European Society for Opinion and Market Research (ESOMAR) and the Market Research Society (MRS), help by providing good guidance about ethics in their codes of practice, but, sad to say, instances of fraud committed by unscrupulous individuals and groups are on the rise.

One of the best examples of good research in this respect was done by a student of one of your authors, a devout Muslim herself who researched what devout Muslim customers in Saudi Arabia wanted from western fashion firms. The answer was definitely NOT fashionable versions of religious wear (which is what the Western companies thought) but rather slightly more modest versions of high fashion for indoor wear, when devout Muslim women are allowed to wear more fashionable items so long as there is no inappropriate male in the room. The customers had a problem – most Western dresses were too short and the sleeves also too short (wives were particularly conscious of the views of the mother in law!). So, the customers would order two of everything and use the fabric from one to extend the other. Perhaps the suppliers could have identified the problem from the fact that every online order from Saudi Arabia was for two items! However, they didn't. They could have emailed the customers. But they didn't. This point also has its cultural implications (see subsequently).

There are many issues relating to mismanagement of information, such as bias, irrationality and scepticism. The role of the marketing researcher as custodian of the truth will still be important, perhaps even more important, as the volume of information threatens to overwhelm clients, who may need guidance as to where to focus. Although there will always be the risk of "shooting the messenger," as senior management denial remains a problem, it is less likely that the researchers themselves will be accused of bias, as it is more likely that they will be able to triangulate their findings using many sources.

User experience in the digital and real world

The last 20 or so years of development in marketing theory and practice have produced many new insights into how we use or should use customer insight.

Customer relationship management (CRM) thinking has taught us that research into users which does not distinguish between, for example, whether the users are new, long-standing, lapsed or prospects and what their likely lifetime value is or that has no regard for the frequency, amount and product category of use/purchase is likely to produce misleading results, so most marketing research in the future will use (where available) data which takes this into account, usually coming from a CRM system.

We have learnt that products and services are effectively multi-layered, with the core product wrapped with several layers of service and other attributes, with physical and other products increasingly supplied on a services basis, with the product itself possibly having been co-created. The user experience of a product cannot be viewed without regard for how the customer is accessing data on it (its features, its price, its channel of availability, and messages about it) and through which device (increasingly a mobile).

We have also learnt that suppliers' attempts to become customer-oriented and to create user experiences and journeys that meet the needs of customers can often by hampered by an internally oriented view. However, we have also learnt that high-quality customer experience rarely comes free, so the more that can be done to make customers responsible for their own experience, the better and lower cost the service will be.

Perhaps most importantly of all, we have learnt that the marketing and customer service experience must be understood in combination with the viewpoints of other business functions, particularly operations and finance, where feasibility and profitability must be considered. The most severe lesson on this comes from low-cost airlines, for whom filling a plane at the right yield and maximising utilisation of planes is what enables them to keep prices very low, so crowded check-ins and delayed flights are part of the normal user experience.

Marketing researchers who have been involved in all this learning will make very good advisors to clients who need more insight and foresight, but this may require some challenging of clients.

Logging people's lives – lifelogging

We have recently seen convergence of technologies to foster the emergence of lifelogging as a mainstream activity. Computer storage has become much cheaper, while advances in sensing technology allow efficient sensing of personal activities, locations and the environment. This is best seen in the growing popularity of quantified self-movement, where life activities are tracked using wearable sensors in the hope of better understanding human performance in a variety of tasks (and in the case of the individual, determining whether enough exercise has taken place!). So far, lifelogging research has focused on visual and movement lifelogging to capture details of life activities. Lifelogging may offer benefits to content-based information retrieval, contextual retrieval, browsing, search, linking, summarisation and user interaction.

In future, lifelogging will pose many challenges to information retrieval scientists. A surrogate memory is akin to a digital library – it is the data from the lifelog and the associated software to organise and manage lifelog data. This poses a new challenge for information retrieval, to develop new retrieval technologies that operate over these enormous new data archives. The term "surrogate memory" does not imply cognitive processes taking place; rather, it is simply the digital library for lifelog data, which so far has focused mainly on maintaining a list of events or episodes from life.

The research tools and techniques now available, both do-it-yourself (DIY) and custom, are allowing more companies than ever to conduct some form of marketing research. Is this not a good thing? In an era of big data, what marketers must do is observe their customers to assess their true desires. We now have an unprecedented opportunity to "observe" many consumers in various locations, engaged in relationships with products and friends. Many marketers have always wanted to immerse themselves in this reality. However, marketers have also been concerned about the cost of research, and this led to DIY research and the tools that make it possible (e.g. online questionnaire services). Marketing researchers and their clients feel liberated by being able to access the views of their clients and customers so directly and easily but must take account of some important developments in consumer lifelogging and DIY research, as follows:

- Data streams will need to be aggregated and curated;
- The right tools will need to be assembled into a usable arsenal that can distinguish the signal from the noise;

- The ultimate needs of the marketer need to be synthesised into the functioning of those tools. They will need to be tuned and tweaked;
- There will need to be institutional memory that makes sense of the insights and correlations over time.

We see the growth of DIY as a demonstration of the split between simple studies, to gain "information" that can be managed by clients and more sophisticated, value-added insight-generating research that agencies and insight departments provide. There is huge potential for research agencies to embrace DIY as another way of gathering data and integrate it with their services to clients. Rather than fight what is already here, agencies should enable clients to design and manage projects using whatever methodology is appropriate.

Changing economics, politics, society and demography

Market researchers have always (or should have) been on top of what could be called these "social science" issues, mainly because of their need to get their sampling frame to match the actual or likely profile of eventual users of a product or service. As these issues of representativeness of samples have gone away due to the high availability of data, another issue has come to the fore – the need to recognise increasing diversity.

This applies to countries, as migration patterns continue to evolve and economic power continues to shift away from Europe and the oil states of the Gulf and East Asia on the one hand to the digital giant-driven economy of the United States and to Asia. Markets for most products and services will be much more culturally diverse not just for these ethnic and geographic reasons or because of the faith reasons mentioned previously but also as diversity based on situations, attitudes and preferences related to age, gender, health, disease, working habits, lifestyle, social class, education and other matters increases. Increasingly, marketing researchers will have to guide clients on how to produce and use insight that reflects the changing nature of their customer base.

Geographical tensions have also started to have an effect, whether through the breakup of trade agreements (like the EU), countries experiencing radical changes to their well-being (e.g. in the Middle East), disruptive behaviour (some would cite Russia as an example) or problems of lack of cooperation (e.g. the China-US stand-off, exacerbated by the coronavirus problem).

Research, insight and foresight are changing

The challenges marketing research faces are similar in many industries. However, there are also big differences in needs and applications. Marketing research projects will change and may not exist as we know them, and the customer-supplier relationship may change.

Who is the customer?

It is conventional to distinguish between business-to-business, business-to-consumer and government-to-citizen marketing. This conventional distinction has already broken down, to some extent. For example, in some countries, much government work has been contracted out to private-sector or not-for-profit organisations. In many consumer and industrial markets, platforms, infomediaries and aggregators have taken over the role once reserved for distributors and retailers, making business-to-business to consumer markets much more transparent, changing the nature of research towards a stronger focus on supplier and customer behaviour towards these new intermediaries, who in many cases take a highly active role in shaping markets rather than just being a place for purchasing and information exchange. Supply chains have become much more transparent to customers, particularly the logistics element. In many markets, customers can now choose not just from a much wider range of products and services from all over the world but also how quickly and in what quantities they want them.

Servitisation

In many markets, servitisation – the conversion of products into services – has become a leading strategy. Much early research focused on industrial market servitisation, but servitisation had been present in many consumer markets for years. Perhaps we had forgotten that in some countries, fire insurance was originally provided by companies who would also put out fires.

Value chain breakup

The breakup of the value chain implied by separating the service of putting out fires from compensating for damage and in some cases advising how to avoid fires is an old story, but this story persists today and is accelerating, as digital technology and services make it much easier to separate parts of the value chain and allocate them to different companies, creating whole new sets of supplier-customer relationships. In many markets, the leading suppliers are the most devoted to value chain breakup, keen to substitute third-party services for their own activities, enabling them to focus on their core business, which often turns out to depend on managing information better than anyone else. Low-cost airlines typically lease their planes, outsource much of their ground handling (passengers, luggage and cargo) and in some cases hire their aircrew from specialist agencies, shrinking even further the definition of core staff. Some of the fastest-growing information technology companies such as Salesforce.com could not achieve their sales success without outsourcing data storage to cloud services companies such as Google and Amazon Web Services (Stone *et al.* 2020)

Outsourcing by government

As mentioned previously, in central and local government, outsourcing of routine services is common, but the frontier keeps moving (forwards and backwards, as sometimes governments discover that outsourcing simply does not work or that for the time being, no suppliers are up to the task). Expensive, uncontrollable overheads can be turned into overheads which can be managed much more tightly, with a stronger focus on quality, for example, in highway maintenance and waste disposal. However, this is an ancient trend – tax farming was a characteristic of ancient civilisations, while the biggest item of pre-modern government expenditure, defence, often used mercenary suppliers. For these suppliers to the public-sector suppliers, it is important to know what the immediate customer (the government) wants and perceives but also how satisfied the end-customer (the citizen or business, for example) is with the service provided, and indeed, this may be a key input into the contract renewal decision.

Many privatisations – common in some parts of the world – can only take place on a contractual, franchised or highly regulated basis, to ensure that the citizen gets a good service at a fair price. This applies particularly in areas such as public utilities, transport services (rail and bus), telecommunications and local environmental services (e.g. waste disposal) but also in more controversial areas such as health and social care. The term "stakeholder management" is commonly used to refer to the need to manage many different groups involved in or with an interest in the successful delivery of services, so marketing researchers can play an important role in identifying, assessing and measuring the perceptions, attitudes and behaviour of different groups of stakeholders.

In all these cases, the three-sided nature of the market opens great opportunities for marketing researchers, but clients will want the research done efficiently and fast and may require it to be integrated, as at the centre of it lies the consumer. For example, how can we justify the separation of assessment of satisfaction of a consumer concerning local government-managed but outsourced refuse collection and recycling from satisfaction with value for money as a local taxpayer? If the same outsourced supplier delivers refuse collection and highway maintenance, should the assessment of their performance for the local government body not be integrated?

User groups

Where an organisation, public or private, delivers products or services to customers on a regular basis, the user group has been an important source of information for suppliers, whether about new needs, satisfaction or perceptions concerning the fulfilment of existing needs. These user groups are now often run digitally. They can be an important source of ideas for new products and services not just at a high-level product definition but also for detailed co-creation. However, special skills are needed to ensure that these groups continue to provide guidance to their suppliers, and here marketing researchers can play an important role in setting up such groups and ensuring that they do guide appropriately.

Project delivery

However, some organisations deliver value to customers through projects in areas as disparate as construction and new product development. In these cases, groups of stakeholders come together for a limited period, from the earliest stages of project planning to the final stages, when whatever was being constructed or developed starts to be used. These temporary stakeholder groups may not have time to learn how to work together before they need to deliver, and in some cases, communication breaks down, or the pursuit of different objectives leads to severe problems with the project. Marketing research is a close relative of communication in these cases, because it is only through staying in touch with the different stakeholders and understanding how they see different aspects of the project that such issues can be avoided (Parnell *et al.* 2020).

Sector analysis

All the previous are issues that we know about today, which we believe will become more important in the delivery of value and where marketing research can play a more important role. However, in many sectors, special factors are at work which increase the demand for insight and foresight and hence for the services of marketing researchers. In this book, we have shown how this applies in areas such as transport and digital entertainment.

The same or similar trends are visible in virtually every area, and in some cases have been accelerated by the coronavirus crisis. For example, pharmaceutical companies, used to long periods of testing of products, in order to minimise or even abolish risk to patients, were suddenly asked to accelerate development and testing of vaccines and remedies, and this meant that the information flow back from patients had to be accelerated, too. Tourism destinations and services companies had to rebuild their propositions and customer bases for a global population which suddenly became wary of rather than excited by leisure pursuits, travel and unfamiliar locations. The statistics relating to infection and survival rates were widely misinterpreted, showing how weak government and media are in statistical analysis. The benefits and costs of working from home and of home education were suddenly of high interest as governments juggled the economic and health pros and cons of lockdown. The world of financial services was turned upside down, with consumers allowed to delay debt repayment, while insurers benefited from the windfall of having customers at home all the time (fewer robberies) and lower road traffic (and so fewer accidents). The question, "What will the new normal be like?", featured often in the media in relation to the coronavirus outbreak, is with us all the time, not just in the management of health.

However, in the case of the coronavirus, at some stage, the new normal will be established, and one thing is certain: whatever digital trends were in place before the coronavirus, they have been accelerated. Very large numbers of people have bought groceries for home delivery or click and collect and have ordered online for the first time. Subscriptions to streaming video services such as Netflix have jumped and will not return to old levels. In these areas, companies are much more closely connected with their customers and use the statistical and related skills that were once the domain just of market research to identify patterns and respond to them. Of course, today they do it partly by artificial intelligence, but as Netflix has demonstrated, they still need people with the right disciplines to support the decision-making. Amazon, such a leader in the use of digital information and customers and analysis of data using artificial intelligence, still needs people who can understand and explain data, particularly as the company moves strongly to selling advertising and therefore has to communicate to potential advertisers how it can use data to improve their sales. Today, marketing researchers more often go under the name of "data scientist" or similar in such companies, but the demand for them can be identified simply by Googling "insight jobs" or "insight teams" along with the company name.

The changing uses of marketing research

In all the previous, the big move, from the perspective of marketing research, has been the move from collection of data to its interpretation (insight) and use in managing the future (foresight) to insight and foresight as seen from the perspective of different business activities. These trends affect different business activities in different ways, with various consequences for marketing research in terms of what insight and foresight are needed and how they may be supplied.

Insight and foresight for marketing planning

Marketing planning conventionally focuses on market analysis and the marketing mix, as a regular (perhaps annually and sometimes now more frequent) process to ensure that brands, products (designs, features, advantages and benefits), propositions, prices, channels and marketing communications deliver what the supplier wants. In some companies, much of the information management side of this process is automated or semi-automated under the description of marketing resource management.

Software that supports this process covers management areas such as strategic planning and budgeting, management of marketing projects (e.g. campaigns), content management (creation, development and distribution – increasingly in digital form), media planning and execution, event coordination and marketing resource management. However, a streamlined marketing process supported by such software does not normally include automated decision-making – it just ensures that everything is in the right place and connected. This is particularly valuable today, when digital techniques allow companies to coherently address a much greater number of segments with different propositions for shorter time periods. The data about what customers need may be represented by past purchasing patterns or marketing research – ideally both – and needs to be in a form that the system can manage.

In practice, many companies have partial systems, and the hype that surrounded marketing resource management systems has largely died away, but this may be because companies who manage marketing resources well prefer to keep quiet about it. For the marketing researcher, it is still important to understand that the demand for marketing research will increasingly come from companies who are using such approaches and who need the data at specific times to input into their systems in specific forms.

Meanwhile, a new view of marketing has emerged, one that is based upon the idea that until data on whether the customer has got what they wanted and is happy with it is feedback into the system (i.e. a closed loop), then marketing cannot be considered to have done its job. This represents a move away from the idea that the job of marketing was to create activity in the marketplace through the marketing mix rather than creating customers and ensuring that they get what they need. This latter view is an essential part of the digital approach to marketing, with testing being a critical component of that approach. Testing is not just a way of finding out what works but a way of understanding customers, and marketing research disciplines of analysis and sampling are used in determining what to test and when. This trend has accelerated as companies partner increasingly with the giant platform companies, for whom such an approach is built into their genes,

Insight and foresight for marketing strategy

The digitalisation of marketing and of business in general has created a new strategic focus to marketing in which the search for competitive advantage is not driven just by issues such as market share and market growth rates but more by the creation of new business models and platforms, as we will see in many chapters of this book. There is much debate about the use of insight and foresight in these approaches, with views ranging from one extreme (you do not need detailed insight to create a new model) to the other (in-depth knowledge of markets and competitors and forecasts of futures are an essential part of the process of business model determination). The use of the business model canvas as a menu for start-ups is part of the latter view. Five of its nine elements relate to marketing (value proposition, channels, customer relationships, segments and revenue streams) and afford plenty of opportunity for marketing research to contribute. Famous cases in which entrepreneurs apparently dismiss marketing research (sometimes referring to the start-up phase) are given the lie by detailed later accounts of how they use marketing research now), though it can be said that often *how* they use research is very different (Insights Association 2020). Of course, businesses using Amazon to distribute still need to do market research, though they are likely to use digital tools to do it (Ecommercefuel 2016).

A particularly important strategic use of marketing research is in the innovation process – idea generation and screening, product testing, launch evaluation, repositioning and product withdrawal. For marketing researchers, these will still provide big opportunities, though always with the need to take into account that the client may have a very accurate view of what their existing customers want and buy, This means that a key differentiator in marketing research projects will be whether the focus is on new or existing customers. Interestingly, this applies particularly to public services, where the need to innovate to create more value for citizens at lower cost and to prioritise between areas is now firmly on the agenda of many governments.

Quality for customer services

It was said towards the end of the twentieth century and the beginning of the twenty-first century that customer satisfaction measurement was a lifesaver for the marketing research industry. Suspect but much-used methodologies such as net promoter score capitalised on this trend, generating enormous volumes of business for marketing research companies and performing the valuable function of increasing the salience of customer satisfaction in senior management discussions.

The need to measure customer satisfaction will always be present, though as the rapid development of technology continues to affect what marketers offer their customers, there will always be scope for marketing researchers to contribute to helping companies understand how best to measure satisfaction with new products and services, often delivered digitally, and whether that satisfaction can be converted into market success.

Sources, analysis and interpretation of data

One of the most interesting developments in marketing research is how sources of information have changed (mostly to digital) and how methods of analysis have changed. Much analysis now is not hypothesis based, and there is more data mining, but there is also more sophisticated statistical analysis for grouping and segmentation and more correlation between the different aspects researched, for example, perceptions and behaviour. In some cases, this has happened because researchers are now dealing with data that is not anonymised, for example, surveys of known customers, who have been shown to be happy to give information with which their identity will be associated. Qualitative market research will continue to play a big role in asking why customers behave as they do, although as we have said, there will be a strong demand to show how this produces foresight and is predictive of what customers will do rather than just providing insight.

New sets of data are becoming available, from videos of customers' behaviour in service usage situations (e.g. stores, airports), to voice records from contact centres (analysed by voice recognition and then text mining), to browsing and purchasing patterns and interactions with social media. Conventional techniques of qualitative and quantitative research can be applied to these new data sources, but it will still require innovativeness by marketing researchers to translate it into useful insight and foresight. The need for speed in decision-making may push companies to seek new and faster ways of achieving the in-depth understanding of customers that was delivered by ethnography, perhaps via cameras and listening devices. The good news in all this is that analytics software providers are very interested in helping clients and agencies do this and are coming up with interesting ideas for data collection, analysis, interpretation, simulation, visualisation and integration into marketing processes (testing and roll-out) using conventional and artificial intelligence-based decision-making.

The challenges facing marketing research

Information management has been transformed by digital techniques and continues to change; marketing research needs to transform itself in the same way not for the sake of change but to meet particular challenges. These are as follows:

- Costs, productivity and quality – marketing research needs to provide insight and foresight at lower cost, commensurate with the low cost and high quality with which clients can now obtain data on product purchase and use;

- Speed – gone are the days when clients were prepared to wait for large reports delivered weeks or even months after surveys took place. They now want the information in weeks or even days, because that is how long their decision cycles last;
- Convenience, accessibility and universality – the insight and foresight must be easily digestible and searchable so that relevant items can be identified and visualised quickly but also available for other uses;
- Creativity – marketing researchers are not just providing information but are supporting decision processes, so they need to use creative techniques, such as storytelling, to communicate their results;
- Integration – the information must be in a form which links easily to other data being used by clients and visualised together with it;
- Comprehensiveness – the marketing research brief will still be issued by some companies, but in some cases, the marketing researcher's overriding brief is to support a decision rather than to produce particular pieces of information, so a comprehensive understanding of the situation being researched is the real need;
- Reliability – truly representative and proof as much as possible against problems of interpretation and bias – difficult to achieve at speed but essential;
- Compliance – not so much with old marketing research requirements of anonymity but more in terms of compliance with the client's promise to customers.

Implications for marketing research and marketing researchers – scenarios

This section takes the scenarios articulated earlier and suggests which scenarios are most likely to apply, to whom. Companies in the industry should review these scenarios, determine which ones are more likely to affect them and strategise accordingly, whether the strategy involves merger, takeover, new activities or seeking new clients with whom they are more likely to make their desired journey.

Scenario 1: business as usual

The industry will continue playing its current roles in different industries and situations and gradually shrink as foresight and insight activities become dominated by other players as described in the previous hypothesis section.

Our forecast for Scenario 1

We think that this scenario is unlikely to apply to most of the industry, partly because so many firms – particularly the larger ones – in the industry are now part of wider marketing services combining and working on projects and clients where marketing research is only part of the deliverable. However, some companies believe that their route to survival is to rename themselves as digital experts and to do lots of research on digital topics without changing in the ways indicated by this chapter and this book. These are the ones at risk.

Scenario 2: gradual shifting and absorbing

The industry will shift gradually from its current position, adapting gradually to changing needs, merging with the other players mentioned previously so that it is no longer identifiable as an industry.

Our forecast for Scenario 2

As indicated in our views about Scenario 1, for many, this is already happening, and it is no bad thing. However, some big marketing services firms have acquired marketing research companies and left them to their own devices, expecting them to exploit the wider client base of the company and that other services can be sold to the marketing research companies' client base. This may be a sensible short-term strategy, but is not sensible in the long term, as it leaves them vulnerable to companies which have adopted a fully integrated approach to digital marketing, such as Accenture Digital.

Scenario 3: the industry wakes up

The industry will wake up and redefine foresight and insight, owning the territory and becoming a much more important part of the marketing services ecosystem, whether as individual firms or merged into other firms.

Our forecast for Scenario 3

Given that some of the leading players have been swallowed up by the large marketing services groups, we think that this scenario is unlikely. However, there is room for start-up companies supplying the full range of marketing services including digital research, and some of these firms are already visible. As is normal in such situations, these start-ups may be established by people who have worked for the digital giants such as Amazon, Google, Facebook and Netflix and understand the new digital model of marketing management.

What the individual marketing researcher should do now

If we are correct, the role of the classic marketing researcher is fading, though it will never fade away completely. There will still be classic marketing research contracts available in many situations, particularly in the interorganisational market where stakeholder-type research will still be very important. However, marketing researchers who want to work in the world of leading-edge digital marketing need to work for the market leaders, understanding their world and getting the digital training they need to be able to broaden the application of their research skills and to add value to the total digital-marketing process. Training in digital marketing is available in-house in these giants and at low cost to external users. We have advised many students that if they want to work in any aspect of digital marketing, they need to learn more about digital marketing from the leading providers, whether in courses supplied directly by them or by training providers who specialise in digital marketing.

Perhaps most importantly of all, researchers should redefine themselves in terms of what they provide – insight and foresight to digital marketers – and not in terms of the activities they undertake – research.

Conclusions

In this brief look at the future of marketing research, we have identified many ways in which the market research industry and marketing researchers could develop and how their relationships with clients may evolve. We hope that the thinking in this chapter and in this book will pervade the boards of marketing research companies and also university and college departments where marketing research is taught.

References

Anderson, K., 2018. Focusing on value – 102 things journal publishers do (2018 Update) [online]. Available from: https://scholarlykitchen.sspnet.org/2018/02/06/focusing-value-102-things-journal-publishers-2018-update/ [Accessed 23 July 2019].

Ecommercefuel, 2016. *Successful Amazon Market Research in 2016* [online]. Available from: www.ecommercefuel.com/amazon-market-research/ [Accessed 6 June 2020].

The Economist, 2020. *Economic Statistics. Crisis Measures* [online]. Available from: www.economist.com/finance-and-economics/2020/05/30/the-pandemic-could-lead-statisticians-to-change-how-they-estimate-gdp [Accessed 26 June 2020].

European Commission, 2018. *2018 Reform of EU Data Protection Rules* [online]. Available from: https://ec.europa.eu/commission/priorities/justice-and-fundamental-rights/data-protection/2018-reform-eu-data-protection-rules_en [Accessed 20 June 2020].

Financial Times, 2020a. *Money Section: Cards and Contactless Used for Most Payments* [online]. Available from: www.ft.com/content/9e7b6428-e357-4547-9379-6c9d48035768 [Accessed 26 June 2020].

Financial Times, 2020b. *Money Section: Sharp Spike in HMRC Coronavirus Tax Scams* [online]. Available from: www.ft.com/content/c0918719-cfcb-4b6b-afa7-a1a6baecaf0b [Accessed 26 June 2020].

Gross, B., 1964. *The Managing of Organizations: The Administrative Struggle, Vols I & II.* New York: Free Press of Glencoe. https://doi.org/10.1177%2F000271626536000140.

Hughes, T., Stone, M., Aravopoulou, E., Wright, L. and Machtynger, L., 2018. Academic research into marketing: Many publications, but little impact? *Cogent Business and Management,* 5(1), 1–18. https://doi.org/10.1080/23311975.2018.1516108.

Insights Association, 2020. *How Amazon Drives Growth Through Agile Market Research* [online]. Available from: www.insightsassociation.org/article/how-amazon-drives-growth-through-agile-market-research [Accessed 20 June 2020].

Johnson, R., Watkinson, A. and Mabe, M., 2018. *The STM Report. An Overview of Scientific and Scholarly Publishing. 1968–2018.* The Hague: Association of Scientific, Technical and Medical Publishers [online]. Available from: www.stm-assoc.org/2018_10_04_STM_Report_2018.pdf [Accessed 26 June 2020].

McDonald, M., 2003. Marketing died in the last decade. *Interactive Marketing,* 5(2), 144–159. https://doi.org/10.1057/palgrave.im.4340229.

McDonald, M., 2009. The future of marketing: Brightest star in the firmament, or a fading meteor? Some hypotheses and a research agenda. *Journal of Marketing Management,* 25(5–6), 431–450. https://doi.org/10.1362/026725709X461786.

Parnell, B., Stone, M. and Aravopoulou, E., 2020. Controlling superprojects – information management requirements. *The Bottom Line,* 33(1), 116–131. https://doi.org/10.1108/BL-11-2019-0126.

Scimago, 2019. *Scimago Journal and Country Rank (Marketing Selected)* [online]. Available from: www.scimagojr.com/journalrank.php?category=1406, Scimago, Madrid [Accessed 20 June 2020].

Stone, M., 2013. Co-operation between academics and practitioners – hope for the future? *Journal of Direct, Data and Digital Marketing Practice,* 15(2), 105–107. https://doi.org/10.1057/dddmp.2013.54.

Stone, M., Kosack, E. and Aravopoulou, E., 2020. Relevance of academic research in information technology and information management. *The Bottom Line,* 33(3), 273–295. https://doi.org/10.1108/BL-05-2020-0034.

Wright, L.T and Crimp, M., 2000. *The Marketing Research Process.* London: Financial Times/Prentice Hall.

2

COMBINING BIG DATA AND MARKETING RESEARCH TO CREATE CUSTOMER INSIGHT

*Len Tiu Wright, Merlin Stone, Robin Robin and
Eleni Aravopoulou*

Summary

The aim of this chapter is to provide a conceptual framework for big data, marketing research and decision-making. Big data refers to the increase in the volume of data that exceeds the capacity of traditional database technologies to store, process and analyse (Hashem *et al.* 2015). Marketing research allows companies to probe beyond what analysis of big data shows to identify why the data says what it does. This has always been the traditional role of research, but in earlier years, the role of marketing research was often to provide much of the data. The case study of Netflix is used to show the kind of big data that can be used to provide insight.

Introduction

The definition of big data keeps evolving, although there are four main characteristics (high volume, high velocity, high variety and high veracity) that commonly define big data (Lau *et al.* 2016). These characteristics and the organizational functions required to support better predictive and prescriptive analyses are considered important in the literature (e.g. George *et al.* 2014). Erevelles *et al.* (2016) also identify the potential use of big data in capturing consumer behaviour and in formulating marketing strategy. The proliferation of mobile devices and social media platforms and their generation of high volumes of data and the development of information platforms for managing these volumes are providing challenges for businesses wishing to exploit big data (Huang 2011; Müller *et al.* 2016; Stone *et al.* 2017).

Customer insight can be defined as knowledge about customers that is or could be valuable to a company (Said *et al.* 2015). This definition is very broad but suits our purpose. It therefore includes understanding from data given to a company by its customers or third-party providers, as well as traditional marketing research (Wright *et al.* 2019).

Without a constructive framework and appropriate analysis tools, researchers may be unable to gain full customer insight (George *et al.* 2016). Hopkins *et al.* (2011) report that the main challenge for organizations and researchers is to identify how the development of big data, its analysis and its combination with marketing research are transformed into applications and actions that benefit customers and companies, in particular creating value for the latter. The case study in this chapter focuses on this.

Customer insight provides opportunities for organizations not only to analyse high volumes of data at speed but also to forecast what may benefit the organizations in the near future (Lee 2018). Forecasting outcomes of strategies is vital to advance organizations' service to customers and to stimulate organizational innovativeness (Antons and Breidbach 2018). This chapter therefore explores situations where organizations implement customer insight approaches to enhance value, competitiveness, and innovativeness, developing a framework to guide understanding of big data characteristics in an innovation context. It also provides a framework highlighting the use of customer insight in supporting marketing innovativeness.

Literature review – big data

In the information-hungry and information-intensive era (Huang and Rust 2013), the use of big data influences the performance of many types of organization. Whether for business process innovation (Wamba 2017) or product innovation (Zhan *et al.* 2017), big data is mined for information to generate critical insights and understanding of customer needs and identification of innovation opportunities (Troilo *et al.* 2017; Chandy *et al.* 2017).

Big data not only leads to commercial innovation but also generates information for social and economic purposes, for example, reducing crime-related risks in money transactions (Economides and Jeziorski 2017) or insurance fraud (Stone and Laughlin 2016). E-commerce and online activities in general have provided new sources of big data which offer opportunities for increasing competitiveness and effectiveness (Kauffman *et al.* 2012). The speed and accuracy with which people can be reached via the Internet and transact using it have increased the availability of data, revolutionizing the environment in which managers operate and how they manage their businesses, both in buying from suppliers and in supplying to customers (Lichtenthal and Eliaz 2003).

The concept of innovation has evolved from merely technological innovation (Utterbuck 1994) to different forms of innovation, such as process innovation (Pisano 1997), service innovation (Gallouj and Weinstein 1997) and strategic innovation (Hamel 1998). In general terms, innovation can be defined as ideas, practice or outputs perceived by the company to be new (Zaltman *et al.* 1973). The features and functionality supported by big data are also often associated with innovativeness. Gobble (2013) identifies that the journey from collecting big data to generating value out of it involves innovativeness. However, poor decisions on big data can cause organizations to suffer delays, misalloction of resources and bankruptcy (Judge and Miller 1991; Miller 2008), so it is important to understand the influence of big data on innovation decision-making processes relating to both customers and business partners (Mueller *et al.* 2007). This includes the process of business model change (Stott *et al.* 2016). The adoption of big data technology requires large investments (Terziovski 2010), while companies using it as the foundation of their business may take years to reach profitability, as in the case of Amazon or Google.

Developing a conceptual framework for big data

The characteristics of big data are shown in Table 2.1.

The attributes of big data are identified in Figure 2.1, which shows how the "decision-making process 'feeds back' (often in real-time) to its big data sources to enhance the next cycle of decision-making using the 4V (volume, velocity, variety and veracity) characteristics of big data." Big data analytics refers to the process of transforming big data into actionable results to improve organizational performance (Wamba *et al.* 2017). The outcomes of applying big data effectively generate more data – hence the feedback loop.

Table 2.1 Characteristics of big data

Characteristic	Explanation
High volume	Much more data is collected, analysed and used than previously, producing more data than marketing research could ever hope to.
High velocity	Data is collected and analysed and results communicated much quickly than previously and much quicker than via traditional marketing research, although acceleration of modes of collection and analysis of data in marketing research has also taken place.
High variety	Big data is collected for various purposes and in all forms and sizes, some by businesses, some by not-for-profit organizations or government agencies. Coverage includes customers, markets, transactions and interactions, populations, resources, climate, facilities, infrastructure and industry changes. The data is heterogeneous; some unstructured, some structured; numerical; in the form of text, audio, still and moving images. In this respect, it has, perhaps surprisingly, much in common with qualitative research.
High veracity	The data must be known to be "true" if an organization is to rely on the data for making decisions.

Source: The authors

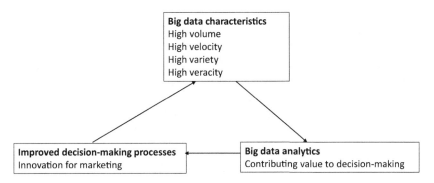

Figure 2.1 Transforming big data into value

Source: The authors

Manyika *et al.* (2011) suggest that big data analytics enables organizations to obtain value from high volumes of heterogeneous data by improving decision-making processes. Wamba *et al.* (2017) demonstrate the direct and indirect effects of the application of big data analytics in influencing the financial form and market performance of an organization. Several other studies (Davenport 2006; Davenport and Harris 2017) highlight the importance of big data analytics in achieving competitive advantage.

Method and conceptual framework

As the aim of this chapter is to provide a conceptual framework for analysing the use of customer insight innovation, an appropriate method is to use information on how organizations use customer insight to innovate by advancing their offerings to businesses and consumers. To illustrate this, a case study (Netflix) was chosen where the information management approaches had severely disrupted markets, whether in terms of new business models, new competition and/or radical improvements to benefits to customers. They are used to highlight the closeness of the relationship between success in achieving strategic objectives and innovating in information management.

Marketing strategy teachers conventionally focus on separate market-focused elements of strategy (products, target markets etc.) rather than information management aspects. The case study fills a gap in the literature by showing the value of an integrated approach. Leadership, innovation and competitiveness are closely related, so it is important to focus on the enablers of innovation, which include information management (Huang 2011).

Value

Successful adoption of the big data-based approach to customer insight requires organizations to invest enough resources to ensure that value can be gained from the data in all aspects of management, from operational use to strategic planning. This may also involve changes to culture, people and technology (Davenport *et al.* 2012). Big data is regarded as one of the most prominent game-changers to marketing in this digital era (Chandy *et al.* 2017). Similarly, Kiron *et al.* (2014) emphasize how successful big data adoption requires a balance between organizational resources, such as employees' analytics skills and technology capabilities and the overall organizational culture.

Big data characteristics, commonly identified as 4Vs, can also be described as 5Vs, with value being the fifth characteristic (Wamba *et al.* 2017; Jin *et al.* 2015; Marr 2015). Its value in contributing to innovation has been described in various ways, such as "the next big thing in innovation" (Gobble 2013) or "the next frontier for innovation, competition, and productivity" (Manyika *et al.* 2011). The implementation of big data analytics can increase marketing return on investment by 15–20% (Court *et al.* 2015). Increased knowledge productivity arises from big data use and may be critical support for economic growth (Jin *et al.* 2015).

Competitiveness

The pressure to be competitive is a crucial determinant of the adoption of innovation and technology (Gatignon and Robertson 1989). Individual competitiveness relates to the desire to win and be better than others (Brown *et al.* 1998). For decision-makers, "trait competitiveness" among management teams implies the drive to take actions to win against rivals. Karatepe *et al.* (2006) investigated the existence of trait competitiveness in an organizational setting, suggesting that the effort devoted to winning against competitors is positively related to competitiveness. Competitiveness has a positive influence on the performance of employees (Karatepe *et al.* 2006) and the organization overall (Schrock *et al.* 2016). This positive impact of competitiveness can be explained by the relationship between market competition and organizational commitment. Schrock *et al.* (2016) examined the role of competitiveness as an antecedent to organizational commitment and found direct and indirect relationships between these two elements. Organizational commitment enhances performance because commitment creates a winning spirit among a firm's stakeholders, driving them to strive to do their jobs well (Schrock *et al.* 2016). Fletcher *et al.* (2008) suggest that the positive and optimistic attitude of competitive individuals boosts their abilities to perform, even when faced with obstacles. If adoption of the big data approach and the techniques and technology needed to deliver competitiveness becomes a central focus for analysis of competitive behaviour, studies of adoption of the big data approach in competitive environments must take into account the previously mentioned "human side" of competitiveness.

Innovativeness

Organizational innovativeness is the desire to succeed and survive through the ability to produce ideas, innovate and be strategic in decision-making (Ruvio *et al.* 2014). An example of the positive impact of innovating comes from a study by Rubera and Kirca (2012), which indicates the positive effect of organizational innovativeness on firm value, market and financial positions. The drive to embrace the use of big data is linked to its functionality in deriving information (e.g. Manyika *et al.* 2011) to support managerial decision-making processes and to communicate decisions to employees, suppliers and customers for implementation. Research by Michaelidou *et al.* (2011) and Siamagka *et al.* (2015) confirms that organizational innovativeness has a significant impact on the adoption rate of other information-based innovations, such as social media. The critical role of leaders in the adoption of innovation has also been noted (Caridi-Zahavi *et al.* 2015; Chen *et al.* 2014).

Resource requirements

Organizations need significant resources to collect, analyze and obtain value from big data (Johnson *et al.* 2017). Many studies of big data resources (Akter *et al.* 2016; Erevelles *et al.* 2016; Wang and Hajli 2017) use resource-based theory (RBT) to evaluate use of big data in organizations. RBT suggests that the rarity, value and imitability of resources determine the ability of the firm to gain competitive advantage (Barney 1991). Our chapter applies a case study approach to arrive at a refinement of a conceptual framework that can be applied to the study of big data in organizations. In the context of big data, the framework takes account of several types of resources needed by organizations. First, adoption requires the equipment to collect, store and analyze big data (unless cloud storage is used). This is especially important due to the high volume, variety and real-time usage of data (Davenport *et al.* 2012). Second, organizations need the expertise and skills to handle and extract value from big data (Erevelles *et al.* 2016). Third, organizations need to innovate to exploit big data investments (Braganza *et al.* 2017) or engage with other businesses to do so. Fourth, organizations that lack resources such as particular IT expertise or appropriate systems might not benefit from big data adoption (Lamberg *et al.* 2009) unless they subcontract or work with other providers.

The balance between big data and marketing research in customer insight

The availability of big data on customers has produced a dramatic advance in the ability of companies to understand their customers. In some cases, this has added to the insight produced by marketing research; in some cases, it has substituted for marketing research; and in other cases, it has produced a merger between the two approaches, such that the boundary between the two becomes fuzzy or disappears altogether. In this section, we examine the main factors that determine the balance between marketing research and big data analysis.

Some of the main factors which influence the balance between the two, in particular the factors likely to tip the balance in favour of big data analysis and against marketing research, are as listed in Table 2.2, together with suggestions as to how they affect the balance between big data analysis and marketing research.

Table 2.2 Factors affecting the balance between usage of big data/analytics and marketing research

Factors	Impact on balance between big data/analysis and marketing research
The data intensity of the typical journey of new customers towards making a first purchase	The more data that is exchanged between the customer and the supplier during the first stages of a purchase or a relationship, the more the supplier will be able to learn directly from the data rather than by using classic marketing research techniques. However, even in very data-intense situations, marketing research will have great value in identifying the choices the customer makes between different kinds of journeys, their attitudes towards the journeys and their requirements for improvements to the journey, for example
Frequency of purchase	The more often the customer purchases from a particular supplier (not just single products or services but any products or services from the supplier), the greater the economies of scale in collection and use of data and the greater the potential for using data analysis to find ways to improve the frequency or amount of purchase. However, if frequency of purchase is inversely correlated with value of purchase, then marketing research can be very valuable in understanding, for example, how the needs of customers change between purchases.
Average value of purchase	The higher the average value of the purchase (whether single items or a bundle of items or services), the lower the cost of data collection from each transaction relative to the value. However, as purchases of higher average value might be more salient or more emotionally involving for customers, they also give great potential for using marketing research to probe reasons for purchase and how to influence purchases.
Nature of relationship between supplier and customer after purchase	If the initial purchase leads to a protracted period of usage and/or after-sales service in which the customer is in a direct relationship with the supplier, this allows the collection of much more data directly from the customer and its analysis to work out how to optimize the relationship. This applies increasingly in a world where the Internet of Things is leading to new streams of data being created that connect the user with the supplier, as in the automotive industry. However, marketing research can be used very productively here to identify customer attitudes to the post-sale relationship and services, particularly if the customer has a choice about with which supplier to conduct the relationship, for example, using third-party service companies.
Channels of communication and distribution which influence the customer before and after purchase, attributability of initial and subsequent purchases to particular marketing communications and the extent to which data from	Given the emergence of platform giants and aggregators and their success in improving the management of markets, the data flowing from and to the customer is often only available to the original product or service supplier via third parties, who often make it part of their role to sell the data to the supplier (or to others) and increasingly to provide the analytics which allows the original supplier to work out which approach is best. This is, of course, of benefit where the third party is making direct revenue from the sale as opposed to merely carrying advertising. However, here marketing research is providing very valuable information about customer preferences between channels and platforms.

(Continued)

Factors	Impact on balance between big data/analysis and marketing research
communication or distribution channels are available to the product or service supplier if they originate with third parties (e.g. distributors or platforms)	
Feasibility and cost (relative to benefits to supplier) of testing different approaches to influencing customer choices	In the digital world, the more that can be learnt from testing, the less dependent a supplier is on marketing research. However, testing in the digital world normally relies on a product or service being fully formed in order to be tested, while marketing research is very valuable for testing concepts.

Source: The authors

Case study – streaming video

Introduction

The streaming video market is now one of the dominant global forms of entertainment. Its origin was with cable TV and satellite broadcasting companies, but the Internet has transformed the market, opening the door to new entrants such as Adobe, Amazon, Hulu (from the Walt Disney Company, Comcast and Twenty-First Century Fox), Google's YouTube, Home Box Office (HBO), Microsoft and Netflix (originally a DVD rental company). Demand is growing, with smartphones increasingly used to watch TV shows, live sports, movies, TV shows and events and to take part in multiplayer games. All providers are supplying wide ranges of streaming services and content, with further progress in 5G mobile networks and other digital technologies supported by partnerships with telecommunications network providers and video streaming providers.

News, sporting events and live concerts still provide the main audiences for television networks, and some streaming service providers, for example, Netflix, do not provide this. However, Hulu and YouTube TV offer live TV streaming alongside video services. Netflix, Hulu and Amazon Prime Video offer a big library of movies and television programs. Agreements with television networks allow them to distribute past and current seasons of popular programs.

Netflix was founded in 1997 but did not launch its streaming service until 2007. It competed with video rental by offering online movies for a low subscription. As technology and video services evolved, Netflix saw the opportunity to allow access via game consoles, Internet-enabled TVs, mobile devices, Apple TV, Roku, Chromecast and the like. As new competitors entered, Netflix differentiated by offering Netflix originals, particularly for series, many of which have become the central focus of binge-watching (Merikivi *et al.* 2019).

Amazon rebranded its video services as Prime Video in 2018. Amazon Prime members can access a library of movies and TV shows. Like Netflix, Prime Video offers instant streaming on Amazon products, game consoles, set-top boxes and devices supporting the Amazon app. Users can download video to watch when an Internet connection is unavailable. Amazon offers HBO content. Prime members can view recent shows and have also started producing their own original content.

How streaming video works

Videos are via adaptive streaming or progressive downloading. In the former, live or on-demand streams are encoded and switched based on network conditions, for example, higher rates of download when connection is good and download rates slowing where connections are not, to maintain the connection. Video-on-demand suits situations where live broadcasting is not required and content can tolerate delivery delay.

Using our categorization of big data, the following picture of this market emerges, as shown in Table 2.3.

The rise of Netflix

Netflix Inc. uses big data technology to understand customers' viewing habits and to support a recommendation engine for customers (Chai and Shih 2017). This business-to-consumer relationship then drives its decisions about what content to acquire and, increasingly, to develop itself as Netflix Originals. In an interview with Netflix's engineering director and vice president of product innovation, Vanderbilt (2013) identifies how volume and velocity of big data algorithms in tracking customer viewing behaviour was fundamental to Netflix's ability to read customer preferences and provide better service to their customers and feedback to content providers (Pääkkönen and Pakkala 2015).

Netflix's entry into the market was disruptive for other companies in the video-on-demand market, particularly cable and satellite TV companies. The choice of Netflix as a case study (and some of the data for it) was based on an in-depth interview with a senior marketing manager in one of the disrupted companies, who identified more specifically the nature of Netflix's big data-based challenge (Parnell *et al.* 2018).

Netflix also hosts some of its data on Amazon Web Services. It has moved away from its own Netflix data centres and data including usage by customers, searching for videos, personalization of recommendations and billing is hosted by Amazon Web Services (AWS) and used to track users, their signing up to the service, their preferences and viewing (including

Table 2.3 Big data characteristics of streaming video market

Characteristics	How demonstrated in streaming video market
High volume	Data is available on hundreds of millions of customers for the largest providers
High velocity	The data is available immediately, with no delay
High variety	Every viewing decision by a customer is available, including not just what they watch but when they watch it, how often they pause it, what they watch before and after, how they rate it and whether they watch recommended selections
High veracity	The data comes directly from interaction with the customer

Source: The authors

whether they are partway through watching) and their clicks, as well as the catalogue of content (Brodkin 2016). However, since Amazon Prime's entry into the video streaming business, this raises some interesting questions about whether this policy will continue (Hoff 2017). However, it took seven years to make the shift, and such is the volume of data concerned and the tough requirements for quality and reliability that it is unlikely that any other supplier can match what AWS delivers. Netflix has several other very large business partners (e.g. in customer relationship management, Salesforce.com and its recent acquisition Tableau – the data visualization specialist), whose software and services it uses because they too are large enough to meet Netflix's needs.

Netflix operates many tens of thousands of servers and many tens of petabytes of storage in the Amazon cloud. However, Netflix operates its own content delivery network called Open Connect. Netflix manages Open Connect from Amazon, but the storage boxes holding videos that stream to houses or mobile devices are in data centres in Internet service providers' networks or at Internet exchange points, facilities where major network operators exchange traffic. Netflix distributes traffic to Comcast, Verizon, AT&T and other large network operators at these exchange points. Amazon's cloud network is spread across 12 regions worldwide, each of which has availability zones consisting of one or more data centres. Netflix has multiple backups of all data within AWS. Netflix was responsible for 15% of the total downstream Internet traffic globally (Armstrong 2018), although this had fallen to 12.6% by 2019 (Spangler 2019), though this decline in share is due to the rise in general streaming not competition from other streaming video services.

The richness of the data

Despite the richness of the big data available to the players in this market, marketing research has proved critical for the main contenders in this market (e.g. Sky, Netflix, Amazon) in understanding the preferences that underlie patterns of viewing and the subscription behaviour of individuals. However, it is worth noting that the creation of customer insight teams and the closeness with which data analysts and researchers must work together to deliver customer insight quickly means that an increasing proportion of marketing research is carried out in-house. This demonstrates the importance of capability – where both marketing researchers and data analysts are concerned. The figure of 60% for internal vs external marketing research has been quoted for Sky (Thomas 2019). The internal staff work in Sky's Strategic Insight Team. Sky also uses its customer base as a research frame to supply customer insight to other companies through its Sky Data arm.

Sky describes the role of its Strategic Insight Team on its recruitment site as follows (Sky TV 2020):

> The Strategic Insight team help the business make key decisions by telling stories about consumers, our customers and the markets we operate in. Leveraging a broad set of behavioural and research data, we are passionate about our customers and how we can better connect them to the things that they love. Within our team we have created a positively challenging culture where we look to get the best out of each other in a collaborative and inclusive way.

Marketing research combined with data analysis also provides essential information on what customers want that they do not currently get, as well as on how many services they use. Companies in the streaming video market carry out research into the choice of provider that customers use. This shows that many customers have several streaming video subscriptions (Bruce 2019). However, as companies grow and begin to dominate markets, the balance between data analysis and marketing research changes. If a company has captured virtually all the customers in the market, it can carry out controlled experiments to help it decide where to innovate, that is, what new products to offer (in terms of product decisions) and what recommendations to make to individual users using machine learning and artificial intelligence techniques (Stone *et al.* 2020). Nonetheless, a company can become too confident that it understands its customers through the data it gathers from its interactions with them rather than using marketing research to understand the reasons for behaviour. Meanwhile, classic questions such as perceptions of branding, of relative pricing, of the strengths and weaknesses of product or content offers or of the intrusiveness of advertising are best answered through marketing research.

Netflix digital data-based research

Netflix is well known in the streaming movie industry and the wider digital marketing world for the quality of its research into techniques to optimize the viewing experience, particularly through choice of programming and recommendation, and publishes summaries of what it does on its website (Netflix 2020a) and in academic articles (Lamkhede and Das 2019). It has been argued that Netflix's approach constitutes a new business model (Rayna and Striukova 2016), based upon its approach to recommendation and content development and delivery, working with new sets of actors (content providers, Netflix itself, primary distribution, secondary distribution and device makers) and with four main flows (video, intellectual property rights, revenue and data) to create a new kind of value (Fagerjord and Kueng 2019).

Netflix's research and analysis approach are summarized in Table 2.4.

Netflix's website also describes its approach to research, stating that research is not centralized but instead is organized into many teams, each carrying out research together with business teams, engineering teams and other researchers, encouraging close partnerships between researchers and the business or engineering teams in each area. This leads to a strong focus on sharing of research across teams. Its website stresses the importance of the Netflix culture (Netflix 2020b), which values curiosity, courage with smart risks, innovation, science, rigor and high impact, and of the focus on experimentation to support hypotheses with evidence. To achieve this, Netflix researchers include neuroscientists, biostatisticians, economists and physicists. They interact frequently with senior managers to ensure that business decisions are as far as possible based on evidence and analysis. These have much in common with the resources required in classic marketing research, but they are used very differently.

Conclusion from Netflix case study

The previous very brief description of how Netflix operates in relation to its data indicates clearly that Netflix has created a series of innovations not just in its business model but in relation to processes for working with its own people and with business partners to create new ways of managing very high volumes of data for commercial advantage and of course for the benefit of users. The long-term value of this innovation remains to be determined, as with many Internet-based companies, the focus of investment on recruiting new customers can erode profits. However, in the last four to five years, Netflix profits has risen substantially, indicating clear creation of value.

Table 2.4 Netflix's research and analysis approach

Aspect	Detail
Machine learning	This is to power recommendation algorithms, to identify what makes content successful, to focus production of original content, to optimize the technical side of content delivery and to identify the best approaches to recruiting new members through advertising spend, channel mix and advertising creativity.
Development and use of very large-scale machine learning platforms	This is required to support the extensive machine learning work.
Personalization and recommendation algorithms	This includes experimentation, collaborative filtering (based on choices made by that users with similar patterns of viewing), A/B testing and long-term satisfaction metrics and finding different ways to present and explain recommendations and create interactions with users – this area is supported by consumer marketing research.
Identification of which markets (geographical or other) to prioritize and what member behaviours help Netflix learn who may or may not benefit from joining Netflix	This includes working with leading online advertisers such as Facebook, Google and YouTube to broaden messaging to potential new members, including identifying which titles make the most sense to include in messaging.
Optimizing marketing communications spend	This is carried out daily to identify the value of particular communications, including identification of extent of cannibalization (who would have joined without receiving communication), working at individual and country levels.
Optimization of social media activity	Including how to stimulate viewing of particular programming and how to maximize "chatter" about particular programmes, creating pre-launch social signals and predicting audience sizes from social activity and using natural language processing and machine learning to analyse social and behavioural data and create tools for those responsible for creating Netflix originals.
Content valuation	Identifying which content is of greatest value to customers.
Streaming optimization	Testing different approaches to video and audio encoding – this includes collaboration with universities, industry partners and standardization bodies to ensure that we continue to innovate and meet the future streaming needs of our members.
A/B experimentation	Testing nearly all proposed changes, including new recommendation algorithms, user interface (UI), content promotion tactics, original launch strategies, streaming algorithms, the new member signup process and payment methods.
Meta-level testing analysis	Identifying the optimum approach to testing (length, timing) taking into account seasonality, holidays, day of the week and time of day effects, novelty and other areas that might affect the validity of tests and to determine how long to persist with a test before implementing the result.

Source: The authors

Limitations

It is hard to measure the value of innovation adoption (Kohli and Devaraj 2003). Successful innovation adoption demands a balance between resources and costs required for adoption and benefits of implementing the innovation (Bunduchi *et al.* 2011). All the players in the market in the case study make investments for two reasons – one is that the investment in the fundamental IT needed to run streaming video is required in order to deliver the product proposition. The second is that investment in analytics has allowed those who have made it to develop their businesses rapidly, because customers view the new products and recommendations provided by the company. The adoption decision requires thorough evaluation from financial, organizational resources and strategic viewpoints, as innovation adoption in information technology is usually risky (Meyer and Goes 1988). As Agarwal and Prasad (1998) show, innovations are intrinsically risky, especially without assurance that they will generate expected results.

Implications for marketing practice

When the first textbooks and articles on information technology marketing were produced in the 1980s, the most advanced information technology products ranged from office productivity software to database software (Stone 1984, 1985). The idea that these systems would be used across companies, up and down supply chains and through entire ecosystems would have been regarded as revolutionary. Indeed, the application of the term "ecosystem" to information technology and application areas such as human resources, operations and marketing only occurred two decades or more later (Stone 2014), while the ideas of cloud storage and platform strategies are even newer, though based on ideas of shared resourcing that have existed for some time (Stone *et al.* 2017).

Today, a central question that product strategists in information technology firms must address relates to which platforms are being used by target customers and how the data on those platforms is stored, accessed and analyzed and how the data and analysis are shared cost-effectively throughout the ecosystem to deliver benefits to customers. Companies that address this question will gain a competitive advantage over companies that see their platform products just as another way of storing and sharing data. Although much of this information is now provided to companies through analysis of their own data, marketing research is still important for identifying consumers' needs. The constant reference to A/B testing in the approaches of Netflix and others indicates a limitation, because customers might want C, and if a company's product planners do not develop C as an option to be tested, a company will never know about the opportunity missed. In an age of co-creation, marketing research has a key role to play in finding the C.

As Wingate (2018) expresses it:

> Amazon's research approach is most clearly evident in its ability to move nimbly during times of adversity or challenge. Despite their massive success, Amazon hasn't avoided failures. Products like Amazon Destinations, Amazon Local and the Fire Phone stumbled quickly after launch. Amazon quickly augmented sales figures with customer feedback and further research to determine the issues and product/market fit. Ultimately, the results were not compelling and Amazon was able to mitigate further losses and scrap the products, shifting energy into higher ROI products and markets.

Conclusions

The chapter addresses the links between big data, organizational innovativeness and marketing, taking account of how changes in the value chain can transform customer value. It contributes to development of a conceptual framework using a case study that highlights the role of big data. This has many implications not just for marketing, sales and customer service staff but also for those who hire them, train them and manage their retention and progression (e.g. human resources, senior line management).

Big data use can be critical in improving decision-making (Davenport 2013; Delen and Demirkan 2013). The conceptual framework and case study show that transforming big data into value depends on organizations' understanding of big data and its characteristics and of how value is delivered through its use. The discussion highlights actions needed to minimize privacy risks. Overall, this chapter opens a new avenue for research to examine decision-making process in marketing innovation and how big data, associated analytics and marketing research support it and can generate new strategies.

Issues for further discussion

The central issue in this case study is the boundary between marketing research as conventionally described and the big data used by Netflix to optimize its operation. The higher the volumes of data accessible by Netflix, the less reliant it will be on conventional market research, but the more important it will be for Netflix to keep a focus on the traditional marketing research questions relating to usage – who views what and when – and attitudes – why do they do it?

Acknowledgements

This chapter is based partly on Wright, L.T., Robin, R., Stone, M. and Aravopoulou, E., 2019. Adoption of big data technology for innovation in B2B marketing. *Journal of Business-to-Business Marketing*, 26(3–4), 281–293.

References

Agarwal, R. and Prasad, J., 1998. The antecedents and consequents of user perceptions in information technology adoption. *Decision Support Systems*, 22(1), 15–29. https://doi.org/10.1016/S0167-9236(97)00006-7.

Akter, S., Wamba, S.F., Gunasekaran, A., Dubey, R. and Childe, S.J., 2016. How to improve firm performance using big data analytics capability and business strategy alignment? *International Journal of Production Economics*, 182, 113–131. http://dx.doi.org/10.1016/j.ijpe.2016.08.018.

Antons, D. and Breidbach, C., 2018. Big data, big insights? Advancing service innovation and design with machine learning. *Journal of Service Research*, 21(1), 17–39. https://doi.org/10.1177/1094670517738373.

Armstrong, M., 2018. Netflix is responsible for 15% of global Internet traffic. *Statista*, 9 October [online]. Available from: www.statista.com/chart/15692/distribution-of-global-downstream-traffic/ [Accessed 27 March 2020].

Barney, J., 1991. Firm resources and sustained competitive advantage. *Journal of Management*, 17(1), 99–120. https://doi.org/10.1177/014920639101700108.

Braganza, A., Brooks, L., Nepelski, D., Ali, M. and Moro, R., 2017. Resource management in big data initiatives: Processes and dynamic capabilities. *Journal of Business Research*, 70, 328–337. https://doi.org/10.1016/j.jbusres.2016.08.006.

Brodkin, J., 2016. Netflix finishes its massive migration to the Amazon cloud. *Ars Technica*, 2 November [online]. Available from: https://arstechnica.com/information-technology/2016/02/netflix-finishes-its-massive-migration-to-the-amazon-cloud/ [Accessed 27 March 2020].

Brown, S., Cron, P. and Slocum, J., 1998. Effects of trait competitiveness and perceived intraorganizational competition on salesperson goal setting and performance. *Journal of Marketing*, 62(40), 88–98. https://doi.org/10.1177/002224299806200407.

Bruce, G., 2019. *How Many Streaming Services Are Americans Willing to Pay For? In Digital & Technology Media Real Time Research: Retail & Consumer* [online]. Available from: https://today.yougov.com/topics/media/articles-reports/2019/10/30/how-many-streaming-services-are-americans-willing [Accessed 19 June 2020].

Bunduchi, R., Weisshaar, C. and Smart, A., 2011. Mapping the benefits and costs associated with process innovation: The case of RFID adoption. *Technovation*, 31(9), 505–521. https://doi.org/10.1016/j.technovation.2011.04.001.

Caridi-Zahavi, O., Carmeli, A. and Arazy, O., 2015. The influence of CEOs' visionary innovation leadership on the performance of high-technology ventures: The mediating roles of connectivity and knowledge integration. *Journal of Product Innovation Management*, 33(3), 356–376. https://doi.org/10.1111/jpim.12275.

Chai, S. and Shih, W., 2017. Why big data isn't enough. *MIT Sloan Management Review*, 58(2) 57–61.

Chandy, R., Hassan, M. and Mukherji, P., 2017. Big data for good: Insights from emerging markets. *Journal of Product Innovation Management*, 34(5), 703–713. https://doi.org/10.1111/jpim.12406.

Chen, Y., Tang, G., Jin, J., Xie, Q. and Li, J., 2014. CEOs' transformational leadership and product innovation performance: The roles of corporate entrepreneurship and technology orientation. *Journal of Product Innovation Management*, 31(1), 2–17. https://doi.org/10.1111/jpim.12188.

Court, D., Perrey, J., McGuire, T., Gordon, J. and Spillecke, D., 2015. *Marketing & Sales: Big Data, Analytics, and the Future of Marketing and Sales*. New York: McKinsey Global Institute [online]. Available from: www.mckinsey.com/~/media/McKinsey/Business%20Functions/Marketing%20and%20Sales/Our%20Insights/EBook%20Big%20data%20analytics%20and%20the%20future%20of%20marketing%20sales/Big-Data-eBook.ashx [Accessed 5 May 2019].

Davenport, T., 2006. Competing on analytics. *Harvard Business Review*, 84(1), 98–107.

Davenport, T., 2013. Analytics 3.0: In the new era, big data will power consumer products and services. *Harvard Business Review*, 91(12), 65–72.

Davenport, T., Barth, P. and Bean, R., 2012. How big data is different. *MIT Sloan Management Review*, 54(1), 43–46.

Davenport, T. and Harris, J., 2017. *Competing on Analytics: The New Science of Winning*. Boston, MA: Harvard Business Review Press.

Delen, D. and Demirkan, H., 2013. Data, information and analytics as services. *Decision Support Systems*, 55(1), 359–363. DOI: 10.1016/j.dss.2012.05.044.

Economides, N. and Jeziorski, P., 2017. Mobile money in Tanzania. *Marketing Science*, 36(6), 815–837. https://doi.org/10.1287/mksc.2017.1027.

Erevelles, S., Fukawa, N. and Swayne, L., 2016. Big data consumer analytics and the transformation of marketing. *Journal of Business Research*, 69(2), 897–904. http://dx.doi.org/10.1016/j.jbusres.2015.07.001.

Fagerjord, A. and Kueng, L., 2019. Mapping the core actors and flows in streaming video services: What Netflix can tell us about these new media networks. *Journal of Media Business Studies*, 16(3), 166–181. https://doi.org/10.1080/16522354.2019.1684717.

Fletcher, T., Major, D. and Davis, D., 2008. The interactive relationship of competitive climate and trait competitiveness with workplace attitudes, stress, and performance. *Journal of Organizational Behavior*, 29(7), 899–922. https://doi.org/10.1002/job.503.

Gallouj, F. and Weinstein, O., 1997. Innovation in services. *Research Policy*, 26(4), 537–556. https://doi.org/10.1016/S0048-7333(97)00030-9.

Gatignon, H. and Robertson, T., 1989. Technology diffusion: An empirical test of competitive effects. *Journal of Marketing*, 53(1), 35–49. https://doi.org/10.1177/002224298905300104.

George, G., Haas, M. and Pentland, A., 2014. Big data and management. *Academy of Management Journal*, 57(2), 321–326. https://doi.org/10.5465/amj.2014.4002.

George, G., Osinga, E., Lavie, D. and Scott, B., 2016. Big data and data science methods for management research. *Academy of Management Journal*, 59(5), 1493–1507. https://doi.org/10.5465/amj.2016.4005.

Gobble, M., 2013. Big data: The next big thing in innovation. *Research Technology Management*, 56(1), 64–66. https://doi.org/10.5437/08956308X5601005.

Hamel, G., 1998. Opinion: Strategy innovation and the quest for value. *Sloan Management Review*, 39(2), 7–14.

Hashem, I., Yaqoob, I., Anuar, N., Mokhtar, S., Gani, A. and Khan, S., 2015. The rise of "big data" on cloud computing: Review and open research issues. *Information Systems*, 47, 98–115. https://doi.org/10.1016/j.is.2014.07.006.

Hoff, T., 2017. *Netflix: What Happens When You Press Play?* [online]. Available from: http://highscalability.com/blog/2017/12/11/netflix-what-happens-when-you-press-play.html [Accessed 1 June 2020].

Hopkins, M., LaValle, S., Lesser, E., Shockley, R. and Kruschwitz, N., 2011. Big data, analytics and the path from insights to value. *Sloan Management Review*, 52(2), 21–32.

Huang, K., 2011. Technology competencies in competitive environment. *Journal of Business Research*, 64(2), 172–179. https://doi.org/10.1016/j.jbusres.2010.02.003.

Huang, M. and Rust, R., 2013. IT-related service: A multidisciplinary perspective. *Journal of Service Research*, 16(3), 251–258. https://doi.org/10.1177/1094670513481853.

Jin, X., Wah, B., Cheng, X. and Wang, Y., 2015. Significance and challenges of big data research. *Big Data Research*, 2(2), 59–64. http://dx.doi.org/10.1016/j.bdr.2015.01.006.

Johnson, J., Friend, S. and Lee, H., 2017. Big data facilitation, utilization, and monetization: Exploring the 3Vs in a new product development process. *Journal of Product Innovation Management*, 34(5), 640–658. https://doi.org/10.1111/jpim.12397.

Judge, W. and Miller, A., 1991. Antecedents and outcomes of decision speed in different environmental contexts. *The Academy of Management Journal*, 34(2), 449–463. DOI: 10.2307/256451.

Karatepe, O., Uludag, O., Menevis, I., Hadzimehmedagic, L. and Baddar, L., 2006. The effects of selected individual characteristics on frontline employee performance and job satisfaction. *Tourism Management*, 27(4), 547–560. DOI: 10.1016/j.tourman.2005.02.009.

Kauffman, R., Srivastava, J. and Vayghan, J., 2012. Business and data analytics: New innovations for the management of e-commerce. *Electronic Commerce Research and Applications*, 11(2), 85–88. DOI: 10.1016/j.elerap.2012.01.001.

Kiron, D., Prentice, P. and Ferguson, R., 2014. The analytics mandate. *MIT Sloan Management Review*, 55(4), 1–25.

Kohli, R. and Devaraj, S., 2003. Measuring information technology payoff: A meta-analysis of structural variables in firm-level empirical research. *Information Systems Research*, 14(2), 127–145. http://dx.doi.org/10.1287/isre.14.2.127.16019.

Lamberg, J., Tikkanen, H., Nokelainen, T. and Suur-Inkeroinen, H., 2009. Competitive dynamics, strategic consistency, and organizational survival. *Strategic Management Journal*, 30(1), 45–60. https://doi.org/10.1002/smj.726.

Lamkhede, S. and Das, S., 2019. *Challenges in Search on Streaming Services: Netflix Case Study*. SIGIR'19, 21–25 July. Paris, France [online]. Available from: https://arxiv.org/pdf/1903.04638.pdf [Accessed 28 March 2020].

Lau, R., Zhao, J., Chen, G. and Guo, X., 2016. Big data commerce. *Information and Management*, 53(8), 929–933. https://doi.org/10.1016/j.im.2016.07.008.

Lee, H., 2018. Big data and the innovation cycle. *Production and Operations Management*, 27(9), 1642–1646. https://doi.org/10.1111/poms.12845.

Lichtenthal, J. and Eliaz, S., 2003. Internet integration in business marketing tactics. *Industrial Marketing Management*, 32(1), 3–13. https://doi.org/10.1016/S0019-8501(01)00198-5.

Manyika, J., Chui, M., Brown, B., Bughin, J., Dobbs, R., Roxburgh, C. and Byers, A., 2011. *Big Data: The Next Frontier for Innovation, Competition, and Productivity*. New York: McKinsey Global Institute [online]. Available from: www.mckinsey.com/~/media/McKinsey/Business%20Functions/McKinsey%20Digital/Our%20Insights/Big%20data%20The%20next%20frontier%20for%20innovation/MGI_big_data_full_report.ashx [Accessed 5 June 2020].

Marr, B., 2015. *Big Data: Using Smart Big Data, Analytics and Metrics to Make Better Decisions and Improve Performance*. Chichester, England: Wiley.

Merikivi, J., Bragge, J., Scornavacca, E. and Verhagen, T., 2019. Binge-watching serialized video content: A transdisciplinary review. *Television & New Media*. https://doi.org/10.1177/1527476419848578.

Meyer, A. and Goes, J., 1988. Organizational assimilation of innovations: A multilevel contextual analysis. *Academy of Management Journal*, 31(4), 897–923. https://doi.org/10.5465/256344.

Michaelidou, N., Siamagka, N. and Christodoulides, G., 2011. Usage, barriers and measurement of social media marketing: An exploratory investigation of small and medium B2B brands. *Industrial Marketing Management*, 40(7), 1153–1159. DOI: 10.1016/j.indmarman.2011.09.009.

Miller, C., 2008. Decisional comprehensiveness and firm performance: Towards a more complete understanding. *Journal of Behavioral Decision Making*, 21(5), 598–620. https://doi.org/10.1002/bdm.607.

Mueller, G., Mone, M. and Barker, V., 2007. Formal strategic analyzes and organizational performance: Decomposing the rational model. *Organization Studies*, 28(6), 853–883. https://doi.org/10.1177/0170840607075262.

Müller, O., Junglas, I., Vom Brocke, J. and Debortoli, S., 2016. Utilizing big data analytics for information systems research: Challenges, promises and guidelines. *European Journal of Information Systems*, 25(4), 289–302. https://doi.org/10.1057/ejis.2016.2.

Netflix, 2020a. *What Is Netflix Research?* [online]. Available from: https://research.netflix.com/ [Accessed 28 March 2020].

Netflix, 2020b. *Netflix Culture* [online]. Available from: https://jobs.netflix.com/culture [Accessed 28 March 2020].

Pääkkönen, P. and Pakkala, D., 2015. Reference architecture and classification of technologies, products and services for big data systems. *Big Data Research*, 2(4), 166–186. https://doi.org/10.1016/j.bdr.2015.01.001.

Parnell, B., Stone, M. and Aravopoulou, E., 2018. How leaders manage their business models using information. *The Bottom Line*, 31(2), 150–167. DOI: 10.1108/BL-04-2018-0017.

Pisano, G., 1997. *The Development Factory: Unlocking the Potential of Process Innovation*. Boston, MA: Harvard Business Review Press.

Rayna, T. and Striukova, L., 2016. 360° business model innovation: Toward an integrated view of business model innovation. *Research Technology Management*, 59(3), 21–28. https://doi.org/10.1080/08956308.2016.1161401.

Rubera, G. and Kirca, A., 2012. Firm innovativeness and its performance outcomes: A meta-analytic review and theoretical integration. *Journal of Marketing*, 76(3), 130–147. https://doi.org/10.1509%2Fjm.10.0494.

Ruvio, A., Shoham, A., Vigoda-Gadot, E. and Schwabsky, N., 2014. Organizational innovativeness: Construct development and cross-cultural validation. *The Journal of Product Innovation Management*, 31(5), 1004–1022. https://doi.org/10.1111/jpim.12141.

Said, E., Macdonald, E., Wilson, H. and Marcos, J., 2015. How organisations generate and use customer insight. *Journal of Marketing Management*, 31(9–10), 1158–1179. https://doi.org/10.1080/0267257X.2015.1037785.

Schrock, W., Hughes, D., Fu, F., Richards, K. and Jones, E., 2016. Better together: Trait competitiveness and competitive psychological climate as antecedents of salesperson organizational commitment and sales performance. *Marketing Letters*, 27(2), 351–360. DOI: 10.1007/s11002-014-9329-7.

Siamagka, N., Christodoulides, G., Michaelidou, N. and Valvi, A., 2015. Determinants of social media adoption by B2B organizations. *Industrial Marketing Management*, 51, 89–99. https://doi.org/10.1016/j.indmarman.2015.05.005.

Sky TV, 2020. *Who Are Our Strategic Insights Team?* [online]. Available from: https://careers.sky.com/2019/07/31/who-are-our-strategic-insights-team/ [Accessed 19 March 2020].

Spangler, T., 2019. *Netflix Bandwidth Consumption Eclipsed by Web Media Streaming Applications*. 10 September [online]. Available from: https://variety.com/2019/digital/news/netflix-loses-title-top-down-stream-bandwidth-application-1203330313/ [Accessed 27 March 2020].

Stone, M., 1985. Strategies for marketing new computer products. *Long Range Planning*, 18(3), 41–54.

Stone, M., 2014. The new (and ever-evolving) direct & digital marketing ecosystem. *Journal of Direct, Data & Digital Marketing Practice*, 16(2), 71–74. DOI: 10.1057/dddmp.2014.58.

Stone, M., Aravopoulou, E., Gerardi, G., Todeva, E., Weinzierl, L., Laughlin, P. and Stott, R., 2017. How platforms are transforming customer information management. *The Bottom Line*, 30(3), 216–235. DOI: 10.1108/BL-08-2017-0024.

Stone, M. and Laughlin, P., 2016. How interactive marketing is changing in consumer financial services. *Journal of Research in Interactive Marketing*, 10(4), 338–356. https://doi.org/10.1108/JRIM-01-2016-0001.

Stone, M. and Macarthur, H., 1984. *How to Market Computers and Office Systems*. Basingstoke, England: Macmillan.

Stone, M., Aravopoulou, E., Ekinci, Y., Evans, G., Hobbs, M., Labib, A., Laughlin, P., Machtynger, J. and Machtynger, L., 2020. Artificial intelligence (AI) in strategic marketing decision-making: A research agenda. *The Bottom Line*, 33(2), 183–200. https://doi.org/10.1108/BL-03-2020-0022.

Stott, R., Stone, M. and Fae, J., 2016. Business models in the business to business and business to consumer worlds – what can each world learn from the other. *Journal of Business and Industrial Marketing*, 31(8), 943–954. DOI: 10.1108/JBIM-10-2016-267.

Terziovski, M., 2010. Innovation practice and its performance implications in small and medium enterprises (SMEs) in the manufacturing sector: A resource-based view. *Strategic Management Journal*, 31(8), 892–902. https://doi.org/10.1002/smj.841.

Thomas, D., 2019. Expectations now sky-high as research tools evolve. *Insight Economy, Sunday Times* [online]. Available from: www.raconteur.net/business-innovation/research-tools' [Accessed 19 March 2020].

Troilo, G., De Luca, L. and Guenzi, P., 2017. Linking data-rich environments with service innovation in incumbent firms: A conceptual framework and research propositions. *Journal of Product Innovation Management*, 34(5), 617–639. https://doi.org/10.1111/jpim.12395.

Utterbuck, J., 1994. *Mastering the Dynamics of Innovation: How Companies Can Seize Opportunities in the Face of Technological Change*. Boston, MA: Harvard Business Review Press.

Vanderbilt, T., 2013. *The Science Behind the Netflix Algorithms That Decide What You'll Watch Next* [online]. Available from: www.wired.com/2013/08/qq_netflix-algorithm/ [Accessed 3 June 2020].

Wamba, F., 2017. Big data analytics and business process innovation. *Business Process Management Journal*, 23(3), 470–476. https://doi.org/10.1108/BPMJ-02-2017-0046.

Wamba, F., Gunasekaran, A., Akter, S., Ren, S., Dubey, R. and Childe, S., 2017. Big data analytics and firm performance: Effects of dynamic capabilities. *Journal of Business Research*, 70, 356–365. https://doi.org/10.1016/j.jbusres.2016.08.009.

Wang, Y. and Hajli, N., 2017. Exploring the path to big data analytics success in healthcare. *Journal of Business Research*, 70, 287–299. DOI: 10.1016/j.jbusres.2016.08.002.

Wingate, M., 2018. How Amazon drives growth through agile market research. *Insights Association* [online]. Available from: www.insightsassociation.org/article/how-amazon-drives-growth-through-agile-market-research [Accessed 20 March 2020].

Wright, L.T., Robin, R., Stone, M. and Aravopoulou, E., 2019. Adoption of big data technology for innovation in B2B marketing. *Journal of Business-to-Business Marketing*, 26(3–4), 281–293. https://doi.org/10.1080/1051712X.2019.1611082.

Zaltman, G., Duncan, R. and Holbek, J., 1973. *Innovations and Organizations*. New York: Wiley & Sons.

Zhan, Y., Tan, K., Ji, G., Chung, L. and Tseng, M., 2017. A big data framework for facilitating product innovation processes. *Business Process Management Journal*, 23(3), 518–536. https://doi.org/10.1108/BPMJ-11-2015-0157.

3

INTERACTIVE MARKETING, CUSTOMER INFORMATION AND MARKETING RESEARCH

Merlin Stone, Eleni Aravopoulou, Neil Woodcock, Paul Laughlin and Ryan Stott

Summary

In this chapter, we explore the impact of the arrival of modern interactive marketing on customer information and marketing research. This chapter explores how the ways in which companies gather and use information about customers has changed radically, sometimes because of their adoption of radically different business models. It considers the impact of developments in customer relationship management on how marketing strategies are developed and implemented, including its impact on different elements of the marketing mix. It investigates how digital approaches have stimulated further significant developments, in particular the rise of platforms which allow companies to manage their information and their interactions with clients very differently from in the past. It explores the rise and development of the customer insight function to manage these developments. It also considers the impact of these developments on the development of business intelligence. The impact on marketing research is investigated, in particular its new roles as custodian of in-depth qualitative information on customers on the one hand, to being experts in the interpretation of social media data on the other hand.

The advent of interactive marketing

Most corporations must now 'market in a digital world'. The 'always on' consumer (and business consumer too) is able, and increasingly likely, to search, enquire, interact, complain, buy and pay through mobile devices. Marketing for most corporations is becoming increasingly interactive and 'always on'. Delivering an efficient (for the customer and the company), relevant (personalised) and engaging experience increasingly relies on a deep knowledge of the consumers: who they are, the devices they use to connect to the company and the content they want to see.

'Always on' marketing differs from 'campaign' marketing, which was the traditional way of managing marketing, involving particular initiatives over a defined period, with a defined objective. A campaign would end, its results would be analysed and conclusions drawn for the next campaign. For 'always on' marketing, the company must develop its people, processes and system capabilities to interact more dynamically with the consumer in all channels – hence the use of the term 'omnichannel', referring to channels customers want to use, rather than 'multichannel', referring to channels suppliers want to use.

Modern interactive marketing demands from companies:

- Deeper understanding of customers and their behaviour and how they prefer to interact with these companies.
- Greater ability on the part of companies to deliver personalised experiences which customers find useful and engaging.

The internet now hosts a rapidly growing proportion of human dialogue in ways that are open to viewing and influencing by companies. This, combined with the growing reach and capacity of mobile telephone networks and the dramatic rise of social media, means that great changes that have taken place in the volumes, frequency and effectiveness of use of the different media by which companies and customers exchange communication. There has also been rapid change in the devices and software used by consumers to exchange communications with companies and individuals and to organise and enjoy their lives. This interactivity is not only in marketing, sales and service. The 'social business', deeply connected with its staff and suppliers, knows how to harness its collective knowledge, enabling information once locked into one channel or department to be shared across a company. Logistics and operations flow through a company have become trackable, constantly, in every process. Non-interactivity and non-trackability are becoming the exception rather than the rule.

How the management of customer information and marketing research has changed

The trends discussed previously have led to many changes in how marketing and the management of customer information and marketing research take place. Interactive marketing is no longer – if it ever was – just a change in how marketing communication takes place. Every aspect of marketing is affected, whether in terms of how customers are affected directly or in terms of how marketing people work with each other; the rest of their company; or distributors, suppliers and other partners. Table 3.1 summarises some of the main changes. Each change leads to new flows of information that need to be managed properly in order to deliver the benefits specified in the table.

Marketing in the value chain

Some companies find that their ability to make the best use of digital and interactive marketing is hampered by the relationship between marketing and the rest of the corporation. We believe that this problem is related to the way the role of marketing has been portrayed in the strategic literature, particularly the value chain literature. Porter's (1985) value chain idea was developed with reference to competitiveness. Marketing and sales were the fourth and service the fifth and final of the primary activities (after inbound logistics, operations and outbound logistics). These were supported by firm infrastructure, human resource management, technology development and procurement. The concept was both helpful and damaging to marketing, sales and service. It helped by focusing managers on the contributions made by the different activities to profit. It damaged by seeming to relegate sales, marketing and service to the status of 'downstream activities', undertaken *after* goods or services were produced. The model did not

Table 3.1 How marketing has changed

Marketing area	Examples of how interactivity affects each area
Marketing mix	
Branding	The locus of many companies' brands has shifted from the real to the virtual world, while the brands of many others are strongly affected by what is said about them in the virtual world.
Product	Customer input into product design (collaborative design) can be obtained much more quickly. Customers can design their own products more easily. Designs can be tested and revised more quickly, while problems can be identified and rectified more quickly and easily.
Price	Prices can be tailored more easily to different customers. Yield management can be applied in many new areas.
Advertising	Website/mobile advertising is gradually usurping advertising in conventional media, allowing greater trackability and better assessment of return on investment. This is leading to a blurring of the distinction between advertising and other marketing communications methods.
Direct marketing	Direct marketing has expanded out of the conventional media of mail and telephone to include virtually all marketing communications
Personal selling	Personal selling now has much stronger information support, while improved sales management systems, sometimes integrated with response management systems, allow much more effective targeting and management of customers and prospects.
Public relations	Electronic word of mouth, or 'word of mouse', is replacing conventional media exposure not solely through social networks but through all aspects of web and mobile dialogue. In some sectors, online reviews have become absolutely critical in determining whether a product will sell.
Sales promotion	The effectiveness of sales promotions can be gauged much more quickly, while online channels facilitate distribution of coupons and other incentives.
Distribution	The web has become a very important channel of distribution for many information-based products and services, as well as some physical products.
Marketing management	
People	Marketing, sales and service people can be much better informed about what they need to know to sell and market better, and results of their work can be obtained and distributed more easily.
Processes, data and systems	Marketing processes can be migrated onto systems, sometimes running on the 'cloud', enhancing the effectiveness and speed of processes. Systems allow much better access to data required for decision-making on everything from individual customers to strategic decisions and then for measurement, review and calculation of return on investment.
Marketing research	Data on what customers have done and what they are now doing is available directly from digital interactions, so the role of marketing research has moved away from the provision of such data – though there are areas where digital data is available less freely, for example, decisions in favour of competitive products. It now focuses much more on trying to understand the reasons for such behaviour using qualitative research disciplines but also on understanding behaviour in new areas, such as social media. In general, the psychological disciplines of marketing researchers have become more valuable. Meanwhile, where it is required, classic marketing research is increasingly carried out online, while customer-initiated feedback is providing a new source of information on how customers think, feel and act.

Source: The authors

cover the importance of marketing in organising the whole corporation's activities to service customer needs.

Porter's book was written nearly 30 years before this chapter. Then, the information needed to organise the whole corporation, as suggested, was simply not available at the right time in the right depth and quality. Then, it might have been necessary to carry out value chain activities in the piecemeal, sequential way that Porter suggested. Today, information systems allow data from all stages of the supply chain to support critical processes for managing the corporation's partners, suppliers and customers. For example, customers can find out where their orders are in the supply chain. This opens new areas for marketing research, for example, covering customer's perceptions of and attitudes towards how they are served by these information systems.

A key question raised by Porter (1985) was, 'What makes for competitive advantage, in the way the whole corporation works?' Today, we might ask 'What is it about a corporation's DNA that makes it competitively successful?' The answer to these questions relates not to a corporation's strategies or policies but to its capabilities and how it deploys them. However, many companies have not even developed one of the most basic capabilities required for interactive marketing: the single customer view (Stone *et al.* 2019).

Business intelligence – the engine room of interactive marketing

Today, marketing is recovering from relegation to downstream status to becoming a key integrator of information to ensure that a company stays competitive. Behind this lies the corporation's business intelligence (BI), a combination of technologies, architectures, people, processes and methodologies that transform raw data into useful business information (Stone and Woodcock 2014). In marketing, the main BI technologies used are reporting, online analytical processing, analytics (past and predictive), data and text mining.

At the heart of successful (interactive) marketing lies a clear view about what BI is needed for marketing to work and how this BI must be created and rapidly deployed to create the insight that marketers need now and will need in the future. A corporation's ability to determine its BI needs and then implement the required BI is an essential part of the maturing of BI management and of marketing. Just as corporations take time to absorb and deploy the best marketing techniques, so they take time to learn how to develop and use BI.

Key aspects of the maturing of marketing are

- The development of a strong data culture (commitment to ensuring that the right BI is available to support decisions and actions);
- The evolution of the relationship between BI people, traditionally located in the IT department but increasingly embedded in commercial decision-making units, and users in marketing, sales and service;
- The emergence of the topic of governance in the development and use of BI.

The latter has become particularly important as increasingly sophisticated data extraction and analysis tools become available. Despite the complexity of their internal workings, they are much easier to use than earlier software, giving rise to 'self-service BI', allowing managers at all levels, from planning through to operational decision-makers to access and analyse data whenever and wherever they need.

Strategic implications

Interactive marketing is strongly linked to, and one output of, an effective business intelligence operation. The areas where a coherent approach to business intelligence management can produce business results include:

*   Customer management (optimising recruitment, retention, development and efficiency strategies);
*   Channels; communications and sales (e.g. digital, web, social, mobile, near real-time customer relationship management [CRM], catalogue, internal sales and contact centre, field sales);
*   Promotions (promoting the right products to the right customers in the most cost-effective way to produce the best results);
*   Product management (optimising product mix, bundles, own/brand and management);
*   Pricing (setting the right prices to make the most revenue/profits and satisfy customers);
*   Purchasing (acquiring the right products for customers and markets);
*   Logistics/supply chain/payment/finance (the flow through the business and delivery to customer);
*   Process (how efficiently, transparently and speedily things are being managed, speed to market);
*   Colleagues (how well people are performing, where improvement is most required);

These cover all areas of the Porter value chain model, not just marketing.

The evolution of customer information – from mail order, through call and contact centres, to the Web

The practice of gathering, holding, analysing and using customer data – their personal details, locations, interactions with media, enquiries, transactions, questionnaire responses and so on, began in the nineteenth century in the mail-order industry. This developed into database marketing (Stone and Shaw 1987). The data was first used to support interactions between customers and companies by post, then by telephone – eventually via large call centres capable of managing conversations with hundreds or even thousands of customers at a time. The rising use of e-mail and the Web (including Web chat) encouraged the transformation of call centres into contact centres, as they began handling several kinds of electronic communications in different digital channels. Along with recording of interactions (including voice files, analysed by voice-to-text software, and website clickstreams), this led to an explosion in customer data volumes.

The CRM approach, especially in electronic form, has revolutionised how many companies market, allowing them to establish an increasingly automated and/or customer-driven dialogue with possibly millions of customers based on customer information management (Stone and Woodcock 2014). Digital data greatly increases the volume of customer data held (Stone and Woodcock 2014), but generally, customers who engage digitally buy more (Sorenson and Adkins 2014), so this has acted as an important incentive for companies to move their dialogue with customers to digital channels. An overview of the information collected and its use has been provided by Stone and Laughlin (2016).

CRM information is used for many purposes, from supporting marketing or business strategy to managing operations and marketing, sales and service processes. It may be integrated with supply chain data (e.g. to identify customers awaiting deliveries) or with financial data (e.g. to identify debtor or other 'bad' customers) (Stone and Laughlin 2016).

Social media can also be used as information platforms (Stone and Woodcock 2013), to manage knowledge from customers or on behalf of customers (Chua and Banerjee 2013; Padula 2008; Sigala 2012). Social media allow real-time sentiment and analysis and the immediate identification of new target customers, while social data is sometimes combined with geospatial weather data or other sources to build a more complete picture of the customer's context (IDC 2016a; Capgemini 2015). However, social media data requires specialist interpretation in some cases, and this has provided a new role for the marketing research industry, particularly in the area of social listening (Tuten and Perotti 2019).

Turning data into insight

Another very important change has been the development of new approaches to turning data into actionable information, commonly referred to as 'customer insight'. This involves using advanced analytics approaches to find correlations in data about customers, their responses and their purchases. These approaches are based on classic (e.g. regression, analysis of variance, cluster analysis) and modern (e.g. neural networks) statistical techniques. Today, software for implementing these techniques usually incorporates visualisation to help busy managers understand their customers. A new category of managers – insight managers – has emerged, along with new categories of software/services (e.g. specialised analytics agencies). Users of customer and market data and analytics may be organised into departments called 'consumer insight' or 'customer intelligence', replacing the older 'market intelligence' or 'marketing information', reflecting the move away from less targeted forms of marketing. Companies are still learning how to manage these volumes of data (WBR Digital 2017) and what to do with so much data, whether owned or non-owned (such as data arising from social media), structured or unstructured (e.g. voice, text, video) (Stone and Woodcock 2014).

An important requirement for creating customer insight is to bring all the data together (Stone *et al.* 2017). This requires:

- Integrating data from many source systems (including transaction processing systems), possibly into a data warehouse (which holds data about current and past transactions);
- Creation of data models to support that integration;
- Creation and application of metadata definitions (e.g. how an 'active customer' is defined using different variables);
- Analysis from straightforward statements on the state of customers, to analysis based on hypotheses about the state of play, to data mining to explore possible interrelationships in the data (Badgett and Stone 2005);
- Providing resulting data and analyses to whomever needs it, wherever they are, by reports or individual data transfers (e.g. data about an individual customer during a transaction), on whatever platform or device users need.

As the idea of the Internet of Things (attaching intelligent devices to objects to enable them to communicate with and receive instructions via the Internet) spreads, many resultant data streams will be associated with individual customers. The same applies in industrial markets, where data streams on customers' usage of products and any variations in performance or quality problems are often transmitted instantly to suppliers, allowing them to help their customers optimise product performance. Another trend that leads to the generation of more data is the move to sell products (hardware, software) as services, when the supplier can constantly monitor the use of the product by the customer (Stone, Cerasale, Adams *et al.* 2003; Stone, Cerasale, Foss *et al.* 2003).

Digitalisation

The previous trends form part of a wider trend, digitalisation – the process by which a business and its people, partners, ecosystems and enabling agencies (in some cases public ones) become interconnected in real time by exchanging digital information and how they use this to commercial benefit (Laudon and Laudon 2020).

Digitalisation is being boosted by six factors:

- Hyper-connectivity – the ability to connect digitally at high speeds, from locally to globally, using everything from highly local communications such as Bluetooth and near field communication to satellite communication and enhanced internet bandwidth through improved transmission and compression technology;
- Virtually unlimited computing power, whether processing or memory, available at low cost;
- Artificial intelligence and machine learning, allowing much smarter management of anything by ensuring that learning takes place quickly and results are immediately implemented;
- Cloud computing, ensuring secure availability of information anywhere for any approved use;
- Sensor proliferation, allowing large amounts of information to be gathered from any point;
- Cybersecurity and advances in security which permit all the previous without prejudicing data security.

One idea of digitalisation is that, where possible and financially justified, a business should integrate all its core processes, systems and data onto a single platform. This makes them easy to manage, particularly as the business grows and serves more customers (without adding complexity). This approach helps provide information (from basics to advanced analytics and machine learning) on customers, products, services, payments, finances and assets to all appropriate business stakeholders – customers, staff, suppliers, business partners and so on. The benefits of digitalisation include improvements in output, sales, customer experience and involvement, staff experience and empowerment and quality and efficiency. This should lead to simplification and streamlining of everything from individual processes to entire work programmes and development of more robust and competitive business models.

Digitalisation is supported by the following information technology strategies:

- Securely connecting all parts of the business – systems, data and tools – by integrating functional systems – human resources, financial, marketing, sales, operations, logistics and so on – into a single system and extending them to partners in the ecosystem, whether on platforms or social media;
- Using the Internet of Things approach by connecting devices to the Internet, including using sensors and mobile devices to provide new and continuous streams of information and new ways of accessing them;
- Providing complete and mobile accessibility to systems and data, ensuring that all employees (and, where appropriate, ecosystem partners and customers or platform users) have the

appropriate and, where needed, mobile access they need to achieve their objectives well and productively;

- Moving to the cloud, ensuring that systems, data and analyses are accessible quickly, flexibly and securely;
- Turning all a business's data, from many sources and analyses, into insight which is real-time, accurate, predictive and easy to understand using smart displays and dashboards, giving the right information to the right people or automated systems, anywhere and everywhere needed and making it easier to identify patterns and trends;
- Converting real-time insight into automated action by connecting insight with systems that trigger actions.

The evolution of the digital marketing ecosystem

Increasingly, to manage the growing volume of data, firms turn to an ecosystem of suppliers, including suppliers of:

- Software to hold the data and make it available or to analyse it;
- Additional data to enhance the value of data the company already holds;
- Data storage and data analysis;
- Customer interaction software and services, who use the data on behalf of the company to manage interactions with customers (e.g. outsourced contact centres, marketing agencies).

Ecosystem evolution allows suppliers to understand and reach their target markets faster, more accurately and more cost effectively, facilitating customer retention and development while paradoxically also making it easier for new entrants to attack incumbents' customers and for bad customers to commit fraud (Stone and Laughlin 2016). An easier digital customer experience tends to lead to customers being more willing to give data (My Customer 2017), so there are additional benefits to using systems which have focused on optimising the customer interface digitally. The evolution of the digital marketing ecosystem (Stone 2014) is complicated by its convergence with the information and communications technology (ICT) ecosystem, itself evolving rapidly. For example, recent developments in the marketing ecosystem include application of artificial intelligence to what would already have been considered advanced software for automating campaign management or for personalising campaign communications to the needs and characteristics of customers.

In marketing, ecosystems have less coherence than in ICT, where ecosystems are defined mainly by groupings of suppliers around the main software or platform providers. At the centre of ICT ecosystems lie software designs, standards and application programming interfaces that allow independent developers to interlock with the leader's software, as well as marketing and service partnerships or (in the case of platforms) the provision of services that allow companies to shift their applications onto a platform easily and cost effectively. The ecosystem leader focuses on building, managing and servicing the ecosystem and defending it from competitive invasion.

The ICT ecosystem continues to evolve due to:

- Rapid development and unconstrained competition and innovation in technology (computing, telecoms – the latter stimulated by privatisation and liberalisation), from components through to final products;

- The rapid development of global ecosystems, helped by open systems and publication of application programming interfaces by the main players, allowing all kinds of suppliers to add value and compete;
- Increasing independence of geography, so anything can be done anywhere (from storage and processing in the cloud to transaction and communicating wherever the individual is).

Intrinsic to the ecosystem idea are co-evolution, co-opetition and value co-creation (Adner 2006; Adner and Kapoor 2010; Mann *et al.* 2012; Brandenburger and Nalebuff 1997; Fjelstad *et al.* 2012; Iansiti and Levien 2004; Kapoor and Lee 2013; Selander *et al.* 2010; Selander *et al.* 2013; Teece 2007) and an 'explosion of alliances' (Dyer and Singh 1998, p. 661). Participation in ecosystems is a necessity (Selander *et al.* 2013). Firms may create digital business ecosystems to achieve competitive advantage (Perry *et al.* 2012; Sarasvathy 2001).

To match this 'external' ecosystem, an 'internal ecosystem' develops in larger companies, merging capabilities of different departments, some of which used to work separately (Stone 2014). People in this internal ecosystem must be kept updated and working with their company's external ecosystem, through training, internal communication, good management and ensuring that senior managers are fully aware of the external and internal ecosystems, how they work and how they are evolving. The part of the external ecosystem with which a given firm connects may be evolving so fast that its people must keep up to date with developments in it, preventing them from looking inwards to colleagues in their internal ecosystem. This good connection with the external ecosystem may ensure that their employer gets the best performance but can lead to poorly integrated performance and conflict. However, the burden of managing the ecosystem can be shifted from a client company to a supplier which takes on the role of ecosystem manager by providing a platform.

The fact that the proposition that a customer buys is often the product of such complex ecosystems provides new opportunities for marketing researchers. Participants in the ecosystem may want to discover their impact on final customers and the extent to which the satisfaction of these customers depends on how well the participants perform. Even awareness that the participant is involved at all may be a subject for research.

The future – the rise of customer information platforms

Recognition that customer information needs to be used more widely, within a complex ecosystem, leads to the development of platforms for managing data (Stone *et al.* 2017). The reasons for this include:

- The need for the company to use the latest, most advanced techniques and capabilities for holding, managing and analysing data and making it available across the company and perhaps to its partners;
- The fact that the company is working with a large business partner that has a much better capability than the company's for gathering, holding, managing and analysing data;
- The company may have changed its business model (Stott *et al.* 2016; Parnell *et al.* 2017) or acquired a business with a different model and adapted it for its own use, with the new model requiring a higher volume or improved use of customer information;
- A commitment or even legal requirement by the company to make some or all of its customer and/or other data available to customers and others, combined with the recognition that the company's own data storage and management capability are not suitable for this (e.g. not enough capacity or security).

In some cases, information may be hosted entirely by platform providers, but a given company's data may also be partly resident on within-company/organisation and shared databases (shared with business partners and in some cases competitors or through open data initiatives, particularly in the public sector). This 'hybrid' approach is not uncommon.

The term 'platform' has many uses in business and information technology (de Reuver *et al.* 2018). In information technology, a platform was originally just the environment (hardware, operating system, web browser or other software) in which program code was executed. The term was then extended to applications (e.g. spreadsheet, accounting), combinations of applications (e.g. office suites), cloud computing or software as a service (allowing users to build software and applications from components not hosted by their own company) and so on. Some platforms require software using them to be adapted to the platform, while others allow an open approach.

Platform concepts are effectively a subset of a much wider topic – co-operation between firms in innovation, which Li and Nguyen (2016) have summarised well. Concepts used to analyse this area include classic competition and innovation theory, dual creation of value, knowledge sharing and management, game theory, spill-overs, transaction costs of collaboration (which we could interpret here as relating to the costs of setting up platforms which other companies can engage with), co-creation, user-innovation and many others. Platforms are therefore a fertile field for investigation of these concepts, as well as being the latest step in the move from products to solutions for many firms (Stone, Cerasale, Adams *et al.* 2003; Stone, Cerasale, Foss *et al.* 2003).

Once a platform is established, value creation can come as much from other companies who use the platform (e.g. content creators) (Aksulu and Wade 2010) as from the company that originated the platform, including for the customers of the platform creator. This can lead to developers inverting the firm (Parker *et al.* 2016), so that firms will choose to innovate using open external resources instead of closed internal ones. In this situation, firms will need to manage external value creation as carefully as they manage internal value creation.

How platforms develop and survive

Platforms can be defined as building blocks that an ecosystem can use to develop complementary technologies, services or products or as components shared between products (Gawer 2009; Boudreau 2010). A platform's components are produced by several firms' efforts or the industry ecosystem. Platforms can be real and/or organisational as well as digital (e.g. business franchises, postal systems, shopping centres and airports). There are degrees of alterability in platforms. Some are open to any user to adopt and adapt, others partially so. A central benefit of platforms is risk reduction, particularly for smaller firms, where risk is a barrier to innovation (Molinillo and Japutra 2017).

To maintain a platform's advantage, third-party developers must be encouraged to develop products that use it. If developers do not provide applications that customers need, another platform may take over, so the platform owner may encourage certain developers to move forward, take them over or develop an in-house capability. A successful platform, such as Amazon's, has big economies of scale and may dominate a whole market, making it hard for other players to compete.

Given the strategic importance of platforms, it is worth considering whether firms strategise to create platforms. Some platforms emerge as a by-product of some other business strategy, and if the strategy is successful, the firm realises that it has created a platform and starts to manage it as a platform. However, as knowledge about the success of platform strategies becomes more widely diffused in industry, firms may create platforms explicitly or at least move quickly from a product or service strategy to a platform strategy.

The rise of platforms is being driven by several transformative digital technologies. Bonchek and Choudary (2013) single out cloud computing, social media and mobile telephony. The cloud enables a global infrastructure for production, so anyone can create content and applications for a global audience. Social networks connect people globally and maintain their identity online. Mobile technology allows connection to this global infrastructure anytime, anywhere. To this we would add 'big data' – the ability to collect, store and use massive volumes of data, some of which arises from increased use of mobile technology and social media. In addition, rapid progress in analytics and artificial intelligence have greatly increased our ability to analyse these much greater data volumes. Meanwhile, progress in communication technology has increased our ability to transmit and receive high volumes of data. The result is a globally accessible network of businesses, workers, consumers and public and third-sector bodies, creating enterprises, contributing content, buying and providing goods and services and improving openness and quality.

Case studies: platforms and clouds

The platform approach to strategy has been facilitated by the arrival of cloud computing, which involves internet delivery of hosted services, so companies can use computing resources rather than their own. This allows companies to manage fluctuating workloads, paying as they use, and move workloads to and from the cloud, according to resource requirements and availability. Cloud computing can be private (user's own), public (third party) or hybrid (a combination). It can be provided as an infrastructure (effectively basic services), platform (where development takes place on the cloud) or software (the cloud hosts software applications). Some firms have moved to buying platform as a service through buying software as a service. A special case of the latter is where advanced analytical software, including artificial intelligence and machine learning, is hosted. Because of perceived security risks of shared use, cloud providers offer very high levels of security, sometimes better than that of a client's own systems.

Platforms can offer shared capabilities or facilities, shared information or both. Examples of digital platforms that exchange data (often customer data) include bank or credit card clearing or accepting systems, travel reservation services, online gaming/gambling and aggregators (e.g. in insurance and travel). When firms collaborate to create information platforms, critical elements for success include economies of scale, knowledge sharing, market size and volatility, strategic partner selection, intellectual property rights, spill-over effects, collaboration costs, trust and commitment, opportunism and overall collaboration strategy (Li and Nguyen 2016). An additional benefit of using a platform can be that legal issues of data sharing and portability (a customer's right to ask for their data to be moved from one company to another when they switch suppliers) and compliance with data protection regulation may be managed by the platform owner. A successful information platform usually requires the platform provider to capture one or more sets of information that are exclusive or nearly so.

On platforms, information is increasingly subject to advanced analysis, using the latest software to identify patterns of segmentation, to forecast and to produce visualisations. In its most recent forms, this includes the deployment of artificial intelligence. This has led to growing demands from large organisations, as they hear of the apparent successes in deploying artificial intelligence on data held by big platform companies, to use the high volumes of data in more productive and faster ways, for example, to provide a more comprehensive and higher-quality context to transactions or to provide suggestions as to how to manage interactions to maximise the opportunity presented by the customer contact.

The combination of cloud, platform and information is proving a very powerful way for firms to redefine their businesses and to enter new businesses. IDC (2016c) predicts that creating industry clouds will become a leading market entry strategy for both IT providers and industrial firms. Industry clouds are defined as cloud-based services that provide broad industry value by aggregating cost reduction, operational benefits, risk mitigation and/or insight creation via pooled information.

The two types of industry clouds are:

- Where a company provides cloud-based services to other companies in their industry (i.e. hospitals providing services to other hospitals);
- A cloud-based platform through which companies in an industry collaborate towards a common goal, such as improving industry insight and/or capability, as shown in the following insurance examples.

Industry clouds are also often sold as a turnkey, multi-tenant, pre-integrated offerings, featuring application programming interfaces (APIs) and a standard user interface that may be customisable, with subscription or usage-based pricing and metering.

Many companies have used cloud computing to create a competitive platform through improved use of customer information. IDC (2016b) tracks the creation of these services. Business-to-business markets also have many such examples, which may share customer information or provide ways to facilitate transactions or check status and performance in the supply chain, check legal compliance, benchmark and manage shared operations or shared problems (e.g. product recalls). Here are two examples from IDC's report:

- In the medical area, Optum One in the United States has a cloud database that contains claims, clinical and demographic data, used for retrospective and prospective analysis of population risk, including care management workflow capabilities to enable risk-based care management. The aim is to support decision-making in care by identifying high-risk patients and gaps in care early and thereby reduce costs and complications for patients. Optum's clients upload their own data, and the platform offers individual analytics as well as community benchmarks;
- In financial services, Pindrop's patented phone-printing technology analyses 147 characteristics of the audio signal for the most precise, accurate analysis of calls available. It can determine true caller location and device type, Caller ID (identity) spoofing, voice distortion and gateway hijacking. Pindrop holds the world's largest database of phone number and automatic number identification (ANI) reputations. Gathered from a consortium of customer attack data, honeypots (numbers specifically designed to attract calls from 'bad' customers) and more, this data includes a number's past fraud attempts, complaints and risk factors. Pindrop solutions analyse voice biometrics to create unique voice prints. Pindrop compares characteristics of a speaker's voice against a database of known attackers to blacklist or whitelist repeat callers. Their product detects more than 80% of fraudulent calls and prevents more than 96% of potential fraud losses.

How marketers collect and consume data has evolved into obtaining digital data from various internal or external sources (IDC 2016a). For example, Unilever developed a People Data Program, collecting data from traditional CRM, social media, contact with customer service and other marketing- or research-related customer data. Twitter is used to produce real-time customer insights to measure the performance of new product launches and the effectiveness of advertising and uncover product or service issues long before customers call in to report them, improving the return on marketing and advertising spend while reducing customer service costs, with all data and analysis being on one platform, ensuring high-quality insights, quicker response and lower costs (Capgemini 2015). A standardised repository has been created based on the most common questions, allowing employees to query the data directly.

Sky TV is an excellent example of the implications for marketing research of the exploding volume of data. It created a customer insight function, which provides data and research to the whole business. Marketing researchers are integrated into data teams, providing information on issues ranging from why customers cancel or change their subscriptions, to problems with home moving, to problems with getting reception. This data is provided to many different parts of the organisation, from customer service and product planning to finance and sales. All these functions want to know not just what is happening or forecast to happen but also why. Finding out why is the main role of the marketing research specialists.

The high volume of customer data and many data collection points make it hard to control and manage customer data effectively, let alone draw coherent insights which can be used to inform strategic customer decision-making (My Customer 2017). Platforms allow multiple sources of data to be imported, tagged, sorted, coded and deployed. Generally, the storage of the customer data is more efficient and secure, but it can also be shared more easily with other companies who are also clients of the same platform company, within the constraints of data protection.

The sharing of customer data, as we have seen, can lead to problems of compliance with data protection requirements. It can also lead to confusion about ownership of the data, which may have been gathered by or for several companies, often using automated processes which not only gather and concentrate the data but also determine which data is worth keeping. This area is being explored in the context of new data protection laws (Actiance 2017) but is likely to become more rather than less problematic.

Customer information platforms often derive their strength from their relative openness to other users of the platform who use it to promote their products (as with Amazon's selling platform or Google's advertising platform). Any seller who wishes to use these platforms must pay the price, but there are many ways to explore the value of the platform information, including using the platform as a consumer to see what results are returned.

If a weakness is detected (in terms, for example, of poor sales results), a firm can try to make its use of the platform more effective or set up a different platform, perhaps using information from the first platform (as do the many sites which extract results from these main platforms). This competition is not just in the form of an alternative customer information platform but may also be an alternative sales platform. For example, Citymapper combines Transport for London's (TfL) real-time data on bus journeys with its own data on journey enquiries (attracted by Citymapper's use of the TfL data) to establish its own bus service. In the airline industry, the openness of data about flights, arrivals, departures and airport usage from various sources, including global distribution systems (like Sabre) and the International Air Transport Association (IATA), gives low-cost airlines a strong basis to plan and set up their own more closed individual platforms.

Conclusions

The rise of digital information management has changed forever how companies learn about and manage their business environment and continues to change rapidly. However, the rise of the digital ecosystem means that companies can cope with this reality without too much difficulty, as new suppliers, software and services are continuously emerging to help them, while cloud computing and information platforms are making it much easier for them to access and manage data. The role of marketing researchers is changing as a result. The deep social and psychological disciplines of marketing research are still much in demand, as they cannot base their strategies just on what customers are doing today. The 'test and learn' discipline of direct and digital marketing is great if a company wants to find out what works today but cannot be the sole basis for longer-term decision-making. Marketing researchers still have a key role to play in helping companies make these decisions. Whether they will still be or should be called marketing researchers is another matter (Nunan 2017). Traditional fieldwork will certainly be a much smaller part of the role of researchers, so expertise in survey design and data collection will need to be balanced by in-depth understanding of how digital data arises and its strengths and weaknesses (Nunan and Di Domenico 2019).

Issues for further discussion

The previous developments mean companies have more options to enter markets or improve management of their customers than previously, especially by using platforms containing information about customers they do not yet have (for market entry) or using platforms which contain information about their existing customers (to sell more to them and defend them from competitors). Effectively, using information platforms such as those described previously opens up the possibility of using new business models (Stott *et al.* 2016). For this to work, marketing directors, managers and leaders of insight and information systems must understand the value of platform information, capitalise on it or create (perhaps working with partners) their own platforms for their own ecosystems – a revisiting of information management as competitive advantage (Porter and Millar 1985). However, we predict that increasing numbers of firms will use information-sharing platforms with strong analytics capabilities, provided platform providers continue to make it attractive financially and easy operationally, as they do today. In the world of marketing research, the platform-based ecosystem creates new business opportunities, as outlined previously – the relationship between the ecosystem and customers becomes more complicated, and the participants in the ecosystem need to understand how their part in the ecosystem is perceived.

We believe that many conventional concepts from marketing – indeed from business strategy – should be re-evaluated in the light of the developments described in this chapter. We would also argue that how we view marketing research should also change, as how companies gather information about their world has changed forever, and marketing research has become in many cases an adjunct to digital information gathering.

Acknowledgements

This chapter is based partly on:

Stone, M. and Woodcock, N., 2014. Interactive, direct and digital marketing – a future that depends on better use of business intelligence. *Journal of Research in Interactive Marketing*, 8(1), 4–17.

Stone, M. and Laughlin, P., 2016. How interactive marketing is changing in consumer financial services. *Journal of Research in Interactive Marketing*, 10(4), 338–356.

Stone, M., 2014. The new (and ever-evolving) direct and digital marketing ecosystem. *Journal of Direct, Data and Digital Marketing Practice*, 16(2), 71–74.

Stone, M., Aravopoulou, E., Gerardi, G., Todeva, E., Weinzierl, L., Laughlin, P. and Stott, R., 2017. How platforms are transforming customer information management. *The Bottom Line*, 30(3), 216–235.

References

Actiance, 2017. *GDPR and the Impact on Data Archiving and Information Governance.* Redwood City, CA: Actiance [online]. Available from: www.actiance.com/wp-content/uploads/2017/03/WP-GDPR-Impact-on-Data-Archiving-and-Information-Governance.pdf [Accessed 19 June 2020].

Adner, R., 2006. Match your innovation strategy to your innovation ecosystem. *Harvard Business Review,* 84(4), 98–107.

Adner, R. and Kapoor, R., 2010. Value creation in innovation ecosystems: How the structure of technological interdependence affects firm performance in new technology generations. *Strategic Management Journal,* 31(3), 306–333. https://doi.org/10.1002/smj.821.

Aksulu, A. and Wade, M., 2010. A comprehensive review and synthesis of open source research. *Journal of the Association for Information Systems,* 11(11), 576–656. DOI: 10.17705/1jais.00245.

Badgett, M. and Stone, M., 2005. Multidimensional segmentation at work. *Journal of Targeting, Analysis and Measurement for Marketing,* 13(2), 103–121. DOI: 10.1057/palgrave.jt.5740137.

Bonchek, M. and Choudary, S., 2013. Three elements of a successful platform strategy. *Harvard Business Review Online* [online]. Available from: https://hbr.org/2013/01/three-elements-of-a-successful-platform [Accessed 20 August 2017].

Boudreau, K., 2010. Open platform strategies and innovation: Granting access versus devolving control. *Management Science,* 56(10), 1849–1872. DOI: 10.1287/mnsc.1100.1215.

Brandenburger, A. and Nalebuff, B., 1997. *Co-Opetition: A Revolutionary Mindset That Combines Competition and Cooperation in the Marketplace: The Game Theory Strategy That's Changing the Game of Business.* New York: Doubleday.

Capgemini, 2015. *Driving the Data Engine: How Unilever Is Using Analytics to Accelerate Customer Understanding.* Paris: CapGemini Consulting [online]. Available from: www.capgemini.com/gb-en/resources/driving-the-data-engine-how-unilever-is-using-analytics-to-accelerate-customer-understanding/ [Accessed 20 June 2020].

Chua, A. and Banerjee, S., 2013. Customer knowledge management via social media: The case of Starbucks. *Journal of Knowledge Management,* 17(2), 237–249. DOI: 10.1108/13673271311315196.

de Reuver, M., Sørensen, C. and Basole, R., 2018. The digital platform: A research agenda. *Journal of Information Technology,* 33(2), 124–135. https://doi.org/10.1057/s41265-016-0033-3.

Dyer, J.H. and Singh, H., 1998. The relational view: Cooperative strategy and sources of interorganizational competitive advantage. *Academy of Management Review,* 23(4), 660–679. DOI: 10.2307/259056.

Fjelstad, Ø., Snow, C., Miles, R. and Lettl, C., 2012. The architecture of collaboration. *Strategic Management Journal,* 33(6), 734–750. https://doi.org/10.1002/smj.1968.

Gawer, A., ed., 2009. *Platforms, Markets and Innovation.* Cheltenham: Edward Elgar Publishing.

Iansiti, M. and Levien, R., 2004. Creating value in your business ecosystem. *Harvard Business Review.*

IDC, 2016a. *CRM on Steroids: Data-Driven Marketing to Enhance the Customer Experience.* Framingham, MA: IDC [online]. Available from: www.marketresearch.com/IDC-v2477/CRM-Steroids-Data-Driven-Enhance-10160097/ [Accessed 20 June 2020].

IDC, 2016b. *Industry Cloud Platform Directory.* Framingham, MA: IDC [online]. Available from: www.idc.com/getdoc.jsp?containerId=US44129219&utm_medium=rss_feed&utm_source=Alert&utm_campaign=rss_syndication [Accessed 20 June 2020].

IDC, 2016c. *Worldwide and Regional Public IT Cloud Services Forecast 2016–2020.* Framingham, MA: IDC [online]. Available from: www.idc.com/getdoc.jsp?containerId=US44202119 [Accessed 20 June 2020].

Kapoor, R. and Lee, J., 2013. Coordinating and competing in ecosystems: How organizational forms shape new technology investments. *Strategic Management Journal,* 34(3), 274–296. https://doi.org/10.1002/smj.2010.

Laudon, K. and Laudon, J., 2020. *Management Information Systems: Managing the Digital Firm,* 17th ed. London: Pearson.

Li, M. and Nguyen, B., 2016. When will firms share information and collaborate to achieve innovation? A review of collaboration strategies. *The Bottom Line,* 30(1), 65–86. https://doi.org/10.1108/BL-12-2016-0039.

Mann, M., Kaufmann, R., Bauer, D., Gopal, S., Baldwin, J. and Vera-Diaz, M., 2012. Ecosystem service value and agricultural conversion in the Amazon: Implications for policy intervention. *Environmental and Resource Economics,* 53(2), 279–295. https://doi.org/10.1007/s10640-012-9562-6.

Molinillo, S. and Japutra, A., 2017. Organizational adoption of digital information and technology: A theoretical review. *The Bottom Line*, 30(1), 33–46. https://doi.org/10.1108/BL-01-2017-0002.

My Customer, 2017. *Winning with GDPR: How to Build Customer Loyalty. The Evolving Role of Identity in Privacy and Consent.* Bristol: My Customer [online]. Available from: https://go.forgerock.com/MyCustomer-Building-Customer-Loyalty-GDPR-RPT.html [Accessed 21 August 2017].

Nunan, D., 2017. Reflections on the future of the marketing research industry: Is marketing research having its 'Kodak moment'? *International Journal of Market Research*, 59(5), 553–555. https://doi.org/10.2501%2FIJMR-2017-043.

Nunan, D. and Di Domenico, M., 2019. Rethinking the marketing research curriculum. *International Journal of Market Research*, 61(1), 22–32. https://doi.org/10.1177%2F1470785318805294.

Padula, G., 2008. Enhancing the innovation performance of firms by balancing cohesiveness and bridging ties. *Long Range Planning*, 41(4), 395–419. DOI: 10.1016/j.lrp.2008.01.004.

Parker, G., Van Alstyne, M.W. and Jiang, X., 2016. Platform ecosystems: How developers invert the firm. *MIS Quarterly*, 41(1), 255–266. DOI: 10.2139/ssrn.2861574.

Parnell, B., Stone, M., Stott, R., Aravopoulou, E. and Timms, L., 2017. Business model innovation, strategic information and the role of analyst firms. *The Bottom Line*, 30(2), 151–162. DOI: 10.1108/BL-06-2017-0012.

Perry, J.T., Chandler, G.N. and Markova, G., 2012. Entrepreneurial effectuation: A review and suggestions for future research. *Entrepreneurship Theory and Practice*, 36(4), 837–861. https://doi.org/10.1111%2Fj.1540-6520.2010.00435.x.

Porter, M., 1985. *Competitive Advantage: Creating and Sustaining Superior Performance.* New York: Free Press.

Porter, M. and Millar, V., 1985. How information gives you competitive advantage. *Harvard Business Review*, 63(4), 149–158.

Sarasvathy, S., 2001. Causation and effectuation: Toward a theoretical shift from economic inevitability to entrepreneurial contingency. *Academy of Management Review*, 26(2), 243–263. https://doi.org/10.5465/amr.2001.4378020.

Selander, L., Henfridsson, O. and Svahn, F., 2010. *Transforming Ecosystem Relationships in Digital Innovation.* Proceedings of the International Conference on Information Systems, ICIS 2010, Saint Louis, MO, 12–15 December.

Selander, L., Henfridsson, O. and Svahn, F., 2013. Capability search and redeem across digital ecosystems. *Journal of Information Technology*, 28(3), 183–197. https://doi.org/10.1057%2Fjit.2013.14.

Sigala, M., 2012. Social networks and customer involvement in new service development (NSD) The case of www. mystarbucksidea.com. *International Journal of Contemporary Hospitality Management*, 24(7), 966–990. DOI: 10.1108/09596111211258874.

Sorenson, S. and Adkins, A., 2014. Why customer engagement matters so much now. *Gallup Business Journal* [online]. Available from: www.gallup.com/businessjournal/172637/why-customer-engagement-matters.aspx [Accessed 19 August 2017].

Stone, M., 2014. The new (and ever-evolving) direct and digital marketing ecosystem. *Journal of Direct, Data and Digital Marketing Practice*, 16(2), 71–74.

Stone, M., Aravopoulou, E., Gerardi, G., Todeva, E., Weinzierl, L., Laughlin, P. and Stott, R., 2017. How platforms are transforming customer information management. *The Bottom Line*, 30(3), 216–235. https://doi.org/10.1108/BL-08-2017-0024.

Stone, M., Cerasale, M., Adams, J. and Clark, A., 2003. From product to solutions: Transforming how companies serve customers Part 1: The development of the solutions market. *Metamorphosis: Journal of the Indian Institute of Management*, 2(1 and 2), 23–46. https://doi.org/10.1177/0972622520030104.

Stone, M., Cerasale, M., Foss, B. and Taylor, G., 2003. From product to solutions: Transforming how companies serve customers Part 2: How solutions are created and delivered. *Metamorphosis: Journal of the Indian Institute of Management*, 2(1 and 2), 46–67. https://doi.org/10.1177/0972622520030105.

Stone, M. and Laughlin, P., 2016. How interactive marketing is changing in consumer financial services. *Journal of Research in Interactive Marketing*, 10(4), 338–356. DOI: 10.1057/dddmp.2014.58.

Stone, M. and Shaw, R., 1987. Database marketing for competitive advantage. *Long Range Planning*, 20(2), 24–39.

Stone, M. and Woodcock, N., 2013. Social intelligence in customer engagement. *Journal of Strategic Marketing*, 21(5), 394–401. https://doi.org/10.1080/0965254X.2013.801613.

Stone, M. and Woodcock, N., 2014. Interactive, direct and digital marketing – a future that depends on better use of business intelligence. *Journal of Research in Interactive Marketing*, 8(1), 4–17. DOI: 10.1108/JRIM-07-2013-0046.

Stone, M., Woodcock, N., Ekinci, Y., Aravopoulou, E. and Parnell, B., 2019. SCHEMA: Information on marketing and customer management performance – reality versus dreams. *The Bottom Line*, 32(1), 98–116. DOI: 10.1108/BL-02-2019-0065.

Stott, R., Stone, M. and Fae, J., 2016. Business models in the business to business and business to consumer worlds – what can each world learn from the other. *Journal of Business and Industrial Marketing*, 31(8), 943–954. DOI: 10.1108/JBIM-10-2016-267.

Teece, D.J., 2007. Explicating dynamic capabilities: The nature and microfoundations of (sustainable) enterprise performance. *Strategic Management Journal*, 28(13), 1319–1350. https://doi.org/10.1002/smj.640.

Tuten, T. and Perotti, V., 2019. Lies, brands and social media. *Qualitative Market Research: An International Journal*, 22(1), 5–13. https://doi.org/10.1108/QMR-02-2017-0063.

WBR Digital, 2017. *Data and Goliath: How New Regulation Is Affecting the Way We Manage Data* [online]. Available from: https://datainsight. wbresearch.com/Data-and-Goliath-How-New-Regulation-Is-Affecting-The-Way-We-Manage-Data-mc [Accessed 7 August 2017].

4

BUSINESS MODELS AND MARKETING RESEARCH

Brett Parnell, Ryan Stott, Merlin Stone and Eleni Aravopoulou

Summary

This chapter investigates how the adoption of different business models affects what marketing researchers do. After defining the concept of business model, it explores the dependence of different business models on marketing research and customer insight. It investigates the implications for analysis of how business leaders use information to review and/or change business models. It identifies that although many large firms have made large investments in customer data and customer insight, they may not use this information appropriately, particularly if a firm's current business model is under threat, whether due to denial by senior management, the problems of changing or adapting business models or the extent to which the firm's financial situation is based upon exploiting its current business model.

Introduction

In recent years, there has been much discussion of the concept of "business model," prompted partly by the success of firms such as Amazon, Netflix, Uber, eBay and Airbnb using disruptive web-based models which have destabilised industries and markets, often by use of new information platforms (Stone *et al.* 2017; Stott *et al.* 2016). For example, Uber has completely revolutionised the "logistics of humans" by the use of a bi-directional information technology platform, putting real-time information in the hands of the customer and connecting an ecosystem of external resources (drivers) to an ecosystem of customers. The sharing of and access to real-time information is at the heart of this model. This type of empowerment of the customer can take place in all markets, whether business or consumer.

The customers in question may be consumers or businesses, while the businesses concerned can be of any size. The many web-based businesses acting as aggregators perform the same function – aggregating demand from consumers and businesses and supply from businesses (and from consumers in the case of second-hand or used goods) to create new markets. In some cases, their business models extend beyond the interface between customer and suppliers into a much smarter approach to the management of logistics and supply chains (including manufacturing), accelerating them, making them more cost-effective and also able to handle a much greater variety of goods and services and in some cases in order sizes and length of production runs much more varied than before. A relatively new business model for product manufacturers is servitisation, which consists of offering a "product as a service" and is based on the flow of information from physical products, the environment, customer usage and supply chains, from the internal operations of a manufacturer's plant, through the external partner and supplier ecosystems. One thing new businesses have in common is that they are technology enabled and based on the flow of information within and between organisations, including partner ecosystems and to and from the customer.

Definition of business model

There are many definitions of "business model." Lambert and Davidson (2013) found that definitions differ in terms of scope and conceptual focus. The scope of business models ranges from being purely internal to the enterprise including the entire partner/channel ecosystem. The conceptual focus of business models ranges from activities, architectures and structures to value and market orientation.

However, most definitions focus on the individual organisation and its value creation and value offerings (Lambert and Davidson 2013). Al-Debei *et al.* (2008) suggest that the business model is used to shape the present and future business, so some elements of the business model are emergent or evolving. Core products and services are included – these are part of the customer value proposition. They refer to business models helping to achieve strategic goals and objectives, showing overlap with strategy. However, the definition must include external networks such as partners and suppliers and a strong customer or market-oriented element.

Academic literature shows how the arrival of the Internet in the mid-1990s and a rise in the frequency of use of the term "business model" coincided. Zott and Amit (2010) analysed literature from 1975 to 2009. They showed that the concept's use grew quickly, particularly in non-academic journals, perhaps due to consultancy firms striving to be seen as thought leaders, particularly in the area of digital transformation.

In the field of marketing, the previous developments led to the articulation of different models of customer management (Stone *et al.* 2002), in which the main dimensions of variation were factors such as the locus of control, the degree of differentiation in how different customers were managed, the depth of the relationship and the frequency and content of contact. The idea of business model was also associated with the idea of playing the competitive game by different rules or even inventing new games, as in the case of the Japanese competitive attack on the West (Stone 1984).

Clarifying the business model concept

Osterwalder *et al.* (2005) found that about half the business model definitions used by businesses had a value/customer or market-oriented ("outward-looking") approach, while the rest were more inward focused. However, different authors refer to different things in writing about business models (Linder and Cantrell 2000). Osterwalder *et al.* (2005) found three different types of reference:

- An abstract overarching business model concept that can describe all businesses. The meta-model covers all the components of a business model (Osterwalder *et al.* 2005; Linder and Cantrell 2000);

- Types of business models and the different taxonomies, for example, freemium, bait and hook, open business models and more (Osterwalder *et al.* 2005). Linder and Cantrell (2000) call these "operating business models" and the logic for creating value, often referred to as "the business model";
- Real-world business models; instance level; Amazon model, Dell model, eBay model. Using the name of a business to reference its business model (Osterwalder *et al.* 2005).

Business model frameworks and components

Osterwalder and Pigneur's (2010) Business Model Canvas consists of four main areas of business: product, customer, infrastructure and finance, which are developed into nine components or building blocks – key partners, cost structure, key activities, key resources, value proposition, customer relationships, customer segments, channels and revenue streams. The canvas includes leveraging external networks or partnering with competitors to increase operational efficiency and finding innovative ways to create customer value (Prahalad and Krishnan 2008; Chesbrough 2006; Mason and Mouzas 2012; Amit and Zott 2001).

The business model concept as a strategic tool

A clear (possibly visual) depiction of a company's business model assists in understanding the model and creates a single view amongst stakeholders (Afuah 2003; Osterwalder and Pigneur 2010) by helping managers communicate and share their understanding of it (Fensel 2001). It allows complex information to be easily understood and digested. It helps identify the different elements and relationships of the business model (Osterwalder *et al.* 2005). Business models aid management decision-making (McGrath 2010). Once the model is captured visually, it is easier to identify metrics for performance measurement and potential risks (Staheler 2002).

The business model is a source of innovation and value creation (Amit and Zott 2001). A company's business model can be compared with those of peers, partners and competitors, providing new insights which stimulate business model innovation (Osterwalder *et al.* 2005).

A defined business model helps align strategy, business processes and technology (Chesbrough and Rosenbloom 2002). Capturing, mapping and understanding the different elements of a business model allows business model designers (senior executives) to adapt elements to external pressures or changing market requirements. Analysing a company via its business model can be better than traditional concepts such as industry positioning (McGrath 2010). The understanding of a business model can lead to new business applications (Veit *et al.* 2014) and improve communications between business and IT (Osterwalder *et al.* 2005). Business models can also be used as a mechanism to facilitate business change (Linder and Cantrell 2000; Osterwalder *et al.* 2005).

Business models, strategy and business processes

The business model concept gives strategists a new way to assess strategic options. This is through a process of discovery rather than an analytical approach, as business model designs can be created and piloted before being rolled out, and in some instances, whole spin-off companies are created to test a new business model before changing the parent company's business model (McGrath 2010). This is where marketing research plays a vital role in identifying customers' perceptions of and satisfaction with the new business model. A continuous customer feedback loop must be created to monitor satisfaction and enable incremental innovation, allowing the business model to evolve in accordance with ever-changing customer expectations and satisfaction. Most technology-enabled business models allow customers to rate suppliers and give feedback in real time, sometimes allowing products or services to adjust according to customer preference.

The business model concept and strategy theory are closely related. Many strategic management concepts overlap with business model themes and concepts (Lambert and Davidson 2013). Porter (2001, p. 71) suggests that "strategy defines how all the elements of what a company does fit together." However, there is still debate on the differences between business models and business strategy (Porter 2001). Business models are a new way of conceiving, creating and executing strategies (McGrath 2010). The business model is an abstract representation of some aspects of a firm's strategy (Seddon and Lewis 2003).

Industrial organisation: business models and the external environment

The "industrial organisation" approach to competitive advantage suggests that a firm's performance depends on how it positions itself and acts in relation to external factors, such as market conditions and competitors. This emphasises the importance of external factors (David 2004). Customer insights are critical to the success of business model design and should be used to guide the design of value propositions, distribution channels, customer relationships and revenue streams (Osterwalder and Pigneur 2010). Gathering customer insights should extend beyond customers to prospects and other segments of the market and include the external environment (Kim and Mauborgne 2015; Osterwalder and Pigneur 2010). Understanding who customers are and what they value is key (Porter and Millar 1985). For a company to deliver customer value through its network, whether or not it has direct contact with the end-customer, it must increase knowledge and understanding of the end-customer (Cairncross 2002; David 2004). Christopher (2000) states that not just the company but the entire network or ecosystem of partners must be able to sense and respond to market changes (Christopher 2000).

When designing new business models, one needs a full analysis of the external environment to gain insight into market trends, customer needs and preferences and competitors, while assessing all political, economic, social, technological, legal and environmental factors as well as carrying out market analysis, forecasting and segmentation activities (Teece 2010; Kim and Mauborgne 2015; Osterwalder and Pigneur 2010; David 2004; McGrath 2010). This normally requires a strong marketing research capability. Timely and co-ordinated information on end-customer behaviour gives companies more flexibility, enabling them to satisfy more completely the changing needs of customers (Hammer 2001). New technologies like big data and analytics, the cloud and mobility help companies to collect and analyse customer and market data from various internal and external sources, enabling firms to build a dynamic view of the customer (Carr *et al.* 2015) and to create flexible and efficient structures that are more responsive to the dynamic needs of the market (Linder and Cantrell 2000; Strohelin 2015). This supplements and can sometimes replace traditional marketing research. It could be argued that the marketing research industry itself needs a new business model. New marketing research platforms will emerge, feeding information directly into management information systems, data models and other strategic planning tools and/or platforms.

Strategic flexibility and business model flexibility

Flexibility is a firm's ability to reposition itself in the market and dismantle old strategies to meet the market's new needs (Sanchez and Mahoney 1996). As a business model is an interface or theoretical layer between strategy and processes (Al-Debei *et al.* 2008; Morris *et al.* 2005), it can give flexibility to strategy and process, allowing businesses to cope with change and uncertainty in the external environment and adapt to achieve strategic goals and objectives (Al-Debei *et al.* 2008). However, with the rise of globalisation and low-cost outsourcing models, some companies are finding that their core resources and capabilities are no longer enough to create a sustainable competitive advantage. To stand out from competition, companies must have flexible product and service offerings that change in line with the market needs (Mason and Mouzas 2012).

However, the view of Prahalad and Krishnan (2008) is customer-centric, where the focus of value creation shifts from products and services to customer experience via understanding the behaviours, needs and skills of individual consumers and co-creating a unique value proposition with them, with customer experience being part of the augmented product that makes up customer value. To deliver customer value, which includes customer experience, services and products, the company must be flexible and constantly realigned to meet individual customer requirements.

Marketing research has always played an important role in identifying the value customers require and whether the value continues to be delivered, and this role is likely to continue. However, as the need for flexibility and speed increases, so traditional marketing research cycles will become tighter. One objective is to deliver "near" real-time market insights, which systems can import and, through powerful machine learning algorithms and AI, make actionable recommendations to leaders or even incremental innovations to the business model itself.

Learning from applying the idea of transforming the business model

The learning from the previous discussion is summarised in Table 4.1, which identifies a series of recommendations for applying the business model concept and deploying marketing research in supporting use of the concept.

Changing business models, competition and the role of leaders

Business models evolve and mature (McGrath 2010). Teece (2010) states that business models must change over time as external factors such as markets, technology and legal environments change. For businesses to survive, business strategy, business model and business process should be treated as one package and reviewed frequently to ensure they stay aligned with the external business environment (Al-Debei *et al.* 2008). Business modelling facilitates emergence of new, more refined strategies (Seddon and Lewis 2003; Margretta 2002). Business models should be reviewed regularly and adjusted to remain aligned with the firm's external environment and strategic objectives. The role of reviewing and changing models normally belongs to a business's leaders.

Little is understood about the role of a business's leader (whether a chief executive officer of a large corporation or a small entrepreneur) in developing a new business model and how that leader may work with members of a new ecosystem of suppliers, partners and customers to create a new business model (Foss and Stieglitz 2015).

Table 4.1 Use of marketing research to support application of business model ideas

Characteristic	Use of business model ideas	Examples of areas where marketing research can be deployed to support business model decisions
Business model definition and understanding	The scope of the business model should be all encompassing and include the internal and external network or ecosystem (partners, suppliers, channels etc.). The focus of the business model must include market and value to customer but also how a business's activities, architectures, processes and structures create value through its different value propositions. Senior executives must have a clear, common understanding of what a business model is and not confuse it with operational or other models.	Identification of different competing models, their markets and customer/prospect attitudes to them. Insight into all external factors: the external ecosystem, customer perceptions and desires, competitors, peers and even adjacent markets from which best practices or new models can be learnt.
Business model components	The business model concept should be formally used in management decision-making. Senior managers should map out the components of their business model, how their functions relate to it and how the overall business model drives the components of the functional models for which they are responsible. This should follow Osterwalder and Pigneur's (2010) nine components: key partners, cost structure, key activities, key resources, value proposition, customer relationships, customer segments, channels and revenue streams. These should be used in strategic reviews, planning and performance measurement. Regular resource audits should be carried out, including identification and assessment of internal and ecosystem (including partners, customers and suppliers) resources, capabilities and capacity (people, process and technology) needed to implement the business model. Key resources that can be leveraged to create value via the business model should be identified. The business model should be featured as an explicit part of the relationship with key customers and suppliers and as underpinning the value delivered to them or obtained from them.	How prospects and customers are exposed to the different components of the model, their perceptions of and attitudes towards them and the alternatives that they use to satisfy the same needs that would be satisfied by the different components. Understanding of market requirements, gaps, opportunities or other challenges being faced, feeding into the value proposition which a firm or partnership needs to deliver so as to meet customer requirements effectively. Marketing research will improve the effectiveness of new value propositions, increase return on business model-related investments and reduce waste due to rework.

Co-creation techniques should be used in planning with key customers and suppliers to allow improvement in the joint business model.

CXOs should continuously assess the entire value chain, internally and through the channel and partner ecosystems, from their functional point of view, to identify opportunities for radical change to functional model.

Critical activities and transactions should be identified, clearly defined and always seen as a part of the entire value chain and not as standalone activities. Activities should be aligned with strategic objectives.

Tailored value chains should be used as a source of competitive advantage.

Critical success activities should be kept in house (retain corporate ownership) to maintain control and minimise risk.

Digital technologies such as social, mobile, big data and analytics should be adopted and be used for activity mapping, value chain analysis and performance measurement.

Companies should have flexible product or service offerings that can change in line with market needs and changes in business models.

Companies should be customer-centric and focus on customer experience/value.

Unique value propositions for customers should be co-created with customers, and unique value inputs should be co-created with suppliers.

Companies should focus on finding new models which combine innovation (increase value) with maintaining efficiency (lowering costs).

(Continued)

Table 4.1 (Continued)

Characteristic	Use of business model ideas	Examples of areas where marketing research can be deployed to support business model decisions
Business model digital and communication aspects	The business model framework, concept and strategic management theories should be used as a blueprint for digital transformation initiatives, ensuring that all elements of the model, processes, ecosystems and external environment are seamlessly connected and synergised through the ongoing process of digital transformation. The organisation's business model should be clearly defined and communicated with all stakeholders, including the most important partners in the ecosystem, and discussed with them as an important philosophy that underlies the relationship with them. Representations of the model should be created, including all nine business model components, and then be shared with all key internal and external stakeholders.	Attitudes towards and perceptions of digital communications techniques used by users of target and competing business models and their effectiveness. This helps to identify critical external stakeholder groups to whom the business model should align, such as regulators or governing bodies (consider the legal fees Uber could have saved had they consulted the regulators on the rollout of their business model).
Business model and strategy	The business model should be used to translate strategy into process and be assessed at the same time as all strategic planning activities. The business model should be compared regularly to the business models of peers, exemplars and competitors. Consideration should be given to divesting parts of the business that are managed using old or past models (for example, as some computer companies did with their hardware businesses as they moved towards a solutions model). The business model should be aligned with strategy, taking into account changes in the external environment, and with business processes to ensure continued successful management of people. The business models of the entire ecosystem of suppliers, partners and customers should be continuously aligned. Part of relationship management should be winning the right to suggest to customers, suppliers and other partners ways to improve mutual strategic alignment and creating processes for doing so. Process, business models and strategy should be complementary and aligned.	Experience of and attitudes towards processes involved in customer management aspects of business model. Marketing research is critical to strategy development, and without it, companies are flying blind, risking developing strategies and business models which do not address the needs of the market. Market insight teams collect, synthesise and feed marketing research into both the functional and corporate strategic planning process.

Management should investigate spin-off products or even businesses with fundamentally different or conflicting business models to the parent organisation to allow the business to compete in new markets, without strategic alignment or major adjustments to the business model of the parent. Thus, several classic all-purpose airlines that wanted to compete on costs created separate companies on the low-cost model. New partnerships, revenue models, marketing and service operations and so on were created and run independently of the parent organisation. Similar model variations have been created successfully in banking and insurance. The business model of any new unit must be strategically aligned with its strategy and processes.

The business model should be reviewed regularly and adjusted to remain aligned with changes in the environment and overall strategic objectives of the firm.

Business model review and analysis should be carried out in all strategic planning cycles, overall and for each function.

Business model, strategy and processes should be seen as one package and changed together.

Businesses creating new models should consider how to create the required new ecosystem.

External environment	The business model should be connected to the external environment (partner, supplier, distributor etc.) ecosystem.	How evolution of the external environment affects appropriateness of different business models.
	Insights about the performance of the ecosystem in supporting success achieved through the business model should be fully available, including success with customers.	The external environment enabled by technology is more dynamic than it has ever been, so marketing research allows firms to track the dynamic marketplace and constantly evolve their business model, maintaining a competitive advantage.
	Firms should regularly fully analyse their external environment and link this activity with business model design adjustments.	
	Firms should receive a continuous flow of customer, competitor and market insights to guide value propositions and business model design.	
	Opportunities and threats arising from the deployment of the model should be regularly identified and prioritised.	
	Third-party platform technologies (social, mobile, cloud, big data and analytics) should be used to support external awareness, analysis and information flows.	

Source: The authors

The link between competitive advantage and choice of business model has been explored extensively (e.g. Zott and Amit 2007; Amit and Zott 2001). Stone (1984) documents how Japanese companies used different models to challenge US and European competitors, using ideas from the military theories of Lanchester (1916), the ideas from which were promoted in the Japanese market (Campbell and Roberts 1986). These ideas included developing an agile and different business model and using it to attack one part of a market at a time by concentrating resources after splitting the enemy force and separating targets, including distinguishing between smaller competitors that can be attacked and larger competitors against which the company must protect itself.

Economists have suggested associations between innovation and business models, leading to "creative destruction" of what we might call old models (Schumpeter 1994). However, they use terms like "modes" and "recipes," rather than "business model," to discuss how industrial revolutions have been defined by changes in those recipes (Baden-Fuller and Mangematin 2013).

Despite advances in thought on the processes, drivers and facilitators of business model change (notably Andries *et al.* 2013; Achtenhagen *et al.* 2013; Willemstein *et al.* 2007; Andries and Debackere 2006, 2007; Mason and Leek 2008; McNamara *et al.* 2013), Saebi *et al.* (2017) suggest that there is not much research on how organisations adapt business models in response to external threats and opportunities, suggesting that failure to adapt business models quickly may occur because managers do not recognise that external changes have occurred. Managerial cognition, especially interpretation in relation to changes in the environment, can be significant in shaping organisational responses (Ginsberg and Venkatraman 1985; Barr *et al.* 1992; Tripsas and Gavetti 2000).

Research is divided on whether negative (perceived threat or weakness) or positive (perceived opportunity or strength) framing of events is more likely to motivate organisational response (Saebi *et al.* 2017). Proponents of threat-rigidity theory argue that perceptions of threat encourage managers to rely on existing routines, while perceptions of opportunity induce more risk-taking behaviour (Dutton and Jackson 1987; Staw *et al.* 1981). However, prospect theory predicts the opposite, that under perceived threat, as opposed to more favourable conditions, managers are seen to be more accepting and motivated to take risks (Barberis 2013; Kahneman and Tversky 1979). This is known popularly as the "burning platform" situation. Research also indicates that an organisation's strategic orientation emerges from its experience, with solutions and heuristics resulting in different approaches to organisational change and adaptability (Gatignon and Xuereb 1997; Lant and Mezias 1992). However, organisations and managers oriented to finding new market opportunities might be more perceptive and so better equipped to adapt their business model in face of emerging threats and opportunities than those with more defensive postures (Teece 2007).

Saebi *et al.* (2017) assert that adapting an existing business model may be difficult and that adaptation might involve changes to market segment, value chain, value proposition and value-capture processes, along with how these are linked in an architecture. However, adapting a business model may involve uncertainty about outcomes (Andries and Debackere 2007; McNamara *et al.* 2013). Saebi *et al.* (2017) suggest that given organisational inertia and outcome uncertainty, organisations are less likely to change model without a strong incentive, even where the need for adaptation is apparent, because an organisation's strategic processes may impede needed model change in response to new market demands or competitive threats.

Research by Foss and Stieglitz (2015) identifies that leadership aspects of business model innovation are poorly addressed in the literature. They suggest that, depending on the innovation, the change could be minor (e.g. market segments, revenue model), or necessitate enterprise-wide change (e.g. processes, activities, employees). So, while different business model innovation types may have different leadership requirements, no analysis was found systematically linking business model innovation types to different leadership competences and organisational design requirements. However, Foss and Stieglitz (2015) point out that some leadership and organisational challenges associated with business models and model innovation have been researched (Teece 2010; Zott and Amit 2010; Amit and Zott 2012; Demil and Lecocq 2010; Doz and Kosonen 2010). Still, the literature does not represent well the heterogeneity of business model innovation and the different leadership challenges created by different kinds of business model innovation (Foss and Stieglitz 2015).

Threats rarely appear from nowhere. Today's leading companies in information and communications technology and associated services, such as Apple, Google and Amazon, took years to grow to where they posed a severe threat to competitors. At some stage, it can be argued that information about their success moved from the "interesting" to the "urgent" for companies whose activities they threatened. One issue is the problem of denial, explored in the competitive strategy and military literature (Stone 2015). Another theme is timing of threats. For example, in an article concerning the media and telecom industry, it was suggested that "on the Internet, it's always better to jump before you're pushed," referring to BSkyB's move to allow consumers to access its content online and if desired on an ad-hoc basis (through NowTV.com) rather than by satellite service subscription, using content from its core business to head off defections to rival services – Netflix, Amazon Prime Video, Apple TV and others.

Empirical study

A study carried out by Parnell *et al.* (2018) focused on board-level leaders from market-leading organisations in six industries – media and communications, financial services, travel, information technology, higher education and retail. Three organisations, with a leader from each, were chosen from each industry, generally with two market-leading organisations and the third a strong challenger in the market. The challenges faced in these sectors are different. For example, one challenge in media industries is the threat of digital business models to print and broadcast businesses and in travel and transport that of low-cost versus scheduled airline models. However, in both cases, digital technology is the underlying basis of threats to incumbents, so this was identified at the beginning of this research, allowing the research and analysis to focus on challenges posed to business models by digital technology. The latter is covered extensively in the grey literature, particularly the disruptive changes created by digital media (Manyika *et al.* 2013).

The research study found that maintaining market share and competitive advantage and the associated degree of business model innovation and disruption is strongly influenced by leadership motivation for model change. This includes board-level acknowledgment and addressing model weaknesses, sharing of model performance and of the relationship between business strategy and model. Understanding business model performance using management information, including partner satisfaction and understanding of client value, facilitates and mitigates the impact of the leaders' motivation for model change. Strategies including partnering and establishing teams to provide management information go some way to supporting board-level motivation for model change. These strategies can lead to improved effectiveness of leadership motivation and decision-making on business model management for competitive advantage.

How companies become aware of the need for information to support decisions on business model change was as an important factor. This stemmed from either the proactive drive by the senior team to grow, maintain and perform better their competition or the need to respond to new or newly identified competitor models and the difficulty, time and expense of doing so. Financial service, transport and information technology organisations were more aware of how to use business model choice information for competitive advantage and growth. The media organisations also tended to be aware, though for different reasons not necessarily wanting to use the information to change the model, because of unwillingness to change from existing "cash cow" business models and difficulty understanding the information to inform the necessary decisions. This appeared to link to the desire of leadership to participate in and support the change and their commitment to it. There were several cases where the information was compelling and readily available and was ignored, and this was often linked to cultural practices and mentalities, or the skills, knowledge and experience of the leaders were simply insufficient to process the information. The latter tended to be in retail and higher education.

Many organisations had some idea of these associated challenges, and some had established dedicated insight teams tasked with staying ahead of trends and competing models, providing high-quality information that was easy to digest and absorb, to equip the boards and leadership with the intelligence needed to rapidly respond rapidly to challenges. More investigation is needed to understand how to encourage leaders to pay attention to the information and then, if required, act upon it, possibly using learnings from the school of thought associated with the psychology of military intelligence and other leadership theories.

A question that also appeared to need answering is whether the quality and detail of the information is important or whether it is "big picture" material that is important ("the elephant in the room"). In several cases, detailed information was available, but leaders remained preoccupied with the minor details and so could not "see the forest for the trees". Again, this may be linked to experience and how to interpret the information but remains a challenge. Appointing a board member focused on insight did appear to remedy this, although one of sufficient experience was not always available.

A clear factor that affected responses was how far an organisation's industry was affected by technological innovation, particularly in information technology, or by other factors such as market, economic, social or demographic change, as was the case with financial services, information technology, travel and media, whose business models and those of their competitors tended to change with greater frequency.

The speed of leaders to respond was, as might be expected, important in determining whether the organisation maintained or gained market share. Those that delayed often lost competitive advantage, and this delay was often a consequence of not having or of ignoring the information. This problem was not insurmountable, and in some cases, the organisation (leadership) learnt from these mistakes and put plans in place to address them, and this paid dividends.

Delays by leadership in acting, for whatever reason, had a direct effect on the extent of business model innovation required (for example, adaptation of model or complete change), the degree of risk and resource commitment required by any change and the company's willingness and ability to take on the risk or degree of change. This highlighted the extent to which the organisation's performance depended on good management of its existing model and how far any new model could leverage existing resources if deployed in a very different way.

In terms of whether management felt capable of managing any new model (whether it knows what to do) and whether it believes its people have the required capabilities and skills, the option of partnering using external suppliers and advisors and widening the ecosystem to help balance and support business functions made a difference, in some cases improving organisational performance by making information available to help leadership be clearer on business model choices.

Another factor appeared to be how the different paradigms of business model innovation and ways of developing business models affect the kind of information required and how it was used by leaders for business model choice, whether resource based (take good resources and do something new), customer based (use existing customers and do something else with them) or products and services (use existing products and services somewhere else).

Conclusions and recommendations

Our main conclusions are these:

- The concept of the business model has become a useful tool in strategic management, both in determining options and how choice about options should be applied.
- However, the information senior managers need to make model choices and to keep their companies competitive needs more research.
- The quality of management information affects leaders' decisions about whether their business model is under threat or needs changing; leaders may or may not choose to use it.
- Although many large firms have made very large investments into areas such as customer insight in the last few years, there may be resistance to using this information, even if it indicates that a firm's current business model is under threat.
- Culture can also play a role if a company's way of doing things is set in stone, bound by a legacy process or tied to rigid systems or processes that were implemented some time before.
- Another cause may be straightforward denial, the inertia associated with factors such as difficulties in changing business models or the extent to which the firm's financial situation is based upon exploiting its current business model, no matter how much that model is under threat from firms with other business models.
- Therefore, in strategic reviews, firms should factor in these risks and seek to mitigate them.
- In public-sector organisations, the risks of denial or inertia may be stronger due to conservatism and lack of willingness to take the risks of change, so public-sector decision-makers need to be particularly aware of these risks and seek to mitigate them.

Issues

One of the key problems in strategic decision-making processes (which include decisions on strategy and on business models) is identification of whether information has strategic implications and, if so, which – the problem of being able (or not) to "see the forest for the trees"). Due to developments in information technology, business leaders now have access to far more information than previously, both about what is happening in their own organisations and about the outside world. Although many easily comprehensible ways of portraying this information have been developed, this does not solve the problem of information overload, although it could be argued that through good processes and learning, leaders will learn to identify which information they need for business model change decisions. However, it could also be argued that the very nature of business model innovation sometimes means that the information required is of a new type and so not routinely accessible to leaders, or else it could be existing information requiring new interpretation. This area therefore needs further research. A key future contribution of marketing researchers will be to help companies identify the need for research to help clarify decisions in this area.

Acknowledgements

This chapter is based partly on:

Stott, R.N., Stone, M. and Fae, J., 2016. Business models in the business-to-business and business-to-consumer worlds – what can each world learn from the other? *Journal of Business and Industrial Marketing*, 31(8), 943–954.

Parnell, B., Stone, M. and Aravopoulou, E., 2018. How leaders manage their business models using information. *The Bottom Line*, 31(2), 150–167.

References

Achtenhagen, L., Melin, L. and Naldi, L., 2013. Dynamics of business models – strategizing, critical capabilities and activities for sustained value creation. *Long Range Planning*, 46(6), 427–442. https://doi.org/10.1016/j.lrp.2013.04.002.

Afuah, A., 2003. *Business Models: A Strategic Management Approach*, 1st ed. New York: McGraw-Hill.

Al-Debei, M., El-Haddadeh, R., Avison, D., 2008. *Defining the Business Model in the New World of Digital Business*. Americas Conference on Information Systems Proceedings, Toronto [online]. Available from: https://pdfs.semanticscholar.org/9f2f/48bdcf94f69cba9df3262fca58988e84b05d.pdf [Accessed 20 June 2020].

Amit, R. and Zott, C., 2001. Value creation in e-business. *Strategic Management Journal*, 22(6/7), 493–520. https://doi.org/10.1002/smj.187.

Amit, R. and Zott, C., 2012. Creating value through business model innovation. *MIT Sloan Management Review*, 53(3), 41–49.

Andries, P. and Debackere, K., 2006. Adaptation in new technology-based ventures: Insights at the company level. *International Journal of Management Reviews*, 8(2), 91–112. https://dx.doi.org/10.1111/j.1468-2370.2006.00122.x.

Andries, P. and Debackere, K., 2007. Adaptation and performance in new businesses: Understanding the moderating effects of independence and industry. *Small Business Economics*, 29(1/2), 81–99. DOI: 10.1007/s11187-005-5640-2.

Andries, P., Debackere, K. and Looy, B., 2013. Simultaneous experimentation as a learning strategy: Business model development under uncertainty. *Strategic Entrepreneurship Journal*, 7(4), 288–310. https://doi.org/10.1002/sej.1170.

Baden-Fuller, C. and Mangematin, V., 2013. Business models: A challenging agenda. *Strategic Organisation*, 11(4), 418–427. https://doi.org/10.1177%2F1476127013510112.

Barberis, N., 2013. Thirty years of prospect theory in economics: A review and assessment. *Journal of Economic Perspectives*, 27(1), 173–196. DOI: 10.1257/jep.27.1.173.

Barr, P., Stimpert, J. and Huff, A., 1992. Cognitive change, strategic action, and organizational renewal. *Strategic Management Journal*, 13(S1), 15–36. https://doi.org/10.1002/smj.4250131004.

Cairncross, F., 2002. *The Company of the Future: Meeting the Management Challenges of the Communications Revolution*. London: Profile Books.

Campbell, N. and Roberts, K., 1986. Lanchester market structures: A Japanese approach to the analysis of business competition. *Strategic Management Journal*, 7(3), 189–200. https://doi.org/10.1002/smj.4250070302.

Carr, M., Miller, P. and Konary, A., 2015. *3rd Platform Ecosystems: Foundational Structures and Business Models*. Framingham, MA: IDC.

Chesbrough, H., 2006. *Open Business Models*. Boston, MA: Harvard Business School Press.

Chesbrough, H. and Rosenbloom, R.S., 2002. The role of the business model in capturing value from innovation: Evidence from Xerox Corporation's technology spin-off companies. *Industrial and Corporate Change*, 11(3), 529–555. https://doi.org/10.1093/icc/11.3.529.

Christopher, M., 2000. The agile supply chain: Competing in volatile markets. *Industrial Marketing Management*, 29(1), 37–44. http://dx.doi.org/10.1016/S0019-8501(99)00110-8.

David, F., 2004. *Strategic Management Concepts*, 10th ed. Upper Saddle River, NJ: Prentice Hall.

Demil, B. and Lecocq, X., 2010. Business model evolution: In search of dynamic consistency. *Long Range Planning*, 43(2/3), 227–246. DOI: 10.1016/j.lrp.2010.02.004.

Doz, Y. and Kosonen, M., 2010. Embedding strategic agility: A leadership agenda for accelerating business model renewal. *Long Range Planning*, 43(2/3), 370–382. https://doi.org/10.1016/j.lrp.2009.07.006.

Dutton, J. and Jackson, S., 1987. Categorizing strategic issues: Links to organizational action. *Academy of Management Review*, 12(1), 76–90. DOI: 10.2307/257995.

Fensel, D., 2001. *Ontologies: Silver Bullet for Knowledge Management and Electronic Commerce*. Heidelberg: Springer. DOI: 10.1007/978-3-662-04396-7.

Foss, N.J. and Stieglitz, N., 2015. Business model innovation: The role of leadership. In N. Foss and T. Saebi, eds. *Business Model Innovation: The Organisational Dimension*. Oxford: Oxford University Press. DOI: 10.1093/acprof:oso/9780198701873.001.0001.

Gatignon, H. and Xuereb, J., 1997. Strategic orientation of the firm and new product performance. *Journal of Marketing Research*, 34(1), 77–90. https://doi.org/10.1177/002224379703400107.

Ginsberg, A. and Venkatraman, N., 1985. Contingency perspectives of organizational strategy: A critical review of the empirical research. *Academy of Management Review*, 10(3), 421–434. https://doi.org/10.5465/amr.1985.4278950.

Hammer, M., 2001. The superefficient company. *Harvard Business Review*, 79(8), 82–91.

Kahneman, D. and Tversky, A., 1979. On the interpretation of intuitive probability: A reply to Jonathan Cohen. *Cognition*, 7(4), 409–411. https://doi.org/10.1016/0010-0277(79)90024-6.

Kim, W. and Mauborgne, R., 2015. *Blue Ocean Strategy: How to Create Uncontested Market Space and Make the Competition Irrelevant*, Expanded ed. Boston, MA: Harvard Business School Press.

Lambert, S. and Davidson, R., 2013. Applications of the business model in studies of success, innovation and classification: An analysis of empirical research from 1996 to 2010. *European Management Journal*, 31(6), 668–681. https://doi.org/10.1016/j.emj.2012.07.007.

Lanchester, F., 1916. *Aircraft in Warfare: The Dawn of the Fourth Arm*. London: Constable and Company.

Lant, T. and Mezias, S., 1992. An organizational learning model of convergence and reorientation. *Organization Science*, 3(1), 47–71. http://dx.doi.org/10.1287/orsc.3.1.47.

Linder, J. and Cantrell, S., 2000. *Changing Business Models*. Chicago: Accenture [online]. Available from: www.businessmodels.eu/images/banners/Articles/Linder_Cantrell.pdf [Accessed 20 June 2020].

Manyika, J., Chui, M., Bughin, J., Dobbs, R., Bisson, P. and Marrs, A., 2013. *Disruptive Technologies: Advances That Will Transform Life, Business, and the Global Economy*. San Francisco, CA: McKinsey Global Institute [online]. Available from: www.mckinsey.com:www.mckinsey.com/business-functions/digital-mckinsey/our-insights/disruptive-technologies [Accessed 2 April 2020].

Margretta, J., 2002. Why Business Models Matter. *Harvard Business Review*, 3–8.

Mason, K. and Leek, S., 2008. Learning to build a supply network: An exploration of dynamic business models. *Journal of Management Studies*, 45(4), 774–799. https://doi.org/10.1111/j.1467-6486.2008.00769.x.

Mason, K. and Mouzas, S., 2012. Flexible business models. *European Journal of Marketing*, 46(10), 1340–1367. DOI: 10.1108/03090561211248062.

McGrath, R., 2010. Business models: A discovery driven approach. *Long Range Planning*, 43(2), 247–261. DOI: 10.1016/j.lrp.2009.07.005.

McNamara, P., Peck, S. and Sasson, A., 2013. Competing business models, value creation and appropriation in English football. *Long Range Planning*, 46(6), 475–487. DOI: 10.1016/j.lrp.2011.10.002.

Morris, M., Schindehutte, M. and Allen, J., 2005. The entrepreneur's business model: Toward a unified perspective." *Journal of Business Research*, 58(6), 726–735. DOI: 10.1016/j.jbusres.2003.11.00.

Osterwalder, A. and Pigneur, Y., 2010. *Business Model Generation*. Hoboken, NJ: John Wiley and Sons, Inc.

Osterwalder, A., Pigneur, Y. and Tucci, C.L., 2005. Clarifying business models: Origins, present, and future of the concept. *Communications of the Association for Information Systems*, 16(1), 1–25. https://doi.org/10.17705/1CAIS.01601.

Parnell, B., Stone, M. and Aravopoulou, E., 2018. How leaders manage their business models using information. *The Bottom Line*, 31(2), 150–167. DOI: 10.1108/BL-04-2018-0017.

Porter, M., 2001. Strategy and the Internet. *Harvard Business Review*, 2–19.

Porter, M. and Millar, V., 1985. How information gives you competitive advantage. *Harvard Business Review*, 63, 149–160.

Prahalad, C. and Krishnan, M., 2008. *The New Age of Innovation: Driving Co-Created Value Through Global Networks*. New York: McGraw-Hill.

Saebi, T., Lien, L. and Foss, N., 2017. What drives business model adaptation? The impact of opportunities, threats and strategic orientation. *Long Range Planning*, 50(5), 567–581. https://doi.org/10.1016/j.lrp.2016.06.006.

Sanchez, R. and Mahoney, J., 1996. Modularity, flexibility and knowledge management in product and organisational design. *Strategic Management Journal*, 17(S2), 63–76. https://doi.org/10.1002/smj.4250171107.

Schumpeter, J., 1994. *Capitalism, Socialism and Democracy*. London: Routledge.

Seddon, P. and Lewis, G., 2003. *Strategy and Business Models: What's the Difference?* 7th Asia Pacific Conference on Information Systems Proceedings, Adelaide [online]. Available from: http://dr-ama.com/wp-content/uploads/2012/12/business-model.pdf [Accessed 20 June 2020].

Staheler, P., 2002. *Business Models as a Unit of Analysis for Strategizing*. In 1st International Workshop on Business Models Proceedings, Lausanne [online]. Available from: www.hec.unil.ch/aosterwa/Documents/workshop/Draft_Staehler.pdf [Accessed 20 June 2020].

Staw, B., Sandelands, L. and Dutton, J., 1981. Threat rigidity effects in organizational behavior: A multilevel analysis. *Administrative Science Quarterly*, 26(4), 501–524. http://dx.doi.org/10.2307/2392337.

Stone, M., 1984. Competing with Japan – the rules of the game. *Long Range Planning*, 17(2), 33–47.

Stone, M., 2015. Competitive marketing intelligence in a digital, data-based world. *Journal of Direct, Data and Digital Marketing Practice*, 17(1), 20–29. https://doi.org/10.1057/dddmp.2015.42.

Stone, M., Laughlin, P., Aravopoulou, E., Gerardi, G., Todeva, E. and Weinzierl, L., 2017. How platforms are transforming customer information management. *The Bottom Line*, 30(3), 216–235. DOI: 10.1108/BL-08-2017-002.

Stone, M., Machtynger, L. and Woodcock, N., 2002. *Customer Relationship Marketing*. London: Kogan Page.

Stott, R.N., Stone, M. and Fae, J., 2016. Business models in the business-to-business and business-to-consumer worlds – what can each world learn from the other? *Journal of Business and Industrial Marketing*, 31(8), 943–954. https://doi.org/10.1108/JBIM-10-2016-267.

Strohelin, M., 2015. *Industry Developments and Models: Seven Practices for Fostering Enterprise Digital Transformation*. Framingham, MA: IDC.

Teece, D., 2007. Explicating dynamic capabilities: The nature and microfoundations of (sustainable) enterprise performance. *Strategic Management Journal*, 28(13), 1319–1350. https://doi.org/10.1002/smj.640.

Teece, D., 2010. Business models, business strategy and innovation. *Long Range Planning*, 43(2–3), 172–194. https://doi.org/10.1016/j.lrp.2009.07.003.

Tripsas, M. and Gavetti, G., 2000. Capabilities, cognition, and inertia: Evidence from digital imaging. *Strategic Management Journal*, 21(10/11), 1147–1161. https://doi.org/10.1002/1097-0266(200010/11)21:10/11%3C1147::AID-SMJ128%3E3.0.CO;2-R.

Veit, D., Clemons, E., Benlian, A. and Buxmann., P., 2014. Business models: An information systems research agenda. *Business and Information Systems Engineering*, 6(1), 45–53. DOI: 10.1007/s12599-013-0308-y.

Willemstein, L., van der Valk, T. and Meeus, M.T., 2007. Dynamics in business models: An empirical analysis of medical biotechnology firms in the Netherlands. *Technovation*, 27(4), 221–232. DOI: 10.1016/j.technovation.2006.08.005.

Zott, C. and Amit, R., 2007. Business model design and the performance of entrepreneurial firms. *Organization Science*, 18(2), 181–199. DOI: 10.1287/orsc.1060.0232.

Zott, C. and Amit, R., 2010. Business model design: An activity system perspective. *Long Range Planning*, 43(2/3), 216–226. DOI: 10.1016/j.lrp.2009.07.004.

PART II

Methods

5

MIXED-METHODS RESEARCH

Why and how to use it

Pantea Foroudi, Maria Palazzo and Merlin Stone

Summary

This chapter explains what mixed methods research is, investigates how researchers should determine whether to use mixed methods in their research and explains how to carry out mixed methods research. It explores in detail the justification of different methods at different stages of the research process. It considers the extent to which practical applicability in business should determine the overall research method, the modelling of the situation being researched, and the choice of statistical tools. It will be particularly valuable for postgraduate researchers in marketing and related business disciplines. The case study of consumers' perceptions towards Hong Kong and Shanghai Banking Corporation's (HSBC) visual identity is employed to illustrate how the mixed-method approach can deliver insight.

Justifying the research methodology

The importance of a paradigm

According to various researchers (e.g. Burrell and Morgan 1979; Deshpande 1983), the marketing paradigm is significant. In academic marketing research, the researcher defines a set of underlying assumptions that serve as a guideline to understand the subject as well as to generate valid and reliable results. A paradigm is a cluster of beliefs which, for scientists in a discipline, influence what should be researched, how study should be done and how the results should be interpreted (Bryman 2004). Tashakkori and Teddlie (1998) indicate that paradigms are opposing worldviews or belief systems that are an indication of and guide the decisions that researchers make.

Paradigms are systems of interrelated ontological, epistemological and methodological assumptions. Ontology is how the researcher regards the nature and form of social reality. Epistemology is the assumption of how people know things and the association between the researcher and the phenomenon studied (nature, sources and limits of knowledge). The methodology paradigm is the technique used by the researcher to discover reality – it relates to the questions and techniques used in a study to collect and validate empirical evidence (the process of conducting the inquiry) (Creswell 2003). According to Lincoln and Guba (2000), these claims can be called "paradigms" or can be considered research methodologies.

Positivism and interpretivism

In social research, two dominant epistemological assumptions are interpretivism-idealism-phenomenology and positivism (e.g. Cassell and Symon 1994; Corbetta 2003; Deshpande 1983; Easterby-Smith *et al.* 2002). Previous studies employed the terms "naturalistic" and "scientific", whereas Tashakkori and Teddlie (1998) use the terms "positivist" and "constructivist". The main classification of each philosophical assumption is presented in Table 5.1.

Interpretivism is social research that aims to develop an understanding of social life and discover how people construct meaning in natural settings (Neuman 2003). Interpretivism addresses the process of interaction between individuals while taking account of the fact that their background shapes their construction of meaning and pragmatism, which deals with actions, situations and consequences rather than antecedent conditions (Creswell 2003). Phenomenology views the world as the qualitative paradigm (Deshpande 1983). The interpretivist approach is concerned with building inductive hypotheses, studying phenomena through direct experience in order to understand the world (Bryman 2004).

Positivism is the oldest and most widely used approach; it is broadly a natural sciences approach. Positivist approaches aim to improve understanding by adopting different methods. Positivism uses the scientific deductive method to conduct empirical and quantitative research (Creswell 2003). The logical positivist view of the world is synonymous with the quantitative paradigm (Deshpande 1983). Furthermore, positivist research employs procedures associated with inferential statistics, hypothesis testing and experimental and quasi-experimental design. Positivism assumes that social reality is external and should be measured by objective methods (Creswell 2003).

To choose which paradigm would lead to a more accurate investigation, the nature of research questions and objectives should be considered. Deshpande (1983) recommends that marketers focus on both paradigms: the positivism and idealism paradigm (theory verification and theory generation) to avoid method bias, which frequently occurs due to focusing on one paradigm. Paradigms should not be considered mutually exclusive (ways of describing these paradigms are illustrated in Table 5.2). Theory generation allows the researcher to develop propositions to be tested later, perhaps using theory verification by quantitative methods.

Pursuing both paradigms has two main results (Table 5.3). The use of qualitative study to obtain preliminary insights into study problems can establish an appropriate scale to measure the

Table 5.1 Research paradigms

	Positivist paradigm	*Phenomenological paradigm*
Basic beliefs	The world is external and objective	The world is socially constructed and subjective
	Observer is independent	Observer is part of what is observed
	Science is value-free	Science is driven by human interests
Preferred methods	Focus on facts	Focus on meanings
	Look for causality and fundamental laws	Try to understand what is happening
	Reduce phenomenon to simplest elements	Look at the totality of each situation
	Formulate hypotheses and then test them	Develop ideas through induction from data
	Taking large samples	Small samples investigated in depth or over time

Source: Easterby-Smith *et al.* (2002)

Table 5.2 Alternative paradigm names

Positivist	Interpretive
Quantitative	Qualitative
Objectivist	Subjectivist
Scientific	Humanistic
Experimentalist	Phenomenological
Traditionalist	Revolutionist

Source: Malhotra and Birks (2000, p. 138)

Table 5.3 Comparison between qualitative and quantitative approaches

	Quantitative research	Qualitative research
Purpose	Deductive: verification and outcome oriented, precise measurement and comparison of variables, establishing relationships between variables, interface from sample to population	Inductive: discovery and process oriented, meaning, context, process Discovering unanticipated events, influences and conditions, inductive development of theory
Research questions	Variance questions, truth of proposition, presence or absence, degree or amount, correlation, hypothesis testing, causality (factual)	Process questions, how and why, meaning, context (holistic), hypotheses as part of conceptual framework, causality (physical)
Research methods		
Relationship	Objectivity/reduction of influence (research as an extraneous variable)	Use of influence as a tool for understanding (research as part of process)
Sampling	Probability sampling, establishing valid comparisons	Purposeful sampling
Data collection	Measures tend to be objective, prior development of instruments, standardisation, measurement/testing-quantitative/categorical	Measures tend to be subjective, inductive development of strategies, adapting to particular situation, collection of textual or visual material
Data analysis	Numerical descriptive analysis (statistics, correlation), estimation of population variables, statistical hypothesis testing, conversion of textual data into numbers or categories	Textual analysis (memos, coding, connecting), grounded theory, narrative approaches
Reliability/validity	Reliable, technology as instrument (the evaluator is removed from the data)	Valid, self as instrument (the evaluator is close to the data)
Generalisability	Generalisable, the outsider's perspective, population oriented	Ungeneralisable, the insider's perspective

Source: Maxwell and Loomis (2003, p. 190), Steckler *et al.* (1992)

focal construct of the research, which can be used later to test theories and hypotheses. It also it helps to identify a new set of scales, which may be useful in measuring marketing constructs. Second, it improves the validity, reliability and generalisability of the research (Bryman 2006; Creswell 2003) by employing a positivist paradigm to test the model and hypotheses and their causal relationship (Shiu *et al.* 2009).

The central research question and the research model

Before deciding on the specific research method, the researcher should determine what type of relationship is under investigation. For example, it is increasingly common for academic marketing researchers to use structured equation modelling, because it is an ideal tool for disentangling the relationship between complex sets of variables. For example, if the researcher wants to find, in a given sample, the relative importance of consumers' perceptions of the quality of customer service in banking, their perceptions of bank brands, whether they use several banks and their loyalty to their main banks, then structured equation modelling would be appropriate to find the relative importance of these variables and whether one or more variables mediate the relationship between a given variable and the object of the study, loyalty to their main bank. However, if the object of the study is to find out for which customers the relationship between perceptions of customer service and loyalty is strong and for which it is weak, then more classic statistical methods might be better.

There is no right answer, but it can be argued than one determinant of the approach should be whether the research study aims to provide practical help to management. In the previous case, for example, it could be argued that management are well aware of the importance of the variables mentioned – they are all important. So, management does not need another study exploring in detail the relationship between variables but would find a study which contributes to segmenting between different types of customers very helpful. Too often, academic researchers decide that they want to study a topic without regard for management implications and then have to force some conclusions about management implications based upon the analysis method or the model that they decided to use. This approach is bound to lead to reduced relevance in their work.

Selection of research approach

To provide a more comprehensive approach to increasing the understanding of the research problem, the best fit was the pluralist research approach (Deshpande 1983; Mingers 2001). Mingers (2001) states, "the different research methods (especially from different paradigms) focus on different aspects of reality and therefore a richer understanding of a research together in a single piece of research or research program . . . combining several methods" (p. 241). Deshpande (1983) and Mingers (2001) believe that ignoring the potential contribution of methods related to non-positivist approaches (e.g. in-depth interviews) probably limits the understanding of researchers who use the positivist approach.

The use of more than one research method (focus group, interview, and questionnaire) enriches the understanding of the phenomenon under study and can reveal new insights (Creswell 2003). Based on the development of research methodology and perceived legitimacy of both quantitative and qualitative research, social and human sciences researchers increasingly use the mixed-methods approach. Creswell (2003) states that the approach is a "quantitative study based on testing a theory in an experiment with a small qualitative interview component in the data collection phase" (p. 177). Qualitative and quantitative approaches may be collected sequentially to confirm, cross-validate or corroborate findings at one stage in the research process.

The phases of research

Four phases can be identified:

- Initiation, before the data collection, for example, when the study problem/measures/ sample are created;
- Implementation – the sequence the researcher uses to collect both quantitative and qualitative data (Creswell 2003);
- Integration – occurs within research questions, data collection, data analysis (Creswell 2003);
- Interpretation, when conclusions are drawn to strengthen the knowledge claims of the research or to explain any lack of convergence that may result.

The mixed-methods approach used to be used mainly in the data collection phase, but now it is used at different stages of the research – problem setting; theory building; and data collection, analysis and interpretation (Bryman 2006; Creswell 2003). The mixed-methods approach increases a construct's reliability and validity (e.g. Bryman 2006; Churchill 1979; Creswell 2003). Also, combining qualitative and quantitative methods often enhances their strengths.

Analysing qualitative data

The analysis of qualitative data can be carried out by content analysis. Bryman (2006) identified two schemes to justify the combination of quantitative and qualitative research based on a content analysis. The significant scheme was developed in the context of assessment research by Greene *et al.* (1989). They coded each article in terms of a primary and a secondary rationale (Bryman 2006). According to Bryman (2006), the scheme developed by Greene *et al.* (1989, p. 259) isolates five justifications for combining qualitative and quantitative research (Table 5.4). According to Bryman (2006), the "advantage of the Greene *et al.* (1989) scheme is its parsimony, in that it boils down the possible reasons for conducting multi-strategy research to just five reasons, although the authors' analysis revealed that initiation was uncommon" (p. 105). In this method, qualitative research is vital for understanding complex social phenomena, helping the researcher develop the theme from the respondents' points of view. Quantitative research summarises a large amount of data for generalisation purposes. The disadvantage is that it only allows primary and secondary data to be coded. For that reason, a more detailed but significantly less parsimonious scheme was devised. Bryman (2006) identified the second scheme with its rationales (see Table 5.4).

Following the positivist perspective, an empirical investigation can be conducted to verify the conceptual model, explain the main concept and generalise the research in a large sample by adopting the quantitative research (questionnaire) (Ageeva *et al.* 2018, 2019a, 2019b). Alternatively, researchers can begin with quantitative methods and move to qualitative research. This approach is similar to an example given by Creswell (2003), where the key approach was quantitative research, based on examining a theory but with a short number of qualitative interviews in the data collection phase. Figure 5.1 illustrates the procedures of mixed methods.

To increase the validity of the study, an inductive approach can be used before the main survey, and the qualitative data collection technique should be used to generate hypotheses and

Table 5.4 Justifications and rationale for combining quantitative and qualitative methods

First scheme	
Triangulation	Convergence, corroboration, correspondence or results from different methods. In coding triangulation, the emphasis was placed on seeking corroboration between quantitative and qualitative data.
Complementarity	Seeks elaboration, enhancement, illustration, clarification of the results from one method with the results from another.
Development	Seeks to use the results from one method to help develop or inform the other method, where development is broadly construed to include sampling and implementation, as well as measurement decisions.
Initiation	Seeks the discovery of paradox and contradiction, new perspectives of [sic] frameworks, the recasting of questions or results from one method with questions or results from the other method.
Expansion	Seeks to extend the breadth and range of enquiry by using different methods for different inquiry components.
Second scheme	
Triangulation or greater validity	Refers to the traditional view that quantitative and qualitative research might be combined to triangulate findings in order that they may be mutually corroborated. If the term was used as a synonym for integrating quantitative and qualitative research, it was not coded as triangulation.
Offset	Refers to the suggestion that the research methods associated with both quantitative and qualitative research have their own strengths and weaknesses so that combining them allows the researcher to offset their weaknesses to draw on the strengths of both.
Completeness	Refers to the notion that the researcher can bring together a more comprehensive account of the area of enquiry in which he or she is interested if both quantitative and qualitative research is employed.
Process	Quantitative research provides an account of structures in social life, but qualitative research provides a sense of process.
Different research questions	This is the argument that quantitative and qualitative research can each answer different research questions, but this item was coded only if the authors explicitly stated that they were doing this.
Explanation	One is used to help explain findings generated by the other.
Unexpected results	Refers to the suggestion that quantitative and qualitative research can be fruitfully combined when one generates surprising results that can be understood by employing the other.
Instrument development	Refers to contexts in which qualitative research is employed to develop questionnaire and scale items – for example, so that better wording or more comprehensive closed answers can be generated.
Sampling	Refers to situations in which one approach is used to facilitate the sampling of respondents or cases.
Credibility	Refers to suggestions that employing both approaches enhances the integrity of findings.
Context	Refers to cases in which the combination is rationalised in terms of qualitative research, providing contextual understanding coupled with either generalisable, externally valid findings or broad relationships among variables uncovered through a survey.
Illustration	Refers to the use of qualitative data to illustrate quantitative findings, often referred to as putting "meat on the bones" of "dry" quantitative findings.

(Continued)

Utility or improving the usefulness of findings	Refers to a suggestion, which is more likely to be prominent among articles with an applied focus, that combining the two approaches will be more useful to practitioners and others.
Confirm and discover	Entails using qualitative data to generate hypotheses and using quantitative research to test them within a single project.
Diversity of views	This includes two slightly different rationales – combining researchers' and participants' perspectives through quantitative and qualitative research, respectively, and uncovering relationships between variables through quantitative research.
Enhancement or building upon quantitative and/or qualitative findings	This entails a reference to making more of or augmenting either quantitative or qualitative findings by gathering data using a qualitative or quantitative research approach.

Source: Bryman (2006, pp. 105–107)

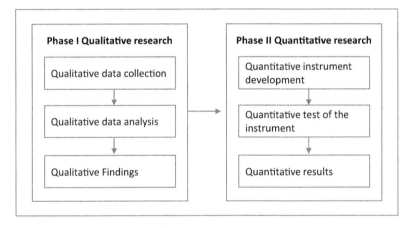

Figure 5.1 Mixed-methods procedures

purify measures for the questionnaire. (Deshpande 1983; Churchill 1979) suggest a quantitative approach with multi-method engagement in the initial stages of an investigation. To examine the research's focal construct, quantitative methods are more suitable than the qualitative method. This method is more appropriate for theory testing than theory generation.

To measure the focal construct, it is suggested that researchers follow Churchill's (1979) approach for developing measures of multiple items for marketing constructs and the approach of Gerbing and Anderson (1988) and DeVellis (2003) in order to construct a set of reliable and valid scales for establishing measurement reliability. This is expected to result in stronger relationships than the use of single-item measures. According to Churchill's (1979) theory, it integrates a qualitative paradigm while being predominantly quantitative in nature. Figure 5.2 illustrates the proposed steps in measurement scale development for marketing constructs. According to Churchill (1979), the first phase of research design is exploratory fieldwork.

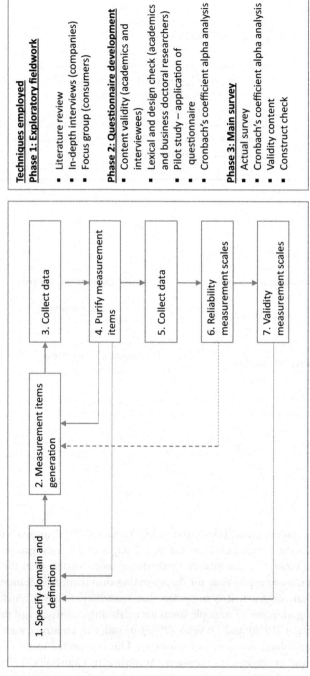

Figure 5.2 Steps in measurement scale development

Source: Based on Churchill (1979, p. 66)

The first phase (qualitative fieldwork)

An initial exploratory study can be carried out for the following reasons:

- To gain an in-depth understanding of the research area (Dacin and Brown 2002);
- To achieve insights into the research context;
- To understand the actual practice in the field in order to gauge whether the proposed research study was relevant;
- To obtain insightful information and understand the proposed research questions, generate hypotheses and purify measures for a questionnaire (Churchill 1979).

Churchill (1979) suggests that the exploratory study, known as an "experience survey", consist of "a judgement sample of persons who can offer ideas and insights into the phenomenon" (p. 66). Exploratory studies tend to begin with a wide study and narrow down to study development (Saunders *et al.* 2007). Churchill (1979) suggests that certain techniques be used to generate sample items and reflect a construct (exploratory research, literature search, interview and focus group).

In-depth interviews and group discussions are very useful in bringing a new perspective to existing data (Ageeva *et al.* 2019a, 2019b; Ritchie *et al.* 2003). The data collected from interviews and focus groups supplies information and insights and adds more data that was not identified in the literature review. However, exploratory research rarely involves large samples (Malhotra and Birks 2000). To minimise any weaknesses, qualitative data can be used to construct a quantitative study, mainly in the form of a questionnaire (Churchill 1979). Table 5.5 illustrates the main benefits of using interviews and focus groups.

Table 5.5 Application of in-depth interviews and focus groups

	In-depth interviews	*Focus groups*
Nature of data	For generating in-depth personal accounts	For generating data that is shaped by group interaction, refined and reflected
	To understand the personal context	To display a social context exploring how people talk about an issue
	For exploring issues in depth and in detail	For creative thinking and solutions, to display and discuss differences within the group
Subject matter	To understand complex processes and issues, for example, motivations, decisions, impacts, outcomes	To tackle abstract and conceptual subjects where enabling or projective techniques are to be used or in different or technical subjects where information is provided
	To explore private subjects or those involving social norms, for sensitive issues	For issues that would be illuminated by the display of social norms, for some sensitive issues, with careful group composition and handling
Study population	For participants who are likely to be willing or able to travel	Where participants are likely to be willing or able to travel to attend a group discussion
	Where the study population is geographically dispersed, where the population is highly diverse	Where the population is geographically clustered, where there is some shared background or relationship to the research topic
	Where there are issues of power or status	For participants who are unlikely to be inhibited by group setting
	Where people have communication difficulties	

Source: Adapted from Ritchie *et al.* (2003)

Planning, management and data interpretation of the qualitative stage

There are many approaches to qualitative data analysis, and these have been widely debated in the literature (Bazeley 2007; Bryman and Burgess 1994; Silverman 1993). One approach is to begin with grounded theory to test the data. To analyse the qualitative data, a process of coding should be used and guided by the conceptual framework developed using the literature. The researcher builds codes by creation of a shared understanding of the focal construct and its dimensions. This sets the framework for coding and analysing the data. The researcher determines that start codes address the research questions, hypotheses, problem areas and/or key variables that the researcher identifies (Ageeva *et al.* 2019a, 2019b; Miles and Huberman 1994, p. 58).

Initially, coding of the narratives is based on the open-code process and the constructs identified in the literature review. According to Miles and Huberman (1994), the start list of codes should be based on a "conceptual framework, list of research questions, hypotheses, problem areas, and/or key variables that the researcher brings to the study" (p. 58). The researcher writes a memo for each interview transcript before coding the transcript. Coding the data makes it easier to search, to make comparisons and to identify any patterns that require further investigation. The process of coding data from interview transcripts situates the process as qualitative analysis (Andriotis *et al.* 2020; Weston *et al.* 2001). Under descriptive codes, the collected data should be gathered and thematic ideas that emerge with the data collected and related to the same content (Brown *et al.* 2019; Malhotra and Birks 2000; Lincoln and Guba 1985). According to Lincoln and Guba (1985), it is vital to "devise rules that describe category properties and that can, ultimately, be used to justify the inclusion of each data bit that remains assigned to the category as well as to provide a basis for later tests of replicability" (p. 347). The process ensures that the theoretical ideas that emerge from the first round of coding can be systematically shown in the data (Esterberg 2002). Codes are analysed in three stages of coding: open coding, axial coding and selective coding (Esterberg 2002; Huberman and Miles 1994). The three stages of coding enhance improve the trustworthiness of the emergent data. The stages of the coding process are explained in Table 5.6.

The first stage of the data analysis is generation of open codes. The open codes are interpreted and categorised into higher concepts until the core categories emerge. The open code begins with reviewing the texts individually (interview transcripts), line by line, and highlighting passages where the focal construct and relationships are discussed and coded using the starting list of new open codes formed during the process. Transcripts should be read twice very carefully to find the patterns in the texts that are relevant to the literature. Each sentence should be compared with earlier sentences and with open codes for differences and similarities. If the codes are the same or very similar, they are coded identically. If the codes are very dissimilar, the

Table 5.6 The stages of the coding process

Stages of the coding process	
Open coding	First stage, through which concepts are identified.
Axial coding	Second stage, through which second-order categories are inductively derived from first-order concepts generated during open coding.
Selective coding	Final stage, through which the emergent theory is identified and refined and the emergent themes are integrated.

Source: Strauss and Corbin (1998)

new sentence is coded using a separate label. The main aim of open coding is to find patterns in the texts that are similar to or different from the related literature review. Following open coding of each interview transcript, the researcher should read the open codes and write more comments and memos to make the analysis more rigorous. This results in the creation of the axial code.

Axial coding is the second stage of data analysis and tries to establish the relationship and contrast between the core categories and sub-categories to enable the identification of patterns within the texts. Systematic axial coding is started after all open coding. Axial coding as a unique approach has the advantage of not misleading the data analysis. Axial codings are maximised by taking into account all of the open codes within one case. The procedure of axial coding is a process of constant comparison. Axial codes are generated based on differences and similarities of the collected data in open coding. After generating the axial code, the open codes are compared with each other and with the generated axial codes. This process assists the researcher in creating a new axial code and changing or merging the existing axial codes.

The final stage of coding is selective coding, which aims to integrate the emerging theory. Selective coding is the most complicated step of grounded theory analysis. To produce a theory that can eventually fit the data, the phenomena must be described in a way that is parsimonious (Strauss and Corbin 1998). According to Spiggle (1994), selective coding "involves moving to a higher level of abstraction with the developed paradigmatic constructs, specifying relationships, and delineating a core category or construct around which the other categories and constructs revolve and that relates them to one another" (p. 495). Strauss and Corbin (1998) state that selective coding begins throughout the axial coding stage by identifying the relationship between these axial codes. This stage is the most difficult and confusing stage of grounded theory analysis, as it is needed to explain the phenomena but must be parsimonious.

In addition to the standard theoretical coding process such as comparison, question asking and writing memos, the researcher employs an extra three techniques:

- Reviewing the research questions as a general guideline;
- Re-considering the open codes and raw data while comparing axial codes,
- Discussing the codes with supervisors and experts to identify the fitness and relationship between the codes.

By reviewing the data, the researcher should able to find the dimensions of the focal construct, its main causes and its consequences. To produce a refined and complete synthesis and interpretation of the material collected, QSR NVivo software is appropriate for data administration and to achieve results. NVivo has tools for recording, data storage, retrieval and linking ideas and exploring the patterns of data and interpretation. It has a wide range of tools in a symmetrical, simple and accurate structure. The use of computer software helps to ensure rigour in the analytic process. NVivo allows the researcher to interrogate the data at a detailed level, addresses the validity and reliability of the study results and also ensures that the researcher work more methodically, thoroughly and attentively (Bazeley 2007). It makes data analysis more reliable, easier, more accurate and more transparent (Gibbs 2002) and manipulation and analysis of the data easier. It is useful for mapping out findings diagrammatically and assists the researcher with viewing the whole text, enabling the inter-relationships between codes to be seen easily (Edirisinghe *et al.* 2019; Welsh 2002). It is also useful for data storage and retrieval (Esterberg 2002).

The researcher should recognise the value of both manual and electronic tools in qualitative data analysis and management and the use of both (Welsh 2002). The data should be checked against the content of specific nodes, as this could affect the inter-relationships of the thematic ideas, reviewing the nodes (themes) for consistency, and proceeding through the qualitative data analysis. To verify the reliability of the coding through content analysis, the code should be established more than once (Weber 1985) by another researcher to gain their agreement on identification of the themes. Content analysis is a research technique for making replicable and valid inferences from data to its context. Patton (2015) states, "the qualitative analyst's effort at uncovering patterns, themes, and categories is a creative process that requires making carefully considered judgments about what is really significant and meaningful in the data" (p. 406). The coding system is used to analyse each word and phrase, allowing consideration of possible meanings assumed or intended by the speaker (Palazzo *et al.* 2020; Weston *et al.* 2001). The researcher should try to locate the phenomenon within the data and mark where the phenomenon begins and ends (Weston *et al.* 2001), based on a prior research-driven code development approach (Patton 2015; Strauss and Corbin 1998). The researcher may collect "rich" data in the form of verbatim transcripts of all interviews with each interviewee, providing the information needed to test the developing scales. This allows consistency of terminology and with previous work. It also facilitates explanation of the data using the relevant research framework.

Validity and reliability

The quality of the data is significant in social sciences because of the diverse philosophical and methodological approaches that are taken to the study of human activity (Ritchie *et al.* 2003). Validity and reliability contribute to designing a study, analysing its results and judging its quality. However, there is no common definition of reliability and validity in qualitative research. To certify the reliability of the research, an assessment of "trustworthiness" is needed. The notion of determining truth through measures of reliability and validity is substantiated by the idea of trustworthiness (Lincoln and Guba 1985). Seale (1999) states that the "trustworthiness of a research report lies at the heart of issues conventionally discussed as validity and reliability" (p. 266). A theoretical sample rather than a statistically random sample can "maximise opportunities for comparing concepts along their properties for the similarities and differences enabling researchers to define categories, to differentiate among them, and to specify their range of variability" (Strauss and Corbin 1998, p. 149). As Lincoln and Guba (1985) stated, "there is no validity without reliability, an expression of the former validity is sufficient to establish the latter reliability" (p. 316). Reliability means sustainable results, and validity means the research is well grounded in the data. Reliability addresses how accurately the research methods and techniques produce data and is a consequence of the validity in a study (Patton 2015). Table 5.7 presents the techniques that could improve trustworthiness.

To examine how the validity and reliability of a study are affected by the qualitative researchers' perceptions and hence to eradicate bias and increase the study's truthfulness, the triangulation method is used. Creswell and Miller (2000) describe triangulation as: "a validity procedure where researchers search for convergence among multiple and different sources of information to form themes or categories in a study" (p. 126). Triangulation improves the validity and reliability of a study and evaluation of its findings. Reliability, validity and triangulation are approaches to establishing truth. To verify the reliability of coding through content analysis, stability is ascertained when content is coded more than once (Vollero *et al.* 2020; Weber 1985). To assess the reliability of emergent categories of the focal construct, one independent coder with considerable qualitative research experience but unfamiliar with the study should be employed.

Table 5.7 Meeting the criteria of trustworthiness

Traditional criteria	Trustworthiness criteria	Techniques employed to ensure trustworthiness
Internal validity	Credibility	Quality access (researcher was provided with an office desk, computer, access to company intranet, email address, freedom of talking to and interviewing anybody, freedom of getting any company documents, including lots of confidential strategic documents) and extensive engagement in the field
		Multiple triangulations
		Peer debriefing
		Constant comparison
External validity	Transferability	Detailed description of the research setting
		Multiple cases and cross-case comparison
Reliability	Dependability	Purposive and theoretical sampling
		Cases and informant confidentiality protected
		Rigorous multiple stages of coding
Objectivity	Confirmability	Separately presenting the exemplar open and axial codes
		Word-by-word interview transcription
		Accurate records of contacts and interviews
		Writing a research journal
		Carefully keeping notes of observation
		Regularly keeping notes of emergent theoretical and methodological ideas

Source: Lincoln and Guba (1985)

Interviews

To meet the research objectives, the research should start with interviews, to identify and operationalise the main elements to measure the focal construct. In-depth interviews can generate a deeper understanding of the subject and collect attitudinal and behavioural data (Shiu *et al.* 2009). A topic guide helps to outline the focal construct as the topic of interest, balance the interview with the key topics and encourage continuity in discussions. The interview can be conducted face to face or digitally, to establish a clear overview of the focal construct and allow deeper understanding of the research objective. The interviews can take place in a location chosen by the participant (Ritchie *et al.* 2003). Usually, interviewers decide the venues and timing of interviews. The interview should be recorded and transcribed verbatim to ensure reliability (Andriopoulos and Lewis 2009). The in-depth interview technique can unveil fundamental motivations, beliefs, attitudes and feelings about the topic. A question sheet should be designed to check whether all areas of interest are covered during the interviews.

Researchers should observe a professional dress code and present themselves as researchers (Easterby-Smith *et al.* 2002). The researcher should develop trust with the respondents through different approaches. In-depth interviews give "the opportunity for the researcher to probe deeply to uncover new clues, open up new dimensions of a problem and to secure vivid, accurate inclusive accounts that are based on personal experience" (Burgess 1982, p. 107). In-depth interviews are flexible and allow questions to be asked on a wide variety of topics. According to Sekaran (2003), personal interviews are extensively used in marketing studies and help to ensure that respondents have understood the questions.

Qualitative studies are based on non-quantified data, such as values, perceptions and attitudes. Attitude is a significant concept often used to understand and predict people's reaction to an object or change. Direct questions can be designed as a fixed-response alternative question that requires selecting from a predetermined set of responses to measure a dimension of attitude (Malhotra and Birks 2000). The obtained data is "more reliable because the responses are limited to the alternatives stated" (Malhotra and Birks 2000, p. 210).

Marketing scholars should place more emphasis on exploratory research and first embark on a situation analysis via interviews with company managers (Churchill 1979). Marketing researchers adopt a qualitative approach to be able to explore in-depth issues in a less structured format and encapsulate the experiences, feeling and beliefs of the respondents in their study (Malhotra and Birks 2000).

Focus groups

Focus groups can be used to understand perceptions about the research. When little is known in advance of investigation, data collected from focus group provides extensive information in a limited time. Focus groups are an effective way of gathering information, testing assumptions or generating information about the research topic, helping the researcher gather information in a shorter time than one-to-one interviews, with the added bonus of the group dynamic. The researcher can be alerted to new ideas. Employing a focus group allows the researcher to gain further insights into what people think about the research (Churchill 1979; Fern 1982; Krueger 1994). Focus groups are used for the following reasons (Fern 1982, p. 1):

- "People are a valuable source of information";
- "People can report on and about themselves, and that they are articulate enough to verbalise their thoughts, feelings, and behaviours";
- "The facilitator who 'focuses' the interview can help people retrieve forgotten information";
- "The dynamics in the group can be used to generate genuine information, rather than the 'group think phenomenon'";
- "Interviewing a group is better than interviewing an individual";
- "Identifying and pretesting questionnaire items".

The venues and timing of focus group interviews can be decided by participants. The researcher should try to provide an environment conducive to respondents feeling comfortable expressing their opinions (Malhotra and Birks 2000). Group discussions provide safety in numbers, allowing participants to communicate more fully (Ritchie *et al.* 2003). The focus group can benefit from diversity in group composition (Churchill 1979; Krueger 1994). To deal with group member(s) dominating the research discussion, the researcher should encourage each group member to speak. Smithson (2000) defined focus group as a "collective voice" which means "a group process of collaboratively constructing a joint perspective, or argument, which emerges very much as a collective procedure which leads to consensus, rather than as any individual's view" (p. 109). The focus group interviews should be recorded and transcribed verbatim. The transcriptions should be cross-checked with the second recorder. For reasons of confidentiality, the names of participants are replaced with a code.

The second phase (research instrument and scale development)

The aim of this phase is to develop valid and reliable measures of the theoretical construct through synthesising insight from the existing literature and qualitative study. When many items are produced in the first phase, some may be identical or equivalent items, so they are excluded for the sake of parsimony. Some academics assess items generated from qualitative research and remove unnecessary measures to ensure that these items are representative of the scale's domain.

Specifying the domain constructs

Specifying the content domain is usually achieved via relevant literature and qualitative studies – the first stage in questionnaire development. When there are few studies on the topic, the researcher can follow Churchill's (1979) paradigm to generate a set of constructs from the literature, from interviews and from researchers who captured the domain of the constructs. For better measurement, the operational definition and dimensions of the focal construct should be specified.

Generation of measurement items

Measurement item generation is the second step in Churchill's (1979) paradigm. The following recommendation by DeVellis (2003, pp. 66–70) can be used to develop the scale:

- Avoid exceptional length;
- Ensure readability of each item;
- Avoid double-barrelled items;
- Avoid ambiguous pronoun references;
- Use positive and negatively worded items.

To generate the measurement items, the researcher should use a combination of literature and a qualitative study (i.e. semi-structured interviews with experts and focus groups with academia) (Churchill 1979). The items representing each construct are a multi-item scale and regenerated from existing literature.

According to Churchill (1979), the single items usually have considerable "uniqueness or specificity in that each item seems to have only a low correlation with the attribute being measured and tends to relate to other attributes" (p. 66). Single items may have significant measurement errors and can produce "unreliable responses in the same way so that the same scale position is unlikely to be checked in successive administrations of an instrument" (Churchill 1979, p. 66). According to Churchill (1979), a multi-item scale should be used for each construct. Researchers (Churchill 1979; Kotabe 1990; Peter 1981; Zaichkowsky 1985) have highlighted the need for explicit attention to be paid to examining the reliability and validity of measurement. The researcher should create reliable and valid scales based on previous studies but keep them to a minimum to avoid redundancy in the measures and a lengthy questionnaire.

Purifying measurement scales

Purifying measurement scales is the third step of Churchill's (1979) paradigm. Purification is related partly to the measurement model used (Churchill 1979; Foroudi 2019, 2020). Validity is "the degree to which what the researcher was trying to measure was actually measured" (McDaniel and Gates 2006, pp. 224–227). Two types of validity are needed before conducting the main survey: face validity and content validity. Both are subjective in nature and provide an indication of the adequacy of the questionnaire. According to Kerlinger (1973), content validity

Table 5.8 Summary of benefits and limitations of content analysis

Benefits	Limitations
Flexibility of research design, that is, types of inferences	Analyses the communication (message) only
Supplements multi-method analyses	Findings may be questionable alone; therefore, verification using another method may be required
Wide variety of analytical application	Underlying premise must be frequency related
May be qualitative and/or quantitative	Reliability – stability, reproducibility, accuracy of judges
May be automated – improves, reliability, reduces cost/time	Validity – construct, hypothesis, predictive and semantic
Range of computer software developed	Less opportunity to pre-test, discuss mechanism with independent judges
Copes with large quantities of data	Undue bias if only part data is analysed, possibly abstracting from context of communication
Unobtrusive, unstructured, context sensitive	Lack of reliability and validity measures reported, raising questions of credibility
Development of standards applicable to specific research, for example, negotiations	

Source: Harwood and Garry (2003, p. 493)

is judgmental and refers to "the extent to which a specific set of items reflects a content domain" (DeVellis 2003, p. 49).

To assess the content validity of questionnaire items, the judgement of experts and academics familiar with the topic can be used (Bearden *et al.* 1993; Zaichkowsky 1985). They are required to comment on the suitability of the items and check the clarity of wording, to check the importance of each statement and to indicate which items should be retained. They should be asked to judge whether the items used in the instrument are representative of the area being investigated and whether the questionnaire items measure what they are intended to measure, perhaps by testing the questionnaire by completing it, as well as checking the wording, layout and ease of competing. Academics can act as judges of a scale's performance in previous studies. The results of this procedure reflect the "informed" judgments of experts in the content field (Green *et al.* 1988). The summary of benefits and limitations of content analysis is illustrated in Table 5.8.

Malhotra and Birks (2000) state that a questionnaire should be pilot tested first, to refine the questionnaire so that respondents have no difficulty answering (Saunders *et al.* 2007). The scale needs to be tested. The Likert scale is commonly used, often with 5 or 7 points (e.g. 1 = strongly disagree, 5 or 7 = strongly agree (Foroudi 2019, 2020), with 7 points recommended to increase construct variance and reduce measurement error (Churchill and Peter 1984). The Likert scale usually is satisfactory in relation to the underlying distribution of responses (Bagozzi 1994). Based on the results of the quantitative assessment, the items can be adjusted and submitted to scale purification.

Quantitative assessment: pilot study

After qualitative assessment, the questionnaire can be revised for use in the actual survey (Malhotra and Birks 2000) to ensure the constructs are valid and the measurement scales are reliable (Saunders *et al.* 2007).

Pilot study

The pilot study aims to assess the requirements for instrument purification, for example, testing question wording, sequence, form and layout; question difficulty and instruction; familiarity with respondents; response rate; questionnaire completion time; and analysis process (Denscombe 2007; Malhotra and Birks 2000; Ticehurst and Veal 2005). According to Malhotra and Birks (2000), the pilot study sample should be 20 to 40 respondents in a small-scale test (Malhotra and Birks 2000). The respondents in the pilot study should not be invited to participate in the final study, as previous participation may affect their responses (Haralambos and Holborn 2000).

The purpose of the pilot study is to clarify the questionnaire so that there are no ambiguously formulated items (Welman and Kruger 2001), that respondents can easily answer the questions, that there are no errors or problems in recording data (Saunders *et al.* 2007; Peter 1979) and to validate the timing and clarity of the survey, the reliability of the constructs and carry out manipulation checks (Malhotra 1999).

Reliability relates to whether a set of variables is consistent in terms of what it is intended to measure and is assessed via Cronbach's alpha (Cronbach 1951). Before conducting the main survey, it is important that the measures used be investigated for reliability. Reliability is a precondition of validity. Exploratory factor analysis (EFA) is performed in the pilot study to reduce the number of questionnaire items and identify any patterns in the data (De Vaus 2002). A Cronbach's alpha value greater than 0.70 shows high suitability for most research purposes (De Vaus 2002; Hair *et al.* 2010; Nunnally 1978).

Exploratory factor analysis is a practical scale for reducing the numbers of observed variables (indicator) to a smaller and more controllable set by examining the factorial structure of scales, taking into account three assumptions underlying EFA – absolute sample size, correlation coefficients and sampling adequacy (Hair *et al.* 2010). This analysis is to make sure that the individual items are loaded onto corresponding factors as intended.

After deleting superfluous items, the researcher should carry out a reliability test to assess whether the constructs, especially the revised items, yield useful results and that the "measures are free from random error" and "provide consistent data" (McDaniel and Gates 2006, p. 222). Examining how respondents answer the survey questions/items related to the constructs in the conceptual framework is important, particularly where the questionnaire examines psychometric properties, which require acceptable reliability and validity (Churchill 1979; Hair *et al.* 2010).

A reliability test is used for the evaluation of consistency between those measurement items measuring single variables (spilt-half method) (Hair *et al.* 2010). This involves correlating the same respondent's score on the same measurement item at two different points in time (test-retest) (Ticehurst and Veal 2005). Reliability helps establish accuracy and consistency of measures, bias avoidance and reproducibility in different samples and time horizons. Cronbach's α coefficient method is the favourite statistical method to measure reliability, as it is easy to calculate and is well accepted in academic research (Cronbach 1951; Nunnally 1978; Tabachnick and Fidell 2006).

Main survey

Target population and sampling

"The segment of population that is selected for investigation is defined as the sample" (Bryman and Bell 2007, p. 182). The larger group of which the sample is a subset is called the "research population". Bryman and Bell (2007) define population as the universe of units (people, nations, cities, regions, firms etc.) from which the sample is to be selected. The group of subjects the investigator actually studies (or collects data on) is the sample, a set of elements selected from a population (Malhotra and Birks 2000) that represents the main area of research and is presumed to have a high external validity (Churchill 1999; Foroudi 2020). Sample design may be biased due to sampling frame error, population specification error and selection error (McDaniel and Gates 1993).

The main reason to sample is to save money and time. The sample should be representative of its population, allowing the researcher to make inferences or generalisations from the sample to the population. However, if sample size is too low, it may not offer reliable answers to the study questions. Sample size of any research must be determined during the design stage. Salant and Dillman (1994) state that the sample should be determined by four main factors:

- How much sampling error can be tolerated;
- Population size;
- How varied the population is with respect to the characteristics of interest;
- The smallest subgroup within the sample for which estimates are required.

There are two main sampling methods, probability and non-probability. A probability sample is selected using random selection, so each population unit has a known chance of selection. This makes the sample more likely to be representative and to keep sampling error low. A non-probability sample has not been selected using a random method, so some units in the population are more likely to be selected. However, in management, convenience samples (simply ones where respondents are chosen based on their ease of inclusion – often used in pilot studies) are common.

A survey rarely achieves a response from every contact (Denscombe 2007), and in many web-based surveys, the number of contacts exposed to the questionnaire is unknown, so there is a strong possibility of bias introduced by self-selection. Churchill (1999) suggests that face-to-face questionnaire collection is the most-used sampling method in large-scale surveys. It also guarantees that the questionnaire is completed by the respondent who was targeted. Non-probability "snowballing" can be used as a distribution method by asking the initial informants to suggest others (Andriopoulos and Lewis 2009; Bryman and Bell 2007; Goodman 1961; Miles and Huberman 1994; Shiu *et al.* 2009; Stevens *et al.* 1997; Zinkhan *et al.* 1983). According to Stevens (1996), a sample should be more than 300 respondents. Bentler and Chou (1987) state that five cases per parameter is acceptable when the data is perfectly distributed and has no missing or outlying cases. Armstrong and Overton (1977) identify that non-response bias "involves the assumption that people who are more interested in the subject of a questionnaire respond more readily and that non-response bias occurs on items in which the subject's answer is related to his interest in the questionnaire" (p. 2).

Appropriate number of participants

The main considerations that determine the number sampled are related to the data analysis processes or techniques (Hair *et al.* 2010), obtaining reliable estimates (Raykov and Widaman 1995) and the "multivariate distribution of the data". In the case of non-normal data, the ratio of respondents to parameters needs to be higher (i.e. 15:1). In other words, five respondents for each parameter is an acceptable number to minimise deviation from normality. If the researcher is using the maximum likelihood (ML) method, the sample size is 150–400 responses. If the researcher is using structural equation modelling (SEM), which is based on the maximum likelihood estimation (MLE) method, the sample size should be 150 to 400 respondents. However, if the sample size exceeds 400, the MLE method becomes more sensitive and the results of goodness-of-fit measures become poorer (Hair *et al.* 2010, p. 3).

For "model complexity", the sample size should be as follows:

- SEM with five or fewer constructs can be estimated with a small sample size of 100 to 150 if each construct is measured by more than three items and the item communalities are higher than 0.6;
- If any of the communalities are modest (0.45 to 0.55) or the model includes a construct with fewer than three items, the required sample size is 200 (Hair *et al.* 2010);
- If the number of factors in the model is more than six, some constructs are measured by fewer than three items and the communalities are low, a large sample size, perhaps exceeding 500, is required;
- Missing data: if more than 10% of data is expected to be missing, sample size should be increased;
- Average error variance of indicator: larger sample sizes are required when construct commonalities are smaller than 0.5.

Roscoe (1975) recommends these rules of thumb for selecting sample sizes based on acceptable confidence levels in behavioural research studies:

- Sample sizes larger than 30 and less than 500 are appropriate for most research;
- If researchers have more than one group (e.g. male and female), researchers need more than 30 participants for each group;
- If researchers use multivariate analysis, the sample size should be at least 10 times or more the number of variables used in the analysis. Stevens (1996) suggests 15 cases per construct to get trustworthy results. Bentler and Chou (1987) advised that if the data is normally distributed, at least five cases per parameter are sufficient;
- If researchers are conducting a simple experiment, the appropriate sample size should be 10 to 20 participants.

Comrey and Lee (1992) state that a sample size of 50 is very poor, 100 is poor, 200 is fair, 300 is good, 500 very good and 1000 excellent.

Data analysis techniques and statistical packages

Data analysis consists of three stages. In the first stage, the content and scales should be refined based on the collected information from the qualitative and quantitative data. The second stage is to validate the scales based on the quantitative data from the main survey. The third stage is to test the final model.

According to Churchill (1979), multi-item scale development is used for each construct to increase reliability and decrease measurement error. Churchill (1979) suggests using multi-item scales rather than single-item scales. Exploratory factor analysis should be performed in the pilot study and the main study to reduce the items and identify any patterns in the data (Tabachnick and Fidell 2006). The alpha coefficient should be checked in the quantitative data to assess the reliability of the scale and quality of the instrument (internal consistency) (Churchill 1979; Peter 1979). Confirmatory factor analysis (CFA) should be carried out on the main survey data to assess the measurement properties of the existing scales' validity (Hair *et al.* 2010). This is useful if scales needed to be constructed for additional examination in structural modelling and applied to confirm the theory of the latent variables (Hair *et al.* 2010). Structural equation modelling is used to test the hypotheses (Hair *et al.* 2010) and to avoid possible connections among structural models and measurements.

The use of SPSS (Statistical Package for Social Sciences) has been confirmed by many researchers (Field 2009; Tabachnick and Fidell 2006). SPSS can be used at the initial stage of data analysis (Norusis 1999, 1993) for several purposes:

- Coding, editing and checking missing data;
- Checking the assumptions of normality, linearity, multi-collinearity and outliers (examining skewness and kurtosis);
- Demonstrating the central tendency and dispersions of the variables, the mean, the standard deviation and analysing frequencies;
- Exploratory factor analysis and descriptive analysis using an overview of the sample (Tabachnick and Fidell 2006);
- Applying reliability tests to the data to assess the validity, reliability and dimensionality of the instrument (Churchill 1979; Peter 1979). The reason for the test is to assess the scales used to measure the constructs and refine the measures (Churchill 1979).

Analysis of moment structure (AMOS), a unique graphical interface, should be used to determine the quality of the proposed measurement model and hypothesised structural model. It should be used to perform confirmatory factor analysis and structural modelling (Byrne 2001).

Exploratory factor analysis and coefficient alpha

Exploratory factor analysis is a fundamental and useful technique for the early stages of scale validity (Netemeyer *et al.* 2003). EFA is a data-driven (exploratory) approach and is a practical way of reducing the numbers of observed variables (indicators) to a smaller and more controllable set (Anderson and Gerbing 1988; Hair *et al.* 2010).

Hair *et al.* (2010) state that exploratory factor analysis ensures that "any individual factor should account for the difference of at least one single variable" (p. 103). It helps the researcher to identify factors that are independent of each other, allowing the structure of a specific field to be understood (Hair *et al.* 2010). The purpose of EFA is to explore the data and provide information to the researcher about the number of possible factors that best represent the data (Hair *et al.* 2010). EFA is useful as an initial analytical technique to prepare data for SEM (Steenkamp and Trijp 1991). The items for each construct should be examined before performing the factor analysis and reliability test. EFA can be performed in the pilot as well as the main study, to reduce the items and identify any pattern in the data (De Vaus 2002; Tabachnick and Fidell 2006). It inspects the factor structure of every variable in the conceptual framework and can be used to propose the dimensions connected with the underlying constructs (Churchill 1979).

The principal components method should be applied for factor extraction (Hair *et al.* 2010; Tabachnick and Fidell 2006). This method examines the total variance (i.e. common, unique and error variances) to predict the minimum number of factors necessary to explain the maximum amount of variance. An orthogonal Varimax rotation method is particularly suitable for reducing the number of variables to a smaller group of uncorrelated variables. These variables are then used in prediction (Hair *et al.* 2010). Eigenvalues are used to identify the number of factors to extract (Hair *et al.* 2010; Nunnally and Bernstein 1994) and defined on the latent root criterion (eigenvalue > 1.00).

Structural equation modelling

To gain insight into the various influences and relationships, SEM should be used to separate relationships for each dependent variable (Hair *et al.* 2010). According to Tabachnick and Fidell (2006), SEM is a collection of statistical techniques that allow a set of associations between one or more independent variables, either continuous or discrete, and one or more dependent variables, either continuous or discrete, to be examined. Exogenous variables and endogenous variables can be either factors or measured variables.

SEM is also referred to as causal modelling, causal analysis, simultaneous equation modelling, analysis of covariance structures, path analysis or confirmatory factor analysis. The latter two are special types of SEM (Tabachnick and Fidell 2006). SEM can be used for the following reasons (Hair *et al.* 2010; Tabachnick and Fidell 2006):

- When the phenomena of interest are complex and multidimensional, SEM is the only analysis that allows several complete and simultaneous dependent associations between observable indicators and the latent variable (i.e. by using the measurement model) and testing of associations among latent variables (i.e. by using the structural model) by calculating multiple regression equations.
- When SEM analysis is the specification of a model, this is a confirmatory rather than an exploratory technique.
- When the researcher needs to calculate unidimensionality, reliability and validity of each construct individually.
- When the researcher needs to estimate direct and indirect correlation.
- When explicit estimates of measurement errors are required or when hypothesis testing is required for inferential purposes.
- When latent variables are needed to account for measurement error to provide the overall goodness of fit to test the measurement model.
- When the researcher needs to answer questions that involve multiple regression analyses of factors (Foroudi 2019; Nazarian *et al.* 2017, 2019).

Stages in structural equation modelling

The first stage tests the measurement properties of the underlying latent variables in the model using confirmatory factor analysis for each construct. The measurement model explains the causal relations among the observed indicators (variables) and respective latent constructs (variables) (Anderson and Gerbing 1982; Chau 1997) to the unidimensionality assumption. Unidimensionality is assessed by the overall fit of the confirmatory model (Garver and Mentzer 1999). Unidimensionality refers to a set of indicators that has only one underlying construct (Hair *et al.* 2010). Confirmatory factor analysis examines another important property, the original unidimensionality of a scale, and is developed by EFA (Steenkamp and Trijp 1991). A confirmatory measurement model should be used at this stage to classify the strong association between observed variables and respective constructs (Anderson and Gerbing 1988) to ensure that the standardised factor loading values are greater than 0.6. Confirmatory factor analysis is computed to examine whether each subset of items is internally consistent (Foroudi 2019). The validity and reliability of the construct are significant for further theory testing. After EFA, CFA allows the computation of an additional estimation of a construct's reliability, namely composite reliability (Gerbing and Anderson 1988; Hair *et al.* 2010).

At the second stage, a structural model can be used to test the development of a measurement that confirms the relationships between a construct and its indicators and to examine the structural model and the casual connection among latent constructs (Anderson and Gerbing 1982). The constructs may all be measured by latent variables, by observed variables or by a combination of the two.

Evaluating the fit of the model

CFA contributes to the confirmatory stage, giving total control over a construct's indicators, allowing a statistical test of goodness of fit and dimensionality for the specific measurement model (Hair *et al.* 2010). The purpose of the CFA is to validate/confirm the measurement factors that exist within a set of variables involved in the theoretical model (Hair *et al.* 2010). According to Bollen (1989), assessing reliability usually assumes unidimensional measures. Novick and Lewis (1967) state that coefficient alpha, the customary index of reliability in marketing, underestimates the reliability of a multidimensional measure. Unidimensionality is required for the effective use of the coefficient alpha (Hunter and Gerbing 1982) and to evaluate the goodness of fit of any model that considers theoretical, statistical and practical deliberations. As recommended in the methodological literature on CFA, incremental fit indices and indices of model parsimony should be used. Absolute fit indices can be used to examine the structural model and measurement models (Hair *et al.* 2010). Absolute fit indices indicate how far the hypothesised model reproduces the sample data. Goodness-of-fit indices are used to examine the nomological validity of the measurement models. Absolute fit indices do not use an alternative model as a base for comparison.

Chi-squared ($\chi 2$) is the most common method of evaluating goodness of fit. Chi-squared statistics are the first measure of fit included in the Amos output. As Hair *et al.* (2010) cited, a low $\chi 2$ value, indicating no significance, would indicate a good fit, because the chi-squared test is used to measure actual and predicted matrices and non-significance means that there is no significant difference among the actual and predicted matrices. In terms of a model's goodness of fit, *p*-values specify whether the model is significantly different from the null model. In statistics, the null is usually 0. A low *p*-value or one close to zero is taken as evidence that the null hypothesis can be rejected with a low probability of being wrong in reaching that conclusion (MacLean and Gray 1998). The discrepancy between the two matrices should not be statistically different ($p > .05$). Hair *et al.* (2010) and Tabachnick and Fidell (2006) state that using this fit to assess the overall goodness of fit of the model has been criticised, as chi-squared is very sensitive to the sample size.

Kline (1998) suggested that a $\chi 2$/df ratio of 3 or less indicates a reasonable fit of the model. The $\chi 2$ is very sensitive to sample size, particularly if the observations are greater than 200. When the data demonstrates deviations from normality, the chi-squared is larger than what is expected from error in the model. There are no clear-cut guidelines for the minimum acceptable norm. Chi-squared is the original fit index for SEM and should be combined with other indices (Hair *et al.* 2010). Chi-squared is routinely reported in SEM results.

The goodness-of-fit index (GFI) was introduced by Joreskog and Sorbom (1982) and was the first measure of a model to create a fit statistic that is less sensitive to sample size. The GFI produces the relative amount of variance and covariance in the sample covariance matrix, the population covariance matrix. GFI values range from zero to one, with values close to one being indicative of a good fit. If the index is greater than one, it is set at one, and if less than zero, it is set to zero. The GFI should be between 0.90 and 1.00. Values between 0.80 and 0.89 are indicative of a reasonable fit (Doll *et al.* 1994). A GFI with less than 0.8 should be discarded.

The adjusted goodness-of-fit Index (AGFI) is useful for comparing competing models and is adjusted for the degrees of freedom of the model to the degrees of freedom for the null model (Hair *et al.* 2010). The GFI and AGFI are chi-squared-based calculations independent of degrees of freedom. AGFI adjusts the GFI for degree of freedom, resulting in lower values for models with more parameters. The AGFI corresponds to the GFI in replacing the total sum of squares by the mean sum of squares. The adjusted goodness-of-fit index should be greater than 0.90, which indicates an adequate fit (Bentler and Bonett 1980). AGFI values range from zero to one, with values equal to or greater than 0.9 considered a good fit (Byrne 2001; Hair *et al.* 2010; Tabachnick and Fidell 2006). Values between 0.90 and 1.00 are considered a good fit. Values ranging from 0.80 to 0.89 indicate a reasonable fit (Doll *et al.* 1994).

Root-mean square error of approximation (RMSEA) measures the discrepancy between the sample and fitted covariance matrices (Steiger 1990) and is sensitive to the number of parameters (MacCallum *et al.* 1996). According to Hair *et al.* (2010), RMSEA represents how well a model fits a population (p. 748). A value of less than 0.05 indicates good fit, up to 0.08 reasonable fit, more than 0.08 a poor and unacceptable fit (Byrne 2001; Hair *et al.* 2010; Tabachnick and Fidell 2006).

Incremental fit indices calculate how a specified model fits a specific null model (Hair *et al.* 2010). The normed fit index (NFI), or Bentler-Bonett index, compares nested models (Tabachnick and Fidell 2006). NFI compares the model with the recommended model without considering degrees of freedom. NFI measures how much a model is improved in terms of fit compared with the base model (Hair *et al.* 2010). NFI compares the $\chi2$ value of the model to the $\chi2$ value of the independence model (Byrne 2001; Hair *et al.* 2010; Tabachnick and Fidell 2006). However, NFI does not control for degrees of freedom and underestimates the fit in small samples (Byrne 2001). The comparative fit index (CFI) is considered an improved version of the NFI (Byrne 2001; Hair *et al.* 2010; Tabachnick and Fidell 2006).

CFI is directly based on the non-centrality measure. If it is greater than one, it is set at one, and if it is less than zero, it is set to zero. A CFI close to one is considered a good fit (Bentler 1990). CFI depends on the average size of the correlations in the data (Byrne 2001; Hair *et al.* 2010; Tabachnick and Fidell 2006). If the average connection among variables is not high, then the CFI will not be very high.

The Tucker-Lewis index (TLI), also known as non-normed fit index (NNFI), compares the $\chi2$ value of the model with that of the independence model and takes degrees of freedom for both models into consideration (Byrne 2001; Hair *et al.* 2010; Tabachnick and Fidell 2006). The Tucker-Lewis index depends on the average size of the correlations in the data. If the average relationship among variables is not high, then the TLI will not be very high. It is a mathematical comparison of a particular theoretical measurement model and a baseline null model (Hair *et al.* 2010). A value of 0.9 or higher is considered good, and a value of 0.8 is considered acceptable (Gerbing and Anderson 1992). TLI is an example of an index that adjusts for parsimony, even though that was not its original intent. The results of the best-fitting model are shown in Table 5.9.

Unidimensionality

Unidimensionality is a significant property for measures because it is essential but not adequate for construct validity (Gerbing and Anderson 1988). As defined by Cronbach (1951), "A set of items is 'unidimensional' if their order of difficulty is the same for everyone in a population of interest" (p. 116). A unidimensional item (indicator) has only one underlying construct, and Anderson and Gerbing (1988) state a unidimensional measure consists of unidimensional items

Table 5.9 Results of the best-fitting model

	Type	Acceptance level in this research
Coefficient alpha (α)	Unidimensionality	α > 0.7 adequate and > 0.5 acceptable
Standardised regression weight ()		Beta > 0.15
Chi-squared (with associated degrees of freedom and probability of significant different) (df, *p*)	Model fit	*p* > 0.05 (at α = 0.05 level)
Normed chi-square (/df)	Absolute fit and model parsimony	< /df < 3.0
Normalised fit index	Incremental fit	Values above 0.08 and close to 0.90 show acceptable fit
Non-normalised fit index	Compare model to baseline independence model	
Comparative fit index		
Goodness-of-fit index	Absolute fit	0.90
Adjusted goodness of fit		0.90
Root-mean square error of approximation		0.08

Source: Developed from Hair *et al.* (2010)

or indicators. Unidimensionality is typically assumed in the specification of a model estimated with structural equation analysis to separate measurement issues (i.e. the association between a construct and its observed variables or indicators) from model structural issues (i.e. the associations or paths between constructs) (Anderson and Gerbing 1988).

Anderson and Gerbing (1982) proposed operationalising unidimensionality by using the structural equation analysis notions of external and internal consistency. Consistency has been described as the structural equation model to fit the data (Kenny 1979). Consistency is defined by Anderson and Gerbing (1982) as two indicators of X, $x1$ and $x2$, which are internally consistent whether the correlation among them is the same as the correlations with their construct X. Correspondingly, an indicator of X and indicators of Z, x and z are externally consistent whether the association between x and z is the same as the three correlations: x with its construct X, z with its construct Z and X with Z. Therefore, if X is internally and externally consistent, it will be unidimensional. External consistency is recommended by items that "cluster together in a matrix of sorted or ordered similarity coefficients" (Anderson and Gerbing 1982, p. 458). According to Gerbing and Anderson (1988), there is little practical difference between the coefficient alpha (α) and latent variable reliability (ρ) for sufficiently unidimensional constructs; the coefficient alpha could be employed to preliminarily assess reliability.

Composite reliability assessment

CFA allows the computation of an additional estimation of a composite reliability, namely a construct's reliability (Gerbing and Anderson 1988; Hair *et al.* 2010). Composite reliability is a measure of reliability and assesses the internal consistency of the measured variables indicating a latent construct (Hair *et al.* 2010). According to Hair *et al.* (2010), composite reliability is a principal measure used in evaluating the overall reliability of the measurement model, for every latent construct in it. Hair *et al.* (2010) note that the minimum value for composite reliability should be 0.7, which indicates that the measures all represent the same latent construct consistently (Nunnally and Bernstein 1994). Construct reliability (Cronbach-alpha) measures the indicators' unidimensionality (inter-correlation) with their latent constructs (Hair *et al.* 2010).

Average variance extracted assessment

The average variance extracted (AVE) is a measure of the common variance in a latent variable (LV), that is, the amount of variance that is captured by the latent variable in relation to the variance due to random measurement error (Dillon and Goldstein 1984; Fornell and Larcker 1981). In different terms, AVE is a measure of the error-free variance of a set of items. According to Fornell and Larcker (1981), AVE represents a stronger indicator of the construct reliability than the composite reliability. The average variance extracted measures the overall amount of variance captured by the indicators relative to measurement error, and it should be equal to or greater than 0.50 to justify using a construct and ensure the validity of the scale under investigation (Hair *et al.* 2010). Fornell and Larcker (1981) state, "if it is less than 0.50, the variance due to measurement error is larger than the variance captured by the construct, and the validity of the construct is questionable" (p. 46).

Nomological validity

In theory development and testing, to achieve construct validity, nomological validity is an essential step (Bagozzi 1980; Gerbing and Anderson 1988; Nunnally 1978; Steenkamp and Trijp 1991). According to Peter (1981) and Peter and Churchill (1986), nomological validity is used to test hypothesised relationships among different constructs and the empirical relationship between measures of different constructs. Nomological validity refers to the expected behaviour of the measure and examines whether constructs behave as expected in theoretical and empirical terms (Peter and Churchill 1986). Goodness-of-fit indices are used to test the nomological validity of the measurement models (Steenkamp and Trijp 1991).

Convergent validity

Convergent validity refers to the homogeneity of the construct and is the extent to which independent measures of the same construct converge or are positively correlated (Gerbing and Anderson 1993; Malhotra and Birks 2000; Peter and Churchill 1986) with other measures of the same construct. Convergent validity may be assessed on the basis of construct reliabilities (Anderson and Gerbing 1988). Convergent validity is related to the internal consistent validity between each construct item, that is, high or low correlations, and is shown by item reliability, composite reliability and average variance extracted (Fornell and Larcker 1981). Convergent validity assesses the *t*-values and level of significance of the factor (Chau 1997). High inter-item correlations within each construct indicate convergent validity (Chau 1997; Shiu *et al.* 2009). Nunnally (1978) suggests that a 0.7 or higher reliability implies convergent validity, while measures with reliabilities above 0.85 include more than a 50% error variance.

Discriminant validity

Discriminant validity is defined as whether measures of one construct are not highly correlated with measures of others (Chau 1997; Malhotra and Birks 2000; Peter and Churchill 1986), that is, when there is a negative correlation between the experiment's measure and the measurement of different constructs (Shiu *et al.* 2009). Since the association between two constructs is significantly lower than 1.00, the presence of discriminant validity is indicated (Anderson and Gerbing 1988; Bagozzi *et al.* 1991). Discriminant validity can be assessed for two estimated constructs by constraining the estimated correlation parameter (φij) between them to 1.00 and then performing a chi-squared difference test on the values obtained for the constrained and unconstrained model (Anderson and Gerbing 1988, p. 416). Foroudi (2019) suggests that where the restricted model shows a poorer fit than the unrestricted model, there is evidence of discriminant validity. Discriminant validity can be measured by the AVE for each construct and compared with the square correlation between them (Fornell and Larcker 1981). If the squared correlation (error-disattenuated or structural equation model) between two LVs is less than either of their individual AVEs, this suggests the constructs each have more error-free (extracted or internal) variance than variance shared with other constructs (R^2). Furthermore, they are more internally correlated than they are with other constructs, and this suggests the discriminant validity of the target variance extracted (Fornell and Larcker 1981).

Validity – summary

In summary, establishing validity is an essential part of the research process (Garver and Mentzer 1999) and should signify the unidimensionality of a construct (Steenkamp and Trijp 1991), reliability, nomological validity, convergent validity and discriminant validity (Peter 1981; Steenkamp and Trijp 1991) for the research to use structural model evaluation.

Ethical considerations

Academic research needs to be aware of the ethics behind the research activity. These are based on the guidelines provided by the university ethics form and the British Educational Research Association. All business and social researchers share several ethical concerns (Jowell 1986). Researchers must conduct their research following these basic rules:

- Protect the statutory rights of respondents by avoiding unnecessary interruption, obtaining permission and protecting privacy;
- Outline the research questions objectively;
- Be aware of social and cultural differences;
- Give full information on the methodologies to respondents;
- Clarify all details of the research in correspondence or communications with respondents;
- Record all interviews and focus group sessions unless one of the participants disagrees.

Case study – HSBC: consumers' perception of visual identity

This case study research was designed to identify the factors that influence how consumers perceive a corporate logo (in this case, that of the bank HSBC) and how this in turn influences their perception of corporate image and corporate reputation. It shows that the main factors that influence perceptions of the corporate logo are corporate name, design and typeface and that the logo does influence consumer perception of corporate image, their attitude to advertisements, their familiarity with the brand, their recognition of it and their perception of corporate reputation.

H1: The more favourably the corporate name is perceived by consumers, the more favourable the attitude consumers have towards the corporate logo.

H2: The more favourably the corporate typeface is perceived by consumers, the more favourable the attitude of the consumers towards the corporate logo.

H3: The more favourably the design of a company's logo is perceived by consumers, the more favourable the attitude consumers have towards the corporate logo.

H4: The more favourably the colour used in a company's logo is perceived by consumers, the more favourable the attitude consumers have towards the corporate logo.

H5: The more favourably the corporate logo of an organisation is perceived by the consumers, the more favourable the image consumers have towards the company.

H6: The more favourable the image consumers have towards the company's corporate image, the more favourably the company's reputation is perceived by consumers.

H7: The more favourably the corporate logo of an organisation is perceived by consumers, the more favourable will be their attitude towards corporate advertisements.

H8: The more favourable the consumers' attitude towards a company's advertisements, the more favourable will be their image of the company.

H9: The more favourably the corporate logo of an organisation is perceived by consumers, the more consumers will feel familiar with the product or the company.

H10: The more consumers feel familiar with the company or product, the more favourable the image consumers have towards the company will be.

H11: The more favourably the corporate logo of an organisation is perceived by consumers, the greater the impact on the product and company recognisability.

H12: The more that consumers recognise the company or the product, the more favourable the image consumers will have towards the company.

The relationship between the hypotheses in the model is shown in Figure 5.3.

Data collection

The sample was drawn from consumers of the Hong Kong and Shanghai Banking Corporation within the United Kingdom: 1352 self-administered questionnaires were distributed

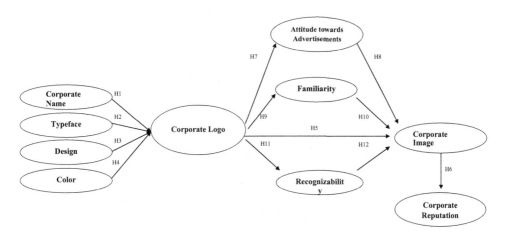

Figure 5.3   The conceptual framework

Source: The author

in London, using convenience sampling, and 332 usable completed questionnaires were received. Prior to this survey, seven interviews were conducted with communication and design consultants, and four focus groups were carried out with marketing lecturers and MBA students. The researchers created a large pool of items for each of the constructs based on literature review and qualitative data and the focus group and interview included in this study. The construct items were examined for appropriateness and clarity of wording by seven faculty members in the researchers' department of marketing who were familiar with the topic, as well as five marketing managers and consultants, and the items were assessed for content validity by using judging procedures The participating faculty members, marketing managers and consultants were also asked to comment on whether the questionnaire appeared to measure the intended construct and if any ambiguity or other difficulty was experienced in responding to the items, as well as asking for any suggestions they deemed suitable. Based on this, some items were eliminated and others modified. The modified questionnaire was critically examined by seven academic experts with respect to domain representativeness, item specificity, and construct clarity. Minor refinements were then made to improve the question specificity and precision, and some questions were eliminated. This was followed by another phase of pre-tests to check that the measurement instrument clearly generated reliable and valid measures (Saunders *et al.* 2007). The questionnaire was completed in the pre-test by 50 academics (lecturers and doctoral researchers); the pre-test respondents were not invited to participate in the final study because it may have impacted their behaviour if they had already been involved in the pilot (exploratory factor analysis [EFA] was performed in the pilot study to reduce the items and identify any patterns in the data; De Vaus 2002). The scale showed a high degree of reliability. Some items were eliminated due to low reliability.

Analysis and results

The research conceptual framework was tested by employing two-stage structural equation modelling. First, multi-item measures were purified and psychometric properties were examined by performing confirmatory factor analysis to assess the measurement properties of the existing scales' validity. The initial CFA confirmed that the absolute correlation between the construct and its measuring of manifest items (i.e. factor loading) was above the minimum threshold criteria of .7 and satisfied the reliability requirements. The Cronbach's α was higher than the required value and satisfied the requirements of the psychometric reliability test. The goodness-of-fit indices of model modification suggested an acceptable fit for the model: The measurement model was nomologically valid, and each criterion of fit thus indicated that the proposed measurement model's fit was acceptable. Therefore, the model fit was adequate (Hair *et al.* 2010). The model's internal structure was examined by testing the discriminant validity, while the homogeneity of the construct was also tested by convergent validity. Two reliability measures for each construct were examined: composite reliability and average variance extracted. These measures satisfied the recommended reliability criteria (Hair *et al.* 2010). The assumed causal and covariance linear relationships among the exogenous (independent) and endogenous (dependent) latent variables were estimated. Based on the structural model, the research hypotheses were examined using the standardised estimate and *t*-value (critical ratio). Goodness-of-fit indices of model modification provided mixed evidence about model fit.

Hypothesis testing

Given the directional nature of the research hypothesis, the importance tests conducted were all one tailed. With regard to the antecedents of the corporate logo, strong support for three of the four hypotheses was found. With regard to corporate name, it was found that the more favourably the corporate name is perceived by consumers, the more favourable is their attitude towards the corporate logo, which supports H1. The outcome is similar to H2, which proposes that the more favourably the corporate typeface is perceived by consumers, the more favourable is their attitude towards the corporate logo. With regard to design, there was strong support for hypothesis H3: the more favourably the design of a company's logo is perceived by consumers, the more favourable is their attitude towards the corporate logo. However, an unexpected result shows that the relationship between colour and corporate logo evaluation was non-significant, and the regression path unexpectedly illustrated a negative relationship between these two variables. Therefore, hypothesis H4 was rejected because the results were not statistically significant.

Concerning the consequences of corporate logo, there was strong support for five out of eight hypotheses. H5 is supported: the more favourably the corporate logo of an organisation is perceived by consumers, then the image consumers have of the company is more favourable. H6 was supported: the more favourably consumers perceive a company's corporate image, the more favourably the company's reputation is perceived by them. There was a strong relationship between the evaluation of corporate logo from consumers' perspective towards an organisation's advertisements (H7), familiarity (H9) and recognisability (H11). Consumers' attitudes towards advertisements, familiarity and recognisability mediated between corporate logo and corporate image (which is in line with the qualitative study and theoretical expectation). However, the relationships between a) consumer attitude towards advertisements and corporate image, b) familiarity and corporate image and c) recognisability and corporate image were not significant, so hypotheses H8, H10 and H12 were rejected, and these relationships were excluded from the model. The results implied that recognisability, attitude towards the advertisements and familiarity did not mediate between corporate logo and corporate image and did not have a significant impact on corporate image. Therefore, hypotheses H8, H10 and H12 were regarded as rejected, and those relationships were excluded from the model.

Issues for further discussion

Further research opportunities could concern a broader analysis of the analysed case. Interdisciplinary issues could also provide relevant insights, particularly in terms of research methods. Future inquiries could be directed towards recognising the research design suitable for carrying out this marketing research study for HSBC, providing a rationale for it, deciding which research method could be used for data collection and explaining the selection of the administrated data collection tool (focusing on the reason for choosing the tool and the pros and cons associated with the chosen method of administration).

References

Ageeva, E., Melewar, T.C., Foroudi, P. and Dennis, C., 2019a. Cues adopted by consumers in examining corporate website favorability: An empirical study of financial institutions in the UK and Russia. *Journal of Business Research*, 98, 15–32. https://doi.org/10.1016/j.jbusres.2018.12.079.

Ageeva, E., Melewar, T.C., Foroudi, P. and Dennis, C., 2019b. Evaluating the factors of corporate website favorability: A case of UK and Russia. *Qualitative Market Research: An International Journal*. https://doi.org/10.1108/qmr-09-2017-0122.

Ageeva, E., Melewar, T.C., Foroudi, P., Dennis, C. and Jin, Z., 2018. Examining the influence of corporate website favorability on corporate image and corporate reputation: Findings from fsQCA. *Journal of Business Research*, 89, 287–304. https://doi.org/10.1016/j.jbusres.2018.01.036.

Anderson, J. and Gerbing, D., 1982. Some methods for respecifying measurement models to obtain unidimensional construct measurement. *Journal of Marketing Research*, 19(4), 453–460. https://doi.org/10.1177/002224378201900407.

Anderson, J. and Gerbing, D., 1988. Structural equation modelling in practice: A review and recommended two-step approach. *Psychological Bulletin*, 103(3), 411–423. https://doi.org/10.1037/0033-2909.103.3.411.

Andriopoulos, C. and Lewis, M., 2009. Exploitation-exploration tensions and organisational ambidexterity: Managing paradoxes of innovation, organisation science. *Special Issue on Ambidextrous Organisations*, 20(4), 696–717. https://doi.org/10.1287/orsc.1080.0406.

Andriotis, K., Foroudi, P. and Marvi, R., 2020. Heritage destination love. *Qualitative Market Research: An International Journal*. https://doi.org/10.1108/qmr-03-2020-0038.

Armstrong, J. and Overton, S., 1977. Estimating nonresponse bias in mail surveys. *Journal of Marketing Research*, 14, 396–402. https://doi.org/10.2307/3150783.

Bagozzi, R., 1980. *Casual Models in Marketing*. New York: Wiley. https://doi.org/10.1002/9781444316568.wiem03016.

Bagozzi, R., 1994. *Principles of Marketing Research*. Cambridge, UK: Blackwell Publishers. https://doi.org/10.2307/3151988.

Bagozzi, R., Yi, Y. and Phillips, L., 1991. Assessing construct validity in organisational research. *Administrative Science Quarterly*, 36(3), 21–58. https://doi.org/10.2307/2393203.

Bazeley, P., 2007. *Qualitative Data Analysis with NVivo*. London: Sage Publication. https://doi.org/10.33151/ajp.5.3.428.

Bearden, W., Netemeyer, R. and Mobley, M., 1993. *Handbook of Marketing Scales*. Newburg Park, CA: Sage Publication. https://doi.org/10.4135/9781412984379.

Bentler, P., 1990. Comparative fit indices in structural models. *Psychological Bulletin*, 107(2), 238–246. https://doi.org/10.1037/0033-2909.107.2.238.

Bentler, P. and Bonett, D., 1980. Significance tests and goodness-of-fit in the analysis of covariance structures. *Psychological Bulletin*, 88(3), 588–600. https://doi.org/10.1037/0033-2909.88.3.588.

Bentler, P. and Chou, C., 1987. Practical issues in structural modeling. *Sociological Methods and Research*, 16(1), 78–117. https://doi.org/10.1177/0049124187016001004.

Bollen, K., 1989. *Structural Equations with Latent Variables*. New York: John Wiley and Sons. https://doi.org/10.1002/9781118619179.

Brown, D., Foroudi, P. and Hafeez, K., 2019. Marketing management capability: The construct, and its dimensions: An examination of managers and entrepreneurs' perception in the retail setting. *Qualitative Market Research: An International Journal*. https://doi.org/10.1108/qmr-10-2017-0131.

Bryman, A., 2004. *Social Research Methods*. Oxford: Oxford University Press.

Bryman, A., 2006. Integrating quantitative and qualitative research: How is it done? *Qualitative Research*, 6(1), 97–113. https://doi.org/10.1177/1468794106058877.

Bryman, A. and Bell, E., 2007. *Business Research Methods*, 2nd ed. Oxford: Oxford University Press.

Bryman, A. and Burgess, R., 1994. *Analysing Qualitative Data*. London: Routledge. https://doi.org/10.4324/9780203413081_chapter_11.

Burgess, R.G., 1982. The unstructured interview as a conversation. In R.G. Burgess, ed. *Field Research: A Sourcebook and Field Manual*. London: George Allen and Unwin. https://doi.org/10.4324/9780203379998.

Burrell, G. and Morgan, G., 1979. *Sociological Paradigms and Organisational Analysis: Elements of the Sociology of Corporate Life*. London: Heinemann. https://doi.org/10.4324/9781315609751.

Byrne, B., 2001. *Structural Equation Modeling with AMOS*. Mahwah, NJ: Lawrence Erlbaum Associates. https://doi.org/10.4324/9781410600219.

Cassell, C. and Symon, G., 1994. *Qualitative Methods in Organisational Research*. London: Sage Publications, 1–13. https://doi.org/10.1108/qrom-10-2015-1332.

Chau, P., 1997. Re-examining a model for evaluating information centre success using a structural equation modelling approach. *Decision Science*, 28(2), 309–334. https://doi.org/10.1111/j.1540-5915.1997.tb01313.x.

Churchill, G., 1979. A paradigm for developing better measures of marketing constructs. *Journal of Marketing Research*, 16(1), 64–74. https://doi.org/10.2307/3150876.

Churchill, G., 1999. *Marketing Research: Methodological Foundations*. Hinsdale, IL: The Dryden Press. https://doi.org/10.2307/3151081.

Churchill, G. and Peter, J., 1984. Research design effects on the reliability of rating scales: A meta-analysis. *Journal of Marketing Research*, 21(4), 360–375. https://doi.org/10.1177/002224378402100402.

Comrey, L. and Lee, H., 1992. *A First Course in Factor Analysis*, 2nd ed. Hillsdale, NJ: Lawrence Erlbaum Associates Inc. https://doi.org/10.1080/10705510701758448.

Corbetta, P., 2003. Social Research, Sage Publication, London.

Creswell, J., 2003. *Research Design: Qualitative, Quantitative, and Mixed Approaches*. Thousand Oaks, CA: Sage Publications. https://doi.org/10.7748/nr.12.1.82.s2.

Creswell, J. and Miller, D.L., 2000. Determining validity in qualitative inquiry. *Theory into Practice*, 39(3), 124–131. https://doi.org/10.1207/s15430421tip3903_2.

Cronbach, L., 1951. Coefficient alpha and the internal structure of tests. *Psychometrika*, 16(3), 297–334. https://doi.org/10.1007/bf02310555.

Dacin, P. and Brown, T., 2002. Corporate identity and corporate associations: A framework for future research. *Corporate Reputation Review*, 5(2/3), 254–263. https://doi.org/10.1057/palgrave.crr.1540178.

De Vaus, D., 2002. *Surveys in Social Research*. London: Routledge. https://doi.org/10.4324/9780203501054.

Denscombe, M., 2007. *The Good Research Guide: For Small-Scale Social Research*. Berkshire: Open University Press.

Deshpande, R., 1983. Paradigms lost: On theory and method in research in marketing. *The Journal of Marketing*, 47(F), 101–110. https://doi.org/10.1177/002224298304700411.

DeVellis, R.F., 2003. *Scale Development: Theory and Application*, 2nd ed. Thousand Oaks, CA: Sage Publications.

Dillon, W. and Goldstein, M., 1984. *Multivariate Analysis, Methods and Applications*. Toronto: John Wiley and Sons. https://doi.org/10.1002/bimj.4710290617.

Doll, W., Xia, W. and Torkzadeh, G., 1994. A confirmatory factor analysis of the end-user computing satisfaction instrument. *MIS Quarterly*, 18(4), 453–461. https://doi.org/10.2307/249524.

Easterby-Smith, M., Thorpe, R. and Lowe, A., 2002. *Management Research: An Introduction*. London: Sage Publications. https://doi.org/10.4135/9781446250488.n3.

Edirisinghe, D., Nazarian, A., Foroudi, P. and Lindridge, A., 2019. Establishing psychological relationship between customers and retailers: A study of the clothing retail industry. *Qualitative Market Research: An International Journal*. https://doi.org/10.1108/qmr-12-2017-0167.

Esterberg, K., 2002. *Qualitative Methods in Social Research*. Boston: McGraw-Hill.

Fern, E.F., 1982. The use of focus groups for idea generation: The effects of group size, acquaintanceship, and moderator on response quantity and quality. *Journal of Marketing Research*, 19(1), 1–13. https://doi.org/10.2307/3151525.

Field, A., 2009. *Discovering Statistics Using SPSS*. London: Sage Publications.

Fornell, C. and Larcker, D., 1981. Structural equation models with unobservable variables and measurement error. *Journal of Marketing Research*, 18(1), 39–50. https://doi.org/10.2307/3150980.

Foroudi, P., 2019. Influence of brand signature, brand awareness, brand attitude, brand reputation on hotel industry's brand performance. *International Journal of Hospitality Management*, 76(January), 271–285. https://doi.org/10.1016/j.ijhm.2018.05.016.

Foroudi, P., 2020. Corporate brand strategy: Drivers and outcomes of corporate brand orientation in international marketing. *International Journal of Hospitality Management* (in print) https://doi.org/10.1016/j.ijhm.2020.102519.

Garver, M. and Mentzer, J., 1999. Logistics research methods: Employing structural equation modeling to test for construct validity. *Journal of Business Logistics*, 20(1), 33–57.

Gerbing, D.W. and Anderson, J.C., 1988. An updated paradigm for scale development incorporating unidimensionality and its assessment. *Journal of Marketing Research*, 25(2), 186–192. https://doi.org/10.1177/002224378802500207.

Gerbing, D.W. and Anderson, J.C., 1992. Monte Carlo evaluation of goodness of fit indices for path analysis models. *Sociological Methods and Research*, 21(2), 131–160. https://doi.org/10.1177/0049124192021002002.

Gerbing, D.W. and Anderson, J.C., 1993. Monte Carlo evaluation of goodness of fit indices for structural equation models. In K.A. Bollen and J.S. Long, eds. *Testing Structural Equation Modems*. Thousand Oaks, CA: Sage Publications, 40–65. https://doi.org/10.1177/0049124192021002002.

Gibbs, G., 2002. *Qualitative Data Analysis: Explorations with NVivo*. London: Open University Press. https://doi.org/10.7748/nr.9.4.86.s3.

Goodman, L., 1961. Snowball sampling. *Annals of Mathematical Statistics*, 32(1), 148–170. https://doi.org/10.1214/aoms/1177705148.

Green, P., Tull, D. and Albaum, G., 1988. *Research for Marketing Decisions*. Englewood Cliffs, NJ: Prentice-Hall. https://doi.org/10.2307/3172616.

Greene, J., Caracelli, V. and Graham, W., 1989. Toward a conceptual framework for mixed-method evaluation designs. *Educational Evaluation and Policy Analysis*, 11(3), 255–274. https://doi.org/10.3102/01623737011003255.

Hair, J., Black, W., Babin, B. and Anderson, R., 2010. *Multivariate Data Analysis: A Global Perspective*, 7th ed. London: Prentice-Hall. https://doi.org/10.1007/978-3-030-06031-2_16.

Haralambos, M. and Holborn, M., 2000. *Sociology: Themes and Perspectives*. London: Collins.

Harwood, T. and Garry, T., 2003. An overview of content analysis. *The Marketing Review*, 3(4), 479–498. https://doi.org/10.1362/146934703771910080.

Huberman, M. and Miles, M., 1994. Data management and analysis methods. In N. Denzin and Y. Lincoln, eds. *Handbook of Qualitative Research*. Thousand Oaks, CA: Sage Publications, 428–444.

Hunter, J. and Gerbing, D., 1982. Unidimensional measurement, second-order factor analysis, and causal models. *Research in Organisational Behaviour*, 4, 267–320.

Joreskog, K. and Sorbom, D., 1982. Recent developments in structural equation modeling, *Journal of Marketing Research*, 19(4), 404–416. https://doi.org/10.2307/3151714.

Jowell, R., 1986. The codification of statistical ethics. *Journal of Official Statistics*, 2(3), 217–253.

Kenny, D.A., 1979. *Correlation and Causality*. New York: Wiley.

Kerlinger, F., 1973. *Foundation of Behavioural Research*, 2nd ed. New York: Holt, Rinehart, Winston Inc.

Kline, R., 1998. *Principles and Practices of Structural Equation Modeling*. New York: Guilford. https://doi.org/10.1080/10705511.2012.687667.

Kotabe, M., 1990. Corporate product policy and innovative behaviour of European and Japanese multinationals: An empirical investigation. *Journal of Marketing*, 54(April), 19–33. https://doi.org/10.1177/002224299005400202.

Krueger, R., 1994. *Focus Groups: A Practical Guide for Applied Research*. London: Sage Publications. https://doi.org/10.1016/0737-6782(96)85709-2.

Lincoln, Y. and Guba, E., 1985. *Naturalistic Inquiry*. Thousand Oaks, CA: Sage Publications. https://doi.org/10.1016/0147-1767(85)90062-8.

Lincoln, Y. and Guba, G., 2000. Paradigmatic controversies, contradictions, and emerging confluences. In N.K. Denzin and Y.S. Lincoln, eds. *Handbook of Qualitative Research*. Thousand Oaks, CA: Sage Publications, 163–188. https://doi.org/10.1176/ps.2007.58.9.1234a.

MacCallum, R., Browne, M. and Sugawara, H., 1996. Power analysis and determination of sample size for covariance structure modeling. *Psychological Methods*, 1(2), 130–149. https://doi.org/10.1037/1082-989x.1.2.130.

MacLean, S. and Gray, K., 1998. Structural equation modeling in market research. *Journal of the Australian Market Research Society*, 6, 17–32. https://doi.org/10.1080/10528008.1993.11488419.

Malhotra, N., 1999. *Marketing Research: An Applied Orientation*, 3rd ed. Englewood Cliffs, NJ: Prentice Hall. https://doi.org/10.2307/1163741.

Malhotra, N. and Birks, D., 2000. *Marketing Research: An Applied Approach*. London: Prentice-Hall.

Maxwell, J. and Loomis, D., 2003. Mixed methods design: An alternative approach. *Handbook of Mixed Methods in Social and Behavioral Research*, 1, 241–272. https://doi.org/10.4135/9781506335193.n6.

McDaniel, C. and Gates, R., 1993. *Contemporary Marketing Research*. New York: West Publishing Company. https://doi.org/10.2307/3172748.

McDaniel, C. and Gates, R., 2006. *Marketing Research Essentials*, 15th ed. Hoboken, NJ: John Wiley. https://doi.org/10.2307/3172748.

Miles, M. and Huberman, A., 1994. *Qualitative Data Analysis: An Expanded Sourcebook*. London: Sage Publications. https://doi.org/10.1177/002076409704300109.

Mingers, J., 2001. Combining IS research methods: Towards a pluralist methodology. *Information Systems Research*, 12(3), 240–259. https://doi.org/10.1287/isre.12.3.240.9709.

Nazarian, A., Atkinson, P. and Foroudi, P., 2017. Influence of national culture and balanced organisational culture on the hotel industry's performance. *International Journal of Hospitality Management*, 63(May), 22–32. https://doi.org/10.1016/j.ijhm.2017.01.003.

Nazarian, A., Atkinson, P., Foroudi, P. and Dennis, K., 2019. Finding the right management approach in independent hotels. *International Journal of Contemporary Hospitality Management*. https://doi.org/10.1108/ijchm-08-2018-0700.

Netemeyer, R., Bearden, W. and Sharma, S., 2003. *Scaling Procedures: Issues and Applications*. Thousand Oaks, CA: Sage Publications. https://doi.org/10.4135/9781412985772.

Neuman, W., 2003. *Social Research Methods*. Boston: Allyn and Bacon. https://doi.org/10.1177/106591297102400434.

Norusis, M., 1993. *SPSS for Windows: Base System User's Guide, Release 6.0*. Chicago, IL: SPSS Inc. https://doi.org/10.1002/mar.4220100307.

Norusis, M., 1999. *SPSS Base 9.0 Applications Guide*. Chicago, IL: SPSS Inc. https://doi.org/10.2307/1318180.

Novick, M. and Lewis, C., 1967. Coefficient alpha and the reliability of composite measurement. *Psychometrika*, 32, 1–13. https://doi.org/10.1007/bf02289400.

Nunnally, J., 1978. *Psychometric Theory*. New York: McGraw-Hill.

Nunnally, J. and Bernstein, I., 1994. *Psychometric Theory*. New York: McGraw-Hill. https://doi.org/10.1177/014662169501900308.

Palazzo, M., Foroudi, P., Kitchen, P. and Siano, A., 2020. Developing corporate communications in Italian firms: An exploratory study. *Qualitative Market Research: An International Journal*. https://doi.org/10.1108/qmr-12-2017-0185.

Patton, M., 2015. *Qualitative Evaluation and Research Methods*, 3rd ed. Thousand Oaks, CA: Sage Publications. https://doi.org/10.1177/10928102005003006.

Peter, J., 1979. Reliability: A review of psychometric basics and recent marketing practices. *Journal of Marketing Research*, 16(1), 6–17.

Peter, J., 1981. Construct validity: A review of basic issues and marketing practices. *Journal of Marketing Research*, 18(2), 133–145.

Peter, J. and Churchill, G., 1986. Relationships among research design choices and psychometric properties of rating scales: A meta-analysis. *Journal of Marketing Research*, 33(February), 1–10. https://doi.org/10.1177/002224378602300101.

Raykov, T. and Widaman, K., 1995. Issues in applied structural equation modeling research. *Structural Equation Modeling*, 2(4), 289–318. https://doi.org/10.1080/10705519509540017.

Ritchie, J., Lewis, J. and Elam, G., 2003. Designing and selecting samples. In J. Ritchie and J. Lewis, eds. *Qualitative Research Practice, a Guide for Social Science Students and Researchers*. Thousand Oaks, CA: Sage Publications, 77–108.

Roscoe, J., 1975. *Fundamental Research Statistics for the Behavioural Sciences*. New York: Rinehart and Winston.

Salant, P. and Dillman, D.A., 1994. *How to Conduct Your Own Survey*. New York: John Wiley and Sons.

Saunders, M., Lewis, P. and Thornhill, A., 2007. *Research Methods for Business Students*. London: Prentice Hall.

Seale, C., 1999. Quality in qualitative research. *Qualitative Inquiry*, 5(4), 465–478. https://doi.org/10.1177/107780049900500402.

Sekaran, U., 2003. *Research Methods for Business – A Skill Building Approach*. Hoboken, NJ: John Wiley and Sons. https://doi.org/10.1108/lodj-06-2013-0079.

Shiu, E., Hair, J.J.F., Bush, R. and Ortinau, D., 2009. *Marketing Research*. London: McGraw-Hill. https://doi.org/10.1108/03090561211189347.

Silverman, D., 1993. *Interpreting Qualitative Data*. London: Sage Publications. https://doi.org/10.1177/1049732308319769.

Smithson, J., 2000. Using and analysing focus groups: Limitations and possibilities. *International Journal of Social Research Methodology*, 3(2), 103–119. https://doi.org/10.1080/136455700405172.

Spiggle, S., 1994. Analysis and interpretation of qualitative data in consumer research. *Journal of Consumer Research*, 21(3), 491–503. https://doi.org/10.1086/209413.

Steckler, A., McLeroy, K., Goodman, R., Bird, S. and McCormick, L., 1992. *Toward Integrating Qualitative and Quantitative Methods: An Introduction*. Newbury Park: Sage Publications. https://doi.org/10.1177/109019819201900101.

Steenkamp, J.B. and van Trijp, H., 1991. The use of Lisrel in validating marketing constructs. *International Journal of Research in Marketing*, 8(4), 283–299. https://doi.org/10.1016/0167-8116(91)90027-5.

Steiger, J., 1990. Structural model evaluation and modification: An interval estimation approach. *Multivariate Behavioural Research*, 25, 173–180. https://doi.org/10.1207/s15327906mbr2502_4.

Stevens, J., 1996. *Applied Multivariate Statistics for the Social Sciences*. Mahwah, NJ: Lawrence Erlbaum. https://doi.org/10.2307/1164712.

Stevens, R., Wrenn, B., Ruddick, M. and Sherwood, P., 1997. *The Marketing Research Guide*. New York: The Haworth Press. https://doi.org/10.4324/9780203050453.

Strauss, A. and Corbin, J., 1998. *Basics of Qualitative Research: Grounded Theory Procedures and Techniques*. Newbury Park, CA: Sage Publications. https://doi.org/10.4135/9781452230153.

Tabachnick, B. and Fidell, L., 2006. *Multivariate Analysis of Grouped Data*. Invited Workshop Presented to the Meeting of the Western Psychological Association. Palm Springs, CA. https://doi.org/10.1007/978-3-642-04898-2_394.

Tashakkori, A. and Teddlie, C., 1998. *Mixed Methodology: Combining the Qualitative and Quantitative Approaches*. Thousand Oaks, CA: Sage Publications. https://doi.org/10.2307/2655606.

Ticehurst, G. and Veal, A., 2005. *Business Research Methods: A Managerial Approach*. Australia: Pearson Education Australia. https://doi.org/10.4324/9781315672489-3.

Vollero, A., Palazzo, M., Siano, A. and Foroudi, P., 2020. From CSR to CSI: Analysing consumers' hostile responses to branding initiatives in social media-scape. *Qualitative Market Research: An International Journal*. https://doi.org/10.1108/qmr-12-2017-0184.

Weber, R., 1985. *Basic Content Analysis*. Beverly Hills, CA: Sage Publications.

Welman, J.C. and Kruger, S.J., 2001. *Research Methodology for the Business and Administrative Sciences*. South Africa: Oxford University Press. https://doi.org/10.24052/jbrmr/v13is04/art-29.

Welsh, E., 2002. Dealing with data: Using NVivo in the qualitative data analysis process. *Forum: Qualitative Social Research*, 3(2), 1–7. https://doi.org/10.7748/nr.9.4.86.s3.

Weston, C., Gandell, T., Beauchamp, J., McAlpine, L., Wiseman, C. and Beauchamp, C., 2001. Analysing interview data: The development and evolution of a coding system. *Qualitative Sociology*, 24(3), 381–400. https://doi.org/10.1023/a:1010690908200.

Zaichkowsky, L., 1985. Measuring the involvement construct. *Journal of Consumer Research*, 12, 341–352. https://doi.org/10.1086/208520.

Zinkhan, G.M., Burton, S. and Wallendorf, M., 1983. Marketing applications for snowball sampling: Potential benefits and problems. In W.R. Darden, K. Monroe and W.R. Dillon, eds. *AMA Winter Educators Conference: Research Methods and Causal Modeling in Marketing*. https://doi.org/10.1177/027347538600800105.

6

CASE STUDIES AS A RESEARCH METHODOLOGY

Abraham Joseph and Suraksha Gupta

Summary

This chapter defines the case study as a methodology and describes how case study research is implemented. It will be particularly valuable to postgraduates in marketing research who are using the case study approach. A systematic and pragmatic approach to designing single and multiple case studies and implementing them is discussed. This includes the use of many different sources of information as the basis for case studies, including expert interviews, observations, archival records and documents. The importance for case study reliability and validity of using a variety of sources and of replicating case studies is discussed. The different data collection instruments, sources and case study analysis are also reviewed. The chapter concludes with a summary of the various ways of reporting a case study.

Epistemological nature

From an epistemological standpoint, case studies are generally based on an interpretivist perspective (Yin 2014). However, the realist perspective, which acknowledges the existence of a single reality independent of any observer, is an alternative paradigm for case study research (Perry 1998). Eisenhardt (1989) advocates a positivistic philosophical stance for case studies, to develop testable propositions that are generalisable. These views are contested in more recent expositions of case study development, such as Piekkari and Welch (2018), who advise the researcher to think about case studies as either theory building (inductive) or theory testing (deductive). The qualitative researcher may design case studies as either exploratory, descriptive or explanatory based on what is appropriate to answer the research questions (Yin 2014).

Table 6.1 Choice of research method and research questions

Research method	Form of research question	Requires control of behaviour events?	Focuses on contemporary events?
Experiment	How, Why?	Yes	Yes
Survey	Who, What, Where?	No	Yes
Archival analysis	Who, What, Where?	No	Yes/No
Case study	How, Why?	No	Yes

Source: Yin (2014)

Designing case studies

A general approach to designing case studies

The research design details the steps to take from designing the research questions to finding the outcomes or answers to the questions posed. In designing a case study, it is important to consider these components (Yin 2014):

- Case study questions;
- Theoretical propositions if any;
- Unit(s) of analysis;
- Logic linking data to the propositions;
- Criteria for interpreting the findings.

Case study questions are usually designed with 'how' or 'why' questions, as explained previously. In developing these questions, a review of the literature is very helpful. If the researcher can find a few studies related closely to their topic of interest, it may help to further dissect and examine those studies to discover new questions that can be posed based on the findings and limitations in them.

Theoretical propositions, based on the literature review, help with setting the focus of the study. Without this, the study may have a very broad scope, leading the researcher in many directions. Propositions bring focus to the identification and collection of the right type of data. These propositions may be considered hypotheses needing to be proved with the help of the data collected. This may lead the researcher to make stronger contributions to theory. This step in the design phase distinguishes case studies from other qualitative research methods such as ethnography (Lincoln and Guba 1985) and grounded theory (Corbin and Strauss 2008).

The next component of the design is defining the unit of analysis or the case. The case, according to Miles and Huberman (1994, p. 25), is a 'phenomenon of some sort occurring in a bounded context' and is the unit of analysis. The case can vary, depending on the type of study, and can be individuals, small groups, communities, decisions, programs and specific events, but the researcher should define the unit of analysis carefully. For example, one cannot consider a whole community the 'case' if the study is about raising children in poorer socio-economic conditions within the community. For such a study, the researcher would need to consider each individual household in a community with such conditions as the unit of analysis. Another way to be sure of the unit of analysis is to consider the research question. If the research question does not point to a specific unit of analysis, then the question may be vague or there may be too many questions (Yin 2014).

Another requirement in deciding the unit of analysis is determining the boundaries of the case so that the researcher is selective about what is considered part of the 'case' or the unit of analysis and what is not (Yin 2014; Baxter and Jack 2008). Boundaries can be set based on i) time and place (Yin 2014), ii) time and activity (Stake 1995) and iii) definition and context (Miles and Huberman 1994). If the case is an organisation, then the researcher must clearly identify the employees to be included or excluded from data collection. Boundaries can also be set in terms of relevant time periods for data collection (Yin 2014).

The next step in the design is to think about the analytic techniques available to analyse the data and make choices based on the study's propositions. This helps in linking the data to the propositions. Recommended analytic techniques are pattern matching, explanation building, time-series analysis, logic models and cross-case synthesis (Yin 2014). Each technique requires a certain quantity and/or quality of data to be effective, and understanding this may help the researcher avoid the extremes of too much or too little data.

Finally, in the research design phase, it is important to consider the rigour of case study findings. One method available to researchers is to identify past theoretical explanations that seem contradictory to the proposed findings of the current study. This helps strengthen the case study's findings once the process is completed. But if such explanations are sought after the data collection is complete, it merely seeks to establish a case for future research.

Single case studies

Case studies based on a single unit of analysis are referred to as single case studies. Single case studies can have a holistic design with a single unit of analysis or an embedded design with multiple subunits of analysis. The choice of design would be based on the topic being investigated and the research question or questions being answered. The selection of the single case is based on various reasons (Yin 2014). A case can be considered critical or unusual if the theory or theoretical propositions under a set of circumstances can be proved true or false and create an anomaly. Another reason is that the case can be a common situation experienced in daily life but which provides valuable lessons based on a theoretical interest. A case may be extremely valuable and revealing when it is studied for the first time due to a lack of previous access or similar reasons. A case can be studied on a longitudinal basis, at two or more points in time, to uncover changes in processes or outcomes over time.

Multiple case studies

When the researcher is studying more than one case, this is referred to as multiple case studies. Multiple case studies may each have a holistic and embedded design as single case studies. Embedded designs require extensive resources and time to complete and so may be hard to complete. The reasons for selecting multiple case studies include seeking i) literal replication where similar results are predicted or ii) theoretical replication where contrasting results are predicted based on theory.

If, for example, in a multiple case study design with 6–10 cases, a researcher found that all the cases produced the predicted results (literal replication), this would be strong evidence for the theoretical propositions. However, if only a few showed literal replications whilst others showed contrasting results (theoretical replication), then the propositions would have to be revised and tested on a new set of cases.

Sampling

When selecting the number of cases, the sampling logic applied in quantitative studies cannot be used. The researcher is not looking for a sample size that is representative of the entire population. As case studies cover both the phenomenon of interest and the context, there may be several potentially relevant constructs or variables of interest. The resulting sample size would be very large, making the study infeasible. The selection of the number of cases or units of analysis will be based on the researcher's discretion and on the number of literal replications needed to make the propositions convincing (Yin 2014).

Preparation and skills of the researcher

Successful completion of a case study, especially in the data collection phase, can depend upon the skills and values of the researcher (Yin 2014). Unlike carrying out a survey using questionnaires, perhaps using research assistants and following a routine approach, a case study requires the researcher's active engagement, as there may be situations demanding a possible change in questions or approach. In addition, the researcher needs to be able to ask pertinent questions, to be an active listener, to interpret responses well, to be flexible and able to adapt, to have sound knowledge of the topic being studied, not to be biased in any way and to behave ethically (Yin 2014, p. 73). From an ethical perspective, care must be taken to ensure that all the participants in the study are informed of the project and consent is sought from them before collecting the data. Participants must also be offered protection from harm and risks and assured as to the privacy and confidentiality of their data.

The data collection process must be encompassed in a case study protocol. Following the case study protocol rigorously ensures case study reliability (Yin 2014). This includes the following:

- There must be documentation giving an overview of the case study project. This should include a background to the case study; details of significant issues that the case study addresses, including theory and/or propositions; any relevant readings on the topic being studied; and an information pack for anyone involved in the study;
- Data collection procedures to be followed in the field, including identifying the various sources of data, logistics, location and access to the data sources or participants. The data can be obtained using interviews, observations, focus groups and so on, and necessary guidelines must be followed. For example, when interviewing, the schedule and availability of the interviewee must be more important than those of the researchers. As the interviews have open-ended questions, it gives less control to the researcher over the direction of the discussion, so the researcher must adapt accordingly.
- Case study questions for the researcher that serve as a reminder of the purpose of the study and the kind of data to be collected.
- A guide to completing the case study report. This should include an outline structure, format of the data to be recorded, use and presentation of documents and other evidence and the extent of documentation to be included. This is helpful when teams of researchers are involved.

Data collection instruments

Various instruments can be used to collect data – interviews, direct observations, participant observations, documentation and archival records.

Interviews

The interviews can be in depth, conducted over a longer period (2 or more hours), where there is no particular order or structure to the questions asked. Interviews can also be shorter, lasting for an hour or so, where the researcher asks a limited number of questions and is more focused. A structured interview allows the researcher to have a set order and number of questions, like in a quantitative survey. There are disadvantages to using interviews – problems with response bias from the participants, poor recall of events and experiences, inaccurate information and the interviewee giving answers the researcher wants to hear (Yin 2014).

Direct and participant observations

Observations of real-life events and experiences can be formal or informal. Using several observers instead of a single observer may increase the reliability of the evidence. In participant observations, the researcher is not a passive observer but can participate in the activity being observed.

Archival records and documentation

Documents can include letters, meeting minutes, diaries, proposals or even what is obtained through the Internet such as news. This can be used as evidence to corroborate or contradict evidence collected by other means such as an interview. Archival records include personnel records, financial statements, statistics and survey data produced by others. Documents are helpful for learning about the cases prior to doing fieldwork, but obtaining access to documents may be a problem, and there may be bias in selection or interpretation by the researcher.

Key principles to be observed in data collection

Irrespective of the data collection instruments, three principles of data collection should be observed.

Data triangulation

It is important to use multiple sources of evidence or instruments to gather the data. The main rationale for using multiple sources of evidence is to triangulate the findings (Patton 2002).

Build a case study database

The researcher should build a database of evidence, including field notes, brochures, photographs and other documents that are organised, labelled and available for later access. This increases the reliability of the case study, so that if the same case study were conducted by a different researcher following the same protocol, the same findings and conclusions would be arrived at (Yin 2014).

Chain of evidence

The evidence that led to the findings and conclusions in the case study report must be properly cited and systematically reported. The case study database should contain the required documents and interviews and must be made accessible. From an external observer or audience's perspective, the chain of evidence must offer a systematic and logical route to examine how the findings were reached, starting from the research question. The case study protocol for data collection should have been followed, showing a link between the case study questions and the propositions (Rowley 2002).

Types of analytic strategies

An analytic strategy should be developed to analyse the data collected and recorded in the case study database. The idea behind the analytic process is to identify the logic that links the data to the propositions developed initially. The strategy should include a way to manipulate data that has been collected. One way to do this is to use computer-assisted software tools such as Atlas.ti, HyperRESEARCH and NVivo. Yin (2014) notes several analytic techniques to use to make sense of the data. They are pattern matching, explanation building, time series analysis, logic model and cross-case synthesis. Three of them are discussed in the following.

Pattern matching

This approach involves comparison of patterns emerging from the qualitative data, with the predicted patterns based on the theoretical propositions. If the results are similar, this supports the case study findings. For explanatory studies, this means checking the patterns emerging for dependent and/or independent variables. If the findings contradict the predicted patterns, the initial propositions should be re-examined, especially in the case of explanatory studies. For multiple case studies, pattern matching can be used to establish literal or theoretical replication.

Explanation building

This type of analysis requires the researcher to build a comprehensive and insightful explanation of the data collected from the case study in the form of a narrative. This technique is especially relevant to explanatory case studies. This is an iterative process and may be more suited to multiple case studies, as it requires the researcher to compare the findings from the case study with the initial propositions to check for congruency and then to revise it if necessary. The revised propositions are then compared with the findings from additional cases until a robust and rigorous explanation can be developed for the case study questions. The allowance for the propositions to be revised and for the final explanation to in a sense be derived makes it different to the pattern-matching technique described earlier. This technique requires that the researcher be skilled or even experienced in generating analytical insights and remain focused on the case study questions and the protocol.

Cross-case synthesis

This technique is only relevant for multiple case studies, while the previous two can be used for both single and multiple case studies. In this approach, each case is considered as a separate study, and the findings from each case are compared for literal replication or contrasting findings.

Identifying and addressing rival explanations or propositions to the study's initial propositions helps in developing a strong argument based on the findings from the case study. This process is also suitable for single case studies with multiple embedded units of analysis.

A good-quality analysis of the case study is made possible by keeping to certain good practices observed in social science research (Yin 2014). First, the case study protocol and analysis strategy must adequately cover the research questions, and all the evidence gathered must have been used in the analysis. Second, the analysis should be able to address all probable rival explanations with the data collected. Third, the analysis should address the most significant issues of your case study without getting lost or diverted because of the findings. Fourth, if possible, the researcher can input their prior knowledge and experience of the topic into the discussion to enhance its depth.

Computer-assisted qualitative data analysis software (CAQDAS) programs

Computer-assisted qualitative data analysis software (CAQDAS) represents various software programmes available to researchers to provide them with an excellent way to store and maintain their qualitative data (Miles *et al.* 2014). Software available to the researchers includes NVivo, ATLAS.ti, MAXQDA and HyperRESEARCH. Basic qualitative analysis such as content analysis or creating complex display tables or adding memos and observations to transcripts can be done using Microsoft Word and Excel. However, software such as that mentioned previously helps the researcher dig deeper into the data and advance theory by testing propositions or creating complex networks connecting various variables (codes) and examining their relationships to a dependent variable.

There are three primary functions that CAQDAS software programs perform – compiling data, disassembling data and reassembling data (Yin 2014). Compiling data involves retrieving and cross-checking words/phrases from field notes; disassembling data involves engaging with the data and assigning codes to similar words. Reassembling data involves synthesising relationships among codes using various combinations and making sense of it (Yin 2015).

There are various capabilities and features in CAQDAS packages. Some can visually display codes assigned to chunks of data, which can then be searched and retrieved to help with creating categories, checking hypotheses or following intuition about the data. MAXQDA can compute quantitative data to help with mixed-methods studies. More advanced packages such as NVivo can also create network displays connecting various nodes to suggest interrelationships between variables. These packages do not automatically compute qualitative data but can create displays of codes assigned in various combinations so that the researcher can engage in deeper analytic thinking. Figure 6.1 shows an example of a word tree to identify themes that can be created using NVivo. Similarly, the researcher can create a word cloud of the most frequently used words in a transcript for analysis purposes. Choice of software depends on the complexity of analysis required (e.g. mixed-methods approach or embedded case studies), the type of data (text, video, photographs etc.) to be coded and analysed, whether it is a longitudinal or large-scale study, functions available such as search and retrieval of data or even compatibility with the researcher's needs or preferences (Miles *et al.* 2014). No single package can do it all.

A brief description about the software and few of the features and functionalities available for two software programmes suitable for qualitative and mixed methods studies are provided in the following.

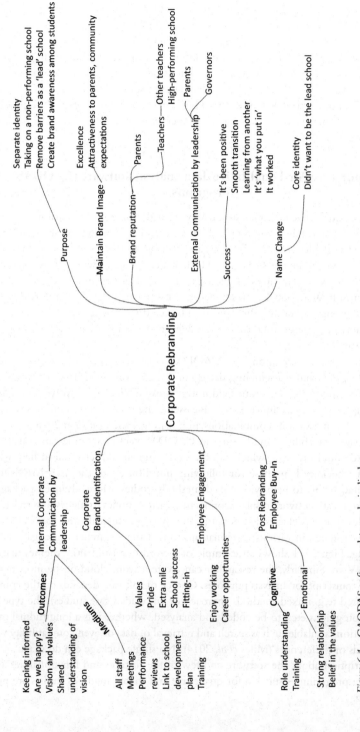

Figure 6.1 CAQDAS software data analysis display

Source: Joseph *et al.* (2020)

NVivo and MAXQDA

NVivo is ideal for researchers conducting qualitative and mixed-methods studies. It can be used to analyse unstructured text, audio, video, images, interviews, surveys and even social media content (NVivo 12). Features include (Yeager 2019):

- Playback audio and video files, so interviews can be transcribed (automatic transcription is available for the latest versions);
- Ability to capture social media content from various social media platforms such as Facebook, Twitter and so on using the 'NCapture' browser plugin;
- Import notes from Evernote;
- Import citations from EndNote, Mendley or other bibliographic software to help with literature reviews;
- User interface and text analysis in various languages.

MAXQDA was developed by researchers for researchers. It offers features and functionalities very similar to NVivo and works with different types of data, including social media posts, and is suitable for various types of qualitative research, such as ethnographic studies or literature reviews and mixed-methods studies. For help using these programs, researchers are advised to refer to books by authors such as Silver and Lewins (2014).

Example of a case study

An example of a multiple case approach is given in the following to give the reader an understanding of the methodological approach required. A similar approach can also be taken for a single case study, except that a cross-case analysis cannot be conducted.

Lee and Bourne (2017) conducted an exploratory multiple case study on ten charities that had recently rebranded. The aim was to determine the determinants of two types of identities, normative and utilitarian, and to explore how managers dealt with the conflicts and tensions that arose in managing these dual identities and in the rebranding process. The research design was guided by two questions, such as 'What drives the adoption of various rebranding strategies?' The authors adopted an inductive approach to building theory by examining the relationship between rebranding and identity by interviewing those involved in the process. Semi-structured in-depth interviews were conducted with ten managers in each of the charities selected. An additional four rebranding consultants were also interviewed. The charities (cases) were selected based on certain criteria – size, degree of change in rebranding and recency of the rebranding event. Interview data was coded and analysed inductively to form theory-building patterns.

Research design and methodology

A within-case analysis was first conducted, and coded data was formed into categories and subcategories that represented significant themes and patterns. A cross-case analysis was then conducted through an iterative look at the data and themes across and within the cases, leading to further refinement of previously identified themes and patterns. The iterations also led to the formation of propositions around the two key issues of rebranding process and identity. These propositions were then tested and refined for uniformity. The final findings were then compared with existing literature on corporate rebranding and organisational identity. The findings are displayed in the form of a process diagram (Figure 6.2) that demonstrates the key

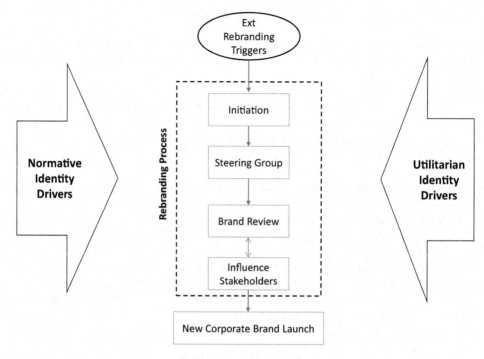

Figure 6.2   Non-profit rebranding process and the dual identities

Source: Adapted from Lee and Bourne (2017, p. 803)

stages followed in implementing the rebranding strategy and practices used by managers to deal with dual-identity tensions.

Findings

The main objective of the researchers was to inductively examine the relationship between rebranding and identity. The findings were structured around three major areas, drivers of different types of identities, common themes in the rebranding process and practices that managers used to manage tensions and conflicting views among stakeholders. Two types of identities were identified, normative and utilitarian. Drivers and motives for each of these identities were singled out from the comments of the participants. Key drivers for normative identity were factors such as brand heritage, communication purpose, values, beliefs and culture, whilst market opportunities, brand awareness and re-positioning were a few of the drivers of a utilitarian identity (Figure 6.2). A typology of non-profit rebranding strategies was also extracted from the data, categorising the ten cases into four quadrants specified by the dominance of these two identities. As an example, the rebranding strategy where both the identities were dominant was termed 'high normative and utilitarian identity'.

The key stages in the rebranding process practiced by managers were identified by the interview data (Figure 6.2). The boxes in the centre of the diagram represent the various sequential phases in implementing the rebranding strategy. The process began with the brand managers' initiation and the formation of a steering group that included the CEO. A brand review was then conducted in consultation with multiple stakeholders. Strong internal communication was identified as necessary to make the transition from the old to the new identity, but it was also an iterative process that moved between brand review and the stakeholder-influencing phase.

To manage tensions, managers used 'justifying' the need to rebrand as an approach to create a sense of urgency. 'Revisioning' was an approach that involved managers in asserting the greater purpose behind the rebrand to stakeholders, to reduce tensions. 'Influencing' was used by managers to facilitate employees to live the brand. This involved the engagement of employees in various internal activities such as the brand launch, roadshows, creating marketing materials and others. This study was thus able to make a theoretical contribution to corporate rebranding.

Reporting and writing a case study

The format for writing case studies depends on whether the researcher is writing it for a journal, a book publisher or in the form of a thesis. For most journal articles and theses, the general sections would include the introduction, literature review, methodology, analysis and findings and then discussion of the findings in the light of the case study questions and theoretical propositions. For single case studies, the individual case study's findings are analysed and discussed. For multiple case studies, the chapters should include findings from each of the individual case studies and a section that deals with cross-case syntheses.

Yin (2014) identifies at least four ways of composing and writing case study reports: linear-analytic, comparative, chronological and theory-building. These can be mixed within a single report or used individually. The linear-analytic structure is a widely used standard structure in which the researcher starts with the issue or problem being investigated, followed by a literature review, methodology, analysis, findings and then conclusions with implications for the problem being studied. The comparative structure uses the same case data repeatedly to suggest various explanations or various conceptualisations of the theory to show how the data fits each conceptualisation. Chronological structures present the findings in a chronological sequence of chapters. Theory-building structures devote separate chapters to each argument or proposition made based on the theory, which is especially useful in explanatory studies.

Conclusions

Case study research is a very useful method to study a phenomenon in its context, using multiple data sources. An element of flexibility exists in crafting the case study research design. For example, the unit of analysis is not restricted to an individual or an organisation, but it depends on the complexity and nature of the phenomenon being studied. The case study approach answers the 'how' and 'why' questions of researchers, allowing them to gain enormous insight. Although the output of the case study approach often seems subjective, various methods such as data triangulation, designing a systematic data collection process and a transparent description of the theory-building process have been suggested for increasing rigour (Eisenhardt and Graebner 2007; Yin 2014). Multiple case studies selected by the researcher with a literal or theoretical replication logic are considered better for generalising findings. Data from case studies should be analysed using CAQDAS software to identify matching patterns in the data to support writing a narrative or synthesising the findings across cases. This helps with theory building. Case study reports generally follow a standard linear structure but can also be written in a manner that establishes the strength of the theory proposed.

Issues

One of the key issues with case study research is the reliability and validity of the data collected and analysed. Four tests recommended to generate reliable outputs and results from the data collected are credibility, trustworthiness, confirmability and dependability (Riege 2003). Some critics of case study research design argue that theory developed from case studies, especially single cases, can be parsimonious. However, Eisenhardt and Graebner (2007) argue that single cases in comparison to multiple cases can be used to create complex theories, provided the researcher fully exploits all of the evidence and its alternative interpretations.

References

Baxter, P. and Jack, S., 2008. Qualitative case study methodology: Study design and implementation for novice researchers. *The Qualitative Report*, 13(4), 544–559.

Corbin, J. and Strauss, A., 2008. *Basics of Qualitative Research (3rd ed.): Techniques and Procedures for Developing Grounded Theory*, 3rd ed. 2455 Teller Road. Thousand Oaks, CA: Sage Publications.

Eisenhardt, K.M., 1989. Building theories from case study research. *Academy of Management Review*, 14(4), 532–550. DOI: 10.5465/amr.1989.4308385.

Eisenhardt, K.M. and Graebner, M.E., 2007. Theory building from cases: Opportunities and challenges. *Academy of Management Journal*, 50(1), 25–32. DOI: 10.5465/amj.2007.24160888.

Joseph, A., Gupta, S., Wang, Y. and Schoefer, K., 2020. Corporate rebranding: An internal perspective. *Journal of Business Research*. DOI: 10.1016/j.jbusres.2020.04.020.

Lee, Z. and Bourne, H., 2017. Managing dual identities in nonprofit rebranding: An exploratory study. *Nonprofit and Voluntary Sector Quarterly*, 46(4), 794–816. DOI: 10.1177/0899764017703705.

Lincoln, Y.S. and Guba, E.G., 1985. *Naturalistic Inquiry*. Newbury Park, CA: Sage Publications.

Miles, M.B. and Huberman, A.M., 1994. *Qualitative Data Analysis: An Expanded Sourcebook*, 2nd ed. Thousand Oaks, CA: Sage Publications.

Miles, M.B., Huberman, A.M. and Saldana, J., 2014. *Qualitative Data Analysis: A Methods Sourcebook*, 3rd ed. Thousand Oaks, CA: Sage Publications.

Patton, M.Q., 2002. Two decades of developments in qualitative inquiry: A personal, experiential perspective. *Qualitative Social Work*, 1(3), 261–283.

Perry, C., 1998. Processes of a case study methodology for postgraduate research in marketing. *European Journal of Marketing*, 32(9/10), 785–802. DOI: 10.1108/03090569810232237.

Piekkari, R. and Welch, C., 2018. The Sage handbook of qualitative business and management research methods: Methods and challenges. In C. Cassell, A. Cunliffe and G. Grandy, eds. *The Sage Handbook of Qualitative Business and Management Research Methods: Methods and Challenges*. 1 Oliver's Yard, 55 City Road London EC1Y 1SP: SAGE Publications, 345–359.

Riege, A.M., 2003. Validity and reliability tests in case study research: A literature review with "hands-on" applications for each research phase. *Qualitative Market Research: An International Journal*, 6(2), 75–86. DOI: 10.1108/13522750310470055.

Rowley, J., 2002. Using case studies in research. *Management Research News*, 25(1), 16–27. DOI: 10.1108/01409170210782990.

Silver, C. and Lewins, A., 2014. *Using Software in Qualitative Research: A Step-by-Step Guide*, 2nd ed. Los Angeles; London: Sage Publications.

Stake, R.E., 1995. *The Art of Case Study Research*. Thousand Oaks, CA; Los Angeles, CA: Sage Publications.

Yeager, K., 2019. *LibGuides: Statistical & Qualitative Data Analysis Software: About NVivo* [online]. Available from: https://libguides.library.kent.edu/statconsulting/NVivo [Accessed 17 July 2019].

Yin, R.K., 2014. *Case Study Research: Design and Methods*, 5th ed. Los Angeles, CA: Sage Publications.

Yin, R.K., 2015. *Qualitative Research from Start to Finish*, 2nd ed. New York: The Guilford Press.

7

ESTABLISHING VALIDITY AND RELIABILITY IN CASE STUDY RESEARCH PROJECTS

Samina Sumrin and Suraksha Gupta

Summary

This chapter investigates in depth the issues of establishing reliability and validity in case study approaches to marketing research. IT will be particularly valuable to postgraduates in marketing research who are using the case study approach. It explores the difference between reliability (replicability of results) and validity (match to the research aim). The tests of validity, credibility and reliability in case studies investigated include construct validity, internal validity, external validity, reliability, credibility, transferability, confirmability and dependability. It identifies that problems with validity and reliability cannot be removed completely, but their negative effects can be reduced by using tests described in the chapter.

Introduction

The case study approach is ideal for research that aims to develop new theories in business and strategic management (Godfrey and Hill 1995; Voss *et al.* 2002), human resource management and organisational behaviour. Yin (2009, p. 14) defines a case study as:

> an empirical inquiry that investigates a contemporary phenomenon within its real-life context; when the boundaries between phenomenon and context are not clearly evident; and in which multiple sources of evidence are used.

This defines case studies as intended studies. Unlike other research methods, it is not primarily a generalising technique but gives a degree of detail and understanding, similar to ethnographic studies.

Darke *et al.* (1998) consider the case study methodology to have the potential to deliver different research results, depending upon data collection methods. Case study findings can develop or test a theory. Case study research can also help the researcher learn more than other types of research in a short time (Yin 1994; Stake 2000). A researcher may use a case study to explore the application of existing theory or to compare different theories using the data from one or more case studies (Cook and Campbell 1979, p. 83). The case study method can be used in exploratory research, descriptive research or explanatory research (Yin 1994).

Stake (2000) defines three kinds of case study – intrinsic, instrumental and collective. An intrinsic case study is where the case study itself is of primary interest and there is no aim to generalise. An instrumental case study is based on a specific case, developed to get more insight and broader knowledge. Collective case studies use different cases to get insight into one phenomenon or a specific problem.

Validity and reliability

Validity and reliability tests are used to determine the accuracy and credibility of case-based research, where research findings may be questioned due to researcher subjectivity. A case study researcher should be familiar with the different factors that increase the risk to research validity and use different strategies at different stages of the research to mitigate the effect of these factors. A researcher should focus on achieving reliability and validity at different stages of research – research design, data collection and data analysis (Patton 2001). This will help the researcher convince readers that the study is important and contains essential knowledge (Lincoln and Guba 1985, p. 290). The researcher should evaluate research quality in terms of credibility, consistency, confirmability, dependability, transferability and applicability (Healy and Perry 2000; Lincoln and Guba 1985).

Validity

According to Winter (2000, p. 1):

> Validity is not a single, fixed or universal concept, but rather a contingent construct, inescapably grounded in the processes and intentions of particular research methodologies and projects.

There are many definitions of validity. Other terms used as synonyms of reliability and validity include truth, value, consistency, trustworthiness and confirmability (Lincoln and Guba 1985). Campbell (1975) separates validity into two types – internal and external. Internal validity refers to the truthfulness of research findings, whether the results represent reality and whether they are affected by any extraneous variables. External validity relates to whether the study findings are appropriate to apply to different groups.

There are various approaches to establishing case study research validity. These include construct validity, internal validity, external validity, credibility, transferability, confirmability and dependability (Riege 2003a).

First set of design tests

Construct validity

Construct validity indicates the nature of the conceptualisation or operationalisation of the applicable idea. Construct validity should be measured during the data collection stage. Construct validity refers to how far a study examines what it aims to research (Denzin and Lincoln

2011). Case study analysts sometimes are not clear concerning measures, and "abstract" decisions are used concerning measures (Yin 1994). The researcher should use operational measures that are suitable for theoretical tests. Because in a case study the researcher may have a personal connection with organisations or individuals being studied, there may be questions of subjectivity. To avoid this and enhance construct validity, the researcher should avoid subjective decisions during the stages of formulation of research design and data collection.

A researcher can ensure construct validity in a case study research by:

- Using different sources to support the study, for example, collecting data in different ways and from different sources, such as recording interviews in tapes, articles and documents to reduce bias (Flick 1992).
- Having a case study database in the form of transcribed interviews, notes of observations during interviews and evidence from other sources (Hirschman 1986).
- Requesting review of the case study report draft by study respondents (Yin 1994)

Internal validity

"Internal validity" is also termed "logical validity" (Cook and Campbell 1979; Yin 1994). This approach is used mainly for explanatory cases rather than exploratory cases, to establish the causal relationship between study constructs. Here, the issue is that although the researcher gives a plausible causal and logical argument, it may not be enough to support the research conclusions. Ensuring internal validity is helped if the researcher anticipates what kind of explanations will be given for real-life experiences. To achieve this, the researcher should describe the similarities and differences of experiences of study respondents but also identify and explain the important patterns in their beliefs. Methods to improve internal validity are (Riege 2003a):

- During the data analysis stage, the researcher should do in-case and cross-case analysis by matching patterns in the design (Miles and Huberman 1994).
- Adding diagrams to explain the study findings of the case study (Miles and Huberman 1994).
- Cross-examination of results to ensure consistency (Yin 1994).

External validity

External validity relates to how far results can be generalised from the findings of the case study. In some cases, this is not the intention, as the aim of the study may be just to focus on the entity being studied. Rather than constructing case studies of various companies or organisations, researchers may create different case studies inside one company (Yin 1994). However, case study analysis can offer outcomes that can be summed up against a specific generalised theory. This is also known as *analytical generalisation*. Case studies can be used in the early stages of theory development. This can be facilitated by various contextual and other investigations to identify the scope for generalisation (Eisenhardt 1989). Methods to improve external validity are (Riege 2003a):

- Using multiple cases for theory replication, such as selecting two different industries or sectors, several cross-industry cases or cases in different countries (Eisenhardt 1989; Parkhe 1993).
- Defining the study scope to facilitate analytical generalisation (Marshall and Rossman 1989).
- Comparing the data collected with the existing literature (Yin 1994).

Reliability

Reliability relates to the consistency and repeatability of research operations and practices, along with the ability of researchers to collect data more accurately. "Consistency" or "repeatability" is associated with the research instrument and how it is deployed, for example, interviewing techniques, and the stability of research results. Reliability in case study analysis means that other researchers could repeat the case study and reach the same conclusion. Case study data is real-life data, possibly covering real-life events, so other researchers may get different results if repeated later. However, later researchers can give additional valuable information concerning, for example, changes in context. Methods to improve reliability are (Riege 2003a):

- Selecting the study design to match the study aim (Yin 1994).
- Using pilot studies to structure appropriate questions (Eisenhardt 1989; Yin 1994).
- Selecting case studies by using appropriate semi-structured or structured procedures (Yin 1994).
- Recording data via electronic equipment (Riege 2003b).

Second set of design tests

These are tests of credibility, transferability, dependability and confirmability (Lincoln and Guba 1985; Denzin and Lincoln 2011).

Credibility

Credibility and internal validity are similar terms. Reality can be interpreted in different ways. Credibility is interpretation of case study findings by different researchers or interviewees to get different interpretations for the study results. Credibility is the answer to the question:

> How can one establish confidence in the "truth" of the findings of a particular inquiry for the subjects (respondents) with which and the context in which the inquiry was carried out?
>
> (Guba 1981, p. 79)

Questions the researcher should answer to increase credibility include (Riege 2003):

- Were the study narratives profound and impenetrable?
- Can the researcher ensure the consistency the case study findings?
- Are there systematic relationships existed between study theories and concepts?

Transferability

Transferability is often referred as generalisability or external validity of the research. Transferability is about attaining parallel or different outcomes of a research phenomenon from similar or different cases, organisations or participants. Transferability relates to the question:

> How can one determine the degree to which the findings of a particular inquiry may have applicability in other contexts or with other subjects (respondents)?
>
> (Guba 1981, pp. 79–80)

To ensure transferability, these questions need answering (Riege 2003):

- Can the researcher's conclusions be used by other researchers focusing on similar phenomena?
- Is the study connected with the prior theory, or does it confirm existing theory?

Dependability

Dependability is an alternative expression of reliability. It refers to the existence of consistency and stability in every step of case study research that allows any other researchers to understand the whole research process and review it easily. It is defined by Guba (1981, p. 80) as:

How can one determine whether the findings of an inquiry would be consistently repeated if the inquiry were replicated with the same (or similar) subjects (respondents) in the same (or similar) context?

Questions that need to be answered to ensure case study dependability include (Riege 2003):

- Are study questions clear and in accordance with the adopted research strategy?
- Have all the research procedures been implemented using necessary precautions?

Confirmability

Confirmability refers to whether study findings can be confirmed by other researchers and whether the conclusions are clearly derived from the information in the case study. Guba (1981, p. 80) defines confirmability as:

How can one establish the degree to which the findings of an inquiry are a function solely of the subjects (respondents) and conditions of the inquiry and not of the biases, motivations, interests, perspectives and so on of the inquirer?

Miles and Huberman (1994, pp. 278–279) identified these questions that a researcher should answer to ensure the confirmability of a case study:

- Are the case study methods and procedures depicted clearly and simply?
- Does the case study researcher have complete knowledge of the background information?
- Did the researcher keep the case study data safe for reanalysis purpose?

Triangulation in case study research

Triangulation refers to using more than one data collection method, researchers, theoretical perspectives or analysis for a single research phenomenon. For case study research, the researcher can use several case studies to get more insight into the analysis. However, the researcher can also use triangulation in single case study by analysing the case at different levels, for example, industry or firm. This increases the amount of data collected and helps the researcher evaluate complex data and shed light on the research question from many perspectives.

Creswell and Miller (2000, p. 126) define triangulation as

a validity procedure where researchers search for convergence among multiple and different sources of information to form themes or categories in a study.

Mathison (1988, p. 13) states:

Triangulation has arisen as an important methodological issue in naturalistic and qualitative approaches to evaluation [to] control bias and establish valid propositions because traditional scientific techniques are incompatible with this alternate epistemology.

The term *triangulation* refers to use of several approaches and sources of data to ensure that research results are valid and credible (Cohen *et al.* 2000). Credibility suggests reliability, while the term validity refers to how far research precisely reflects or assesses the idea or thoughts being explored. Triangulation by combining data sources and collection methods can help to overcome the biases due to the use of a single method. Each researcher can use their own triangulation method (Golafshani 2003). Denzin (1970, p. 301) and Patton (2001) introduced four types of triangulations:

- Data: Different periods of time, space and people;
- Investigator: Using several different researchers;
- Theory: Using different theories to facilitate understanding of a phenomenon;
- Methodological: Using different data collection (e.g. interviews, observations) and interpretation methods.

Data triangulation

Data triangulation simply means collecting different types of data. Any weakness due to use of one data source can be compensated for by the quality of other information, expanding the authenticity and reliability of the study. This strengthens conclusions about outcomes and minimises the danger of false translation.

Example

Non-governmental organisations (NGOs) were running their projects in different cities to study the customers' decision-making concerning environmentally friendly products. Interviews were conducted with buyers across four cities, and data was triangulated across four cities with very different characteristics. This provided deeper insight for the study and provided conclusions.

Investigator triangulation

This involves using more than one investigator, interviewer, observer, researcher or data analyst in a study. Confirming findings across investigators, without earlier communication or co-operation between them, can improve result validity. Investigator triangulation is especially important for reducing bias in data collection, communication or analysis.

Example

A cold drink company was focusing on advertising and consumer buying behaviour. The company hired three different investigators for this study. Each investigator found different advertising impacts on buying decision. Triangulating the outcomes from the three researchers allowed their methodologies, predispositions and discoveries to be analysed and the investigation to be improved.

Theory triangulation

This refers to applying more than one theory or hypothesis in the research to examine a phenomenon or condition from different points of view using different theories or approaches. The more different the theories are, the more likely they are to distinguish unique issues as well as concerns.

Example

A study for a clothing brand focused on young consumers' online buying behaviour and whether the buyer's culture and their elders' habits had an impact. Another study focused on the effect of online advertisements on multiple platforms. A third study examined the impact of the cost of travel to retail stores and the time taken in online buying. Triangulation allowed comparison of the outcomes using different theories.

Methodological triangulation

This refers to using different research techniques to reduce the drawbacks of using just one technique, with one technique's strengths making up for another's shortcomings. Methodological triangulation is like mixed-methods research, where a combination of data collection methods is used to support study findings. It is like information triangulation.

Example

A study of brand loyalty assessed the impact of corporate social responsibility (CSR) practices on a brand. It used different methods for collecting data, including interviews, questionnaires and third-party reports to assess the impact of CSR activities on brand loyalty. This gave the company deeper understanding than any one method.

Validity and reliability – summary

Table 7.1 summarises the previous discussion.

Tests for determining case study validity and reliability – example

Here, we take the example of a research project conducted by an employee of a packaging company, focused on corporate social responsibility practices in the packaging industry. The study focuses on the spot packaging market, that is, that part of the market which is not under contract between suppliers and users of packaging. The first stage of the research was formulation of the research question. A review of the literature indicated several variables that might affect a company's CSR practices. The researcher organised the themes from the literature to create a consistent line of reasoning and a tentative conceptual framework. Next, the researcher created a working hypothesis and model and based predictions on it to be tested in the fieldwork, which covered all the variables tentatively

Table 7.1 Establishing validity and reliability in the case study research

Focus of test	Corresponding design tests	Case study techniques	Qualitative techniques	Research phase
Construct validity	Confirmability (corresponding to objectivity and neutrality of positivism)	Collection of data evidence from more than one resource		Data collection
		Form a chain of evidence		Data collection
		Keeping the reviews of the study participants as case study draft reports		Researcher's diary and report writing
			Confirmability assessment (examining the data, findings, interpretations and recommendations)	Data collection and data analysis
Internal validity	Credibility	First conduct within case assessment, then check if case pattern identical		Data analysis
		Write understandable description		Data analysis
		Ensure internal consistency of analytically correlated study results and concepts		Data analysis
			Triangulations (informants, researchers and approaches)	Data collection and data analysis
			Peer examining	Data analysis
			Participant checks	Researcher's diary and report writing
			Investigators' theories, world views, theoretical assimilation	Research design
			Researcher self-scrutinising	Data collection and data analysis

Focus of test	Corresponding design tests	Case study techniques	Qualitative techniques	Research phase
External validity	Transferability	Use repetition logic in various case studies		Data collection and data analysis
		Define scope and limitations		Research design
		Investigative simplification for the research		Research design
		Assess data with existing literature		Data analysis
			Determined questions	Research design
			Deep narrative (develop case-study database)	Data collection
			Cross-case analysis	Data analysis
			Specific procedures for coding and analysis	Data analysis
Reliability	Dependability	Give full information of theories and ideas		Research design to data analysis
		Ensure similarity between research problems and elements of study design		Research design
		Build up and improve case-study procedure		Research design
		Use several investigators		Data collection
		Record statements and activities as faithfully as possible		Data collection
		Record data, automatically develop database		Data collection
		Confirm significant parallelism of outcomes across multiple data sources		Data collection

(Continued)

Table 7.1 (Continued)

Focus of test	Corresponding design tests	Case study techniques	Qualitative techniques	Research phase
		Use peer review/ examination		Data collection
			Reliability assessment (examine and document the process of enquiry	Research design
			Clarify researcher's theoretical positioning and preferences	Research design

Source: Adapted from Riege A. M. (2003a)

Table 7.2 Assessment of case study data collection and analysis (based on Dubé and Paré 2003)

Good practice	How good practice is achieved
Data collection	
Explanation of data collection process (reliability, replication, validity)	The data collection process is discussed in detail. The findings from each case are recorded in a checklist to enable the reader to follow the development of the argument and monitor progress
Multiple data collection methods	The data collected are mainly qualitative. The study relies
Mix of qualitative and quantitative methods (reliability)	on multiple sources of evidence and data collection techniques, and these are shown in a table at the beginning of the fieldwork description
Triangulation (reliability)	The study uses triangulation of data sources and theories
Case study protocol and case study database (reliability, replication)	The case study database and organisation of the material are discussed in some detail in the study before introducing the fieldwork
Data analysis	
Clarification of analysis process (reliability)	Data collection and analysis have been carried out in parallel. Care has been taken to document the process, substantiate statements and clearly display the evidence
General good practice	
Field notes, coding, data displays (replication, external validity)	Data was mostly collected informally during the normal course of business. Case selection was partly opportunistic, allowing the researcher to use participant observation. Field notes were taken and filed electronically. The study includes a sample of sketches of practice and photographs to illustrate concepts and substantiate statements
Logical chain of evidence (internal validity)	Evidence was presented in a readable and accessible manner, so the reader can follow the argument but ultimately form his/her own opinion

(Continued)

Good practice	How good practice is achieved
Empirical testing and time series analysis (internal validity)	Research objectives were discussed and stated at the beginning of the study, as theory description and theory testing
Cross-case comparisons (internal validity)	Within-case and cross-case analysis and pattern matching were used
Use of natural controls (internal validity)	The researcher used naturally occurring variations in the variables
Quotes (reliability)	All cases quote extensively from academic literature and business press, industry sources and company files
Project reviews (reliability)	Emerging themes were discussed with informants. The project was a doctoral thesis, so it was reviewed by supervisors and internal and external examiners
Comparison with literature (validity)	Emerging themes from the fieldwork were constantly referred to and compared with the literature

Source: Adapted from Iacono *et al.* (2011)

identified as contributing to the packaging industry's CSR practices. The model was then tested and improved through the fieldwork and recommended for further testing in other industries.

Multiple cases (based on theoretical sampling) were used, along with multiple levels of assessment within cases. The cases covered packaging characteristics, industry structure, business practices and the perspective of customers and sellers. There were seven cases, three from the primary market, where packaging is made to the specifications of the buyer, and four from secondary markets, where packaging is received by the buyer with the product, that is, fast-moving consumer goods (FMCG). Table 7.2 explains the how the study achieved validity and reliability, based on the criteria of Dubé and Paré (2003) and Yin (2009).

Conclusions

The case study method is a very valuable method for research but is vulnerable to a range of criticisms concerning validity and reliability. These criticisms can be countered by following a wide range of recommendations designed to improve validity and reliability.

Issues for further discussion

- Is there a difference in the validity and reliability of case studies in different disciplines, that is, education and management?
- Can the use of case study methods be compared between different research paradigms?
- How can validity and reliability be estimated for longitudinal case studies?
- Can credibility be used as an interchangeable term for reliability and validity? If so, what strategies can a researcher use to make study findings more credible?

References

Campbell, D.T., 1975. Degrees of freedom and the case study. *Comparative Political Studies*, 8(2), 178–193.

Cohen, L., Manion, L. and Morrison, K., 2000. Research methods in education. *British Journal of Educational Studies*, 48, 446. https://doi.org/10.4324/9780203720967.

Cook, T. and Campbell, D., 1979. *Quasi-Experimental Design: Design and Analysis Issues for Field Settings*. Skokie, IL: Rand McNally. https://doi.org/10.1207/s15327752jpa4601_16.

Creswell, J. and Miller, D., 2000. Determining validity in qualitative inquiry. *Theory into Practice*, 39(3), 124–131. https://doi.org/10.1207/s15430421tip3903_2.

Darke, P., Shanks, G. and Broadbent, M., 1998. Successfully completing case study research: Combining rigour, relevance and pragmatism. *Information Systems Journal*, 8, 273–289. https://doi.org/10.1046/j.1365-2575.1998.00040.x.

Denzin, N., 1970. *The Research Act: A Theoretical Introduction to Sociological Methods*. Englewood Cliffs, NJ: Transaction Publishers. https://doi.org/10.4324/9781315134543.

Denzin, N.K. and Lincoln, Y.S., eds., 2011. *The Sage Handbook of Qualitative Research*. Thousand Oaks, CA: Sage.

Donnellan, E., 1995. Changing perspectives on research methodology in marketing. *Irish Marketing Review-Dublin*, 8, 81–90.

Dubé, L. and Paré, G., 2003. Rigor in information systems positivist case research: Current practices: Trends and recommendations. *MIS Quarterly*, 27(4), 597. https://doi.org/10.2307/30036550.

Eisenhardt, K., 1989. Building theories from case study research. *Academy of Management Review*, 14(4), 532–550. https://doi.org/10.2307/258557.

Flick, U., 1992. Triangulation revisited: Strategy of validation and alternative? *Journal of the Theory of Social Behaviour*, 22, 175–198. https://doi.org/10.1111/j.1468-5914.1992.tb00215.x.

Godfrey, P. and Hill, C., 1995. The problem of unobservable in strategic management research. *Strategic Management Journal*, 16(7), 519–533. https://doi.org/10.1002/smj.4250160703.

Golafshani, N., 2003. Understanding reliability and validity in qualitative research. *The Qualitative Report*, 8(4), 597–607. Available from: https://nsuworks.nova.edu/tqr/vol8/iss4/6/.

Guba, E.G., 1981. Criteria for assessing the trustworthiness of naturalistic inquiries. *Educational Technology Research and Development*, 29, 75–91. https://doi.org/10.1007/BF02766777.

Healy, M. and Perry, C., 2000. Comprehensive criteria to judge validity and reliability of qualitative research within the realism paradigm. *Qualitative Market Research*, 3(3), 118–126. https://doi.org/10.1108/13522750010333861.

Hirschman, E.C., 1986. Humanistic enquiry in human research: Philosophy, method and criteria. *Journal of Marketing Research*, 23, 237–249. https://doi.org/10.1177/002224378602300304.

Iacono, J., Brown, A. and Holtham, C., 2011. The use of the case study method in theory testing: The example of steel e marketplaces. *The Electronic Journal of Business Research Methods*, 9(1), 57–65. http://doi.org/10.1046/j.1365-2575.1998.00040.x.

Lincoln, Y. and Guba, E., 1985. *Naturalistic Inquiry*. Beverly Hills, CA: Sage Publications. https://doi.org/10.1002/9781405165518.wbeosn006.

Marshall, S. and Rossman, G., 1989. *Designing Qualitative Research*. Newbury Park, CA: Sage Publications. ISSN 1050-4273.

Mathison, S., 1988. Why triangulate? *Educational Researcher*, 17(2), 13–17. http://doi.org/10.2307/1174583.

Miles, M.B. and Huberman, A.M., 1994. *Qualitative Data Analysis: An Expanded Sourcebook*. London: Sage.

Parkhe, A., 1993. Messy research, methodological preposition and theory development in international joint ventures. *Academy of Management Review*, 18(2), 491–500. http://doi.org/10.5465/amr.1993.3997515.

Patton, M., 2001. *Qualitative Research and Evaluation Methods*, 2nd ed. Thousand Oaks, CA: Sage Publications.

Riege, A.M., 2003a. Validity and reliability tests in case study research. *Qualitative Market Research: An International Journal*, 6(2), 75–86. DOI: 10.1108/13522750310470055.

Riege, A.M. 2003b. Convergent interviewing: A structured approach to defining market research problems. *Australasian Journal of Market Research*, 11(2), 13–25.

Stake, R., 2000. *Case Studies, Denzin and Lincoln (ed), Handbook of Qualitative Research*, 2nd ed. Ch. 16, Thousand Oaks, CA: Sage Publications. https://doi.org/10.1111/j.1365-2648.2001.0472a.x.

Voss, C., Tsikriktsis, N. and Frohlich, M., 2002. Case research in operations management. *International Journal of Operations and Production Management*, 22(2), 195–219. DOI: 10.1108/01443570210414329.

Winter, G., 2000. A comparative discussion of the notion of validity in qualitative and quantitative research. *The Qualitative Report*, 4(3), 1–14.

Yin, R.K., 1994. *Case Study Research: Design and Methods*. London: Sage Publications.

Yin, R.K., 2009. *Case Study Research. Design and Methods*, 4th ed. Thousand Oaks, CA: Sage Publications. https://doi.org/10.33524/cjar.v14i1.73.

8

ENCOURAGING INFORMATION DISCLOSURE ON SOCIAL MEDIA PLATFORMS IN CONSUMER MARKETING RESEARCH

Robin Robin, Hazem Gaber and Len Tiu Wright

Summary

This chapter explores issues of trust, privacy and information security as they apply to new types of consumer data arising from digital marketing and social media. It identifies how consumers might be concerned about the extent of disclosure, and what their motivations to disclose their data and their attitudes to subsequent use of that data might be. and attitudes. The chapter investigates in depth the issue of user-generated content. It examines the relevance of theories of social gratification and social identity. It then moves on to the wider context in building profiles, communities, sharing of information, institutional trust, brand image, technological innovation and personalisation. It considers the implications of these issues for marketing researchers.

Introduction

Consumer marketing research draws from a broad range of perspectives within the social sciences relating to the study of consumer attitudes, motivations and behaviour, for example, from psychology, sociology, marketing and economics disciplines. It has long been enriched by the knowledge and insights of published studies (Wright and Wright 2006) from research on people. Quantitative and qualitative consumer data collected from the interactions and exchanges between organisations and consumers has aided the rise of consumer research. Now helped by social media using new technologies, the value of consumer research can be seen from the estimates of the growth of the worldwide marketing research industry, now valued at well over $47 billion (Palazzo 2020; ESOMAR 2020). The demand for marketing research shows the importance of the value of information disclosure to an industry whose value of billions of dollars arises mostly from its use of such data.

What is the critical role of information disclosure in social media? For a start, on these social media platforms, users *sign up for free* with email addresses and passwords. They can *immediately engage* in brand-related conversations with each other and with organisations, demonstrating the *ease of use, without having prior specialist knowledge.* If the user likes the platform, they will *continue giving information on their personal experiences, knowledge and behaviour as customers, for free,* including what they used and consumed at high, moderate and low prices for different qualities of products bought and experienced. Social media platforms gather their information from daily consumer information disclosure, but information is also shared by consumers giving personal information on a range of their life activities, including local and overseas bookings and purchases for hotels, travel, insurance and finance.

User engagement can become addictive, a way of life; witness the rise in the popularity of social media sites, as evidenced by the hundreds of millions and in some cases billions of users fuelling global sites such as Facebook, YouTube, Twitter, Instagram, Pinterest, Snapchat, LinkedIn, Tumblr and Reddit, followed by the growing popularity of Tik Tok during the Coronavirus pandemic. Review42.com (2020) estimates that with 4.39 billion global Internet users and Google's search engine market share at over 90%, the number of Google users worldwide is close to 4 billion. There are also an estimated 2.5 billion Android-powered devices. These and other information platforms have transformed the approach of many companies to customer information management (Stone *et al.* 2017)

This makes social media a very important ultimate place for marketing research and customer relationship management. There is a need to distinguish between social media and social activity, for example, on aggregator/comparison or supplier sites such as AirBnB, GoCompare and Moneysupermarket. Information-giving by consumers in entering their search preferences is very specific to the categories they need and an essential part of the value-added context for firms. Product reviews are posted by consumers about what, how and where they consume and the quality and uniqueness of what they experienced.

Despite such disclosures, organisations face many challenges concerning their social media platforms. These challenges include the resistance of users to part with more personal data due to fears of breaches of their privacy and concerns over how their active participation could have a positive impact on organisational performance when faced with more brands being produced of similar me-too products competing for their attention.

There are external environmental factors, such as demographic, cultural, psychological, social, economic, political, legal and regulatory factors, that affect how consumers' ultimate decisions become interrelated and complicated. These factors profoundly and fundamentally influence perceptions and expectations relating to online purchasing, including choice of shopping platform. Researchers aim to construct consumer behaviour models to understand, explain and then predict consumers' purchasing behaviour in terms of purchase timing, place, reason, quantity and value. Consumer marketers use their marketing resources, such as communication, pricing and branding, to change how they present their products to take account of these variables

Big data boosts the importance of social media platforms for marketers. The social media platforms referred to previously fuel four dimensions of big data – volume, variety, velocity and veracity. Analysis of data from these social media platforms can improve the effectiveness of their marketing. Marketers have always faced problems in conducting qualitative and quantitative marketing research, from poor response rates to ensuring the reliability and validity of the results. The data from social media platforms gives marketers vital insights into consumer behaviour as well as real-time data about the dynamic marketing environment, so companies need to encourage users to participate actively and create content on those platforms. This applies to international, national and local platforms – the latter having risen dramatically in importance due to the improved local targeting capability afforded by mobile and Internet technology and the consequent rise of locally focused social media.

Marketers have recognised the critical role of information on social media. On these platforms, users can engage in brand-related conversations with each other and with organisations. This makes social media the ultimate place for marketing research and customer relationship management. However, organisations face many challenges in encouraging information disclosure on various social media platforms. These challenges include the resistance of users to sharing information for different reasons, such as the fear of breach of their privacy.

User-generated content

User-generated content (UGC) has been at the centre of how organisations capitalise on the existence of social media platforms. UGC refers to content that users create on digital platforms. It conveys their identity and individuality as well as their preferences and needs. Social media platforms, as the main enabler of UGC, provide various instruments for customers to express themselves, from simple posting and other uploading capabilities to using augmented reality to provide an image of an individual as a basis for trying on clothes. From Web 1.0 to Web 4.0, social media platforms steadily improved these capabilities. Earlier versions of the web (Web 1.0) focused on the digital platform as a publication platform. Web 2.0 was characterised by the enhanced role of the audience, allowing user participation through conversation and content augmentation via commenting, rating, editing and sharing (Tuten and Solomon 2017). Web 3.0, or the semantic web, is based on the idea that the web "understands" the information it stores and can make logical connections with it, and Web 4.0, or the symbiotic web, is based on the idea of humans and machines interacting using the web. An example of a Web 4.0 social medium is Waze (now owned by Google), which allows drivers to share data using mobile phone signals to find the best routes and report traffic congestion.

Creating and disclosing information

To enable the generation of high volumes of data on social media platforms, companies need to ensure that customers consistently create and disclose information on them. The generation of information on social media platforms allows brands and organisations to cultivate insights into consumers' preferences, propensities and attitudes. These insights are fundamental for marketing research, to discern the value that consumers seek when they generate content and information on those platforms. Organisations can use social media to get immediate feedback on consumers' beliefs and experiences and can ask consumers to give their opinions on potential products and services improvements. Another important role for big data is that it allows marketers to understand which consumers are worth communicating with; which content type converts users from passive (e.g. non-commenting, non-posting, non-reviewing) to active, from uncommitted to committed; and which social media platforms are more effective and at what times. This data also allows organisations to execute fully personalised marketing strategies with communication tailored to individual users. All these result in more effective marketing campaigns.

Customer engagement

The term "consumer engagement" has been increasingly used to describe the nature of consumers' interactive experiences on social media (Oh and Sundar 2016). This arises from marketers' eagerness to use social media platforms to engage consumers using the platform's two-way communication capabilities. Customer engagement marketing goes beyond just selling brands to consumers, aiming to make brands a meaningful part of consumers' conversations and lives (Kotler and Armstrong 2016). Consumer engagement with brand-related content on social media usually encompasses emotional, cognitive and behavioural components (Gaber *et al.* 2019b). Emotional engagement refers to the enjoyment and enthusiasm consumers feel towards the content. Cognitive engagement results from the high levels of attention and absorption consumers have for the social media content. Finally, behavioural engagement relates to behaviours of consumers on different social media platforms, such as consuming, endorsing or sharing content. On social media, consumers can join their favourite brand pages, share or create brand narratives and advocate consumption experiences, within a triad of online communications between consumers and brands, other consumers and suppliers (Gaber *et al.* 2019a). There is a downside in that social media can become a hotbed of disinformation and re-crafted or re-created fake news, making it hard for people to know what is real and what to believe. So, marketing researchers must grapple with fake news, particularly when it relates to their products or brands or their consumption contexts (Yang *et al.* 2019).

Customer engagement performance

Social media sites allow consumers to contribute to content by enabling them to post comments and interact with other consumers as well as with companies, turning consumers into active participants. This contrasts with traditional mass media, where consumers were passive recipients of marketing messages. Many companies use Facebook brand pages to increase brand awareness and gain access to new audiences in a more targeted way, delivering information to their current and prospective customers and engaging customers with their brands. Companies that have not yet developed significant online activity are missing an important course of information for marketing research.

Instagram, now owned by Facebook, provides filters to change how its users portray themselves, with visual effects that are both aesthetically pleasing and unconventional. This type of innovation is just one example of incentives to create more content. Companies encourage consumers to be active contributors to the content on a platform by ensuring that their brand-related content has an element of interactivity. Interactive or engaging content can include posts (sometimes with incentives) that ask consumers to give feedback about products or services or to share content to their friends. Converting passive to active contributors may require diversifying the content types of their posts and using unconventional posting strategies. In general, social media platforms have been used to enhance the quality of customer relationship management (Ma *et al.* 2015). This approach will not succeed unless consumers believe that social media platforms can help in handling their complaints and answering their questions.

In summary, consumer engagement on different media platforms is a key factor in boosting UGC. However, many marketers cannot yet determine the best ways to engage consumers on social media consumers and convert them into active participants (Social Media Examiner 2019).

Social gratifications to encourage disclosure

Consuming and creating on social media platforms allow users to achieve social gratification, such as the ability to attract attention and be idiosyncratic. Social gratification is the type of gratification associated with collective and social enterprise that reflect personal connections. The pursuit of social gratification eventually encourages information disclosure and content creation on social media platforms and is related to the notion of social identity of a customer as an idiosyncratic individual.

Social identity theory

Tajfel and Turner (1979) introduced social identity theory (SIT) to explain how people create their identity by association with social groups. It argues that people tend to categorise themselves and others into homogenous groups that share common characteristics. These groups, for example, family, social class, football team, nationality, can be an important source of pride and self-esteem for people and can give them a sense of belonging to a particular social world. These groups facilitate individuals' self-definition in their social environments. People tend to perceive huge differences between themselves and other social groups that they do not belong to and small differences between themselves and other people in the group into which they have categorised themselves.

Through the association of identity with products and services they use, or portrayal of predisposition towards a certain group, customers can build their identity in a digital environment. Organisations can facilitate this by encouraging association with their brand image. For instance, using a product endorsed by an opinion leader or a celebrity can improve the user's social identity. Similarly, using a product that is sustainable and eco-friendly can strengthen one's identity as an environmentally conscious individual. These examples imply that if companies understand how customers assert their identity through the content and information that they create and disclose, they will find it easier to deliver marketing strategies that align with customer values (Wallace-Williams 2017).

Uses and gratifications theory

Another theory used to explain why people use social media is uses and gratifications theory, which argues that users of different communication media have different uses for various media to fulfil their needs and that this leads to ultimate gratifications (Palmgreen and Rayburn 1979). Whiting and Williams (2013) identified ten uses and gratifications users have for social media – social interaction, information seeking, passing time, entertainment, relaxation, communicatory utility, convenience utility, expression of opinion, information sharing, and surveillance/knowledge about others. Understanding the motives behind the usage of different social media platforms can help marketers to diversify content to satisfy different motives and engage consumers with brand-related content.

Building images, profiles and communities

Social media, with its interactive nature, allows people to create desirable images of themselves by posting pictures and other information on their profiles, enhancing their social image and building their social identity through online interactions with others (Wang *et al.* 2015). These platforms allow consumers to join online brand communities to interact with like-minded consumers. So, brand identification is one of the main motives encouraging users to join brand communities, where they can show others that they belong to a certain social group (the users of the brand).

Marketing researchers can observe brand communities and the creativity of their members in producing images and videos with news, personal stories and short narratives, which are easily accessible on portable devices such as smartphones and tablets. Poynter (2017) noted that with accessibility of images and videos, new business start-ups relating to them are common, for example, Voxpopme, Living Lens and GlimpzIt (acquired by Forrester Research).

Sharing information

Social networking uses particular techniques to enhance the power of brand identification. For example, when a user presses the like button on a certain brand page, other users can see that this user joined that group. They allow users to share posts on their platforms that are visible to other members of the social network and allows other to join in, for example, by commenting and reposting (Mosseri 2018). This creates a set of perceptions of brand community members towards each other and towards non-members.

Subjective norms in information disclosure

Encouraging information disclosure and content creation also requires an understanding of how subjective norms influence this information disclosure. One kind of social gratification that customers may seek from participating in content creation is the sense of belonging to a particular group or trend. The notion of subjective norms is an integral part of the classic theory of planned behaviour (Ajzen 1991), which suggests that there are prominent people who influence an individual's behaviour, particularly role models, for example, celebrities from the world of sport or entertainment. The type of information and content disclosed can be influenced by consumers' role models. Social media influencers can shape the behaviour of their followers, including purchasing and consumption behaviours. Influencers play a unique role in fulfilment of social gratification of users of social media platforms, from association with their role models to portraying identity through association with the influencers and brands. Enhancing social image is one of the strongest motives for users to actively participate in social media platforms. Thus, companies should aim to create a unique image for their brands, encouraging consumers to join their online communities to enhance their social identity. Social media-based brand communities can be a critical place for satisfying consumers' need to belong.

Institutional trust and brand image

Social media platforms allow brands and organisations to amplify their message to customers. The effectiveness of this depends on images of brands and organisations. Consumers are less likely to create content and share information with negatively branded organisations, such as those the consumer perceives to suffer from social, ethical or environmental issues. One important determinant of the image of brands and organisations is institutional trust relating to data, defined as the level of confidence in the data-collecting institution not to misuse personal data within its possession. The concept of brand trust is very important in the context of social media and virtual brand communities, as consumers perceive higher risk in interacting with companies online. As consumers rely on social networks in their search for information and in making buying choices, the trustworthiness of the information and updates on these networks are important for them (Kehr *et al.* 2015; Social Media Examiner 2019).

Customers who are willing to share their information and generate content on platforms need reassurance from platforms concerning how their information is collected and used. Institutional trust creates willingness not just to give information but also to co-create content with brands and organisations. Often, willingness to share and create content depends on how comfortable customers feel with the platform and its corporate image. An individual customer's trust may seem unimportant, but the viral power of the Internet allows consumers to combine their power through features such as petitions and hashtags on social media platforms.

Critical mass to encourage disclosure

The concept of critical mass has been used to study the number of users needed for a new technology to succeed (Morris and Ogan 1996). It refers to the point at which a minimum number of users adopt an innovation. At this point, the rate of the adoption of the new communication suddenly dramatically increases (Rogers 2010). Consumers perceive a critical mass in a community when the number of participants and interactions exceeds a certain level (Lim 2014). Although it is hard for consumers to identify a brand community's critical mass, they can see achievement of critical mass by observation of online interactions in the community and perhaps decide to participate. One assumption of critical mass theory is that people may be influenced by other people who came before them (Markus 1987). Although most members of online communities are passive, their presence is important to shape other consumers' attitudes towards the brand and its community.

The influence of consumer perception of critical mass on intention to disclose information on social media can be seen from the finding that the number of likes that Facebook brand pages receive affects the number of users who like the page and actively engage with other users (Gaber *et al.* 2019a). New consumers join these online communities to benefit from the huge numbers of interactions that take place inside them. This would not happen without interactive and engaging posts that encourage consumers to participate in meaningful conversations, encouraging other users to join the communities (Tuten and Solomon 2017).

Technological innovation and data collection

Innovation in digital technology has changed business models and marketing strategies. We have witnessed the rise of Uber against traditional taxis, of Airbnb against the long-established concept of bed-and-breakfast and of the ingenious sharing-economy business model of food delivery from Deliveroo. The constant connectivity of our digital devices allows us to experience the products and services provided using these new business models. Organisations can capitalise on our incessant attachment to our digital devices, for either utilitarian or hedonistic purposes, by providing platforms to allow information disclosure that helps them achieve their marketing objectives. Customer data feeds into organisation's pool of big data, which supports more rigorous marketing approaches (Wright et al. 2018).

Technology innovation in marketing

Although the concept of personalised and targeted communication existed long ago, the latest advances in technology have increased the accuracy, effectiveness and impact of marketing.

Industry leaders in marketing research, such as Nielsen or Gallup, have embraced current technology developments to support this. Nielsen, for instance, has developed the Nielsen Marketing Cloud that increases response rate to real-time behavioural changes in customers in order to optimise customer engagement and return on investment (Nielsen 2017). This machine-learning technology can extract insights from complex data sets, helping predict future trends and behaviour.

Understanding human behaviour using new techniques

Technological innovation in marketing is also visible in the development of scientific methods in understanding human behaviours, such as neuromarketing. Neuromarketing uses neuroscience to understand the interaction between human behaviours and neuropsychology in influencing neurological – cognitive and affective – responses to marketing stimuli. In neuromarketing, responses to various stimuli based on electrical brain activity are evaluated in order to measure the attention, arousal, appraisal and preference towards certain products/brands and eventually purchasing behaviour and recognition of products/brands (Thomas *et al.* 2016). The existence of technological innovation to gather and analyse real-time data has facilitated progress in neuromarketing. One innovation that complements neuromarketing is facial recognition software. The combination of neuromarketing with facial recognition software can help marketers to understand conscious and unconscious responses of customers to marketing stimuli.

Natural language processing (NLP) and artificial intelligence have led to the development of *chatbots* which digitally mimic human interaction. One example of the effective use of chatbots to increase brand awareness is the UK tea brand PG Tips and its monkey mascot. The Facebook Messenger platform was used for this monkey mascot to serve as a *chatbot* in raising funds for the national charity event Red Nose Day while promoting its own brand.

NLP and AI techniques work very well in driving the popularity of voice-activated virtual assistants, which are an important part of innovations such as smart homes and other "smart" devices. These devices transform mundane activities such as turning on/off devices and obtaining real-time weather forecast into more futuristic and entertaining activities They are instrumental for marketing purposes, as they function as platforms to disseminate information and can also act as a point of purchase. Marketers can use them to spread subtle marketing communication and to promote their products or organisations. Companies such as Uber and JustEat use their partnerships with Amazon through Amazon Echo's Alexa to make sure that their services get priority for owners of Amazon Echo devices. Here, technological innovation has become an important part of marketing evolution.

Data collection to improve personalisation

One similarity that connects technological innovations such as facial recognition software, chatbots, and voice-activated devices is the use of customer data. From an organisational perspective, the generation of customer data is a pivotal part of value co-creation. The concept of value co-creation refers to active interaction and resource integration between customers and firms to create value (Lusch and Vargo 2014). Value co-creation in the context of technological innovations lies in the reciprocal use of customer data, when businesses render personalised services to consumers from their expressed preferences. Smart devices enable businesses to make personalised or tailor-made recommendations to consumers to more accurately address their preferences and needs.

The value co-created based on collected and disclosed data allows businesses to identify attitudinal and behavioural patterns of their consumers and tailor their product and service offerings to these patterns. This allows firms to provide value that is relevant to customers instead of value that the business *perceives* to be relevant. Consumers prefer to receive customised content that is relevant to them and matches their interests (Wali *et al.* 2020). Personalised marketing strategies based on individual customer data on attitudes and behaviour have replaced – to a degree – traditional market segmentation strategy. However, where customers actively and deliberately disclose their data for personalisation purposes, too high a level of personalisation can trigger cognitive overload. The process of co-creating value can backfire because customers may feel overwhelmed by the cognitive effort spent in personalisation. This cognitive overload is manageable by providing standardised options based on their popularity. Amazon, for example, balances between highlighting personalisation for each customer and recommending popular and highly rated products that have been highly reviewed and rated by other customers.

Another issue that might emerge from personalisation is privacy. Firms can collect customer data covertly from any online information disclosure, from consumers' purchase histories to their likes on posts or their hashtags on Instagram, Twitter or Facebook accounts. The problem emerges when customers perceive that their data is being collected and used without consent, resulting in intrusive and aggravating advertisements or other marketing initiatives. This can create negative feelings. For instance, likes can transform into banner advertisements every time consumers go online, while inadvertent clicks on a product thumbnail can create constant reminders about those products. Customer may see this intrusiveness and irritation as a result of privacy invasion.

Privacy and information disclosure

As constructive and positive content favours brands and organisations, content and information with an unfriendly tone can also create retaliation by consumers. So, organisations need to understand how to encourage disclosure of information that is both valuable in generating insights into market trends and favourable to brands and organisations. The collection of data and information is an important part of service delivery for customers. To enable customers to enjoy the personalisation of products and services provided, customers need to provide their data. The data may be covertly extracted from information belonging to customers, such as their location, generated from their digital devices by positioning systems. So, organisations must abide by ethics that the collected data should be treated discreetly and with consent from their consumers.

Privacy and control

Although there are various definitions of privacy, the core tenet of privacy relates to limiting access to and controlling information. Creating content that signifies a consumer's identity and preference requires a leap of faith as well as a social contract between an organisation and its customers that specifies the privacy of their information will be guaranteed, that the organisations who collect the information will not misuse the information and that the latter will ask for consent before using such information for any purpose. This relates to control over how the information is collected and used.

For social media platforms, customers derive an elementary sense of control from how they can adjust who can see the content that they share, for example, privacy and sharing settings. Is this enough to provide a sense of control and privacy? Perhaps the answer is yes for most customers. However, with the spotlight on how organisations use customer data and the many cases of data misuse and mistreatment, the answer to that question may have changed. Privacy in a social media context is more than just controlling access to one's profile. Privacy should encompass all activities related to the data disclosed by customers and stored by organisations.

Terms and conditions

Savvy customers may be aware of the many pages of user agreement that we scroll through until we reach the end of the page so that we can click on the "accept" button and use a service provided. This is a covert way for organisations to obtain consent from consumers on use of their information. Lengthy documents filled with legal jargon and esoteric language distract and dissuade consumers from reading terms and conditions. The need for instant use of the product or service provided by an organisation may encourage consumers to avoid inspection of terms and conditions, which effectively becomes a way of covertly collecting information from customers with a single consent. This has led to consumer protection authorities to require commitment from organisations to be more transparent and straightforward in how their users' information is collected and used.

Protecting customers' privacy

Facebook, as one of the leading social media platforms to date, has been in the spotlight since the Cambridge Analytica case. As a result, Facebook CEO Mark Zuckerberg vowed to protect customers' privacy and information, due to pressure from government bodies and customers. Apart from a conscious endeavour to improve how social media platforms with billions of active users treat their users' personal information and privacy, the European Union (EU) also reformed its data protection regulation with the implementation of General Data Protection Regulation (GDPR) on 25 May 2018. GDPR provides clear guidelines of how information is collected, used and stored by businesses operating in the EU. Customers should have total control in terms of knowing who processes their information, of being able to access the information they disclose and of being able to ask that their information be deleted and forgotten.

The GDPR regulates how organisations manage the information that they need from their customers. This framework of data protection regulations is an important element of organisational strategy, especially regarding how organisations personalise their marketing strategies from the insights distilled from personal data of customers. The GDPR provides a clear framework that standardises data protection regulations for any organisations that operate in the EU with its Data Protection Authority (DPA). According to the European Commission (2018), the framework of the GDPR includes obligations for organisations such as:

1   Obtain consent in order to use personal data, which should be presented in an informed and unambiguous manner through plain language and given through an affirmative action such as ticking a box or signing a form;
2   Protect individual rights to control their personal information, which includes the availability of information on who collects the information, why the information is collected and how the information is processed;
3   Rectify inaccurate or incomplete information when requested;
4   Stop processing the personal information when requested;
5   Appoint a data protection officer (DPO) as circumstances require;
6   Ensure the presence of data protection by design and data protection by default;

7   Implement measures to avoid data breaches and provide notifications in the case of a data breach.

Regulations such as the GDPR have a positive impact on organisational relationships with customers and on trust. They give customers a sense of external support, as noncompliance with the GDPR can lead to a significant fine for the organisation, up to 4% of an organisation's worldwide annual turnover or up to 20 million Euro, whichever is higher. In February 2019, nine months after the GDPR was implemented, the total administrative fines had reached nearly 56 million Euro (European Data Protection Board 2019). This demonstrates both the severity of privacy breach cases and the effectiveness of the GDPR in its role of protecting personal information in the EU.

Case study – Facebook and its data collection empire

Facebook takes whatever personal consumer data individuals want to enter, for example, from age and marital status to interests and hobbies. Add to this paid promotions by firms popping up on users' feeds, and these generate more two-way traffic between individuals and firms.

However, Aleksandr Kogan, a neuroscientist and psychologist, played a key role in the 2014 Cambridge Analytica scandal by using a "personality test" app on the Facebook platform to harvest the data of millions of Facebook users for dubious political campaigns (Graham-Harrison and Cadwalladr 2018) This scandal propelled the data collection and consumer privacy issue into the spotlight and also led Mark Zuckerberg to attend a US Congress hearing in April 2018 as the chief executive of Facebook (The Washington Post 2018). During the five-hour hearing, Mr. Zuckerberg admitted that Facebook made a mistake by not banning Cambridge Analytica's activities on the Facebook platform.

> I believe it's important to tell people exactly how the information that they share on Facebook is going to be used.
>
> Mark Zuckerberg

This scandal highlights the emergence of social media platforms such as Facebook functioning as data collection platforms for marketing purposes – an initially unintended function for platforms built to enable social networking. However, data collection for market research is common and, if conducted properly, should not involve any unethical practices. The question, then, is why data collection on social media platforms tends to have a negative connotation.

To answer that question, first we need to look at how social networking sites provide data for marketers and organisations. For instance, Facebook provides a platform that accommodates the disclosure of characteristic information such as your name, age, location or education or observational information such as your opinions and likes/dislikes, as well as images or videos to enrich user experience on the platform. Both types of information represent demographic and psychographic information that allows marketers and firms to understand who their consumers are through their online personas (Mosseri 2018). With over two billion users disclosing these types of information, it is unsurprising that social networking sites have been one of the biggest contributors to the volume of big data for marketers and organisations.

A combination of negative experiences from social media users, an emphasis on intricate and lengthy terms and conditions and the issue of ownership over data disclosed on social media platforms has probably contributed to the negative connotation of data collection practices on social network platforms. Violation of data privacy still occurs.

Regarding efforts to protect users' privacy, Mark Zuckerberg has gone to great lengths to highlight his company's utmost support for such efforts, using public relations and advertisements showing how users can control their data disclosure settings or through his own personal accounts. In an article for the Washington Post (Zuckerberg 2019), Zuckerberg strongly advocated that regulations prescribe their ability to protect users' privacy, and, without stronger regulations, they are unable to maximise their efforts to protect users' privacy. It is an odd assertion that Facebook does not have the power to stop itself from collecting data *on its own platform* and capitalising on it.

Following widespread privacy concerns, the EU established GDPR in 2018 to protect the data privacy of users and consumers of EU consumers. This automatically covers social media platforms such as Facebook. However, Facebook made an unprecedented response to GDPR implementation by moving its international headquarters from Ireland to its main offices in California (Hern 2018), taking itself out of the jurisdiction of EU laws. This contradicted the supportive comments that Mark Zuckerberg (2019) made concerning GDPR as step towards a safer Internet and social media use.

As social media platforms enable UGC in various forms, including opinions and "likes," their algorithms can push more relevant posts to users based on their data (Mosseri 2018). Facebook wants to ensure that you will see posts that will spark users' conversations or active engagement. The more actively a consumer engages with posts on Facebook, the better the algorithms can predict what may cause the consumer to be even more interactive. This type of insight can be invaluable for market researchers and organisations, as they can collect information from a targeted group of individuals and derive a better personalisation strategy.

Personalisation on Facebook and the capitalisation of information with better algorithms do not always receive positive feedback from their users. Sparked by the Cambridge Analytica scandal, issues related to election interference have become a top priority for Facebook in the US 2020 presidential election. The ability to target a specific group of individuals with political posts that may provoke, mislead or misinform is alarming. Facebook reacted to the Cambridge Analytica scandal by taking down interference activities from Russia and Iran (Wong 2019). However, this does not mean that Facebook is going to neglect its paid political advertisement business willingly, considering that the projected revenue from that alone can reach $420 million in 2020 (Ivanova 2019). While there may not be anything unethical about running political campaigns on Facebook, critiques focused on Facebook's inaction towards any misinformation that may be included in paid political advertisements. Although from an organisational perspective, Facebook's inaction can be interpreted as a neutral response to advertisements from various political ideologies, it can also be interpreted as an unethical practice of allowing misinformation to be circulated.

It is fascinating to see how Facebook evolved from a social networking platform built by university students to a giant networking platform with billions of global users. Perhaps the world, especially government institutions and regulators, is not prepared to face the challenges posed by the evolution of Facebook into a data collection empire. Facebook is an advertiser, and its use of marketing research is integrated into its advertising targeting. Whilst companies can capitalise on information on platforms such as Facebook, the concept of privacy inevitably contrasts with the data collection practices of Facebook and other social media sites (Hern 2018; Mosseri 2018). For marketing researchers, the benefits from big data generated by social media platforms are apparent, but measures to check unethical data practices should be a priority. Regulations such as GDPR may provide a robust framework to protect consumer privacy, but organisations also have a responsibility to ensure their data collection practice is ethical.

Conclusion

While there are many benefits for organisations in collecting information via social media, care should be taken to ensure that this is done ethically. Consumer marketing researchers can mitigate anxieties consumers have about parting with their personal information if researchers clarify why the information is needed for businesses and organisations to provide benefits to consumers.

References

Ajzen, I., 1991. The theory of planned behavior. *Organizational Behavior and Human Decision Processes*, 50(2), 179–211. DOI: 10.1016/0749-5978(91)90020-T.

ESOMAR B.V., 2020. Global market research 2020. Available from: https://ana.esomar.org/documents/global-market-research-2020 [Accessed 3 October 2020].

European Commission, 2018. Reform of EU data protection rules [online]. Available from: https://ec.europa.eu/commission/priorities/justice-and-fundamental-rights/data-protection/2018-reform-eu-data-protection-rules_en [Accessed 5 January 2020].

European Data Protection Board, 2019. First overview on the implementation of the GDPR and the roles and means of the national supervisory authorities. *European Data Protection Board* [online]. Available from: https://edpb.europa.eu/sites/edpb/files/files/file1/19_2019_edpb_written_report_to_libe_en.pdf [Accessed 5 January 2020].

Gaber, H.R., Elsamadicy, A.M. and Wright, L.T., 2019a. Why do consumers use Facebook brand pages? A case study of a leading fast-food brand fan page in Egypt. *Journal of Global Scholars of Marketing Science*, 29(3), 293–310.

Gaber, H.R., Wright, L.T. and Kooli, K., 2019b. Consumer attitudes towards Instagram advertisements in Egypt: The role of the perceived advertising value and personalization. *Cogent Business & Management*, 6(1), 1618431.

Graham-Harrison, E. and Cadwalladr, C., 2018. Revealed: 50 million Facebook profiles harvested for Cambridge Analytica in major data breach. *The Guardian* [online]. Available from: www.theguardian.com/news/2018/mar/17/cambridge-analytica-facebook-influence-us-election [Accessed 6 December 2019].

Hern, A., 2018. *Facebook Moves 1.5bn Users Out of Reach of New European Privacy Law. The Guardian* [online]. Available from: www.theguardian.com/technology/2018/apr/19/facebook-moves-15bn-users-out-of-reach-of-new-european-privacy-law [Accessed 6 December 2019].

Instagram, 2019. *Our Story* [online]. Available from: https://instagram-press.com/our-story/ [Accessed 5 January 2020].

Ivanova, I., 2019. Facebook expects to sell over $400 million of political ads next year. *CBS News* [online]. Available from: www.cbsnews.com/news/facebook-earnings-call-political-ads-to-bring-in-350-million-this-year/ [Accessed 6 December 2019].

Kehr, F., Kowatsch, T., Wentzel, D. and Fleisch, E., 2015. Blissfully ignorant: The effects of general privacy concerns, general institutional trust and affect in the privacy calculus: Privacy calculus: Dispositions and affect. *Information Systems Journal*, 25(6), 607–635. DOI: 10.1111/isj.12062.

Kotler, P. and Armstrong, G., 2016. *Principles of Marketing (Vol. 16th), Global*. Harlow: Pearson Education.

Lim, W.M., 2014. Sense of virtual community and perceived critical mass in online group buying. *Journal of Strategic Marketing*, 22(3), 268–283. https://doi.org/10.1080/0965254X.2013.876068.

Lusch, R.F. and Vargo, S.L., 2014. *Service-Dominant Logic: Premises, Perspectives, Possibilities*. Cambridge: Cambridge University Press. https://doi.org/10.1017/CBO9781139043120.

Ma, L., Sun, B. and Kekre, S., 2015. The squeaky wheel gets the grease – An empirical analysis of customer voice and firm intervention on Twitter. *Marketing Science*, 34(5), 627–645. http://dx.doi.org/10.1287/mksc.2015.0912.

Markus, M.L., 1987. Toward a "critical mass" theory of interactive media: Universal access, interdependence and diffusion. *Communication Research*, 14(5), 491–511. https://doi.org/10.1177%2F009365087014005003.

Morris, M. and Ogan, C., 1996. The Internet as mass medium. *Journal of Computer-Mediated Communication*, 1(4), JCMC141. https://doi.org/10.1111/j.1083-6101.1996.tb00174.x.

Mosseri, A., 2018. Bringing people closer together – about Facebook. *About Facebook* [online]. Available from: https://about.fb.com/news/2018/01/news-feed-fyi-bringing-people-closer-together/ [Accessed 6 December 2019].

Nielsen, 2017. *Nielsen Launches Artificial Intelligence Technology* [online]. Available from: www.nielsen.com/uk/en/press-room/2017/nielsen-launches-artificial-intelligence-technology.html [Accessed 5 January 2020].

Oh, J. and Sundar, S.S., 2016. User engagement with interactive media: A communication perspective. In H O'Brien and P. Carins (eds), *Why Engagement Matters*. Cham: Springer, 177–198. https://doi.org/10.1007/978-3-319-27446-1_8.

Palazzo, X., 2020. *Esomar's Latest Global Market Research Report Values Global Research and Data Industry Market at Us$80 Billion* [online]. Available from: www.researchworld.com/esomars-latest-global-market-research-report-values-global-research-and-data-industry-market-at-us-80-billion/ [Accessed 3 October 2020].

Palmgreen, P. and Rayburn, J.D., 1979. Uses and gratifications and exposure to public television: A discrepancy approach. *Communication Research*, 6(2), 155–179. https://doi.org/10.1177%2F009365027900600203.

Poynter, 2017. The state of the global MR industry. *Research News*, November–December, 18–19 [online]. Available from: https://newmr.org/wp-content/uploads/sites/2/2017/11/RN_Nov-Dec17_Ray-Poynter.pdf [Accessed 3 October 2020].

Rogers, E.M., 2010. *Diffusion of Innovations*. New York: Simon and Schuster. DOI: 10.4236/jep.2011.24038.

Social Media Examiner, 2019. *2019 Social Media Marketing Industry Report* [online]. Available from: www.socialmediaexaminer.com/social-media-marketing-industry-report-2019/ [Accessed 5 January 2020].

Stone, M., Laughlin, P., Aravopoulou, E., Gerardi, G., Todeva, E. and Weinzierl, L., 2017. How platforms are transforming customer information management. *The Bottom Line*, 30(3), 216–235.

Tajfel, H. and Turner, J.C., 1979. An integrative theory of intergroup conflict. *The Social Psychology of Intergroup Relations*, 33(47), 74. https://doi.org/10.1007/978-1-4614-5583-7_289.

Thomas, A.R., Pop, N.A., Iorga, A.M. and Ducu, C., 2016. *Ethics and Neuromarketing: Implications for Market Research and Business Practice*. Cham: Springer International Publishing. DOI: 10.1007/978-3-319-45609-6.

Tuten, T.L. and Solomon, M.R., 2017. *Social Media Marketing*. New Delhi: Sage Publications.

Wali, A.F., Cyprian, J. and Nkpurukwe, O.I., 2020. Influences of social media marketing tools towards online purchases: Nuances from undergraduate students in Nigeria Public Universities. *Paradigm*, 24(2), 239–253.

Wallace-Williams, D., 2017. *Consumption practices, conflict resolution and behaviour change in the UK smokers market*. Masters thesis, University of Huddersfield. http://eprints.hud.ac.uk/id/eprint/34671/

Wang, Y., Ma, S.S. and Li, D., 2015. Customer participation in virtual brand communities: The self-construal perspective. *Information and Management*, 52(5), 577–587. DOI: 10.1108/QMR-06-2013-0041.

The Washington Post, 2018. Transcript of Mark Zuckerberg's Senate hearing. Transcript Courtesy of Bloomberg Government [online]. Available from: www.washingtonpost.com/news/the-switch/wp/2018/04/10/transcript-of-mark-zuckerbergs-senate-hearing/ [Accessed 6 December 2019].

Whiting, A. and Williams, D., 2013. Why people use social media: A uses and gratifications approach. *Qualitative Market Research: An International Journal*, 16(4), 362–369. DOI: 10.1108/QMR-06-2013-0041.

Wong, J., 2019. Facebook discloses operations by Russia and Iran to meddle in 2020 election. *The Guardian* [online]. Available from: www.theguardian.com/technology/2019/oct/21/facebook-us-2020-elections-foreign-interference-russia [Accessed 6 December 2019].

Wright, A. and Wright, L.T. 2006. Book review: The Sage Handbook of Qualitative Research (3rd ed.). European Journal of Marketing, 40(9/10), 1145-1147. https://doi.org/10.1108/0309056061 0681050

Wright L.T., Wright R. and Kooli K. 2018. Book review: Business Marketing Concepts and Cases. Journal of Business & Industrial Marketing, 31(8), 1017-1018, DOI: https://doi.org/10.1108/JBIM-10-2016-274.

Yang, S., Shu, K., Wang, S., Gu, R., Wu, F. and Liu, H., 2019. Unsupervised fake news detection on social media: A generative approach. *Association for the Advancement of Artificial Intelligence: Thirty-Third AAAI*

Conference on Artificial Intelligence (AAAI-19) AAAI Technical Track: Machine Learning, 33(1), 5644–5651. https://doi.org/10.1609/aaai.v33i01.33015644.

Zuckerberg, M., 2019. Mark Zuckerberg: The Internet needs new rules. Let's start in these four areas. *The Washington Post* [online]. Available from: www.washingtonpost.com/opinions/mark-zuckerberg-the-Internet-needs-new-rules-lets-start-in-these-four-areas/2019/03/29/9e6f0504-521a-11e9-a3f7-78b7525a8d5f_story.html [Accessed 6 December 2019].

9

ARTIFICIAL INTELLIGENCE IN MARKETING AND MARKETING RESEARCH

Merlin Stone, Luiz Moutinho, Yuksel Ekinci, Ashraf Labib,
Geraint Evans, Eleni Aravopoulou, Paul Laughlin, Matt Hobbs,
Jon Machtynger and Liz Machtynger

Summary

This chapter focuses on the evolution of marketing practice and on the application of artificial intelligence (AI) to strategic marketing decision-making, in managing the marketing mix, and in marketing research. It concludes that the use of artificial intelligence offers opportunities to marketing researchers, but that it may also disrupt the business models of marketing research companies and change how they conduct marketing research.

Introduction

In marketing – and in other disciplines – the boundary between humans and computers in decision-making is shifting. Today, artificial intelligence (AI) is increasingly deployed in operational marketing, for example, identification of risks and contact centre response management, as well as in marketing, including analysis and targeting of customers, design and selection of advertising copy to match target customers and pricing to maximise yield from individual customers (Marinchak *et al.* 2018). Tomorrow, we expect that AI will be employed in strategic decision-making (e.g. which business models to use, which strategies to follow, which markets to target, which products to market, which channels of communication and distribution to use, overall pricing strategy, competitive positioning etc.) (Stone *et al.* 2020). However, the use of AI in marketing strategy has not been much discussed in the public domain. Our contacts with industry indicate that some companies have made great progress in this area, but these projects are kept secret and treated as a source of competitive advantage (Stone *et al.* 2020).

It should be emphasised at this point that the focus is not primarily on the replacement of human decision-making in strategic decisions but on the creation of a higher-quality decision-making mechanism using AI in which marketers are provided with quicker, more complete and more fully worked out options from which to choose and the creation of the associated theoretical framework.

Much of the writing about AI and marketing focuses on strategies for extending the use of AI in organisations, often in operational marketing areas, as Kiron and Schrage (2019) point out. However, as researchers start to focus on how AI can be used to develop new business models – a possible outcome of business and/or marketing planning (e.g. Lee *et al.* 2019; Valter *et al.* 2018), this may lead to the extension that Kiron and Schrage (2019) focus on, the use of AI in determining strategy.

AI in management decision-making

The frontier between humans and computers in management is moving from operational to strategic. A good synthesis is provided by Jarrahi (2018). A particularly relevant article, based on empirical research, is that of Kolbjørnsrud *et al.* (2016), which focuses on the use of AI in redefining management. Another application of AI in management decision-making is classification and incorporation of various stakeholders' views using the AI technique of fuzzy logic (Poplawska *et al.* 2015) and group decision-making using a machine learning method (Chakhar *et al.* 2016).

Claudé and Combe (2018) identify that today, AI is seen primarily as a support to major business decisions rather than a decision-maker but attribute this to the fact that AI as currently constituted is relatively weak, compared to what will be the strong AI of the future. As computational capacity and speed increase, and as data sets available to support decisions grow, the frontier of substitutability of AI for human decision-making shifts. Shrestha *et al.* (2019) suggest several possibilities, as follows:

- Full human-to-AI delegation, for example, recommender systems, digital advertising, online fraud detection, dynamic pricing;
- Hybrid 1: AI-to-human sequential decision-making, for example, idea evaluation, hiring;
- Hybrid 2: Human-to-AI sequential decision-making, for example, sports analytics, health monitoring;
- Aggregated human-AI decision-making, for example, top management teams, boards.

Shrestha *et al.* (2019) also suggest that the appropriateness of these alternatives, in particular the likelihood of appropriateness of full delegation to AI, depends upon:

- Decision search space specificity – the more specific the required decisions, the more suitable AI is;
- Interpretability – how easy it is to understand the reasons for decisions/recommendations (this relates to whether the AI approach used is "black box" or can "explain" its decisions);
- Size of the alternative set – the larger the size, the greater the problems humans have in dealing with them;
- Decision-making speed required – the faster it is, the more suitable AI is;
- Replicability – the higher the commonality of data/decisions and so on, the more suitable AI is, given that AI depends partly on learning from other cases.

In strategic decisions, the time it can take to see if a particular approach works, the lack of specificity, possible diversity of interpretations, the fact that speed is less of the essence and a relative lack of replicability mean that aggregated human-AI decision-making may be more appropriate, although Hybrid 1 may be used, too. In terms of evidence on implementation of AI in strategy, this seems to be secret, though there is evidence of a battle between the two main relevant digital players, Amazon and Google, to extend AI use using the enormous data sets available to both companies (Kiron and Schrage 2019).

This section mainly covers the perspective of business-to-consumer (B2C) and businesses selling to consumers via other businesses (known as B2B2C). We have covered some aspects of these developments in Wright *et al.* (2019), Parnell *et al.* (2018), Stone and Aravopoulou (2018) and Stone *et al.* (2017a, 2017b, 2018).

The evolution of marketing analytics towards AI

There is a fashion element to discussions about AI, particularly in marketing, where the boundary between advanced analytics and AI is fuzzy. Sometimes, quite basic analytics is claimed to show evidence of deployment of AI. Analytics has evolved to where it can handle problems which are relatively unstructured and come up with suggestions in a way that would once have been considered "expert" and even defined as AI.

One essential characteristic of AI that distinguishes it from classic "advanced analytics" is automation of feedback loops and improvement, that is, learning by the system (machine learning) about how to do things better, and this in turn implies that conclusions are being tested and assessed against certain criteria, as opposed to being reviewed by humans who then make decisions about what to do next. Where the action being "managed" by AI is precise and contained, implemented quickly and with the results also being measurable and assessable quickly, AI is generally very productive. But where decisions are more wide-ranging and take time to implement and time elapses before the results of the decisions are apparent, let alone measurable and assessable, deployment of AI can be more complicated. It may be hybrid, with parts of the cycle being undertaken by AI and part by human decision-makers. The latter applies to marketing strategy. However, one technique which may be usable to improve applicability is back-casting, in which decisions taken earlier and of which the results are now known are used along with data from the period of analysis to application to train the system. This approach can also be used to capture the "historic expertise" of strategic marketers by rule elicitation or case-based reasoning.

The rise of AI in marketing is not taking place in isolation from the rapid, wider advance of marketing technology, whether in front-line marketing operations such as contact centres or the management of marketing resources. This advance helps in the deployment of AI in marketing in the sense that it computerises other aspects of marketing and generates data which can be used to support AI. However, this also means that AI use should be integrated with these applications, taking data feeds automatically and making recommendations back to these other areas.

Ethical and data protection issues

Marketing involves doing things to customers and using their data. Both have important ethical considerations. Asking computers to decide which customers shall be offered which products, or which customers seem to have committed fraud, is already normal in industries such as financial services but has already raised problems of equity and trust. Where customers' data is concerned, legislation makes it paramount that AI-based processing does not lead to infringement of increasingly stringent data protection legislation or of basic ethical rules which marketers should observe.

Ethical rules are not, however, universally or consistently understood. Some organisations are overt in their claims to consciously opt out of certain activities. That something can be (technically) achieved is not by itself a justification for doing it. Microsoft's AETHER board and process is designed to consider ethical implications from a top-down perspective. Some organisations have publicly distanced themselves from certain military or policing applications of AI technology. Google in 2019 announced that it would end involvement with Project Maven (a Pentagon program aimed at using AI to improve object recognition in military drones) after employees signed an open protest letter. On the other hand, companies such as Palentir have caused controversy by using face recognition deployed by the US Immigration and Customs Enforcement. Despite employee protests at the separation of families resulting from the technology, this was rationalised as helping fight crime and reduce drug offences.

Marketing planning processes

Research into this topic goes back to the 1960s, when the first marketing planning texts were produced, first by management consultants, then by academics, becoming integrated into university teaching a decade or so later. The leading author, McDonald (2016a, 2016b), has researched marketing planning for 40 years and focuses on logical (e.g. from objectives, through strategies, to tactics), analytical and functional or cross-functional (especially finance) and other processes deemed necessary to produce a marketing plan appropriate for a firm's context. His work includes ideas about appropriate marketing research, customer information management and competitive intelligence.

The data content of planning has been changed by the advent of customer relationship management and digital marketing, with data about individual customers, their behaviour and needs becoming more widely used compared to "classic" marketing research (Stone *et al.* 1996; Stone and Woodcock 2014). Digitally supported marketing allows an initiative to move from an idea or concept to execution in weeks or even days, compared to the months or years suggested in classic marketing (Chaffey and Ellis-Chadwick 2019). More generally, the impact of big data on board decisions has been researched by Merendino *et al.* (2018). The impact of the digitisation of data on board decisions has been explored by Dibb *et al.* (2015). The impact of digitisation on the role of strategists is discussed by Åberg *et al.* (2017), while the problem posed by data overload and the impossibility of articulating all data is covered by Quinn *et al.* (2018). One of the most relevant points emphasised by Lee *et al.* (2019) is the dependence of AI on data quality and quantity and the issue of shortage of AI skills, pointing out that even in relatively straightforward operational implementation on AI, shortage of AI skills may hinder progress. Blending the relatively high-level skills of business/marketing planning with AI skills may prove an even greater challenge.

The benefits of AI in marketing decision-making

The benefits of applying AI to strategic marketing decision-making are expected to include these:

- Increased speed of decision-making, especially in response to new data being available or competitive threats emerging, allowing companies to capture the benefits of stronger market positions earlier;
- Identification of missing data;
- Increased rationality, particularly via removal or reduction of cognitive bias by decision-makers;
- Creation of a common basis for decision-making;
- Incorporation of learning from experience;
- Higher-quality management of marketing projects;
- Stronger ability to align to partnerships (particularly ones with shared ethical cultures);
- Ability to produce clarity for customers, including a clear rationale for the benefit of data;
- Improved responsiveness and collaboration between departments.

Examples of application

In this section, we consider some of the ways in which AI might be used in different areas of marketing decision-making and planning. It is based on the analysis framework proposed by Stone and Woodcock (2014) for analysing the impact of digitalisation but applied to AI.

A similar matrix of needs could be developed for corporate strategy. There is not always a clear separation between marketing strategy and business strategy. Nor is there a clear separation between overall marketing strategy and strategy for different elements of the marketing mix. For example, decisions about marketing channels have strategic aspects (Stone *et al.* 2002) as well as tactical aspects, particularly as digital approaches change the balance between channels and the roles that different channels play. These decisions can affect every aspect of marketing. However, Tables 9.1 to 9.3 present an attempt to show the main changes that digital marketing has made to different marketing activities, as digitalisation of marketing is a

Table 9.1 Deployment of AI in marketing strategy

Marketing area	Changes made by digital marketing	Examples of how AI can be used in each area
Overall strategy – target markets, marketing mix for each, objectives, key performance indicators (KPIs), goals etc.	This allows information for decision-making to be assembled quickly and be automated and results of different strategies to be analysed more quickly so strategy can be revised in a "test and learn" approach.	Quickly assessing different outcomes based on alternative strategies; assisting in rapid decision-making to choose those most likely to produce best results.
Business model of customer management	This relates to which customers the company wants to acquire, retain, develop (up-sell and cross-sell) and divest, with what resulting revenues and costs, to achieve its strategic objectives rather than to meet the goals of certain elements of the marketing mix in isolation.	Using technology such as machine learning to assist in "reaching" look-alike audiences. Quantifying and exploring consequences of different business models.
Overall branding and proposition	Depending on whether the company is involved in many different types of product and market, this may apply to the whole company or to parts of it but at a higher level than individual products and services – with different branding approaches taken on different channels.	Identifying results of brand investments, recommending future investments and channel strategy.
Developing new revenue streams	This refers to developing revenue using a way or introducing a new product or service that is in some sense different from existing ways – it may involve any or all elements of the marketing mix and different markets.	Identifying revenue streams for existing customer base and for new markets in order to accelerate launch.

(Continued)

Table 9.1 (Continued)

Marketing area	Changes made by digital marketing	Examples of how AI can be used in each area
Ecosystem management, partnering, outsourcing and value chain redefinition	This relates to how companies and partners (i.e. suppliers and manufacturers!) that are not owned by the client but work very closely with it are organised to ensure that the company's overall marketing (and business) strategy is developed and delivered and how the gains from working together are shared.	Identifying most productive parts of ecosystem and gaps in ecosystem development.
Competitive strategy – who main competitors are, targeting for winning and defence	This relates to how direct and indirect competitors are identified, their strategies discovered and understood and how the company strategises so as to avoid where possible the negative effects of competition.	Identifying weak signals of impending competition. Identifying weaknesses in own and competitor's strategy.
Resource management	This allows overall costs and benefits of different strategies to be measured and analysed more quickly in order to adjust resourcing (i.e. for periods of peak demand).	Analysis of the data to identify risks, rewards and outcomes/possible planning scenarios.

Source: The authors

Table 9.2 Deployment of AI in the marketing mix

Marketing area	Changes made by digital marketing	Examples of how AI can be used in each area
Branding	The locus of many companies' brands has shifted from the real to the virtual world, with many brands of many others strongly affected by what is said about them in the virtual world.	Tracking shifting brand image using evidence from the web, particularly social media. Finding evidence of the causes of brand shift and loss of market share.
Product	Customer input into product design (collaborative design) can be obtained much more quickly. Customers can design their own products more easily. Designs can be tested and revised more quickly, while problems can be identified and rectified more quickly and easily using a variety of digital channels and collaboration tools.	Synthesising input from customers. Simulating results of new product designs of formulations.

Marketing area	Changes made by digital marketing	Examples of how AI can be used in each area
Proposition	The proposition can be more closely attuned to target markets, and the engagement of customers with different propositions can be understood more quickly, with iterative changes made and tested for further feedback.	Identifying which propositions work best though customer feedback and testing.
Price	Prices can be tailored more easily to different customers. Yield management can be applied in many new areas.	Resetting pricing strategies based on results of different yield management approaches.
Advertising	Website/mobile/digital advertising is gradually usurping advertising in conventional physical media, allowing greater trackability and better assessment of return on investment. This is leading to a blurring of the distinction between advertising, digital and other marketing communications methods. The automation applied to advertising via programmatic and similar approaches is greatly increasing the opportunity for applying AI approaches.	Choosing/designing text, images and videos to suit market segments and individuals in different channels and platforms.
Direct marketing	Direct marketing has expanded out of the conventional media of mail and telephone to include virtually all marketing communications, especially digital and customer relationship management (CRM), so that in some ways, it appears in all marketing, whether initiated by the company or its customers. Referrals, always valuable, have been transformed into recommendations for many companies.	Choosing which forms/combinations of contact types/channels/content are appropriate for different target markets and individuals.
Personal selling	Personal selling now has much stronger information support, while improved sales management systems, sometimes integrated with response management systems, allow much more effective targeting, prospecting and management of customers and prospects.	Providing personalised response to individuals. Analysing the results. Recommending different ways to personalise.
Public relations	Electronic word of mouth, or "word of mouse," is replacing conventional media exposure, not solely through social networks but through all aspects of web and mobile dialogue – and often developing rapidly and in real time ("trending"). In some sectors, online reviews have become critical in determining whether a product will sell, while social influencers have become a very important part of marketing in some sectors, such as travel, clothing, cosmetics and automotive.	Identifying patterns of word of mouth, reasons for them, suggested actions and underlying sentiment.

(Continued)

Table 9.2 (Continued)

Marketing area	Changes made by digital marketing	Examples of how AI can be used in each area
Sales promotion	The effectiveness of sales promotions can be gauged much more quickly than ever before, while online channels facilitate distribution of buying incentives (such as coupons, discounts and other incentives).	Identifying which promotions work best and quickest with which customers/ market segments. Identifying which offers should be used and when.
Content	The increase in the number of channels and the importance of content (text, audio, image, video) in persuading and influencing customers has come to the fore, particularly given the possibility of customising all kinds of content to market segments and now individual customers, supported by the ability to search for, classify and analyse all kinds of content. The rapid rise in video content, facilitated by significant improvements in mobile bandwidth (with more to come with the advent of 5G), is both a challenge and an opportunity, multiplied by using messaging to communicate content. Extended (virtual and augmented) reality is changing the approach to content, allowing the blending of real and digital experiences. Brand and product storytelling are being used much more, partly because they support the development of much richer content that can be used across all communication channels. However, an issue which remains controversial is the extent to which the use of AI can support and encourage creativity and increase the returns from it.	Serving content to the right customers and prospects at the right time and analysing results of serving it. Customising content to target segments and customers.
Customer management (acquisition, retention, development, customer service, customer experience)	This relates to how the customer inventory is built for particular products or groups of them, from the targets set to the techniques used to achieve desired results and track fulfilment of commitment and customer promises following transaction.	Optimising inventory levels in real time and helping the customer react to different segments of demand. Automating interaction with the customer (bots).

(Continued)

Marketing area	Changes made by digital marketing	Examples of how AI can be used in each area
Distribution	The web has become a very important channel of distribution for many information-based products and services, as well as some physical products, and in many markets the dominant channel for marketing communication, so that distribution and the communication decisions become closely tied to each other, with customers seeking an immediate response to their requests or a simple method in which to purchase when they are ready.	Optimising channels. Identifying missing channels. Improving transaction times and streamlining fulfilment.

Source: The authors

Table 9.3 Deployment of AI in marketing management

Marketing area	Changes made by digital marketing	Examples of how AI can be used in each area
People	Marketing, sales and service people can be much better informed about what they need to know to sell and market better, and results of their work can be obtained and distributed more easily. They can also benefit professionally from having more training on new digital marketing tools and how to apply the technology personally.	Identifying what information should be used to support different types of decisions. Identifying where managers are not using the right information, have not got access to the right information or are misinterpreting the information they have. Providing tools and frameworks to better use the opportunities created by new AI technology.
Marketing analysis	Using the huge volumes of data now available to some companies and customers growing increasingly impatient for rapid response targeting of outbound messaging and rapid response to inbound messaging can be much more accurate and timelier. Timing has become critically important to capture buying intent, as customers may be in the market for a very short time as they make their comparisons and reach their conclusions using the mountains of content available from firms and their competitors.	Accelerating analysis and its application – both from a "reactive" internal perspective and also from the point of view of customers accessing information relevant to a purchase.

(Continued)

Table 9.3 (Continued)

Marketing area	Changes made by digital marketing	Examples of how AI can be used in each area
Market research	Market research is increasingly online, while gaining insight from both customer-initiated feedback and sentiment analysis (with the appropriate permissions) is providing a new source of information to marketers on how their current and prospective customers think, feel and act.	Gaining and analysing larger data sets. Analysis of results of research, especially when combined across different studies.
Market targeting	Due to its growing complexity, market targeting is becoming increasingly automated. The results of recent changes in targets and deployment of different elements of marketing mix to produce appropriate response rates and sales.	AI can assist with more accurate targeting, including allowing for real-time changes to strategy.
Data and systems	Marketing processes can be migrated onto systems, increasingly running on the "cloud" and allowing the marketing and wider team to collaborate and enhance their effectiveness and speed of processes such as workflow/project management. Systems allow much better access to data required for decision-making on everything from individual customers to strategic decisions and then for measurement, review and calculation of return on investment. Personalisation and location-based marketing have moved on from becoming watchwords to being "business as usual" for the most effective marketing teams. However, they pose significant privacy risks, as data protection requirements have become a central focus for marketing management. Meanwhile, the requirements for integrating data from different sources so as to maximise marketing effectiveness, particularly the integration of data management platforms (centralised systems for collecting and analysing large data sets from disparate sources) with demand-side platforms (systems that allow buyers of digital advertising to coordinate their activity, including bidding) are essential to keep up with competitors.	Identifying opportunities for improving returns to systems deployment. Identifying new ways to accelerate workflow and collaboration to assist in developing speed to market and increased compliance.

Marketing area	Changes made by digital marketing	Examples of how AI can be used in each area
Marketing resource management	Marketing automation allows marketing processes to be managed more effectively as the return on investment for different marketing expenditures can be calculated and forecast with more accuracy than traditional channels.	Optimising resource management is key, with business being more stretched than ever by a hypercompetitive market.
Content management	Managing the increasing volume and variety of content requires maintaining various systems, and constantly customising content to the needs and use cases of specific situations is particularly important, given the rising possibility of exposing the wrong customer to the wrong content. Matching content to the right end customer (at the right time) uses significantly more marketing resources, so the return on the additional cost improving content management must be measured and acted upon.	Detailed optimisation for individual customers. Provision of tools that speed up delivery of content and improve its optimisation.
Managing marketing people	This relates to how marketing people are recruited, trained, developed, targeted and assessed as marketing professionals. This is particularly important in a rapidly changing landscape of digital technology which is necessitating an entirely new skill set from traditional marketing channels and disciplines.	Identifying the most productive marketers and assisting the resolution of problems associated with the decision-making of others.
Marketing operating model	With digitalisation, the marketing operating model is changing. One of the best examples of this is the rise of programmatic advertising, which is helping companies use technology to move beyond manual management of advertising to use technology to reach the nirvana of attributing the correct value to different advertising interventions, given the possession and use of the right analytics tools to reach the right target audience automatically.	Optimising the efficient working of model, including using machine learning to make real-time decisions on appropriate audiences and investment levels.

(Continued)

Table 9.3 (Continued)

Marketing area	Changes made by digital marketing	Examples of how AI can be used in each area
Marketing resource management	Marketing automation allows marketing processes to be managed more effectively as the return on investment for different marketing expenditures can be calculated and forecast with more accuracy than traditional channels.	Optimising resource management is key, with business being more stretched than ever by a hypercompetitive market.
Marketing finance	Identifying where revenue and, crucially, profit come from while operating in a complex multi-channel, multi-product/service business is essential. Given the reduction in barriers to entry online and the increasing speed of change in the market, whether a business is acting in a sustainable manner needs to be ascertained much more quickly. New measures are being used, not just the classic financial ones, that take into account portfolio approaches and digital traction.	Identifying returns accurately, more rapidly and with greater impartiality than human analysis.

Source: The authors

precondition for the data to be made available for AI to be deployed, and examples of possible AI deployment. The tables cover in turn marketing strategy, marketing mix and marketing management.

Progress to date

The use of AI in marketing operations has been extensively publicised by suppliers of systems which are either ones where AI can be deployed or which provide the AI component, for example, from the leading supplier of customer relationship management software, Salesforce.com (Garvin 2019). However, the use of AI in making strategic marketing decisions has been researched very little, with the most recent comprehensive report being from Accenture (Awalegaonkar *et al.* 2019). This report, based on interviews with 1500 C-suite executives from companies with a minimum revenue of US$1 billion in 12 countries in 16 industries, focused on the factors required to scale artificial intelligence. The report used the concepts of piloting and scaling to segment users of AI. It defined a "pilot" as rolling out a capability with real data, users and processes in a production environment (using a subset of the relevant scope). The purpose of piloting is to test how the capability performs with a limited scope and to then make any needed modifications before expanding to the full applicable scope. It defined "scale" as extension of the piloted capability across the full applicable scope with all relevant data, end users, customers and processes.

The main findings of the report were as follows:

- 84% of C-suite executives believe they need to use artificial intelligence to achieve their growth objectives. Nearly all C-suite executives view AI as an enabler of their strategic priorities and think achieving a positive return on AI investments requires scaling across the organisation;
- 76% acknowledge that they struggle in scaling AI across the business and that if they do not scale AI in the next five years, they risk going out of business;
- Companies that successfully scale AI achieve much better financial returns from their investment in it.

The report suggested that users of AI fell into three groups:

- Those at proof-of-concept stage (80–85% of companies), with a low scaling success rate, a low return on their AI investments and their efforts usually siloed within a department or team, often IT-led, with no connection to a business imperative and difficult to scale.
- Those engaged in strategic scaling (15–20% of companies), having moved beyond proof of concept, with a higher success rate for AI, with a clear AI strategy and operating model linked to the company's business objectives; with an experimental mindset; with their efforts supported by a larger, multi-dimensional team championed by the chief AI, data or analytics officer, but with the scaled AI generally applied to individual applications such as personalisation, intelligent automation and predictive reporting.
- Those (at most 5%) who have industrialised their use of AI, creating a culture of AI, a clear enterprise vision based on strategy and competitive advantage that resists siloed applications, with strong accountability, metrics and governance, with thousands of models in use within an AI framework, using it to promote product and service innovation, using "what-if" analysis enabling improved acquisition, service and satisfaction and re-using digital assets. They recognise the importance of business-critical data – identifying financial, marketing, consumer and master data as a priority, investing in structuring and managing data, data quality, data management and data governance frameworks on the cloud, with clear operating models for generation versus consumption of data, integrating internal and external data sets as a standard practice and understand the importance of using more diverse datasets to support initiatives.

The report cites two case studies, as follows:

- A brewing firm which uses AI to develop more accurate forecasting models, improved consumer and customer segmentations and enhanced sales, deploying advanced analytics capabilities on more than one hundred global datasets, including sales and forecast data, social media, trade spend, customer and product master data and weather data;
- A convenience store chain which uses AI in pricing to match customer demand across the world, using virtual agents to interact with global category management teams to drive adoption of the new pricing approach, supported by multi-disciplinary teams with skills in areas like data engineering, visualisation, data quality and human-centred design.

How AI will disrupt marketing research

General benefits

AI-driven marketing research can now bring together a range of research methodologies, data types and machine learning techniques to automate the research process from design to delivery. By putting AI at the core of a platform and layering methodologies and frameworks around it, AI can not only drive research design to generate insights but also can provide recommendations that inform business decisions.

Researchers say that AI will bring greater data accuracy, increase the size of the market-research industry, and create or maintain more jobs than it destroys. Making room for the expected advancements of AI means adapting to a major new presence in the industry. Automating insight generation not only saves marketing research professionals time and money but also offers the opportunity to find patterns in data at a scale never possible before. One way that AI helps marketers is in its ability to mine data and find insights in data that has already been collected. What started from simpler server logs, then evolved into more complex analytics software, then into big data-driven business intelligence platforms, grows increasingly complex and broad in its ability to gather, process and analyse sets of data.

The use of algorithms and AI makes marketing research faster and cheaper, cutting down project timelines from weeks and months to hours and days. That change alone is making the use of market research feasible beyond big decisions. With quick results, one can apply AI-driven market research to day-to-day decisions. So, one of the most important outcomes of combining marketing research with AI includes the impact on insights and research productivity. While AI is great for data collection, its primary purpose is to quickly learn from data and adjust itself, while marketing research wants to take those learnings and apply additional action outside of the data. Being able to collect more robust data sets that can quickly incorporate the who, what, when, where and how of the data allows marketing researchers to focus on more important aspects like why, saving time and cost. Also, more data means better data quality and less bias.

AI-driven marketing research is accessible because it does not require a team of experts to develop a study and interpret results. Users can go to a portal and simply ask a business question, and natural language processing (NLP) capabilities enable the AI solution to access the right data and return actionable recommendations in language anyone can understand, meaning more people in an organisation can use marketing research.

Which research questions are facilitated by AI?

What research questions are best answered with AI? At its core, AI is a data reduction technique. It can analyse thousands, even millions, of records. We commonly recommend AI for a company that has broad questions to answer. For example, what needs exist in the marketplace? What insights in our category could we have missed with prior research? What insights can we gather from adjacent categories that might help inform our strategy?

Automation, insight generation and natural language processing enable businesses to survey the market continually rather than dedicating specific time, labour and money to the process. AI solutions take seconds to produce insights that used to take teams of people days or even weeks to produce. Using AI also means data can be digested in real time. AI in marketing research can unearth, read and analyse data far more quickly than humans. The ability to extract real insights from written comments is a great example of how AI in marketing research can reduce insight time. AI excels at storing and remembering huge amounts of data and making very complex calculations based on large data sets.

An expected evolution relates to what we refer to as "deep learning segmentation" – a segmentation system that has been enhanced using artificial intelligence to identify patterns that are too complex for human comprehension. This is a way to break through the barriers and realise the opportunities that big data affords. Traditional data analytics are based on linear patterns and testing hypotheses such as "Is this true or not?" But in this more complex world, there are far more predictive and insightful patterns outside of the linear. Deep learning also finds patterns without human bias or preconceptions, combining many types of data and allowing organisations to deal with complex and missing data. It also unifies disparate data, breaking down the silos that exist in organisations and providing a common language to describe the customers which can be used across all business units.

AI also gives market researchers access to tools like powerful automated text analysis, which can analyse millions of comments, both voice and text, in minutes and emerge with a nuanced understanding of what customers think and want. Powerful algorithms can learn from respondents and ask the right follow-up questions, micro-targeting the questions to be specific to a single respondent's interests and needs.

The ability to include real-time data from a variety of sources in marketing research projects is another fundamental change. Now, one can analyse up-to-the-minute data from sources like sales, texts, social media, behavioural information, and passive data, transforming market research from a backward-looking analytics function to a future-focused discipline.

Removal of bias

AI can produce accurate data simply because it reduces the chances of human bias. In a focus group, information is collected by interacting with people. The person doing the interviewing will remember things in a certain way, therefore creating a chance for bias to show in the report. With AI, human bias is basically eliminated because the program processes informational factoids only.

One kind of bias is in the person being researched. Our memories have a funny way of presenting some things more clearly than others when we recall them. However, software designed to gather data about user behaviour and actions remembers all points equally. Using AI tools, researchers can create a more accurate representation of what people are really thinking and doing. This is because the methods used to do the research are based on real human interactions (such as collecting eye movement, usage of a mobile app or their path through a retail environment) as opposed to a research participants' ability to recall what they said, did or thought.

Further developments

With the continued development of different AI features like natural language processing and natural language generation (NLG), AI is growing its capability to help understand different qualitative and quantitative data fed to it. This means programs can write individualised reports based on keywords or subject areas that a client is interested in, which can save many hours.

AI will democratise market research by expanding access and eliminating research skill requirements. It will make market research more broadly applicable, extending use cases beyond strategic decisions to inform tactical choices. For all these reasons and more, AI will change everything about market research, and companies that get in on the ground floor will benefit the most.

Issues

Where does this leave us? Our view is that there is an urgent need for deeper research to guide how marketing research academics teach their students – both about marketing decision-making and marketing research.

Other areas that need more research include:

* Impact of culture on attitudes to possible changes in decision-making;
* Applicability of AI-supported decision-making to transformational decisions, for example, switching to a new business model or dealing with "wicked" problems (Foss and Saebi 2018) or in turbulent environments (Vecchiato 2015);
* How to maintain innovativeness in marketing research in an AI-driven world.

Acknowledgements

This chapter is based partly on:
Stone, M., Aravopoulou, E., Ekinci, Y., Evans, G., Hobbs, M., Labib, A., Laughlin, P., Machtynger, J. and Machtynger, L., 2020. Artificial intelligence (AI) in strategic marketing decision-making: A research agenda. *The Bottom Line*, 33(2), 183–200.

References

Åberg, C., Kazemargi, N. and Bankewitz, M., 2017. Strategists on the board in a digital era. *Business and Management Research*, 6(2), 40–51. https://doi.org/10.5430/bmr.v6n2p40.

Awalegaonkar, K., Berkey, R., Douglass, G. and Reilly, A., 2019. *AI: Built to Scale*. London: Accenture [online]. Available from: www.accenture.com/gb-en/insights/artificial-intelligence/ai-investments [Accessed 20 June 2020].

Chaffey, D. and Ellis-Chadwick, F., 2019. *Digital Marketing*. London: Pearson.

Chakhar, S., Ishizaka, A., Labib, A. and Saad, I., 2016. Dominance-based rough set approach for group decisions. *European Journal of Operational Research*, 251(1), 206–224. https://doi.org/10.1016/j.ejor.2015.10.060.

Claudé, M. and Combe, D., 2018. *The Roles of Artificial Intelligence and Humans in Decision-Making: Towards Augmented Humans*. Master's Thesis, Umeå University School of Business, Economics and Statistics, Sweden.

Dibb, S., Meadows, M. and Wilson, D., 2015. *Digitisation and Decision Making in the Boardroom* [online]. Available from: www.nemode.ac.uk/?page_id=1524 [Accessed 18 October 2019].

Foss, N.J. and Saebi, T., 2018. Business models and business model innovation: Between wicked and paradigmatic problems. *Long Range Planning*, 51(1), 9–21.

Garvin, K., 2019. *Artificial Intelligence in Marketing Is What Customers Want* [online]. Available from: www.salesforce.com/products/marketing-cloud/best-practices/artificial-intelligence-for-marketing/ [Accessed 27 December 2019].

Jarrahi, M., 2018. Artificial intelligence and the future of work: Human-AI symbiosis in organizational decision making. *Business Horizons*, 61(4), 577–586. DOI: 10.1016/j.bushor.2018.03.007.

Kiron, D. and Schrage, M., 2019. Strategy for and with AI. *MIT Sloan Management Review Magazine*.

Kolbjørnsrud, V., Amico, R. and Thomas, R.J., 2016. How artificial intelligence will redefine management. *Harvard Business Review*.

Lee, J., Suh, T., Roy, D. and Baucus, M., 2019. Emerging technology and business model innovation: The case of artificial intelligence. *Journal of Open Innovation: Technology, Market, and Complexity*, 5, 44. DOI: 10.3390/joitmc5030044.

Marinchak, C., Forrest, E. and Hoanca, B., 2018. Artificial intelligence: Redefining marketing management and the customer experience. *International Journal of E-Entrepreneurship and Innovation*, 8(2), 14–24. DOI: 10.4018/IJEEI.2018070102.

McDonald, M., 2016a. *Marketing Plans: How to Prepare Them, How to Profit from Them*. Chichester: Wiley.

McDonald, M., 2016b. Strategic marketing planning: Theory and practice. In M. Baker and S. Hart, eds. *The Marketing Book*. London: Routledge, 108–142.

Merendino, A., Dibb, S., Meadows, M., Quinn, L., Wilson, D., Simkin, L. and Canhoto, A., 2018. Big data, big decisions: The impact of big data on board level decision-making. *Journal of Business Research*, 93, 67–78. DOI: 10.1016/j.jbusres.2018.08.029.

Parnell, B., Stone, M. and Aravopoulou, E., 2018. How leaders manage their business models using information. *The Bottom Line*, 31(2), 150–167. https://doi.org/10.1108/BL-04-2018-0017.

Poplawska, J., Labib, A., Reed, D. and Ishizaka, A., 2015. Stakeholder profile definition and salience measurement with fuzzy logic and visual analytics applied to corporate social responsibility case study. *Journal of Cleaner Production*, 105, 103–115. DOI: 10.1016/j.jclepro.2014.10.095.

Quinn, L., Ardley, B. and Dibb, S., 2018. *Unravelling the Tacit in a Digital Age: The Inescapable Role of Inarticulable Insight*. Paper Presented at the Data, Organisations and Society Conference, Coventry University [online]. Available from: http://eprints.lincoln.ac.uk/id/eprint/34332/ [Accessed 20 June 2020].

Shrestha, Y., Ben-Menahem, S. and von Krogh, G., 2019. Organizational decision-making structures in the age of artificial intelligence. *California Management Review*, 61(4), 66–83. https://doi.org/10.1177/0008125619862257.

Stone, M. and Aravopoulou, E., 2018. Improving journeys by opening data: The case of Transport for London (TfL). *The Bottom Line*, 31(1), 2–15. DOI: 10.1108/BL-12-2017-0035.

Stone, M., Aravopoulou, E., Ekinci, Y., Evans, G., Hobbs, M., Labib, A., Laughlin, P., Machtynger, J. and Machtynger, L., 2020. Artificial intelligence (AI) in strategic marketing decision-making: A research agenda. *The Bottom Line*, 33(2), 183–200. https://doi.org/10.1108/BL-03-2020-0022.

Stone, M., Hobbs, M. and Khaleeli, M., 2002. Multichannel customer management: The benefits and challenges. *Journal of Database Marketing*, 10(1), 39–52.

Stone, M., Laughlin, P., Aravopoulou, E., Gerardi, G., Todeva, E. and Weinzierl, L., 2017a. How platforms are transforming customer information management. *The Bottom Line*, 30(3), 216–235. DOI: 10.1108/BL-08-2017-0024.

Stone, M., Machtynger, L. and Machtynger, J., 2018. Managing customer insight creatively through storytelling. *Journal of Direct, Data & Digital Marketing*, 17(2), 77–83. DOI: 10.1057/dddmp.2015.45.

Stone, M., Parnell, B., Stott, R., Aravopoulou, E. and Timms, L., 2017b. Business model innovation, strategic information & the role of analyst firms. *The Bottom Line*, 30(2), 151–162. https://doi.org/10.1108/BL-06-2017-0012.

Stone, M. and Woodcock, N., 2014. Interactive, direct and digital marketing: A future that depends on better use of business intelligence. *Journal of Research in Interactive Marketing*, 8(1), 4–17. DOI: 10.1108/JRIM-07-2013-0046.

Stone, M., Woodcock, N. and Wilson, M., 1996. Managing the change from marketing planning to customer relationship management. *Long Range Planning*, 29(5), 675–683. https://doi.org/10.1016/0024-6301(96)00061-1.

Valter, P., Lindgren, P. and Prasad, R., 2018. Advanced business model innovation supported by artificial intelligence and deep learning. *Wireless Personal Communications*, 100(1), 97–111. https://doi.org/10.1007/s11277-018-5612-x.

Vecchiato, R., 2015. Strategic planning and organizational flexibility in turbulent environments. *Foresight*, 17(3), 257–273. https://doi.org/10.1108/FS-05-2014-0032.

Wright, L., Robin, R., Stone, M. and Aravopoulou, E., 2019. Adoption of big data technology for innovation in B2B marketing. *Journal of Business-to-Business Marketing*, 26(3/4), 281–293. https://doi.org/10.1080/1051712X.2019.1611082.

10

DATA MANAGEMENT AND MARKETING RESEARCH

Merlin Stone, Tony Mooney and Paul Laughlin

Summary

This chapter outlines recent developments in the availability and use of marketing and customer data. It aims to give marketing researchers some insights into the processes at work that generate new sets of data which may be used to provide commercial researchers with some insights as to how they should use data. It discusses a wide range of data issues, technical, operational, strategic and legal, and how they are changing under the impact of the internet. The chapter also briefly discusses the difference social media is making in the way marketing research is being conducted, identifying the area as one where marketing researchers are already making a significant contribution to turning social media into one of the most important sources of marketing research information for companies.

Introduction

Behavioural versus stated data

Data can be divided into two categories: behavioural and stated. Behavioural data is collected as the result of people or machines doing things. Examples are transactions, interactions, browsing and viewing. Stated data is gathered from processes that collect or monitor humans expressing attitudes, views and opinions. Surveys, focus groups, customer satisfaction scores, reviews and blogs are examples of this. Ideally, both types of data are required to provide robust insight. A reliance on insight derived just from stated preferences or opinions can be problematic, as people may not think what they feel, say what they think or do what they say.

Connected pervasive computing has created huge volumes of behavioural data as well as new stated data. Although there remain many situations where stated data is the only source available (new product development, for example), building your research foundation on behavioural data, before embarking on stated data, is desirable whenever possible. This enables the researcher to understand the 'what happened' and objectively diagnose the behaviours that caused it (the 'why it happened') to help focus the collection of stated data either from primary or secondary sources. This represents the best opportunity to integrate what people say and what they do and avoid cognitive biases.

The importance of understanding data provenance, context and recency

Collection of data is not a competitive advantage; it is what you can do with it. Not all data is valuable. Some data is much more valuable than other data. Organisations often do not have the data or do not have it in a format to do what they want. So, it is important to know where data was collected, when it was collected, how it was collected and from whom it was collected. All these things can make a fundamental difference to the insight derived.

Here are some examples:

- Survey data collected by email or online compared to telephone or face-to-face interviews;
- Evaluating Amazon review data without knowing whether reviews have been incentivised;
- Respondents to a prize draw or incentivised questionnaire;
- Browsing click-through or call data that hasn't deduplicated repeated interactions; that is, one individual could have called many times;
- Coronavirus tests in hospitals or laboratories compared with those taken in tents in public car parks;
- Website behavioural data collected before and after significant changes have been made to a website.

Recency of data can be critical, depending on the decisions required from the insight. In particular, the rapid changes and developments associated with the digital world often make data redundant unless it is up to date.

Another factor that is widely overlooked is the need for temporal consistency in data. There are two aspects to this. First, if the fundamental nature of any data changes over time, these changes need to be captured, documented and understood. Without this, any research and analysis will be open to misinterpretation. An example would be where a company makes changes to a product or service offering where such changes involuntarily impact customer eligibility or usage. The second consideration is when an understanding of a journey through time offers valuable and important insight. This is most obviously required for trend analysis, but the biggest benefit is where temporal data enables an understanding of discrete, or individual, lifecycle. Talking a snapshot from a data set at any moment in time does not produce any insight of what happened previously to create that snapshot. Some common applications of this are in path-to-purchase analysis, customer lifecycle analysis and longitudinal research. An understanding of customer journeys, for example, requires all the data associated with an individual customer to be time stamped to enable analysis of the drivers, triggers and events that have contributed to the customer moving over time from one state to another. Data without time stamping makes journey analysis very challenging, if not impossible. Similar issues occur in market research, where data is either captured for specific one-off purposes or taken from different populations across time, which compromises accurate research and understanding about the longitudinal development and change of attitudes and opinions of the individual.

Some research studies create data sets from the aggregation of other studies. This may be insightful and valid but may lead to erroneous conclusions when one multiplies the compound effects of averages and aggregates, let alone the dangers of poor representativeness.

The role of data quality and data integrity in completeness and accuracy

Generally, organisations underestimate the challenges of data management. There is often a preference to play with the new cool toys rather than fixing the data. The issue is platform independent; problems with data quality or integrity are the same whether one has on-premise databases or cloud capability.

Data quality

This is the process and governance by which any data captured has been subject to checks for accuracy and completeness. It is a vital step in the insight process. Does the captured data meet the qualitative requirements demanded by the decisions that will be made using it? Perhaps the simplest example is a personal name and address. If this is incorrectly captured, then all downstream uses of the data are compromised. Data quality management is a business process. Most organisations have huge issues with data quality. It is an often-overlooked area, regarded as rather dull and boring. Yet many studies have been done to show the significant monetary risks and benefits of data quality. There are several good tools available to organisations to deploy in data ecosystems that monitor and measure data quality and help reduce negative impacts.

Data integrity

This is the governance process that ensures any data that is moved across an enterprise remains consistent. This is the role of the information technology function in an organisation. Data integrity is required to prevent data being lost, corrupted or changed as it moves from system to system around the organisation. In practice, this happens a lot. One of the more common instances of data integrity failure is where a change is made to a source system without any downstream system owners or insight users being aware. This has the effect of changing the underlying data and compromising any resultant reporting and research.

If data is inaccurate, then any analysis or research is compromised. However, incomplete data sets can still provide value so long as the nature of the incompleteness is clearly understood. It will depend on the decision-making required (and particularly whether supporting insight needs to be directional or absolute), but sampling methodologies can be applied to make data sets suitably representative. For example, television viewing around the world is still largely determined using primary data gathered from small sample sets. BARB in the United Kingdom predicts the TV viewing of 26 million homes from a panel of just 5000 homes.

The broadening and deepening of data

The broadening and deepening of the insight that users want has led to a widening of the scope of the primary and secondary data that a given user may be interested in, whether this is data from within the user's organisation or external. While quantitative data is still very important, there has been increasing interest in the story behind the quantitative data, that is, qualitative information in comments, narratives, observation and the like, although these are often converted into quantitative data, for example, sentiment analysis for in social media. However, qualitative data, whether primary or secondary, in its relatively raw form is still very important in these ways, for example:

*   It can be the focus of commentary on how customers respond to a business initiative, because verbatim comments from customers often bring home to senior managers how these customers feel about the company and its products much more effectively than tables summarising positive and negative comments;
*   It may form part of action research or ethnographic studies of consumers and their responses to products, communication and so on;

- It may be used as the basis for thematic analysis in academic research, to support certain theories or findings in academic research;
- It may form part of a case study used for teaching purposes.

Where this data is secondary, attention needs to be paid to how it is collected. The same applies at the other extreme of research-generated information, for quantitative, logically explained studies, measured with recurring samples over years, for example, drug trials, consumer attitude and usage studies or panel studies. However, we argue that we can be relaxed about the definitional issue, because, as we shall see, it does not create problems where turning the data into information is concerned. Whether collected before or collected for some other objective, the same issues of analysis and interpretation apply.

What is clear is that the availability and comprehensiveness of primary and secondary data has expanded very quickly, so that, whether for researchers or practitioners, it makes sense to identify and review the sources and content of available data before and during any research initiative in order to identify whether any research question has already been partially or completely answered or whether it might change what should be or is being researched.

The new data

The data that is available today and will be available tomorrow has been and is being transformed by developments in digital technology. It is collected by from many sources, which include:

- The increasingly complex transactions and interactions between organisations and their stakeholders – whether customers, employees, suppliers, business partners, investors, regulators or others, many of which are captured electronically, from methods as unstructured as email trails and social media to formal interactions which are captured in structured forms. The rise of this form has been accelerated by the focus of many organisations on digitally transforming every aspect of their business, whether in internal interactions or interactions with all these stakeholders. In one of the newest developments, it is becoming possible to directly measure activities in the human brain (e.g. emotions) and associate them with more commercial variables, for example, the extent to which commercial messages are received. This 'affective computing' may change the conventional role of the researcher in gathering primary data;
- Interactions between organisations and devices, such as mobile telephones, cars, domestic appliances and of course computers. Many of these overlap with the previous, but not all do, for example, a smart meter telling a utility about energy consumption in a household;
- Interactions between the stakeholders themselves, for example, in calls, correspondence and social media, which then become available to the organisation, whether it be a company wanting to track positive and negative comments about its brands on social media, an insurance company wanting to track networks of potential fraudsters or a government security organisation wanting to track the existence and content of contacts between suspects.

This data is available much more quickly than previously. We no longer have to wait for reports, documents, even computer print-outs (which used to be the earliest version available to researchers), Many kinds of data are available as soon as they are created and can be shared with users immediately, too, whether on their computers or their mobile phones. During the Covid-19 epidemic, many aggregators have arisen to collect the data and publish it immediately, saving users the trouble of collecting it. For example, as soon as data on numbers of cases and deaths were published anywhere in the world, it was made available all over the world by aggregators and translated into information through tracking charts and tables.

Types of data

There are many ways of categorising data in general, and most of them can be applied to both primary and secondary data, simply because data which is primary becomes secondary as soon as it is used differently in some way – by different people, for different purposes or in different forms. For example, in marketing, data relates to contacts (whether known or anonymous, transactional data (purchases, enquiries or information exchange – which may now be as much machine to machine as machine to person or person to person), collected or surveyed data, inferred data (based on analysing combinations of variables) or modelled/forecast (e.g. propensities to enquire but remain loyal or likely responses to particular scenarios). The data may therefore be relatively raw (e.g. the fact that a customer logged on to a website and clicked on certain parts of it or pages) or more processed (e.g. the fact that the customer visited the website several times, then enquired about a product and bought it). This data could be made available as primary data to the marketing or sales person responsible for managing that customer, then perhaps as secondary data (depending on the definition of the term) to a customer service manager who has to handle a problem the customer experienced – and all this might be within a few minutes!

Some data does not fit easily into primary or secondary data categories. For example, where does content fit? Content, for example, an advertising video or a blog, is clearly data. It is usually created for a clear purpose, and at its point of creation, it could be argued that it is primary. However, conventionally it is classified as secondary, as we have discussed in relation to blogs. Content that has already been formally published is of course secondary data, but even here the immediacy with which other researchers are notified of it has removed the time lag which was once held to apply to secondary data.

Some content data is relatively formalised, that is, provided in a standard format (e.g. company financial accounts) so that it can be extracted and repurposed (e.g. as in databases of company directorship or finances, tax returns, some health diagnostic reports) with different degrees of ease (depending on the extent to which the required or recommended formats have been observed). More general repositories of data also exist – these may be as general as the Archive of Market and Social Research or government statistical repositories (such as the UK's Office of National Statistics). There are simply too many different levels of aggregation and summarisation and of variations in focus for us to list here.

However, a particularly important type of data which is nearly always secondary is data which measures the results of actions of organisations or of interactions between organisations and their stakeholders. This data may be of several types, for example:

- Economic (e.g. have people worked more hours as a result of tax incentives or found employment more easily as a result of interventions in the labour market?);
- Financial (e.g. are more small businesses taking out loans as a result of a government scheme to facilitate small business loans?);
- Health (e.g. are citizens receiving the right immunisations, are fewer cases of heart disease being reported as a result of an initiative to improve diet, are particular therapies working?);
- Educational (e.g. are children from deprived neighbourhoods increasing their attendance at school as a result of outreach programmes, are more students receiving higher classification degrees as a result of them being asked to pay higher fees and universities treating them as customers?);
- Social (e.g. are there fewer cases of crime among young adults as a result of sporting initiatives?).

These types of secondary data, which require connecting between policy initiatives and their supposed outcomes, are commonly the focus of academic research, but in marketing, they are often a central focus of studies, whether initially or when data is used for secondary purposes, whether to see which products are successful with which customers, whether customers are sensitive to prices, how they respond to marketing communications, which channels of distribution they prefer, whether competitive actions are affecting marketing results and the like.

The uses of data

In summary, data can be of the following kinds:

- Descriptive (what actually is – although here one must guard against assuming that the terms used to describe represent an objective reality rather than an interpretation of it, for example, wealth);
- Diagnostic or analytical (what has caused something or what relationship exists between different variables, perhaps represented as a meta-variable);
- Predictive (what will be);
- Prescriptive (what should be).

This data is used in varying mixes, mainly to:

- Understand, forecast and predict business performance and allocate overall business resources, typically in analyses taking some time to perform and digest;
- Optimise the deployment of business resources for the benefit of particular customers, given the value or risk attached to them, and improve customer experience through more relevant and/or personalised interaction, typically working in real time (at the speed of the individual customer).

Social media and social sources

Social media data includes not only data from dedicated social media sites such as Facebook but also customer comments and reviews on sites which range from the providers of the products and services that are being reviewed, to aggregator or intermediary sites. This data has been made much more accessible by the rise of infomediaries that specialise in gathering or interpreting social media data.

Social media resources currently contain a vast amount of unstructured data, clearly open for processing with marketing predictive analytics tools. Some existing cognitive computing systems allow researchers to uncover and handle interdependencies within unstructured data, turning them into structured ones. Cognitive computer systems are rapidly developing and have huge potential to change the way information is used in marketing research applications. Evolution of cognitive computing information systems is still ongoing, yet they are already used in the business and marketing areas. Social networks are an excellent backdrop for most swift and immediate reactions by customers to various marketing activities. Analysis of such types of data therefore provides interesting, relevant and important insights on how people perceive different products and brands.

Social media management has three main components – identifying which pieces of data to focus on, analysing it and then interpreting it. Much social media data in unstructured and so requires significant work to categorise and structure it before it can be analysed, but this task is made much easier by the rise of infomediaries such as Social Baker and Hootsuite and agencies that specialise in the interpretation of social media data and provide services that can give researchers and companies insights into what individuals are saying what about relevant topics, their sentiments and how what they are saying may be related to other pieces of data which relate to the context, for example, product launches and advertising campaigns. However, analytics on raw data is always fraught with issues, and unstructured data requires preparation and categorisation. If this preparation step is done poorly, it can result in a biased data set which undermines any subsequent analysis.

Despite the very large number of users of social media, they do not include the whole population. This means that there can be a problem of selection bias when using social media data sets. For example, in the United Kingdom, many organisations consider Twitter a representative sample of the population, so although in principle it is possible to record and analyse every message on Twitter and use it to draw conclusions about the public mood (or use a subset of data), it should be recognised that only about one-fifth of the whole population uses it.

Some providers also provide interpretations of the information gathered – needed because of the very large volume of information. This interpretation may relate to anything from market segmentation, to identification of topics of interest to customers, brand sentiment, product or service adoption, estimates of exposure to social media and its subsequent impact, to identification of loyal customers and identification of advocates, influencers and detractors.

The ability to handle social media professionally has become an essential capability for marketing researchers, particularly those involved in customer relationship management projects. The term 'social CRM' has been coined to describe the associated marketing communications capability (Wang and Kim 2017; Alves *et al.* 2016; Alalwan *et al.* 2017; Felix *et al.* 2017). The role of marketing research disciplines in interpreting and indeed soliciting feedback via social media has become important, particularly in relation to customer engagement. The rise of a new channel, social media influencers, has added a new dimension to the concept of word of mouth, particularly where these influencers are celebrities or become so because of the success of their influencing, usually through blogging (Khamis *et al.* 2017).

A new term, 'earned media', has been coined to express the idea that social media comment is earned rather than paid for, as distinguished from paid media (conventional advertising) and owned media (on channels owned by companies, such as their own website). There is of course some overlap between owned and earned, as a well-designed website can host significant social activity by customers. One of the results of this is companies are more able to access customers in different modes and environments where responses and input may vary due to trust earned through different platforms, with different audiences and through responses by companies to customers' queries. The rise of social media has shown that customers are willing to provide truthful inputs to many kinds of organisations and to other customers, provided trust is present – hence the importance of trust indices such as that from Edelman, itself based on marketing research.

Several years ago, the role of social media in marketing research was identified as including (Patino *et al.* 2011) measurement of share of public opinion, construction and use of consumer panels and focus groups, gaining responses to surveys, interviewing, identification of the power of opinion leaders, creation of dedicated marketing research online groups for particular purposes, social listening and geo-tagging of locations of consumers while engaging in specific actions. These views are echoed by a study of the use of social media in marketing research for small businesses by Mahajan (2015). Today, all leading marketing research agencies offer social media services, with subsidiaries or departments with the term "social" in their name, offering services which range from research into broad categories of markets or consumers using social data, tracking (social listening) of specific brands and topics and customer engagement analysis.

One of the consequences of the rise of the Internet and social media is that there has been a big cultural shift in terms of customers believing they are more knowledgeable, experienced and 'street-savvy' than previously. Much of this is driven by a larger younger audience who are more prone to what has been described as the Dunning-Kruger effect (Kruger and Dunning 1999), in which people believe that they are smarter than they are, and much is driven by people's perceptions of their own success in simple near-automated decision-making for tasks that require little or no substantial decision-making (e.g. social media, passive attention via targeted ads etc.). This leads to a focus on the excitement of decision-making and communication, not the reasons for it or the outcomes. Marketing researchers, while enjoying these new sources of data, need to be cautious about what they represent. However, in some cases, customers are getting smarter, deploying a range of analysis and other tools to evaluate decisions and their consequences, using new sources of data available to them, such as information from very large numbers of other customers about the quality of the product or service, after-sales service, value for money and so on.

Social media tracking and analysis (e.g. of comments, positive and negative statements, likes, forwards, time spent on sites, purchasing via sites) has provided a significant income stream for marketing research agencies, allowing them to recover from a long period of decline of traditional research, supported mainly by the explosion of customer satisfaction studies. It has also opened opportunities for new aggregator businesses, such as Social Baker or Hootsuite. The depth of understanding of the attitudes, perceptions, behaviour and engagement of very large numbers of customers, many more than in conventional marketing research, is a gold mine for marketing researchers, providing them with their own 'big data' which is analysable using conventional and new marketing research techniques, based on the traditional marketing research disciplines of the social sciences. It has its pitfalls, is subject to the problems of fake news and can create ethical problems, but given the massive switch of marketing expenditure to digital techniques and the continuing success of giant social media companies, it is clear that the future of the marketing research industry lies in this direction.

Social media sources contain vast amount of unstructured data, clearly open for processing with predictive analytics tools. Some existing cognitive computing systems allow researchers to uncover and handle interdependencies within unstructured data, turning them into structured ones. Cognitive computer systems are rapidly developing and have huge potential to change the way information is used in marketing research applications, particularly social media analytics. Evolution of cognitive computing information systems is still ongoing, yet they are already used in the business and marketing areas. Social networks are an excellent source for swift identification of reactions by customers to various marketing activities, providing interesting, relevant and important insights into how people perceive different products and brands.

Data warehouses and data marts

This problem of data fragmentation has created a demand for a more holistic or less fragmented view of a company's primary and secondary data on a single platform, sometimes referred to as a data warehouse or, when it concerns customers, a customer data platform, Creating these is not easy and usually involves some compromise about what data to include, but even reducing fragmentation can produce significant benefits in terms of translating the data into information that can be used to manage customers or any aspect of the marketing mix, particularly in companies committed to digital transformation. However, as we shall see, the move to cloud storage has mitigated some fragmentation problems.

The techniques and technologies of storing and exploiting data have changed considerably over the past 20 years, and the explosion of digital data has accelerated the adoption of new approaches into the mainstream. Data warehouses have been a popular application for data storage and use for some time. Data is extracted, transformed and loaded (ETL) from internal and external systems into the data warehouse or warehouses and made accessible to a large variety of business users. Data warehouses are large, structured data environments with the advantage of ensuring consistency and repeatability of queries. Hence, they are most often used in business intelligence (BI) applications.

The disadvantages of data warehouses are:

*   Time to ETL data is usually relatively slow and therefore not very agile;
*   The rigidity and IT governance of data warehousing does not lend itself to analytics use (where agile data manipulation and modelling requirements come to the fore);
*   Data warehouses are not good at handling unstructured data;
*   Data warehouse technologies are expensive. And expensive (and relatively slow) to expand and scale.

Data marts are designed to meet specific business applications, such as customer analytics, direct campaign management and various finance processes. Their use is a well-established practice. A data mart can be any size. Whilst most are smaller applications, some, such as customer marts, can sometimes be larger than data warehouses. Whilst data marts also require an extract, transform and load process (and sometimes the 'transform' happens after the 'load'), they are usually far more agile environments than data warehouses and allow more user data manipulation and data derivation (e.g. the creation of propensity models). In some technology systems, data marts will sit as satellites to a central data warehouse system.

Data marts and data warehouses are both highly structured repositories, where data is stored and managed until it is needed. However, they differ in the scope of data stored: data warehouses are built to serve as the central store of data for the entire business, whereas a data mart fulfils the request of a specific division or business function. Thus, the primary purpose of a data mart is to partition a smaller set of data from a whole to provide easier data access for a group of end consumers. However, with the explosion of structured and unstructured data from digital channels, both data warehousing and data mart approaches have been found wanting. Neither manages the huge volume and variety of data and the particular demands of unstructured data.

Big data (in or out of the cloud)

The rise of big data

The explosion of data availability is one aspect of what is called 'big data'. The volume and variety of the data; the speed at which it is created, made available and analysed; problems with establishing its veracity and interconnectedness; and the issue of whether it pays to collect and analyse it are all issues of which the researcher should be aware when contemplating its use and when trying to avoid drowning in it. Where storage of data is concerned, the problems organisations face have been partly but not completely resolved by the rise of cloud computing and of suppliers who claim to be able to resolve problems of managing big data 'off-premise', that is, on their own storage systems. However, researchers and users face the problem of what is called 'mass data fragmentation'. This refers to how unstructured data can be scattered everywhere, in the cloud and on-premises. With mass data fragmentation, massive volumes of what is called secondary data are stored in a complex array of computer systems, often separated from each other and not integrated with each other and so very difficult and costly to manage, with IT staff not being resourced or even technically competent to manage it. Instead of being a support to digital transformation, it may become a hindrance to it.

As the new technology companies found with the development of online propositions, such as web search, conventional data management techniques could not meet the new demands for speed and capacity. Consequently, other database applications and techniques were developed, and the term 'big data' was born. However, like any new development, big data has suffered from its share of success, hype and disappointment. The term 'big data' describes a sophisticated information ecosystem comprising high-performance computing platforms and analytical capabilities to capture, process, transform, discover and derive business insights and value within a reasonable elapsed time (and usually real time).

The primary goal of big data is to help companies make better business decisions by enabling data scientists and other users to analyse huge volumes of data and/or other data sources that may be left untapped by conventional business intelligence programs to uncover hidden patterns, unknown correlations and other useful information. Proponents argue that such information can provide competitive advantages over rival organisations and result in business benefits, such as more effective marketing and increased revenue.

Attributes, applications and benefits of big data

Big data has the potential to offer benefits in applications where there is:

- Volume – there are very large amounts of data to work with;
- Variety – the data is in structured and unstructured form (such as social media comments);
- Velocity – the requirement is for very fast (real-time) decisions or on-the-fly analysis.

Relevant applications include search; recommendations; fraud; security; real-time ad bidding; web logs; social data; internet text and documents; call detail records; astronomy; atmospheric science; genomics; biogeochemical, biological and other complex and often interdisciplinary scientific research; military surveillance; medical records; and large-scale e-commerce.

Proponents of big data suggest the approach offers benefits in these areas:

- Costs (software is open source);
- Flexibility (good for changing things on the fly);
- Speed (it uses a bigger computing installation, which should mean faster performance).

The original proponents for big data made claims that:

- Data analytics produces uncannily accurate results;
- Every single data point can be captured, making old statistical sampling techniques obsolete;
- There is no need to worry about what causes what, because statistical correlation tells us what we need to know;
- Statistical models are not needed because with enough data, the numbers speak for themselves.

Unfortunately, none of these points are valid, and this has been demonstrated many times, often after significant investment. There are many small data problems that occur in big data, and they do not disappear when an organisation has a lot of data. They get worse.

For example, Google once announced that, without needing the results of a single medical check-up, they were nevertheless able to track the spread of influenza across the US. What was more, they could do it more quickly than the US Centers for Disease Control and Prevention (CDC). Google's tracking had only a day's delay, compared with the week or more it took for the CDC to assemble a picture based on reports from doctors' surgeries. Google was faster because it was tracking the outbreak by finding a correlation between what people searched for online and whether they had flu symptoms. Not only was Google Flu Trends quick, accurate and cheap, it was theory free. Google's engineers did not bother to develop a hypothesis about what search terms – "flu symptoms" or "pharmacies near me" – might be correlated with the spread of the disease itself. The Google team just took their top 50 million search terms and let the algorithms do the work. After reliably providing a swift and accurate account of flu out-breaks for several winters, the theory-free, data-rich model had lost its nose for where flu was going. Google's model pointed to a severe outbreak, but when the slow-and-steady data from the CDC arrived, they showed that Google's estimates of the spread of flu-like illnesses were overstated by almost a factor of two. The problem was that Google did not know – could not begin to know – what linked the search terms with the spread of flu. Google's engineers were not trying to figure out what caused what. They were merely finding statistical patterns in the data. They cared about correlation rather than causation. This is common in big data analysis. Figuring out what causes what is hard. Figuring out what is correlated with what is much cheaper and easier.

Despite the concerns about how users access data, the bringing together of primary and secondary data, and their understanding of the characteristics and significance of the big data and secondary data, users in an organisation that repeatedly uses the same secondary data set or similar sets of secondary data, should develop learning about its characteristics and meaning. In some cases, the meaning may be relatively transparent. For example, one of the key pieces of data arising from the use of mobile phones is where users are (not just at the time they make calls but whenever their mobile phone is switched on). This data has been used to sharpen tar-geting of retail promotions (e.g. when the customer is near the store) but also to help transport organisations manage road networks and help users avoid traffic jams (as in Waze or Google maps) or to check whether citizens are complying with health recommendations (as in the case of tracking whether Swedish citizens were complying with recommendations not to go on holiday during the Covid-19 outbreak).

Because found data sets (for example, from searches or social media) are so messy, it can be hard to figure out what biases are inside them – and because they are so large, some analysts seem to have decided the sampling problem isn't worth worrying about. It is.

Big data does not necessarily produce big insights

Big data may have arrived, but big insights have not. Data set size is secondary to inferring what is going on and working out how to intervene to change a system or behaviour for the better. The challenge is to gain new answers without making the old statistical mistakes on a grander scale.

Big data is not the answer to everything – simply pulling data together and getting it in one place does not solve business problems. Fewer organisations have seen tangible returns than most advocates/reports suggest, and there is a paucity of real, material use cases outside one or two high-profile applications. Many companies lack the required domain/business experience for business decision-making. The real power of better decisions is in the analysis, the combination and interpretation of data in relation to business objectives.

Costs are not necessarily lower, as licences might be cheaper, but lots of hardware is still needed. Big data has evolved as a technology to deploy and use more hardware, not necessarily to make efficient use of hardware. Big data is typically less efficient than traditional analytical database platforms where a good data model is present.

Using the cloud

Big data applications can be on-premise, hosted in the cloud (public or private) or a mixture of the two. The significant growth of cloud providers such as Amazon, Microsoft Azure and Google and improved connectivity and security have brought cloud computing into the mainstream, with even financial services institutions now willing to host their data in the cloud. Proponents of cloud computing insist that it is a more cost-effective, scalable and flexible solution to data storage and use than on-premise approaches. It also has a further advantage of easy accessibility from any location and free-to-use data management and analytical toolsets. Certainly, most organisations are either using or seriously considering cloud capabilities. It remains to be seen whether the cost savings and productivity benefits will be proven over the long term.

Data aggregation

One partial solution to the issue of fragmentation is offered by data aggregators – companies which bring a variety of data sources together. For marketers, these traditionally included credit referencing agencies and providers of consumer profiles which include credit referencing data and a variety of additional data, such as social and economic data, sourced from censuses, surveys and data sharing with other organisations. This information could be appended to a company's customer data so that much more was known about individual customers. This data has been massively expanded to include a host of digital sources, including web usage patterns, often attuned to the needs of specific industries, and provided not just as raw data but as information resulting from complex analyses. This aggregator role has appeared in many areas not just in the customer-related aspects of marketing but in areas that are closely related to marketing, such as economic, financial, health, innovation – the list is virtually endless. This means that one of the first tasks of any researcher is to find out whether there are any aggregators active in areas relevant to the research, what they cover and the terms under which the data is available – in many cases, it is completely or partially open access, with the aggregator either being a public interest body or making its money through advertising on sites. These aggregators now include meta-aggregators, which provide listings of aggregators, including the major digital platform providers, such as Google (Google Data), as well as open source statistical software providers such as Gretel, which provides lists of data available for analysis.

Aggregators and meta-aggregators provide a great service in making secondary data available, but they may put a kind of filter between the marketing researcher and the data so that the researcher is less aware of the status of the data – the definitions used, how the data was collected or assembled and privacy issues.

BI, data warehousing and data marts

BI has various definitions, but most commonly it is used to refer to both the technology that is used to collect, store and analyse data, most of which is internal and arises from what the company does, for example, its transactions, and sometimes to the data and information that are produced by the technology, Generally, BI activities translate the business's data into outputs like reports, measures of performance and trends to support management decisions. Businesses rely on the quality of their BI approach to ensure that decisions are based on the right data, data which is timely and accurate (Stone and Woodcock 2014). The activities of BI people include finding ways to capture and analyse data that the organisation needs to support its analyses and decisions that is not already being managed through BI processes and systems. BI specialists tend to focus almost entirely on internal company data, but as external, secondary data becomes more critical to understanding how the organisation is doing and what it should be doing, BI specialists need to understand these secondary data sources and work out how they should be integrated with data from the organisation's own sources to facilitate analysis and decision-making. In most large organisations, this issue has already been addressed through integration of data from companies offering data to enhance customer records but with the variety of sources expanding rapidly,

As identified previously, the move of data storage to the cloud and the presence of many companies offering services to integrate internal and external sources is helping companies resolve some BI issues. The term 'data warehouse', which used to be in very common use and mainly applied to the 'on-premise' storage of data, is now less commonly heard, and some would regard the days of data warehouses as being over, with the focus being more on the different streams of data that are being stored in the cloud. In some cases, the idea of a single integrated database has been abandoned, given the technical problems associated with it, and the idea of separate databases serving different functions has been accepted.

The facilitation of access to data is a critical function of cloud storage companies, and for some organisations, this has resolved some of the tensions that previously existed between those working in BI and those working in customer insight. In the most advanced companies, customer insight people can access primary and secondary data combined and hosted in the cloud as easily as specialist BI people. Where special subsets of data need to be combined and analysed separately, a common practice is to create a special 'data mart', which serves a specific purpose (e.g. analysing marketing campaign success) and is usually not updated in real time because this is not needed for analysis purposes (though advances in computing are now making real-time updating easier).

Decision support

Insight and decisions

The main purpose of data is to create better insight, and the main purpose of this is to make better decisions. Data should produce insight to support decision-making, so it is important to understand what decisions are to be made before determining what insight is required and when and what data best inform this.

Decision-making can be conveniently divided into:

- Big decisions (decision support);
- Small decisions (automated decision management).

Big decisions include the traditional processes and methodologies that deliver insight to human beings, who subsequently make decisions. Traditional techniques include reporting/ BI, marketing research, research analytics and econometrics. The growth of digital channels, with increased complexity and velocity, has meant that these techniques alone are no longer enough. Automated decision management, in which computer cognition drives every interaction between an enterprise and its consumers (or machines), without human employee intermediation, includes machine learning, AI and real-time decisioning. Human involvement is re-engineered to sit at the 'head-end' of the process, focused on review, evaluation, diagnosis, planning, forecasting and scenario modelling. Decision support still has a vital place in this new decision ecosystem, feeding insight to human employees in this 'offline' head-end process, but these big decisions are then often disaggregated, deployed and, importantly, modified in automated systems that manage billions of individual interactions.

Decision support definitions

The terms used in decision support are summarised in Table 10.1.

Table 10.1 Decision support terms

	Reporting examples	*Analysis examples*	*Insight examples*
Typical starting point	Monitoring drop-out rates in the provisioning process on a weekly basis Accurate, simple and consistent view of trends in new customer acquisitions?	Does product-holding impact customer attrition? Do customers with certain products call the call centre more? Has customer satisfaction among customers increased in the last year?	How can customer attrition be reduced? How can upgrade rates be improved? Is customer satisfaction important?
Typical output	'The data' Numbers and graphs only Clearly presented Transparent definitions Consistent with other reports Trustworthy and accurate	'The answer' A layman's description of what the data is telling us Output is primarily numeric and graphical but often includes commentary and recommendations	'The decision' A clear recommendation for action Justification for action A forecast of the impact of that action Output is primarily prose, not numeric or graphical
Process characteristics	Key document = report specification Waterfall or agile development approach	Key document = analysis brief Generally, ad-hoc requests + small projects Most effort goes to number-crunching Smaller number of iterations Consumer is the decision-maker's representative	Key document is the problem statement Generally, ad-hoc projects More effort on conclusions and recommendations Larger number of iterations Consumer is the decision-maker

(Continued)

Table 10.1 (Continued)

	Reporting examples	*Analysis examples*	*Insight examples*
Typical professional background	BI Finance	Statistics Operational Research BI	Finance/commercial Pricing/economics Management consultancy
Key skills	Definition of metrics and business rules Data manipulation Database querying Report design and user interface Quality assurance Service management	Data manipulation Statistical techniques Database querying Workflow management Communication skills	Commercially minded Understanding business objectives, strategies and value model Advanced influencing skills Framing a business problem or objective as an analysis problem Asking the right questions

Source: The authors

Skills dependency

The role of the data scientist has emerged but has brought with it several issues:

- Supply and demand imbalances for these skills has inflated data science salaries and head-count costs;
- Data science myopia and a lack of understanding of business and consumer contexts;
- Business users have been further intermediated from data;
- Increased dependencies on specific human resources as data scientists can hold critical enterprise knowledge.

The rise of self-service

One of the consequences of the previous developments in data availability to end-users, such as marketing researchers or marketing managers, has been the rise of what is called 'self-service', in which managers at all levels, from planning through to operational decision-makers, can access and analyse data whenever and wherever they need, as opposed to asking specialist BI or insight professionals to do it for them (Stone and Woodcock 2014). In many organisations, users of BI are organised into departments like Consumer Insight or Customer Intelligence, replacing the older Market Intelligence or Marketing Information, reflecting the move from less targeted forms of marketing towards precision marketing and creating personalised customer experiences. However, the BI community is not always good at managing customer insight (CI) users. CI has emerged as a powerful BI user but is still learning what to do with so much data, whether owned or non-owned (such as data arising from social media), structured or unstructured (e.g. voice, text, video). For some corporations, markets – customer needs, channels used and competition, devices – are changing fast. Capabilities are changing, too – witness the move towards real-time or near real-time marketing.

The CI community is right to demand better self-service, but an unrestrained and unplanned drive to self-service may lead to wrong conclusions due to poor understanding of how data arises or to use of the wrong analyses or tools. Improved planning and governance are needed to cope with a powerful, self-servicing CI community. Self-service therefore needs to be implemented in a careful, prioritised and targeted way, using criteria of need and competence. BI's experts, who know the software and are in command of metadata development and data definitions, should work across both communities. Their knowledge of what works well and what does not is crucial to the interface. Governance is needed at all levels of the organisation.

Where BI and CI communities move in different directions or have different priorities, CI users may not get the support they need, while the BI community may take the route of technological optimisation rather than meeting users' needs. If this is so, the company should either slow down deployment of new BI technologies and/or ensure better alignment in plans and operational delivery for the two communities. Applying maturity modelling to the relationship between them helps, whether to look backwards to see how the relationship developed or forwards to see how to improve it, towards the nirvana of CI and BI marching in step, along a road where each step's value is understood by the business and supported throughout it.

As excellent BI self-service tools become common and as users such as CI become more competent at using them, the question, 'Who guards the guardians?' must be asked. In many corporations, the BI community's role is to support users with data and tools for 'self-serve' data access and analysis. But what if users get it wrong? What happens if they are looking in the wrong direction when a tsunami comes, as many financial services companies were? Or should the BI community abdicate its role as custodian of ensuring that users use data correctly in the face of a well-organised CI community which professes expertise in using BI in marketing, sales and service, keeping the BI community busy with demands for new self-service tools to model, analyse, explore, view, measure, collaborate, virtualise and then write back results, citing the advantages of more agile decision-making, reduced delays and frustration for users and so on and reports that show a strong correlation between self-service and good business results? These questions can only be resolved by partnership between IT and user communities. However, partnering processes often evolve over years, without careful consideration and analysis of how well they work, and meet the demands of the user community or of the governance needed to supervise the partnerships. This must change.

Meanwhile, wherever the question 'how far should self-service users be allowed to go' is asked, in circumstances where users are highly motivated to use self-service tools and where central BI teams are limited in resources (which seems to be the norm!), then a good strategy is for the central teams to use modern toolsets to provide users with many different ways of selecting, analysing and forecasting using given data sets but for the central BI team to maintain some control over the content of the dataset, so that the corporation as a whole can be sure of the validity of the results. In our view, there should be a strong focus on how users should use secondary data, partly because users may be familiar with the characteristics of the organisation's own (primary) data but less familiar with the characteristics of secondary data and so need some education. To take a simple example, a marketer may understand the value of a customer in terms of likely future sales but not understand the value of a 'like' by a customer on social media.

In most organisations, the data-to-insight process is slower, more costly and more fragmented than it needs to be. This is usually due to the intermediation between business decision-makers and data caused by the existence of a variety of insight production teams and processes. This can cause considerable internal conflict and tension. Insight production teams often feel bombarded by business users with unconnected requests and queries, many of them of dubious materiality. Business users feel frustrated with the pace and quality of outputs.

Whilst it may seem easy to resolve this by bringing business users 'closer to the data' through direct access to data or through interrogation tools, in practice, this does not work. There are a number of reasons for this, including:

- Even well-curated databases contain traps for the unwary, and deep data knowledge is usually needed to navigate successfully and avoid erroneous outputs;
- Despite stated desires for data access, most business users have little appetite for the grind of analysis, research or insight production;
- Most business users lack the quality of analysis and research skills required to produce multivariate insight and therefore actionable performance improvement and transformation;
- There are dangers in allowing business user groups to 'mark their own homework' by extracting and presenting data that illustrates their desired view rather than any objective truth;
- Giving wide access to data to a distributed user base provides no repository of insight learning or corporate memory;
- It further enables the development of cottage industries of insight with attendant internal conflicts and competition.

If the over-intermediation in the data-to-insight process is ineffective but allowing business users unfettered access to data is problematic, what might the answer be?

One means of solving this conundrum is to segment business user needs. For example, executives don't want access to data, they want clear insight answers. A finance analyst, on the other hand, may have the need for detailed analysis and data manipulation on a specific area and have the query skills and knowledge to do this.

This leads to a tripartite classification of self-service capabilities:

1 **Expert self-service:** qualified business users, trained in basic query and BI skills, given access to curated and managed data universes;
2 **BI self-service:** business users trained in specific BI tools and/or Excel who have access to highly pre-configured data sets (e.g. data cubes). This allows them to interrogate data sets (behavioural or attitudinal) using a variety of predetermined variables to support their regular business processes or routines;
3 **Insight repository:** a corporate memory of all published reports, analyses and research available to a wide range of business users to search and retrieve. Content can be collateral (the result of a piece of work commissioned by one user and made available to all) or pushed (an insight produced centrally for common consumption). The repository can take the form of a portal or web intranet and have the capability to publish newsworthy insights to business user groups and executives through desktop and mobile devices.

This view has the advantage of:

- Giving 'power users' fast and flexible access to data to carry out specific functional tasks;
- Giving trained business users a safe environment to interrogate and explore data sets without the risks of definitional inaccuracy and invalid insight;
- Establishing a living, highly accessible library of what an enterprise knows about a topic, allowing all these business users who prefer to deploy the insight rather than have to produce it to focus on the productive part of their jobs;
- Distributing and communicating a single version of the truth on any topic to align an enterprise around a common understanding;

- Making connections between insights that may otherwise be missed;
- Codifying subject matter expert knowledge for distribution;
- Reducing ad hoc and repetitive queries being levied on the insight production teams and releasing skilled resources to tackle more complex and material business issues.

The role of metadata

This brings us to a more important general point: that raw data should always be accompanied by sound metadata explaining what the data items mean and information on collection, completeness, accuracy and context.

Any insight creation techniques depend on a sound and consistent understanding of what the data means. This becomes particularly acute when data has been processed, transformed or conflated. Examples include:

- What defines a 'customer'?
- When is a subscriber deemed to have 'churned'?
- At what level of usage does a pre-pay mobile phone user become 'dormant'?
- Is a positive test for coronavirus a medical 'case'?

Whilst the phrase 'data is the new oil' has been rather over-used, it does describe rather well one of the big limitations of data: it's not that useful in its raw state. Like oil, it usually needs some processing to turn it into a useful basis for analysis or research. Such processing, or transformation, must be clearly understood by the user to avoid misinterpretation. A data dictionary should provide the guidebook for any user of data. Unfortunately, surprisingly, many databases and datasets lack adequate data dictionaries and robust governance, which often contributes to conflicting insights being derived from seemingly common data.

One of the most common abuses of data use by enterprises, organisations and governments is where data definitions are manipulated to deliver desired outcomes. Changing the time period that a non-bill-paying customer stays in a pending state would have an impact on a reported churn number, for example. Shifting the definition of what a product is would change the products per customer metric. And moving the thresholds of calls and texts that determine that a mobile phone is being used will change the reported active customer base of a mobile operator. A more recent example: a change in the UK definition of a Covid-19 death, such that those who die within 28 days of a positive test are counted (previously, anyone testing positive would be counted in Covid-19 deaths, even if they died months later of something else) reduced the Covid-19 death toll by 5000 people at a stroke.

Metadata is a term used to describe data about data. As well as its use in data dictionaries, metadata is also crucially important in data labelling. Poor capture of metadata is a common data quality issue and presents huge problems for those in analysis and research. It is usually associated with opaque or partial product or service taxonomies used in source systems that inadequately describe the artefact itself. Here is an example from TV programme data. A data field that describes a particular broadcast as 'Football Super Sunday' without any indication of which teams were playing is not very useful for analysis. Nor is just labelling every episode of a multi-part series with its title without including the episode number.

The preparation of data for speech and text analytics provides particular challenges, as raw data has to be transformed into a usable and meaningful data set before analysis and research can be carried out. Determining how to describe and categorise this kind of data is both and art and a science and will have large consequences if it is not done well.

Business-to-business versus business-to-consumer data

Much of the discussion about whether data is secondary or primary takes place in the context of consumer data, but much marketing research focuses on business customers, particularly ones who are large or very important to a product or services supplier. Here, the data situation can be very different, with relatively intimate connections between customers and suppliers, particularly in the case of very large or very important clients and much of the data being qualitative and resident in sales, marketing contact and customer service or logistics records, key account profiles and the like. In such situations, analysis of the data requires use of BI tools such as analysis of frequency and type of contact, which products and services have been ordered and used, what the outcomes of their use have been, whether customer service problems arose, what the quality of the relationship has been and likely future requirements – not just of products and services but also relationships and the like. The complexity of the customer's decision-making unit is a critical factor in this situation – we are rarely focusing on a single decision-maker or user but usually several and possibly even hundreds or thousands of them. Marketing research in these situations is likely to include a very strong qualitative focus, probing not just what customers need and whether they are satisfied but the reasons that lie behind these points (Hale 2020).

Data quality

The researcher or manager who is creating primary data should be very clear about – and document – what is being collected. Without this, any subsequent user of the data is prone to errors of definition and interpretation. There is a view that a data dictionary should always be created when data is first collected and then accompany secondary data usage, to enable secondary users to examine data collection processes, data definitions applied, metadata, completeness and accuracy and so forth, Without this, secondary users will be subject to inaccurate or misleading definitions, misleading terminology, lack of contextual information and lack of basis for assessing the quality, accuracy and completeness of the data and no measure of accuracy or completeness. In short, it will not be possible to assess whether the data is to be trusted. While there may be genuine errors caused by collection methods or the circumstances under which data has been collected, there may also be deliberate falsification because the original data collector wanted to present a certain picture. In the case of data collected in order to produce a public position, for example, a government statement or a company public relations statement, secondary users should be particularly suspicious.

Legal and ethical issues

The legal position

The main area in which legal issues encounter data issues is in the area of data protection and privacy, but existing data may be used in legal cases involving marketing, sales or customer service, for example, to establish whether a company's claims to have followed a policy can be substantiated by evidence or whether a company was prevented from doing something with its customers because of a failure by one or more of its suppliers. In such cases, individual customer data is rarely required. However, in both business-to-business and business-to-consumer cases, individual data, whether arising from contacts, transactions or research, might be used where the issue relates to what was done or not done with a given customer.

Privacy issues

Where it comes to the use of data which does identify individual customers, most organisations play safe and try to ensure that they have consent from the customer. However, the customer must understand how the data to whose use they are consenting is going to be used, and if the use changes, consent needs to be given. For example, a company might want to combine customer satisfaction survey data with details of transactions or contacts in order to determine which customer should receive which promotional message, for example, not to send promotional messages to high-value customers whose complaints have not yet been resolved. In the EU, for example, this action would require positive consent by the individual. This means that marketing researchers, or indeed marketers in general, should realise that using existing data which identifies customers in ways that were not originally consented to may be illegal, so they need to check what permissions were given at the time of collection of the data

Whether the data is primary or secondary, privacy issues have become a central issue in the collection and subsequent management of data when it relates to people. Whether for marketing researchers gathering data directly from consumers or for data specialists in organisations, the focus on data protection of many governments in the last few years, the resulting legislation and the very large fines for organisations in breach of the legislation have all made it essential for organisations to ensure compliance with it. In the case of market researchers, there are additional requirements in terms of commitments to those from whom data is gathered about themselves to comply with fixed requirements, such as anonymity, that go beyond legal requirements. This is not the place to list these requirements, which are easily available in terms of the codes of practice and the laws, However, fundamental data protection requirements include:

- Personal data not to be used for purposes beyond those for the original capture;
- The right to anonymisation or at a minimum pseudonymisation of data;
- The right to have personal data erased;
- The right not to be profiled due to automated data processing.

Profiling

From an organisational point of view, efficient management of customers depends partly on bringing all the data about them together so that any action taken or planned in relation to a customer uses all that data and using the customers' information along with other information (usually about other customers) to classify the customer – usually to assess the likely result of those actions in the case of the individual customer – in other words, profiling. This has become common practice to support automated customer management actions. Data protection laws in some countries now give customers the right not to be subject to decisions based just on automated means (with some exceptions, often financial, such as fraud detection, but also where the customer gives consent) if the decision produces legal or certain other effects, such as influencing circumstances, behaviour or choices (e.g. whether it leads to the customer not receiving an offer). These automated decisions are often based on algorithms, and this has led to significant controversies about who is responsible for creating and using algorithms which may lead to discrimination between customers.

Anonymisation

All this means that secondary users of personal data need to be particularly aware of legal requirements and to ensure that they are not breached. A particular threat in this situation is when combinations of secondary data can be used to reidentify customers who have been anonymised (e.g. by removing their name, address and contact details and replacing them with, for example, a number). In the United Kingdom, for example, with about 1.8 million postcodes in use and around 27 million households, the average number of households per postcode is 15 but in some cases much fewer. So individual households are in some cases quite easy to identify, and it does not take many variables (in some cases as few as three or four) to identify an individual. Users of secondary data need to be particularly aware of this and manage it by being very careful about what data sets they create and pass on.

In the case of internet use, where an individual is providing very high volumes of data about what they are doing and who they are, the need to ensure privacy has led to the use of what are called privacy-enhancing technologies, which minimise the personal data collected and used by companies using pseudonyms or anonymous data credentials, and to a focus on achieving informed consent. However, Sroujui and Mechier (2020) point out that the legal penalties for breach of privacy are encouraging organisations to take the approach of 'privacy by design', in which privacy requirements are built into the design and architecture of information technology systems and business practices, using the various technologies available to help with this, such as dashboards which give data subjects visibility of the collection and processing of their personal data, data tracking technologies which record which information has been disclosed to whom, access control technologies and technologies that allow minimisation of data collection and anonymisation of data collected.

Do customers worry about privacy?

It can be argued that the legal and institutional requirements are way ahead of the requirements of customers, who in many surveys have been shown to be unconcerned about their privacy, possibly being prepared to trade their data for value, and only concerned in very sensitive areas (such as health), although this contrasts with their propensity to discuss sensitive matters with other individuals whom they only know through internet contact.

Issues

In this rapid tour through how companies manage data, there are issues which companies now face. These include:

- Validity and quality of the source data – which takes time to check and which can be put at risk in accelerated or automated collection or delivery processes;
- Permissioning of data use is a constant problem, particularly when the sources of existing data are unclear or when permissions given at time of collection have not been well stored or managed;
- Integration – with increasing automation of the marketing process, users increasingly expect that the data used to support decision-making be integrated into the decision-making process, and this can be difficult with existing data.

Acknowledgements

This chapter is based partly on:
Stone, M. and Woodcock, N., 2014. Interactive, direct and digital marketing – a future that depends on better use of business intelligence. *Journal of Research in Interactive Marketing*, 8(1), 4–17.

References

Alalwan, A., Rana, N., Dwivedi, Y. and Algharabat, R., 2017. Social media in marketing: A review and analysis of the existing literature. *Telematics and Informatics*, 34(7), 1177–1190. http://dx.doi.org/10.1016/j.tele.2017.05.008.

Alves, H., Fernandes, C. and Raposo, M., 2016. Social media marketing: A literature review and implications. *Psychology & Marketing*, 33(11), 1029–1038. https://doi.org/10.1002/mar.20936.

Felix, R., Rauschnabel, P. and Hinsch, C., 2017. Elements of strategic social media marketing: A holistic framework. *Journal of Business Research*, 70(C), 118–126. DOI: 10.1016/j.jbusres.2016.05.001.

Hale, A., 2020. Not so similar: How B2B research is different from B2C. *Quirk's Marketing Research Review*, March–April 50–54 [online]. Available from: www.quirks.com/storage/attachments/5e5d242c21b49d0efe4176f1/5e5ead1f21b49d1d6b08eaa3/original/202003_quirks.pdf [Accessed 23 September 2020].

Khamis, S., Ang, L. and Welling, R., 2017. Self-branding,'micro-celebrity'and the rise of social media influencers. *Celebrity Studies*, 8(2), 191–208. DOI: 10.1080/19392397.2016.1218292.

Kruger, J. and Dunning, D., 1999. Unskilled and unaware of it: How difficulties in recognizing one's own incompetence lead to inflated self-assessments. *Journal of Personality and Social Psychology*, 77(6), 1111–1134. https://psycnet.apa.org/doi/10.1037/0022-3514.77.6.1111.

Mahajan, R., 2015. Use of social media as a new investigative tool in marketing research for small business. *International Journal of e-Education, e-Business, e-Management and e-Learning*, 5(3), 119–135. DOI: 10.17706/ijeeee.2015.5.3.119-135.

Patino, A., Pitta, D. and Quinones, R., 2011. Social media's emerging importance in marketing research: Implications and concerns. *Journal of Consumer Marketing*, 29(3), 233–237. DOI: 10.1108/07363761111121800.

Sroujui, J. and Mechier, T., 2020. How privacy-enhancing technologies are transforming privacy by design and default: Perspectives for today and tomorrow. *Journal of Data Protection and Privacy*, 3(3), 268–280.

Stone, M. and Woodcock, N., 2014. Interactive, direct and digital marketing – a future that depends on better use of business intelligence. *Journal of Research in Interactive Marketing*, 8(1), 4–17.

Wang, Z. and Kim, H., 2017. Can social media marketing improve customer relationship capabilities and firm performance? Dynamic capability perspective. *Journal of Interactive Marketing*, 39, 15–26. DOI: 10.1016/j.intmar.2017.02.004.

11

DECIDING ON AND USING RESEARCH DATA

Merlin Stone, Len Tiu Wright, Robin Birn and Luiz Moutinho

Summary

This chapter is aimed at academics carrying out marketing research projects. It investigates in detail the difference between primary and secondary data and how the interpretation of these definitions is changing under the impact of digital marketing. It suggests how both primary and secondary data can be and will be used in the future to support academic and commercial research. It considers how different statistical techniques can be used to interpret data, and the use and sources of case studies. It also includes brief coverage of the use of story-telling rather than standard statistical reporting to explain marketing research findings. It concludes with a case study of the use of secondary data to identify how well different countries managed their early response to COVID-19.

Primary or secondary data?

One of the most significant developments in the world of data is the explosion in the quantity and availability of secondary data and the way in which, even inside organisations, data can be made much more available for use beyond its original purpose, that is, a secondary use. The classic definition of secondary data is data created by somebody else for prior objectives (not those of the researcher). However, while this definition works for the individual academic researcher, it does not work so well for a researcher who works in an organisation in which someone else has collected the data and with whom some objectives may be shared.

For example, in one case in which one of the authors was involved, the market research team regularly collected data from customers who had ended their subscription to the company's services. The data was then used as part of a legal submission in relation to the failed development of customer relationship management to estimate how many customers left as a result of the company having to continue to use its old system, which could only hold details of transactions rather than other information about the relationship with the customer. If we define prior objectives as finding out why customers left, then this second use could be called primary rather than secondary. However, this usage had all the characteristics of secondary use, such as the secondary users needing to investigate how and when the data was collected, definitions of the terms, how the responses were captured and so on. So sometimes a simpler and older definition of secondary data may be useful, such as data that already exists or was collected by somebody else rather than data that is being captured as a result of a given researcher's initiatives.

One of the defining characteristics of primary data is that it is collected direct from the source. However, what is the difference between an interviewer asking someone's opinion (which would normally be classified as primary data) and a blogger asking for responses to a blog (which would conventionally be classified as secondary data)? Is this primary data from the blogger and secondary data for anyone else viewing the blog and responses?

Another issue relating to the definition is what we mean by "data". Do we mean "data", the numbers, words, even bits and bytes of information, or "information", which is the result of applying analysis, however simple, to the data? In some cases, the data is secondary but the information can be regarded as primary, because the data might not have been analysed at all before or might have been analysed in different ways by the person or organisation that created it in the first place so that the secondary use produces very different information.

The problem of definition arises partly because the term "secondary data" was created in a world in which "researchers" were a distinct group, often working in the social sciences and investigating phenomena, sometimes on behalf of a separate group, the "users". The researchers created primary data for one or more users, and other users or researchers who used that data became secondary users, Today, the information is not just research information, as we shall see, but any information that is available, whether externally or internally. Some would argue that rather than applying the term "secondary" to the data itself, we should apply it to the use of the data or the purpose for which it was originally collected, with primary being used to describe the first purpose or use and secondary being any other use,

Data may also become secondary because primary data is analysed or processed in some way and made available in a different form. For example, income and turnover data may be gathered by tax authorities for the purposes of taxing individuals or companies and aggregated and used by economists for analysing and planning the whole economy. Large numbers of likes or dislikes of users of social media may be aggregated into indices of positive or negative sentiments. Individual reports of cases can be aggregated into higher levels, for example, market segments, regions and countries, and transformed to make it easy for non-specialist users to understand and digest it. It should also be mentioned that data empowers people (whether people in a business or individual consumers) in a way not seen before, because they can access it quickly – even consumers can quickly see who else is recommending a product or service that they plan to buy.

Grey sources of data

From the point of view of academic researchers, one recent trend in management literature has been the strengthening of what academics disparaging call "grey" literature (Adams *et al.* 2017; Tzempelikos *et al.* 2020), publications outside traditional academic peer-reviewed papers. This covers a range of different outputs, such as academic articles and discussion papers which were not or have not yet been published or were rejected; articles in non-academic media; bibliographies; book chapters; company reports; conference abstracts; data sets; dissertations, theses and other student research reports; emails; personal correspondence; wiki articles; blogs; newsletters; and other less formal communications, among other categories.

Incorporating grey literature – the diverse and heterogeneous body of material available outside, and not subject to, traditional academic peer-review processes – can make a variety of positive contributions to subsequent inquiry and practice. Several scholars have used grey literature to extend the scope of findings in their studies by incorporating relevant contemporary material in dynamic and applied topic areas where scholarship lags; they have explored novel fields of enquiry, and have validated or corroborated findings from the academic literature (c.f. Adams *et al.* 2017). In addition, many scholars use grey literature to make their work more impactful and bridge the research-practice gap (Deadrick and Gibson 2007; Huff 2000). Grey literature has been described as a means of gathering and analysing evidence that can answer practice-relevant research questions (Tranfield *et al.* 2003). Although high-quality, peer-reviewed articles should be a source of information for both researchers and students, we believe that the variety and relevance of academic inquiry can be increased by considering the diverse wisdom gained from grey literature.

In line with the previous discussion, an emerging literature category worthy of attention is so-called "thought-leadership" literature, produced by consultancy, research, analyst and many other types of organisations to influence – directly or indirectly – their target markets (Ernst *et al.* 2011). Much of this research is very practical, focusing on current issues faced by management and recommendations as to how to deal with them.

An example of this can be seen in the rise of think tanks, such as the McKinsey Global Institute (MGI), established in 1990, with the specific objective of providing research to inform business leaders. Such think tanks have become so common that they are now analysed and indexed (McGann 2019), with MGI rated as the leader. McGann identifies over 2000 think tanks in North America and a slightly larger number in Europe, with the number in Asia slightly smaller but growing rapidly and a slightly smaller number again in the rest of the world. They are not all business focused, with some focused on public policy issues. These think tanks may issue anything from a few to hundreds of reports a year.

Increased richness

The richness of data – whether primary or secondary – that researchers and organisations can use is partly due to the enormous variety of sources, many of which (from individuals, groups and organisations up to regions and whole countries) are now recording some or all of their data digitally (or asking all the individuals within a group to do so) and therefore able to make it available more easily. For example, the move to online-only income tax collection makes income data available more accurately and more quickly.

Information mapping

In any research project, before deciding on an information collection strategy, it makes sense to draw up an information map, enumerating all the possible sources of data on the topic in question. These include individuals and organisations (public, private and not-for-profit) themselves and their partners and intermediaries (for primary data), organised groups with an interest in collecting and analysing the data (e.g. governments, not-for-profit organisations interested in the area), experts with knowledge and experience, trade associations and professional institutes (e.g. registers of members), consultancies and analysts. The data may be available in every form, from a digital database to a printed or PDF report, or in the case of content, anything from a lecture or a podcast to a printed report, e-book or book (of which the availability has been increased dramatically by initiatives such as Google Books and its work with national libraries). Academic studies may be available (articles, dissertations, theses and books). A recent development is the digitisation of hundreds of thousands of out-of-copyright books in the British Library/Google Books initiative – Books for All.

The original sources of the data will vary from data collected as a result of interactions between companies and individuals, between individuals, surveys (from quantitative to qualitative, including ethnography and netnography), audits (specially retail), censuses, reports from data providers (such as credit referencing agencies), legal documents (e.g. company reports, court cases), media circulation reports, social media, feedback from staff in contact with customers and other stake-holders and so forth – the list is virtually endless. The data may be used and interpreted by many of these in a secondary form by the media, which now includes individuals such as bloggers.

The role of data aggregators and meta-aggregators

Marketers are familiar with the classic role of infomediaries, typically in the provision of demographic and similar information to enhance customer databases. However, marketing researchers need not just customer information but a wide a variety of contextual information, particularly economic, social and even political. The internet has facilitated the rise of a whole new set of information providers, ranging from those that track corruption and innovation at country level to those that provide survey data about a whole range of topics. Searching for these data sources has been made much easier by the rise of meta-aggregators such as Google Data (which allows searching for any data source) and the practice of statistical software companies or their users of providing search facilities to identify databases to which the statistical software can be applied. These should be consulted as a routine part of information mapping before a research project is defined in detail.

Existing data and research help you decide what to research

The aims, objectives and scope of research projects, whether academic or practitioner, should be based partly on an appraisal of what data and studies are already available. In academic projects, one approach, particularly for doctoral students, is to identify what is called a "research gap", defined as a missing element in the literature. The gap is defined irrespective of its usefulness to practitioners and of its contribution to broader academic understanding of the topic and has led to a proliferation of very narrow studies which are of limited use. This limited usefulness is visible in the arcane attempts of the researcher to find management implications at the end of the project. Too often, these implications amount to little more than that "practitioners should read this thesis and take it into account" rather than a careful analysis of what practitioners know already and how the additional knowledge and/or frameworks produced by the research is useful to them. However, in some cases, the purpose of the research is to demonstrate the validity of a research approach or to demonstrate the researcher's capability in handling a certain technical approach, so these reservations might not apply. Still, this chapter takes the approach that whatever the purpose of the research, if it aims to be of use to management or in management studies, the researcher or the research team should develop a clear idea of its practical usefulness through a review of the data and research already available.

Determining what data and analyses already exist is a critical part of deciding what to research. Using what already exists may allow greater coverage at lower cost, creating or extending a basis for generalisation or increasing validity by drawing conclusions from a larger number of studies. Where the aim of the research is to identify what works, in terms of management or other policies, existing data is often past data (though, as we have seen, it may only just have been produced) and so can see not only the relationship between different entities or factors but also the results of policies, such as marketing policies (campaigns, changes in the marketing mix) or other interventions which may affect marketing, for example, medical, economic, legal.

We can also find out whether past forecasts were accurate and, if not, why they were not. It can be argued that there is a general problem in academic and practical research projects in that not enough attention is paid to returning to thoroughly analyse past forecasts and initiatives. For example, in some countries, there is a strong focus in the public sector (and parts of the private sector) on what is called "evidence-based policy making", which refers to the idea that decision-making must use rigorous and objective evidence and evidence which is not selected to support a particular policy but drawn from a relevant and scientifically based selection of evidence, as opposed to being based solely on ideology, theory or "common sense". Sadly, often the pressure to move on to the next decision or policy rather than review what worked often precludes serious analysis of what did work, and in some cases this refusal to use existing data to see what worked is coloured by a desire to avoid finding out what went wrong.

A secondary data-based approach would be particularly useful in exploring some of the simplified tenets of marketing. For example, the phrase "it costs more to acquire a customer than to retain an existing one" is often quoted in both commercial and academic research. However, in an internet world, where customer acquisition can be very cheap, the cost of retaining a specific existing customer, who might not want a product or service as much as a new customer, could be higher. In some situations, existing customers become expert in extracting value from suppliers and paying as little as possible for it. So, from a supplier's point of view, it might be better to focus on optimising the product or service and its promotion and just attract whichever customers most want the product or service at the time, whether or not they are existing customers. Putting additional effort into marketing specifically to existing customers might cost more. This assertion might therefore be best explored through secondary data, reviewing the costs, revenues and resulting profits from new and existing customers in different situations.

There is also an important role for existing data and research at the exploratory stage, that is, before the specific area for focus is identified, to identify the general relationships between concepts, to see how the subjects of the research, for example, consumers, behave in general and what the trends are in that behaviour and also what is known or unknown, what puzzles suppliers, governments or others.

Existing data and research help you decide how to research

At the most basic level, existing data about the situation that is the focus of research provides a basis for sampling, weighting and stratification and may provide a basis for checking for bias. Over 80 human biases in decision-making have been identified. This is not the place to review them, but these biases can apply to everything from selection of research topic to the choice of method and interpretation of results. These biases are often very simple and easily identified. It is easy for academic researchers to convince themselves that what they are researching is relevant to practitioners by avoiding looking for evidence of practical usefulness. Worse, they might decide that something they wanted to research was relevant, even though the research would contribute nothing because the phenomenon was already well understood. A few years before this chapter was written, at an academic conference on marketing that one of your authors attended, the suggestion was made that more research was needed into the use of artificial intelligence in designing email copy and customising it to the recipient. Your author responded that there were already several established companies providing such services to their clients. The researcher who made the comment had simply not explored commercial practice, in particular, the thought leadership reports produced by the suppliers in question detailing their methods, but had focused solely on academic articles.

Existing research and data can help the researcher identify concepts that are already in use by researchers or users of research or by the subjects of the research (particularly the language they use). For example, the term "customer loyalty" is in common use amongst practitioners, but in some markets, customers rarely use it, so questionnaires using the term are to be avoided, with a better option being to describe the behaviours and attitudes which are deemed the components of customer loyalty. Even amongst practitioners, the meaning of the term varies dramatically, depending partly on the market. For example, in situations where it is only possible to have one supplier, for example, domestic electricity, loyalty means staying with that supplier (but for how long and how much to use electricity rather than gas?). Even here, in deregulated situations, intermediaries may exist which allow the consumer or business to switch between suppliers (sometimes hourly) based upon pricing. In this case, the customer may be loyal to the intermediary rather than the power supplier.

At a more basic level, existing data normally helps researchers to identify the target sample for research and may help the researcher identify how best to obtain a valid sample, including the sampling method – particularly whether to stratify the sample or use some other basis for sampling. It also helps the researcher determine what variables to include as determinants or independent variables, such as demographics. As researchers explore the secondary data and research, different research objectives and goals may seem appropriate, as some variables are found to be well understood but others are found to need clarification and further investigation and as some relationships between variables turn out to be well established but others questionable. Missing variables may become apparent, and secondary research will help identify whether they have not been researched because data on them is simply too hard to get or controversial or simply because nobody has deemed it important (and this may be incorrect).

Before embarking on any study and investing time and effort in determining research questions, it makes sense to investigate the academic and practitioner literature for published studies and any publicly available secondary data. The academic literature and secondary data become important when academics and practitioners need to find answers out there for their marketing and marketing research problems at hand. It makes sense "not to reinvent the wheel" if there are similar studies already accessible that could provide some or, with luck, all of the needed information a researcher needs. In the case of academic research, publishers such as Taylor & Francis provide information not only about the content of articles but also about their impact, the authors, countries of origin and so forth. Investigating citations can be a very fruitful activity, leading to identification of further relevant research and possibly additional case studies. Even if such sources are not used as the main source of information, they can be very useful for triangulation, providing additional validity. This applies particularly to case studies, where it could be argued that while academics have made significant progress in establishing criteria for the validity of case studies, business researchers tend to use them in a biased and selective way to support particular viewpoints.

The outcome of the previous should be to firm up central research question(s) and objective(s). The idea of central research question(s) is common in academic research, while often in commercial research, the question(s) may be more open or implicit, while the objectives may be clear, for example, we need to find out more about which customers are loyal, why they are and how they demonstrate their loyalty.

Searching wider and deeper

Given the almost bewildering variety of data sources available, it is critical for marketing researchers – whether academic or practitioner – to be extremely thorough and well organised in their search for data at the beginning of a research project. Too often, academic researchers confine their searches to the outputs of other academics. This has two major disadvantages. The first is that the information and research likely to be found may be out of date due to time lags not just in publication but also in academics identifying issues as worth researching. The second is that they are likely to omit non-academic sources of great value, of the kind identified earlier. Today, searching has become much easier, with so many search facilities available, ranging from standard web browsers and browsers focused on certain sources (such as Google Scholar), as well as the presence of meta-aggregators in providing database search facilities. Also, as the use of search facilities like Google Scholar becomes more widespread, non-academic producers of research are learning to ensure that Google Scholar indexes their publications.

However, your authors' experience of reviewing submissions to academic journals indicates that many academic authors still fail to pick up vital non-academic secondary sources. In some cases, it is clear that the authors are simply not very good at browsing, with a narrow choice of key terms and poor learning about which search terms are best for their particular project. They may also be very impatient browsers.

Organising and evaluating sources

Once the data sources have been identified, then it is important to check their quality and validity both of the source itself and the individual pieces of data and research, particularly the validity of the research or collection process and the likely accuracy of the outcome. We live in an era of "fake news", but also an era where there is much greater awareness of bias, so we owe it to ourselves as researchers to investigate possible bias, whether in sampling, data collection or interpretation.

Other rules for ensuring that sources are well classified and used include not just the simple one of organising the courses properly in some kind of database or spreadsheet so that they are analysable and classifiable rather than in a word-processed table but also ensuring that the sources are classified not just according to their coverage but also according to the concepts, definitions and theories used (whether explicitly or implicitly). For example, if a study or a database claims to explain customer loyalty or rank the loyalty of different types of customers to particular companies or products, what definition of loyalty has been used and how has information to infer it been gathered?

Existing data should also be classified according to standard data quality criteria, which include:

- Accessibility;
- Accuracy;
- Adequacy – fit for purpose;
- Applicability;
- Authenticity;
- Clarity of definitions and sources;
- Completeness;
- Cost of access and use – if any;
- Ease of processing;
- Reliability;
- Validity.

It may be the case that the search turns up some excellent sources which match the researcher's objectives but not completely. In some cases, this might call not for leaving these sources aside but for revision of research objectives. In the case of academic research, these sources might reveal a slightly different research gap, and in the case of commercial research, they might reveal a much more useful ser of information or ideas. In other words, it might make sense not to be inflexible but to consider "sailing with the wind" and anchoring the research on strong existing data sets.

Where existing numerical data is concerned, it is particularly important to check sources and how the data has been transferred to the source, including whether any errors or biases have been discovered by other researchers using the same data set. In the case of qualitative data, such as company annual reports or blogs, it is important to check the validity of sources but also whether it is searchable or classifiable using standard digital techniques. In an example encountered by one of your authors, who was trying to see whether a particular company's annual report mentioned the concept of market segmentation, he discovered that not all references to the term in the report were picked up by a simple search, as some of the words visible on the digital page were actually represented by digital codes – a different set of characters which were not picked up by a word search. Companies offering search services covering such documents have learnt of the need to take a digital image of a report to ensure that it is fully searchable. The occasional researcher might miss such a point. Once such issues have been resolved, this kind of secondary qualitative data can be analysed using standard classification approaches, such as digital thematic analysis.

Building a research database

Where several existing data sources are used, the researcher may need to build a research database, with data from different sources combined to give a more complex picture of the entity being researched. For example, the researcher might want to combine data from different sources using a geographical classification, for example, country or town, or a classification combining social, economic and demographic variables (e.g. young consumers with certain income levels and social backgrounds). Here, it is particularly important to check whether the classificatory variables are defined in the same way or whether adjustments need to be made in order to ensure that bringing the data together does not introduce bias. This may seem obvious, but it is very easy for serious research errors to creep in because of failure in this area. Some sources themselves carry out the data combination process, for example, combining census and financial data, but it is important for the researcher to understand the methodologies they use.

Triangulation

Exact matching is not always necessary. The technique of triangulation is very useful when comparing sources, so that even if there is not an exact match of variable definitions, different sources can be combined to infer conclusions through triangulation. While a conclusion from triangulation is still an inference rather than a logical deduction, the more varied and comprehensive the different data types, sources, definitions, investigators and theoretical bases, the stronger the inference. Such triangulation can also be very useful in helping the researcher decide what variable definitions to use for primary research, based not just on theoretical match with objectives but also on feasibility of collection and quality of resulting data.

Building the research model

Reviewing existing data and research is a critical part of building a model of relationship. The requirement to build an explicit model is common in academic research, while in commercial research, the model is more often implicit – but nonetheless present.

Modelling the relationships is a critical step, in which questions such as the following are resolved:

- Is the prime purpose of the research to understand more about a particular situation or to see the results of actions taken in the situation?
- Is the audience for the research primarily academic or commercial?
- Which are the most important variables and what is the hypothesised relationship between them?

- Is the interest primarily in the relationships between variables which determine a particular outcome or in how these relationships vary for different subjects, leading to the question as to whether the situation calls for different approaches to different subjects of market segments, or are the relationships between variables being investigated for all subjects?
- Are there some variables which are categorical, requiring specific statistical treatment (e.g. as dummy variables in a regression)?
- Are there issues of time dependence as well as logical dependence; for example, are there lags in supposed relationships?
- Is the data available from known existing data to apply the model in practice, or can it be made available through further investigation of secondary data or through primary research?
- Is there an implied direction of causation between the variables, and might it be bi-directional?
- Is the resulting model coherent and explainable to those for whom it is intended?
- How sensitive are the different relationships in the model to other variables and to contextual variables which may not be included in the model?

A particularly valuable use of existing research and data is to help the researcher decide the statistical approach to representing models. Alternatives include:

- Structured equation modelling (primarily used by academic researchers or analysing relationships between concepts);
- Classic statistical techniques, such as analysis of variance, regression analysis and factor analysis, often used to find out which relationships between concepts apply to which subjects of research;
- More open-ended approaches, perhaps using artificial intelligence or machine learning approaches (where the research is more open ended and perhaps does not require pre-specifying of the model) – these are particularly good at finding complex patterns in multiple large data sets – and textual analysis, in some cases used to automate model development or application or to automate decision-making associated with use of the model;
- Propensity modelling – focused specifically on the likelihood of subjects behaving in particular ways or responding in particular ways to policies or marketing initiatives;
- Forecasting – which may be related to propensity but may be aimed at identifying how a whole system is likely to change based on relationships established by the research and future values of independent variables that are obtained from other forecasts;
- Qualitative analysis, perhaps based on thematic analysis, inferring relationships between variables or subjects.

Advanced statistical analysis in marketing research

Generalised linear modelling

The general linear model (GLM) underlies most statistical analyses used in applied and social research. It is the foundation for the *t*-test, analysis of variance (ANOVA), analysis of covariance (ANCOVA), regression analysis and many multivariate methods, including factor analysis, cluster analysis, multidimensional scaling, discriminant function analysis, canonical correlation and others. Because of its generality, the model is important for marketing research and provides a general framework for many models whose common goal is to explain or predict a quantitative dependent variable by a set of independent variables that can be categorical or quantitative.

The term generalised linear model (GLIM or GLM) refers to a larger class of models popularised by McCullagh and Nelder (1989). In these models, the dependent variable Yi is assumed to follow an exponential family distribution with mean μi, which is assumed to be some (often nonlinear) function of the independent variables $xTi\beta$. Some would call these "nonlinear" because μi is often a nonlinear function of the covariates, but McCullagh and Nelder consider them linear, because the covariates affect the distribution of the dependent variable yi only through the linear combination of the independent variables $xTi\beta$. Such an approach might be used, for example, to disentangle the separate and combined effects of the independent variables – consumer income, temperature and price on the dependent variable: the demand for a particular category of food.

The first widely used software package for fitting these models was called GLIM. Because of this program, GLIM became a well-accepted abbreviation for generalised linear models, as opposed to GLM, which often is used for general linear models. Today, GLIMs are fitted by many packages, including SAS Proc Genmod and the R function glm.

The GLM is adequate only for fixed-effect models. To take into account random-effect models, the GLM needs to be extended and becomes the mixed-effect model. The term general linear model usually refers to conventional linear regression models for a continuous response variable given continuous and/or categorical predictors. It includes multiple linear regression, as well as ANOVA and ANCOVA (with fixed effects only).

Marketing researchers increasingly recognise the importance of investigating phenomena at multiple levels. However, the analysis methods that currently dominate in marketing may not be appropriate for dealing with multilevel or nested data structures. Multilevel models are known by several names, such as hierarchical linear models, mixed models and random-effects models, and are used in medical research, economics, sociology, marketing, educational psychology and numerous other fields.

Multilevel modelling

The term "multilevel" refers to a hierarchical or nested data structure, usually subjects within organisational groups, but nesting may also consist of repeated measures within subjects or respondents within clusters, as in cluster sampling. The expression *multilevel model* is used as a generic term for all models for nested data. Multilevel analysis is used to examine relations between variables measured at different levels of the multilevel data structure. Multilevel modelling has contributed to the analysis of traditional individuals within group data, repeated measures and longitudinal data, sociometric modelling, twin studies, meta-analysis and analysis of cluster randomised trials. In multilevel research, the data structure in the population is hierarchical, and the sample data is a sample from this hierarchical population.

For example, the implementation of sales force automation (SFA) often fails owing to the lack of adoption by salespeople. Previous studies investigating drivers of salespeople's SFA adoption have mainly examined predictors that relate just to the salespeople themselves (within-level analysis) and have mostly neglected the social influence of co-workers' and superiors' SFA adoption on salespeople's SFA adoption. When a multilevel framework of SFA adoption is used, the findings demonstrate that co-workers' and superiors' SFA adoption has a positive effect on subordinates' SFA adoption which goes beyond the commonly tested determinants (Homburg *et al.* 2010). Also, results reveal differences among predictors of the technology acceptance model (within-level effects) examined at three different hierarchical levels.

Multilevel modelling (MLM) is a regression-based approach for handling nested and clustered data. Nested data (sometimes referred to as person–period data) occurs when research designs include multiple measurements for each individual, and this approach allows researchers to examine how participants differ, as well as how individuals vary across measurement periods. A good example of nested data is repeated measurements taken from people over time. In this situation, the repeated measurements are nested under each person. Clustered data involves a hierarchical structure such that individuals in the same group are hypothesised to be more similar to each other than to other groups.

In multilevel research, variables can be defined at any level of the hierarchy. Some of these variables may be measured directly at their "own" natural level. In addition, we may move variables from one level to another by aggregation or disaggregation. Aggregation means that the variables at a level are moved to a higher level. Disaggregation means moving variables to a lower level.

The relevance of multilevel research is that it can help to bridge this gap by integrating disciplines and levels of analysis. Multilevel research emphasises the joint analysis of variables located at different levels, examining relationships between them. Many multilevel studies examine variables at the micro (individual or group) level and variables at the macro (organisation) level and then integrate these levels, bridging the micro-macro gap. Multilevel research can be also used to analyse longitudinal data. In previous examples, the macro levels referred to context variables that could influence variables at the micro levels.

Hierarchical linear modelling

Hierarchical linear modelling (HLM) is a statistical technique available to researchers that is ideally suited for the study of cross-level issues. Marketing data often take on a panel structure, with multiple responses (e.g. purchases) per respondent, which allows estimation of parameters associated with each model component. Hierarchical Bayesian (HB) analysis models are hierarchical models analysed using Bayesian methods. HB analysis is commonly used to analyse the results of choice exercises such as conjoint or maximum difference analysis (MaxDiff). In these choice exercises, respondents make decisions about which items (or attributes, products, services, etc.) are most preferred. The strength of HB is that robust estimates of preferences can be created from survey instruments in which respondents provide relatively little information (set up through balanced survey designs). So respondent fatigue is at a minimum while producing abundant information regarding preferences.

Choice modelling is an "as if" statistical model. It is assumed that people behave as if they assigned utility to the attribute levels varied in a choice design. Products are attribute bundles, so the value of the product is a function of the utilities of its component attribute levels. One should be able to look at the proportions in the previous table and infer what utilities would have produced such data. That is, Brand A tends to be selected more often than Brand B; therefore, Brand A must have a higher utility than Brand B. Similarly, one can observe price sensitivity in the decreasing proportions selecting each brand as that brand's price increases.

The problems associated with long questionnaires call for experimental designs and estimation methods that recover heterogeneity with shorter questionnaires. Unlike more popular estimation methods, HB random effects models do not require that individual-level design matrices be of full rank, which leads to the possibility of using fewer profiles per subject than currently used. One can reduce the steepness of the researcher's learning curve by learning how to use one function from the R package bayesm to analyse one type of choice data.

Artificial neural networks

Artificial neural networks (ANNs) are an important subset of machine learning. They are used by computer scientists to work on complex tasks, such as making predictions, strategising and recognising trends. Unlike other machine learning algorithms, which may organise data or crunch numbers, neural networks learn from experience, like humans. Neural networks, as the name suggests, are modelled after the neural networks of the human brain, which are responsible for human decision-making. The brain takes in information and then attempts to connect the dots to come up with a conclusion. We do not always get it right at first, nor do machine learning algorithms. However, through trial and error, we and the artificial neural networks start producing better outputs.

A neural network is a series of algorithms that endeavours to recognise underlying relationships in a set of data through a process that mimics the way the human brain operates. In this sense, neural networks refer to systems of neurons, either organic or artificial in nature. Neural networks work similarly to the human brain's neural network. A "neuron" in a neural network is a mathematical function that collects and classifies information according to a specific architecture. The network bears a strong resemblance to statistical methods such as curve fitting and regression analysis.

Neural networks can adapt to changing input, so the network generates the best possible result without needing to redesign the output criteria. Today, most ANNs are relatively simple when compared to the complex neural interactions that take place when a human mind makes decisions. There is an input layer, an output layer and a hidden layer sandwiched in between – where there are hundreds of virtual nodes the algorithm connects and reconnects to when trying to reach an outcome. To "learn" with each input experience, the algorithm alters the internal connections until it figures out how to achieve a desired output within a specified level of accuracy. Once the algorithm has learned, more inputs can be entered, and the ANN provides a workable prediction.

A multi-layer perceptron neural network (MLP) is an acyclic forward network. Neurons can be divided into disjunctive layers so that the outputs of each neuron of one layer are connected to the inputs of each neuron layer following. There are no links between non-neighbouring layers of neurons or between neurons in the same layer. Each neuron has as many inputs as there are neurons in the lower layer. The input layer serves only to distribute input values to the first hidden layer. The most widely used application of artificial neural networks is in the field of predictive analytics.

Evolutionary algorithms

An evolutionary algorithm is a type of machine learning algorithm used for artificial intelligence, which uses mechanisms inspired by biological evolution, such as reproduction, mutation, recombination and selection. It is a type of metaheuristic algorithm; that is, it employs a high-level procedure or heuristic to find, generate or choose a heuristic that provides an approximate solution to an optimisation problem. Evolutionary algorithms are often used to find good approximate solutions that cannot be easily solved by other techniques. Optimisation problems often do not have an exact solution, as it may be too time consuming and computationally intensive to find an optimal solution. However, evolutionary algorithms are ideal in such situations, as they can be used to find a near-optimal solution which is often sufficient.

A new approach to optimisation is based on the principles of genetic evolution. One starts with a quasi-random initial set of variants, presents them to respondents and, based on their feedback, selects the better-performing ones as parents for breeding purposes. The genetic algorithm then uses genetic crossover to combine traits from two parents and breed new subject of analysis candidates (offspring), mutation to introduce traits that were not present in either parent and replacement to eliminate poor-performing members of the population and make room for the offspring. Step by step, in survival-of-the-fittest fashion, the population of new entities/concepts evolves to reflect the preferences of the respondents, and one will end up with perhaps four or five top entities/concepts that can be further investigated. The genetic algorithm is essentially a search and optimisation process that is guided by human feedback every step of the way and acts as a learning system. It does not require modelling complex human behaviour – and solving the difficult mathematical problems that come with such models – and yet it implicitly accounts for all that complexity.

Memetic algorithms

Memetic algorithms (MAs) provide one of the most effective and flexible metaheuristic approaches for tackling hard optimisation problems. MAs address the difficulty of developing high-performance universal heuristics by encouraging the exploitation of multiple heuristics acting in concert, making use of all available sources of information for a problem. This approach has resulted in a rich arsenal of heuristic algorithms and metaheuristic frameworks for many problems. MAs are optimisation techniques based on the synergistic combination of ideas taken from different algorithmic solvers, such as population-based search (as in evolutionary techniques) and local search (as in gradient-ascent techniques). They are a meta-heuristic approach that combines problem-specific solvers with evolutionary algorithms. The problem solvers can be implemented using exact methods, approximation algorithms or local search heuristics. The hybridisation aims to accelerate the discovery of good solutions or to find the solutions that are unreachable by evolutionary algorithms or the local search methods alone.

Metaheuristics

Marketing models and problems are becoming increasingly complex, requiring the use of sophisticated solution procedures. This is leading to an increasing utilisation of metaheuristics. For example, one could present three population-based metaheuristics: genetic, memetic and electromagnetism-like algorithms. The use of these metaheuristics is in different phases of maturity. Genetic algorithms have a wide range of applications in the marketing field. Memetic algorithms have many applications in different fields of management, but very few in marketing. Electromagnetism-like algorithms are now starting to be applied in a wide variety of fields.

Statistical software

There are many kinds of statistical software available to help the marketing researcher. There are many packages available for statistical analysis of data. Today, all such packages have easy user interfaces, so that even those who are relatively inexpert in using them can do so with ease. The functionality of statistical software includes:

- Importing data from different sources
- Preparing data, including sampling, conversion of variables into different forms, distribution sampling and coding
- Modelling data, including fitting distributions, regression analysis and analysis of variance

- Dashboards and visualisation
- Analysis and reporting

In this section, we provide a brief profile of one of the recent favourites among marketing research academics, R programming, and then even shorter profiles of some other common packages.

R programming

Developed from the earlier S, R is a programming language for statistical computing. The open-source R software has gained massive popularity in the past decade as the tool of choice for data analysts. The language is used as part of the data analysis toolchain in some of the biggest companies in the world. Researchers can apply logistic regression, customer segmentation, hierarchical linear modelling, market basket analysis, structural equation modelling, artificial neural networks, GLMs and conjoint analysis in R, as well as a huge number of other statistical and mathematical techniques.

R is a great choice for marketing analysis. It offers unique capabilities for fitting statistical models. It is extensible and can process data from many different systems, in a variety of forms, for both small and large datasets. The R ecosystem includes the widest available range of established and emerging statistical methods as well as visualisation techniques. Yet the use of R in marketing lags other fields such as statistics, econometrics, psychology and bioinformatics.

Gretl

Gretl is an open-source package built primarily for econometrics but incorporating many of the statistical functions required by marketing researchers, written in the C programming language, with the interface available in the languages of many countries and many datasets available that have been provided by Gretl users. Its use in empirical research is explained by Tarassow (2019). It is distinguished by its extreme ease of use, particularly in reading and manipulating data extracted from many other programmes, such as spreadsheets. Many add-ons have been developed to add to its functionality, and it supports machine learning.

SPSS

IBM SPSS Statistics is the world's leading statistical software, used by marketing researchers for decades. Approaches to using it in marketing research have been well documented (Charry *et al.* 2016; Aljandali 2017; Wagner 2019). It is particularly strong at making sense of complex patterns and associations and integrates with open source software such as R and Python. Its SPSS Modeler is a visual data science and machine-learning solution that helps in data preparation and discovery, model management and deployment, predictive analytics and machine learning. It is particularly useful for hypothesis and model generation and for combining data from different sources.

SAS

SAS software allows users to mine, alter, manage and retrieve data from different sources and carry out statistical analysis on it. Its use in statistics has been explained by Der and Everitt (2007). It is particularly strong at combining and analysing very large (e.g. enterprise-wide) data sets (BI – where it competes with a range of other BI packages such as SAP Business Objects, IBM Cognos, Oracle Hyperion and Microsoft Power BI), and many large companies in the world use it for this purpose. It now includes text mining, social media analytics, customer intelligence and other applications designed to help in customer interaction management, as well as fraud identification applications.

Presenting data

So far in this chapter, we have focused on how to collect and analyse data. One of the problems associated with leaving research to the specialist researcher is that these researchers may not know how to present data findings to non-specialists. This problem has been addressed, though not completely resolved, by the attention paid by specialist analytical and related software companies to visualisation, which includes not just static presentation of data in graphical, tabular, heat maps, moving images, equations and other forms but also giving the user (whether the specialist researcher or the self-servicing user) the ability to "drill down" into the data to explore why the top level results are as they are. Other important areas of development include more conceptual ideas, such as how to express complex findings through infographics and rich pictures, as well as the art of using data to tell a story (storytelling).

The art of storytelling using data is one very few academic researchers master (Stone *et al.* 2015). Figure 11.1 suggests some areas for telling customer stories. The storytelling process can involve the following steps:

- Decide why you need a story;
- Decide what is tellable and find it;
- Decide on the target audience and what you want them to feel, think or do;
- Decide how you want your story to work;
- Decide on the domain/overall content;
- Decide on the plot and message;
- Write the brief for the story;
- Create the story – the medium;
- Create the story – the storyboard and testing;
- Create the story – delivery;
- Save the story;
- Communicate the story – channel/media;
- Evaluate the story.

Issues

In this rapid tour through the issues associated with using data in marketing research, there are many other issues which require focus. They include the following:

- Speed, convenience, cost and quality of delivery/implementation of research and data plans – the required speed of decision-making in digital marketing leads to a requirement for rapid knowledge production. The long cycles of researching and reporting that were normal in the last century are no longer acceptable, while any problems in quality are immediately reflected in much more trackable marketing activity, so errors are not so quickly or easily forgiven;

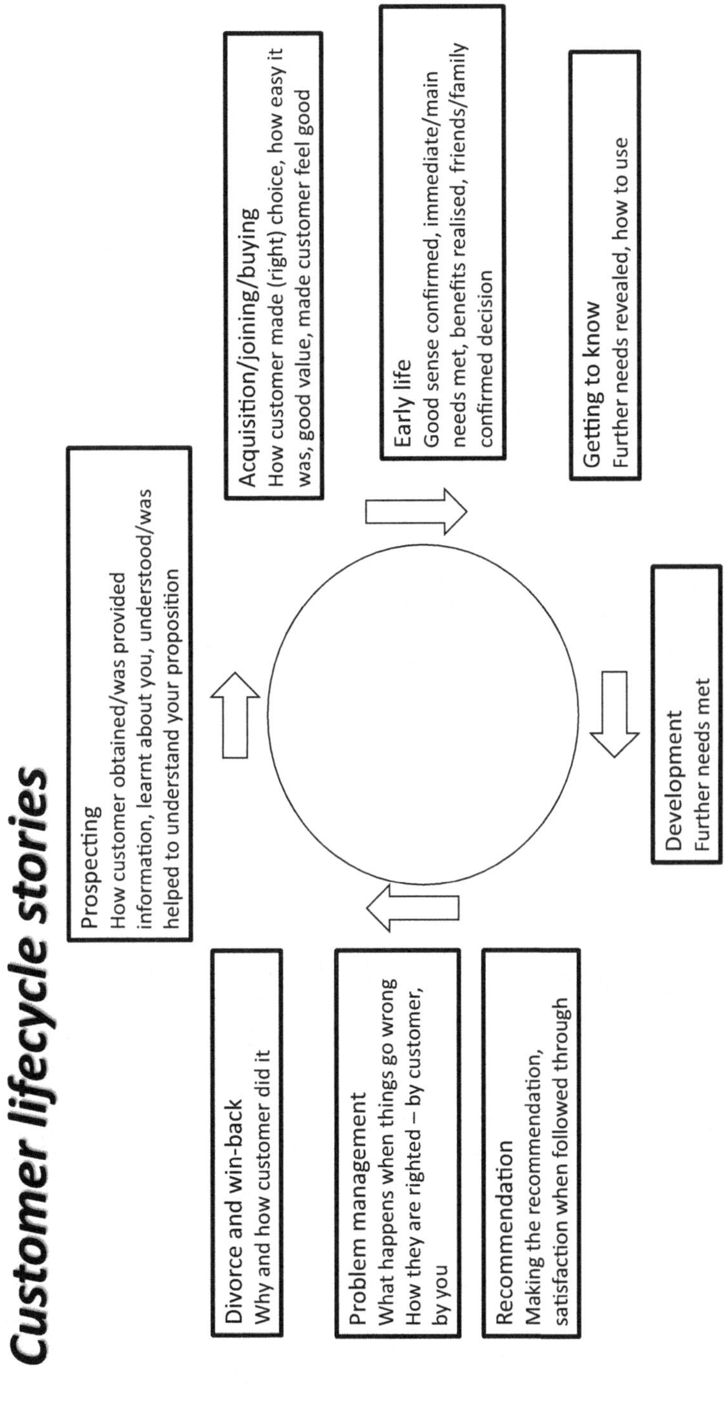

Customer lifecycle stories

Prospecting
How customer obtained/was provided information, learnt about you, understood/was helped to understand your proposition

Acquisition/joining/buying
How customer made (right) choice, how easy it was, good value, made customer feel good

Early life
Good sense confirmed, immediate/main needs met, benefits realised, friends/family confirmed decision

Getting to know
Further needs revealed, how to use

Development
Further needs met

Divorce and win-back
Why and how customer did it

Problem management
What happens when things go wrong. How they are righted – by customer, by you

Recommendation
Making the recommendation, satisfaction when followed through

Figure 11.1 Storytelling opportunities

Source: The authors

- Data overload and confusion – users and researchers often feel that they are drowning in data, although if they had taken a more structured and critical approach to data as described in this chapter, they might find that they have not got the data they need and that it was already available directly or indirectly (through triangulation) from other sources or even that they did not need the data that they thought they did. This problem may be caused simply by the fact that it does take significant time to search for and digest data (particularly if an unstructured approach has been taken);
- The need to learn from other disciplines – some outside management – where it is common to produce meta-studies identifying important contributory factors or outcomes, using formalised methodologies, such as health/medicine;
- The need in academic research for much more critical appraisals of prior research (not just the recitations of prior authorities);
- The need for researchers to make much more adventurous and exciting use of existing data.

The future of marketing research data management

We see the future as continuing trends that are already in place, such as:

- Continued acceleration of availability;
- Further application of AI/ML techniques;
- Continued broadening and deepening of sources;
- Increased concerns concerning reliability and validity;
- More blurring of the boundary between secondary and primary data;
- More substitution of secondary for primary data, with primary often to validate secondary (in some areas);
- More creation of aggregated datasets.

Case studies

Sources of cases

We had such a rich selection of case studies available that it was hard to choose which ones to describe. This is partly because of your authors' own involvement in many projects using existing data but also because much existing data, by its nature, is published along with examples of its application. For this reason, we refer the readers to these institutions for examples of good use of secondary data:

- Consultancies such as McKinsey, Boston Consulting Group, Accenture, Deloitte and PwC and information technology analysts such as IDC, Gartner, Forrester and HFS, as well as the many financial analysts – a simple browse including terms like "research", "report", and "pdf" will usually yield a rich harvest, perhaps also including in the browse term the field in which the researcher is interested, for example, "consumer buying behaviour", retailing";
- The digital giants themselves, which produce many reports exploring the relationship between what they do and marketing outcomes – Facebook, Amazon, Netflix, Google, eBay and so on;
- Government and international inter-government providers of data – government statistical services, regulators (particularly of communications and broadcasting, utilities and financial

services); the European Union and similar geographical entities; international organisations such as the International Monetary Fund, the World Bank and the various agencies of the United Nations;

- National and international industry associations, for example, sectors such as retailing, financial services and industry associations and their related organisations, particularly in marketing, such as (in the United Kingdom) the Archive of Market and Social Research, the Data and Marketing Association;
- Not-for-profit organisations, whether charities aiming to make improvements in different domains or charities committed to ensuring greater clarity of information, for example, Transparency, Global Innovation Index.

Case study

Rather than duplicate these sources, we decided to cover an example in which one of your authors has been involved, a study of how different countries reacted to the early stages of the Covid-19 pandemic (Stone *et al.* 2020). The aim of the research was to identify whether very early stage actions by governments affected the speed with which the pandemic spread in their countries. The data was sourced from one of the leading data aggregators on the topic, Worldometer, which has a large dedicated section on the pandemic, mainly using sources from the governments of the individual countries or press reports stimulated by data releases by governments, with all the problems of possible fake news and weak data collection methods that that is known to entail.

Reviewing the literature on the topic led us to identify four key dates (Table 11.1).

To understand government actions using these dates, we built a database by country (covering 136 countries, which included 98% of the world's population) of the dates, mortality rates at time of writing (by which time all countries had passed their peak death rate in the first wave) and variables which might determine the infection spread, for example, air travel intensity, obesity, longevity, population structure, income per head, vaccination rates, corruption perceptions and distance from Wuhan. The only variable which we had trouble sourcing data on and which we knew to be important was any statistic on crowding in housing.

Table 11.1 Early date definitions

Term	Date	Comment
Lockdown	When first introduced	Some lockdowns began partially, for example, specific regions or activities
Border/flight closure	When first closed	Some initial closures were for one or more regions or against certain countries, for example, land borders with/flights from China or countries with early spikes
First death	When happened	Subject to mortality interpretation and honest reporting
Take-off	When deaths reached or exceeded one millionth of the population.	Subject to mortality interpretation and honest reporting

Source: The authors

We used Gretl open-source econometrics software to analyse the result. We reached these conclusions:

- As first death is likely to be preceded by infection by around two weeks, to be effective, border closure should precede first death by (say) over 14 days, while lockdown should precede take-off (a clear sign that the disease is spreading) by over 14 days;
- First death occurred by 15 March for 40 countries, by March 31 for 100 countries;
- Take-off occurred by March 31 for 35 countries, by April 30 for 94 countries;
- Countries furthest from Wuhan had higher mortality (broadly the Americas), while those nearest – more experienced in viral outbreaks – acted quickly. Africa is different, with younger populations, and is more isolated (with less air travel);
- Countries with older populations had higher mortality;
- Countries which reached take-off earlier had higher final mortality;
- Border closures took place late – 45 countries closed borders on or after the first death, and 15 did not close, while only 34 countries closed borders more than 14 days before first death;
- Lockdowns took place late – 47 countries locked down less than 14 days before take-off, and 25 did not lock down;
- The earlier a country closed its borders and/or locked down, relative to when the first death occurred, the more delayed the take-off was and the lower the mortality.

These indicated the need to absorb information and act quickly. We used 25 country case studies that show that this did not usually take place, with slow realisation of the outbreak's severity and piecemeal and fragmented action.

Acknowledgement

This chapter uses part of the following article:
Tzempelikos, N., Kooli, K., Stone, M., Aravopoulou, E., Birn, R. and Kosack, E., 2020. Distribution of marketing research material to universities: The case of archive of market and social research (AMSR). *Journal of Business-to-Business Marketing*, 27(2), 187–202.

References

Adams, R., Smart, P. and Huff, A., 2017. Shades of grey: Guidelines for working with the grey literature in systematic reviews for management and organizational studies. *International Journal of Management Reviews*, 19(4), 432–454. https://doi.org/10.1111/ijmr.11102.

Aljandali, A., 2017. *Multivariate Methods and Forecasting with IBM® SPSS® Statistics*. New York: Springer.

Charry, K., Coussement, K., Demoulin, N. and Heuvinck, N., 2016. *Marketing Research with IBM® SPSS Statistics: A Practical Guide*. London: Routledge.

Deadrick, D. and Gibson, P., 2007. An examination of the research – practice gap in HR: Comparing topics of interest to HR academics and HR professionals. *Human Resource Management Review*, 17(2), 131–139. DOI: 10.1016/j.hrmr.2007.03.001.

Der, G. and Everitt, B., 2007. *Basic Statistics Using SAS Enterprise Guide® a Primer*. London: SAS Institute Inc.

Ernst, J., Cooperstein, D. and Dernoga, M., 2011. *Thought Leadership: The Next Wave of Differentiation in B2B Marketing*. Cambridge, MA: Forrester Research.

Homburg, C., Wieseke, J. and Kuehnl, C., 2010. Social influence on salespeople's adoption of sales technology: A multilevel analysis. *Journal of the Academy of Marketing Sciences*, 38, 159–168. https://doi.org/10.1007/s11747-009-0157-x.

Huff, A., 2000. 1999 presidential address: Changes in organizational knowledge production. *Academy of Management Review*, 25(2), 288–293. DOI: 10.2307/259014.

McCullagh, P. and Nelder, J., 1989. *Generalized Linear Models*. London: Chapman and Hall.

McGann, J., 2019. *2018 Global Go to Think Tank Index Report* [online]. Available from: https://repository.upenn.edu/think_tanks/16 [Accessed 23 September 2020].

Stone, M., Machtynger, L. and Machtynger, J., 2015. Managing customer insight creatively through storytelling. *Journal of Direct, Data and Digital Marketing Practice*, 17(2), 7–83. https://doi.org/10.1057/dddmp.2015.45.

Stone, M., Sanders, K., Biron, D., Aravopoulou, E., Brodsky, S., Kosack, E., Al Dhaen, E., Mahmood, M. and Usacheva, A., 2020. Information management in the early stages of the COVID-19 pandemic. *The Bottom Line* [online]. Available from   https://doi.org/10.1108/BL-09-2020-0062.

Tarassow, A., 2019. Practical empirical research using Gretl and Hansl. *Australian Economic Review*, 52(2), 255–271. https://doi.org/10.1111/1467-8462.11324.

Tranfield, D., Denyer, D. and Smart, P., 2003. Towards a methodology for developing evidence-informed management knowledge by means of systematic review. *British Journal of Management*, 14(3), 207–222. https://doi.org/10.1111/1467-8551.00375.

Tzempelikos, N., Kooli, K., Stone, M., Aravopoulou, E., Birn, R. and Kosack, E., 2020. Distribution of marketing research material to universities: The case of archive of market and social research (AMSR). *Journal of Business-to-Business Marketing*, 27(2), 187–202.

Wagner III, W., 2019. *Using IBM SPSS Statistics for Research Methods and Social Science Statistics*. London: Sage Publications.

12

THE ARCHIVE OF MARKET AND SOCIAL RESEARCH

Looking backwards to look forwards

Robin Birn, Merlin Stone, Nektarios Tzempelikos, Kaouther Kooli and Emmanuel Kosack

Summary

This chapter relates to the work of the Archive of Market and Social Research (AMSR), which liberates a rich set of data and commentary generated since the 1950s by the market and social research industry to support commercial and social progress. The AMSR was initially focused on the marketing services sector. A series of qualitative and quantitative research projects carried out to identify the market for the Archive showed that the information could usefully be made available to universities, to enhance research and learning in business and social science disciplines and to prepare graduates for their careers. The chapter reviews in full the contents of the Archive and suggests how it (and similar archives and material) could be used in developing academic understanding of marketing research.

What the AMSR is

The AMSR is a living, searchable archive of high-quality research, trend data and commentary, regularly updated and accumulated over many decades. The AMSR was set up by several senior members of the marketing research industry, concerned that the knowledge gained over the preceding 70 years was in danger of being lost to future researchers. Drawn from the output of practitioners over many decades, it forms an inspiring source of insight for those seeking to explore the dynamics of change – in the past, the present and, crucially, the future. The AMSR is established as a charity under UK law, overseen by a Board of Trustees, with day-to-day management being the responsibility of the Executive Committee (AMSR 2020).

The Archive consists of reports and data from market, social, political and economic researchers in research agencies, such as MORI, TGI, NOP Millward Brown and the Market Research Society, and in companies that use the data. This digital resource provides direct access to the complete Archive. For the first time, a comprehensive collection of historic research materials was drawn together and held in one place, showing how the marketing research and customer insight industry developed and the role played by significant individuals, organisations and companies. The development of techniques is catalogued and made available for reference and study (AMSR 2020).

The core proposition was clearly stated as "Market and social insight set free". Its purpose was:

- Building and providing free access to the Archive for as wide a range of audiences as possible.
- Developing thought leadership pieces, writing papers, presented at conferences and published in journals – drawing from the past to inform the present and the future.
- Fostering links with key academic institutions and academics: providing access to academics and students and sponsoring student research projects.
- Fostering links with key industry associations and other marketing research Archives.

The Archive is designed to be used by:

- Educators and students in academic institutions;
- Research practitioners;
- Business and marketing consultants;
- Industry associations.

The sources and form of AMSR information

Since World War II, the United Kingdom has been one of the leading countries in the development and use of qualitative and quantitative survey research to measure people's behaviour and attitudes. Such research has now become a major part of everyday life, affecting all activities, including food, drink, lifestyle, media, finance, travel and social attitudes. The AMSR provides access to major studies detailing UK business and social history. Its research continues to collect as much material as possible relating to its areas of interest, professionally housing and curating it for the benefit of the research community and wider audiences.

The Archive is divided into a number of groups, called 'collections'. When accessing the Archive website, users see these listed, with a brief description of what they contain. For example, if a researcher is looking for a book, a simple click links the user to the detailed pages for that collection. Collections are defined by the type of document they contain (books, papers, reports etc.) rather than by subject (since most items in the Archive span a range of subjects). Where there is a clearly recognisable group or series, such as the UK Marker Research Society Newsletter or the MORI British Public Opinion series, that can be a separate collection.

The Archive of Market and Social Research contains several significant studies, technical developments, survey results and biographical details and key documents, including published papers, journals, books and newsletters covering the fields of UK market and social research over the last 70 years.

Users can also find:

- Longitudinal surveys covering commercial, social and attitudinal topics;
- Case studies showing how marketing research and customer insight has been used to effect commercial and social change;
- Published thinking on qualitative and quantitative research techniques and their uses available from a single source;

- A long run of general election polling statistics;
- Historical documents charting the story of the market and social research industries.

Forms of content

The user can see the following content:

Books

The AMSR contains books on market or social research and research-related topics. They include textbooks on research methods and statistical techniques, as well as books written for less specialist audiences on subjects such as how marketing and advertising work, on the result of research into various topics and on the history of marketing research. They include *The Making of an Industry* (Blythe 2005), a 230-page history of UK marketing research published in 2005 by the Market Research Society, and the *Dictionary of Market Research* (Talmage 1988), published by the Market Research Society and the Incorporated Society of British Advertisers (ISBA).

BBC World Service Audience Research

This includes a collection of audience research reports and papers relating to the operations of the BBC World Service between 1990 and 2001. These studies were undertaken in all parts of the world covered by the World Service, many of them during periods of crisis in the countries concerned. BBC World Service Audience Research was donated to the Archive by Graham Mytton, who was head of the BBC International Audience Research Department during those years.

Census

This includes documents about censuses, mainly the UK Census. It includes discussion papers and analyses, selected papers in journals and a small number of conference papers and press cuttings.

Conference papers

This includes volumes of papers from research conferences from the 1960s onwards. Most are conferences and seminars organised by the UK's Market Research Society (MRS) and the Industrial Market Research Association (IMRA), later the Business & Industrial Group (BIG). There are also some papers from specialist groups such as qualitative researchers, academic bodies and international organisations, though most international conference papers are not currently available to this Archive.

Company reports and PR

This includes promotional reports and brochures from commercial research companies, company annual reports, membership directories and other information from UK-based research organisations such as the Market Research Society and the Association of Market Survey Organisations (AMSO).

The CRAM Peter Cooper Collection

Peter Cooper (1936–2010) was co-founder of Cooper Research & Marketing, later CRAM International, with his wife Jackie French. Cooper studied clinical psychology at the University of Manchester, where he became a lecturer in the early 1960s. He became involved in commercial motivational research and in 1968 opened Cooper Research & Marketing in Manchester. Cooper was one of the most important pioneers of what we now know as qualitative research. The collection includes commercial research reports and early academic papers.

Geodemographics

Geodemographics is the science of linking variables from the census to local areas and using cluster analysis methods to group areas with similar profiles. Developed in the United Kingdom by Richard Webber in the 1970s, the system was commercially launched by CACI in the United Kingdom (under the name Acorn), parallel to Claritas' Prizm in the United States. Since then, several other organisations have entered the market.

Guides and rulebooks

This includes practical manuals, guides, handbooks, how-to documents, training course handouts, quality standards and codes of practice on research methodology. Many of these were produced by the Market Research Society and other UK-based and international research organisations, by research buying organisations such as the UK-based Association of Users of Research Agencies (AURA) and by research agencies and others conducting marketing research. Topics covered include commissioning research, writing research proposals, research design, sampling, questionnaire design, interview standards, analysis, presentations and report writing, plus standardised systems for measuring audiences and classifying population groups (e.g. social grading).

Journals and other documents

This includes miscellaneous issues of journals, mainly from publishers outside the United Kingdom, for which the Archive does not keep a series. For some issues, only the title and contents pages have been digitised and the actual volumes can be viewed at the History of Advertising Trust. There is also a collection of miscellaneous qualitative research.

Market Research Abstracts (1963–1997)

A complete collection of volumes of Market Research Abstracts which were produced and published by the Market Research Society twice a year from 1963 to 1997. They contain abstracts of papers relevant to marketing research, from a range of journals and conference papers, both UK and international, on topics including research, statistics, psychology and sociology, economics, marketing, advertising and business management. Each volume includes a list of the titles covered, an extensive subject index of the abstracts included and an author index. Publication ceased in 1997, as by then it had been overtaken by online searching.

Market Research Development Fund

These are reports, reviews and papers produced by the Market Research Development Fund between 1982 and 1987. These are mainly in-depth reports on topics of importance to the marketing research industry at the time, including response rates, interview methods, qualitative research, employee research and data fusion.

MRS Newsletter (1966–1992)

The *Market Research Society Newsletter* was published monthly from 1966 to 1992. It contained news on companies, people, meetings and events, training courses, seminars, conferences, plus correspondence and advertisements for jobs in marketing research in the United Kingdom and elsewhere. Later it expanded to include feature articles on topics of current interest. In 1992 it was replaced by *Research Magazine* (see subsequently).

AURA Newsletter

These are issues of short newsletters produced between 1993 and 1997 by the UK Association of Users of Research Agencies for its members, typically research buyers (clients) of research providers and research agencies. Each newsletter lists meetings and events, personnel changes and other items of interest to the membership.

Millward Brown

Short papers, most from 2006 onwards, from the research agency Millward Brown (later Kantar Millward Brown), an advertising and brand research specialist. The papers are all about successful advertising and branding strategies. They are based on information drawn from Millward Brown's Knowledge Bank, a large database of its research on brands and advertising, plus case studies, conference papers, magazine articles and learnings documents.

Miscellaneous newsletters

These are newsletters from various mainly UK-based research organisations, including:

- The Industrial Market Research Association;
- The Business and Industrial Research Group;
- The Association of Qualitative Research Practitioners (AQRP), the British Market Research Association (BMRA) (an association of research suppliers formed in 1998 from a merger of the Association of Market Survey Organisations and the Association of British Market Research Companies [ABMRC]);
- The Independent Consultants Group of the Market Research Society;
- The Market Research Development Fund (MRDF).

At the time of writing, the Archive did not have a complete series of any of these newsletters, but more will be added if and when they become available.

MORI British Public Opinion

British Public Opinion was published by MORI (Market and Opinion Research International), the company founded by Sir Robert Worcester, from 1979 to 2003. These highly detailed journals contain a mass of information from polls and surveys giving a fascinating insight into the political topics of the time. These were made available by the top polling expert, Sir Robert Worcester. This collection can be searched by topic, context, location, research method and publication date.

MORI Reports

This is a selection of over 50 reports on research conducted by the opinion polling and research company Market and Opinion Research International. These have been made available by the Ipsos MORI archive, cover a wide range of topics and are dated from 1982 to 2009. Only a summary of the contents is available in the digital archive. Copies of these reports are not held by the Archive, and the full reports may be viewed only with the permission and at the discretion of Ipsos MORI. As the reports are held in a storage facility, there is a charge to cover retrieval costs.

NOP Reports

This is a continuous series of monthly reports on their public opinion polling from National Opinion Polls (NOP) Ltd. The series began in 1963 under the title *Political Bulletin* but in 1975 became *Political, Economic & Social Review*. Each volume contains the results of polling on voting intentions and satisfaction with politicians and policies. Most volumes also contain a collection of press cuttings showing how the polls were reported and special features on research on other topics which were prominent at the time. They offer a very interesting insight into public opinion at the time on many issues.

Opinion Polling Reports

This is a collection of reports of or about opinion polling from various sources. The material about opinion polls, including results, can also be found in some of the other collections, including the *British Public Opinion* journal and the Political Bulletins from National Opinion Poll. This collection is one that can be searched by topic, context, location, research method and publication date. The collection includes:

- A 1939 report on opinion polling techniques from the British Institute of Public Opinion;
- Reports on public opinion surveys on various topics conducted by Louis Harris Research Limited between 1969 and 1972;
- The Market Research Society's review of opinion polling and the 1992 general election.

Papers and offprints

This includes papers and offprints from a very wide range of journals, magazines, conferences and other sources, both UK and international, dating from 1948 onwards. These papers were donated to AMSR by research practitioners who collected them during their careers. The topics covered are very wide ranging, but many are about development in research methodology and statistical techniques. This collection is one that can be searched by topic, context, location, research method and publication date.

Papers – Ehrenberg collection

This is a special collection of papers from, or relating to, the work of Andrew Ehrenberg, Gerald Goodhardt and their colleagues over many years at London Business School, Southbank University, Aske Research and so on to develop a scientific understanding of consumer behaviour. They come largely from the files left by the late Andrew Ehrenberg, supplemented by donations from other sources, and deal with a wide range of subjects, especially analytical and modelling techniques and statistics. This collection can also be searched by topic, context, location, research method and publication date.

Press cuttings and articles

This includes cuttings from a wide range of publications (UK and international) about marketing research practice or practitioners, plus other ephemera. These items were donated to AMSR by research practitioners who accumulated them during the course of their careers. They are mainly cuttings from the marketing press or national newspapers.

Proposals and tenders

This is a miscellaneous collection of bid documents proposing or tendering for research projects. These date from the 1970s onwards. In most cases, the bid is for research to a single research buyer, but in some cases, it is for syndicated research, that is, research where the costs would be shared between multiple buyers.

Qualitative journals

These are journals specialising in qualitative research (i.e. in-depth research using techniques such as group discussions, focus groups and depth interviews). The main titles included are:

- *Qualitative Market Research: An International Journal* (1998–2014);
- *Qualitative Methods in Psychology* (QMIP) newsletter (British Psychological Society) (2006–2011);
- For each journal, only the title and contents pages have been digitised, and the actual volumes can be viewed at the History of Advertising Trust.

Reports of projects

These are reports on research projects. These documents were donated to the AMSR by research practitioners who worked on them or acquired them during their careers. These reports, the oldest of which dates from 1925, cover a very wide range of topics, from food purchasing to social housing, from magazine readership to car advertising, plus reports on the marketing research industry itself. In a few of the reports, only the title and contents pages have been digitised, and the actual reports can be viewed at the History of Advertising Trust (www. hatads.org.uk/).

Research Magazine

Research Magazine was published monthly by the Market Research Society from 1992 to 2012 as the successor to the *MRS Newsletter* (see separate collection). This Archive holds issues from 1992 to 2002; issues from 2003 to 2012 are available from the MRS. Like the *Newsletter*, it contained news on companies, people, meetings and events, training courses, seminars, conferences, correspondence, feature articles on research topics and advertisements for omnibus surveys and for jobs in marketing research in the United Kingdom and elsewhere. Issues frequently had an accompanying, separate supplement on subjects of interest such as research on specific markets, on different continents or different types of research. In 2001, an accompanying, separate newsletter hiving off the news element was created. *Research Magazine* was replaced in 2013 by *Impact Magazine*, published quarterly with a focus on research effectiveness and available online via the Market Research Society.

Statistics journals

This covers the title and contents pages of 25 volumes of statistics journals, mostly from the UK-based Royal Statistical Society and Institute of Statisticians. The complete volumes can be viewed at the History of Advertising Trust or other sources.

Survey Magazine (1983–1991)

Survey Magazine was published quarterly by the Market Research Society from 1983 to 1991. It was intended to provide more detailed articles and analyses on research topics than were found in the monthly MRS members' newsletter Publication ceased when the *Newsletter and Survey Magazine* were replaced by *Research Magazine* in 1992.

Survey methods

Survey Methods newsletters were produced three times a year by Social & Community Planning Research (SCPR), later the Joint Centre for Survey Methods. In October 1980, the research company Social & Community Planning Research, in association with City University, set up the Survey Methods Centre (one of five national Designated Research Centres funded by the Social Science Research Council [SSRC]) and began publishing the newsletters. Their aim was to promote good practice in survey methodology, disseminate relevant research findings and encourage discussion and debate. They include reports on methodological seminars held by the organisation plus short papers on other topics of current interest, news, conference reports, book reviews and so on. The Archive contains volumes 1–18, published from 1980 to 1998. SCPR is now the National Centre for Social Research (NATCEN), and since 2004 (volume 22), the newsletter has been published on its website.

TGI

The Target Group Index (TGI) is a continuous survey carried out in Great Britain since 1969 and in Northern Ireland since 1992. It comprises completed self-completion questionnaires from 25,000 adults aged 15-plus in Great Britain per annum. Each respondent provides information on his or her use or purchase of all major products, brands and services. Exposure to different media is measured, as well as attitudinal and demographic data. The reports in the Archive so far include:

- Trackback studies on specific product areas using 25 years' data up to 1993.

The MRS Journal

The journal is the main publication of the Market Research Society, recognised as a peer-reviewed academic journal, although its editors and contributors were traditionally practitioners in the research industry rather than academics. Founded in 1956 under the title *Commentary*, it became the *Journal of the Market Research Society* (JMRS) in 1968 and the *International Journal of Market Research* in winter 1999–2000. It was issued quarterly up to 2004 and changed to bi-monthly in 2005. Issues up to and including 1990 can be read online. Issues from 1991 and later can be accessed online at the World Advertising Research Centre (www.warc.com). Physical copies of both periods are held at the History of Advertising Trust.

AMSRS demonstration

Research News is the journal of the Australian Market and Social Research Society (AMSRS).

Use of AMSR

Other examples of stories on the Archive website at the time of writing include those listed subsequently.

The UK National Health Service: changing attitudes and expectations – AMSR

Given the events of the coronavirus pandemic, belief in the care and capabilities of the UK's National Health Service (NHS) is an increasingly important issue. This is confirmed by an Ipsos MORI poll completed nationwide on 30 March 2020 in which people were asked how confident they were in the ability of the NHS to deal with those who are ill as a result of getting coronavirus. Seventy-one percent said they were very or fairly confident, while only 25% were not so confident.

However, earlier poll data in the Archive showed that this confidence in the competence and durability of the NHS has not always been present. In 1988, MORI also found that although 64% rated the NHS a Good or Fairly Good, only 35% expected it would deserve a similar rating in five years' time. This declining optimism was further evident in the fact that while 47% thought in 2000 that the NHS would get better, only 28% thought similarly in 2005. In 2001, MORI found as many as 60% thought it likely that within their lifetime, healthcare would no longer be free on the NHS. Also, in 1988, more than 70% rated nurses, GPs and hospital doctors as Good, but only 39% were willing to say the same of NHS administrators. More recently, in 2017, negative expectations of the NHS were still prevalent. According to a British Medical Association survey, 43% were dissatisfied with the NHS and only 33% satisfied, 82% were worried about its future, and 62% expected it to get worse. Clearly all these negative attitudes and expectations have been overtaken by the Covid-19 crisis in which the NHS has reasserted its central role in our lives.

British reservations about Europe have been apparent for at least 50 years

Historical evidence shows that the British people have always had strong reservations about their links with Europe. As shown by results accessible via the AMSR website, in September 1969, the Harris Poll found that 54% of voters were against Britain joining the Common Market, while only 30% were in favour. By February 1970, a further poll found that this difference had increased, with a 63% to 19% negative result. Then in a poll on the eve of the House of Commons vote in October 1971, the difference narrowed, but still 49% were found to be against joining the EU, while only 30% were in favour. Despite that, 84% assumed that Britain *would* join. Among many other questions covered in these polls, in the last of them, voters were asked whether they thought the government had given enough time and opportunity for full nationwide discussion on the issues: as many as 59% thought it had not. So, for 50 years, the divide over Europe has clearly been a sore spot, not only in the Tory party but also across the nation as a whole.

A simple measure of the growth in environmental awareness

The continuous consumer study Target Group Index has asked for respondents' opinions on a range of topics since the mid-1980s. Some of its attitude statements have remained constant; others have been added or removed to reflect changing times. The area of greatest change has been in measuring attitudes to the environment. Examining the statements included in the 1987 and 2012 TGI datasets is very revealing. In 1987, only one of about 200 TGI statements was environmentally themed: "I disapprove of aerosols because of their effect on the atmosphere." In those days, CFCs and their impact on the ozone layer were a regular news topic. CFCs were to be banned internationally by 1996, but in 1987, the balance of the UK population were not persuaded. More people disagreed with the statement (34%) than agreed (26%).

The changing face of our eating habits – AMSR

Several market research studies have tracked the changes in our eating habits which we now take for granted. For example, an article in *Survey* Spring 1989 reports on the studies conducted by the then Ministry of Agriculture, Fisheries and Food, which for half a century collected data monitoring the nations' eating patterns. The National Food Survey was conceived in the 1930s, drawing on the food baskets of the past-depression years and World War II, and it continued to provide a monitor of the changing larders and fridges of British households.

The Family Food Panel was established by Taylor Nelson in 1974, with the objective of filling a gap in the availability of continuous research tracking the nation's eating habits. The Food Panel identified changing trends in eating habits and behaviour such as convenience/time saving and healthy diets. An article in *Survey* January 1985 discussed how changing patterns of work, leisure and personal relationships and attitudes towards health and well-being affected eating habits. It also focused on the changing habits of eating out and 'grazing' and snacking throughout the day. In Spring 1989, an article discussed the demise of 'tea-time' with cakes and sandwiches and a 30% decline in cooked breakfasts. It reported a huge increase in awareness and consumption of foods like curries, pasta and pizza. In 1989, microwave ownership, now a staple in most kitchens, was approaching 50%. The trend towards divergent individual tastes within families had begun, and no longer were members of the family necessarily sitting down together and eating the same meal. They were exercising autonomy over what they eat.

In 1986, to mark the 40th anniversary of the founding of the Market Research Society, Gallup, on behalf of the Society, interviewed a nationally representative cross-section of people throughout Great Britain. The question put to them was: "If expense was no object and you could have anything you wanted, what would you choose for a perfect meal?" The ideal menus for 1986 were compared with those of 1947, in the days of post-war austerity. In 1986, respondents chose vegetable soup, prawn/shrimp cocktail, steak and chips and gateau; in 1947, it was tomato soup, sole, roast chicken and roast potatoes and trifle. Chips had taken over from roast as the most popular choice of potatoes. The change in drinking habits was most remarkable: in 1986, 61% would like wine with their meal; in 1947, only 4% chose wine. Coffee had supplanted tea as the British favourite after-dinner drink.

Why the AMSR is important for marketing academics and students

Students constantly voice their desire for business and marketing lecturers to provide examples and case studies which are practical and realistic and more up to date or detailed than available from textbooks or academic articles. The AMSR provides data for students who want to support their projects, assessments and dissertations or even to use research data such as that available in the AMSR database. Much academic journal writing consists of articles written by marketing academics, usually using relatively small-scale surveys rather than data of the breadth and depth included in the Archive. The Scimago (2019) ranking gives nearly 178 marketing journals. The globalisation of enterprise and the rise of the digital economy have posed challenges to academics to make it more relevant to industrial needs, but according to McDonald (2003, 2009), Hughes *et al.* (2018), Stone (2013), Tzempelikos *et al.* (2020) and others, the result has not been research that is more relevant to industry.

The causes of the problem where marketing research is concerned were summarised by Tzempelikos *et al.* (2020) as including divorce from commercial practice, focus on techniques which are academically attractive but of limited value to business, focus on explaining reality through preconceived theory and delay in understanding the new problems of business. As Tzempelikos *et al.* (2020) point out, this contrasts with the high volume of grey literature (surveys, thought leadership, consulting comment, analyst reports) that has emerged from management consultancies and think tanks, which has added new and relevant sources to academics. However, their lack of academic "credibility" and failure to index them means that they are either not accessible to students or not valued as sources by their lecturers.

The risk of not making historical market research known to students and academic researchers is that their view of marketing research will always be what they produce at university – small studies, often with invalid data sets such as other students or academics, using analysis techniques which are commercially inappropriate. Therefore, we consider it important that more be done to make material such as that held by the AMSR available to and used by academics – students, lecturers and researchers.

Making the AMSR known to and available to students.

Tzempelikos *et al.* (2020) identified a number of actions that need to be taken to make the AMSR more known and available to students. These include:

*   Indexing (especially on Google Scholar, students' preferred search engine);
*   Creating awareness among university librarians and academics;

- Allowing the archive to form part of the contracts now the norm between universities and publishers, possibly involving information aggregators;
- Creating and using feedback on the use of AMSR content to guide further development of the AMSR;
- Providing short versions of content, including regularly posted newsletters to keep subscribers up to date and related blogs to highlight new and existing documents.

Conclusions

Research is necessary to ensure the effectiveness of marketing, and so it is not only a service of the marketing function but also a means of directing the company to a successful future. Research helps management to "win by indicating the action it needs to take" (Birn 2004). Therefore, there is still an opportunity for marketing education to prepare students for the practical world, and indeed academics also need to understand the transformation of the marketing research sector to the customer insight industry. The transformation of the customer insight function is in a sense returning to its roots. Forty years ago, marketing researchers were considered revolutionary voices within major global brands – experimental thinkers happy to try new things, searching for new answers about consumers. For example, both qualitative research and marketing analytic techniques emerged from groups of creative planners and researchers in the 1970s and 1980s.

As marketing researchers and customer insight specialists develop knowledge of the market sector and their brand in the sector, they tend to work across all brands, so the insight role tends to be the only one (other than the marketing director) that has a perspective of the entire portfolio.

The Archive of Market Research has now helped this process by providing the history and story of the brands in all markets. AMSR provides much of this thought leadership and the history and origins for theories and concepts which need to be developed as thought leadership focuses on changes in marketing research education and its practical application.

Acknowledgements

This chapter uses part of the following article:
Tzempelikos, N., Kooli, K., Stone, M., Aravopoulou, E., Birn, R. and Kosack, E., 2020. Distribution of marketing research material to universities: The case of archive of market and social research (AMSR). *Journal of Business-to-Business Marketing*, 27(2), 187–202.

References

AMSR, 2020. *The Archive of Market and Social Research* [online]. Available from: www.amsr.org.uk/ [Accessed 25 March 2020].

Birn, R., 2004. *The Effective Use of Market Research*, 4th ed. London: Kogan Page. EAN: 9780749442002.

Blythe, I., 2005. *The Making of an Industry: The Market Research Society 1946–1986; A History of Growing Achievement*. London: Ashgate.

Hughes, T., Stone, M., Aravopoulou, E., Wright, L.T. and Machtynger, L., 2018. Academic research into marketing: Many publications, but little impact? *Cogent Business & Management*, 5(1), 1–18. https://doi. org/10.1080/23311975.2018.1516108.

McDonald, M., 2003. Marketing died in the last decade. *Interactive Marketing*, 5(2), 144–159. https://doi. org/10.1057/palgrave.im.4340229.

McDonald, M., 2009. The future of marketing: Brightest star in the firmament, or a fading meteor? Some hypotheses and a research agenda. *Journal of Marketing Management*, 25(5–6), 431–450. https://doi. org/10.1362/026725709X461786.

Robin Birn et al.

Scimago, 2019. *Scimago Journal and Country Rank* [online]. Available from: www.scimagojr.com/journal-rank.php?category=1406 [Accessed 1 April 2020].

Stone, M., 2013. Co-operation between academics and practitioners – hope for the future? *Journal of Direct, Data and Digital Marketing Practice*, 15(2), 105–107. https://doi.org/10.1057/dddmp.2013.54.

Talmage, P.A., 1988. *Dictionary of Market Research*. London: Market Research Society/Incorporated Society of British Advertisers.

Tzempelikos, N., Kooli, K., Birn, R., Stone, M., Aravopoulou, E. and Kosack, E., 2020. Distribution of marketing research material to universities: The case of archive of market and social research (AMSR). *Journal of Business to Business Marketing*, 27(2), 187–202. https://doi.org/10.1080/10517 12X.2020.1748376.

218

13

KEY ISSUES IN MANAGING MARKETING RESEARCH AND CUSTOMER INSIGHT

Robin Birn and Merlin Stone

Summary

This chapter explores the evolution of marketing information systems and the requirement of companies to use marketing information to understand customers' needs and behaviour and to monitor customer engagement and quality of service. This chapter provides a guide to the key issues relating to how marketing research leads – or should lead – company decision-making. It includes information on classic marketing research techniques and which techniques are essential for a company to identify growth, solve problems and use effectively in competitive marketing. It also covers the issue of forecasting n marketing research. It explores the different sources used in marketing research and how these are evolving. The chapter also provides a timeline for the evolution of marketing research in industry. The issue of ethics and standards is also explored. This chapter also explains how the development and management of customer insight has changed the role of information and made it a critically important information management technique used to support marketing strategy and marketing mix decisions.

Introduction

As Birn (1994, pp. 184–185) suggests, 'research provides the means of getting a clear understanding of the market and the focus on market needs. It provides the mechanism for feedback and monitoring management decisions and their effectiveness.' This text sets the scene for the rest of this chapter:

> Growing the business may present its complexities and uncertainties. Using marketing research to grow the business does not just reduce the risk, it helps management to confirm that their decisions have a competitive edge and will result in achieving new sales, and eventually committed customers.

This chapter will therefore help senior management to understand why investment in marketing research provides a good return but also why the use of data ensures that the company as a whole and its marketing management can understand the behaviour and engagement of customers.

Background

The value a business gets from marketing research and customer insight

Over the 75 years in which marketing research has been used by companies, its purpose has been to gather and evaluate information about the industry, a company's markets and its competitors and the performance of product or service being sold to target customers. However, when the Information Highway caused the explosion of information, companies benefited from referring to much greater volumes and variety of internal and external information but also discovered that they had too much information to analyse and interpret. After trying to organise this information – and in some cases succeeding – most companies realised the deploying the information productively partly depended on understanding the contribution made by marketing research and customer insight and how, used together, they help the company to answer quickly and accurately key questions such as:

- What is the current demand for my product or service?
- What consumer or customer pain point or issue does my product or service address?
- Who and what are my customer segments, what is the profile of the customers in these segments and what is their behaviour?
- How do our regular customers buy our product or service, and when is the best time to sell my product or service to them?
- How profitable is our market and market segments for all or some of our brands?
- Is our business succeeding relative to competitors in the market?
- How can our business best deal with competitive rivalry in the market in general and in specific the market segments, and where are the main risks of competitive entry into markets the company currently serves?
- Are there opportunities to enter new markets, nationally or globally?
- Are there opportunities for new products or services in these national and global markets?
- What are the main opportunities for expansion or growth within our market and market segments?

Marketing research is essential for decision-making on marketing strategies and programmes. The techniques of marketing research are therefore very important for identifying any changes in the market or market segment environment and providing information to understand customers' needs and market activities and changes.

Customer insight and marketing research

However, as there is now more information to analyse, customer insight has provided businesses with an added benefit. The main benefit has been learning by companies as to how to analyse data about customers, sometimes coming directly from interactions with customers, to improve their understanding of their customers, their journeys and their engagement with the company and its brands and to help management to make better decisions about what, when and how (through which channels and with what communication) to sell to their customers at what prices and how to communicate with them. These decisions result in marketing and communications strategies and campaigns which are not just more effective but also provide more profitability for the business.

There are many different definitions of customer and consumer insight, but few can define it in detail, which is curious considering that it has become a critical input into marketing decisions. A good definition for consumer insight is that it is an interpretation used by businesses to gain a deeper understanding of how their audience thinks and feels. It includes analysing human behaviours, which allows companies to really understand what their consumers want and need and, more importantly, why.

As businesses have developed their information resources and formed both marketing research and customer insight departments – sometimes merged – the role of both departments has become more strategic in their contribution, and the customer insight manager and marketing research manager have become more important. This has meant that companies have in the last two decades become more adept at creating market-led strategies rather than just effective communications strategies and tactics designed just to attract customers' attention irrespective of their needs, as they have understood much better the needs of their customers. Put simply, marketing research and customer insight help a company to be aware of what is happening around it, how it can remain competitive and provide many long-lasting benefits, identified subsequently.

Ensuring that the company and its employees 'live the brand'

Marketing research provides detailed information on how a company's product or service is being 'talked about' within the industry by consumers and even competitors. Understanding the conversation and the language taking place around a brand can reinforce:

- Knowing more about customer needs;
- Reactions to the current communication strategy and the target audiences;
- Supporting decisions to make any necessary changes to counteract any negative sentiments about a brand, typically now fed back through social media.

Identifying opportunities for growth in new and existing markets

As industries and companies restructure to adapt to changing consumer needs as a result of the coronavirus pandemic, marketing research and customer insight can help companies stay ahead of the product development curve and use research and insight to identify new market and product opportunities.

Researching with 'trade off' techniques helps a company to make decisions easier and, for some, faster. It helps companies understand how a consumer may be prepared to sacrifice some or all of one quality, aspect or benefit of a product in exchange for another quality, aspect or benefit. This process helps a company determine what a salesperson or a marketing communication campaign should focus on – known as customer pain points. Once these are understood in more depth through marketing research and customer insight, then expansion and growth opportunities can be identified, plans made to capture them and initiatives designed to launch them.

Evaluating product and market investment risk

The research industry has grown as more companies use marketing research techniques to test new markets or expand product and service offerings and to identify risks when, for example, making investments in production or service capacity or marketing technologies. Although it has been well known since the 1950s by the marketing directors of the large fast-moving packaged consumer goods companies, the high failure rate is a cause for concern (Schneider and Hall 2011).

Marketing research may alert a company to potential problems with the product or service or issues with distributing them or just reveal that the consumer is not interested in the product and that it is the wrong time to launch it. For example, although Sir Clive Sinclair invested in market research which identified a small market for two products, he produced the TV80, a flat-screen portable mini television, too early for the market, and also the Sinclair 5, a battery vehicle, which also failed to reach a profitable volume for production.

Competitive benchmarking

Conducting marketing research can help businesses assess their relative level of success in the industry by comparing themselves to competitors. Knowing how the competition is performing enables a company to set business and marketing goals for the future. Competitive analysis also helps identify comparative weaknesses that can be turned into strengths with the appropriate marketing mix.

Strategic planning

Now that companies have an enormous amount of internal and external data, analysing and interpreting it can change decision-making and help management plan, ensuring that customer needs are satisfied. Marketers have as a result moved from years of reactive analysis of data and management to being more proactive by understanding market trends, customer satisfaction and behaviour and developing strategic plans based on robust data. The value of marketing research and customer insight has therefore risen, and as this value has been more appreciated, more users have emerged to use research to take their important and strategic business decisions.

Companies have been encouraging and training their sales teams to draw on the resources of marketing research and customer insight departments to learn more about customer needs. This has given sales teams a better opportunity to align their negotiations with known customer needs and find new customers with needs that the company can satisfy. This has supported the development of the sales function and encouraged many sales forces to pursue a consultative sales approach.

Rather than just assessing a market and its competitiveness and rivalry, marketing research has given more tools to entrepreneurs and venture capitalists. These have followed the example of the major food and drink companies and of direct marketers and adopted a 'test and learn approach' by evaluating product or service investments in more detail. One of the most important tools they have used has been trend analyses, to ensure that the investment is being made at the best time in any trend cycle.

From sales information to marketing information systems – customer relationship management and customer experience systems

Marketing research and customer insight are encouraging management to be more cautious by checking on the market situation before making commitments and investments but also more confident that by understanding customer behaviour and engagement better, they can make the right decisions. Companies are increasingly combining all their information sources, such as those listed subsequently.

Sales information

Feedback from frontline staff – sales and customer service teams – can alert a business to changes in customer needs or competitor activities. However, this information is usually limited and may prevent management from understanding 'the bigger picture' of market activities and trends, because:

- Clients only give salespeople the information they want to provide without giving too much confidential data and may be concerned about providing too much detailed information;
- The information tends to focus on changes in the relationship a salesperson has with a client;
- The information tends to be focused on pricing and discounting and so restricts understanding of other factors that customers are concerned about or may be hiding, which salespeople may not discover due to poor questioning and analytical skills.

Marketing information systems

Developing a marketing information system requires investment in systems and the staff needed to run and manage the information coming into and leaving the business to create a more systematic approach to collecting, storing and using data. The main benefit of a marketing information system is to integrate market-monitoring systems with strategy development and the strategic implementation of policies and processes. This helps to drive the strategic marketing planning and monitoring processes and to move a company from depending on sales information to using 'market intelligence', expanding the use of up-to-date information to support customer relationship management and customer service, helping managers develop and implement market-based plans and campaigns.

Marketing information systems enable businesses to use information in three different ways:

- Collect more published research and commission more survey research analysis and store it to understand customers' needs;
- Understand better what motivates consumers to buy and become more committed to a brand;
- Understand competitive activity and develop competitor response strategies.

A good marketing information system should have the following characteristics:

- Clearly define internal data and its source, how it is different from external data and where that data is sourced from relevant management information data;
- Cover information on trends and consumer preferences so that it can be interpreted to either solve a marketing or communications problem or provide the 'alarm system' to stop any problem affecting the business;
- Be accessible by marketing and communications teams at any time and be updated and 'cleaned' regularly;

- Provide trend information that can inform a company on how the future may develop and be used to develop forecasts.

Customer relationship management systems evolved as the customer-focused part of management information systems, becoming as far as possible automated and integrated with other systems (e.g. logistics, supply chain, financial, human resources). In general, their main focus is on customer communications and the success of sales efforts, from evaluation of sales opportunities to achieving purchase and repeat purchase. They give the business the following benefits:

- More knowledge of the profile of customers and their needs, buying preferences and buying habits;
- An understanding of customer behaviour and engagement – the key to knowing the characteristics of regular and loyal customers;
- The opportunity to analyse data and cluster it into the relevant market and customer segments;
- Developing trend analyses, helping management to anticipate customer needs;
- Fostering a faster exchange of data within an organisation to take more agile decisions;
- Provide the technological means of collecting and protecting confidential and customer data.

Some refer to these systems as customer experience systems, with a focus on how the system manages the customer – particularly important in an era of self-service. This brings together all customer-facing touchpoints; organises, synchronises and automates all the data; and provides customers with all the services they require, solves their problems or sells them more products or services. An effective customer experience management system includes ways to track customer feedback by sending out and analysing returns for all types of surveys:

- Web surveys;
- Mobile telephone text surveys;
- Interactive voice response;
- Live chat;
- Net Promoter Score surveys.

The best customer experience (CX) systems are customised to the company and have dashboards created for easy reference by anyone in the company. Management can see the metrics that matter most to them to complete their role in the company. The type of data and analysis sourced from a CX system includes the following:

- Key driver analysis for analysing both qualitative and quantitative data, giving indications of the key drivers that consumers consider when buying a brand and focusing on the drivers that continue to encourage customer to buy more products to make profitable revenues for businesses;
- Statistical analysis for comparing customer types with other classifications of customers, analysing Net Promoter Score data and how it varies by department and function and using multivariate analysis to identify the variables that are significant for decision-making;
- Content analysis, combining social media, website and customer service centre feedback, analysing the comments and responses and clustering them into topics, issues, problems or positive feedback about the brand.

Using a customer experience system generally leads to improved customer retention, customer experience with the brand and customer commitment to the brand. A customer experience system can provide the foundation for loyalty programmes, in-store or online, with promotions and coupons designed to encourage customers to engage regularly with the brand and promotions for emails, text messages and loyalty cards customised to customers' regular purchasing.

The emergence of lean marketing research

As businesses now have both the internal and external data, many review it, but few make the most of it by delivering what their customers want. This shows that there is still a problem with marketing research departments and customer insight departments interpreting customer insights. This is because there is so much data to absorb that many companies find it hard to find high-quality insights, which can be used to develop customer-focused propositions. Companies that have allocated resources and time to collect valuable insights for lower cost than before have been identified as 'lean marketing researchers'. They tend to follow these guidelines:

- Focusing on carefully selected surveys and their results;
- Ensuring that key markets and segments are researched continuously, particularly using panels to monitor three-year trends to help identify problems quickly and find new business opportunities;
- Surveys being completed by marketing research teams within the company rather than subcontracting the project to an expert research agency or research consultancy, not just to save money but to build internal intelligence and knowledge;
- Integrating marketing research and customer insight into decision-making so that the marketing team understands the 'language' of the customers, uses the 'voice of the customer' and develops insights which increase business and reassure loyal customers.

Lean marketing research has been stimulated by instant access to social media; by observation techniques in retailers; and by other collaboration tools, better analysis of the CX system and better segmentation of customers. There has also been the growth of services such as Lightspeed (now Kantar), UK Datahouse, Marketscan Online, Businesslists UK, Data.com and NetProspex, which provide sample lists which are more cost effective than samples developed by marketing research agencies.

General lessons reinforced by use of these systems

One lesson learnt has been to carry out qualitative research before quantitative research, to identify the key drivers and motivations of customers and use their language to capture the phrases and insights, which then form the language of marketing and communications content and campaigns. This also helps a company to focus on the key parts of the marketing mix by concentrating on those parts of the mix that need developing or adjusting to meet the challenge of competition. It then rests on the skills of the creative part of the marketing team to develop examples or mock-ups of marketing and communications to share the intended thoughts of the marketer with the loyal customer. This becomes effective when a representative sample of customers are asked to opt in (under current data regulations) to be a permanent panel to be consulted with regularly.

Companies can plan their marketing research better by reviewing secondary research, which has become easier to find on the internet. This includes search patterns, for example, sourced from Google on the results of Google AdWords. This secondary data includes detailed consumer and client analysis, providing consumer profiles, which can be defined as similar or different by reviewing the traditional elements of customer classification, age, gender, education, lifestyle values, income, occupations, cultural habits and how they behave and engage with brands.

Changing views and use of information, marketing research and insight

Marketing and direct marketing techniques have a longer history than many people realise, originating with paper promotions, progressing to radio and TV promotions and then more recently to computer and iPad app and website promotions. As marketing databases and the internet have been developed, there have been significant developments in software and technology for cost-effective marketing.

In the first 75 years of the marketing research industry, the role and use of market and marketing research techniques has also been through many changes, developments and improvements. The technique started with door-to-door personal interviewing and has expanded to include online surveys and digital tools that provide data at the click of a link.

The significant timelines since the Doomsday Book for marketing, direct marketing, market research and customer insight are shown in Table 13.1.

Table 13.1 Key milestones in marketing research

	Key milestones in marketing, market research and customer insight
Pre 1900	
1000 BC	The first known direct marketing advert by a member of the Egyptian Royal household, offering a gold reward for the return of a runaway slave.
1434	Gutenberg creates the first low-cost mass printed literature in Europe.
1680	William Penn encourages investment in Pennsylvania using printed leaflets, posters and brochures.
1801	The first UK Census is completed, directed by Thomas Malthus.
1800s	A number of US businesses spend more than $1 million per year on direct mail.
1824	First opinion poll – conducted by the *Harrisburg Pennsylvanian*, PA, USA, predicts Andrew Jackson's victory as US president in the presidential elections.
1938	Journal of the Royal Statistical Society founded.
1843	Aaron-Montgomery Ward (1843–1913) founds both direct mail and direct marketing.
1851	William Farr classifies the population of London by both age and occupation.
1890	Herman Hollerith uses punch cards to speed up tabulation and analysis of the US Census.
1893	The definition 'standard deviation' in statistical analysis is created.
1900–39	
1923	AC Nielsen, the information, data and measurement firm, founded in Chicago.
1924	J Walter Thompson (now a WPP member company) develops a system for demographic profiling.
1931	Audit Bureau of Circulation (ABC) established.
1932	George Gallup creates his opinion poll tool.
1932	Rensis Likert develops the Likert scale, introducing psychology into market and social research.
1933	British Marketing Research Bureau established, the first research agency in the UK.
1937	Mass Observation established as an agency, using ethnography for the first time.

	Key milestones in marketing, market research and customer insight
1940–50	
1941	Robert K Merton and Paul Lazarsfield create the focus group as part of a radio research project.
1941	UK Central Statistical Office (now Office of National Statistics) includes all clothing categories and provides details of each type of men's and ladies' underwear by number and volume.
1942	AC Nielsen creates an index to measure radio audiences.
1946	Ernest Dichter founds the first Institute for Motivational Research, the first qualitative research agency.
1947	ESOMAR (European Society for Opinion and Marketing Research) is founded in Amsterdam.
1950–60	
1950s	Computers first arrive and are marketed using direct marketing techniques.
1952	AC Nielsen creates a machine-based rating system for TV audience measurement.
1953	UK Marketing Research Society established.
1956	UK National Readership Survey established.
1957	Charles Osgood's 'semantic space' method created for quantifying highly qualitative data.
1958	Jack Kilby and Robert Noyce co-invent the silicon microchip.
1958	*The International Journal of Market Research* founded.
1960–70	
1962	Bill Schlackman establishes the Institute for Motivational Research in London, using projective techniques for the first time in the UK.
1962	Profusion of marketing research agencies and specialist 'qualitative shops' established.
1963	*Market Research Abstracts* established by the Market Research Society.
1964	*The Journal of Marketing Research* established by the American Marketing Association.
1967	Lester Wunderman, considered the father of direct marketing, coins the phrase 'direct marketing' in a 1976 speech at the Massachusetts Institute of Technology.
1968	File-based systems manufactured: predecessor of databases. Data maintained in a flat file with the processing characteristics determined by common use of magnetic tape medium.
1968	Era of non-relational database started to 1980: A database which provides integrated and structured collection of stored operational data, which can be used or shared by application systems. Computerised databases are set up, including Codasyl, IMS and Sabre, which IBM set up specifically for American Airlines.
1969	Target Group Index established by BMRB.
1970–80	
1970s	1970 to present day: Era of relational database and database management systems (DBMSs). Based on relational calculus, shared collection of logically related data and a description of the data, designed to meet the information needs of an organisation.
1974–1997	Two major relational database system prototypes are created: Ingres, which was developed at UBC, and System R, created at IBM San Jose. Relational database management systems, or RDBMSs, becomes a recognised term.
1970	Jim Inglis and Doug Johnson design the computer for multivariate analysis.
1970	EF Codd publishes an important paper to propose the use of a relational database model.
1970	MAS and the Omnimas Survey established, a method of quantitative marketing research, where data on a wide variety of subjects is collected in the same interview.
1973	*The Journal of Business Research* established by Elsevier.
1974	*The Journal of Consumer Research* established by Oxford Academic Journals.

(Continued)

Table 13.1 (Continued)

	Key milestones in marketing, market research and customer insight
1975	Mark Abrams establishes the 'Quality of Life in Britain' survey, including the innovative use of 'subjective social indicators', to gain perceptions of social change. As research director at The Age Concern Institute of Gerontology, he also completes studies of living standards amongst people aged 65+.
1975	The computer-aided telephone interview (CATI) revolution established, with many agencies establishing CATI interviewing centres.
1975	Many marketing research agencies develop specific testing and tracking surveys.
1976	A new database model called entity-relationship, or ER, is proposed by P Chen, making it possible for designers to focus on data application instead of logical table structure.
1978	Enhanced competition following the Airline Deregulation Act of 1978 encourages airline marketing professionals to set up ways to reward repeat clients and drive brand loyalty. American Airlines is the first to offer free tickets in first class, upgrades for companions or discounted coach tickets. United Airlines takes less than a week to launch its Mileage Plus initiative. Other airlines follow in the ensuing months and years.
Mid 1970s	Credit card loyalty programs also emerge when the Discover card is introduced, to offer cash rebates to customers once a certain minimum level is spent. After Discover gains market share, Visa, Diner's Club and MasterCard respond with loyalty programs in the early 80s.
1979	Semiotics, the study of signs and symbols and their use or interpretation, established.
1980–90	
1980s	Structured Query Language, or SQL, becomes the standard query computer language. Relational database systems become a commercial success, and the introduction of the IBM PC results in the establishment of many new database companies.
1983	*Survey Magazine* established by The Market Research Society.
1984	UK Data Protection Legislation established.
1980 onwards	The growth of global agencies, such as TNS, MBL and GFK.
1980 onwards	Market and marketing research begins to be considered a valued service, as it starts to explore the value of a brand to a customer.
1989	Tim Berners-Lee creates HTML, leading to the emergence of the World Wide Web.
1980s	Direct mail boom, with mail order sales growing 10% per year, twice the average growth of retail stores.
1980s	Customer loyalty programs established, such as 'green stamp' programs where customers collect stamps from retailers, marking the first time retailers had loyalty initiatives to get the customer back into the store.
1998	*Qualitative Research – An International Journal* (QMR) launched.
1990–2000	
1990	Internet polling introduced.
1990s	New tools for software application development released, including Oracle Developer, PowerBuilder, VB and others. A number of tools for personal productivity, such as ODBC and Excel/Access, are also developed.
1990s	The advent of the Internet leads to exponential growth of the database industry, with client-server database systems used to access computer systems that contain legacy data.
1992	*The Journal of Consumer Psychology* established.

	Key milestones in marketing, market research and customer insight
1992	*Research Magazine* established by the Market Research Society.
1993	Mark Andreessen and Jim Clark found Netscape Communications with Netscape Navigator.
1994	The growth of medium-sized marketing research agencies, developing consultancy services on the impact of the research to the company commissioning a project.
1994	The emergence of data analysis and understanding of customer and consumer insight from consultancies.
1994 onwards	The publication of books in the Market Research Society Market Research in Practice Series, Kogan Page, including Stone *et al.* (2004), Birn (1994) and Callingham (2004).
1995	Qualitative research methods develop techniques to research behavioural and anthropological consumer behaviour.
1998	Data fusion, merging data from different sources, and data mining, the practice of examining large pre-existing databases, to generate new information.
Late 90s	Email and digital marketing introduced.
2000–present	
2001	Increasing use of the Internet as a source for sampling and a data collection method.
2003	Fred Reichheld invents the net promoter score.
2005	Ethnography rediscovered as researchers start to focus on consumer behaviour and engagement both online and in retail outlets.
2000s	Although the Internet industry experiences a decline in the early 2000s, database applications continue to grow, with new interactive applications developed for PDAs, point-of-sale transactions and consolidation of vendors.

Source: The authors

(We are grateful to Phyllis Vangelder, former editor of the *MRS Newsletter* and *MRS Survey Magazine*, for her advice on key milestones for the research industry, and John Kelly, managing director, Ceallaigh Associates Limited, and former president of ESOMAR, for giving permission to quote some of the key timelines from his presentation, 'A Little History, It's Not That New!', May 2011.)

Over the last decade, one of the most significant developments in marketing research has been the arrival of on-demand insights. As a result of the proportion of people owning smartphones, access to consumers has been transformed. Prior to the arrival of on-demand insights, managers of any brand wanting to conduct a large-scale consumer survey would need to work with a marketing research agency. Getting results often took a lot of time and money. Today, marketers can get answers to their burning questions in hours, not weeks or months, meaning important decisions can be always be grounded in reliable data. The development of consumer and business-to-business marketing research has been a major investment by both marketing and academia. Marketing research no longer needs to be a long and costly process. These new tools mean any person, in any brand, can ask their target customers questions and get actionable insights in the space of a few clicks. With so much power to know, some might say there has never been a more exciting time to be in marketing.

Today, databases are everywhere and are used to enhance our day-to-day life. From personal cloud storage to predicting the weather, many of the services we utilise today are likely to be due to databases. Trends are also emerging that focus on making powerful technology accessible to everyone via online database platforms built on a relational database, which gives users of any skill level the ability to create custom applications using the power of a relational database but with the simplicity of a point-and-click user interface.

Effective marketing research and customer insight

Marketing research and customer insight have proved themselves techniques which can reduce risk to make important decisions – they are no longer the domain of those who want to prove or disprove their own ideas. If marketing research and customer insight are analysed properly, then a company can understand how actual and potential consumers behave and plan business and marketing more accurately.

Applying marketing research and analysing it is only effective if it is relevant to the brand as it is performing. It requires a combination of various techniques, including:

- Regular personal interviews, one to one or online;
- Referring to trends in panel research;
- Ethnography and observations;
- Social media monitoring;
- Profile matching and customer journey monitoring;
- Insights emerge if the purchasing habits in relation to quantity and frequency are interpreted;
- An assessment of consumers' relationships with the brand and the degree to which they have a need for the brand;
- Consumers' interests and personal lives and how they use the brand in these scenarios;
- Media used and preferred and depended on for information relating to the brand;
- Consumers' satisfaction with the brand, which is a good measure of customer retention and the impact on the performance of the brand. This can be measured via straightforward customer satisfaction surveys, but increasingly, companies are using particular simplified versions of these, such as net promoter scores, with all their attendant problems of validity (Fisher and Kordupleski 2019).

Good marketing research and customer insight provide direction and feedback on success through methods identified subsequently.

Brand research

This focuses on ensuring that there is assessment and monitoring of those that engage with brands at all stages of their lifecycles. The use of information on branding is particularly helpful for:

- Brand awareness – which profiles or target consumers are aware of the brand;
- Brand penetration – what the proportions are of the different target consumers who are both buying and using brands;
- Brand loyalty – which of the target consumers are repeat customers;
- Brand perception and positioning – what the unique selling points of the brand are and how the brand can be differentiated from competing brands;
- Brand advocacy – now often measured through recommendation scores;
- Brand value – the absolute monetary contribution made by the brand to the total value of their group companies.

The value of marketing research and customer insight is that they determine the features and benefits that differentiate a brand from competing brands, but if data about customer behaviour and engagement is analysed professionally, the research is translated into consumer language for impactful propositions.

Customer insight has removed some of the uncertainty concerning the value of promotional expenditure, as there is now a clearer understanding that the information collected through marketing research is 100% valuable if:

- Research confirms the advertising message provides the desired result – increasing awareness, sales or brand switching;
- Data confirms the expenditure on the research provides a good return on the investment;
- Information confirms the good and bad aspects of a campaign.

Competitive analysis

Marketing research is increasingly being used to assess competitors' campaigns. Comparative analyses are developed, showing:

- The strengths and weaknesses of their brand;
- Whether competitors are taking a share of existing markets or entering new markets or market segments.

Developing insight

When data is collected, it is developed into insight, with actual and potential customers being clearly segmented, often using behaviour personas with similar characteristics – this helps to improve targeting and planning how to improve marketing performance. Then the work starts – the marketing team needs to review the segments and personalise campaigns – this is more than just cultural marketing in different parts of the world; it is behavioural marketing, which reassures customers they are related to the brand and that they can live the brand experience.

The consumer insight team then needs to develop the research with the defined consumer personas and complete further research on the product. The stages of the product life cycle that have proved to be successful to develop deeper insights, if the research is completed at the correct time, are:

- New product concept testing, which helps to confirm or delay the market or marketing opportunities for the defined new concept;
- Testing and learning about a prototype concept, to check that the value proposition is appealing to the target customer;
- Product introduction, monitoring the sales of the product at all stages of distribution, both through direct and online research monitoring and eye-tracking studies;
- Product revision, tweaking the benefits that are most important to the target customer in the different customer segments;
- Monitoring the customer journey, either via a retail store, via an app or online and additional online surveys;
- Tracking the same customers' behaviour on the company's website – clicking for information, clicking for purchase or clicking for referral to others.

Whether it is with algorithms, internal data or a mixture of internal and external data, consumer insights help refine the way companies communicate to their customers. Obtaining consumer insights is hard work but can pay off in the long run.

It is important to understand the difference between marketing research and customer insight, which can be summarised as follows:

- There is plenty of marketing research on brands, but there is much less actionable insight;
- Research delivers facts, knowledge and statistics;
- Insight delivers knowledge but focuses on the customer journey to help the marketer better understand consumers' behaviour and engagement with brands;
- There is a view that research departments deliver data and statistics, and customer insight departments deliver data plus narrative and storytelling – but this may relate to a handful of companies.

In conclusion, research tells the research manager *what* is happening through both qualitative and quantitative research – whereas insight tells the insight manager *why* it is happening by interpreting the competitive behaviour of a consumer and their loyalty to the brand. More importantly, insight helps companies understand what to do about consumer reactions. Insight gives direction to decide to take marketing actions to:

- Increase customer satisfaction;
- Develop customer loyalty and help boost the bottom line.

Both are equally important elements of any business, but, if marketing management creates solutions to problems, they need deeper and more actionable insight.

From knowing to forecasting

A customer-focused company invests in strategic, marketing and communications research, which assists management with planning, monitoring and reviewing the effectiveness of the marketing mix. The business is then in a good position to use this internal and external data for forecasting. This is the use of historic data to determine future market trends and sales to facilitate financial and business planning. This chapter does not investigate the technical content or application of forecasting techniques but suggests how forecasting techniques benefit the company, as follows.

Historical analogy

This is a sales forecasting technique in which past sales of products are used to predict the likely sales of future products – it can be used for all products or individual products if certain market activities are focused on.

Delphi method

This is a forecasting process framework based on the results of many surveys sent to a panel of experts or defined committed customers. The aim of the method is to clarify and expand on issues, identify areas of agreement or disagreement and then analyse the answers to the questions to find consensus. Delphi techniques can usually achieve satisfactory results in three rounds. This required number is a function of the number of participants, how much work is involved for them to develop their forecasts and their speed of responding. The Delphi method is very useful when there is no historical data from which to develop statistical models – when judgment or opinion, based on experience and study of market, industry or scientific developments, is the only basis for making informed projections. This technique tends to be used to develop long-range forecasts of product demand, new product sales projections and technological forecasting.

Time series analysis

The time-series forecasting technique tries to predict the future of a variable based on past data about it. For instance, sales figures collected for each of the past, say, four weeks can be used for the fifth week. The methods of time-series analysis focus on average, trend and seasonal influence characteristics of time series. The task of analysts is to try to replicate these characteristics while projecting future demand. The classical times series forecasting methods are:

- Autoregression;
- Moving average;
- Autoregressive moving average;
- Autoregressive integrated moving average;
- Seasonal autoregressive integrated moving-average;
- Seasonal autoregressive moving average with exogenous regressors;
- Vector autoregression;
- Vector autoregression moving average;
- Vector autoregression moving average with exogenous regressors;
- Simple exponential smoothing;
- Holt Winter's exponential smoothing.

Exponential smoothing

This is a technique to smooth out data to make forecasts, usually used for finance and economics rather than marketing, marketing research and customer insight. If the data has a time series with a clear pattern, it is possible to use moving averages – but if there is not a clear pattern, then it is appropriate to use exponential smoothing. These models tend to be very accurate, are easy to implement and are good for tests for accuracy.

Linear regression analysis

This is used to show or predict the relationship between two or more variables or factors. It is the most commonly used type of predictive analysis. Using a linear regression model will allow a company to discover whether a relationship between variables exists at all. But to understand what the relationship is, and whether one variable causes another, additional research and statistical analysis are needed.

Causal relationship forecasting

Causal methods are the most sophisticated forecasting tools. They are used when historical data are available and the relationship between the factor to be forecasted and other external and internal factors can be identified. Causal methods are the best for predicting turning points in demand and preparing long-range forecasts.

Choosing a forecasting method

A business uses forecasting in planning its inventory and production levels, as well as for new product development investment and resource planning. At the product level, it is inexpensive to develop forecasts using simple moving averages, weighted moving averages or exponential smoothing. These methods would apply to large bulk of standard inventory items carried by a firm. The choice of which of these three methods to use is based partly on market conditions. Moving averages weight each period the same, exponential smoothening weights the recent past more and weighted moving average allows the weights to be determined by the forecaster.

Increasing complexity of primary and secondary research

As research has been completed and published, and as the Internet has grown as a means of accessing published information faster, a variety of sources have developed. These are either articles from specific journals or newsletters, news information published on company websites or data published by government and commercial research organisations monitoring the different market sectors.

In the 1950s to 1970s, when marketing research was mainly used only by very large companies, there were few published sources of information. From the 1980s onwards, marketing research companies started to publish research data, so more secondary data was used, particularly to help to design primary research to focus on specific issues. Many companies were also encouraged to engage with both marketing and market research, particularly those who lacked internal expertise or budgets to commission consultants or agencies to support them with these techniques, through government and industry body support and guidance. In the United Kingdom and United States, particularly in the era of Margaret Thatcher and Ronald Reagan, their years running their respective countries became the decade in which the enterprise culture emerged as a central objective in government policies. In the United Kingdom, in 1985, Lord Young became Secretary of State for Employment, and he developed a programme with an enterprise message. In 1988, the Department of Trade and Industry launched a series of 'enterprise initiatives', which included the Enterprise Allowance Scheme and the Private and Business Enterprise programme. Lord Young said, 'Enterprise involves generating and taking ideas and putting them to work, taking decisions and talking responsibility, taking considered risks, welcoming change and helping to shape it and creating wealth'.

In the United States, the Reagan government introduced a series of executive orders to implement similar strategies and policies, which focused on free markets, limiting state control, reducing regulation and encouraging enterprise/entrepreneurship – so in the United Kingdom, there was a growth of privatisation and in the United States an anti-trust approach.

In the United Kingdom, in 1997, the Labour government continued to promote enterprise and in 2000 set up the Small Business Service, 'to drive progress towards the Government's aims, to make the UK the best place in the world to start and grow a business'. In 2010, a Back to Work Allowance scheme was also set up.

In the 1980s, the Department of Trade and Industry launched the Export Marketing Research Scheme, which in July 2016 was replaced as one of the sections of the Department of International Trade.

The significance of this government activity was that the enterprise culture was introduced to small and medium-sized businesses. The Thatcher Government Scheme ran a programme with the Chartered Institute of Marketing to send professional marketers to small and medium-sized enterprises to develop marketing plans, with the consultancy time funded by the government. This increased awareness amongst entrepreneurs and small business owners of secondary research, to help develop their plans and primary research as part of the programme to implement the agreed-upon strategies and actions.

Today the world of secondary research is driven by researchers' use of the Internet. But there are a variety of very important sources of information accessed by search engines to focus on the subjects being researched. The best sources of information are as shown in the following discussions.

Google

Google is now the natural main port of call to start secondary research searches, as it accesses the worldwide web. But accessing this information needs to done taking note of the following points:

- The information is published without being reviewed by any authoritative assessor;
- All research results tend to be disorganised and are not listed in any logical order or any degree of importance, with paid-for or sponsored listings prioritised;
- Google's algorithms rank the results by what it thinks you want to see, and the algorithm is constantly evolving, so advanced secondary researchers need to keep updated on changes in the algorithm;
- A text may be identified, but then a request is often given to the researcher to pay for a full text.

Subscriptions to specialist and university libraries

These sources of information tend to be relied on because:

- There is reassurance that the information has been reviewed by someone in authority;
- The research results are organised and in a chronological order;
- Results tend to be ranked by relevance;
- The information is accessed via a library, and there is likely to be free access to full texts.

Published research

The main sources of information that provide authoritative secondary research are published by management consultancies, market research agencies and online search resources and government departments and bodies as follows:

Management consultancies, for example:

- Bain & Co
- Harvard Business Review
- McKinsey & Co

Market research agencies and online search resources, for example:

- Euromonitor
- Fame

- Forrester
- Gartner
- GlobalData
- IDC Research
- JISC
- Kantar surveys
- Kantar Worldpanel
- MarketLine
- Mintel
- PrivCo
- Statista
- Timetric
- The Economist
- The Archive of Market and Social Research

Government and inter-government departments and bodies, for example:

- Eurostat
- International Monetary Fund Statistics
- Office of National Statistics
- OECD Statistics
- UN Statistics
- World Bank Statistics
- World Market Intelligence

Each of these organisations should to be reviewed by a researcher to identify information relevant to their research topic, subject or need to access data. A few are commented on for their importance in marketing, marketing research and customer insight.

Mintel

As one of the world's leading market intelligence agencies, Mintel's analysis of consumers, markets, new products and competitive landscapes provides a perspective on global and local economies. Its core services are as follows:

- Market intelligence: market analysis, competitive intelligence, product intelligence;
- Marketing research: research on trade, industry and government data, integrating them into meaningful sizing models and value forecasts for thousands of sectors worldwide;
- Product intelligence and competitive intelligence.

The company publishes reports from all market sectors, including food, retail, health and well-being, leisure and retail.

Kantar

Kantar is the world's leading data, insights and consulting company. It is a data- and evidence-based agency providing insights and actionable recommendations to companies, worldwide.

Kantar collects data digitally and shares insights in real time. The company uses AI and machine learning to make existing offerings faster and cheaper. Kantar inspires, informs and works with researchers to create strategies, such as:

- Improving brand awareness;
- Attracting more consumers;
- Increasing brand penetration;
- Financial success or growing peoples' confidence in public services.

The Archive of Market and Social Research

The Archive of Market and Social Research is both a history of UK marketing research and UK history through marketing research. Its aim is to liberate the rich data and commentary generated since the 1950s by the market and social research industry in the United Kingdom, making it available to be harnessed and applied for future social and commercial progress. For the first time, a comprehensive collection of historic research materials has been drawn together and held in one place, available free of charge. It demonstrates how the industry in the United Kingdom developed and the role played by significant individuals, organisations and companies. The development of techniques is to be catalogued and made available for reference and study. The Archive contains significant studies, technical developments, survey results and biographical details and key documents, including published papers, journals, books and newsletters covering the fields of UK market and social research over the last 70 years. The Archive includes:

- Longitudinal surveys covering commercial, social and attitudinal topics;
- Case studies showing how research has been used to effect commercial and social change;
- Published thinking on research techniques and their uses available from a single source;
- A long run of polling statistics;
- Historical documents charting the story of the market and social research industry.

Financial issues

Secondary research is either free from the Internet or is purchased in the form of datasets and reports from commercial research organisations. As for ad-hoc research, there are no clear guidelines for costing marketing research as part of a marketing budget, which covers other marketing mix expenditure, such as public relations and advertising and digital marketing costs.

Ad-hoc surveys

Ad-hoc surveys are purpose-built surveys. Their costs are calculated on the basis of the following:

- The time invested in the project;
- The design of the survey;
- The cost of preparing the sample information and designing the contact process;
- Administration of the survey;
- Analysis of the survey;
- The time invested in presenting results.

Definitive costs tend to be for:

- Published survey reports – which can be priced from £1,000 to £10,000;
- Online panels – which can be priced from £5,000 to £75,000.

The briefing and proposal process – how it has changed

The main constituents of a good brief are (Birn 1994):

- An introduction, providing background company and market information and the reasons for the project;
- A review of the sales, marketing or communications issues and the research hypothesis and how it relates to the situation or the reason for the research;
- Details of the target market to be researched and whether the company will provide the sample or specifications for the research company to work on when completing the sample for the interview;
- Comments on previous research data or statistics that might help in planning the research project. This includes the market universe, penetration of products in the market, awareness of the company and so on;
- Any specific information requirements and areas that need detailed probing and analysis;
- The schedule needed for the publication of results;
- The budget and financial specifications for the business relationship;
- Any data or company information that is required to illustrate the brief and what is contained in it.

This professional briefing approach to developing the business relationship with researchers acts as a firm basis for making comparisons between companies and deciding which company to commission to complete the project. It identifies the parameters to be used in judging which company to use. If a busy manager already knows which research company to use, the document is a detailed briefing, which lays out how the research project is to be carried out so all members of the marketing team are clear as to what can be achieved; it becomes the basis for a project management plan.

The final commitment to the business relationship has to come from the research company proposing to do the project. It must lay out how it will organise the project and how it will deliver the requirements to the commissioning company. However, even these documents should not be totally definitive. It is important for the research company that during the project there be the opportunity to develop and revise the ideas and methodology.

Today, the brief is often delivered verbally in meetings or via videocalls and short catch-ups – it is rare to see a clearly written brief! As there is also an increasing trend for brands managers to work with their internal research managers and insight managers, so the brief changes into a regular meeting between internal clients and suppliers.

Ethics, law and trust

Business, marketing and communications ethics are becoming more important, as data privacy needs to be a priority. Regulation for data protection has caused companies to operate in a more ethical manner and keep their customers reassured that they are conforming to the regulations. Some believe that ethical marketing and communications is not so much a marketing or communications strategy but more a philosophy which defines the standards of all marketing activities.

Before looking at the codes of practice for marketing and customer insight, it is important to review the guidelines for being ethical in marketing and communications from both the Chartered Institute of Marketing and the Market Research Society. These guidelines include:

- All marketing communications and its content must 'share the common standard to truth';
- Marketing professionals must abide by the highest standard of personal ethics;
- Advertising content must be distinguished from news content;
- Marketers must declare who endorses or sponsors their products;
- Consumers should be treated fairly based on the nature and the claims of the product benefit;
- The privacy of consumers should never be compromised, as there are laws for general data protection and processes for implementing them;
- Marketing must comply with regulations and standards established by governmental and professional organisations;
- Ethics should be reviewed and discussed honestly in all decisions about the marketing mix.

The reality of business is that decisions are taken very fast, and therefore a business may not be totally ethical in all its activities. But every company should now review risk and in this process have the opportunity to check on whether its activities are ethical. As there are codes of practice, it is now the role of the marketing manager to ensure that the marketing research, advertising, social media and analysis of marketing metrics are being completed ethically.

There are two essential sources of ethical information for marketing researchers, identified subsequently.

The General Data Protection Regulation (EU), 2016

This is a European Union law on data protection and privacy. It addresses the transfer of personal data outside the EU. The GDPR aims primarily to give control to individuals over their personal data. It superseded the Data Protection Directive.

GDPR (2016, Article 1) states:

1   This Regulation lays down rules relating to the protection of natural persons with regard to the free movement of personal data.
2   This Regulation protects fundamental rights and freedoms of natural persons and in particular their right to the protection of personal data.
3   The free movement of personal data within the Union shall be neither restricted nor prohibited for reasons connected with the protection of natural persons with regard to the processing of personal data.

There are seven principles for a business to conform to under GDPR:

- Lawfulness, fairness and transparency;
- Purpose limitation;
- Data minimisation;
- Accuracy;

- Storage limitation;
- Integrity and confidentiality (security);
- Accountability.

Standards and Guidelines of the UK Market Research Society

The Market Research Society (MRS) champions the highest ethical, commercial and methodological practices in market and social research. It provides 'fair regulation', clear guidance and practical advice, with the goal that research must flourish. The standards of the MRS are embodied in its Code of Conduct and other Guidelines.

The Code of Conduct of the Marketing Research Society (Market Research Society 2020) was created to support all those engaged in research, insight and data analytics in maintaining professional standards. The MRS Code of Conduct has been expanded to cover all professional activities being undertaken by MRS members and MRS company partners. The Code is also intended to reassure the general public and other interested parties that activities undertaken by MRS members and MRS company partners are carried out in a professional and ethical manner. The MRS Guidelines help businesses interpret and apply the MRS Code of Conduct and provide advice on best practice.

MRS Guidelines include the following:

- MRS regulations for the use of predictive diallers, produced to aid MRS members in applying Sections 128 to 130 of the Communications Act 2003, which give the Office of Communications (Ofcom) powers to take action against persons or companies who persistently misuse electronic communications networks or services in any way that causes or is likely to cause unnecessary annoyance, inconvenience or anxiety;
- MRS regulations for using research techniques for non-research purposes, which set out the legal and ethical responsibilities of MRS Members and MRS Company Partners working outside the scope of traditional research projects;
- MRS regulations for administering incentives and free prize draws, which are binding on all MRS Members and MRS Company Partners. In cases where additional legal requirements apply the most stringent set of rules must be applied;
- Data Protection and Research: Guidance for MRS members and company partners, designed to help researchers understand the impact of the General Data Protection Regulation and Data Protection Act 2018 on research policies and practices. It was developed through informal consultation with the Information Commissioner's Office (ICO);
- Guidelines on the Privacy and Electronic Communications Regulations, covering use of unsolicited emails and text messages and require the consent for the use of 'cookies' by websites;
- Guidelines and frequently answered questions on the operation of the Freedom of Information Act, including how to deal with requests and how to help protect sensitive commercial information.

There are also three joint guidelines:

- Chartered Institute of Public Relations, MRS, Royal Statistical Society Guidelines for using statistics in Communications;
- MRS, The Local Authorities Research and Intelligence Association (LARIA) Guidelines for using surveys for consultation;
- MRS/Interviewer Quality Control Guidelines for Interviewer Health and Safety.

Research in practice guidelines include:

- Guidance on polling and insider dealing;
- Advice for non-researchers on how to interpret opinion polls;
- Guidelines for business-to-business research;
- Guidelines for mystery shopping research;
- Guidelines for online research;
- Guidelines for qualitative research;
- Guidelines for questionnaire design;
- Guidelines for researching children and young people;
- Viewing facilities – commitments to participants.

Conclusion

The evolution of marketing research and insight in organisations has developed into a model for knowledge management. This model depends on a company having a marketing information system managing internal and external information. Consumer and shopper insight has evolved by analysing both types of information, as companies have focused on how it provides the best insight into customer behaviour.

A consumer insight-led company is likely to be one that combines data and information from transactions, published marketing research and intelligence collected by the sales team and management at trade shows and conferences and applies it to marketing planning from the most strategic to the most operational level. The company's insight team needs to understand the marketing strategy and plan and planning and implementation processes well enough to create insight from data and use it to support those processes and be involved in the collection and interpretation of data resulting from interactions with customers as a result of the implementation of marketing policy, to provide input concerning whether the marketing actually worked.

The changes in technologies used to gather and interpret data have helped managers to interpret all types of data and the marketing research and customer insight department to report it and present it effectively. Effective reporting is now done to a high standard, as most marketing information systems have 'dashboards' to monitor key measures. Marketing research and customer insight have become more professional, and their development continues apace.

Issues for marketers for using market research and customer insight

In Stone *et al.* (2004, p. 4), the scene is set for the professional contribution of consumer insight:

> Professionally, the domain of consumer insight stretches from market research into database marketing, into customer service, into any function that deals directly with consumers – and into some that do not, but still have a strong interest in how consumers are managed, such as supply chain management.

The key issue for marketers is to use data to plan and monitor every aspect of this domain, but many marketers still find it a challenge to identify and influence what drives customers' attitudes and behaviour. They also have:

- Lack of confidence in market research, as they may not have been trained in market research techniques and may not know how to interpret research findings effectively;

- A belief that there is lack of trust in what consumers say, as consumers rely on their memories to answer surveys;
- Concern about Internet transactions, as they were only a small proportion of consumer purchase and survey responses before the pandemic and so were not considered totally representative of consumers' engagement with a brand.

As a result, the re-emergence of ethnographic research has given marketers increased confidence in data, as consumers' individual behaviour is 'shadowed'. But many marketers have also questioned the value of this technique, as the consumer is observed by the researcher while the data is being collected.

As we continue to use traditional market research techniques, clearly the example of companies such as Unilever, BSkyB, Microsoft and many other global companies has added real-time experience tracking (RET) to the collection of consumer data. Insights from real-time experience can be acted on immediately, which benefits marketers in product launches or marketing campaigns in what are now fast-changing, very competitive markets. RET covers the complete customer journey, generating data useful for every customer-facing part of a business – marketing planning, marketing communications, public relations, direct marketing, customer operations and customer service delivery.

Examples of real-time experiences are:

- VoIP (voice over Internet protocol);
- Videoconference applications;
- Online gaming;
- E-commerce transactions;
- Online chatting;
- Instant messaging.

The issues for marketers for using market research and consumer and customer insight in the future are:

- Meaningful analysis and reporting – to be able to turn data into impact stories, which provide feedback on customer journeys, identifying trends to plan for change;
- Changing technology – ensuring fast-changing hardware and software continue to provide reliable data;
- Management of all data in the business – making sense of data collected at the business and market's data points and how this information relates to customer journeys being monitored;
- Using social media and mobile technologies for data analysis and being able to react fast and make changes if necessary, whether the feedback is positive or negative;
- Getting consumers to both opt into surveys and also receive information from businesses, as privacy has become regulated to manage the relationship of a consumer with a brand.

But the main challenge for businesses is to have the confidence to take all their decisions based on better insight into customer behaviour. Post the pandemic, it is hoped that this challenge will be met by those companies that recognise they need to change the way that they deliver their products and services, knowing that consumer and customer behaviour has had to change and adapt to a new way of life.

References

Birn, R., 1994. *Using Market Research to Grow Your Business*. London: Pitman Publishing.

Callingham, M., 2004. *Market Intelligence*. London: Kogan Page.

Fisher, N.I. and Kordupleski, R.E., 2019. Good and bad market research: A critical review of net promoter score. *Applied Stochastic Models in Business and Industry*, 35(1), 138–151.

GDPR (www.gdpr-info.eu), 2016. *Article 1, Subject-Matter and Objectives* [online]. Available from: https://gdpr-info.eu/art-1-gdpr/ [Accessed 24 September 2020].

Market Research Society, 2020. *Code of Conduct* [online]. Available from: www.mrs.org.uk/pdf/mrs%20code%20of%20conduct%202014.pdf#:~:text=The%20Code%20of%20Conduct%20is%20designed%20to%20support,and%20ethical%20manner.%205%20MRS%20Regulations%20and%20Guidelines [Accessed 24 September 2020].

Schneider, J. and Hall, J., 2011. Why most product launches fail. *Harvard Business Review*, April [online]. Available from: https://hbr.org/2011/04/why-most-product-launches-fail [Accessed 25 September 2020].

Stone, M., Bond, A. and Foss, B., 2004. *Consumer Insight, How to Use Data and Market Research to Get Closer to Your Customer*. London: Kogan Page.

PART III

Techniques

14

BRAIN'S VALUATION NETWORKS AND CONSUMERS' NEUROSCIENCE METHODS IN THE FUZZY FRONT-END INNOVATION PROCESS

Jyrki Suomala and Pekka Berg

Summary

This chapter explains how analysis of the structure and activities of the human brain can help develop our understanding of consumers' responses to marketing actions. It explains how the brain's semantic pointers (SPs) are products of binding of sub-representations. The valuation network is a SP and fuzzy front-end (FFE) innovation process that can be reinforced by taking it into account. Neuroscientific methods are presented from the FFE point of view. IT identifies that confidence between stakeholders is the key for success when applying neuroscience and how to achieve that confidence.

Introduction

There is growing evidence that the human brain is a complex system that considers the flow of internal and surrounding environments by using distributed mental representations. The semantic pointer (SP) model describes mental representations in terms of the activities of large numbers of individually spiking neurons (Blouw *et al.* 2016). By SPs, people can form a multimodal coherent experience about surrounding events and behave in optimal ways in the constantly changing environment.

The SP of a specific concept contains a wide range of information in various modalities, such as verbal, visual, tactual and emotional (Fernandino *et al.* 2016). For example, the concept "smartphone" includes both low- and high-level features. Colour, shape, sound, emotion, the feeling of motion and even the feeling of a vibration alarm or screen-touch are examples of low-level features of a smartphone, while brand, the feeling of uniqueness, aesthetics, modernity and functionality are examples of high-level features of a smartphone (Pombo and Velasco 2019). When a human being creates the mental representation of a smartphone, SP maintains "the movie in his/her head" about a smartphone. The richness of human concepts suggests that it is unlikely that all of the aspects of a concepts are actively represented at the same time (Eliasmith 2013).

The main processing mechanism in the brain is the convolution, which helps limit both the memory and processing requirements for building mental representation (Eliasmith 2013). It uses high-dimensional vectors to store structured information and algebraic operations to manipulate these representations. By using convolution, the high dimensionality of mental representations does not lead to an unlimited explosion of dimensions as representations get more complicated (Stewart and Eliasmith 2013).

The valuation network in the brain is one of the most important networks from the decision point of view. This network computes the necessary information by convolution (Chib *et al.* 2009; Levy and Glimcher 2012). The valuation network is a SP, which uses information from different brain areas and acts as the gatekeeper for an individual's choice, constantly computing, consciously and subconsciously, values for different items in the human's environment.

People in companies and other organisations make many decisions every day (Iyengar 2011). One of the most critical strategic decisions is how much a company should invest in a new offering, that is, the innovation process. Despite an improved understanding of the innovation process, game-changing offerings remain hard to come by (Bouquet *et al.* 2018).

The brain's valuation network

In the current high-choice market environment, consumers are exposed to diverse content and messages every day, so it is essential for innovators to understand how consumers compare different offerings and make decisions. We use the term "offering" in this article to include products and services. The growing evidence from decision neuroscience shows that there are general valuation networks in the brain, which compute the subjective value for different offerings as well as executing behaviour in favour of the most valuable items. According to this view (Levy and Glimcher 2012; McNamee *et al.* 2013), the values of offerings are presented and processed in the networks formed mainly from the medial prefrontal cortex (MPFC) and the striatum. The activation change in this valuation network has been shown to correlate reliably with goods' values using a wide class of objects, including biological needs like food (Levy and Glimcher 2012) and clothes (Lim *et al.* 2013) and abstract cultural values like money (Glimcher and Fehr 2014) and charitable donations (Hare *et al.* 2010).

The activation changes in the valuation network during the presentation of a stimulus predict behaviourally observed decision-making and choice (Berkman and Falk 2013). For example, a sunscreen study showed that the neural signals in the MPFC, when subjects are exposed to persuasive messages concerning sun exposure, can predict changes in sunscreen use one week following the experiment (Falk *et al.* 2016). Unexpectedly, these neural signals in the MPFC predicted the variability in behaviour better than self-reported measures like intentions and attitudes measures by themselves. Moreover, MPFC activation when subjects were exposed to antismoking messages predicted quitting from smoking one month after initial fMRI better than traditional behavioural measurements (Falk *et al.* 2011). Therefore, activation of the critical valuation network in the brain serves as an indirect marker of future behaviour change and provides information that is not conveyed by participants' self-reports (Falk *et al.* 2012).

Consistent with these studies, a recent study (Kühn *et al.* 2016) showed that the mean brain activation change in a small group of consumers during a fMRI experiment predicted real sales in a supermarket. So, incorporating neural data with self-reported measures provides additional information for developing predictive models and gives new opportunities for testing of innovative concepts with users and consumers as early as possible.

It is difficult for humans to express subjective value only on a linguistic level, because valuation consideration requires several cognitive operations, many of which are subconscious (Venkatraman *et al.* 2015). This applies especially to innovative products, which have high market failure rates (Hauser *et al.* 2006), because they often have high risks resulting from uncertainty concerning consumer acceptance (Joshi and Sharma 2004). Over half of new products fail commercially (Iyengar 2011).

The development of decision neuroscience gives new opportunities to solve the problems that innovators face when they try to understand consumer preferences (Ariely and Berns 2010; Venkatraman *et al.* 2015). Over the last decade, there is growing evidence that neuroimaging can reveal unique information about consumer preferences.

The process of innovation

Innovations are an important part of company operations and are key to the dynamic growth of enterprises and profit creation (Suomala *et al.* 2006; Taatila *et al.* 2006). The innovation process starts with a novel idea, continuing to an idea implementation. It should be profitable from commercial or peoples' welfare points of view (Taatila *et al.* 2006). Companies usually organise innovation processes in two parts, fuzzy front-end (FFE) innovation and its implementation (Berg *et al.* 2009, 2008). The innovation process often includes pretesting new offerings con-cepts, mock-ups, prototypes or marketing campaign ideas. Many behavioural methods have been developed for this, ranging from interviews and focus groups to self-reported measures such as recall, liking, purchase intent and surveys (Venkatraman *et al.* 2015). However, predict-ing consumers' preferences in response to new offerings remains a difficult task (Falk *et al.* 2016). Consumers cannot fully articulate their preferences when asked for them explicitly (Boksem and Smidts 2015). The reason for this is that many important mental processes occur subcon-sciously (Dijksterhuis *et al.* 2006), limiting consumers' ability to predict their own behaviour and to accurately reproduce their mental states by verbal or written self-reports (Falk *et al.* 2016).

While neuroscientific methods have been seen as essential tools in the development of an advertisements and marketing campaigns in the business-to-consumer contexts (Morin 2011), their applications in the business-to-business context also have potential commercial benefits (Ariely and Berns 2010). So, neuroscientific methods are suitable tools for understanding how people behave in both different contexts.

Brain responses to new offerings in valuation networks are likely to reflect subjective valu-ation and may yield measurements that are more confident than traditional self-reports (Ariely and Berns 2010; Berkman and Falk 2013). The act of rating something by using behavioural methods requires metacognition – the brain response during the consumption of the offers – and the latter may prove superior to rating approaches. In the high-choice marketing environ-ment, companies try to reach consumers by producing popular new offerings and by advertising them using messages drawing attention to attractive features.

Integration of consumers into the innovation process in general (Gassmann *et al.* 2010) and especially by using neuroscientific tools (Kopton and Kenning 2014) has been become increas-ingly essential. Decision neuroscience tools can provide less biased data on consumers' prefer-ences, giving accurate information for innovation processes and successful marketing campaigns.

The neuroscientific methods essential to innovation

Modern neurophysiological tools allow innovators to measure consumers' brain activation pat-terns of the valuation network relating to offering concepts when a consumer participates in experiments, making it possible to study how different features of new products and services correlate to the brain's valuation network activation and the relationship between messages and consumers' behavioural changes. Using neuroimaging tools – functional magnetic resonance imaging (fMRI), electroencephalography (EEG) and functional near-infrared spectroscopy (fNIRS) – it is possible to measure the hemodynamic response related to neural activity in the valuation network when subjects are exposed to persuasive messages. These non-invasive tools measure the hemodynamic response to the cerebral cortex (Naseer and Hong 2013).

While fMRI can measure the hemodynamic activation from the whole brain, fNIRS only detects signals from the cerebral cortex. Because fNIRS is more practical to use than EEG or fMRI, it is a promising tool to measure brain activation in the real-life context, when a participant uses a computer or walks in a shopping centre (Naseer *et al.* 2014). However, this technology is new, and there are only few scientific studies using it. fMRI, EEG and fNIRS are most promising tools to accurately measure activation of the brain's valuation system, so this chapter does not focus on other biometric methods – for this, see Ruff and Huettel (2014) and Suomala (2018a, 2018b).

Functional magnetic resonance imaging (fMRI)

With fMRI, it is possible to measure the blood oxygen level-dependent (BOLD) signal, which is a measure of the ratio of oxygenated to deoxygenated haemoglobin (Ashby 2011). It uses the principle that active brain areas consume more oxygen and sugar than inactive areas. Neural responses when participants are processing messages or choosing different options can be measured, and it is possible to infer how the brain compounds several neurocognitive networks simultaneously (Falk *et al.* 2013). fMRI has been used to study several different mental processes, such as conformity (Klucharev *et al.* 2009), responsiveness to social tagging of stimuli (Plassmann *et al.* 2008) and other persuasive inputs (Berns and Moore 2012; Falk *et al.* 2016; Kühn *et al.* 2016).

The constantly growing scientific knowledge about the brain's architecture and mechanisms is mostly based on scientific research using fMRI. Information from fMRI is reliable and valid from a scientific perspective (Genevsky *et al.* 2017). Understanding the mechanisms and other properties of the brain's valuation network has been based on studies using fMRI. However, although using fMRI allows unique and reliable information about consumers' valuation networks to be obtained, a limitation of fMRI from the innovation perspective is that it can be difficult to create naturalistic situations in the fMRI measurement environment.

Electroencephalography (EEG)

Neural responses change the electrical potential of cell membranes and can produce action potentials. When many neurons express similar action potentials and share similar spatial locations, then the coherent electrical current can be detected by electrodes positioned on the scalp (Ruff and Huettel 2014). The EEG can measure this electrical current. Typical EEG studies record changes in action potential using electrodes positioned on the scalp. The electrical action potential reflects changes in the group of the neurons when an individual participates in an experiment (Ruff and Huettel 2014).

The conventional way to interpret the electrical potential is to classify commonly observed signals into frequency bands, that is, activity. Frequency bands describe how many action potentials the neuron produces in one second (Hertz = Hz). Delta activity (4 Hz or less) is typical in dreamless sleep. Theta activity (4 to 8 Hz) is associated with internally focused information processing. Alpha activity (8 to 12 Hz) is dominant when the brain is in a relaxed state, for example, when eyes are closed. Beta activity (13 to 30 Hz) is associated with active attention, alertness and has also been found to be associated with reward processing. Gamma activity (over 30 Hz) is associated with emotional processing and learning (Boksem and Smidts 2015; Genco *et al.* 2013).

EEG is used to measure the coherence and power of brain-wave frequencies. Coherence measures the consistency of brain-wave frequencies across different regions of the brain, whereas power measures the degree of activity within a particular frequency band over a specified period of time (Genco *et al.* 2013). EEG provides access to the electrical activity of the brain and is a common choice for scientific laboratories and companies involved in innovation and decision neuroscience.

High beta activity (16–18 Hz) during viewing of a movie trailer has been shown to be related to a high stated preference for that movie, and a cluster of EEG activity in the gamma range (60–100Hz) was a significant predictor of U.S. box office. The higher this gamma activity in participants during trailer viewing, the more box office money the movie generated (Boksem and Smidts 2015). So, based on a small sample's brain activation profile during movie trailer viewing, it is possible to predict the success of movies.

EEG machinery is moderately expensive and allows relatively naturalistic viewing conditions. Participants can sit in a comfortable chair and view a large screen with high-quality audio (Boksem and Smidts 2015). However, a limitation of EEG measurement compared to fMRI and fNIRS is that the EEG cannot localise activity inside the brain with the same precision as fMRI and fNIRS. The EEG signal is attenuated greatly by the skull and the scalp, and the activity recorded by scalp electrodes could be generated by any of an infinite number of potential sources (Ruff and Huettel 2014). Brain networks below the cortex have an essential role in human behaviour (Levy and Glimcher 2012), but the EEG cannot capture these signals precisely.

Functional near-infrared spectroscopy (fNIRS)

Although the application of fNIRS to decision neuroscience is still rare, it has good potential for applicability in both experimental and in field studies. fNRIS is a non-invasive optical brain imaging technique that investigates cerebral blood flow (CBF) as well as the hemodynamic response in a brain region during neural activity (Jackson and Kennedy 2013). Previous studies have demonstrated that, as with fMRI, the fNIRS method is a valid measurement for cortical activations (Ernst *et al.* 2013). Its weakness is that it cannot measure activation patterns of subcortical areas. The striatum is an essential component of the valuation network, so future studies are needed to clarify whether the signals from the MPFC are a sufficient indicator of consumer's subjective preferences, that is, the need valuation network.

Jöbsis (1977) describes how the optical measurement for the cerebral hemodynamic response known as near-infrared spectroscopy (NIRS) is performed by the irradiation of near-infrared light into a participants' head and its scattering positions. Near-infrared light (650–950 nanometres [nm]) passes through biological tissue and can non-invasively illuminate reliably 2 to 3 centimetres of the tissue. In this way, fNIRS opens an "optical window" to the human brain (Jöbsis-vanderVliet 1999; Kopton and Kenning 2014). It has been suggested that oxy- and deoxy-haemoglobin (HHb) are the main absorbers, so that changes in oxy- and deoxy-HHb can be measured, allowing for reliable quantification of neural activity (Jackson and Kennedy 2013). In fNIRS, laser-emitted diodes are near-infrared light sources placed directly onto a participant's scalp. Diodes send a "banana-shaped" form to the detectors, called optodes. The precision of measurement depends on the distance between the source and the detector.

Human decision-making has studied using both stationary and wireless mobile fNIRS. In one stationary fNIRS study, part of the valuation network (anterior lateral orbitofrontal cortex – part of MPFC) showed stronger activation in terms of increased oxygenated HHb while approaching attractive stimuli compared to avoiding pictures (Ernst *et al.* 2013). In other studies (Shimokawa *et al.* 2009, 2012), investors' decision-making processes were investigated. These studies showed that the orbitofrontal cortex (OFC) is sensitive to loss prediction, while the MPFC is sensitive to reward prediction. MPFC activations measured by fNIRS have been found to have strong associations with participants' subjective product preferences (Luu and

Chau 2009). These studies confirm the results of previous fMRI-studies (Chib *et al.* 2009; Levy and Glimcher 2012), that the valuation networks in the brain have an essential role in human decision-making and choices.

Wireless mobile fNIRS has been applied successfully. Holper *et al.* (2014) found that increased activity of the lateral prefrontal cortex is related to high-risk decisions and reduced activation in this area with low-risk decisions. Another study – not directly related to decision-making – showed that vehicle deceleration requires more brain activation in the prefrontal cortex than does vehicle acceleration (Yoshino *et al.* 2013).

Although mobile wireless fNIRS technology is still new, these prototype studies generally show interesting new tendencies, providing a foundation for applications of this technique as a potential measurement methodology for innovation studies. Studies in decision neuroscience have shown that the activation patterns of the brain's valuation system – measured mainly by fMRI – predict real behavioural changes in only a sample of participants rather than at population level, so an important future research question is whether fNRIS data predicts participants' behaviour. Different prior studies have demonstrated that, compared to fMRI, fNIRS is a reliable and valid way to measure cortical activations (Ernst *et al.* 2013; Kopton and Kenning 2014). fNIRS is cheaper and easier to use than fMRI and may open new opportunities for the applications in FFE innovation.

Reinforcing innovativeness with neuroscientific methods during the FFE innovation process

FFE innovation is creative and uncertain and includes many design processes (Berg *et al.* 2009). Typically, innovators describe functions and other requirements of new offerings based on their intuition and expertise. Neuroscientific tools give us the opportunity to measure consumers response from the human brain valuation network point of view.

The creative process includes almost endless possibilities, and designers can manipulate things in many ways. So, experts in FFE innovation should use their intuition in these creative processes. It is important for them to use as much scientific evidence as possible during this process (Lilienfeld *et al.* 2013; Pfeffer and Sutton 2006a). Neuroscientific tools can help them to use their intuition in more effective ways (Ariely and Berns 2010). New knowledge about human decision-making and its association with the brain's valuation network can have a transformative impact on creative industries (Noble *et al.* 2019).

Neuroimaging methods allow testing of new concepts created during FFE throughout the development process, predicting how consumers will react while validating the gut instincts of a companies' creative agency team. This neuroscientific insight supports the creation of distinctive imagery to ensure to the customers (Noble *et al.* 2019).

Figure 14.1 shows how neuroscientific tools can reinforce creative processes during FFE innovation. The creative team first creates many different concepts (prototypes, new radical features for old goods etc.) based on their expertise and intuition. When perceptive (video, picture, drawings, 3D model) or tactile forms are created, the neuro team can help the creative team choose the best possible concepts for development. It is important that the creative and neuro teams be confident in each other and work together to find the concepts that fit best with consumer preferences, as measured by neuroscientific tools from brain's valuation network. A company can choose a sample of consumers for a neurofocus group from its customer database or from the non-customer population, depending on the purpose of the creative process. If the goal is to strengthen the loyalty of existing customers, the company's own database may be a good source for the sample. However, if the goal is sales to new customers, the sample for

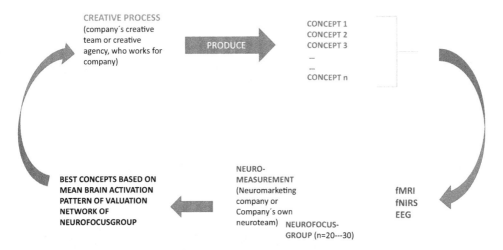

Figure 14.1 The application of the neuroscientific methods during FFE innovation

Source: The authors

the neurofocus group should be selected from outside the company's customer database. Of course, two samples can be tested in the same study to increase understanding of loyal and new consumers.

When the sample is ready, the neuro team usually invites participants to the neuromeasurement. In the measurement, a participant sees pictures, videos or audios relating to concepts produced by creative team. A typical decision neuroscience experiment by fMRI lasts one hour. During this time, one can present 30–40 different concepts for one participant, depending on the protocol (Suomala *et al.* 2012). By using fMRI, one can get reliable signals from all parts of the valuation networks and so give companies unique and reliable information about the potential success of concepts. The limitation of fMRI is that one cannot interact with concepts in real situations (touch, use etc.), as the measurement is based on visual and auditive information about concepts.

New EEG and fNRIS equipment operate via wireless, so it is possible to use these tools in naturalistic environments like shopping centres. The limitation of EEG is that it is hard to get reliable signals from the valuation network, which is the most important source of human preference. By using fNRIS, it is possible to measure part of valuation network, especially the activation of MPFC.

After neuromeasurement, the neuro team presents the results to the company's creative team. Based on this information, the team decides how to continue. It is possible to continue to the development process or use the neuroinformation in an iterative way until the best concepts are found.

The biggest barrier for companies is that it is difficult to understand the benefits of scientific evidence as part of companies' processes (Lilienfeld *et al.* 2013; Pfeffer and Sutton 2006a, 2006b). Thus, the first step toward neuroscience evidence-based innovations will be that decision neuroscience experts educate creative agency staff on the neuroscience and its applications. After that, it is beneficial to run some pilot experiments with the creative agency and neuro team. Then it is possible to begin use these tools in daily based in companies' FFE innovation processes.

Conclusion

The brain's valuation network is the semantic pointer (Eliasmith 2013), which computes total values for different items in the individuals' inner and outer environment. Neuroscientific studies have found that the brain's valuation network assign values to goods using a common currency (Hytönen 2011; Levy & Glimcher 2012; McNamee *et al.* 2013). This brain-as-prediction approach has found that value-encoding areas in the MPFC and in the striatum represent coherently the value of nearly all stimulus types on a common scale (Falk *et al.* 2013; Levy & Glimcher 2012). These brain activation changes during a good presentation in the experiments predict behaviourally observed decision-making and choice.

Decision neuroscience no longer faces critical technological barriers. The critical barrier is the difficulty different stakeholders have in collaborating and trusting each other during the innovation process. When creative people in companies understand the benefits of decision neuroscience during new concept development, they also begin to trust neuroexperts and learn to apply objective neuroscientific data to make better decisions. They begin to see neuroscientific data as an essential source to produce valuable information about consumers' hidden preferences. The hope is that innovators can apply these ideas in their own work in order to improve prediction of consumers' behaviour.

References

Ariely, D. and Berns, G., 2010. Neuromarketing: The hope and hype of neuroimaging in business. *Nature Review: Neuroscience*, 11 284–292. https://doi.org/10.1038/nrn2795.

Ashby, F., 2011. *Statistical Analysis of fMRI Data*. Cambridge, MA: MIT Press.

Berg, P., Pihlajamaa, J., Poskela, J., Lempiala, T., Haner, U. and Mabogunje, A., 2008. *Measurement of the Innovation Front End: Viewpoint of Process, Social Environment and Physical Environment*. PIC-MET'08–2008 Portland International Conference on Management of Engineering and Technology, Presented at the Technology, IEEE, Cape Town, South Africa, 1112–1120. https://doi.org/10.1109/PICMET.2008.4599721.

Berg, P., Pihlajamaa, J., Poskela, J., Lempiala, T., Haner, U. and Mabogunje, A., 2009. *Balanced Innovation Front End Measurement: Discontinuous Innovation Approach*. PICMET'09–2009 Portland International Conference on Management of Engineering & Technology, Presented at the Technology, IEEE, Portland, OR, 746–753. https://doi.org/10.1109/PICMET.2009.5262065.

Berkman, E. and Falk, E., 2013. Beyond brain mapping: Using neural measures to predict real-world outcomes. *Current Directions in Psychological. Science*, 22, 45–50. https://doi.org/10.1177/0963721412469394.

Berns, G.S. and Moore, S.E., 2012. A neural predictor of cultural popularity. *Journal of Consumer Psychology*, 22, 154–160. https://doi.org/10.1016/j.jcps.2011.05.001.

Blouw, P., Solodkin, E., Thagard, P. and Eliasmith, C., 2016. Concepts as semantic pointers: A framework and computational model. *Cognitive Science*. 40, 1128–1162. https://doi.org/10.1111/cogs.12265.

Boksem, M.A.S. and Smidts, A., 2015. Brain responses to movie trailers predict individual preferences for movies and their population-wide commercial success. *Journal of Marketing Research*, 52, 482–492. https://doi.org/10.1509/jmr.13.0572.

Bouquet, C., Barsoux, J.-L. and Wade, M., 2018. Bring your breakthrough ideas to life. *Harvard Business Review*, 96, 102–113.

Chib, V., Rangel, A., Shimojo, S. and O'Doherty, J.P., 2009. Evidence for a common representation of decision values for dissimilar goods in human ventromedial prefrontal cortex. *Journal of Neuroscience*, 29, 12315–12320. https://doi.org/10.1523/JNEUROSCI.2575-09.2009.

Dijksterhuis, A., Bos, M., Nordgren, L. and van Baaren, R., 2006. On making the right choice: The deliberation-without-attention effect. *Science*, 311, 1005–1007. https://doi.org/10.1126/science.1121629.

Eliasmith, C., 2013. *How to Build a Brain: A Neural Architecture for Biological Cognition*. Oxford: Oxford University Press. DOI: 10.1093/acprof:oso/9780199794546.001.0001.

Ernst, L., Plichta, M., Lutz, E., Zesewitz, A.K., Tupak, S., Dresler, T., Ehlis, A. and Fallgatter, A., 2013. Prefrontal activation patterns of automatic and regulated approach-avoidance reactions – a functional near-infrared spectroscopy (fNIRS) study. *Cortex*, 49, 131–142. https://doi.org/10.1016/j.cortex. 2011.09.013.

Falk, E.B., Berkman, E.T., Whalen, D. and Lieberman, M., 2011. Neural activity during health messaging predicts reductions in smoking above and beyond self-report. *Health Psychology*, 30, 177–185. https:// doi.org/10.1037/a0022259.

Falk, E.B., Morelli, S.A., Welborn, B.L., Dambacher, K. and Lieberman, M.D., 2013. Creating buzz: The neural correlates of effective message propagation. *Psychological Science*, 24, 1234–1242. https://doi. org/10.1177/0956797612474670.

Falk, E.B., O'Donnell, M.B. and Lieberman, M.D., 2012. Getting the word out: Neural correlates of enthusiastic message propagation. *Frontiers in Human Neuroscience*, 6, Art 313. https://doi.org/10.3389/ fnhum.2012.00313.

Falk, E.B., O'Donnell, M.B., Tompson, S., Gonzalez, R., Dal Cin, S., Strecher, V., Cummings, K.M. and An, L., 2016. Functional brain imaging predicts public health campaign success. *Social, Cognitive and Affective Neuroscience*, 11(2), 204–214. https://doi.org/10.1093/scan/nsv108.

Fernandino, L., Binder, J.R., Desai, R.H., Pendl, S.L., Humphries, C.J., Gross, W.L., Conant, L.L. and Seidenberg, M.S., 2016. Concept representation reflects multimodal abstraction: A framework for embodied semantics. *Cerebral Cortex*, 26(5), 2018–2034. https://doi.org/10.1093/cercor/bhv020.

Gassmann, O., Enkel, E. and Chesbrough, H., 2010. The future of open innovation. *R&D Management*, 40(3), 213–221. https://doi.org/10.1111/j.1467-9310.2010.00605.x.

Genco, S., Pohlmann, A. and Steidl, P., 2013. *Neuromarketing for Dummies. For Dummies*. Mississauga: Wiley.

Genevsky, A., Yoon, C. and Knutson, B., 2017. When brain beats behavior: Neuroforecasting crowdfunding outcomes. *Journal of Neuroscience*, 37(36), 8625–8634. https://doi.org/10.1523/ JNEUROSCI.1633-16.2017.

Glimcher, P. and Fehr, E., eds., 2014. *Neuroeconomics: Decision Making and the Brain*, 2nd ed. Amsterdam; Boston: Elsevier Academic Press.

Hare, T., Camerer, C., Knoepfle, D., O'Doherty, J. and Rangel, A., 2010. Value computations in ventral medial prefrontal cortex during charitable decision-making incorporate input from regions involved in social cognition. *Journal of Neuroscience*, 30(2), 583–590. https://doi.org/10.1523/ JNEUROSCI.4089-09.2010.

Hauser, J., Tellis, G.J. and Griffin, A., 2006. Research on innovation: A review and agenda for marketing science. *Marketing Science*, 25(6), 687–717. https://doi.org/10.1287/mksc.1050.0144.

Holper, L., Wolf, M. and Tobler, P., 2014. Comparison of functional near-infrared spectroscopy and electrodermal activity in assessing objective versus subjective risk during risky financial decisions. *Neuroimage*, 84, 833–842. https://doi.org/10.1016/j.neuroimage.2013.09.047.

Hytönen, K., 2011. *Context Effects in Valuation, Judgment and Choice: A Neuroscientific Approach*. PhD Thesis, Erasmus Univraity, Rotterdam (No. EPS-2011-252-MKT).

Iyengar, S., 2011. *The Art of Choosing*. New York: Twelve.

Jackson, P. and Kennedy, D., 2013. The application of near infrared spectroscopy in nutritional intervention studies. *Frontiers in Human Neuroscience*, 7. Art. 473. https://doi.org/10.3389/fnhum.2013.00473.

Jöbsis, F., 1977. Noninvasive, infrared monitoring of cerebral and myocardial oxygen sufficiency and circulatory parameters. *Science*, 198(4323), 1264–1267. https://doi.org/10.1126/science.929199.

Jöbsis-vanderVliet, F., 1999. Discovery of the near-infrared window into the body and the early development of near-infrared spectroscopy. *Journal of Biomedical Optics*, 4(4), 392. https://doi.org/10.1117/ 1.429952.

Joshi, A. and Sharma, S., 2004. Customer knowledge development: Antecedents and impact on new product performance. *Journal of Marketing*, 68(4), 47–59. https://doi.org/10.1509/jmkg.68.4.47.42722.

Klucharev, V., Hytönen, K., Rijpkema, M., Smidts, A. and Fernández, G., 2009. Reinforcement learning signal predicts social conformity. *Neuron*, 61, 140–151. https://doi.org/10.1016/j.neuron. 2008.11.027.

Kopton, I. and Kenning, P., 2014. Near-infrared spectroscopy (NIRS) as a new tool for neuroeconomic research. *Frontiers in Human Neuroscience*, 8. Art. 549. https://doi.org/10.3389/fnhum.2014.00549.

Kühn, S., Strelow, E. and Gallinat, J., 2016. Multiple "buy buttons" in the brain: Forecasting chocolate sales at point-of-sale based on functional brain activation using fMRI. *Neuroimage*, 136, 122–128. https://doi.org/10.1016/j.neuroimage.2016.05.021.

Levy, D. and Glimcher, P., 2012. The root of all value: A neural common currency for choice. *Current Opinion in Neurobiology*, 22(6), 1027–1038. https://doi.org/10.1016/j.conb.2012.06.001.

Lilienfeld, S., Ritschel, L., Lynn, S., Cautin, R. and Latzman, R., 2013. Why many clinical psychologists are resistant to evidence-based practice: Root causes and constructive remedies. *Clinical Psychology Review*, 33(7), 883–900. https://doi.org/10.1016/j.cpr.2012.09.008.

Lim, S., O'Doherty, J. and Rangel, A., 2013. Stimulus value signals in ventromedial PFC reflect the integration of attribute value signals computed in fusiform gyrus and posterior superior temporal gyrus. *Journal of Neuroscience*, 33(20), 8729–8741. https://doi.org/10.1523/JNEUROSCI.4809-12.2013.

Luu, S. and Chau, T., 2009. Decoding subjective preference from single-trial near-infrared spectroscopy signals. *Journal of Neural Engineering*, 6(1), 016003. https://doi.org/10.1088/1741-2560/6/1/016003.

McNamee, D., Rangel, A. and O'Doherty, J., 2013. Category-dependent and category-independent goal-value codes in human ventromedial prefrontal cortex. *Nature Neuroscience*, 16, 479–485. https://doi.org/10.1038/nn.3337.

Morin, C., 2011. Neuromarketing: The new science of consumer behavior. *Society*, 48, 131–135. https://doi.org/10.1007/s12115-010-9408-1.

Naseer, N. and Hong, K., 2013. Classification of functional near-infrared spectroscopy signals corresponding to the right- and left-wrist motor imagery for development of a brain-computer interface. *Neuroscience Letters*, 553, 84–89. https://doi.org/10.1016/j.neulet.2013.08.021.

Naseer, N., Hong, M. and Hong, K., 2014. Online binary decision decoding using functional near-infrared spectroscopy for the development of brain-computer interface. *Experimental Brain Research*, 232, 555–564. https://doi.org/10.1007/s00221-013-3764-1.

Noble, S., Scheinost, D. and Constable, R.T., 2019. A decade of test-retest reliability of functional connectivity: A systematic review and meta-analysis. *Neuroimage*, 203, 116157. https://doi.org/10.1016/j.neuroimage.2019.116157.

Pfeffer, J. and Sutton, R., 2006a. Evidence-based management. *Harvard Business Review*, January.

Pfeffer, J. and Sutton, R., 2006b. *Hard Facts, Dangerous Half-Truths, and Total Nonsense: Profiting from Evidence-Based Management*. Boston, MA: Harvard Business School Press.

Plassmann, H., O'Doherty, J., Shiv, B. and Rangel, A., 2008. Marketing actions can modulate neural representations of experienced pleasantness. *Proceedings of the National Academy of Sciences*, 105(3), 1050–1054. https://doi.org/10.1073/pnas.0706929105.

Pombo, M. and Velasco, C., 2019. How aesthetic features convey the concept of brand premiumness. *PsyArXiv* (August). DOI: 10.31234/osf.io/7kpwz.

Ruff, C.C. and Huettel, S.A., 2014. Experimental methods in cognitive neuroscience. In *Neuroeconomics*. Elsevier, 77–108. https://doi.org/10.1016/B978-0-12-416008-8.00006-1.

Shimokawa, T., Kinoshita, K., Miyagawa, K. and Misawa, T., 2012. A brain information-aided intelligent investment system. *Decision Support Systems*, 54(1), 336–344. https://doi.org/10.1016/j.dss.2012.05.041.

Shimokawa, T., Suzuki, K., Misawa, T. and Miyagawa, K., 2009. Predictability of investment behavior from brain information measured by functional near-infrared spectroscopy: A Bayesian neural network model. *Neuroscience*, 161(2), 347–358. https://doi.org/10.1016/j.neuroscience.2009.02.079.

Stewart, T. and Eliasmith, C., 2013. Realistic neurons can compute the operations needed by quantum probability theory and other vector symbolic architectures. *Behavioral and Brain Sciences*, 36(3), 307–308. https://doi.org/10.1017/S0140525X12003111.

Suomala, J., 2018a. The neuroscience research methods in management. In L. Moutinho and M. Sokele, eds. *Innovative Research Methodologies in Management*. Cham: Springer International Publishing, 135–158. https://doi.org/10.1007/978-3-319-64400-4_6.

Suomala, J., 2018b. Benefits of neuromarketing in the product/service innovation process and creative marketing campaign. In L. Moutinho and M. Sokele, eds. *Innovative Research Methodologies in Management*. Cham: Springer International Publishing, 159–177. https://doi.org/10.1007/978-3-319-64400-4_7.

Suomala, J., Palokangas, L., Leminen, S., Westerlund, M., Heinonen, J. and Numminen, J., 2012. Neuromarketing: Understanding customers: Subconscious responses to marketing. *Technological Innovation Management Review*, 2(12), 12–21. DOI: 10.22215/timreview/634.

Suomala, J., Taatila, V., Siltala, R. and Keskinen, S., 2006. Chance discovery as a first step to economic innovation. In *Proceedings of the 28th Annual Conference of the Cognitive Science Society*. Vancouver, BC: Cognitive Science Society, 2204–2209.

Taatila, V.P., Suomala, J., Siltala, R. and Keskinen, S., 2006. Framework to study the social innovation networks. *European Journal of Innovation Management*, 9(3), 312–326. https://doi.org/10.1108/14601060610678176.

Venkatraman, V., Dimoka, A., Pavlou, P., Vo, K., Hampton, W., Bollinger, B., Hershfield, H., Ishihara, M. and Winer, R., 2015. Predicting advertising success beyond traditional measures: New insights from neurophysiological methods and market response modeling. *Journal of Marketing Research*, 52(4), 436–452. https://doi.org/10.1509/jmr.13.0593.

Yoshino, K., Oka, N., Yamamoto, K., Takahashi, H. and Kato, T., 2013. Correlation of prefrontal cortical activation with changing vehicle speeds in actual driving: A vector-based functional near-infrared spectroscopy study. *Frontiers in Human Neuroscience*, 7. Art. 595. https://doi.org/10.3389/fnhum.2013.00895.

15

AN INTRODUCTION TO THE USE OF EEG IN MARKETING RESEARCH

Reem Refai A. Mahmoud and Richard P. Bagozzi

Summary

Academic research is flourishing in the interface between behavioural marketing and the use of functional imaging techniques such as hemodynamic measurements (fMRI) and electromagnetic measurements (EEG and MEG). Electrophysiology (EEG) is one of the oldest non-invasive and convenient imaging techniques. EEG involves attaching an array of electrodes on the scalp to record dynamic electrical activity along the brain surface in the sub-second time range. EEG delivers precise topographical maps of brain activation. High-density EEG systems, when combined with anatomical and structural information about the brain, can be used to infer source localisation in the brain with respect to information processing, emotions, and decision-making. This chapter intends to walk you through EEG basics, how different it is from other imaging techniques, and what a typical EEG experimental protocol would be. Examples of state-of-the-art studies and future trends are presented briefly at the end of this chapter.

Introduction

> Advances in science can often be attributed to the "marriage" between two apparently unrelated disciplines. These marriages frequently lead to paradigm changes in which the concepts, methods, and procedures of one discipline are applied to answer the questions of another discipline . . . within psychology, considerable progress has been made following the marriage between cognitive psychology and linguistics and between engineering and experimental psychology.
>
> Coles (1989, p. 251), in the opening of his paper entitled
"Modern Mind-Brain Reading: Psychophysiology,
Physiology, and Cognition"

Cognitive neuroscience, neuroeconomics, social neuroscience, and consumer neuroscience are all examples of contemporary interdisciplinary fields emerging as a result of the marriage of their parent disciplines and social sciences disciplines including psychology, consumer behaviour, and economics. Finding a link between cognitive, emotional, and social processes and underlying neural processes —or more generally between behaviour and brain – by utilising tools and concepts from neuroscience is the main aim of such emergent fields. Importantly, findings from current research in the previously listed interdisciplinary fields seems to be very promising. The main focus of our chapter is on the interdisciplinary field of consumer neuroscience, which represents a modern and vibrant field incorporating research across neuroscience, psychology, decision-making, and marketing disciplines (Plassmann *et al.* 2011; Shaw and Bagozzi 2018). The integration of theories, methods, and tools from these other disciplines enables consumer behaviour researchers to understand marketing phenomena that they could not fully understand before (for recent reviews, see Harris *et al.* 2018; Karmarkar and Plassmann 2019). The extraordinary advances in neuroscientific methods and brain imaging techniques have profoundly paved the way for the recent growth in interdisciplinary fields in general and more specifically in consumer neuroscience. Examples of currently available brain imaging techniques include but are not limited to functional magnetic resonance imaging (fMRI), positron emission tomography (PET), electroencephalography, and magnetoencephalography (MEG). The current chapter mainly concerns EEG measurement.

We begin with a quick review of brain physiology to provide basic background information regarding relevant human brain structure and functions. This review is followed by an introduction of EEG and covers its definition, concise history, and generation. A comprehensive survey of different available brain imaging techniques is provided. We then provide an overview of typical EEG protocols, experimental design, and signal pre-processing and analysis routines. This overview, however, is not meant to serve as a primer for basic design and analysis steps but rather is meant to delineate the path typically followed by scholars and researchers in this domain. Toward the end of the chapter, examples of recent marketing studies which utilised EEG systems are outlined. Finally, the authors' perspectives regarding directions for future research in this specific domain are presented.

Brain physiology

Neuroimaging techniques, including EEG, measure neural activity of the brain, either directly or indirectly. Therefore, before going deeper into the fundamentals of EEG and its application to marketing research, it is beneficial to review *brain physiology* very briefly.

Major areas of the brain

The major brain regions are the brain stem (which holds the medulla oblongata and the pons), the midbrain, the limbic system, the basal ganglia, the cerebellum, and the cerebrum (Abhang *et al.* 2016). Each region executes a particular set of functions (see Figure 15.1).

The cerebrum

The cerebrum is the largest and most significant portion of the brain, where the cerebral cortex and other subcortical structures are located. The outer layer of the cerebrum is the cerebral cortex. The cerebral cortex is divided into two hemispheres, which are further divided into four cerebral lobes named the frontal, temporal, parietal, and occipital lobes (Abhang *et al.* 2016). Each cerebral lobe performs a distinct set of functions, as illustrated in Table 15.1.

The cerebral hemispheres

The cerebrum is divided into two anatomically asymmetrical cortical hemispheres by the longitudinal fissure called the right and left hemispheres. Each hemisphere is dominant and more active for a specific function. Such differences in activation between the two hemispheres are

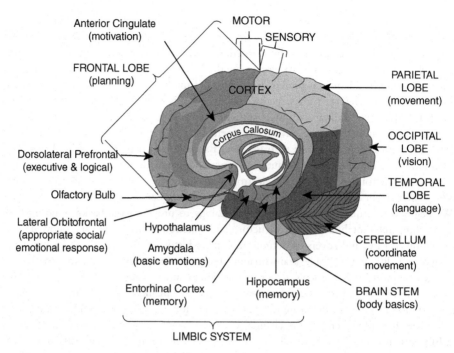

Figure 15.1 Major brain areas
Source: Abhang *et al.* (2016)

Table 15.1 Cerebral lobes and their functions

Cerebral lobes	Cerebral lobe functions
The frontal lobe	is the anterior lobe and houses the primary motor cortex, the medial cortex, and the prefrontal cortex (PFC). The frontal lobe is associated with motor function, cognition, problem solving, planning, organising, and short-term memory (Abhang *et al.* 2016). The PFC is the largest and the anterior-most portion of the frontal lobe located just behind the forebrain and contains two main sub-regions: the ventro-medial PFC (vmPFC) and dorsolateral PFC (dlPFC) regions (Abhang *et al.* 2016). The PFC is accountable for regulating social behaviour and emotions, shaping personality, and influencing decisions (Abhang *et al.* 2016).
The parietal lobe	is involved with regulating and processing the body's five senses. It integrates sensory information (such as pain, temperature, pressure, and touch) from different modalities (Abhang *et al.* 2016; Sanei and Chambers 2007).
The temporal lobe	is dedicated to the perception and recognition of auditory sounds and also to formation of long-term visual and verbal memories (Abhang *et al.* 2016).
The occipital lobe	is the posterior and smallest region of the cerebral cortex, typically processes visual information, and is the part of the brain associated with movement and colour recognition (Abhang *et al.* 2016).

Source: Authors

termed "functional lateralization" (Abhang *et al.* 2016). Typically and speaking loosely, the left hemisphere is dominant for sequential processing and other higher cognitive functions, such as sequencing of written and spoken languages and mathematical reasoning, whereas the right hemisphere is the holistic creative hemisphere that dominates simultaneous processing, such as registration or as detection of emotions and recognition of unfamiliar objects, faces, and metaphors (Abhang *et al.* 2016).

Electroencephalography

Definition

EEG is one of the oldest brain imaging techniques. EEG involves attaching multiple electrodes on the scalp to record dynamic electrical activity along the brain surface. The acronym EEG is an abbreviation of "electroencephalogram" where electro- denotes registration of brain electrical activities, encephalo- denotes emitting the signals from the head, and finally -gram or -graphy conveys drawing or writing (Sanei and Chambers 2007). The EEG signals can be measurable only when tens of thousands of cortical pyramidal neuronal populations are synchronously active (Lopes da Silva 2010; Luck 2014). That is, EEG signals reflect the summed excitatory and inhibitory postsynaptic electrical potentials of these populations of neurons (Lopes da Silva 2010; Luck 2014). For more in-depth treatment of the mechanisms generating the EEG signals, interested readers may refer to specialist books such as Luck (2014) and Lopes da Silva (2010).

History

In his 1875 article published in the *British Medical Journal*, the English physiologist Richard Caton (1824–1926) disclosed the presence of cerebral cortical electrical activity (EEG signals) induced as a response by exposing rabbits to sensory stimulation (Laureys *et al.* 2002). Fifty-four years later, in 1929, the journey of recording the electrical activity of the brain took an incredible advance when Hans Berger (1873–1941), a German psychiatrist, successfully performed the first human electroencephalographic recording (Luck 2014; Cox and Savoy 2003). Berger recorded the brain's electrical activity by placing electrodes on the scalp of an intact skull and plotting the voltage changes over time (Luck 2014; Cox and Savoy 2003). Berger's seminal research was then replicated and extended by many physiologist researchers, who even discovered additional dimensions of EEG recording. Since then, EEG has become a useful method for tracking brain activation. Nowadays, EEG is widely used in clinical and academic research.

EEG paradigms

Neuroelectric brain activity detected by EEG recordings takes two forms: (1) spontaneous brain activity and (2) event-related potentials (ERPs). The first form represents continuous EEG electrical activity recorded without any outer stimulation and is known as brainwaves or rhythms. The second form denotes EEG electrical activity recorded in a time-locked way to multiple presentations of the same stimuli, event, or cognitive process (Savoy 2001; Srinivasan 2007).

Spontaneous EEG

Continuous EEG recordings show "oscillating electrical voltages" that vacillate over time and possess different frequencies (speed in Hz, number of cycles per second), power (strength or amount of energy), and phase (timing of the activity) (see Fig 15.2) (Abhang *et al.* 2016; Cohen 2014; Nisar and Yeap 2014). These oscillations are not time locked or related to any external stimuli and are commonly termed brainwaves or brain rhythms (Nisar and Yeap 2014).

Brain rhythms provide potentially useful indicators of a subject's global brain state such as alertness, sleep, stress, and resting state (Nisar and Yeap 2014). Nearly a century ago, four traditional brain rhythms/bands were identified: Delta (δ), Theta (θ), Alpha (α), and Beta (β) (Weiergräber *et al.* 2016). Later, additional frequency bands and sub-bands were further identified including Gamma (γ), theta-alpha, Mu, and the sigma band (Weiergräber *et al.* 2016). Tables 15.2 and 15.3 summarise the five typical EEG bands in normal adults along with their description, images, and putative functional roles.

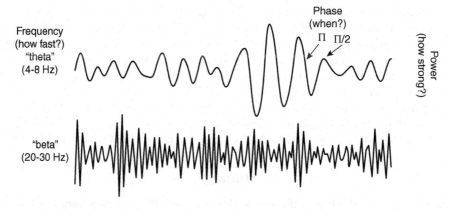

Figure 15.2 Oscillations dimensions: frequency, power, and phase
Source: Adapted from Cohen (2014)

Table 15.2 Typical human EEG waveforms in normal adult: their descriptions and putative functional roles

Band name	Amplitude/voltage	Bandwidth	Main scalp area	Brain states associated with bandwidth
Delta *(δ)*	20–400 (μV)	0.5–4 Hz	Variable	Deep sleep, brain lesions tumours and during anaesthesia
Theta *(θ)*	5–100	4–7.5 Hz	Frontal and temporal	Drowsiness, impaired information processing, focused attention, mental effort, and effective stimulus processing.
Alpha *(α)*	5–100	8–13 Hz	Posterior (occipital-parietal)	Relaxed wakefulness (eyes closed).
A beta *(β)*	2–20	14–26 Hz	Precentral and frontal	Excitatory activity (mostly during diffuse arousal and focused attention).
Gamma *(γ)*	2–10	> 30 Hz	Precentral and frontal	Attention, arousal, object recognition, and top-down modulation of sensory processes.

Source: Based on Sanei and Chambers (2007), Pizzagalli (2007, p. 60), Lewine and Orrison (1995)

Table 15.3 Images of typical human EEG waveforms in normal adult

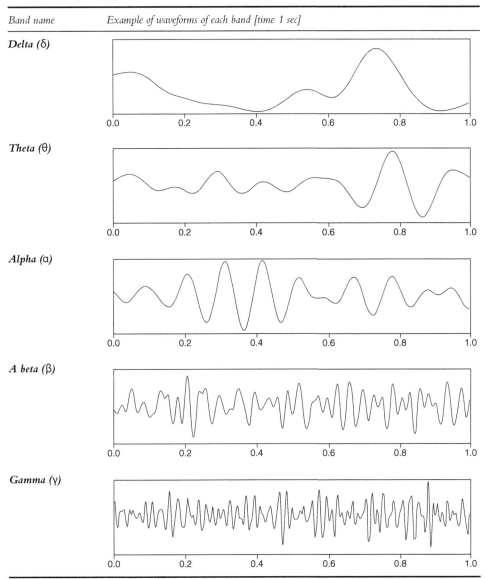

Band name	Example of waveforms of each band [time 1 sec]
Delta (δ)	
Theta (θ)	
Alpha (α)	
A beta (β)	
Gamma (γ)	

Source: The waveforms images are raw EEG signals at sampling rate of 256 HZ created by Gamboa (2005)

Event-related potentials

The term "event-related potential" refers to the electrical response of the brain to a specific stimulus or cognitive process (Menon and Crottaz-Herbette 2005, p. 293).

ERPs are extracted from spontaneous EEG activation by means of signal-averaging techniques (Lewine and Orrison 1995). The signal-averaging techniques typically entail the presentation of the exact same stimulus many times (so-called trails), recording the electrical responses from each trial, and then averaging them (Savoy 2001; Srinivasan 2007). The averaging process makes it possible to visualise and extract reliable ERPs (Menon and Crottaz-Herbette 2005). The rationale for using the signal-averaging techniques for extracting ERPs is as follows. The EEG data of a single trial consists of an ERP waveform with tiny amplitudes in the range of a few microvolts and random noise (i.e. non-event related and background EEG activity) with much larger amplitudes (Menon and Crottaz-Herbette 2005; Jiang 2014; Srinivasan 2007). The ERP waveform is elicited by the stimulus, and it is assumed to be identical in shape and phase, whereas the noise is assumed to be completely unrelated to the time-locking event (Jiang 2014, p. 74). Accordingly, averaging several trails (e.g. 30 to 100 trails for cognitive processes) tends to decrease the noise and retain only the consistent event-related activities (the ERPs) (Menon and Crottaz-Herbette 2005).

ERP waveforms consists of a series of peaks and deflections with different latency, morphology, and topography, termed "ERP components" (Jiang 2014). These components are named by their polarity (P for positive, N for negative) and either their ordinal position (in the waveform) after stimulus onset (P1 is the first positive peak) or their latency after stimulus onset (measured in milliseconds) (N4 or N400 is a negative-going component peaking at 400 ms, for example) (Menon and Crottaz-Herbette 2005, p. 294). Figure 15.3 depicts a graphical example of ERP components of a typical grand average waveform (the average of extracted ERPs between subjects).

Components are classified based on latency to early-latency components (occurring before 100ms), mid-latency components (occurring between 100 and 200ms), and late-latency components (occurring after 250ms) (Menon and Crottaz-Herbette 2005). Components in each category are believed to serve as an index for a certain level of cognitive, affective, sensory, or perceptual processes (Menon and Crottaz-Herbette 2005). Although the investigation and interpretation of ERP components began about 1970, it was not until the mid-1980s that attempts were made to use ERP components to address complicated questions in cognitive

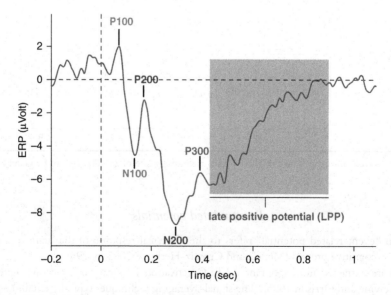

Figure 15.3   ERP components of a typical grand average waveform

Source: Adapted from Lithari *et al.* (2010, p. 31)

neuroscience (Kropotov 2010; Shiv *et al*. 2005). The ability to monitor the online processing of information is one of the greatest advantages of the ERP technique (Kropotov 2010).

EEG versus other brain imaging techniques

Currently, several brain-imaging techniques are available to researchers for investigating brain functions or, more broadly, dynamics of brain activity. Hence, a researcher intending to incorporate neuroimaging techniques into his/her research must make an educated decision concerning which neuroimaging techniques best suits his/her research purpose. To be able to make the right decision, researchers need to understand the capabilities, key differences, advantages, and disadvantages of each brain imaging technique. For this reason, a detailed presentation and comparison of the different techniques is provided in this section.

Pizzagalli (2007) proposed that functional imaging techniques presently available can be grouped into three categories:

- Techniques based on hemodynamic measurements: functional magnetic resonance imaging;
- Techniques based on metabolic measurements: positron emission tomography;
- Techniques based on electromagnetic measurements: electroencephalography and magnetoencephalography.

Functional neuroimaging techniques are further classified into either (Savoy 2001):

- Direct measures of neural activity (i.e. EEG and MEG);
- Indirect measures of neural activity (i.e. PET and fMRI).

The former classification is used subsequently to compare the different techniques along many dimensions: measurement, invasiveness, temporal resolution, spatial resolution, source localisation, cost and availability, safety, setup and mobility, signal to noise ratio, and devices.

Tables 15.4 and 15.5 demonstrate the basic differences between the most commonly used functional neuroimaging techniques. Clearly, differences in spatial and temporal resolution are the most important ones due to the implications they impose on the ability of each technique to answer a specific type of research question.

EEG systems provide topographical mapping for the brain by showing the neural activation along the surface of the brain (Michel and Brunet 2019). Most clinical and research studies use the EEG system to obtain this high-resolution topographical localisation. On the other hand, due to poor spatial resolution, EEG systems are typically unable to capture brain or source localisation well. In other words, inferring which specific location inside the brain generated the neural activation detected by the sensors on the scalp is not possible using EEG (Cohen 2014). This problem is known in the literature as the "inverse problem". The EEG inverse problem refers to the incapability of currently used algorithms and mathematical models to specify the exact source that generates the recorded electrical potentials (Lopes da Silva 2010). The inverse problem arises from insufficient information and the use of many assumptions about the nature of the source of the neural activation (e.g. assumptions regarding the structure of the head and electrical conductivity of the sensors) (Cohen 2014; Lopes da Silva 2010). To date, the scientific community does not offer a definite solution to the EEG inverse problem.

However, recent developments in EEG devices and analysis algorithms have led to improvements in its capability to depict brain localisation. More specifically, combining high-density EEG systems with anatomical and structural information about the brain can allow researcher

Table 15.4 Direct measures of neural activity: EEG and MEG

Measurement	EEG measures the electrical potentials of the brain, while MEG measures very tiny magnetic fields produced by the brain's electrical activity (Bunge and Kahn 2009).
Scope	EEG measures the activity of pyramidal cells in cortical gyri and the depths of the sulci, whereas MEG is sensitive primarily to the activity of pyramidal cells in the superficial parts of the sulci, and it is therefore more limited in its scope (Bunge and Kahn 2009, p. 1064).
Signal-to-noise ratio (SNR)	EEG is more sensitive to signal distortion than MEG (Bunge and Kahn 2009). EEG is susceptible to both biological and non-biological artefacts.
Invasiveness	Both MEG and EEG are non-invasive brain-imaging techniques.
Temporal resolution	Unlike the indirect measures, both EEG and MEG offer excellent temporal resolution (in the range of milliseconds).
Spatial resolution	EEG and MEG share the weakness of poor three-dimensional spatial resolution. MEG has even lower spatial resolution relative to EEG.
Source localisation	Unlike fMRI and PET systems, EEG and MEG systems are not capable of spatially localising brain activity (Kabl 2011). Yet MEG has more accurate localisation capabilities than EEG, as it can show activity in deeper brain areas (Kenning *et al.* 2007).
Cost and availability	MEG is much more expensive and less available to researchers than EEG (Shiv *et al.* 2005). EEG is also less expensive than fMRI and PET.
Safety	Both MEG and EEG are safe to use with subjects (Savoy 2001). EEG does not aggravate claustrophobia and is tolerant of subjects' movements, which is not the case for MEG, PET, and fMRI.
Setup	The EEG setup time varies according to the type of the EEG device being used, with a minimum estimation of 30 minutes. MEG as well as fMRI require shorter setup times than medical-grade EEG systems.
Mobility	MEG uses bulky and immobile equipment, whereas both fixed and portable EEG devices are currently available in the market.
Devices	EEG researchers can use either medical-grade devices or the currently more available commercial EEG devices. Some of them are equipped with wireless amplifiers, and their caps are compatible with the conventional gel-based or dry electrodes (Malik and Amin 2017). Every EEG device comes with its own acquisition software. On the other hand, MEG can be measured by special medical grade devices called superconducting quantum interference devices (SQUIDs).

Source: Authors

to infer which area of the brain generated the detected neural activity (for review, see Michel and Brunet 2019).

Research studies have also utilised EEG systems to identify the timing of responses following the presentation of a cognitive stimulus. By contrast, fMRI is incapable of answering such questions due to its poor temporal resolution. To understand the reason for the poor temporal resolution of fMRI, a very brief description of fMRI is provided hereafter.

The most powerful and commonly used functional MRI technique is known as the blood oxygenation level-dependent (BOLD) contrast, oxygen-rich (oxygenated) versus oxygen-depleted (deoxygenated) mechanism. The BOLD fMRI technique captures the hemodynamic response (HDR) to neuronal activation in a brain area as induced by a

Table 15.5 Indirect measures of neural activity: PET and fMRI

Measurement	fMRI uses an indirect proxy of brain activity, that is, blood flow, while PET uses metabolic activity as a proxy.
Scope	A BOLD fMRI signal is not an absolute measure of blood oxygenation levels but rather a relative measure of the intensity of BOLD signals across conditions (Dimoka *et al.* 2012). That is, it only provides relative local neural activity. fMRI cannot answer questions regarding the necessity of a given brain region for a specific task.
Signal to noise ratio	FMRI is vulnerable to artefacts produced by subject movement (Shiv *et al.* 2005).
Invasiveness	fMRI is a non-invasive method, while PET is a much more invasive technique than fMRI due to the need to inject subjects with a radioactive tracer (Savoy 2001).
Temporal resolution	fMRI and PET temporal resolution is relatively poor compared to EEG and MEG. PET temporal resolution is even poorer, on the order of 1 min compared to 2 to 8 sec. for fMRI.
Spatial resolution	PET spatial resolution is decent and much better than the spatial resolution of EEG or MEG, yet it is worse than fMRI resolution (Shiv *et al.* 2005).
Source localisation	PET and fMRI yield highly localised measures of brain activation.
Cost and availability	PET facility costs are higher than that of fMRI (Shiv *et al.* 2005, p. 382). Relative to PET, FMRI is moderately expensive. The cost of one session could be about \$400–800, whereas PET is extremely expensive due to the need for radioactive isotopes (Luck 2014). Both MRI and PET scanners and technology are readily available.
Safety	fMRI and PET scanners have confined interior space constraining subjects' movements and possibly triggering panic reactions for subjects with claustrophobia (Dimoka *et al.* 2012). Furthermore, subjects maybe bothered by the load noise due to beeping and hammering fMRI scanner sounds. Yet fMRI scanners provide few risks for subjects (Savoy 2001). On the contrary, PET requires the use of radioactive substance, which makes its application to test persons restricted (Kenning *et al.* 2007; Shiv *et al.* 2005).
Setup and mobility	PET and fMRI equipment is generally bulky and immobile.
Devices	fMRI uses the same machinery as conventional MRI.

Source: Author elaboration

specific stimulation (Dimoka *et al.* 2012). An increase in HDR reflects an increase in cerebral blood flow and the use of glucose in response to elevated neuronal activity. HDR occurs over several seconds, typically about 4 or 5 seconds after the onset of neural activity, because it takes time for the vascular system to respond to the brain's need for glucose (Dimoka *et al.* 2012). Due to this hemodynamic lag – the amount of time it takes for HDR to peak – fMRI temporal resolution is limited to several seconds (Menon and Crottaz-Herbette 2005). Figure 15.4 depicts the timing of EEG vs fMRI responses following the presentation of a stimulus. As shown in the figure, the EEG response peaks immediately after stimulus presentation in about 1 second post-stimulus. The BOLD fMRI response peaks after 2–3 seconds and reaches a maximum after about 5–6 seconds post-stimulus (Menon and Crottaz-Herbette 2005).

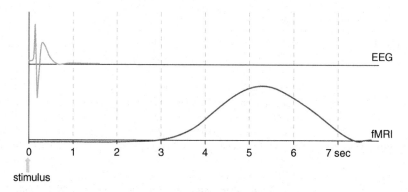

Figure 15.4 Relative timing of EEG and fMRI responses following the presentation of a stimulus
Source: Menon and Crottaz-Herbette (2005, p. 295)

EEG experimental design

This section reviews three major issues: EEG data acquisition and recording, EEG experimental protocol, and EEG preprocessing and analysis. This review only explores typical practices followed by EEG research and is not intended to serve as a basic primer for a specific study.

Data acquisition and recording

EEG data are captured by multiple-electrode EEG devices and recorded in different formats using either accompanying data acquisition software, which comes with the EEG device, or other available computing software such as MATLAB (Mathworks, Inc.). Two computers are usually used in EEG experiments. One computer is used for stimulus presentation and collection of behavioural data post stimulus, while the other computer is used for collection of the raw EEG data and for online monitoring of the signal quality while recording. Then the obtained raw signal goes through certain relevant pre-processing and analysis steps to transform it into metrics that can be merged with other collected behavioural data, if any, and putatively linked to the phenomena under investigations.

EEG devices

Nowadays, numerous EEG devices are available for both clinical and research purposes. EEG systems consist of electrodes, amplifiers with filters, analogue to digital (A/D) converters, and computers. EEG systems differ from each other in many aspects, including modality, density, electrodes (type of the conductive media), amplifier, acquisition software, and sampling rate (see Table 15.6).

When deciding which device best suits a certain project or research question under investigation, the previously listed features should be taken into considerations. Currently, several EEG hardware companies market medical-grade EEG systems, as well as so-called consumer-grade EEG systems, making EEG technology more accessible for purposes of interdisciplinary research. In April 2017, the iMotions company blog listed the top 14 most-used EEG hardware companies ranked according to the number of publications they were associated with as retrieved from Google Scholar. The list is: NeuroScan, Brain Products, BioSemi, Electrical Geodesic Incorporated (EGI), Emotiv, NeuroSky, Advanced Brain Monitoring (ABM), g.tec,

Table 15.6 EEG systems

Modality	EEG devices can be either portable (wireless) devices or fixed (non-wireless) ones.
Density	Currently, available EEG devices ranging from low–density EEG devices with 8-channel, 21-channel, 25-channel, and 32-channel EEG, to high-density EEG with 40-channel EEG and above. The 32-channel EEG system is the most widely used presently.
Electrodes (type of the conductive media)	EEG devices are equipped with either dry electrodes or gel-based electrodes.
Amplifier	The amplifier can be either an independent unit or integrated into the electrodes. Amplifiers differ on such characteristics as linearity, bandpass, and connection (wired, Bluetooth, or USB connection to computer).
Acquisition software	Contemporary EEG systems are equipped with their own acquisition software with simple signal processing tools, as well as topographical brain visualisation tools (Sanei and Chambers 2007).
Sampling rate	EEG devices should be at least capable of recording with high sampling rates (250 Hz is the least acceptable sampling rate generally).

Source: Author elaboration

ANT Neuro, Neuroelectrics, Muse, OpenBCI, Cognionics, and finally mBrainTrain (Farnsworth 2017).

Recording: electrode placement

Use of a standardised system for electrode placement on the scalp is necessary for comparing results of different research studies. The commonly used standardised system is known as the international 10/20 system (see Figure 15.5), which was designed and recommended by the International Federation of Societies for Electroencephalography and Clinical Neuro-physiology.

In this system, each electrode site is identified by a letter and a number. Letters are used to identify the brain lobe, where "F" refers to frontal lobe, "T" to temporal lobe, "P" to parietal lobe, and "O" to occipital lobe. The letter "C" stands for "central" (there is no central lobe). The letter "Z" stands for electrodes placed on the midline. The anterior is represented by the symbol "A". Numbers are used to identify the hemisphere location, where even numbers denote electrode positions on the right hemisphere, and odd numbers denote electrode positions on the left hemisphere. The earlobe electrodes (A1) and (A2) are used as reference electrodes (Srinivasan 2007).

Recording: sampling rate

The sampling rate, expressed in Hertz, is the number of samples per second, that is, the number of physically recorded data points per second (Weiergräber *et al.* 2016). Considerable attention should be paid to the sampling rate of the EEG recording system due to the great influence it has on the nature of the subsequent analysis. The EEG recording system specifies whether the system sampling rate is adjustable by the end user or if it is a technical constant and cannot be

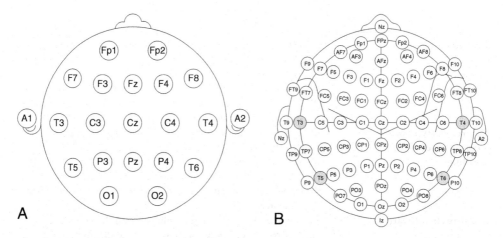

Figure 15.5   The International 1020 (A) and 1010 (B) electrode placement systems
Source: Maskeliunas *et al.* (2016, p. 5)

adjusted (Weiergräber *et al.* 2016). For example, BioSemi, a commercial EEG system, has four user-selectable sample rate options, as demonstrated in Table 15.7.

Best practice in specifying the sufficient sampling rate for a specific experimental design is to follow the *Nyquist Theorem*, which states that the sampling rate should be at least twice the highest frequency one intends to record (Pizzagalli 2007). Using too low a sampling rate could cause aliasing (misidentification of a signal frequency), while oversampling could produce more data, which requires higher storage and could slow down further data processing. The nominal sampling rate is 5 times higher than the bandwidth (frequency range in Hz); thus, for a 250-Hz nominal sampling rate system, the bandwidth (B) would be (1–50 Hz) (Weiergräber 2016). In other words, the highest attainable frequency in this case is 50 Hz. Hence, increasing the sampling rate allows the recording of higher EEG frequencies and the investigation of early sensory ERP components as well (Pizzagalli 2007; Weiergräber 2016).

EEG recording rooms

It is preferable to record EEG sessions in an electrically shielded room or chamber to eliminate any electrical noise that may disturb the signals. Recording in normal unshielded rooms is also possible. This possibility is conditional on the proper elimination of any source of electromagnetic interference such as large motors, elevators, or A/C equipment. Recording rooms should be at least 50 feet away from these sources. Special consideration should also be given to the room environmental conditions. The light, temperature, and humidity must be balanced and stable for example.

Experimental protocol/design

This section discusses several fundamental issues concerning the design of an EEG experiment. Most design issues are unique to the type of brain responses or phenomena under investigation.

Table 15.7 BioSemi EEG system specification

Sample rate: (adjustable by user)	2048 Hz	4096 Hz	8192 Hz	16,384 Hz
Maximum number of channels at selected sample rate	256	128	64	32
Bandwidth (–3dB)	DC – 400 Hz	DC – 800 Hz	DC – 1600	DC – 3200 Hz

Source: Adapted from BioSemi (n.d.)

However, numerous principles are relevant to most EEG studies. The following briefings describe these common principles.

Participants

For enhancing the quality of recorded signals (mainly by minimising impedance and artefacts), certain instructions should be provided before and during the recording sessions. For example, an experimenter should keenly inform participants that they should, if possible, arrive to the laboratory with their hair washed and refrain from using any hair products. Participants should be informed of the importance of avoiding eye blinking, raising eyebrows, clenching the jaw, and tightening forehead muscles as much as possible during the session. Finally, participants should refrain from drinking coffee/alcohol prior to the experiment.

Materials/stimuli

Selecting and/or designing a study stimulus is a critical task for experimenters. A wide variety of stimuli of different modalities (e.g. auditory, visual, audio-visual stimulation [AVS], somatosensory, olfactory etc.) have been employed by experimental and behavioural psychologists for years in the study of stimulus-response associations. When it comes to the domain of interdisciplinary research, such as social and consumer neuroscience, there is a genuine need for more novel stimuli. For example, watching a relatively short video to assess how consumers respond to a specific advertising stimulus may be needed. Also, reading scenarios or whole sentences instead of only single words is another kind of unconventional stimulus used in consumer neuroscience. Using such stimuli requires modifications in the experimental design and represents a major challenge for researchers.

Experimental paradigm and procedures

Designing an experimental EEG study involves making a wide range of decisions and choices, starting with defining the number of conditions, the order of stimulus presentation, and whether the stimulus will be perfectly randomised or counterbalanced across conditions. For an ERP study, additional choices should be clarified such as the number and sequence/order of trials (number of times the stimulus will be presented in each condition). Marketing researchers considering using EEG in their research are recommended to review the experimental conventions section in the relevant literature, learn how to use specialised stimulus presentation programs such as E-prime, and consult EEG specialists prior to designing and running their experiments.

Baseline recording

To establish a person's baseline neurological activity during the EEG recording session, researchers need to record at least 10 seconds with eyes open and a following period of 10 seconds with eyes closed. The necessity of such practice varies depending on the research question and design.

Presentation software

A variety of presentation software packages are available for researchers to use to control stimuli exposed to the participants. One of the most used in social psychology and cognitive neuroscience studies is E-Prime, which provides a precise and powerful stimulus delivery environment and has very good timing accuracy. A researcher may also use other available software such as Psyscope X (http://psy.ck.sissa.it/), EventIDE (http://okazolab.com/), psychToolbox (http://psychtoolbox.org/), PsychoPy (www.psychopy.org/), and OpenSesame (http://osdoc.cogsci.nl/). Each software package works on a specific operating system (Mac or Windows), some are free open source, others must be purchased, and, finally, some require advanced programming skills. Briefly, each program has its own merits and demerits with which researchers have to take educated decisions regarding which program to select according to their own skills and the nature of their research design.

Event markers

Experiment event markers, or triggers, are timestamps sent from the stimulus presentation PC to the EEG acquisition system and are typically logged as a separate channel in the raw data file (Cohen 2014). Event markers are very important for precise synchronisation of the EEG data with events of interest (e.g. the onset of a trial in ERP studies). Each EEG recording system utilises a different method for logging and integrating event triggers with the EEG data, including the use of a parallel data port and/or serial data port, where the former is more preferable (for review, see Hairston *et al.* 2014). Commercial software packages (e.g. Presentation or E-Prime) as well as MATLAB software open-source toolboxes can deliver event markers to the EEG acquisition system (Cohen 2014). The E-prime software package, for instance, has many options to stamp certain events on EEG recordings, such as fixation onset, stimulus onset, stimulus, and subjects' responses (Malik and Amin 2017).

EEG data preprocessing

Preprocessing refers to "any transformations or reorganizations that occur between collecting the data and analyzing the data" (Bunge and Kahn 2009, p. 73). The preprocessing steps could vary from simple organisation of the data to some more radical steps that involve removing bad channels and/or epochs or even modifying clean data via applying, for example, temporal filters (Bunge and Kahn 2009). Although preprocessing steps are by no means standardised or automated, some basic and commonly performed steps include: data conversion and importing, montage mapping, filtering, further artifact removal (removing and interpolating bad channels if necessary), down-sampling if necessary, referencing, segmentation, epoching, running ICA if necessary, and rejection of bad epochs, if any. The sequence and necessity of each of these mentioned steps may differ according to the quality of the recorded raw EEG signals and the type of intended analyses. In the following, we will briefly outline methods of artefact detection, attenuation, and correction.

Artefacts

EEG signals are unfortunately often contaminated by various artefacts. Signals with no cerebral origin are termed "artifacts" (Fisch and Spehlmann 1999). Artefacts can be grouped according to their origin into two main categories; physiological artefacts or non-physiological artefacts, or, in other words, biological subject-related and non-biological technical artefacts (Fisch and Spehlmann 1999; Pizzagalli 2007).

Non-biological artefacts arise from (1) external electrical interference derived from either power lines (50/60 Hz) or electrical noise from, for example, a nearby telephone ringing, and (2) internal electrical malfunctioning of the recording system itself derived from detached electrodes, poor or dried conductive media, and defective electrodes (Fisch and Spehlmann 1999; Pizzagalli 2007; Tatum 2014).

Biological subject-related artefacts arise from three main sources: movements, bioelectrical potential, and skin potential (Fisch and Spehlmann 1999). Examples are:

- Movements: subjects' head or body movements;
- Bioelectrical potential: blinks and eye movements, muscle activities (e.g. chewing), heartbeats;
- Skin potential: perspiration, sweat gland activity and galvanic skin response (GSR).

Artefact attenuation and correction

The literature tackling de-noising techniques is too immense to be appropriately reviewed in this chapter. Hence, a selective review of commonly employed methods is presented here:

- Filtering is the most standard method for attenuating or removing artefacts. Several types of filtering are available, including low-pass, high-pass, band-stop, and bandpass filters, each performing a different task (Srinivasan 2007). High-pass filtering at 0.1 or 0.5 Hz removes low frequencies and retains high frequencies, while low-pass filtering removes high frequencies (Cohen 2014; Srinivasan 2007). High-pass filters should be applied only to continuous data and not to epoched data (Cohen 2014, p. 80). If there is frequency band signal overlap, researchers should switch from these standard filtering techniques to techniques such as Wiener or Bayes filtering (Srinivasan 2007);
- Notch filters (50 or 60 Hz), which are used to diminish interference and noise from non-biological sources (Pizzagalli 2007);
- Independent component analysis (ICA), which is a technique that decomposes the EEG time series data into a set of components based on their statistical properties and which allows researchers to identify and subtract components with artefacts from the recorded data (Cohen 2014). ICA-extracted components, however, may have signal or noise or both at the same time; therefore, researchers should be careful and seek only to remove components containing artefacts and no or very little signal (Cohen 2014). ICA is mostly utilised to eliminate electrocardiogram (ECG) activation from the raw EEG data, typically before averaging (Pizzagalli 2007).

Concurrent recording of the electrocardiogram, electrooculogram (EOG), and electromyogram (EMG) is a highly recommended tactic for handling biological subject-related artefacts (Baillet 2011). Researchers need to be able to identify artefacts contaminating their raw EEG data visually (Fisch and Spehlmann 1999). EEG specialists might also be able to understand what causes such artefacts.

EEG feature extraction and data analysis

Analyses of time series are often carried out by extracting features from the signal of interest. Features can be defined as "parameters which provide information about the underlying structure of a signal" (Motamedi-Fakhr *et al.* 2014, p. 25). A considerable number of EEG feature extraction techniques have been reported in the literature, ranging from time, frequency, and time-frequency to complexity systems modelling, neural networks, and expert systems (see Table 15.8). The most-used methods for EEG feature extraction are reviewed subsequently.

Time-series domain

Temporal features (such as amplitude, mean, median, mode, standard deviation, variance, skewness, and kurtosis) are obtained by applying standard statistical techniques applied to EEG signals in the time domain (Motamedi-Fakhr *et al.* 2014).

Frequency (spectral) domain

Spectral analyses are performed using fast Fourier transform (FFT) to estimate the various frequency composition of EEG signal oscillations, for example, estimating 8–13 Hz for the alpha band (see Figure 15.6) (Pizzagalli 2007). Spectral analysis is only suitable for processing

Table 15.8 Most frequently used EEG feature extraction techniques

Feature	Technique
Frequency (spectral) domain	Non-parametric spectral analysis (periodogram and Welch method).
	Parametric spectral analysis (Autoregressive [AR], AAR, Kalman filtering).
	Higher-order spectral analysis (bispectrum, bicoherence, etc.).
	Coherence analysis (Normalised cross-spectral density [CSD]).
Time-frequency domain	Wavelet transform (wavelet coefficients).
	Matching pursuits (MPs).
	Short-time Fourier transform (STFT).
	Wigner-Ville distribution.
	Fast-time frequency transform (FTFT).
Complexity measures/nonlinear parameters	Correlation dimension (or its estimate: dimensional complexity).
	Lyapunov exponents.
	Fractal dimension.
	Synchronisation likelihood.
Spatial features/source localisation	Independent component analysis.
	Low resolution electro-magnetic tomography (LORETA).
	Principle component analysis (PCA).

Source: Adapted from Motamedi-Fakhr *et al.* (2014)

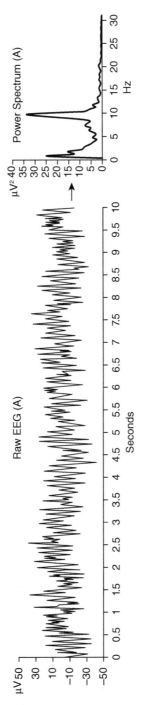

Figure 15.6 A signal (raw EEG data) collected in the time domain (left side) and converted to a frequency-domain representation in the form of a power spectrum (right side)

Source: Allen *et al.* (2004, p. 185)

stationary EEG signals that have relatively stable statistical proprieties (e.g. mean, variance) (Motamedi-Fakhr *et al.* 2014; Pizzagalli 2007). A host of measurements (e.g. absolute or relative power) can be driven from spectral analyses (Pizzagalli 2007).

Most spectral analysis methods are power spectral density (PSD) estimation and asymmetry indices.

Power spectral density: PSD can be performed by parametric and nonparametric methods. Periodogram and Welch methods are the two most-used nonparametric methods that use the fast Fourier transform (FFT) algorithm to estimate the power spectrum (Motamedi-Fakhr *et al.* 2014). The drawbacks of nonparametric methods include their limited time frequency resolution and assumption of the stationarity of the recorded EEG signals, which is likely to be violated in real EEG data (Motamedi-Fakhr *et al.* 2014). To overcome such limitations, you may consider using parametric methods of PSD estimation instead.

Asymmetry indices: Considerable research effort has been devoted to the investigation of asymmetrical activity over the frontal cortex, typically in the alpha frequency band. Reznik and Allen (2018, p. 2) defined frontal EEG asymmetry as "a measure of the difference in EEG alpha power between homologous right and left frontal electrodes". Asymmetry scores are often computed by subtracting the natural log transformed scores for each homologous left and right pair [Asymmetry Score = ln (Alpha Power$_{right}$) − ln (Alpha Power$_{left}$)] (Allen *et al.* 2004). Building upon the assumption that alpha power is inversely related to brain activation, higher scores imply relatively greater left frontal cortical activity, whereas lower scores imply relatively greater right frontal cortical activity (Allen *et al.* 2004; Pizzagalli 2007). The literature draws an essential distinction between resting and state frontal EEG asymmetry. Frontal EEG asymmetry recorded at rest is considered a *trait measure* of psychological phenomena and is referred to as "frontal EEG activity", while frontal EEG asymmetry recorded during emotionally evocative tasks reflects a *state measure* of current emotion or behaviour and is referred to as "frontal EEG activation" (Reznik and Allen 2018). More specifically, frontal EEG activation refers to a change in EEG activity in response to stimuli, tasks, or emotional manipulation (e.g. the difference from rest to activation of the emotion state) (Reznik and Allen 2018). Frontal EEG asymmetry trait measures, deemed to designate *trait predispositions* to respond to or engage with specific types of emotions, have been called an index of individual differences (Coan and Allen 2004).

Time-frequency domain

EEG time-frequency analyses demonstrate which frequencies have the most power at specific points in time and space (Roach and Mathalon 2008). Time-frequently analyses have many approaches including for example:

- **Short time Fourier transform:** STFT is based on the fast Fourier transform and uses fixed size windowing technique for all frequencies, which limit its frequency resolution (Roach and Mathalon 2008);
- **Wavelet transform:** The wavelet transform extracts the frequency components of EEG signals and identifies where a certain frequency exists in the temporal or spatial domain as well (Roach and Mathalon 2008). Wavelet analysis, unlike STFT, uses a windowing technique but with variable window size rather than fixed, which can optimise temporal resolution (Roach and Mathalon 2008). The rule of thumb is that "the larger the time window used to estimate the complex data for a given time point, the greater the frequency resolution but the poorer the temporal resolution" (Roach and Mathalon 2008, p. 912).

Examples of state-of-the-art studies

The following section reviews a group of studies that are relevant to our current discussion and reflects contemporary illustrative examples of how the use of the EEG method can inform and enrich our understanding of consumers affective (e.g. emotional engagement, pleasure and arousal), cognitive (e.g. information processing, memory and attention), and motivational processes as well as brands and product choices and preferences. These studies are also methodologically interesting because they employed diverse EEG paradigms. Therefore, the following review will be broadly divided into three categories based on the employed EEG paradigms. The fist category will include examples of studies which utilised *non-hemispheric brain wave analysis*, whereas the second category will cover EEG asymmetric frontal cortical activity (AFCA) studies, and the last category will cover studies which employed *event-related brain potentials*.

Examples of non-hemispheric brain wave analysis studies

Considering its potential in providing bias-free data, EEG has been used in research that attempts to predict behaviour in the health domain such as smoking or physical activities as well as in research trying to predict ethical and environmental consumption behaviours. EEG and other neuroimaging techniques might provide valuable insights in addressing such research topics where there is a kind of attitude-behaviour or value-action gap. Building on that, Lee *et al.* (2014) expected that "neural indicator of green engagement could potentially be a more proximal indicator of impending green action" (p. 513). They carried out an experiment where 19 participants viewed two versions of text advertisements, one for an environmentally friendly (green) product and one for a conventional product. After reading the content of each advertisement, respondents were provided with the price information for each product option as well. The green product option had a premium price of 10%. Afterwards, respondents were asked to select one of the two products to purchase. Respondents were then divided into a green consumers group or non-green consumers group based on their product selection in this choice task. Throughout the two phases of this choice task (the product massage phase and the price information phase), participant brain activity was recorded using a 19-channel EEG system (WEEG-32, Laxtha Inc., Daejeon, Korea). Theta rhythm from three frontal channels (Fz, F3, and F4) was extracted via EEG power spectral analysis. The findings disclosed that, during the product message phase, frontal theta activations were significantly higher among green consumers compared to non-green consumers. The authors argued that when green consumers were confronted with product choice, they needed to evaluate this choice according to their values and higher-order goals, which increases the demand for working memory resources. This explanation is backed by evidence from neuroscience literature, which pointed out that frontal cortex theta activation is associated with increased attention, task load, and processing efficiency. Furthermore, prior literature reported a possible role for frontal cortex theta activation during the encoding and retaining of information in working memory. Theories of goal-directed and self-regulatory behaviour also provide evidence for increased cognitive engagement of consumers when making choices related to their personal goals and values.

In a similar vein, Gountas *el al.* (2019) used EEG to examine how consumers respond to and process social marketing advertisements in terms of their content and style. In study 2 by Gountas *el al.* (2019), participants watched five anti-drinking and anti-social behaviour short video advertisements while EEG was recorded. Two EEG analysis techniques were employed. The first technique was global field power (GFP), which measures fluctuation of cognitive attention during the watching of advertisements. GFP analysis shows significant millisecond-by-millisecond fluctuations in the theta and alpha EEG bands (calculated from frontal electrodes) for each video. The z-scores of frontal alpha GFP were used to index attention processes, and z-scores of theta GFP were used to index memorisation processes for the whole video. Then the two indexes were combined to produce an overall impression index. Two out of the five tested social marketing video advertisements (video 4 portrayed a shocking situation and video 5 portrayed a familiar situation) obtained the highest overall impression index and were considered more effective in conveying massages to the target audiences. The second EEG technique was standardised low-resolution electromagnetic tomography (sLORETA), which identifies brain regions which contribute to decision-making at the peak of the attention or memorisation process. sLORETA images show the same pattern as GFP, indicating that the same two videos (videos 4 and 5) generated stronger brain activation, which implies heightened cognitive and emotional processing by the participants. Gountas *et al.* (2019) posited that GFP is more powerful and informative relative to sLORETA. These results can help marketers in designing more effective social marketing campaigns and promoting pro-social behaviour.

EEG has been also used to study consumers' preferences and choices. For example, Boksem and Smidts (2015) conducted one of the first experiments using electroencephalography to investigate consumers' preferences and choices. The aim of the study was twofold. First, the authors aimed to identify the specific components of the EEG oscillation that are associated with individual preferences for movies and their population-wide preferences (i.e. commercial success). Second, the authors intended to examine whether neural measures have greater potential to predict consumer preferences and choice compared to conventional (i.e. stated preference) behavioural measures. Twenty-nine participants viewed 18 movie trailers in a random order while EEG was recording (using a Biosemi ActiveTwo high-density, high-sampling-rate EEG system). After each trailer, participants responded to two stated preferences measures: (1) how much they liked the movie and (2) how much they would be willing to pay (WTP) for the DVD of the movie. Finally, after the 18 movie trailers were viewed, participants sorted them in descending order according to their own preferences.

The findings revealed that heightened medial-frontal beta (16–18 Hz) activity during viewing of the trailer is associated with a high preference for that movie, whereas heightened frontocentral gamma activity during viewing of the trailer is related to population-wide preference (i.e. the more money this movie will make at the box office). These findings align with the extant literature, which reported that reward-related stimuli elicit enhanced frontal beta activity and might also reflect a neural mechanism for "coupling systems involved in memory, attention, and motivation" (Hosseini and Holroyd 2015, p. 3). Consequently, Boksem and Smidts (2015) concluded that "the increased amplitudes of beta oscillations evoked by movie trailers seem to indicate that these trailers may be experienced as motivationally rewarding" (p. 489). Also, Boksem and Smidts (2015) tested two regression models, one model that included only WTP as a predictor of individual preferences and choices and one model that had both WTP and frontocentral beta as predictors of individual preferences and choices. The second model with both the neural and stated measures showed a limited but highly significant improvement in the overall model fit. The same results were also obtained for the model assessing population-wide preferences using frontal gamma as a predictor. Thus, the overall results proved the added predictive power of neural markers to stated preference measures and established the unique contribution of neural measures to the prediction of choice behaviour. The authors call for more experiments to be conducted to further validate and establish the robustness of their findings.

Given that visual aesthetics of products is thought to influence consumer preferences and choices, Guo *et al.* (2019) conducted a multi-method study using EEG and eye tracking to better understand neural patterns of the brain during evaluating visual aesthetics of a product. They used EEG oscillations in alpha and gamma frequency ranges to distinguish between high, middle, and low visual aesthetics of a product, given that alpha and gamma bands are reported in the literature to be possibly associated with perceptual and conceptual representations. Overall, the results revealed that low aesthetic products (3D desk lamps) evoked significantly weakened relative alpha power and enhanced relative gamma power.

Examples of EEG frontal asymmetry studies

As a sub-field of emotion and motivation, the study of frontal EEG asymmetry holds substantial promise.

(Coan and Allen 2004, p. 43, emphasis added)

We will include a brief summary of the most powerful frontal EEG asymmetry theoretical frameworks in the literature before presenting this stream of research.

Davidson's (1992, 2004) model represents the most dominant theoretical formulation guiding most EEG frontal asymmetry studies and conceptual arguments, as well as data analysis and interpretation (Cacioppo 2004). Davidson's model postulates that "high levels of relative left frontal activity are associated with the expression and experience of positive, approach-related emotions, and high levels of relative right frontal activity are associated with the experience and expression of negative, withdrawal-related emotions" (Cacioppo 2004, pp. 236–237). In the years since the Davidson (1992) study, there has been tremendous growth in the number of studies investigating the utility of EEG frontal asymmetry in motivational, emotional, and cognitive processes.

EEG frontal asymmetry literature cites other theoretical frameworks than Davidson's model, including, for example, Harmon-Jones's (2004) valence and motivational direction model and Heller's (1993) affective valence and arousal model. These models follow the Davidson model in illustrating that greater relative left frontal activity is linked to the processing of positive emotions and greater relative right frontal activity is linked to the processing of negative emotions. However, these models attempt to draw more distinction between the emotional, motivational, and valence components of frontal EEG asymmetry. For example, the Heller (1993) model distinguishes between the patterns of EEG asymmetry in different cortical regions. He postulates that EEG asymmetry in the frontal region reflects emotional valence, while EEG asymmetry in the right parietal region is involved in regulating autonomic and behavioural arousal (i.e. the intensity of emotions) (Schmidt and Trainor 2001) (for a review, see Davidson 2004; Harmon-Jones 2004; Heller 1993; Spielberg *et al.* 2008; Sutton and Davidson 1997).

The influential article by Coan and Allen (2004), "Frontal EEG Asymmetry as Moderator and Mediator of Emotion", represents an early contribution to the conceptual, methodological, and statistical considerations that guide the field in investigating whether frontal EEG asymmetry serves as a moderator or mediator of emotional processes. According to Cacioppo (2004, p. 239), frontal EEG asymmetry is conceptualised as a mediator when the neural processes underlying the differential frontal activation are thought to be instrumental in the production of tonic affective states or state changes (e.g. more or less pleasant or unpleasant feelings about a stimulus) or approach- or withdrawal-motivational tendencies. By contrast, frontal EEG asymmetry is conceptualised as a moderator when the neural processes underlying it are thought to dampen or augment the processes instrumental in the production of tonic affective states or state changes (Cacioppo 2004, p. 239). See Harmon-Jones and Gable (2018) and Reznik and Allen

(2018) for a comprehensive recent review of the role of frontal EEG asymmetry in emotional and motivational processes.

Recently, cortical frontal asymmetries have been used in studying a wide range of behaviours, including, for example, emotions and approach/avoidance behavioural tendencies (e.g. Ohme *et al.* 2010; Ravaja *et al.* 2013; Tullett *et al.* 2012; Vecchiato *et al.* 2011; Walsh *et al.* 2017) and product preferences and choices (Garczarek-Bąk and Disterheft 2018; Ramsøy *et al.* 2018).

In the context of consumer approach/withdrawal motivation and purchase decisions, Ravaja *et al.* (2013) conducted a study where EEG asymmetry over the prefrontal cortex was employed as an index for approach motivation to predict purchase decisions. Participants (33 business students) viewed seven grocery private label products and seven national brand products whose prices were increased and decreased while their EEG activity was recorded. The findings showed that alpha asymmetry is a significant predictor for purchase decision, as such greater left frontal activation reflects higher approach motivation and higher probability that the participants will buy the product. The finding also revealed that frontal EEG alpha asymmetry was more positively associated with purchase decision for national brand products but not private label products. It was also positively associated with purchase decision when the price of a product was below the normal price but not when it was above the normal price. The authors also examined the EEG asymmetry indices over the central and temporal regions (not only the prefrontal region) and found no relationship between those indices and purchase decision.

Vecchiato and co-authors (2011) examined EEG frontal asymmetrical activations recorded while participants were watching a neutral documentary which was interrupted by TV commercial advertisements. Eleven undergraduate students participated in the study. High-density EEG system (BrainAmp, Brainproducts GmbH, Germany) was utilised for EEG data acquisition. Participants rated the degree to which they perceived each commercial as pleasant and unpleasant. The findings showed that right frontal activity is significantly greater than left frontal activity in theta and alpha bands. Furthermore, the findings also showed that the left frontal and pre-frontal scalp regions are activated when participants watch a pleasant video clip, while the right frontal regions are typically activated while an unpleasant video clip is presented. These results are highly consistent with the reported EEG asymmetric patterns in the literature.

Understanding what shapes consumer food choices and experiences is vital for achieving customer satisfaction. A huge body of literature in the psychology and marketing domains has tried to find an answer to this question. What are the affective, cognitive, and motivational processes that shape consumer food choices? Does the aesthetic appearance of the food products and packaging play a role? Does visual sense also influence their choices? Can EEG inform us about these processes and choices? In an attempt to enlighten our understanding of these processes, Walsh *et al.* (2017) assessed consumers' emotional and motivational behaviours in response to food stimuli using both implicit and explicit measures simultaneously. They measured approach/withdrawal tendencies toward food stimuli using EEG frontal cortex asymmetries along with facial expression (AFEA: index for liking and emotions), heart rate (ECG: index for arousal), and self-report measures. Walsh *et al.* (2017) created two video stimuli averaging 40s in length. The first was "evented" stimuli and contained emotion-eliciting events (foods with spoilage, hygiene and safety characteristics). The second was "control" stimuli and contained non-emotion-eliciting events (i.e. no food concern). After calculating EEG frontal cortex asymmetry scores, a paired sample *t*-test was performed to compare the evented and control stimuli. The results revealed a significant difference in the asymmetric scores between the two stimuli. The evented stimuli elicited greater right hemisphere activation, reflecting withdrawal motivational behaviour. The authors went one step further and performed an exploratory time series analysis on the EEG data. The results showed an approach behaviour tendency

5 seconds prior to viewing the evented stimuli and a shift to withdrawal behaviour tendency during the 5 seconds after the presentation of the evented stimuli. Overall, the EEG findings aligned with the results from the other implicit measures used in the study.

Ramsøy *et al.* (2018) did one of the first studies to investigate the role of prefrontal EEG asymmetry in the context of consumer decision-making and choices. They tried to assess the underlying neural processes of consumers' willingness to pay in exchange for a product or service by means of prefrontal EEG asymmetry. Sixteen women viewed images of products from four categories (bags, clothes, women's shoes, and fast-moving consumer goods) while EEG was recording. Afterwards, participants reported their willingness to pay using a bid task. The Emotiv EPOC EEG system was utilised for raw EEG data acquisition. Data analysis was performed using the EEGLAB toolbox in MATLAB. Prefrontal asymmetry for alpha, beta, and gamma frequencies was calculated and included in the analysis. Findings indicated that pre-frontal asymmetry in both the gamma and beta ranges was significantly related to willingness-to-pay choices. However, unexpectedly their findings showed that there was no significant relationship between frontal asymmetry in the alpha band and willingness-to-pay decisions. This finding should be interpreted in the light of Davidson's (2004) recommendation to go forward carefully in examining other frequency bands, as these may provide additional information not reflected in alpha power. Moreover, differences in methodology could be the reason behind the inconsistent findings in the literature. The type of task used (i.e. resting or emotionally evocative and the extent to which cognition is involved), aspects of the experimental interaction, personal relevance of the stimuli to the participants, time of day or year, type of EEG device, recording montage, site utilised in the analyses of the manner of EEG data preprocessing, and the method in which data was subsequently analyzed, among other factors, might also impact relative left frontal activity findings (Allen *et al.* 2004; Reznik and Allen 2018; Smith *et al.* 2016). To date, none of the published studies in consumer neuroscience have used the Coan and Allen (2004) frontal EEG asymmetry mediator and moderator framework to our knowledge.

Mahmoud (2017) conducted an EEG study, as part of her PhD thesis, where she adapted Coan and Allen's (2004) frontal EEG asymmetry mediator and moderator framework. The aim of the study was to explore the moderating role of frontal EEG alpha asymmetry on the link between co-creation of value and emotions. A between-subjects experimental design was employed. Participants were randomly assigned to either the treatment condition (high co-creation) or the control condition (no co-creation). A sample of 77 graduate and undergraduate students took part in the study. All participants were right-handed, had normal or corrected-to-normal vision, and were not wearing eyeglasses. Raw electroencephalogram data was recorded using the Emotiv Systems Inc. (San Francisco, USA) EPOC 16-electrode cap and accompanying SDK software (TestBuch). MATLAB was used for EEG data filtering and visualisation. The study hypotheses were tested within a moderated mediation analysis framework using the Hayes PROCESS macro in SPSS. Overall, the findings revealed that frontal EEG asymmetries serve as significant moderators of the link between co-creation and emotions.

Examples of event-related potential studies

ERP is considered a well-established EEG paradigm in the literature and has been used in marketing and consumer behaviour to study emotional responses (Pozharliev *et al.* 2015; Stothart *et al.* 2016), attentional and motivational processes (e.g. Liao *et al.* 2019), information processing (e.g. Jones *et al.* 2012), brand perception and preferences (Jin *et al.* 2015), and consumer purchasing decisions (Jones *et al.* 2012; Özkara and Bagozzi 2021).

Stothart *et al.* (2016) recorded EEG from smokers and non-smokers to compare their visual perception of pictorial health warning labels. Four event-related potentials components were extracted from their EEG data. Smokers showed reduced attentional orientation and emotional responses evident in the delayed and lower-amplitude late positive potential (LPP) response. The authors recommended increasing the emotional salience of pictorial health warning content to trigger a stronger emotional response among smokers. Wang *et al.* (2015) is another example of how EEG has been used in research on brain responses to emotionally graphic cigarette warning labels.

Evidence of the utility of ERP in investigating motivational and affective processes related to product endorsement comes from a study by Liao *et al.* (2019). Participants viewed positive or negative gossip about different endorsers (a celebrity, a friend, or a complete stranger) while EEG was recorded. The gossip was simply a sentence describing positive or negative social behaviour of an endorser. Liao *et al.* (2019) extracted two ERP components: (1) the centro-posterior N400 in the 350–500 ms time window and (2) centro-parietal late positive potential in the 500–700 ms time window. The extant ERP literature posits that that N400 component is associated with evaluative processes and typically evoked with the increased cognitive effort needed to update the stored knowledge base after exposure to unforeseen information, or, in other words, information that violates the norm. On the other hand, the late positive potential reflects sustained attention toward emotionally evoking stimuli and is deemed to be driven by motivational salience (for a review, see Hajcak and Olvet 2008). Accordingly, the authors expected that the N400 component would respond more strongly to negative gossip and to gossip about a friend (vs a celebrity or stranger). Further, they expected a larger LPP during friend endorsement relative to celebrity endorsement. The findings illustrate the motivational significance of gossip about friends from a social learning perspective. The findings turned out to be in line with the ERP literature and confirmed the authors' expectations.

Jones *et al.* (2012) used event-related potential to investigate consumer buying decisions. They examined how gender and level of consumer math anxiety (high vs low) interact to influence their decisions to buy discount and non-discount products. They tested a four-way interaction model: buys (yes vs no) × (math anxiety: high vs low) × (condition: no promotion vs promotion) × (gender: male vs female). P200, P3, and frontal N400 (FN400) ERP components were extracted and included in the four-way interaction comparisons. Prior studies postulated that increased frontal P200 and frontocentral P300 are speculatively linked to subjective feeling of knowing, or perceptual fluency, while the FN400 index increases familiarity and reduces conceptual processing (Jones *et al.* 2012). The findings revealed that high math-anxious females show greater P200 amplitudes when they choose to buy non-discounted products. High math-anxious males show greater P3 amplitudes when they decide to buy non-discounted products, while low math-anxious males show greater P3 amplitudes when they decide not to buy non-discounted products. When respondents decide to buy products that are offered at a reduced price, larger FN400 amplitudes are depicted among high math-anxious females and low-math anxious males. Jones and co-authors provided valuable discussion and interpretations of their findings in the light of the neuroscience literature and relevant behavioural and cognitive theories. Overall, they concluded that perceptual and conceptual processes interact with anxiety and gender to modulate brain responses during consumer choices.

Özkara and Bagozzi (2021) studied consumer purchasing decisions that involve both conscious and unconscious processes. The ability to measure mental changes with high temporal resolution makes the EEG-based event-related potential method very useful in studying the distinction between consciousness and unconsciousness. Although experiences with brands significantly affect the awareness or unconsciousness of decisions to purchase, ERP studies have ignored experiences of consumers in relation to brand purchases. For this purpose, EEG recordings of participants were taken in the order they saw brand names: experienced brands, brands with reviews by consumers, and unknown brands. Participants chose one of the three options for the brands they saw on the screen: buying, not buying, and no idea. A total of 35 people participated in the study. The results indicate that early ERPs, which are unconscious mental reactions, related to purchase decisions for previously unknown brands. Late ERPs associated with conscious mental reactions related to purchasing review-based brands or experienced brands. The authors concluded that purchasing decisions about unknown brands occur as a result of automatic, unconscious mental processes, whereas purchasing decisions about previously experienced brands and based on consumer reviews result from conscious mental processes. This study is the first that demonstrates the relationship between ERPs and purchasing decisions, with an experimental design focused on consumer experience and consciousness. The EEG method can thus be used to discover how consumers process information consciously and unconsciously. Results from such studies can provide guidelines concerning advertising strategy and copy, as well as providing insight into estimating consumer receptivity to products.

In closing, the previous section presented examples of pioneering marketing research which utilised EEG systems to provide a more comprehensive and deeper understanding about consumers' affective and motivational behaviour, cognition, and preferences and choices. Next, we will present some ideas for future research.

Directions for future research

Over the last decades, research on how social contexts influence human behaviours and responses has increased dramatically, generating a rich body of literature in the area. However, the study of the neural mechanisms underpinning such influence is a quite untapped area of research. To date, studies examining different brain processes underpinning responses to a specific stimulus were conducted in non-social situations rather than social ones. Only in the last few years have researchers in the field of social neuroscience started to recognise the importance of conducting such studies. EEG recording in such research is called multisubject EEG or hyperscanning EEG.

Verbeke *et al*.s (2014) were among early scholars to incorporate social interaction in studying attachment theory using EEG-based methodology. They probed how attachment styles (secure, avoidant, anxious) modulate cortical brain oscillations occurring in different frequency bands when a person in a task-free resting state, either alone or with another person (that is, when a person is awake in a resting state and sitting passively with another person vs when a person is awake in a resting state and sitting alone). The findings of Verbeke *et al.* (2014) interestingly revealed that only high-anxious attachment participants experienced greater alpha (only over the frontal and parietal regions), beta, and theta power when they were in the resting state together with another person compared to when they were alone. Verbeke *et al.* (2014) revealed that the reasoning behind such results is that sitting passively in resting state and in the presence of others makes anxious attachment style participants preoccupied with how other persons judge them. which is an anxiety-provoking condition given their relative sensitivity to feedback from others. By contrast, avoidant attached people are less social and less concerned with judgments of others, so such situations are not anxiety provoking. Thus, alpha power will be moderated significantly by individuals' scores on anxious attachment, unlike individuals' scores on avoidant attachment.

In a study by Pozharliev *et al.* (2015), two forms of social context were examined using EEG. The study investigated brain responses during mere observation of emotionally salient cues (luxury vs basic branded products) when participants were either alone or in a situation where another person was passively co-present. According to the authors' expectations, in situations that did not involve the stress and commitment experienced during actual buying decisions (e.g. passive viewing situations), images of luxury-branded products are more likely to evoke intense positive emotions like pleasure and joy relative to images of basic branded products. Additionally, based on social facilitation theory, they predicted that the mere presence of others can produce nondirective arousal. Event-related potentials were recorded and three ERP components were extracted: P2 (positive waveform peaking around 150–250 ms after stimulus onset, thought to index early selective attention and modulated by emotional arousal), P3 (positive waveform peaking around 250–450 ms after stimulus onset and thought to be enhanced by exposure to affective motivationally relevant stimuli), and late positive potential (positive waveform peaking around 500–700 ms after stimulus onset and believed to designate prolonged enhanced attention allocation and motivational significance to emotional visual stimuli) (Pozharliev *et al.* 2015). Overall, the study findings confirmed the authors' expectations and revealed heightened LPP amplitudes for luxury than for basic branded products only in the mere presence of another person.

In 2017, Pozharliev and co-authors, in their article tackling consumer neuroscience in advertising contexts, coined the term "social consumer neuroscience". Social consumer neuroscience can be considered a branch of consumer neuroscience where the study of the different brain processes is done while people view relevant marketing stimuli with others rather than in isolation. Social consumer neuroscience is expected to generate salient insights and implications for marketing scholars and professionals. It represents an active and promising area for future research. In the advertising context, Pozharliev *et al.* (2017) advised marketers to carry out research where a group of participants process advertising materials in isolation and another group of participants process the same ad materials but in a dynamic social context. Comparing EEG activation across the two groups might provide novel insights regarding the effects that TV advertisements have on viewers' emotional engagement of marketing stimuli in various social contexts.

To recap, social consumer neuroscience, the study of the different brain processes happening when people view relevant marketing stimuli with others, rather than alone in, holds substantial promise for marketing research.

Another promising direction for future research is the use of asymmetric frontal cortical activity in the study of self-conscious emotions. Harmon-Jones *et al.* (2010) suggested that "asymmetric frontal cortical activity fluctuates with changes in approach motivation even when these changes occur over relatively short periods of time" (p. 458). Given that the experience of some types of self-conscious emotions, such as guilt, may also generate fluctuation in approach/avoidance motivations, this raises the possibility of using asymmetric frontal cortical activity as an index of such fluctuation. Harmon-Jones *et al.*'s (2010) exploratory study confirmed such a prediction by revealing that the initial experience of guilt results in a decreased relative left frontal activation (i.e. a decrease in approach motivation). The feelings of guilt, however, were associated with greater relative left frontal activity when participants were given a chance to perform correction behaviour. Such interesting findings open the door to using frontal EEG to understand the underlying neural activation of the brain while experiencing one of the self-conscious emotions.

Conclusion

Our purpose has been to introduce how electrophysiological systems can be employed in the marketing domain. EEG studies provide more comprehensive understating of how consumers process information and respond to different marketing stimuli. Marketers need to realise the advantages and limitations of EEG systems and how to use them appropriately to obtain reliable, valuable, and genuine insights from their studies. It is beyond the scope of this chapter to deal with issues of reliability and validity (for more details in this regard, see Bagozzi and Lee 2019; Towers and Allen 2009). As we pointed out before, recent developments in EEG devices and analysis algorithms have led to improvement in its capability to depict not only brain activation but also brain localisation. This implies that the potential of EEG methods in marketing research is still not fully realised, and more studies need to be conducted.

References

Abhang, P.A., Gawali, B.W. and Mehrotra, S.C., 2016. *Introduction to EEG-and Speech-Based Emotion Recognition*. Academic Press.

Allen, J.J., Coan, J.A. and Nazarian, M., 2004. Issues and assumptions on the road from raw signals to metrics of frontal EEG asymmetry in emotion. *Biological Psychology*, 67(1), 183–218. DOI: 10.1016/j.biopsycho.2004.03.007.

Bagozzi, R.P. and Lee, N., 2019. Philosophical foundations of neuroscience in organizational research: Functional and nonfunctional approaches. *Organizational Research Methods*, 22(1), 299–331. DOI: 10.1177/1094428117697042.

Baillet, S., 2011. Electromagnetic brain mapping using MEG and EEG. In J. Decety and J.T. Cacioppo, eds. *The Oxford Handbook of Social Neuroscience*. Oxford Library of Psychology, 97–133.

Biosemi.com, n.d. *Biosemi EEG ECG EMG BSPM NEURO Amplifiers Systems* [online]. Available from: www.biosemi.com/faq/adjust_samplerate.htm [Accessed 23 June 2020].

Boksem, M.A.S. and Smidts, A., 2015. Brain responses to movie trailers predict individual preferences for movies and their population-wide commercial success. *Journal of Marketing Research*, 52(4), 482–492. DOI: 10.1509/jmr.13.0572.

Bunge, S.A. and Kahn, I., 2009. Cognition: An overview of neuroimaging techniques. *Encyclopedia of Neuroscience*, 1063–1067. DOI: 10.1016/B978-008045046-9.00298-9.

Cacioppo, J.T., 2004. Feelings and emotions: Roles for electrophysiological markers. *Biological Psychology*, 67(1–2), 235–243. DOI: 10.1016/j.biopsycho.2004.03.009.

Coan, J.A. and Allen, J.J., 2004. Frontal EEG asymmetry as a moderator and mediator of emotion. *Biological psychology*, 67(1–2), 7–49. DOI: 10.1016/j.biopsycho.2004.03.002.

Cohen, M.X., 2014. *Analyzing Neural Time Series Data: Theory and Practice*. MIT Press.

Coles, M.G., 1989. Modern mind-brain reading: Psychophysiology, physiology, and cognition. *Psychophysiology*, 26(3), 251–269.

Cox, D.D. and Savoy, R.L., 2003. Functional magnetic resonance imaging (fMRI) "brain reading": Detecting and classifying distributed patterns of fMRI activity in human visual cortex. *Neuroimage*, 19(2), 261–270. DOI: 10.1016/s1053-8119(03)00049-1.

Davidson, R.J., 1992. Anterior cerebral asymmetry and the nature of emotion. *Brain and Cognition*, 20(1), 125–151.

Davidson, R.J., 2004. What does the prefrontal cortex "do" in affect: Perspectives on frontal EEG asymmetry research. *Biological Psychology*, 67(1–2), 219–234. DOI: 10.1016/j.biopsycho.2004.03.008.

Dimoka, A., Davis, F.D., Gupta, A., Pavlou, P.A., Banker, R.D., Dennis, A.R., Ischebeck, A., Müller-Putz, G., Benbasat, I., Gefen, D. and Kenning, P.H., 2012. On the use of neurophysiological tools in IS research: Developing a research agenda for NeuroIS. *MIS Quarterly*, 679–702. DOI: 10.2307/41703475. DOI: 10.1201/b17605.

Farnsworth, B., 2020. *Top 14 EEG Hardware Companies [Ranked] – Imotions. Imotions* [online]. Available from: https://imotions.com/blog/top-14-eeg-hardware-companies-ranked/ [Accessed 12 August 2017].

Fisch, B.J. and Spehlmann, R., 1999. *Fisch and Spehlmann's EEG Primer: Basic Principles of Digital and Analog EEG*. Elsevier Health Sciences.

Gamboa, H., 2005. File: Eeg Raw.Svg – Wikimedia commons. *Commons.wikimedia.org* [online]. Available from: https://commons.wikimedia.org/wiki/File:Eeg_raw.svg [Accessed August 2017].

Garczarek-Bąk, U. and Disterheft, A., 2018. EEG frontal asymmetry predicts product purchase differently for national brands and private labels. *Journal of Neuroscience, Psychology, and Economics*, 11(3), 182–195. DOI: 10.1037/npe0000094.

Gountas, J., Gountas, S., Ciorciari, J. and Sharma, P., 2019. Looking beyond traditional measures of advertising impact: Using neuroscientific methods to evaluate social marketing messages. *Journal of Business Research*, 105, 121–135. DOI: 10.1016/j.jbusres.2019.07.011.

Guo, F., Li, M., Hu, M., Li, F. and Lin, B., 2019. Distinguishing and quantifying the visual aesthetics of a product: An integrated approach of eye-tracking and EEG. *International Journal of Industrial Ergonomics*, 71, 47–56. DOI: 10.1016/j.ergon.2019.02.006.

Hairston, W.D., Whitaker, K.W., Ries, A.J., Vettel, J.M., Bradford, J.C., Kerick, S.E. and McDowell, K., 2014. Usability of four commercially-oriented EEG systems. *Journal of Neural Engineering*, 11(4), 046018. DOI: 10.1088/1741-2560/11/4/046018.

Hajcak, G. and Olvet, D.M., 2008. The persistence of attention to emotion: Brain potentials during and after picture presentation. *Emotion*, 8(2), 250. DOI: 10.1037/1528-3542.8.2.250.

Harmon-Jones, E., 2004. Contributions from research on anger and cognitive dissonance to understanding the motivational functions of asymmetrical frontal brain activity. *Biological Psychology*, 67(1–2), 51–76. DOI: 10.1016/j.biopsycho.2004.03.003.

Harmon-Jones, E. and Gable, P.A., 2018. On the role of asymmetric frontal cortical activity in approach and withdrawal motivation: An updated review of the evidence. *Psychophysiology*, 55(1), e12879. DOI: 10.1111/psyp.12879.

Harmon-Jones, E., Gable, P.A. and Peterson, C.K., 2010. The role of asymmetric frontal cortical activity in emotion-related phenomena: A review and update. *Biological Psychology*, 84(3), 451–462. DOI: 10.1016/j.biopsycho.2009.08.010.

Harris, J.M., Ciorciari, J. and Gountas, J., 2018. Consumer neuroscience for marketing researchers. *Journal of Consumer Behaviour*, 17(3), 239–252. DOI: 10.1002/cb.1710.

Heller, W., 1993. Neuropsychological mechanisms of individual differences in emotion, personality, and arousal. *Neuropsychology*, 7(4), 476. DOI: 10.1037/0894-4105.7.4.476.

Hosseini, A.H. and Holroyd, C.B., 2015. Reward feedback stimuli elicit high-beta EEG oscillations in human dorsolateral prefrontal cortex. *Scientific Reports*, 5, 13021. DOI: 10.1038/srep13021.

Jiang, Z., 2014. Event related potentials. In K. Nidal and A.S. Malik, eds. *EEG/ERP Analysis: Methods and Applications*. CRC Press, 3–90. DOI: 10.1201/b17605.

Jin, J., Wang, C., Yu, L. and Ma, Q., 2015. Extending or creating a new brand: Evidence from a study on event-related potentials. *NeuroReport*, 26(10), 572–577. DOI: 10.1097/WNR.0000000000 000390.

Jones, W.J., Childers, T.L. and Jiang, Y., 2012. The shopping brain: Math anxiety modulates brain responses to buying decisions. *Biological Psychology*, 89(1), 201–213.

Kable, J.W., 2011. The cognitive neuroscience toolkit for the neuroeconomist: A functional overview. *Journal of Neuroscience, Psychology, and Economics*, 4(2), 63. DOI: 10.1037/a0023555.

Karmarkar, U.R. and Plassmann, H., 2019. Consumer neuroscience: Past, present, and future. *Organizational Research Methods*, 22(1), 174–195. DOI: 10.1177/1094428117730598.

Kenning, P., Plassmann, H. and Ahlert, D., 2007. Applications of functional magnetic resonance imaging for market research. *Qualitative Market Research: An International Journal*, 10(2), 135–152. DOI: 10.1108/13522750710740817.

Kropotov, J.D., 2010. *Quantitative EEG, Event-Related Potentials and Neurotherapy*. Academic Press. DOI: 10.1016/B978-0-12-374512-5.50038-3.

Laureys, S., Peigneux, P. and Goldman, S., 2002. Brain imaging. In H. D'haenen, J.A. den Boer and P. Willner, eds. *Biological Psychiatry*, Vol. 1. New York: Wiley, 155–166. DOI: 10.1002/0470854871.chxi.

Lee, E.J., Kwon, G., Shin, H.J., Yang, S., Lee, S. and Suh, M., 2014. The spell of green: Can frontal EEG activations identify green consumers? *Journal of Business Ethics*, 122(3), 511–521. DOI: 10.1007/s10551-013-1775-2.

Lewine, J.D. and Orrison, W.W., 1995. Clinical electroencephalography and event related potentials. In W.W. Orrison, J.D. Lewine, J.A. Sanders and M.F. Hartshorne, eds. *Functional Brain Imaging*. St. Louis: Moshby, 327–368.

Liao, W., Zhang, Y. and Peng, X., 2019. Neurophysiological effect of exposure to gossip on product endorsement and willingness-to-pay. *Neuropsychologia*, 132, 107123. DOI: 10.1016/j.neuropsychologia.2019.107123.

Lithari, C., Frantzidis, C.A., Papadelis, C., Vivas, A.B., Klados, M.A., Kourtidou-Papadeli, C., Pappas, C., Ioannides, A.A. and Bamidis, P.D., 2010. Are females more responsive to emotional stimuli? A neurophysiological study across arousal and valence dimensions. *Brain topography*, 23(1), 27–40. DOI: 10.1007/s10548-009-0130-5.

Lopes da Silva, F., 2010. EEG: Origin and measurement. In C. Mulert and L. Lemieux, eds. *EEG-fMRI: Physiological Basis, Technique, and Applications*. New York: Springer, 19–38.

Luck, S.J., 2014. *An Introduction to the Event-Related Potential Technique*. MIT Press, Cambridge.

Mahmoud, R.R.A., 2017. *The Use of Neuromarketing Research to Explore Consumers' Co-Creation Experiences: Applied on Higher Education Market*. Unpublished (PhD) dissertation, Faculty of Commerce, English Section, Suez Canal University, Ismailia, Egypt.

Malik, A.S. and Amin, H.U., 2017. *Designing EEG Experiments for Studying the Brain: Design Code and Example Datasets*. Academic Press. DOI: 10.1016/B978-0-12-811140-6.00001-1.

Maskeliunas, R., Damasevicius, R., Martisius, I. and Vasiljevas, M., 2016. Consumer-grade EEG devices: Are they usable for control tasks? *PeerJ*, 4, e1746. DOI: 10.7717/peerj.1746.

Menon, V. and Crottaz-Herbette, S., 2005. Combined EEG and fMRI studies of human brain function. *International Review of Neurobiology*, 66(5), 291–321. DOI: 10.1016/S0074-7742(05)66010-2.

Michel, C.M. and Brunet, D., 2019. EEG source imaging: A practical review of the analysis steps. *Frontiers in neurology*, 10. DOI: 10.3389/fneur.2019.00325.

Motamedi-Fakhr, S., Moshrefi-Torbati, M., Hill, M., Hill, C.M. and White, P.R., 2014. Signal processing techniques applied to human sleep EEG signals – a review. *Biomedical Signal Processing and Control*, 10, 21–33. DOI: 10.1016/j.bspc.2013.12.003.

Nisar, H. and Yeap, K.H., 2014. Introduction. In K. Nidal and A.S. Malik, eds. *EEG/ERP Analysis: Methods and Applications*. Boca Raton: CRC Press, 1–20.

Ohme, R., Reykowska, D., Wiener, D. and Choromanska, A., 2010. Application of frontal EEG asymmetry to advertising research. *Journal of Economic Psychology*, 31(5), 785–793. DOI: 10.1016/j.joep.2010.03.008.

Özkara, B. and Bagozzi, R.P., 2021. Using event-related potentials brain methods to study conscious and unconscious consumer decisions. *Journal of Retailing and Consumer Services*, 58. https://doi.org/10.1016/j.jretconser.2020.102202.

Pizzagalli, D.A., 2007. Electroencephalography and high-density electrophysiological source localization. In J.T. Cacioppo, L.G. Tassinary and G. Berntson, eds. *Handbook of Psychophysiology*. Cambridge: Cambridge University Press, 56–84.

Plassmann, H., Carolyn Yoon, C., Fred Feinberg, F. and Baba Shiv, B., 2011. Consumer neuroscience. In R.P. Bagozzi and A. Ruvio, eds. *Wiley International Encyclopedia of Marketing*, Vol. 3. West Sussex: John Wiley and Sons, 115–122. DOI: 10.1002/9781444316568.wiem03051.

Pozharliev, R., Verbeke, W.J. and Bagozzi, R.P., 2017. Social consumer neuroscience: Neurophysiological measures of advertising effectiveness in a social context. *Journal of Advertising*, 46(3), 351–362. DOI: 10.1080/00913367.2017.1343162.

Pozharliev, R., Verbeke, W.J., Van Strien, J.W. and Bagozzi, R.P., 2015. Merely being with you increases my attention to luxury products: Using EEG to understand consumers' emotional experience with luxury branded products. *Journal of Marketing Research*, 52(4), 546–558. DOI: 10.1509/jmr.13.0560.

Ramsøy, T.Z., Skov, M., Christensen, M.K. and Stahlhut, C., 2018. Frontal brain asymmetry and willingness to pay. *Frontiers in Neuroscience*, 12, 138. DOI: 10.3389/fnins.2018.00138.

Ravaja, N., Somervuori, O. and Salminen, M., 2013. Predicting purchase decision: The role of hemispheric asymmetry over the frontal cortex. *Journal of Neuroscience, Psychology, and Economics*, 6(1), 1–13. DOI: 10.1037/a0029949.

Reznik, S.J. and Allen, J.J., 2018. Frontal asymmetry as a mediator and moderator of emotion: An updated review. *Psychophysiology*, 55(1), e12965. DOI: 10.1111/psyp.12965.

Roach, B.J. and Mathalon, D.H., 2008. Event-related EEG time-frequency analysis: An overview of measures and an analysis of early gamma band phase locking in schizophrenia. *Schizophrenia bulletin*, 34(5), 907–926. DOI: 10.1093/schbul/sbn093.

Sanei, S. and Chambers, J.A., 2007. Introduction to EEG. In *EEG Signal Processing*. John Wiley and Sons Ltd., 1–34. DOI: 10.1002/9780470511923.ch1.

Savoy, R.L., 2001. History and future directions of human brain mapping and functional neuroimaging. *Acta Psychologica*, 107(1), 9–42. DOI: 10.1016/s0001-6918(01)00018-x.

Schmidt, L.A. and Trainor, L.J., 2001. Frontal brain electrical activity (EEG) distinguishes valence and intensity of musical emotions. *Cognition and Emotion*, 15(4), 487–500. DOI: 10.1080/0269993 0126048.

Shaw, S.D. and Bagozzi, R.P., 2018. The neuropsychology of consumer behavior and marketing. *Consumer Psychology Review*, 1(1), 22–40. DOI: 10.1002/arcp.1006.

Shiv, B., Bechara, A., Levin, I., Alba, J.W., Bettman, J.R., Dube, L., Isen, A., Mellers, B., Smidts, A., Grant, S.J. and McGraw, A.P., 2005. Decision neuroscience. *Marketing Letters*, 16(3–4), 375–386. DOI: 10.1007/s11002-005-5899-8.

Smith, E.E., Reznik, S.J., Stewart, J.L. and Allen, J.J.B., 2016. Assessing and conceptualizing frontal EEG asymmetry: An updated primer on recording, processing, analyzing, and interpreting frontal alpha asymmetry. *International Journal of Psychophysiology*, 111, 98–114. DOI: 10.1016/j.ijpsycho.2016.11.005.

Spielberg, J.M., Stewart, J.L., Levin, R.L., Miller, G.A. and Heller, W., 2008. Prefrontal cortex, emotion, and approach/withdrawal motivation. *Social and Personality Psychology Compass*, 2(1), 135–153. DOI: 10.1111/j.1751-9004.2007.00064.x.

Srinivasan, N., 2007. Cognitive neuroscience of creativity: EEG based approaches. *Methods*, 42(1), 109–116. DOI: 10.1016/j.ymeth.2006.12.008.

Stothart, G., Maynard, O., Lavis, R. and Munafò, M., 2016. Neural correlates of cigarette health warning avoidance among smokers. *Drug and Alcohol Dependence*, 161, 155–162. DOI: 10.1016/j.drugalcdep.2016.01.025.

Sutton, S.K. and Davidson, R.J., 1997. Prefrontal brain asymmetry: A biological substrate of the behavioral approach and inhibition systems. *Psychological Science*, 8(3), 204–210. DOI: 10.1111/j.1467-9280.1997.tb00413.x.

Tatum IV, W., 2014. Normal EEG. In W.O. Tatum IV, ed. *Handbook of EEG Interpretation*, 2nd ed. Demos Medical Publishing, 1–56.

Towers, D.N. and Allen, J.J., 2009. A better estimate of the internal consistency reliability of frontal EEG asymmetry scores. *Psychophysiology*, 46(1), 132–142. DOI: 10.1111/j.1469-8986.2008.00759.x.

Tullett, A.M., Harmon-Jones, E. and Inzlicht, M., 2012. Right frontal cortical asymmetry predicts empathic reactions: Support for a link between withdrawal motivation and empathy. *Psychophysiology*, 49, 1145–1153. DOI: 10.1111/j.1469-8986.2012.01395.x.

Vecchiato, G., Toppi, J., Astolfi, L., Fallani, F.D.V., Cincotti, F., Mattia, D., Bez, F. and Babiloni, F., 2011. Spectral EEG frontal asymmetries correlate with the experienced pleasantness of TV commercial advertisements. *Medical and Biological Engineering and Computing*, 49(5), 579–583. DOI: 10.1007/s11517-011-0747-x.

Verbeke, W.J., Pozharliev, R., Van Strien, J.W., Belschak, F. and Bagozzi, R.P., 2014. "I am resting but rest less well with you." The moderating effect of anxious attachment style on alpha power during EEG resting state in a social context. *Frontiers in Human Neuroscience*, 8, 486. DOI: 10.3389/fnhum.2014.00486.

Walsh, A.M., Duncan, S.E., Bell, M.A., O'Keefe, S.F. and Gallagher, D.L., 2017. Integrating implicit and explicit emotional assessment of food quality and safety concerns. *Food Quality and Preference*, 56, 212–224. DOI: 10.1016/j.foodqual.2016.11.002.

Wang, A.L., Romer, D., Elman, I., Turetsky, B.I., Gur, R.C. and Langleben, D.D., 2015. Emotional graphic cigarette warning labels reduce the electrophysiological brain response to smoking cues. *Addiction biology*, 20(2), 368–376. DOI: 10.1111/adb.12117.

Weiergräber, M., Papazoglou, A., Broich, K. and Müller, R., 2016. Sampling rate, signal bandwidth and related pitfalls in EEG analysis. *Journal of Neuroscience Methods*, 268, 53–55. DOI: 10.1016/j.jneumeth.2016.05.010.

16

HOW BRAND INTEREST MEDIATES THE RELATIONSHIP BETWEEN CROSS-MEDIA INVESTMENTS AND WORD-OF-MOUTH AND PURCHASE INTENTION

A mixture-amount moderated mediation model

Patrick De Pelsmacker, Nathalie Dens, Peter Goos and Leonids Aleksandrovs

Summary

Consumers' media usage patterns interact with the advertising media mix to affect brand interest and, purchase and word-of-mouth intention. This chapter explains the use of mixture-amount modelling, a novel methodology in marketing research, to analyse the impact of advertising effort and allocation of this effort across magazines and television on purchase and word-of-mouth intention and to test the mediating role of brand interest and the moderating role of consumers' media usage. It uses illustrative data from 52 beauty care product advertising campaigns that ran in the Netherlands and Belgium, we illustrate mixture-amount modelling. It also shows how to quantify the synergy or cannibalization between magazine and television advertising. It shows how the optimal media mix differs depending on total advertising investment and consumers' media usage patterns. The chapter shows that positive and negative synergistic effects differ for different advertising budgets and media usage patterns.

Introduction

Advertisers repeatedly have to decide on the total amount of advertising effort to invest (i.e. budget, gross rating points, or GRPs) and on how to allocate this effort across different media. A large number of studies indicate that marketers can create positive synergy effects by spreading their effort across different media (Naik and Raman 2003; Chang and Thorson 2004; Vakratsas and Ma 2005; Havlena *et al.* 2007; Reynar *et al.* 2010; Voorveld *et al.* 2011). Positive synergy is created when advertising investments in multiple media produce a joint effect greater than the same investments in any single medium. At the same time, other studies detect poor or no synergistic effects (Wakolbinger *et al.* 2009; Pfeiffer and Zinnbauer 2010; Frison *et al.* 2014) or even negative effects (Tsao and Sibley 2004; Dijkstra *et al.* 2005; Godfrey *et al.* 2011). According to Assael (2011), the largest void in the literature on advertising is research on media allocation guidelines that can optimize synergistic cross-media effects.

Despite its relevance to advertisers and media planners, a sound methodology to investigate the optimal allocation of advertising budgets across different media is lacking (Schultz *et al.* 2012). This chapter's objective is to partly fill this void by proposing such a new methodology, mixture-amount modelling (MAM), to investigate how advertisers can maximize campaign effectiveness in terms of activation (i.e. word-of-mouth and purchase intentions) by optimizing their advertising effort across different media, and this for different levels of total investments. The novelty of this model is that it explicitly allows simulation of how the optimal media mix allocation changes for varying amounts of advertising investment. To our knowledge, there are no other models in contemporary literature that explicitly allow for the derivation of different optima for different total amounts of advertising effort.

Mixture-amount models have a long history in industrial statistics, bio-science engineering, medicine and agriculture (Cornell 2002; Smith 2005). This chapter represents one of the first applications to marketing that we are aware of. We provide a proof of concept based on real-life observational data involving individual responses to 52 advertising campaigns with a large spread in advertising effort and allocations to different media. In his overview article of 50 years of media mix research, Assael (2011) stresses that the key requirement for identifying synergies in cross-media advertising is to measure the effect of interactions between media at the individual consumer level. This has been identified as an important research topic by several other authors as well (Hung *et al.* 2005; Pilotta and Schultz 2005; Wendel and Dellaert 2005; Wang 2006; Hallward 2008; Enoch and Johnson 2010; Schultz *et al.* 2012). In the present study, we measure brand activation and consumer media usage at the individual respondent level.

According to the traditional hierarchy-of-effects principle, advertising campaigns lead to behavioural (intention) outcomes through the effect they have on intermediary evaluative brand responses of consumers (Barry 1987, 2002; Barry and Howard 1990). Evaluative brand effects thus mediate the relationship between campaign characteristics and behavioural advertising outcomes. However, no study has yet explored how brand evaluation mediates the effect of different media advertising effort allocations on behavioural outcomes. The importance of studying mediating processes for media effects has been stressed by a number of studies (McLeod and Reeves 1980; McGuire 1986; Holbert and Stephenson 2003). Therefore, in this chapter, we test the mediating effect of brand interest on the relationship between campaign characteristics (the advertising effort and its allocation across two types of media) on behavioural outcomes, more particularly word-of-mouth and purchase intentions towards the advertised brands.

Compared to more traditional regression models (e.g. Gatignon and Hanssens 1987; Danaher and Dagger 2013), mixture-amount models not only allow for optimization but also for simulations to predict responses for different combinations of advertising effort and cross-media allocation across consumer groups. Indeed, the model can be extended to include different moderators. Therefore, we use the same modelling approach to explore how consumers' media usage moderates this mediation effect. We investigate how the optimal allocation (and the resulting responses) change for consumers with different media usage patterns. This extension enables us to gain insight into the way in which consumers with different media usage profiles differ in their response to cross-media advertising efforts and how cross-media synergy interacts with consumers' media usage profile to affect outcomes. Finally, we propose a method to

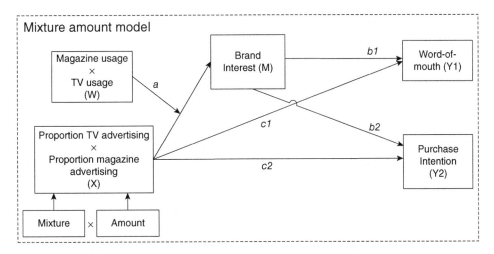

Figure 16.1 Moderated mediation MAM structure

Source: The authors

formally quantify the synergistic effects of cross-media investments for different levels of advertising investments and media usage profiles.

In sum, the proposed new method has the potential to answer important questions advertisers may have: What is the impact of the total advertising effort on advertising effectiveness, and does this depend on the media mix utilized? What is the optimal media mix for every possible total advertising effort, and how does this mix impact outcomes? Is the optimal media mix also different for different target groups? Does a positive synergy exist between different media? If yes, does the synergy depend on the total advertising effort, and is it different for different target groups? Is brand interest a relevant consumer response for explaining activation?

The conceptual model tested in this chapter is presented in Figure 16.1.

Cross-media advertising synergy effects

Many studies, either experimental or those based on real-life data, have been devoted to studying interactions or synergy between different media. Most of these studies indicate that advertising campaigns involving multiple media produce better results than campaigns using a single medium; that is, they find a positive synergistic effect. For example, in an experimental study, Chang and Thorson (2004) found that showing an advertisement on both TV and the Internet was superior to repeating that advertisement in either of the media in terms of attention, perceived message credibility and number of total and positive thoughts. In an experimental study by Voorveld *et al.* (2011), exposure to cross-media advertising (TV and the Internet) resulted in a more positive attitude toward the brand, attitude toward the TV commercial and purchase intention than repetitive single-medium exposure (TV or the Internet). Naik and Raman (2003) show that sales for Dockers benefit from positive synergy between magazine and TV advertising. Reynar *et al.* (2010) optimized media spending and allocations of the advertising budget for packaged consumer goods across a variety of media to maximize revenues and profits. Their results support the existence of positive synergy effects through the indirect effect one medium has on another.

At the same time, other studies have detected poor or no cross-media synergistic effects or even negative effects (cannibalization). For example, Havlena *et al.* (2007) find little or no synergy effects when online banner advertising is added to the media mix. Frison *et al.* (2014) found no evidence of short- or long-run synergistic effects between billboard and cinema advertising. An experimental study by Dijkstra *et al.* (2005) demonstrates the superiority of TV-only campaigns over multiple-media campaigns in evoking cognitive responses and that print-only campaigns are as effective as multiple-media campaigns for most responses.

A large number of prior studies on synergy effects are experimental (Tsao and Sibley 2004; Dijkstra *et al.* 2005; Bronner and Neijens 2006; Wang 2006). As a result, they involve only a limited number of allocations to different media and usually suffer from limited ecological validity. At the same time, modelling papers on sales data often involve aggregated sales responses, generalizing across effects that occur at the individual level. Our methodological approach allows for a systematic estimation of synergy effects for different levels of advertising effort based on a large selection of real campaigns and individual consumer responses to these campaigns.

The mediating effect of brand interest

According to the classical hierarchy-of-effects principle, advertising campaigns lead to behavioural outcomes through the effect they have on cognitive and affective responses of consumers (Barry 1987, 2002; Barry and Howard 1990). First, consumers learn about a campaign and the brand in the campaign (cognitive response), then they develop positive attitudes and evaluations (affective response) and finally they develop behavioural intentions and ultimately behaviour. Previous responses in the hierarchy are considered necessary conditions for subsequent responses to occur. In advertising strategy and advertising research, cognitive and affective responses are therefore referred to as 'intermediary' effects, that is, effects of advertising campaigns that mediate the effect of the campaign on behavioural outcomes. Intermediary brand effects are an indication of how the campaign has affected brand cognitions and attitudes. Brand knowledge (cognitive) and brand attitude or interest (affective) are examples of such intermediary brand effects. There is ample evidence that evaluative brand effects (such as brand attitudes or brand interest) mediate the relationship between campaign characteristics and advertising outcomes (Hoyle and Kenny 1999; Zarantonello and Schmitt 2013). However, none of the previous studies explored how brand interest mediates different media advertising effort allocations on behavioural outcomes. Therefore, in this chapter, we test the mediating effect of brand interest (an evaluative intermediary brand response) on the relationship between campaign characteristics (the advertising effort and its allocation across two types of media) on behavioural outcomes, more particularly word-of-mouth and purchase intentions towards the advertised brands. We hypothesize that brand interest will positively mediate the effects of cross-media advertising efforts on purchase intention (PI) and word-of-mouth (WoM).

The moderating effect of consumer media usage

There is ample evidence that people frequently consume several media simultaneously (Lin *et al.* 2013). For example, Nielsen (2014) reports that 84% of smartphone and tablet owners use their devices as second screens while watching TV at the same time. Advertisers exploit consumers' use of multiple media by using multiple channels to increase the reach and frequency of exposure to a campaign. Most previous studies that have investigated the impact of consumer media usage on advertising responses have used an experimental approach to study the effect of individuals' usage of a single medium on advertising responses. For instance, Krugman *et al.*

(1995) found that the longer a person attends to TV, the more TV ads he or she remembers. Danaher and Mullarkey (2003) examined how factors such as webpage viewing duration impact web advertising recall and recognition.

Importantly, none of these studies have investigated the impact of varying allocations of advertising efforts across multiple media on advertising effectiveness for consumer groups differing in media usage. Nevertheless, being able to tailor an advertising strategy, and more particularly the media mix allocation, to a target group is essential to maximize advertising efficiency. In this study, we not only study how cross-media synergy effects differ across advertising investment levels but also across audiences. On the one hand, targeting logic would suggest that a relatively higher proportion of magazine advertising would be best for heavy magazine readers (and likewise for heavy television users). On the other hand, heavy users of one medium tend to be heavy users of many media (Enoch and Johnson 2010). Therefore, the outcome in terms of optimal media mix is not that straightforward. Different media mixes may also be appropriate depending on the size of the campaign. Specifically, we investigate how the optimal media mix depends on the total advertising effort as well as consumers' media usage. We also quantify how synergy effects change as a function of the investment effort and the consumer group.

Mixture-amount model specification

Basic model structure

The type of regression model we use in this chapter is inspired by research in industrial statistics, bio-science engineering, medicine and agriculture (Cornell 2002; Smith 2005). In agriculture, for instance, fertilizers and pesticides are commonly used to enhance the yield of a crop. The fertilizers and pesticides are mixtures of various ingredients. Statistical models for studying the yield of a crop not only use the amount of fertilizer as an independent variable but also the proportions of the different ingredients. These models are commonly referred to as mixture-amount models (Cornell 2002) and allow the optimal proportion of the ingredients to depend on the dose of fertilizer or pesticide. For instance, choosing the right amount of fertilizer and the right proportion of the different ingredients given the amount of fertilizer may lead to improved plant growth (Niedz and Evens 2011).

Just like farmers and food scientists must decide on how much fertilizer to use and what its composition should be, marketers must decide on how much effort to spend on an advertising campaign and on how to allocate this effort across different media. The effect of a campaign is influenced by the total advertising effort as well as by the allocation of this effort to the different media. So, conceptually, the decision problem of marketers, on the one hand, and farmers and food scientists, on the other hand, is the same. Therefore, MAMs are very suitable for studying the impact of advertising effort and its allocation across different media on advertising effectiveness measures.

The basic specification of a mixture-amount model (1) recognizes that advertising in magazines and on television might have a different impact, (2) allows for a possible interaction effect between magazine and television advertising (i.e. allows for [positive or negative] synergistic effects) and (3) allows for a possible interaction effect between the amount of advertising and the proportion of magazine or television advertising. Therefore, the model allows one to determine an optimal media mix allocation for each advertising amount, including interpolation to advertising amounts not present in the dataset. The basic model structure thus looks at follows. Assume we have q ingredients in a mixture and denote the proportion of the ith ingredient by x_i

and the total amount of the mixture (or a transformation of it) by A. A MAM allowing for linear and nonlinear mixing effects among the q mixture components, can be formulated as follows:

$$\eta = \sum_{i=1}^{q} \beta_i x_i + \sum_{i=1}^{q-1} \sum_{j=i+1}^{q} \beta_{ij} x_i x_j + A(\sum_{i=1}^{q} \gamma_i x_i + \sum_{i=1}^{q-1} \sum_{j=i+1}^{q} \gamma_{ij} x_i x_j), \tag{1}$$

where η represents the linear predictor of an outcome, β_i and β_{ij} represent the effects of the mixture composition, and γ_i and γ_{ij} represent the interaction effects of the (transformation of the) amount A with the mixture's composition. The MAM in Equation (1) involves several terms which capture interaction effects between different ingredient proportions and interaction effects between the total amount and the ingredient proportions. This allows cross-media synergy to be captured and the optimal values of the proportions to depend on the total amount. In the context of advertising, q corresponds to the number of media types utilized, x_i corresponds to the proportion of advertising in the ith medium, A is a measure of the total advertising effort and η is the outcome.

The model can also include fixed effects to allow for different intercepts between, for instance, countries. To capture all the dependencies between responses in the data, a number of random effects can be included, for instance, to control for the fact that the data include measurements at different points in time, to model the dependency between answers from the same respondent or to capture the dependency between all answers for the same campaign and for the same brand. Hence, we adopt a multilevel generalized linear model (GLM) approach.

Regression models for mixture data do not involve an intercept because the sum of all ingredient proportions equals 1. Also, in the presence of interactions between the ingredient proportions, it is impossible to include the proportions' quadratic effects in the model. These technical issues with models for mixture data are explained in detail in Goos and Jones (2011). Regression models for data from mixtures are characterized by a large degree of multicollinearity, because the ingredient proportions cannot be changed independently: when one proportion goes up, at least one other proportion has to go down. This makes most of the usual significance tests for individual coefficients, which implicitly assume that all the regression coefficients can be interpreted independently, useless. The models are, however, useful for making predictions and for determining the optimal proportions of the ingredients for any given total amount.

The inclusion of moderators

In this study, we include respondent information in the MAM, that is, their media usage, and treat the variables quantifying that information as moderators. The resulting model is akin to mixture-process variable models in Næs *et al.* (1998), Cornell (2002), Kowalski *et al.* (2002), Smith (2005) and Goos and Jones (2011). An appropriate model for the impact of q ingredient proportions and l moderating variables $z_1, \ldots, z_l$ on a response η is given by

$$\eta = \sum_{i=1}^{q} \beta_i x_i + \sum_{i=1}^{q-1} \sum_{j=i+1}^{q} \beta_{ij} x_i x_j + \sum_{k=1}^{l} z_k (\sum_{i=1}^{q} \gamma_{ik} x_i + \sum_{i=1}^{q-1} \sum_{j=i+1}^{q} \gamma_{ijk} x_i x_j), \tag{2}$$

In the context of the current chapter, the process variables $z_1, \ldots, z_l$ correspond to the usage of magazines and television.

Model specification for the present study

The model structure displayed in Figure 16.1 was tested through a series of regressions, following the procedure proposed by Baron and Kenny (1986) and Sobel (1982). In the first step, we analyze the effects of the media mix on word-of-mouth and purchase intention (paths *c1 and c2* in Figure 16.1) by means of two mixture amount models formulated as follows:

$$\eta = \beta_{mag}x_{mag} + \beta_{TV}x_{TV} + \gamma_{mag}x_{mag}A + \gamma_{TV}x_{TV}A + \beta_{int}x_{mag}x_{TV} + \gamma_{int}x_{mag}x_{TV}A, \tag{3}$$

where η represents word-of-mouth and purchase intention, x_{mg} and x_{TV} represent the proportions of magazine and TV advertising and the amount A is a measure for the total advertising effort (in natural logarithm of GRPs).

In the second step, we estimate a second MAM for the effects of the media mix on the mediator, brand interest (path *a* in Figure 16.1). Because our model involves a moderated mediation, we also added the effects of the moderators (magazine and TV usage [W]). Ignoring the random effects, the linear predictor in our MAM is given by:

$$\begin{aligned}
\eta = {} & \beta_{mg}x_{mg} + \beta_{TV}x_{TV} + \gamma_{mg}x_{mg}A + \gamma_{TV}x_{TV}A + \beta_{int}x_{mg}x_{TV} + \gamma_{int}x_{mg}x_{TV}A \\
& + \lambda_{mg}x_{mg}m_{mg} + \lambda_{TV}x_{TV}m_{mg} + \varphi_{mg}x_{mg}Am_{mg} + \varphi_{TV}x_{TV}Am_{mg} + \lambda_{int}x_{mg}x_{TV}m_{mg} + \varphi_{int}x_{mg}x_{TV}Am_{mg} \\
& + \kappa_{mg}x_{mg}m_{TV} + \kappa_{TV}x_{TV}m_{TV} + \phi_{mg}x_{mg}Am_{TV} + \phi_{TV}x_{TV}Am_{TV} + \kappa_{int}x_{mg}x_{TV}m_{TV} + \phi_{int}x_{mg}x_{TV}Am_{TV} \\
& + \iota_{mg}x_{mg}m_{mg}m_{TV} + \iota_{TV}x_{TV}m_{mg}m_{TV} + \vartheta_{mg}x_{mg}Am_{mg}m_{TV} + \vartheta_{TV}x_{TV}Am_{mg}m_{TV} + \iota_{int}x_{mg}x_{TV}m_{mg}m_{TV} + \vartheta_{int}x_{mg}x_{TV}Am_{mg}m_{TV},
\end{aligned} \tag{4}$$

where η represents brand interest, x_{mg} and x_{TV} represent the proportions of magazine and TV advertising and the amount A is a measure for the total advertising effort (in natural logarithm of GRPs). The second and third lines in Equation (4) describe how the media mix effects and the effect of the amount of advertising are moderated by magazine usage m_{mg} and TV usage m_{TV}, respectively. The fourth line in Equation (4) adds the magazine usage m_{mg} and TV usage m_{TV} interaction effects.

In the third step, we regressed purchase intention and word-of-mouth on brand interest with all random effects, using a generalized linear mixed model (path *b1* and *b2*, in Figure 16.1). Since word-of-mouth outcome is binary, we used a generalized linear mixed model with a logit link function to estimate path *b1*.

All regressions include random effects to model the dependency between answers from the same respondent (as each respondent scored multiple campaigns) and between answers for the same campaign, the same brand, the regions and the waves. Hence, we adopt a multilevel regression approach when estimating the mediation model. Our dataset is sufficiently large to assume that there is enough power to apply a Sobel test (Zhao *et al.* 2010). Therefore, we rely on Sobel tests to test the significance of the conditional indirect paths (Sobel 1982; Baron and Kenny 1986).

Data and measures

Advertising effort data and consumer responses were collected for 52 skin and hair care (shampoo, facial cream, soap) campaigns that ran in magazines and/or on TV in the Netherlands and Belgium between June and December 2011. We selected 19 campaigns which ran in the Netherlands, 18 campaigns which ran in Flanders (the northern Dutch-speaking part of Belgium) and 15 campaigns which ran in Wallonia (the southern French-speaking part of Belgium). The campaigns in the Netherlands involved 15 brands from 6 mother brands (e.g. the brands Youth Code and Revitalift from the mother brand L'Oréal Paris). The campaigns in Flanders involved 13 brands from 4 mother brands, while the campaigns in Wallonia involved 11 brands from 4 mother brands. Some brands had multiple campaigns in the tested period and were included several times.

To quantify the advertising effort in each campaign, we use gross rating point indicators. A GRP value is the number of contacts of a campaign expressed as a percentage of the target audience. We use GRP values rather than campaign budgets expressed in monetary terms because campaign budgets are biased by the discounts offered by media companies, which typically vary across campaigns, brands and media. Moreover, a euro spent on TV advertising is certainly not equivalent to a euro spent on advertising in a given magazine. In terms of advertising effort, a GRP, on the other hand, is always worth the same, since it represents contacts with the target group regardless of the medium vehicle used. That is why GRPs, as a standardized measure for the number of contacts with the target group, are better suited for our purposes. GRP values were also used by Danaher and Dagger (2013), for example, for the same reason and were also advocated as a suitable measure in a multi-media context (Fulgoni 2015).

The different campaigns were selected at five different time points, which we refer to as waves. For each campaign, data was available on the number of GRPs that were invested in TV and magazine advertising. We used the GRP values in the six weeks preceding the data collection as input for our analyses. Table 16.1 provides examples of the data. In the table, x_{mag} and x_{TV} represent the proportions of magazine and TV advertising investments, respectively.

For the dependent variable and the moderators in the model, we used panel data collected through GfK. The data contains detailed respondent feedback on the 52 campaigns. As the selected campaigns involve skin and hair products for women, the respondents in the study were randomly selected women in the age range of 20 to 50 (the target group), who were representative of the Dutch and Belgian population in terms of education and social status. In each wave, about 500 respondents were recruited for the Netherlands, Flanders and Wallonia to evaluate

Table 16.1 Input data examples (advertising campaigns)

Campaign	Brand	Mother brand	Region	Wave	Advertising effort: GRPs	Proportion of magazine advertising x_{mag}	Proportion of TV advertising x_{TV}
1	1	1	The Netherlands	1	582.1	1	0
2	2	2	The Netherlands	2	87.1	0.25	0.75
3	3	4	The Netherlands	2	347.7	0.02	0.98
4	4	1	The Netherlands	4	71.0	0.11	0.89
...	...	...	...	...	...	...	...
19	1	1	The Netherlands	5	349.4	0.11	0.89
20	4	1	Flanders	1	227.4	0.14	0.86
21	5	4	Flanders	2	497.8	0.20	0.80
22	1	1	Flanders	3	359	0	1
23	6	2	Flanders	4	115.7	0.32	0.68
...	...	...	...	...	...	...	...
37	1	1	Flanders	5	48.8	0.25	0.75
38	4	1	Wallonia	1	255.6	0	1
39	1	1	Wallonia	3	36.6	0	1
40	6	2	Wallonia	4	190.6	0.24	0.76
41	1	1	Wallonia	5	624.4	0.28	0.72
...	...	...	...	...	...	...	...

Source: Authors

between two and four campaigns. As a result, the dataset contains repeated measurements for each respondent. In total, the analyzed dataset contains 26785 responses from 6679 respondents.

Word-of-mouth intention was measured using eight binary questions, where 1 means that the respondent had initiated or would consider initiating this WoM activity (e.g. 1 = "start a conversation with friends, family, colleagues or acquaintances about the campaign", 0 = "respondent has not initiated or would not consider initiating this type of WoM"). The WoM variable used in the analysis is a 0–1 variable: 0 if the respondent has not initiated or has not considered initiating any of the eight WoM activities; 1 if the respondent has initiated or would consider initiating at least one of the eight WoM activities. Purchase intention (PI) was measured using a single-item 7-point semantic differential (not at all likely–very likely). Brand interest (BI) was measured using a 10-item 7-point Likert scale (e.g. "This campaign has led me to pay more attention to the brand in the store", "This campaign has encouraged me to try the brand", $\alpha = 0.97$). To obtain a single score for BI, we averaged respondents' scores across the ten items. In this chapter, respondents' magazine usage was measured on a 5-point scale (1 = leaf through magazines without actually reading them; 5 = read them thoroughly from cover to cover). The TV usage measure was a 9-point scale (1 = less than 30 minutes per day; 9 = eight or more hours per day).

Results

The models' overall F-tests are displayed in Table 16.2. Coefficient estimates and significance tests are displayed in Tables 16.3 to 16.5. However, due to the MAM requirement that the sum of all ingredient proportions must equal 1, together with the large number of interactions in our MAM (five-way interaction), it is not useful to interpret the individual estimates of the MAM-coefficients in Table 16.3 because of multicollinearity. However, one can predict and optimize responses perfectly well, even in the presence of multicollinearity (see e.g. Goos *et al.* 2016). To interpret the results, we therefore depict them in the prediction profiler embedded in the software package JMP.

The analysis in the first step shows that the direct effects of the media mix (X) on WoM and PI (paths $c1$ and $c2$) are not significant (F-tests in Table 16.2). However, the presence of a direct effect is not a prerequisite for mediation (Zhao *et al.* 2010). The second step shows that the media mix (X) has a significant impact on brand interest (M) (path a) as the overall F-statistic in Table 2 is significant ($p < .001$). The third step, which tests paths $b1$ and $b2$ (generalized linear mixed models) shows a positive and significant effect of brand interest on purchase intention ($\theta_M x_M = .561$, $p < .001$), and on WoM ($\theta_M x_M = 1.158$, $p < .001$). Based on the results for

Table 16.2 Significance tests (overall F-tests)

Model	F value	Pr > F
Path $c1$: Word-of-mouth (Y1) on media mix (X)	1.25	0.288
Path $c2$: Purchase intention (Y2) on media mix (X)	1.42	0.214
Path a: Brand interest (M) on media mix (X) moderated by media usage (W)	9.32	<.001
Path $b1$: Word-of-mouth (Y1) on brand interest (M)	1323.09	<.001
Path $b2$: Purchase intention (Y2) on brand interest (M)	2753.96	<.001

Source: Authors

Table 16.3 Brand interest (M) on media mix (X) moderated by media usage (W)

Effect	Estimate	Standard error	F Value	Pr > F
$\beta_{mg} x_{mg}$	3.346	1.516	4.87	.027
$\beta_{TV} x_{TV}$	.488	1.822	.07	.789
$\gamma_{mg} x_{mg} A$	.022	.334	.00	.947
$\gamma_{TV} x_{TV} A$	.486	.323	2.27	.132
$\beta_{int} x_{mg} x_{TV}$	12.614	8.304	2.31	.129
$\gamma_{int} x_{mg} x_{TV} A$	−2.070	1.536	1.82	.178
$\lambda_{mg} x_{mg} m_{mg}$	−.029	.394	.01	.942
$\lambda_{TV} x_{TV} m_{mg}$	1.209	.478	6.38	.012
$\varphi_{mg} x_{mg} A m_{mg}$	−.002	.087	.00	.980
$\varphi_{TV} x_{TV} A m_{mg}$	−.214	.085	6.33	.012
$\lambda_{int} x_{mg} x_{TV} m_{mg}$	−5.365	2.175	6.09	.014
$\varphi_{int} x_{mg} x_{TV} A m_{mg}$	.965	.402	5.75	.017
$\kappa_{mag} x_{mag} m_{TV}$	.162	.323	.25	.616
$\kappa_{TV} x_{TV} m_{TV}$	.582	.370	2.48	.116
$\phi_{mag} x_{mag} A m_{TV}$	−.044	.071	.38	.538
$\phi_{TV} x_{TV} A m_{TV}$	−.105	.066	2.56	.110
$\kappa_{int} x_{mag} x_{TV} m_{TV}$	−2.732	1.670	2.67	.102
$\phi_{int} x_{mag} x_{TV} A m_{TV}$	.495	.310	2.54	.111
$l_{mg} x_{mg} m_{mg} m_{TV}$	−.048	.083	.33	.563
$l_{TV} x_{TV} m_{mg} m_{TV}$	−.193	.098	3.92	.048
$\vartheta_{mg} x_{mg} A m_{mg} m_{TV}$	.017	.019	.80	.370
$\vartheta_{TV} x_{TV} A m_{mg} m_{TV}$	.038	.017	4.84	.028
$l_{int} x_{mg} x_{TV} m_{mg} m_{TV}$	1.028	.439	5.50	.019
$\vartheta_{int} x_{mg} x_{TV} A m_{mg} m_{TV}$	−.193	.081	5.64	.018

Source: Authors

paths a and b (Tables 16.3–16.5), a Sobel tests confirms that the indirect effect is significant for PI ($z = -2.373$; $p = .018$) and WoM ($z = -2.378$; $p = .017$). Based on the fact that the direct effects of the media mix on WoM and PI are not significant (paths $c1$ and $c2$), this indicates indirect-only mediation (Zhao *et al.* 2010).

In Figures 16.2 to 16.4, we display prediction profiler outputs for various scenarios representing different GRP inputs and levels of media usage on PI. Using the estimates from Tables 16.3–16.5, the prediction profiler allows us to show the combined direct and indirect effect (media mix effects on PI through BI) for different levels of media usage and GRPs. We show PI outcomes in Figures 16.3–16.5, but the outcomes for WoM are similar. We show the corresponding BI, PI and WoM outcomes and summarize the key indicators for different scenarios in Table 16.6.

The first scenario listed in Table 16.6 involves a relatively low advertising effort of 150 GRPs for respondents with moderate levels of magazine (3) and TV usage (5). In this scenario, an allocation of 48% to magazine advertising and 52% to TV advertising maximizes the predicted PI (3.68) and WoM (5%). If an advertiser would increase the campaign weight to 620 GRPs (Scenario 2, Table 6), given the same consumer media usage levels as in Scenario 1, the maximum PI would increase to 3.74 and WoM to 6%. Under this scenario, the optimal media mix also shifts from 52% for TV and 48% for magazines to 38% for TV and 62% for magazines. In case

Table 16.4 Word-of-mouth (Y1) on brand interest (M) $(\theta_M x_M)$

Effect	Estimate	Standard error	t Value	Pr > |t|
Intercept	−7.168	0.248	−28.86	<.001
$\theta_M x_M$	1.158	0.032	36.37	<.001

Source: Authors

Table 16.5 Purchase intention (Y2) on brand interest (M) $(\theta_M x_M)$

Effect	Estimate	Standard error	t Value	Pr > |t|
Intercept	1.638	.174	9.42	<.001
$\theta_M x_M$	.561	.011	52.48	<.001

Source: Authors

Table 16.6 BI, PI and WoM for five example scenarios

Scenario	1	2	3	4	5
GRP	150	620	620	620	620
Magazine usage	3 (moderate)	3 (moderate)	5 (high)	1 (low)	5 (high)
TV usage	5 (moderate)	5 (moderate)	9 (high)	9 (high)	1 (low)
Optimal mag. proportion	48%	62%	100%	46%	59%
Optimal TV proportion	52%	38%	0	54%	41%
Brand interest	3.64	3.75	4.81	3.54	3.95
Purchase Intention	3.68	3.74	4.33	3.63	3.84
Word-of-mouth	5%	6%	17%	4%	7%

Source: Authors

of high levels of magazine (5) and TV (9) usage, for a campaign weight of 620 GRPs (Scenario 3, Table 6), the optimal media mix of 100% of magazine advertising and 0% of TV advertising leads to a predicted PI of 4.33 and a WoM of 17%. In case of a low level of magazine usage (1), a high level of TV usage (9) and a campaign weight of 620 GRPs (Scenario 4, Table 16.6), the maximum predicted PI drops to 3.63 and WoM to 4%, while the optimal media mix changes to 46% of magazine advertising and 54% of TV advertising. When consumers use magazines with high intensity (5) and TV with low (1) intensity (Scenario 5, Table 6), the optimal media mix changes to 59% for magazines and 41% for TV, and the maximum predicted PI becomes 3.84 and WoM 7%.

Figure 16.2 represents Scenario 1 of Table 16.5. The vertical axis represents the level of PI on a 7-point scale. The horizontal axis shows the levels of the five explanatory variables in the MAM: the proportion of magazine advertising, the proportion of TV advertising, GRPs, magazine usage and TV usage. In each of the panels of the figure, dashed vertical lines indicate the level of the explanatory variables. The solid convex curved lines in the first two panels show how PI changes as a function of the allocation of campaign spends. Figure 16.2 shows that, in

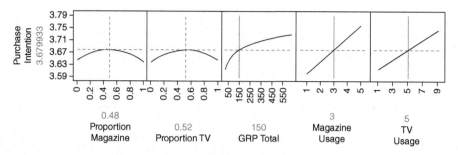

Figure 16.2   Prediction profiler for Scenario 1

Source: The authors

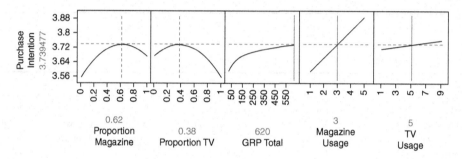

Figure 16.3   Prediction profiler for Scenario 2

Source: The authors

this scenario, a media mix of 48% magazines and 52% TV maximizes PI (3.68). The shape of the convex curves in the first two panels shows a positive synergistic effect – if the allocation is different, PI will drop. If campaign weight is increased to 620 GRPs (Scenario 2), the maximal PI would increase to 3.74 (38% TV and 62% magazines; Figure 16.3). The convex curves in the first two panels of Figure 16.3 show that a different allocation of the advertising effort of 620 GRPs to the two media under study would lead to a drop in the PI. For instance, if all 620 GRPs were invested in magazines, the predicted PI would drop to 3.67. In case of Scenario 3, the optimal proportions of 100% magazine and 0% TV advertising lead to a PI of 4.33. The inverted shape of the convex curves in the first two panes of Figure 16.4 indicate a media cannibalization (negative synergistic) effect.

Synergistic effects measure

To measure the synergistic effect of cross-media advertising, we calculate a media mix synergy coefficient that we define as the difference between the value of the dependent variable for the optimal media mix and the maximum of all scenarios involving a single medium investment, in the case of a positive synergistic effect. In case of cross-media cannibalization, we define the coefficient to be the difference between the value of the dependent variable for the worst media

Table 16.7 Synergy coefficient for five example scenarios

Scenario	1	2	3	4	5
GRP	150	620	620	620	620
Magazine usage	3 (moderate)	3 (moderate)	5 (high)	1 (low)	5 (high)
TV usage	5 (moderate)	5 (moderate)	9 (high)	9 (high)	1 (low)
Optimal mag. proportion	48%	62%	100%	46%	59%
Optimal TV proportion	52%	38%	0	54%	41%
BI synergy coefficient	3.64	3.75	4.81	3.54	3.95
PI synergy coefficient	0.03	0.07	0.31	0.26	0.27
WoM synergy coefficient	0.003	0.007	0.098	0.019	0.0285

Source: Authors

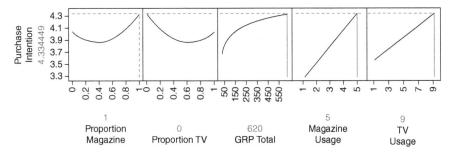

Figure 16.4   Prediction profiler for Scenario 3

Source: The authors

mix and the minimum of all scenarios involving a single medium investment. The mathematical expression for the synergy coefficient is:

$$\varsigma_m = \begin{cases} \tau_{opt} - \max(v_1, v_2, ..., v_i, ..., v_n), \tilde{\rho}_{opt} \neq \% \\ \tau_{min} - \min(v_1, v_2, ..., v_i, ..., v_n), \tilde{\rho}_{opt} = \% \end{cases} \tag{5}$$

where τ_{opt} represents the value of the dependent variable for the optimal media mix allocation, τ_{min} is the value of the dependent variable for the worst media mix allocation and v_i is the response in the case where the entire campaign budget is invested in medium i. For example, in Scenario 4, the optimal media mix resulted in a predicted PI of 3.63. If an advertiser fully invested the 620 GRPs in TV (and thus no GRPs in magazines), the predicted PI would be 3.36. If only magazines were used, PI would be 3.26. Therefore, the synergy coefficient for PI under this scenario equals 3.63 − 3.36 = 0.27. This means that, in the given scenario, by spreading their efforts across magazine and TV advertising according to the optimal media mix derived from the estimated MAM, advertisers can increase PI by 0.27 points, compared to the situation in which they allocated the entire advertising effort to the "best" single medium (in this case, TV). Figure 16.5 shows how the synergy coefficient for PI changes as a function of GRP for different levels of media usage. When advertisers invest a relatively low number of GRPs and consumers are light magazine users, the synergy is highest when consumers are also light users of TV. For intensive TV users under this scenario, the synergy is negative. With

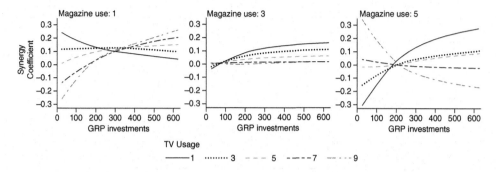

Figure 16.5   Synergy coefficient as a function of GRP, grouped by magazine usage and TV usage

Source: The authors

increasing GRPs, the synergy becomes most positive for intensive TV users. For moderate to high magazine users, the synergy increases with increasing GRPs when consumers are low TV users. For consumers with a high usage of both media, the synergistic effect decreases with the number of GRPs (and eventually becomes negative). Table 16.7 summarizes key scenario synergy coefficients for PI and WoM.

Discussion

We applied a mixture-amount modelling approach in a multilevel moderated mediation framework for advertisement investment optimization. We found that consumers' media usage patterns interact with the total advertising effort and the media mix to have an effect on brand interest. Not surprisingly, for consumers with low magazine usage and high TV usage, proportionally more advertising should be done on TV in order to maximize brand interest, purchase intention and word-of-mouth. Conversely, for consumers with high magazine usage and low TV usage, more advertising investments should be allocated to magazines in order to maximize outcomes.

In addition, brand interest acts as a full mediator for the effect of the advertising effort and the media mix on word-of-mouth and purchase intention. It should be noted that increasing advertising investment in terms of GRP only results in a minor increase in brand interest and as a result in word-of-mouth and purchase intention regardless of the media mix and consumers' media usage. This could be because the brands used in our study are all well-established brands. Attitudes toward such brands are stable and hard to affect through advertising (Machleit *et al.* 1993). This is because consumers are already familiar with the brand and have already formed expectations regarding its advertising (Alden *et al.* 2000; Dahlén and Lange 2005). Our results show a relatively low impact of advertising efforts on word-of-mouth. Word-of-mouth, however, is typically hard to influence (Dellarocas 2003; Jansen *et al.* 2009). Typically, advertised products rarely create buzz (Berger and Schwartz 2011). For instance, a study by Niederhoffer *et al.* (2007) showed that 10% of consumer packaged goods account for 85% of the buzz. Practitioners also often argue that products need to be novel or surprising to be talked about (Dye 1999; Berger and Schwartz 2011). The products in our study are all well-established brands, which might subdue word-of-mouth effectiveness.

We developed a synergy coefficient and studied how synergy effects change with investment efforts and across consumer groups. Consistent with the majority of previous studies, a positive synergistic effect of a TV and magazine advertising mix on outcomes was found. However, our results also show negative synergistic effects of TV and magazine advertising. The synergy coefficient is more positive for consumers with high magazine usage and low TV usage and for consumers with high TV usage and low magazine usage when more GRPs are invested. For consumers with high usage of both media, the synergy coefficient becomes negative when advertisers invest more than 150 GRPs (Figure 16.5). This could be due to ceiling effects: consumers who watch television intensively may be more likely to notice a campaign there, and so the added value of magazine advertising may be limited as a result thereof. This may result in so-called media cannibalization (Rice 1987). Our results also show that for consumers with low usage of both media, synergistic effects also become lower with more GRP (Figure 16.5).

Typically, an advertiser defines a target group, decides on a budget and, with the assistance of a media planner, allocates this budget across media vehicles to optimize the effect of the campaign in terms of GRPs. Consequently, traditional media planning decisions do not take responses to advertising into account. They are aimed at maximizing potential contacts with the target group, not at campaign effectiveness. As a conceptual and methodological contribution, we proposed and tested a novel modelling approach that allows estimation of the direct and indirect effects of advertising efforts and media allocation across different consumer groups on behavioural advertising outcomes using real-life campaign data and individual measurements of media usage, brand interest, word-of-mouth and purchase intention. The predicted response values obtained from an estimated MAM can also be used to quantify how synergy effects change with investment effort and across consumer groups.

Raman (2010) already suggested that an optimal allocation can enhance a firm's profitability by as much as 400%. Our modelling approach allows one to improve the efficiency of media planning, in terms of evaluative and behavioural advertising effects. The results of our study can help practitioners optimize their advertising efforts and media allocation decisions in terms of achieving optimal attitudinal and behavioural responses to their campaigns. They further allow them to differentiate their media mix for consumer groups that vary in the degree of media usage. Obviously, campaign effectiveness also depends on factors other than advertising budgets and media allocation. Future research should try to include these factors, such as advertising creativity, originality or the quality of advertising executions.

References

Alden, D., Mukherjee, A. and Hoyer, W.D., 2000. The effects of incongruity, surprise and positive moderators on perceived humor in television advertising. *Journal of Advertising*, 29(2), 1–15. DOI: 10.1080/00913367.2000.10673599.

Assael, H., 2011. From silos to synergy. A fifty-year review of cross-media research shows synergy has yet to achieve its full potential. *Journal of Advertising Research*, 51(1, 50th Anniversary Supplement), 42–48. DOI: 10.2501/JAR-51-1-042-058.

Baron, R. and Kenny, D., 1986. The moderator–mediator variable distinction in social psychological research: Conceptual, strategic, and statistical considerations. *Journal of Personality and Social Psychology*, 51(6), 1173–1182. DOI: 10.1037/0022-3514.51.6.1173.

Barry, T., 1987. The development of the hierarchy of effects: An historical perspective. *Current Issues and Research in Advertising*, 10(1–2), 251–295. DOI: 10.1080/01633392.1987.10504921.

Barry, T., 2002. In defense of the hierarchy of effects: A rejoinder to Weilbacher. *Journal of Advertising Research*, 42(3), 44–47. DOI: 10.2501/JAR-42-3-44-47.

Barry, T. and Howard, D., 1990. A review and critique of the hierarchy of effects in advertising. *International Journal of Advertising*, 9(2), 121–135. DOI: 10.1080/02650487.1990.11107138.

Berger, J. and Schwartz, E., 2011. What drives immediate and ongoing word of mouth? *Journal of Marketing Research*, 48(5), 869–880. DOI: 10.1509/jmkr.48.5.869.

Bronner, F. and Neijens, P.C., 2006. Audience experiences of media context and embedded advertising: A comparison of eight media. *International Journal of Market Research*, 48(1), 81–100. DOI: 10.1177/147078530604800106.

Chang, Y. and Thorson, E., 2004. Television and web advertising synergies. *Journal of Advertising*, 33(2), 75–84. DOI: 10.1080/00913367.2004.10639161.

Cornell, J., 2002. Experiments with mixtures: Designs, models, and the analysis of mixture data, 3rd ed. New York: Wiley.

Dahlén, M. and Lange, F., 2005. Advertising weak and strong brands: Who gains? *Psychology and Marketing*, 22(6), 473–488. DOI: 10.1002/mar.20069.

Danaher, P. and Dagger, T., 2013. Comparing the relative effectiveness of advertising channels: A case study of a multimedia blitz campaign. *Journal of Marketing Research*, 50(4), 517–534. DOI: 10.1509/jmr.12.0241.

Danaher, P. and Mullarkey, G., 2003. Factors affecting online advertising recall: A study of students. *Journal of Advertising Research*, 43(3), 252–267. DOI: 10.2501/JAR-43-3-252-267.

Dellarocas, C., 2003. The digitization of word of mouth: Promise and challenges of online feedback mechanisms. *Management Science*, 49(10), 1407–1424. DOI: 10.1287/mnsc.49.10.1407.17308.

Dijkstra, M., Buijtels, H. and van Raaij, W.F., 2005. Separate and joint effects of medium type on consumer responses: A comparison of television, print, and the Internet. *Journal of Business Research*, 58(3), 377–386. DOI: 10.1016/S0148-2963(03)00105-X.

Dye, R., 1999. The buzz on buzz. *Harvard Business Review*, 78(6), 139–146.

Enoch, G. and Johnson, K., 2010. Cracking the cross-media code: How to use single-source measures to examine media cannibalization and convergence. *Journal of Advertising Research*, 50(2), 125–136. DOI: 10.2501/S0021849910091294.

Frison, S., Dekimpe, M.G., Croux, C. and De Maeyer, P., 2014. Billboard and cinema advertising: Missed opportunity or spoiled arms? *International Journal of Research in Marketing*, 31(4), 425–433. DOI: 10.1016/j.ijresmar.2014.05.004.

Fulgoni, G., 2015. Is the GRP really dead in a cross-platform ecosystem? Why the gross rating point metric should thrive in today's fragmented media world. *Journal of Advertising Research*, 55(4), 358–361. DOI: 10.2501/JAR-2015-019.

Gatignon, H. and Hanssens, D., 1987. Modeling marketing interactions with application to salesforce effectiveness. *Journal of Marketing Research*, 24(3), 247–257. DOI: 10.1177/002224378702400301.

Godfrey, A., Seiders, K. and Voss, G., 2011. Enough is enough! The fine line in executing multichannel relational communication. *Journal of Marketing*, 75(4), 94–109. DOI: 10.1509/jmkg.75.4.94.

Goos, P. and Jones, B., 2011. *Optimal Design of Experiments: A Case Study Approach*. Southern Gate, UK: John Wiley and Sons.

Goos, P., Jones, B. and Syafitri, U., 2016. I-optimal design of mixture experiments. *Journal of the American Statistical Association*, 111(514), 899–911. DOI: 10.1080/01621459.2015.1136632.

Hallward, J., 2008. "Make measurable what is not so": Consumer mix modeling for the evolving media world. *Journal of Advertising Research*, 48(3), 339–351. DOI: 10.2501/S0021849908080392.

Havlena, W., Cardarelli, R. and De Montigny, M., 2007. Quantifying the isolated and synergistic effects of exposure frequency for TV, print, and Internet advertising. *Journal of Advertising Research*, 47(3), 215–221. DOI: 10.2501/S0021849907070262.

Holbert, R. and Stephenson, M., 2003. The importance of indirect effects in media effects research: Testing for mediation in structural equation modeling. *Journal of Broadcasting and Electronic Media*, 47(4), 556–572. DOI: 10.1207/s15506878jobem4704_5.

Hoyle, R. and Kenny, D., 1999. Sample size, reliability, and tests of statistical mediation. In R. Hoyle, ed. *Statistical Strategies for Small Sample Research*, Vol. 1. Thousand Oaks, CA: Sage Publications, 195–222.

Hung, K., Gu, F. and Tse, D., 2005. Improving media decisions in China: A targetability and cost-benefit analysis. *Journal of Advertising*, 34(1), 49–63. DOI: 10.1080/00913367.2005.10639186.

Jansen, B., Zhang, M., Sobel, K. and Chowdury, A., 2009. Twitter power: Tweets as electronic word of mouth. *Journal of the American Society for Information Science and Technology*, 60(11), 2169–2188. DOI: 10.1002/asi.21149.

Kowalski, S., Cornell, J. and Vining, G., 2002. Split-plot designs and estimation methods for mixture experiments with process variables. *Technometrics*, 44(1), 72–79. DOI: 10.1198/004017002753398344.

Krugman, D., Cameron, G. and White, C., 1995. Visual attention to programming and commercials: The use of in-home observations. *Journal of Advertising*, 24(1), 1–12. DOI: 10.1080/00913367.1995.10673464.

Lin, C., Venkataraman, S. and Jap, S., 2013. Media multiplexing behavior: Implications for targeting and media planning. *Marketing Science*, 32(2), 310–324. DOI: 10.1287/mksc.1120.0759.

Machleit, K., Allen, C. and Madden, T., 1993. The mature brand and brand interest: An alternative consequence of ad-evoked affect. *Journal of Marketing*, 57(4), 72–82. DOI: 10.1177/002224299305700406.

McGuire, W., 1986. The myth of massive media impact: Savagings and salvagings. In G. Comstock, ed. *Public Communication and Behavior*. Orlando, FL: Academic Press, 173–257.

McLeod, J. and Reeves, B., 1980. On the nature of mass media effects. In S.B. Withey and R.P. Ables, eds. *Television and Social Behavior: Beyond Violence and Children*. Hillsdale, NJ: Erbaum.

Næs, T., Færgestad, E. and Cornell, J., 1998. A comparison of methods for analyzing data from a three component mixture experiment in the presence of variation created by two process variables. *Chemometrics and Intelligent Laboratory Systems*, 41(2), 221–235. DOI: 10.1016/S0169-7439(98)00056-2.

Naik, P. and Raman, K., 2003. Understanding the impact of synergy in multimedia communications. *Journal of Marketing Research*, 40(4), 375–388. DOI: 10.1509/jmkr.40.4.375.19385.

Niederhoffer, K., Mooth, R., Wiesenfeld, D. and Gordon, J., 2007. The origin and impact of CPG new-product buzz: Emerging trends and implications. *Journal of Advertising Research*, 47(4), 420–426. DOI: 10.2501/S0021849907070432.

Niedz, R. and Evens, T., 2011. Mixture screening and mixture-amount designs to determine plant growth regulator effects on shoot regeneration from grapefruit (citrus paradisi macf. Epicotyls). *In Vitro Cellular and Developmental Biology-Plant*, 47(6), 682–694. DOI: 10.1007/s11627-011-9381-4.

Nielsen, 2014. *The Digital Consumer* [online]. Available from: www.nielsen.com/us/en/insights/reports/2014/the-us-digital-consumer-report.html [Accessed 5 January 2016].

Pfeiffer, M. and Zinnbauer, M., 2010. Can old media enhance new media? How traditional advertising pays off for an online social network. *Journal of Advertising Research*, 50(1), 42–49. DOI: 10.2501/S0021849910091166.

Pilotta, J. and Schultz, D., 2005. Simultaneous media experience and synesthesia. *Journal of Advertising Research*, 45(1), 19–26. DOI: 10.1017/S0021849905050087.

Raman, K., 2010. Resource allocation in marketing. *Journal of Research and Management*, 1, 51–62. DOI: 10.15358/0344-1369-2010-JRM-1-81.

Reynar, A., Phillips, J. and Heumann, S., 2010. New technologies drive CPG media mix optimization. *Journal of Advertising Research*, 50(4), 416–427. DOI: 10.2501/S002184991009156.

Rice, M., 1987. A comparison of unidimensional and multidimensional television exposure distribution models. *International Journal of Research in Marketing*, 4(2), 147–156. DOI: 10.1016/0167–8116(87)90005-X.

Schultz, D., Block, M. and Raman, K., 2012. Understanding consumer-created media synergy. *Journal of Marketing Communications*, 18(3), 173–187. DOI: 10.1080/13527266.2011.567453.

Smith, W., 2005. *Experimental Design for Formulation*. Philadelphia: University City Science Center, Siam.

Sobel, M., 1982. Asymptotic confidence intervals for indirect effects in structural equation models. *Sociological Methodology*, 13, 290–312. DOI: 10.2307/270723.

Tsao, J. and Sibley, S., 2004. Displacement and reinforcement effects of the Internet and other media as sources of advertising information. *Journal of Advertising Research*, 44(1), 126–142. DOI: 10.1017/S0021849904040073.

Vakratsas, D. and Ma, Z., 2005. A look at the long-run effectiveness of multimedia advertising and its implications for budget allocation decisions. *Journal of Advertising Research*, 45(2), 241–254. DOI: 10.1017/S0021849905050269.

Voorveld, H., Neijens, P. and Smit, E., 2011. Opening the black box: Understanding cross-media effects. *Journal of Marketing Communications*, 17(2), 69–85. DOI: 10.1080/13527260903160460.

Wakolbinger, L., Denk, M. and Oberecker, K., 2009. The effectiveness of combining online and print advertisements: Is the whole better than the individual parts? *Journal of Advertising Research*, 49(3), 360–372. DOI: 10.2501/S0021849909090436.

Wang, A., 2006. When synergy in marketing communication online enhances audience response: The effects of varying advertising and product publicity messages. *Journal of Advertising Research*, 46(2), 160–170. DOI: 10.2501/S0021849906060181.

Wendel, S. and Dellaert, B., 2005. Situation variation in consumers' media channel consideration. *Journal of the Academy of Marketing Science*, 33(4), 575–584. DOI: 10.1177/0092070305277447.

Zarantonello, L. and Schmitt, B., 2013. The impact of event marketing on brand equity: The mediating roles of brand experience and brand attitude. *International Journal of Advertising*, 32(2), 255–280. DOI: 10.2501/IJA-32-2-255-280.

Zhao, X., Lynch, J. and Chen, Q., 2010. Reconsidering Baron and Kenny: Myths and truths about mediation analysis. *Journal of Consumer Research*, 37(2), 197–206. DOI: 10.1086/651257.

17

THE EFFECT OF VOICE EMOTION RESPONSE ON BRAND RECALL BY GENDER

Wan-Chen Wang, Maria Helena Pestana and Luiz Moutinho

Summary

This chapter analyses the effect of voice emotion responses on brand recall by gender. Using Taiwan as a case study, it explains how voice emotion software and audio-recording equipment were deployed in a laboratory and field environment and. The research found that brand recall in Mandarin speech is positively associated with emotions and varies by products and gender. Men have better recall scores for cars, whereas women scored higher for soft drinks and fast food.

Introduction

Emotions can be defined as expressions, embodiments, outcomes of cognitive appraisals, social constructs and products of neural circuitry (Calvo and D'Mello 2010). Darwin was the first to scientifically explore emotions as expressions in 1872, noticing that some facial and body expressions of humans were like those of other animals and concluding that behavioural correlates of emotional experience were the result of evolutionary processes (Darwin *et al.* 1998). James (1884) proposed a model of emotions as embodiments that combined expression with the interpretation of the perception of physiological changes as the emotion itself. Arnold (1960) is considered the pioneer of the cognitive approach to emotions, holding for a person to experience an emotion, an object or event must be appraised as directly affecting the person based on their experience, goals and opportunity for action. Averill (1980, pp. 305–339) claimed that emotions are primarily social constructs.

Affective neuroscience helps us to understand the neural circuitry that underlies emotional experience and the ethology of certain mental health pathologies and offers new perspectives on how emotional states and their development influence our health and life outcomes (Damasio 2003; Davidson *et al.* 2009; Dalgleish *et al.* 2009). Affective neuroscience also provides evidence that elements of emotional learning can occur without awareness (Öhman and Soares 1998), that they do not require explicit processing (Calvo and Nummenmaa 2007) and also that self-reports of emotion might not reflect more subtle phenomena that do not make it to consciousness (Chamberlain and Broderick 2007). Wang *et al.* (2015) show that emotions are better captured using voice emotion response than self-reported measures. The relevance of voice emotion response can also be seen in Glenberg *et al.* (2005), who identify that the relationship between emotion and language is a vital part of the experience of emotion as social construct.

Lang (2010) shows that the measurement of emotions is critical for commercial purposes, often conveyed by an advertising slogan, where an appealing campaign arouses positive consumer emotion toward the message being communicated. Teixeira *et al.* (2012) state that it helps to deliver the desired image of brand position which could generate enormous profit.

Emotions vary with gender Guimond *et al.* (2007). Women tend to be more external in expressing their emotions (Gallois 1994; Brody 1997) and more emotionally sensitive (Bradley *et al.* 2001; Becht and Vingerhoets 2002; Chentsova-Dutton and Tsai 2007), reporting greater impulse intensity and greater positive and negative expressivity, while men mask their emotions (Kring and Gordon 1998; Chentsova-Dutton and Tsai 2007). Women are more emotion sensitive and more willing to communicate their internal emotional states verbally and non-verbally than men, who normally use more extreme ratings of arousal than women (Becht and Vingerhoets 2002; Burriss *et al.* 2007). Younger women tend to have more emotional connection with brands, while men have a more rational connection with brands, but as time passes, this gender difference narrows (Sahay *et al.* 2012),

The impact of automatic preferences (for instance, indulging in impulse purchases) is stronger when people focus on affect, whereas cognition has greater impact when people focus on reason for choice (Scarabis *et al.* 2006). Men are, in general, selective information processors and focus on visual and tangible cues while shopping (Meyers-Levy 1988), while women are more comprehensive and detailed processors, helping them to distinguish more finely between products (Laroche *et al.* 2003). Women generally engage in a greater degree of elaborative processing of personal, real-life emotional experiences than men (Davis 1999). Thus, women have in-depth knowledge structures about the products they use. In addition, the memories that women have consist of greater emotional feelings and experiences, which is very unlikely to be so with men (Kring and Gordon 1998). Women directly recall actual experience when faced with an evaluation task, in addition to drawing on subjective knowledge (Laroche *et al.* 2003, p. 256). Women recall more autobiographical memories of emotional events and generally do so faster, strongly suggesting that they engage in a greater degree of elaborative processing of personal, real-life emotional experiences than men do (Davis 1999). Meanwhile, a study exploring men's brand relationships found that the relationships that men form are more oriented towards achieving certain goals; men do form relationships but are very functional in extracting benefits from a brand (Zayer and Neier 2011).

Following these findings, this research goes deeper by analysing by gender the recall of emotions obtained by advertising slogans captured through voice emotion software, an affective computing tool. Due to the small size of the sample, the robust methodology of optimal data analysis (Yarnold and Soltysik 2005) was used.

Affective computing aims to reduce the communication gap between the highly emotional human and the computer, with computer systems that respond to the user's affective states (Calvo and D'Mello 2010), allowing the detection of users' mental states, revealing which features customers enjoy and excluding those that receive negative feedback. It shows great potential to enhance companies' customer relationship management capabilities and marketing strategies through collecting customers' attitudes towards their products and brands (Rukavina *et al.* 2016).

The basic principle behind most affective computing systems is that automatically recognizing and responding to a user's affective states with a computer can enhance interaction quality, making a computer interface more usable and effective by measuring multimodal signals, namely speech, facial expressions and/or psychobiology. Emotions play an important role in successful and effective human-human communication, as well as in humans' rational learning (Cambria 2016). Affective computing focuses on extracting a set of emotion labels (Picard 1997; Zeng 2009; Calvo and D'Mello 2010; Schuller *et al.* 2011; Gunes and Schuller 2013) and polarity detection, usually a binary classification task with output such as positive versus negative or like versus dislike (Pang and Lee 2008; Liu 2012; Cambria 2013).

Literature review

Spoken language is between 200,000 and 2 million years old (Gibson *et al.* 1993), and speech is indispensable for sharing ideas, observations and feelings (Furnas *et al.* 1987). Ambady and Rosenthal (1992) suggest that voice is very important in the human judgment of behavioural cues. Many judgments we make about others in our everyday lives are based on cues from these expressive behaviours. We communicate our interpersonal expectancies and biases through very subtle, almost imperceptible, nonverbal cues. These cues are so subtle that they are neither encoded nor decoded at an intentional, conscious level of awareness (Christensen and Rosenthal 1982; Harris and Rosenthal 1985) Brief clips of behaviour have been used to successfully identify the subtle expressive cues conveying interpersonal expectancies that are very influential in the interpersonal influence process (Chaikin *et al.* 1974; Rosenthal and Rubin 1978). For example, studies conducted by Bugental and her colleagues revealed that parents' expectancies, identified from brief clips of their tone of voice, are related to their children's behaviour (Bugental *et al.* 1980, 1971, 1976; Bugental and Love 1975).

Picard (1997) considered emotional states generally associated with certain physiological features, which produce mechanical and therefore measurable properties in speech, particularly in pitch, timing, frequency and voice quality. For example, in a state of fear, anger or joy, the sympathetic nervous system is aroused, blood pressure and heart rate increase and the mouth becomes dry. Speech is then loud, fast and voiced with strong high-frequency energy (Breazeal 2003).

A connection exists between language processing and emotions, most obviously with spoken language (Wurm *et al.* 2001). The accuracy of human emotion recognition has been improved through advanced analysis methods and techniques including voice recognition, natural language processing, image processing and electroencephalography devices (Cambria 2016). Emotion modulates almost all modes of human communication (e.g. word choice, tone of voice (Picard *et al.* 2001) and can significantly change the message. Sometimes it is not what was said that was most important but how it was said. Cowie *et al.* (2001) analyse how emotions could be recognized in human-computer interactions, providing a comprehensive summary of qualitative acoustic correlations for prototypical emotions.

Comparing affect recognition to speech recognition is useful for highlighting how nascent and challenging the research is (Picard 2003). Pantic and Rothkrantz (2003) discussed how to integrate into computers several components of human behaviour in the context-constrained analysis of multimodal behavioural signals, producing a more naturalistic interaction aimed at discrete emotion recognition from auditory features like pitch, intensity and speech rate.

Other researchers show some reliable correlates of emotion in the acoustic characteristics of the signal (Banse and Scherer 1996; Burkhardt *et al.* 2005). Ambady and Rosenthal (1992) suggest that voice and body correlates well with facial expression, and many studies in psychology and linguistic confirm the correlation between prototypical emotions, including happiness, sadness, fear, anger, disgust and surprise, and specific audio and visual signals (e.g. Russell *et al.* 2003). Although many systems still focus on detecting the basic emotions, there are some marked efforts aimed at detecting other states, such as frustration (Kapoor *et al.* 2007). Zeng *et al.* (2009) show the advantage over single modalities of the integration of multiple modalities like vocal and visual expression in human affect perception, and when compared to vision-based detection, speech-based detection systems are more apt to meet the needs of real-world applications. According to Calvo and D'Mello (2010), speech transmits affective information through the explicit linguistic message (what is said) and the implicit paralinguistic features of the expression (how it is said), while pitch appears to be an index into arousal. Koelstra *et al.* (2012) showed that recent advances in emotion recognition have motivated the creation of novel databases containing emotional expressions in different modalities, like speech.

The top ten most cited, innovative and central references about affective computing, discussed previously, are shown in Table 17.1, by title, author, year and source, none of them in the field of marketing. These are the results of a scientometric review from CiteSpace (Chen 2013) on 5078 bibliographical records published between 1991–2016 from Web-of-Science of Thomson Reuters records on affective computing.

Since the 1980s, little research has related voice pitch analysis to marketing studies (Wang and Minor 2008). Compared to other psychophysiological techniques, voice pitch analysis has two notable advantages for marketing research: the experimental procedure only requires oral responses and unobtrusive audio-recording equipment, which in controlled and unnatural experimental settings is less likely to influence individuals than bulky apparatus (Klebba 1985).

In pursuing these ideas, an investigation centred on slogans is helpful. Slogans are short phrases that communicate ideas with a themed affective position, which are used to increase a brand's likeability and memorability (Boush 1993; O'Guinn *et al.* 2003). However, not all successful brands utilize slogans as positioning strategy to communicate brand attributes that are differentiated from competitors. For instance, Burberry, Zara and Chanel employ non-verbal marketing messages using visual, textural and atmosphere cues instead of verbal speech. Nevertheless, as a verbal form of emotional expression that most consumers have no difficulty recognizing, slogans can deliver emotional messages more easily and proactively than non-verbal communication can.

Signal-based evaluation tools make it possible to capture and analyse speech signals of advertising slogans and elicit emotions from the signal data – a more natural way to measure emotions than analysing the recalled data from self-report measures. Hence, this research proposes a

Table 17.1 References most cited, innovative and central in affective computing

References	Year	Source	Citations	Centrality	Sigma
Zeng ZH *et al.*	2009	IEEE T PATTERN ANAL	79	0.24	5.09
Calvo RA and D'Mello S	2010	IEEE T AFFECT COMPUT	61	0.15	4.66
Cowie R *et al.*	2001	IEEE SIGNAL PROC MAG	38	0.14	7.42
Picard RW *et al.*	2001	IEEE T PATTERN ANAL	38	0.5	334.24
Picard RW	1997	AFFECTIVE COMPUTING	35	0.35	688.39
Pantic M and Rothkrantz LJM	2003	P IEEE	34	0.4	15.22
Kim J and André E	2008	IEEE T PATTERN ANAL	31	0.04	1.22
Kapoor A *et al.*	2007	INT J HUM-COMPUT ST	30	0.12	1.56
Picard RW and Liu KK	2007	INT J HUM-COMPUT ST	28	0.03	1.24
Koelstra S *et al.*	2012	IEEE T AFFECT COMPUT	26	0.02	1.18

Source: The authors

different method for analysing voice expression and emotions so that marketing researchers can access an uncomplicated and easy-to-operate computer-based instrument for assessing emotions embedded in advertising slogans.

Example of use of methodology with a case study

Voice emotion response

The purpose of the voice emotion response is to give computers affect recognition abilities, ideally at a level that enables researchers to label the emotional states of other people. However, researchers face complex problems when they attempt to teach computers how to do this, and the complexities involved could be enormous. So, only partial solutions may be obtained, but these partial solutions can still be of value. Picard (2003) argues that infants recognize some kinds of affect in speech, obviously long before they recognize what is said. Researchers in the Department of Computer Science and Engineering at Tatung University, Taiwan, developed a user interface (a human-computer interface) – the voice emotion response – to classify emotion. Its graphical user interface (GUI) is shown in Figure 17.1.

It includes short utterances covering five full-blown emotions in Mandarin speech: happiness, anger, sadness, boredom and neutrality (unemotional) (Murray and Arnott 1993). The term "full-blown emotion" is used to describe a fully developed emotional expression, which

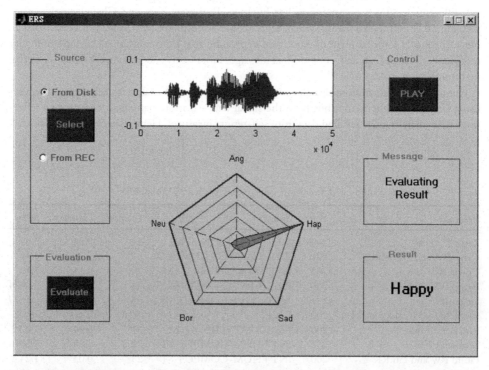

Figure 17.1 Graphical user interface (GUI) of the voice emotion response

Source: Adapted from Wang *et al.* (2015)

is typically impassioned and has inherent factors considered relevant to emotional expression. When emotion is used in this sense, a positive or negative orientation can be conveyed to others (Plutchik 1994). The core architecture of this interface was developed through four stages of computer engineering.

In the first stage, pre-processing, the interface locates the endpoints of the input speech signal, and a high-pass filter filters the speech signal, which is then partitioned into frame pieces. A Hamming window is applied to each frame, minimizing the signal discontinuities at both the beginning and the end of each frame and converting the frames into several types of parametric representations.

The second stage extracts possible candidates from speech features. Feature extraction methods include mel-frequency cepstral coefficients (MFCC) and linear prediction cepstral coefficients (LPCC).

The third stage is the feature vector quantization stage, which occurs when 20 MFCCs and 12 LPCCs of each speech frame extract the parameters of each utterance as a feature vector. A vector quantization method obtains the mean of the feature parameters corresponding to each frame in one utterance.

The fourth stage is a classification algorithm designed to evaluate the emotions in the speech data. A weighted distance K-nearest neighbour (D-KNN) is used to find a vector of real-valued weights that would optimize the classification accuracy of the recognition system by assigning lower weights to less relevant features and higher weights to features that provide more reliable information.

In this study, the experiment required the author to record the voice of each participant as he or she spoke the slogan, then used the voice emotion response to analyse the recorded emotions. In the voice emotion response, each axis of the radar chart represents emotions in the designated key performance dimensions and examines these five primary emotions. A radar chart visualizes the consumer's evaluated emotion results, analysing several factors at once and presenting them simultaneously. By analysing speech patterns, emotional speech processing recognizes the consumer's emotional state. Vocal properties and prosody features such as pitch variables and speech rate are analysed through pattern recognition. The source of the speech signals, whether the recorded utterances in the corpus or the real-time recorded utterances from the users, is the source frame. The interface then plots the evaluation results on the radar chart, from the least extent of the emotion at the central point to the greatest extent of the same emotion on the edges. The message frame indicates the progression of the evaluation or error messages. The resulting frame shows the recognition result (Figure 17.2).

Voice emotion response can capture and analyse speech signals and their underlying emotions directly and can collect consumers' emotional response more naturally than self-reported measures. Park and Thorson (1990) suggest that the consumer's emotional response toward the advertisement can greatly persuade post-exposure attitudes and recall. Hazlett and Hazlett (1999) compare results of facial electromyography (EMG) and self-report on participants' emotional responses to TV commercials, finding that EMG measures are more connected to brand recall.

Optimal data analysis

Optimal data analysis (ODA) is a method developed by Yarnold and Soltysik (2005) that offers maximum predictive accuracy to data, even when the assumptions of the alternative statistical models are not applied. This method is used to identify patterns in the data that distinguish the effect of voice emotion response on brand recall by gender.

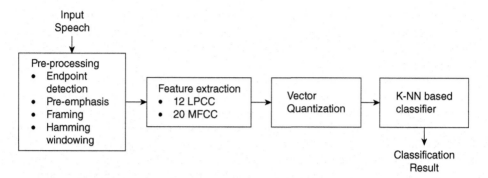

Figure 17.2 Four-stage K-NN based emotion recognition system.

Source: Based on Chien *et al.* (2007)

The accuracy of ODA is obtained by calculating the following measures:

- Sensitivity, the proportion of actual women who are correctly predicted by the model;
- Specificity, the proportion of actual men who are correctly predicted by the model;
- Effect size sensitivity (ESS), an index of predictive accuracy relative to chance, where values less than 25% indicates a relative weak effect; 25%–50% indicates a moderate effect, 50%–75% indicates a relatively strong effect, and 75% or greater indicates a strong effect over chance.

To assess generalizability, ODA first estimates using the entire sample (training set), calculating accuracy measures as described previously. Next, the model is cross-validated, and the accuracy measures are recalculated. If the accuracy measures remain consistent with those of the original model using the entire sample, then it can be said that the model is generalizable. The current study applies the approach of 'leave-one-out' (LOO) cross-validation, which is simply an n-fold cross-validation, where $n = 141$ observations in the dataset. Each observation in turn is left out, and the model is estimated for all remaining observations. The predicted value is then calculated for the hold-out observation, and the accuracy is determined as women or men in predicting the outcome for that observation.

The results of all predictions are used to calculate the final accuracy estimates. Model accuracy measures are calculated using the average values across all hold-out models. All variables included in the ODA model were constrained to achieve identical classification accuracy in training (total sample) and LOO validity analysis. To ensure adequate statistical power, inhibit over-fitting and increase the likelihood of cross-validation when the model is applied to classify a smaller independent sample, model endpoints were constrained to have $N \geq 10\%$ of the total sample (Yarnold and Soltysik 2016).

Results

The study in Taiwan involved a sample of 141 participants, from 18 to 55 years old, with 80 women and 61 men and a mix of salespeople, librarians, university staff, working professionals and graduate students. Several studies indicate that gender is associated with brand commitment

(Tifferet and Herstein 2012), which explains the analysis of voice emotion response and its effect on brand recall by gender, applying optimal data analysis due to its robustness with small samples (Yarnold and Soltysik 2016).

Participants were presented with eight slogans to be classified into five categories of emotion, registered by voice emotion response, to determine the effect of the emotion on brand recall by gender.

With the exceptions of Family Mart and 7-Eleven, the other slogans have two patterns regarding recall by gender: men feel happier with cars (Suzuki and SYM), showing greater recall than women. In the remaining four slogans, Coca-Cola, Pepsi-Cola, KFC and Burger King, the opposite occurs, with women being happier and showing better recall than men. The results are in line with those found by other researchers (Teixeira *et al.* 2012; Martensen *et al.* 2007; Faseur and Geuens 2006; Janssens and De Pelsmacker 2005; Vakratsas and Ambler 1999), who state that a significant relationship exists between advertising effectiveness and positive emotions.

The brand recall is higher when associated with positive emotions, as shown in Table 17.2, which reveals the ODA performance indices to be better than chance for all brands: 8.38% for Burger King (exact $p = 0.02$), 8.77% for KFC (exact $p = 0.003$), 13.31% for Coca-Cola ($p < 0.00001$), 15.1% for Pepsi ($p < 0.00001$), 15.96% for Suzuki ($p < 0.00001$) and 26.57% for SYM ($p < 0.00001$).

The observed values of the relationship between brand recall by gender are shown in Table 17.3. Women's recall is higher than men's for Coca-Cola (98.75% vs 72.13%), KFC (92.94% vs 75.4%), Pepsi (92.50% vs 62.30%) and Burger King (72.50% vs 55.73%). Men's recall is higher than women's for SYM (86.89% vs 33.75%) and Suzuki (60.66% vs 28.75%).

Except for Family Mart and 7-Eleven, where there is a high recall – 95.74%, almost equal between genders – all other brands have a statistically significant relationship with gender.

For Suzuki, men have at least 1.886 (=1/0.530) more chance of recall than women, while for Coca-Cola, women have at least 3.929 times more chance of recall than men.

The magnitude of recall by substitute brands are: SYM (56.74%) higher than Suzuki (42.55%), Coca-Cola (87.23%) higher than Pepsi-Cola (79.43%), KFC (85.11%) higher than Burger King (65.25%), and Family Mart and 7-Eleven are equal (both 95.74%). This can be explained by the fact that in the Taiwanese market, SYM motorcycles are more popular than Suzuki motorcycles and Coca-Cola is still the leading soft drink brand. KFC came to Taiwan in 1985 and Burger King in 1990, so KFC is much more well known and loved by Taiwanese consumers. Finally, Family Mart and 7-Eleven are the top two popular brands of convenience store.

Table 17.2 ODA performance indices by slogans

Indexes/brands	Coca	KFC	Pepsi	Burger King	SYM	Suzuki
Overall accuracy	68.09%	64.38%	68.79%	60.28%	75.18%	66.67%
Sens column 1: % recall	98.75%	92.94%	92.50%	72.50%	86.89%	86.89%
Modal gender for recall	Female	Female	Female	Female	Male	Male
Sens column 2: % of no recall	27.87%	24.59%	37.70%	44.26%	66.25%	71.25%
Modal gender for no recall	Male	Male	Male	Male	Female	Female
ESS	26.62%	17.53%	30.20%	16.76%	53.14%	31.91%
Above chance	13.31%	8.77%	15.1%	8.38%	26.57%	15.96%

Source: The authors

Table 17.3 Voice emotion recall by gender and slogans

Voice Emotion recall	Coca-Cola		Pepsi-Cola		FamilyMart		Seven-Eleven	
	Female	Male	Female	Male	Female	Male	Female	Male
	N(%)	N(%)						
Yes	79	44	74	38	74	61	74	61
	(98.75%)	(72.1%)	(92.5%)	(62.3%)	(92.5%)	(100%)	(92.5%)	(100%)
No	1	17	6	23	6	0	6	0
	(1.3%)	(27.9%)	(7.5%)	(37.7%)	(7.5%)	0%	(7.5%)	0%

Voice Emotion recall	Burger King		KFC		Suzuki		SYM	
	Female	Male	Female	Male	Female	Male	Female	Male
Yes	58	34	74	46	23	37	27	53
	(72.5%)	(55.7%)	(92.5%)	(75.4%)	(28.7%)	(60.7%)	(33.8%)	(86.9%)
No	22	27	6	15	57	24	53	8
	(27.5%)	(44.3%)	(7.5%)	(24.6%)	(71.3%)	(39.3%)	(66.3%)	(13.1%)

Source: The authors

Conclusions

This study analyses emotions associated with repeating a slogan in Mandarin Chinese, applies emotions as social constructs and identifies their effects on brand recall. Men felt happier when referring their personalities to the use of automobiles, whereas women consumers felt happier when developing associations with brands marketing both soft drinks and fast-food products.

There has been always a clear association between the memorization process of advertisements and the triggering of an emotional state towards brands. It has been confirmed using optimal data analysis that a positive relationship between consumers' recall and brand stimuli does exist.

Issues for further discussion

International marketers view Taiwan as an entry for other Asian markets, and the understanding of Taiwanese consumers is valuable not only in targeting China but also in gaining access to other Asian markets with high concentrations of ethnic Chinese people (Javalgi *et al.* 2013). This study offers international marketing managers practical suggestions for engaging in the Chinese consumer market, which is growing in significance.

Given the preliminary nature of this study, the voice emotion response can so far only recognize five basic emotions, which critically constrains the effort. Hence, researchers at Tatung University are developing further techniques to recognize more emotions that better suit marketing research. More research dedicated to translating the Mandarin Chinese Emotional Corpus into other languages and replicating the voice recognition method of the WD-KNN algorithm should provide more evidence of voice emotion.

The difficulty of measuring emotions should not, however, be overlooked (Ambler 2000), and diversity among methods improves the robustness of marketing research. Therefore, future research should involve other psychophysiological measures to test the consistency of results with the aim of generating a deeper understanding of the construct of emotions. Computer systems are now attempting to interact more naturally with the users as human beings. The application of recognizing affect in a context-specific response would form another level of work in affective computing.

The numerous perspectives on conceptualizing emotions are being further challenged by emerging neuroscience evidence. Some of this evidence challenges the common view that the organization of neural circuits in the brain is why indicators of emotion covary. This evidence, together with progress in complex systems theory, has increased the interest in models where emotions do not cause, but rather are caused by, the measured indicators of emotion (Calvo and D'Mello 2010).

References

Ambady, N. and Rosenthal, R., 1992. Thin slices of expressive behavior as predictors of interpersonal consequences: A meta-analysis. *Psychological Bulletin*, 111(2), 256–274. https://psycnet.apa.org/doi/10.1037/0033-2909.111.2.256.

Ambler, T., 2000. Persuasion, pride and prejudice: How ads work. *International Journal of Advertising*, 19(3), 299–315. https://doi.org/10.1080/02650487.2000.11104803.

Arnold, M.B., 1960. *Emotion and Personality*. New York: Columbia University Press.

Averill, J., 1980. A constructivist view of emotion in emotion: Theory, research and experience. Ch 12 in R. Plutchik and H. Kellerman, eds. *Theories of Emotion*. London: Elsevier, pp.305–339.

Banse, R. and Scherer, K., 1996. Acoustic profiles in vocal emotion expression. *Journal of Personality and Social Psychology*, 70(3), 614–636. DOI: 10.1037/0022-3514.70.3.614.

Becht, M. and Vingerhoets, A., 2002. Crying and mood change: A cross-cultural study. *Cognition and Emotion*, 16(1), 87–101. DOI: 10.1080/02699930143000149.

Boush, D., 1993. How advertising slogans can prime evaluations of brand extensions. *Psychology and Marketing*, 10(1), 67–78. DOI: 10.1002/mar.4220100106.

Bradley, M., Codispoti, M., Sabatinelli, D. and Lang, P., 2001. Emotion and motivation II: Sex differences in picture processing. *Emotion*, 1(3), 300–319. DOI: 10.1037/1528-3542.1.3.300.

Brody, L., 1997. Gender and emotion: Beyond stereotypes. *Journal of Social Issues*, 53(2), 369–393. https://doi.org/10.1111/j.1540-4560.1997.tb02448.x.

Bugental, D.B., Caporael, L. and Shennum, W.A., 1980. Experimentally produced child uncontrollability: Effects on the potency of adult communication patterns. *Child Development*, 51(2), 520–528. https://doi.org/10.2307/1129287.

Bugental, D.B., Henker, B. and Whalen, C.K., 1976. Attributional antecedents of verbal and vocal assertiveness. *Journal of Personality and Social Psychology*, 34(3), 405–411. https://doi.org/10.1037/0022-3514.34.3.405.

Bugental, D.B. and Love, L., 1975. Nonassertive expression of parental approval and disapproval and its relationship to child disturbance. *Child Development*, 46(3), 747–752. https://doi.org/10.2307/1128573.

Bugental, D.E., Love, L.R., Kaswan, J.W. and April, C., 1971. Verbal-nonverbal conflict in parental messages to normal and disturbed children. *Journal of Abnormal Psychology*, 77(1), 6–10. https://doi.org/10.1037/h0030497.

Burkhardt, F., Paeschke, A., Rolfes, M., Sendlmeier, W. and Weiss, B., 2005. A database of German emotional speech. *Interspeech*, 5, 1517–1520. 9th European Conference on Speech Communication and Technology, Lisbon, Portugal.

Burriss, L., Powell, D. and White, J., 2007. Psychophysiological and subjective indices of emotion as a function of age and gender. *Cognition and Emotion*, 21(1), 182–210. https://doi.org/10.1080/02699930600562235.

Calvo, R. and D'Mello, S., 2010. Affect detection: An interdisciplinary review of models, methods, and their applications. *IEEE Transactions on Affective Computing*, 1(1), 18–37. DOI: 10.1109/T-AFFC.2010.1.

Calvo, M. and Nummenmaa, L., 2007. Processing of unattended emotional visual scenes. *Journal of Experimental Psychology: General*, 136(3), 347–369. DOI: 10.1037/0096-3445.136.3.347.

Cambria, E., 2016. Affective computing and sentiment analysis. *IEEE Intelligent Systems*, 31(2), 102–107. DOI: 10.1109/MIS.2016.31.

Cambria, E., Schuller, B., Xia, Y. and Havasi, C., 2013. New avenues in opinion mining and sentiment analysis. *IEEE Intelligent Systems*, 28(2), 15–21. DOI: 10.1109/MIS.2013.30.

Chaikin, A.L., Sigler, E. and Derlega, V.J., 1974. Nonverbal mediators of teacher expectancy effects. *Journal of Personality and Social Psychology*, 30(1), 144–149. https://doi.org/10.1037/h0036738.

Chamberlain, L. and Broderick, A.J., 2007. The application of physiological observation methods to emotion research. *Qualitative Market Research: An International Journal*, 10(2), 199–216. http://dx.doi.org/10.1108/13522750710740853.

Chen, C., 2013. The structure and dynamics of scientific knowledge. In C. Chen, ed. *Doi: Mapping Scientific Frontiers*. London: Springer, 163–199. DOI: 10.1007/978-1-4471-0051-5.

Chentsova-Dutton, Y. and Tsai, L., 2007. Gender differences in emotional response among European Americans and Hmong Americans. *Cognition and emotion*, 21(1), 162–181. https://doi.org/10.1080/02699930600911333.

Chien, C.S., Wan-Chen, W., Moutinho, L., Cheng, Y.M., Pao, T.L., Yu-Te, C. and Jun-Heng, Y., 2007. Applying recognition of emotions in speech to extend the impact of brand slogan research. *Portuguese Journal of Management Studies*, 12(2), 115–132.

Christensen, D. and Rosenthal, R., 1982. Gender and nonverbal decoding skill as determinants of interpersonal expectancy effects. *Journal of Personality and Social Psychology*, 42(1), 75–87. https://doi.org/10.1037/0022-3514.42.1.75.

Cowie, R., Douglas-Cowie, E., Tsapatsoulis, N., Votsis, G., Kollias, S., Fellenz, W. and Taylor, J., 2001. Emotion recognition in human-computer interaction. *IEEE Signal Processing Magazine*, 18(1), 32–80. DOI: 10.1109/79.911197.

Dalgleish, T., Dunn, B. and Mobbs, D., 2009. Affective neuroscience: Past, present, and future. *Emotion Review*, 1(4), 355–368. https://doi.org/10.1177/1754073909338307.

Damasio, A., 2003. *Looking for Spinoza: Joy, Sorrow, and the Feeling Brain*. Houghton Mifflin Harcourt.

Darwin, C., Ekman, P. and Prodger, P., 1998. *The Expression of the Emotions in Man and Animals*. Oxford University Press.

Davidson, R., Sherer, K. and Goldsmith, H., 2009. *Series in Affective Science. Handbook of Affective Sciences*. Oxford University Press.

Davis, P.J., 1999. Gender differences in autobiographical memory for childhood emotional experiences. *Journal of Personality and Social Psychology*, 76(3), 498–510. https://doi.org/10.1037/0022-3514.76.3.498.

Faseur, T. and Geuens, M., 2006. Different positive feelings leading to different ad evaluations: The case of coziness, excitement, and romance. *Journal of Advertising*, 35(4), 129–142. Available from: www.jstor.org/stable/20460760.

Furnas, G., Landauer, T., Gomez, L. and Dumais, S., 1987. The vocabulary problem in human-system communication. *Communications of the ACM*, 30(11), 964–971. https://doi.org/10.1145/32206.32212.

Gallois, C., 1994. Group membership, social rules, and power: A social-psychological perspective on emotional communication. *Journal of Pragmatics*, 22(3–4), 301–324. https://doi.org/10.1016/0378-2166(94)90114-7.

Gibson, K. and Ingold, T., 1993. *Tools, Language and Cognition in Human Evolution*. Cambridge: Cambridge University Press. https://doi.org/10.1002/bs.3830380308.

Glenberg, A., Havas, D., Becker, R. and Rinck, M., 2005. Grounding language in bodily states. In D. Pcher, ed. *Grounding Cognition: The Role of Perception and Action in Memory, Language, and Thinking*. 115–128. https://doi.org/10.1017/CBO9780511499968.006.

Guimond, S., Branscombe, N., Brunot, S., Buunk, A., Chatard, A., Désert, M. and Yzerbyt, V., 2007. Culture, gender, and the self: Variations and impact of social comparison processes. *Journal of Personality and Social Psychology*, 92(6), 1118–1134. DOI: 10.1037/0022-3514.92.6.1118.

Gunes, H. and Schuller, B., 2013. Categorical and dimensional affect analysis in continuous input: Current trends and future directions. *Image and Vision Computing*, 31(2), 120–136.

Harris, M.J. and Rosenthal, R., 1985. Mediation of interpersonal expectancy effects: 31 meta-analyses. *Psychological Bulletin*, 97(3), 363–386. https://doi.org/10.1037/0033-2909.97.3.363.

Hazlett, R. and Hazlett, S., 1999. Emotional response to television commercials: Facial EMG vs. self-report. *Journal of Advertising Research*, 39(2), 7–23.

James, W., 1884. What is an emotion? *Mind*, 9(34), 188–205. https://doi.org/10.1093/mind/os-IX.34.188.

Janssens, W. and De Pelsmacker, P., 2005. Advertising for new and existing brands: The impact of media context and type of advertisement. *Journal of Marketing Communications*, 11(2), 113–128. DOI: 10.1080/1352726042000306847.

Javalgi, R., Park, J., Lee, O., Prasad, V. and Vernon, I., 2013. Antecedents of Taiwan Chinese consumers' purchase intentions toward US-and Japanese-made household appliances. *Journal of Global Marketing*, 26(4), 203–223. https://doi.org/10.1080/08911762.2013.814820.

Kapoor, A., Burleson, W. and Picard, R., 2007. Automatic prediction of frustration. *International Journal of Human-Computer Studies*, 65(8), 724–736. DOI: 10.1016/j.ijhcs.2007.02.003.

Kim, J. and André, E., 2008. Emotion recognition based on physiological changes in music listening. *IEEE Transactions on Pattern Analysis and Machine Intelligence*, 30(12), 2067–2083.

Klebba, J., 1985. Physiological measures of research: A review of brain activity, electrodermal response, pupil dilation, and voice analysis methods and studies. *Current Issues and Research in Advertising*, 8(1), 53–76. DOI: 10.1080/01633392.1985.10505372.

Koelstra, S., Muhl, C., Soleymani, M., Lee, J., Yazdani, A., Ebrahimi, T. and Patras, I., 2012. Deap: A database for emotion analysis; using physiological signals. *IEEE Transactions on Affective Computing*, 3(1), 18–31. DOI: 10.1109/T-AFFC.2011.15.

Kring, A. and Gordon, A., 1998. Sex differences in emotion: Expression, experience, and physiology. *Journal of Personality and Social Psychology*, 74(3), 686–703. DOI: 10.1037//0022-3514.74.3.686.

Lang, P., 2010. Emotion and motivation: Toward consensus definitions and a common research purpose. *Emotion Review*, 2(3), 229–233. https://doi.org/10.1177%2F1754073910361984.

Laroche, M., Cleveland, M., Bergeron, J. and Goutaland, C., 2003. The knowledge-experience-evaluation relationship: A structural equations modeling test of gender differences. *Canadian Journal of Administrative Sciences/Revue Canadienne des Sciences de l'Administration*, 20(3), 246–259. https://doi.org/10.1111/j.1936-4490.2003.tb00315.x.

Liu, B., 2012. Sentiment analysis and opinion mining. *Synthesis Lectures on Human Language Technologies*, 5(1), 1–167. DOI: 10.2200/S00416ED1V01Y201204HLT016.

Martensen, A., Grønholdt, L., Bendtsen, L. and Jensen, M.J., 2007. Application of a model for the effectiveness of event marketing. *Journal of Advertising Research*, 47(3), 283–301. DOI: 10.2501/S0021849907070316.

Meyers-Levy, J., 1988. The influence of sex roles on judgment. *Journal of Consumer Research*, 14(4), 522–530.

Murray, I. and Arnott, J., 1993. Toward the simulation of emotion in synthetic speech: A review of the literature on human vocal emotion. *The Journal of the Acoustical Society of America*, 93(2), 1097–1108. DOI: 10.1121/1.405558.

O'Guinn, A.T. and Semenik, R., 2003. *Advertising and Integrated Brand Promotion*, 3rd ed. Mason, OH: Thomson; New York: South-Western College Publishing.

Öhman, A. and Soares, J.J., 1998. Emotional conditioning to masked stimuli: Expectancies for aversive outcomes following nonrecognized fear-relevant stimuli. *Journal of Experimental Psychology: General*, 127(1), 69–82.

Pang, B. and Lee, L., 2008. Opinion mining and sentiment analysis. *Foundations and Trends® in Information Retrieval*, 2(1–2), 1–135. DOI: 10.1561/1500000011.

Pantic, M. and Rothkrantz, L., 2003. Towards an affect-sensitive multimodal human-computer interaction. *P IEEE, Proceedings of the IEEE*, 91(9), 1370–1390. DOI: 10.1109/JPROC.2003.817122.

Park, C. and Thorson, E., 1990. *Influences on Emotional Response to Commercials of Different Executional Styles. Emotion in Advertising: Theoretical and Practical Explorations*. Westport: Quorum Books.

Picard, R., 1997. *Affective Computing*. Cambridge: The MIT Press.

Picard, R., 2003. Affective computing: Challenges. *International Journal of Human-Computer Studies*, 59(1), 55–64. DOI: 10.1016/S1071-5819(03)00052-1.

Picard, R. and Liu, K.K., 2007. Relative subjective count and assessment of interruptive technologies applied to mobile monitoring of stress. *International Journal of Human-Computer Studies*, 65(4), 361–375. https://doi.org/10.1016/j.ijhcs.2006.11.019.

Picard, R., Vyzas, E. and Healey, J., 2001. Toward machine emotional intelligence: Analysis of affective physiological state. *IEEE Transactions on Pattern Analysis and Machine Intelligence*, 23(10), 1175–1191. DOI: 10.1109/34.954607.

Plutchik, R., 1994. *The Psychology and Biology of Emotion*. HarperCollins College Publishers.

Rosenthal, R. and Rubin, D.B., 1978. Interpersonal expectancy effects: The first 345 studies. *Behavioral and Brain Sciences*, (3), 377–386. https://doi.org/10.1017/S0140525X00075506.

Rukavina, S., Gruss, S., Hoffmann, H., Tan, J., Walter, S. and Traue, H., 2016. Affective computing and the impact of gender and age. *PLoS ONE*, 11(3), e0150584. https://doi.org/10.1371/journal.pone.0150584.

Russell, J., 2003. Core affect and the psychological construction of emotion. *Psychological Review*, 110(1), 145–172. DOI: 10.1037//0033-295X.110.1.145.

Sahay, A., Sharma, N. and Mehta, K., 2012. Role of affect and cognition in consumer brand relationship: Exploring gender differences. *Journal of Indian Business Research*, 4(1), 36–60. DOI: 10.1108/17554191211206799.

Scarabis, M., Florack, A. and Gosejohann, S., 2006. When consumers follow their feelings: The impact of affective or cognitive focus on the basis of consumers' choice. *Psychology & Marketing*, 23(12), 1015–1034. https://doi.org/10.1002/mar.20144.

Schuller, B., Batliner, A., Steidl, S. and Seppi, D., 2011. Recognising realistic emotions and affect in speech: State of the art and lessons learnt from the first challenge. *Speech Communication*, 53(9), 1062–1087. DOI: 10.1016/j.specom.2011.01.011.

Teixeira, T., Wedel, M. and Pieters, R., 2012. Emotion-induced engagement in Internet video advertisements. *Journal of Marketing Research*, 49(2), 144–159. DOI: 10.1509/jmr.10.0207.

Tifferet, S. and Herstein, R., 2012. Gender differences in brand commitment, impulse buying, and hedonic consumption. *Journal of Product & Brand Management*, 21(3) 176–182. https://doi.org/10.1108/10610421211228793.

Vakratsas, D. and Ambler, T., 1999. How advertising works: What do we really know? *The Journal of Marketing*, 26–43. DOI: 10.2307/1251999.

Wang, W., Chien, C. and Moutinho, L., 2015. Do you really feel happy? Some implications of voice emotion response in Mandarin Chinese. *Marketing Letters*, 26(3), 391–409. DOI: 10.1007/s11002-015-9357-y.

Wang, Y. and Minor, M., 2008. Validity, reliability, and applicability of psychophysiological techniques in marketing research. *Psychology and Marketing*, 25(2), 197–232. DOI: 10.1002/mar.20206.

Wurm, L., Vakoch, D., Strasser, M., Calin-Jageman, R. and Ross, S., 2001. Speech perception and vocal expression of emotion. *Cognition and Emotion*, 15(6), 831–852. DOI: 10.1080/02699930143000086.

Yarnold, P.R. and Soltysik, R.C., 2005. *Optimal Data Analysis. A Guidebook with Software for Windows*. Washington, DC: American Psychological Association.

Yarnold, P.R. and Soltysik, R.C., 2016. *Maximizing Predictive Accuracy*. Chicago, IL: ODA Books. DOI: 10.13140/RG.2.1.1368.3286.

Zayer, L.T. and Neier, S., 2011. An exploration of men's brand relationships. *Qualitative Market Research: An International Journal*, 14(1), 83–104. DOI: 10.1108/13522751111099337.

Zeng, Z., Pantic, M., Roisman, G.I. and Huang, T.S., 2009. A survey of affect recognition methods: Audio, visual, and spontaneous expressions. *IEEE Transactions on Pattern Analysis and Machine Intelligence*, 31(1), 39–58. DOI: 10.1109/TPAMI.2008.52.

18

IDENTIFYING THE DRIVERS OF SHOPPER ATTENTION, ENGAGEMENT, AND PURCHASE

Raymond R. Burke and Alex Leykin

Summary

This chapter explains new research techniques which can help marketers to understand how customers allocate their attention in a complex, competitive environment and to assess the impact of in-store factors on shopper behaviour. It summarizes studies using observational research, virtual reality simulations, and eye tracking to identify the drivers of shopper attention, product engagement, and purchase conversion. The research reveals that small changes in a product's appearance and presentation, such as showing the right product on window signs, straightening store shelves, using a distinctive product package, grouping products into solutions, folding items to encourage touch, and offering a compliment to the shopper, can have a powerful impact on shopper engagement and purchase conversion.

Introduction

Today's shoppers must be selective in processing in-store information. They usually have a limited amount of time available and must decide which departments to visit, categories to shop, and specific brands and items to purchase based on their shopping plans and level of engagement with the merchandise. Sorensen (2017) reports that, of the 30,000 to 50,000 items carried by a typical grocery store, the average household buys just 300 different items during the course of a year. On an average trip, half of shoppers purchase five items or less. In a study by Marsh Supermarkets, product category penetration ranged from a low of 5 to 25% for general merchandise, health and beauty care, and flowers to a high of 60% for the meat department (Burke 1993).

Once they choose to shop in a specific department and category, shoppers continue to be frugal with their time and attention. In a field study of consumer purchases of laundry detergent, Hoyer (1984) found that the median time per purchase decision was 8.5 seconds (including the time taken to walk down the grocery aisle), and only 28% of shoppers looked at, and 17% picked up, two or more brands. Dickson and Sawyer (1990) found that, for coffee, toothpaste, margarine, and cold cereal, the mean category shopping time was less than 12 seconds, with 42% of shoppers spending 5 seconds or less. Shoppers examined an average of 1.2 brands. Young (2010, pp. 22, 34–36) reports that category shoppers actively see and consider only about 50% of the brands on the shelf, with new products seen less than 33% of the time. If shoppers do not find what they're looking for in 8–10 seconds, they often walk away.

For marketers to be successful in this environment, they need to understand how shoppers allocate their attention across the available products and displays in the store and identify the factors that drive shopper engagement and interest. This new focus on measuring shopper behaviour has fuelled several recent research trends. The first is the increased use of *observational and ethnographic research* (see e.g. Underhill 1999, 2004). Merchants have found that by watching how customers shop their stores, they can identify locations where shoppers are open to communication, isolate points of friction in the shopping process, and discover opportunities to improve shopping convenience. This research is usually executed by setting up one or more video cameras within the store, recording consumer shopping activity for several hours a day, and then manually coding shopper behaviour later (Musalem *et al.* 2020). Video observation is often combined with intercept interviews to identify both how and why consumers buy.

The second trend is the increased use of *customer tracking technologies* in both online and conventional retail shopping environments. Unlike traditional ethnographic research, which can be very time consuming and subjective, tracking technologies provide an efficient and reliable means to collect and analyse data on the consumer shopping process. In online environments, detailed clickstream data allows retailers to analyse the path that shoppers take through a site and assess how consumer and marketing variables affect click-through rates and purchase likelihood (see e.g. Bucklin and Sismeiro 2003; Moe 2003; Montgomery *et al.* 2004). In conventional retail stores, WiFi, Bluetooth, RFID, handheld barcode scanner, and video-based customer tracking solutions have been developed which permit retailers to track how shoppers navigate through stores and respond to changes in the store environment (Burke 2006; Hui *et al.* 2009a, 2009b; Hui, Huang *et al.* 2013; Larson *et al.* 2005; Sorensen 2017; Stilley *et al.* 2010). The shopping path data encode the sequence of events leading up to a purchase. By counting the number of customers who enter the store and walk through each aisle, department, and product category, retailers can create thermal maps showing the percentage of customers who penetrate each section of the store. When traffic data are combined with transaction log data, retailers can calculate overall and category-specific purchase conversion rates, reflecting the store's ability to turn consumer demand into purchase.

A third trend is the use of laboratory or online *virtual reality simulations* to explore how changes in the store environment affect shopper behaviour. Recent innovations in computer graphics permit researchers to create highly realistic simulations of the retail shopping environment (Baker *et al.* 2002; Bigné *et al.* 2016; Burke *et al.* 1992; Burke 1996, 2018; Meißner *et al.* 2020; Van Herpen 2016). These simulations provide tremendous flexibility, allowing retailers to go beyond existing conventions and explore new approaches for improving the shopping experience. Like in-store tracking solutions, computer simulations can record detailed information about consumers' shopping patterns and purchase behaviour, and the results can be used to forecast future sales and profitability. Commercial applications are discussed in Breen (2009).

The fourth recent trend is the use of *eye-tracking technologies* to measure patterns of visual attention in the online, laboratory, or physical store environment to understand how product presentation, merchandising, and packaging drive shopper attention (e.g. Meißner *et al.* 2016; Grewal *et al.* 2020). Wedel and Pieters (2007, 2008), Chandon *et al.* (2009) and Orquin and Loose (2013) summarize academic research investigating bottom–up and top–down effects on visual attention in marketing contexts. Yang *et al.* (2018), in a series of eye-tracking experiments, show that as the choice probability increases, consumers become less novelty seeking and more price sensitive. Walter *et al.* (2020) show that a disordered product arrangement prompts shoppers to expand their visual search to unfamiliar products due to a greater *perceptual disfluency*. Eye tracking has also gained popularity in commercial shopper marketing research and is used in virtual shopping simulations, mock store studies, and field experiments in retail stores (Klingensmith 2013; Young 2010).

In the following sections, we provide an overview of the psychological process involved in directing visual attention, and then discuss several studies investigating how shopper attention, engagement, and purchase are influenced by the store environment using a combination of customer observation, virtual shopping simulations, and eye tracking.

The psychology of visual attention

As shoppers enter a retail store and walk the aisles, a tremendous amount of information enters the brain through the lens of the eye and is perceived and understood in the context of their expectations and prior knowledge. Attention is a mechanism that helps to filter and selectively process this flow of information (Lynch and Srull 1982). Focusing on what to look at can be thought of as the first step in seeing. Vision scientists have identified a number of low-level features of the visual stimulus, such as colour, contrast, and orientation, which either guide or modulate attention, what is called "bottom-up" processing (Wolfe and Horowitz 2004). Another class of processing, called "top-down," involves the interaction of higher-level mental processes with the scene. These can range from mental goals and plans to emotional states and expectations (Baluch and Itti 2011). When shoppers have specific goals and expectations in mind that narrow the focus of their attention, they can easily miss other information in the scene, a phenomenon called "inattentional blindness" (Simons and Chabris 1999; Most *et al.* 2005).

Human vision operates as a sequence of relatively steady gaze fixations separated by transitional saccades. Saccades have speeds of up to 1000 degrees of visual field per second and are relatively short in duration – on the order of 50 milliseconds (Fischer and Ramsperger 1984). Fixations are much longer, typically in the range of 100 to 500 milliseconds. During these intervals, the human gaze focuses on specific locations, and this is when the major part of visual processing is believed to take place. In the human eye, the fovea – an area of the retina where the most photoreceptive cells are concentrated – covers only the central two to three degrees of the visual field, which is roughly equivalent to twice the width of your thumbnail at arm's length (Smythies 1996). Around this area, there is a parafoveal region of reduced acuity which extends to an additional five degrees of visual angle and usually includes the target point for the subsequent saccade.

Shoppers are often searching for specific products from the complex array of merchandise displayed on store shelves. For the last 25 years, there has been a debate among cognitive scientists about the mechanisms behind this visual search process. On the one hand, there are several empirical studies showing that visual objects within the field of view are selected and processed at the same time, that is, in parallel (Eckstein 1998). On the other hand, proponents of a "serial processing" approach have demonstrated that some visual features are processed one after the other (Treisman 1996). In recent years, there is a growing body of evidence that object search happens in a hybrid serial-parallel process (Wolfe *et al.* 2011). One can think of the visual image as a sort of importance map, which, while varying for each scene type, still usually marks more interesting or common objects as more salient (Elazary and Itti 2008).

The psychology literature has identified a number of low-level stimulus features that guide the visual attention process. In targeted search experiments, an object's colour, orientation, size, and motion have all been shown to reliably direct attention (Treisman and Gormican 1988; Czerwinski *et al.* 1992; Wolfe and Horowitz 2004). For example, it is easy to find a green object among a set of red objects, and a small object stands out from a field of large ones. Similarly, an object with a distinctive shape can be located more quickly (Treisman and Gormican 1988). Higher-level features such as faces, text, and even houses can quickly draw attention toward them (Cerf *et al.* 2009; Kanwisher and Wojciulik 2000). A flickering or flashing stimulus, where there are abrupt changes in luminance, also attracts attention, but curiously, similar changes in colour do not have a matching effect (Theeuwes 1995).

The anatomy of the eye also appears to affect the direction of attention. Tatler and Vincent (2009) argue that there are significant oculomotor behavioural biases that influence where people look. For example, there appears to be a strong central bias corresponding to where the gaze would fall when the eye is in a relaxed position (cf. Atalay *et al.* 2012).

In addition to the visual characteristics of the target stimulus, the surrounding visual field has a major impact on the shopper's ability to find an object quickly and reliably. The greater the visual heterogeneity of the background (i.e. the higher the level of "clutter"), the longer the search times. Search times usually directly correlate with the number and variety of visual distractions in the scene. Subjects are faster at finding a green dot among the red ones than among a set of varying colours (Wolfe and Horowitz 2004). The task of creating a balanced visual scene becomes an optimization problem of trying to maximize the saliency of individual target objects while keeping the clutter at a minimum. In natural scenes, the task is even more complex, since the number of objects (set size) is not clearly defined and can vary depending on the scale of consideration. Perceptual organization of the items is another factor affecting clutter. A seemingly diverse set of items can be sorted, for instance, by colour, creating a much cleaner visual presentation and thus reducing search times (Rosenholtz *et al.* 2007).

Since real-world images usually present a complex combination of guiding features along with the high variability of visual distractors, Duncan and Humphreys (1989) have proposed to approach the task as an information theory problem. Increasing the difference between targets and distractors would aid the search, while increasing the variety of distractors would create more noise, thus decreasing the efficiency of visual search.

While it is often possible to isolate the individual guiding features in a carefully crafted lab experiment, guided search fails in natural scenes where a complex mix of low-level features interact with the higher-level rules and knowledge of the real world. The latter is often referred to as contextual or scene-based guidance (Torralba *et al.* 2006). For example, if you are in a retail store, you automatically assume that you will see certain types of objects: price tags, checkouts, navigational signs, and so on. Moreover, you would have a set of inherent rules as to where these objects are located (Eckstein *et al.* 2006). One would expect to see price tags next to the merchandise in the aisles and navigational signs higher up between the aisles. Indeed, location seems to be an important factor based on analyses of the neural workings of the brain (Bisley 2011).

Memory also plays a role in visual search. Objects in a familiar scene are usually easier to find due to "semantic-guidance." A familiar scene raises the probability of seeing specific objects at specific locations based on prior knowledge (Hollingworth 2006). It is important to note that, unlike context-driven attention, semantic guidance is not generalizable across environments and only applies to the specific, concrete scene observed in the past.

Neurophysiological evidence also suggests that attentional processes must achieve a balance between data-driven and knowledge-driven processes (Colby 1991). Applied to natural scenes, the top-down guidance is somewhat modulated by the visual features but is clearly demonstrated to play a more dominant role (Henderson *et al.* 2009). Another interesting feature of visual attention is the ability to "see the forest without recognizing individual trees," a.k.a. the "gist" of the scene (Green and Oliva 2009). This type of processing makes it possible to categorize the scene (e.g. urban or natural) with a single fixation.

Based on the research to date, one would expect that shopper attention will be a function of both high-level goals and expectations (as expressed in a shopping list or primed by an advertisement or prior experience) and the low-level visual features of the store environment. Several researchers in psychology (e.g. Zelinsky *et al.* 2005; Kanan *et al.* 2009; Torralba *et al.* 2006; Bruce and Tsotos 2009) and marketing (e.g. van der Lans *et al.* 2008a, 2008b; Chandon *et al.* 2008, 2009) have developed models using a combination of top-down features with low-level saliency to predict visual attention.

Managing shopper attention

In a complex and cluttered store environment, it is critical for marketers to make it easy for shoppers to find the products that meet their needs. In some cases, shoppers are looking for something specific, and the retailer must organize and display products in a way that helps shoppers to "see what there is to see" and connect what they have in mind with what is physically available in the store. In others, shoppers are "just browsing" (Bloch *et al.* 1989), so the retailer has to draw the shoppers' attention to relevant products and "activate" latent needs and desires. Once the shopper is engaged, the shelf presentation must clearly communicate the benefits and value of the available products and minimize purchase obstacles to convert demand into purchase (Burke 2005).

In either case, it's important to identify the factors driving visual attention as shoppers walk the store aisles and visit the various departments and categories and to understand how the presentation of products affects shoppers' ability to visually connect with the merchandise and find what they're looking for. As Wedel and Pieters (2007) note, most of the eye-tracking research by marketing academics has focused on print ads. However, there have been a few academic studies that have analyzed visual attention in a retail context, including Russo and Leclerc's (1994) study of the stages of consumer choice (orientation, evaluation, and verification), Pieters and Warlop's (1999) study of time pressure and task motivation effects on package examination and choice, and Chandon *et al.*'s (2009) study of the effects of shelf position and number of facings on brand attention and evaluation. There are also commercial studies using eye tracking, including packaging studies by Young (2010) and mobile eye-tracking research by Hendrickson and Ailawadi (2014).

In the following sections, we present five studies conducted at Indiana University's Kelley School of Business, with support from the school's Customer Interface Laboratory and Centre for Education and Research in Retailing. The first two studies use computer graphic simulations and eye-tracking technology to identify in-store factors affecting visual attention for both planned and unplanned purchases. The remaining three studies observe shopper behaviour in laboratory and field settings and explore how store signage, product presentation, and salesperson interactions can engage shoppers and drive sales.

Study 1: what do shoppers "see" as they walk through the store?

The objective of the first study is to determine where shoppers direct their attention as they enter a grocery store, walk the aisles, and shop the various departments and categories. The study was conducted in a simulated shopping context, where participants shopped for a basket of goods in a visually familiar, self-service shopping environment modelled after a local super-market chain.

Research method

A total of 323 adults, age 18–65, were recruited to participate in this study; 201 respondents provided reliable eye-tracking data (60 in Phase 1 and 141 in Phase 2). All participants were screened to be the primary grocery shoppers in the household. After giving their informed consent, participants were instructed on how to use the computer interface, presented with a shopping list, and asked to take several "trips" through a computer-simulated store environment. On each trip, visual attention was measured using an Eye Tech eye-tracking device attached to a high-resolution (1920 × 1280) video monitor.

Each shopper took a total of six separate trips through the shopping simulation, with a different shopping list for each trip. These "time compressed" trips helped shoppers to become familiar with the virtual store environment and encouraged them to adopt the same routine shopping mindset as during a typical grocery store visit (cf. Burke *et al.* 1992). The target categories included lemons, instant coffee, tomatoes, ground coffee, donuts, Spray n Wash, pudding cups, detergent, cereal bars, paper towels, Pop-tarts, aluminium foil, and magazines. The order of the six shopping trips was rotated across respondents. (For example, on the first shopping trip, respondent 1 was asked to shop for lemons and instant coffee, while respondent 2 shopped for tomatoes and ground coffee.) The manipulation of shopping list allowed the comparison of goal-directed product search versus browsing behaviour. While shoppers could not actually pick up and purchase products in the virtual store, they could click on displayed products to indicate their purchase interest.

Shoppers had the opportunity to travel around the store's perimeter and enter the aisles to shop for perishable products (e.g. produce, bakery, and refrigerated items), edible grocery items (cereal, breakfast bars, coffee, etc.), and non-edible grocery items (laundry detergent, cleaning products, aluminium foil, paper towels, etc.) and then visited the checkout area. In categories of interest, product shelf positions were counterbalanced across conditions to balance the effects of product appeal and shelf position. The study measured the sequence of eye fixations and dwell time for each shopper, their purchase intentions, and ratings of trip shoppability.

Results

Several patterns of shopper attention consistently emerged in the findings. First, shoppers navigating through the store tend to look ahead and scan horizontally across the visual field as they search for desired products, as shown in the plots in Figure 18.1. They typically pause in a department for just 3 to 4 seconds and fixate on 8 to 10 different shelf locations before deciding to move on to another department. Visual attention is distributed from about 2 to 6 feet above the floor and concentrated at a height of about 4 feet, just below eye level. We observed that shopper attention is often drawn to distinctive signs and product displays. For example, large signs offering discounted prices and in-aisle secondary displays attracted attention, as did the presence of other shoppers (Figure 18.2).

When shoppers first glance at a shelf fixture, they tend to focus on the centre of the shelf display. If shoppers are not engaged in the category, they may only look at a few products on the middle shelves. However, if they pause to shop from the set of displayed items, their visual attention expands outward as they scan the shelves (see Figure 18.3). This central bias has also been reported by Chandon *et al.* (2009) and Atalay *et al.* (2012).

Figure 18.1 Visual attention during store navigation

Source: The authors

Note: Heatmap regions shown in red are the areas of highest visual attention. When shoppers pause in a specific location of the store to examine merchandise, statistics are calculated for the average number of fixations, dwell time, and number of "clicks." Shoppers indicate purchase interest by clicking on products, displayed as green crosses.

Figure 18.2 Visual attention to product promotions and displays

Source: The authors

Note: Promotional signs (e.g. "Buy one, get one free") and in-aisle temporary displays attract two to four times the visual attention of surrounding merchandise.

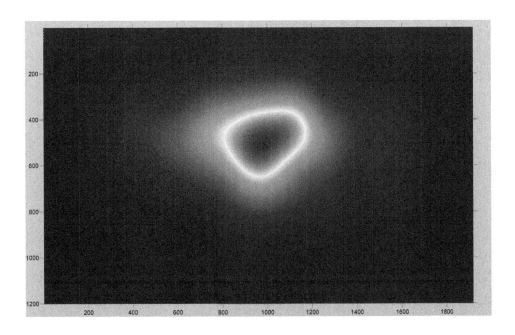

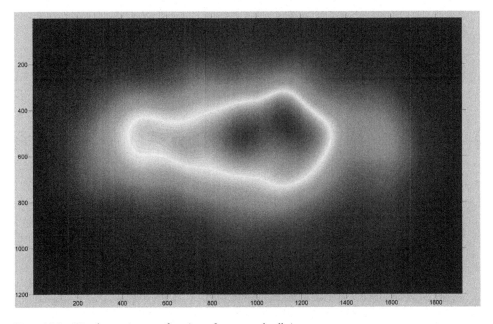

Figure 18.3 Visual attention as a function of category dwell time

Source: The authors

Note: The heatmaps show the density of attention across the visual field as a function of the shopper's dwell time. For brief fixations (less than a second), shoppers tend to focus on the centre of the product display. If they are engaged by the category, their visual attention expands outward as they scan the shelves.

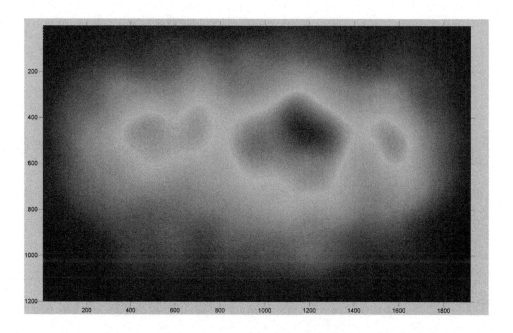

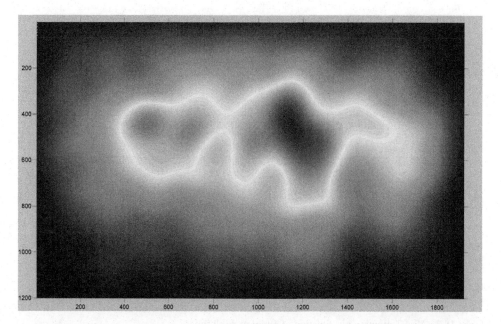

Figure 18.3   Continued

Shoppers' goals have a strong influence on visual attention and purchase interest. When shoppers plan to purchase an item, they spend significantly longer in the category and examine a larger set of products, as illustrated in Figures 18.4a, b, and c. For example, for the perishable products used in the study (lemons, tomatoes, donuts, and pudding cups), the mean time to shop

Figure 18.4a: The influence of shopper goals on visual attention to produce items

Source: The authors

in each category increased from 3.9 to 11.8 seconds, and the average number of fixations jumped from 10 to 29 when the item appeared on the shopper's list (all $p < .001$). This is consistent with past findings that individuals who observe the same stimuli with different goals will have different scan paths based on the goal-relevance of the stimuli (see, e.g. Pieters and Wedel 2007).

Figure 18.4b: The influence of shopper goals on visual attention to bakery items

Source: The authors

As shoppers approach the checkout lanes, the centre of the endcap fixtures receives the most visual attention. When shoppers walk closer to the display, their angle of view changes and their attention shifts towards the higher shelves, closer to eye level. Attention to the various product categories is influenced by adjacent categories and merchandising. For example, shoppers are less likely to look at magazines if they are positioned next to a soft drink cooler, a shelf of snacks, or items promoted as being "new," unless shoppers are specifically planning to purchase something in the magazine category. The black frame of the beverage cooler's door seemed particularly effective at focusing the shopper's attention on soft drinks and away from the adjacent magazines and candy (Figure 18.4c).

Figure 18.4c: The influence of shopper goals on visual attention to checkout items

Source: The authors

In summary, shoppers scan the visual field and rapidly decide if a product category or display is relevant. Shopper goals are critical in determining the breadth and duration of visual search. When shoppers are just browsing, a product's shelf position, visual distinctiveness, presentation, and product adjacencies are key drivers of attention.

Study 2: what affects shoppers' ability to find what they want?

Given the proliferation of products in retail stores, it can be difficult for shoppers to find the products they desire. This is especially true for modern supermarkets, discount stores, and supercentres, which can carry tens of thousands of different items. The second study investigates how the visual appearance and complexity of a shelf display and the mental representation of shopper goals affect how quickly shoppers can find a desired product.

Research method

Eighty-four undergraduate students participated in a computer-controlled, laboratory study of grocery shopping. Participants were asked to take a series of 40 "shopping trips" through a simulated grocery store. On each trip, the shopper was first shown either the name of a specific product (e.g. "Corn Chex") or an image of the product's package for 5 seconds and then shown a shelf display that may or may not contain the item. The shelf display featured an assortment of 32 different brands of cereal, with eight different brands positioned on each of four shelves; two facings per brand. (The positions of brands were counterbalanced across conditions.) Participants were asked to locate the target item from the available selection of products as quickly as possible. As soon as the respondent found the product on the shelf, he or she would press the right Shift key. If the specified product was not found, the respondent would press the left Shift key. Two example trials were conducted before the main data collection. On each trip, visual attention was measured using an Eye Tech eye-tracking device attached to a high-resolution (1920 × 1280) video monitor.

Four factors were manipulated in the experimental design: the target brand to be located (10 levels), the shelf configuration (10 levels), whether the search target was specified with text or a package image (2 levels), and shelf permutation (2 levels). Each respondent was asked to find one of 10 different targets (Corn Chex, Frosted Cheerios, Golden Grahams, Kellogg's Apple Jacks, Kellogg's Corn Flakes, Kellogg's Raisin Bran, Nabisco Shredded Wheat, Post Bran Flakes, Post Honey Comb, Rice Chex) from each of 10 different shelf configurations: (1) default organization by brand, (2) products grouped by package colour, (3) products grouped by common visual features (e.g. presence of large spoon, bowl, cartoon characters), (4) products grouped by similar size and orientation of text, (5) angled shelf to simulate walking down aisle, (6) angled product packages to simulate disorganized shelves, (7) increased number of facings – 4 facings per brand for 16 brands, (8) 30% out-of-stock condition with search target present, (9) 30% out-of-stock condition with search target absent, and (10) product facings distributed randomly on the shelf. The specific pairings of brands and shelves were determined by a 10 × 10 Latin-square design, which was rotated across respondents and trials.

Across the 40 trials, respondents were presented with two different search prompts (textual or visual) and two shelf permutations for each of the 10 brand/shelf combinations. Across all respondents, a total of 400 unique target-brand/shelf-configuration shopping scenarios were tested. Eye fixation, latency, and accuracy data were recorded for each trial, and then a survey was administered at the end of the procedure. Product search times were highly correlated with the number of eye fixations ($r = 0.89$) and gaze trajectory length ($r = 0.88$) across trips and respondents, and all three measures yielded similar results. We therefore focus on search times in the following discussion.

Results

The manipulations of the target object and shelf appearance had a significant impact on the speed with which shoppers could find the desired products. In the following discussion, the reported means and significance tests summarize data from the full set of 400 unique shopping scenarios, and the 3360 (40 trips × 84 respondents) search trials. Only data where targets were present and identified are reported. To help illustrate the findings, example maps of visual attention are presented reflecting specific combinations of shelf organization and search target.

When shoppers have a picture of the desired product in mind, they are much faster at finding the item ($p < .001$). It took an average of 4.9 seconds for shoppers to successfully locate a product with a textual target and only 3.0 seconds with a visual target. Figure 18.5 shows this effect for one of the 10 target brands (Frosted Cheerios). These findings are consistent with research in psychology on feature priming, which demonstrates that visual search for a unique target item is quicker when the property that defines this object is repeated between trials (e.g. Maljkovic and Nakayama 1994).

Looking at the relative performance of the various brands, a distinctive package appeared to improve brand findability, cutting search times from 20 to 40%. Compared to the average search time for the category (3.9 seconds), packages with a distinctive colour, like the bright green Apple Jacks box or the purple Raisin Bran box, had significantly shorter search times of 2.3 and 3.0 seconds, respectively ($p < .01$; see e.g. Figure 18.6). These findings parallel the results of van der Lans *et al.* (2008a), who find that a distinctive package improves brand salience, which helps the product to be identified faster and more accurately.

Additional shelf facings also improve brand findability. When the number of facings was doubled, search times dropped 26%, from an average of 3.9 seconds for two facings to 2.9 seconds for four facings ($p < .001$). Figure 18.7 illustrates this effect for the visual search target Post Bran Flakes. Looking across the experimental conditions, the additional shelf space seems to have the greatest positive impact when the target product is not positioned in the centre of the shelf fixture. Chandon *et al.* (2009) similarly report that the number of facings has a strong influence on visual attention, and this can drive choice for brands that might otherwise not have been noticed.

Neat shelves appear to improve shopping efficiency, while packages that are not arranged in a consistent way can slow down the search process. When the packages on the shelf were not aligned with the shelf edge, but rotated slightly to the left or right, the search times increased 10%, from 4.0 to 4.4 seconds ($p < .05$). This effect was magnified when shoppers had just the name of the brand in mind rather than the package image. Comparing the standard brand organization with alternative product groupings (by package colour, similarity of visual features, and text orientation), there were no significant differences in search times. Also, as expected, there were no differences in search times for the counter-balanced shelf arrangements; $p = .42$.

Packages that were out of stock dramatically increased search times ($p < .001$). When a desired product was "sold out," it took shoppers almost 9 seconds to realize that the item was missing from the shelf. The more interesting result occurred when a desired item was actually *in stock* but the shelves looked depleted (with 30% of items out of stock). In this case, respondents were 50% more likely to conclude that the item they were looking for was unavailable than when the shelves were fully stocked. They also spent less time looking for the target item ($p < .02$) and looked at fewer items ($p < .08$).

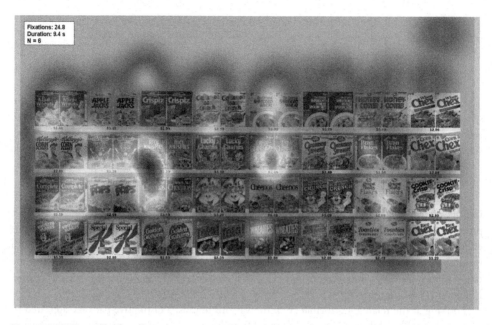

Text target: Frosted Cheerios

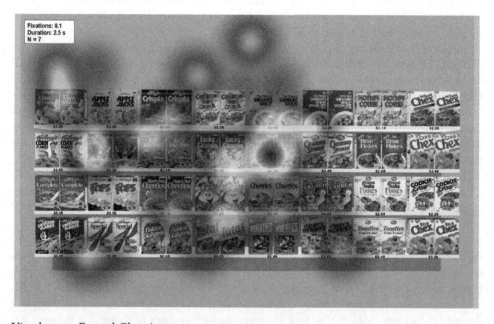

Visual target: Frosted Cheerios

Figure 18.5 Search speed and visual attention as a function of target type (textual/visual)
Source: The authors

Visual target: Golden Grahams

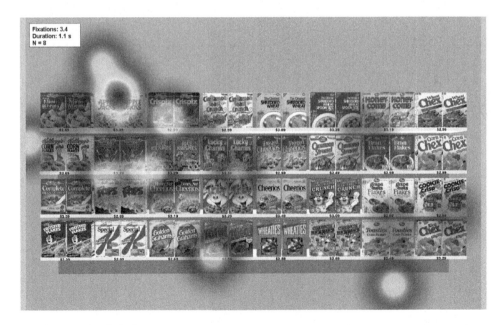

Visual target: Apple Jacks

Figure 18.6 Search speed and visual attention as a function of target brand

Source: The authors

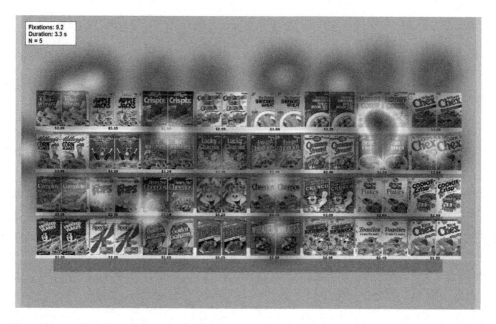

Visual target: Post Bran Flakes – two facings

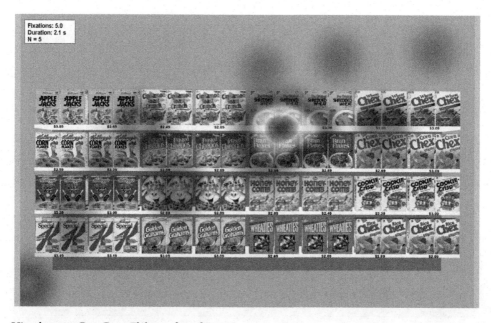

Visual target: Post Bran Flakes – four facings

Figure 18.7   Search speed and visual attention as a function of number of shelf facings

Source: The authors

Managing shopper engagement and purchase

The next three studies explore how marketers can connect with shoppers' needs through relevant signage, store organization, product presentation, and sales assistance. All three studies were conducted in the context of a retail apparel store. The first study uses a computer-simulated shopping environment while the second and third studies report on field experiments conducted in a physical retail store.

Study 3: how do a store's signage and layout affect store penetration and purchase?

Retailers often attempt to connect with shoppers' needs and desires and improve shopping convenience through relevant signage and navigational aids positioned in the store windows and throughout the store. Edwards and Shackley (1992) report that placing displays in the windows of drug stores – especially displays that are relevant to the target audience, feature new products, and use colour and contrast – boost product interest, recall, and sales. Burke (2006, 2009) reports that digital signs can drive store traffic and lift product sales, especially when they feature "news" (new items, promotions, seasonal information) and hedonic products (e.g. food and entertainment).

Once shoppers enter a store, a familiar and well-organized layout can help them find their way through the complex array of products to locate the desired items (Park *et al.* 1989). The effective organization of store interiors and the presence of navigational aids can enhance the perceived "environmental legibility" of the store (Titus and Everett 1995; Weisman 1981), resulting in fewer errors in navigation and lower stress among consumers (Nelson-Shulman 1984; Wener and Kaminoff 1982). The design and layout of stores can aid or hinder consumer movement inside the store and reduce or add to the time spent in locating desired products (Sadalla and Montello 1989; Weisman 1981).

When consumers shop in stores with low environmental legibility, this can increase the time and effort required to find the desired products. In such difficult and time-constrained environments, people are more likely to engage in heuristic and non-compensatory processing (Chaiken 1980; Payne *et al.* 1988), focusing on easily processed and distinctive cues, such as price, to decide (cf. Dhar and Nowlis 1999). One would therefore expect to see higher consumer price sensitivity in stores with low rather than high legibility.

To explore these issues in more detail, the first author collaborated with Professors Saurabh Mishra (George Mason University) and Alex Rusetski (York University) on a project to simulate a specialty apparel store and measure the influence of exterior signage, store organization and navigational aids, and price on shoppers' penetration of the store and purchase likelihood (Mishra *et al.* 2008).

Research method

One hundred and fifty-one undergraduate students, enrolled in introductory marketing courses at a major university, participated in the study. Individuals were told that the purpose of the study was to understand how consumers shop in retail stores and the role that consumer goals and the shopping environment play in the shopping process. After giving their approval to participate, people were seated in front of computer displays used to simulate the retail shopping environment, present information, and take measurements. The three-dimensional interactive model of the retail context was created with the AutoDesSys FormZ software package based on the layout of an actual retail store. The interactive simulation and electronic survey were programmed using Macromedia Authorware and software plug-ins.

Participants were asked to assume that they had travelled to another city to attend a business-casual meeting. Because of the warm weather, they would like to wear a polo shirt but forgot to pack one and so visited a nearby shopping mall to look for a shirt. Participants entered a simulated shopping mall environment and arrived at the first apparel store, called Elements.

At the first stage of the shopping simulation, individuals could visually scan the exterior of the store, "walking" closer or farther from the window display. They were asked to decide whether they would like to enter the store to look for a polo shirt or shop somewhere else, rating their entry likelihood on a scale from 0% to 100%. At the second stage, individuals entered the Elements store and were asked whether they would like to continue walking through the store to look for the shirt or turn around and leave, shopping somewhere else. Once again, they rated the likelihood on a scale from 0% to 100%. At the third stage in the simulation, participants entered the polo shirt department and could scan the shelf fixture stocked with ladies' and men's shirts in various colours. They were asked if they would like to buy one of the shirts at the price shown (assuming the store carried the appropriate size) or shop somewhere else and rated their purchase likelihood on a 0% to 100% scale, with additional questions about the shopping experience and their personal background. Figure 18.8 illustrates the manipulation of the store's exterior and interior appearance.

Stage 1: exterior window display

Low relevance/high relevance

Stage 2: store interior

Low legibility/high legibility

Stage 3: product category

Price: $24.95/price: $34.95

Figure 18.8   Store context manipulations

Source: The authors

Participants were randomly assigned to one of eight treatment conditions in a $2 \times 2 \times 2$ full factorial between-subject design. The first factor was a manipulation of the goal relevance of the exterior window display. The store windows featured a total of four posters, two each for men's and women's fashions. In the high-relevance condition, two of the posters featured models wearing polo shirts, while two displayed models wearing other styles of clothing. In the low-relevance condition, all four models were wearing non-polo-style shirts (see Figure 18.6). A change was also made to the semi-transparent banner that appeared just inside the store. In the high-relevance condition, the male model was wearing a polo shirt, while both the male and female models were wearing other fashions in the low-relevance condition. In all other respects, the posters were identical across the two conditions.

The second factor in the design was a manipulation of the environmental legibility of the store's interior (Titus and Everett 1995). In the high-legibility condition, the store used a "race-track" format, with wide aisles and department signs to facilitate visual and physical navigation. In the low-legibility condition, the store had a more conventional appearance, with fixtures placed throughout the store, and there were no department signs. (This format was similar to many existing specialty apparel stores.) To simulate the effects of store legibility on the time needed to navigate the store, participants in the high-legibility condition experienced a 10-second delay before they found the polo shirt category, while individuals in the low-legibility condition took 60 seconds to reach the polo shirt category.

The third factor in the design was product price. In the low-price condition, polo shirts were featured at $24.95, and in the high-price condition, the same shirts were featured for $34.95. These values reflected the prevailing range of prices in the marketplace at the time of the study.

Results

The manipulation of the store's window display had a significant impact on shoppers' reported likelihood of penetrating the store. The mean entry likelihood increased from 64% in the "low relevance" condition to 73% in the "high relevance" condition, $F(1, 149) = 9.79$, $p < .01$. If one assumes that only those shoppers with store entry likelihoods greater than 50% would actually enter the store, the window display manipulation would increase the conversion of mall customers to store traffic from 65% to 83% ($\chi^2 = 6.42$, $p < .02$). When display attractiveness was included as a covariate in the analysis of the effects of window display on store entry likelihood, the coefficient was statistically significant; $F(1, 148) = 56.11$, $p < .001$. However, the manipulation of display relevance still had a significant positive impact on store entry likelihood; $F(1, 148) = 5.55$, $p < .05$.

In the second stage of the shopping trip, respondents were shown a panoramic interior view of the retail environment and asked if they would like to walk through the store to look for a polo shirt or turn around and leave, shopping elsewhere. The manipulation of store organization and signage did not have a significant effect on shoppers' judgments; $F(1, 147) = .02$, $p > .10$. The mean shopping likelihood ratings were 64% and 65% in the low- and high-legibility conditions, respectively. Those consumers who chose to enter the store may have felt committed to shop in the store despite what appeared to be a difficult shopping environment. The incremental effort to shop a relatively small (approximately 6000 square feet) store would be minimal. Supporting this, over 80% of the people who entered the store indicated that they would continue shopping rather than going somewhere else. The correlation between the probability of entering the store and walking through the store was .539 ($p < .001$).

In the third stage of the shopping trip, respondents were shown a panoramic image of the polo shirt category and asked to decide whether to buy one of the shirts at the price shown or to leave and shop somewhere else. As one would expect, the manipulation of price had a significant main effect on purchase likelihood; $F(1, 143) = 15.88$, $p < .001$. The mean purchase likelihood was 60% when shirts were priced at $24.95 but only 44% when they were sold at $34.95.

The more interesting result was the interaction between store legibility and price. For the 111 customers who chose to enter the store, their likelihood of buying in the two price conditions depended on the ease with which they could shop the store; $F(1, 107) = 6.60$, $p < .02$. When customers visited a store that was well organized and clearly signed, with quick access to the desired product, a $10 increase in price produced a small but statistically insignificant drop in purchase likelihood ($M_{\$24.95} = 64\%$, $M_{\$34.95} = 55\%$, $p > .10$). However, when the store environment was not as well organized and the shopping process took much longer, the same price change caused a dramatic decrease in purchase likelihood ($M_{\$24.95} = 69\%$, $M_{\$34.95} = 38\%$, $p < .001$; see Figure 18.9). This effect was mirrored by interactions between legibility and price for customer ratings of overall store value ($F(1, 147) = 4.11$, $p < .05$; see Figure 18.10) and the shopper's likelihood of recommending the store to a friend; $F(1, 147) = 8.99$, $p < .01$. Once again, price increases only produced a negative effect in the low-legibility conditions.

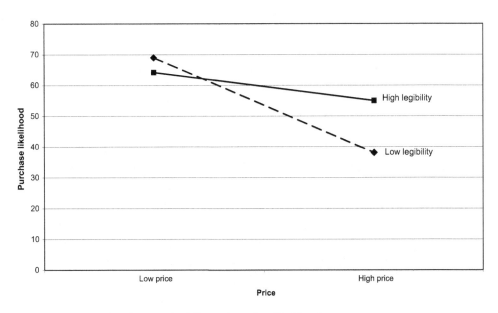

Figure 18.9   Interactions between legibility and purchase likelihood

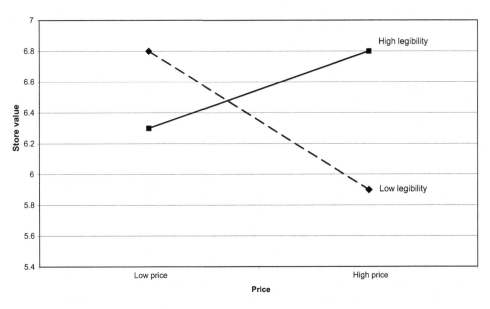

Figure 18.10   Interactions between legibility and price

In summary, the results reveal that a store's signage and layout have direct effects on store penetration and purchase likelihood, as well as carryover effects on consumer price response and value perceptions. Consumers are willing to pay a higher price for products in stores with high environmental legibility, where product organization and signage make it easy and less time consuming to find the desired items.

Study 4: how does product presentation affect shopper engagement and purchase?

While the store environment plays an important role in creating a convenient and enjoyable shopping experience, the primary focus of the shopper is on the *physical product*, and its presentation can have a powerful effect on shopper engagement and purchase likelihood (Burke 2005). The objective of this study is to explore how merchandising products as "solutions" and folding apparel items to facilitate mental simulation can help retailers to connect with shoppers' needs and desires and increase sales.

Research method

This study was conducted in cooperation with a retailer selling private-label apparel to young adults (aged 15 to 25) through a chain of mall-based specialty stores. In this particular chain, almost half of the store's floor space was allocated to men's merchandise, but men represented less than 30% of the chain's customers and 20% of yearly dollar sales. To help identify the reasons for the poor performance with male customers, observational data were collected to measure how customers shopped the men's section of the store and identify points of engagement and friction in the shopping process. Fifty-three hours of observation were conducted in a local store, and the activities of 440 customers (305 men and 135 women) were recorded. (Only data for male shoppers who shopped on the men's side of the store are reported here.) Trained observers coded each shopper's path through the store and the sequence and degree of interaction with shelf fixtures and employees. Purchase transactions were recorded using the point-of-sale system. Shoppers were randomly selected as they exited the store and asked to complete a short survey with questions about their perceptions of the shopping experience and reasons for not buying.

Of the shoppers observed during the study, over 25% of men stopped to examine merchandise on the lead fixture as they entered the store. Many of them walked past the various displays in the centre area to the back of the store, arriving at the clearance racks, which again had a high rate of product interaction (+25%). Levels of engagement were much lower with the various product display tables, rounders, and wall displays in the middle part of the store (less than 10%). This appeared to be a missed opportunity, as the category-level purchase conversion rates for shoppers who stopped at these fixtures were relatively high (13 to 25%).

When male shoppers were intercepted and asked why they did not make a purchase, most reported that they could not find what they were looking for. This echoes the results of a survey conducted by the Verde Group and Wharton faculty, which found that young men have more problems than women with store navigation and item selection and will walk away rather than ask for assistance if they can't find the desired product (Verde Group 2007). When male shoppers were asked why they did not stop to interact with more of the merchandise, a few commented that they could not fold and put back the clothing the way they found it.

Two techniques were used to increase shopper engagement. The first was to group related products together as "solutions." Complementary products were identified through an analysis of two years of historical purchase data, collected from 54,511 of the retailer's customers. The analysis revealed that certain combinations of products were often purchased together, including men's shorts with graphic tees ($r = .413$) and active tops (.346); men's denim with sport shirts (.379), knit tops (.389), and active tops (.414); and men's footwear with active tops (.280), graphic tees (.276), sports shirts (.274), and shorts (.262). To help men put together outfits, a "Men's Style Centre" was created using six bust forms featuring popular combinations of men's shirts, shorts, and flip-flops, positioned in close proximity to tables with product inventory (see Figure 18.11). The Style Centre was located near the centre of the store and would be seen by shoppers as they passed the lead fixtures.

Baseline condition

Initial product presentation

Test condition

Men's Style Centre

Adjacent products (half fold)

Figure 18.11   Product merchandising manipulations

Source: The authors

The second technique for encouraging product interaction was to change how products were folded on tables. Instead of using the conventional creased fold, shirts and pants were simply folded in half and stacked. The goal was to make it easier for shoppers to imagine picking up, examining, and returning a product to the shelf (see Elder and Krishna's 2012 discussion of embodied mental simulation).

A field experiment was conducted in one of the retailer's stores to test the impact of the presentation manipulations on shopper behaviour. The study was run during the May/June time frame, when sales were traditionally stable and not affected by major promotions, clearance events, or "back to school" shopping. During the one-month baseline period, products were displayed in their conventional locations as prescribed by the retailer's standard floor set and planograms for the season. During the subsequent one-month test period, the Men's Style Centre was assembled in the centre of the men's section, with merchandised products available for sale on adjacent tables. Sales data were collected using point-of-sale terminals, customer traffic was recorded using ShopperTrak Orbit sensors, and product fixture interaction was captured through covert observation by trained observers. (Cash purchases were not captured in this database. In a typical store, 80 to 90% of transactions are completed with a credit card, so the dataset should provide a representative sample of the kinds of products customers purchased at the chain.)

Results

The findings support the prediction that enhanced product displays make it easier for customers to shop, driving store traffic, product interaction, and sales. Compared to the baseline period, total store traffic increased 11% during the test period (from 537 to 596 customers per day), transactions increased 20% (from 129 to 154 per day, $p < .05$), and unit sales increased 18% (from 266 to 313 units per day, $p < .05$).

The Men's Style Centre had an even more dramatic impact on shopper interaction with the featured products. The percent of shoppers who stopped to examine the men's shirts and cargo shorts jumped from 2.9% to 13.3%; and examination of the accompanying flip-flops had a similar increase from 2.0% to 10.3% ($p < .05$). This increase in attention translated into significantly higher sales. The unit sale of men's knit tops increased 54% (from 13 to 20 per day, $p < .05$), and dollar sales increased 74% (from $219 to $380 per day, $p < .01$). The unit sales of men's shorts increased 36% (from 14 to 19 units per day, $p < .05$), and dollar sales increased 20% (from $432 to $518). In contrast, sales in these categories were flat or declined during the same period in the previous year. Note that there were no changes to the prices or assortment of products. The store simply did a better job of connecting what was in the mind of the shopper with what was physically available in the store.

Study 5: what role do salespeople play in influencing shopper behaviour?

When a customer can't find the product that he or she is looking for, a salesperson can intervene in the shopping process and play an active role in clarifying and addressing the shopper's needs (Pennington 1968; Weitz 1981). Interactions with salespeople can enhance shopper engagement by slowing down the shopper, encouraging a longer store visit, and increasing product interaction and purchase (Zhang *et al.* 2014). Retail sales associates have various selling tactics at their disposal but often with limited knowledge about which of these will be most effective. The objective of the next study was to investigate the different selling approaches that are used by sales associates and identify which are most (and least) effective at converting customers into buyers. This study was conducted by Professors Katie Hartman and Rosann Spiro (2006) and described here with their permission.

Research method

In the fall of 2005, a study of sales associate-customer interaction was conducted in a mall-based specialty apparel store. During this period, sales associates were asked to wear concealed microphones to record their conversations with shoppers. Each device could record conversations for a two-hour interval, and then the audio data were saved and the device was passed along to another sales associate to wear for the next two hours. Two or three different sales associates stationed in the main selling area of the store (not the fitting room or cash wrap) might wear a device during a given day.

At the completion of each shopper's store visit, the number of items purchased was recorded by the sales associate. Shoppers were then given a "customer appreciation card" which offered them a gift card ($10 off the next purchase over $50) if they completed an online survey and entered their unique customer ID number. This short (10–15 minute) "exit interview" asked about the shopper's reasons for visiting the store, shopping companions, items purchased, recollections of the sales interaction, satisfaction with the shopping experience, repeat patronage intentions, and demographics.

Results

The research team transcribed and coded the audio recordings of the conversations and merged the data with the survey responses. A total of 46 "tracked" conversations (matched to customer surveys) were coded. There was considerable variability in the length of conversations between sales associates and customers, ranging from 30 seconds to 19 minutes. Most interactions were relatively short, with an average length of 4.5 minutes. About half of the conversations lasted less than 2.5 minutes. A typical conversation between a sales associate and customer is as follows:

1   A sales associate makes an inquiry as an opening statement (e.g. "Is there something I can help you find today?" "How are you doing today?");
2   A series of questions are asked to identify customer product interests ("What colours do you like?" "Do you want a small or medium?");
3   A series of statements provide product information ("We have this style in brown and green," "The jeans we carry are available in different washes and cuts");
4   A conversation closer ("Here you go," "Would you like me to get you into a fitting room?"); and
5   When necessary, a follow-up inquiry ("How's that working out for you?" "Can I get you a different size?").

A content analysis of the conversations revealed that sales associates were most likely to ask shoppers questions to elicit additional information (92% of conversations), provide the customer with product information (87%), and offer assistance or aid to the customer (80%). Less frequent comments involved sales associates sharing their personal opinions (which were always positive, 48%); recommending a particular product, style, or size (25%); describing personal experiences with a specific product (25%); passing along the opinions of other customers (15%); and/or suggesting a different (or additional) product, style, or size than what the customer was currently considering (12%).

In some conversations, the sales associate attempted to *proactively address or anticipate the customer's needs and wants* by making product suggestions, sharing personal experiences about the product, offering to get the customer into a fitting room, making a product recommendation, and so on. For example, the associate might say, "I found the dark jeans you were looking for in a size 6. I also found other jeans in a size 6 that you might like. Would you like to take a look at these?" In other conversations, the sales associate was more reactive, simply responding to the customer's verbalized needs. For example, "I found the dark jeans you were looking for in a size 6. Let me know if you need anything else."

When proactive conversations were compared to reactive conversations, the former produced significantly higher average sales ($97 vs. $62), and shoppers who engaged in these conversations felt that the salesperson was more persuasive (although their satisfaction levels were not higher). The content analysis revealed several specific comments that seemed to drive higher shopping baskets, as listed in Table 18.1.

The data indicate that sales associates frequently missed opportunities to personalize conversations with individual shoppers. Personalization could include general comments such as making small talk or sharing personal information and product-specific comments like complimenting the customer on his/her appearance, asking personal questions, or sharing personal

Table 18.1 The influence of salesperson comments on customer behaviour

Conversation content	Conversations with content	Avg. sales w/ content	Avg. sales without
The sales associate working with a customer *specifically recommends a particular product, style, or size.* Statements that provided a product recommendation were characterized by an explicit expression suggesting a particular product.	25%	$107	$75
The sales associate working with a customer explains *his or her own experiences with a particular product.* Product experience provided information about product purchases, product wear, and/or product care.	25%	$92	$80
The sales associate working with a customer *suggests a different (or additional) product, style, or size than what the customer is currently considering.*	12%	$91	$83

Source: The authors

product experience. Surprisingly, the study revealed only three instances in which a sales associate directly or indirectly complimented or flattered the customer (e.g. "That looks nice on you," "Cute," "That's a good colour for you"). In all three instances, customers reported the highest level of satisfaction with the employee at the time of purchase (5 on a 5-point scale), the highest level of influence attributed to the sales associate, and the highest level of satisfaction with store employees during all past shopping experiences. Chan and Sengupta (2013) also find that salesperson flattery can lead to higher sales, even for customers who overhear the conversation.

Other social factors can also play an important role in the shopping process, affecting the time shoppers spend in the store; the departments they visit; and the specific products they notice, pick up, and purchase. For example, Hui *et al.* (2009) find that grocery shoppers are drawn to areas of the store with high shopper density but spend less time visiting these regions. Zhang *et al.* (2014) report that crowds in a mall store can sometimes be beneficial, as a busy store can attract shoppers into its departments and encourage product interaction, but higher levels of shopper density can interfere with the shopping process, reducing the likelihood of purchase. Zhang *et al.* (2018) find that shoppers in groups walk slower and visit more departments than their solo counterparts and that conversations between group members encourage shoppers to return to departments and spend more.

Conclusions

Retailers typically assess store performance using measures like change in same-store sales, gross margin, direct product profit, sales per square foot, and return on inventory investment. While these metrics can help guide store operations and improve productivity, they provide little insight into the unmet demand of shoppers and the obstacles they face when attempting to find and buy desired products. Several new research techniques have become available – including video-based customer tracking, virtual reality simulations, and eye tracking – which measure how shoppers allocate their attention across the available products and displays in the store. Merchants can leverage these tools to identify the factors that drive shopper engagement and purchase, as well as the points of friction in the shopping process, and create store environments that better connect with shoppers' needs and desires.

This chapter summarizes several studies which use these tools to begin to map out how various elements of the store environment can facilitate or impede the shopper's journey. Critical factors include the interaction between shoppers' goals and the available product assortment, package appearance, price, and merchandising; shelf space allocation, organization, and adjacencies; and salesperson interaction and crowding conditions. The research reveals that small changes to the shopping environment, such as showing the right product on window signs, grouping products into solutions, folding items to encourage touch, and offering a compliment to the shopper, can have a powerful impact on shopper engagement and purchase conversion.

The research also suggests several promising avenues for future research. For example, the simulation research demonstrates that shoppers who have a picture of a desired brand in mind are faster at finding the item on a store shelf. However, additional research is needed to determine if this mental picture makes shoppers more susceptible to distraction from similar-looking competitors (cf. van Horen and Pieters 2012). We observed that shoppers are more willing to pay a higher price for merchandise in a store that is well organized and signed, but it is still unclear if this is because the psychological costs of shopping are lower or such stores convey a higher-quality image that casts a positive halo on the products (cf. Baker *et al.* 2002). Classical surveying of customers can also be used to better understand their requirements, their perceptions of the store environment, and opportunities for improving the shopping experience. Researchers can use personal interviews, focus groups, and questionnaires, alone or in combination with tools discussed in this article, to explore how customer characteristics interact with attributes of the store and product categories (e.g. Inman *et al.* 2009).

In the future, observational research technologies will continue to evolve to capture more detailed information about shoppers and their behaviour. For example, using computer vision techniques, we can automatically code the demographic characteristics of shoppers (e.g. gender, age category, and ethnicity), estimate their height and weight, trace their path through the store, record their interactions with products and displays, and analyse their facial expressions to measure their emotional reactions. As marketers begin to deploy these new tools, it is important to consider issues of consumer privacy and shopper reactance. Companies must act responsibly to protect shoppers' identities and personal information and to secure their informed consent if any risks are involved.

Acknowledgements

This is an updated version of the following book chapter:

Burke, R.R. and Leykin, A., 2014. Identifying the drivers of shopper attention, engagement, and purchase. In D. Grewal, A. Roggeveen and J. Nordfält, eds., 2014. *Review of marketing research, Volume 11: Shopper marketing and the role of in-store marketing.* Bingley, UK: Emerald Group, 147–187. http://doi.org/10.1108/S1548-643520140000011006.

References

Atalay, A.S., Bodur, H.O. and Rasolofoarison, D., 2012. Shining in the center: Central gaze cascade effect on product choice. *Journal of Consumer Research*, 39 (December), 848–866. https://doi.org/10.1086/665984.

Baker, J., Parasuraman, A., Grewal, D. and Voss, G.B., 2002. The influence of multiple store environment cues on perceived merchandise value and patronage intentions. *Journal of Marketing*, 66(April), 120–141. https://doi.org/10.1509%2Fjmkg.66.2.120.18470.

Baluch, F. and Itti, L., 2011. Mechanisms of top-down attention. *Trends in Neurosciences*, 34(4), 210–224. https://doi.org/10.1016/j.tins.2011.02.003.

Bigné, E., Llinares, C. and Torrecilla, C., 2016. Elapsed time on first buying triggers brand choices within a category: A virtual reality-based study. *Journal of Business Research*, 69(4), 1423–1427. https://doi.org/10.1016/j.jbusres.2015.10.119.

Bisley, J.W., 2011. The neural basis of visual attention. *The Journal of Physiology*, 589 (Pt 1), 49–57. https://doi.org/10.1113/jphysiol.2010.192666.

Bloch, P.H., Ridgway, N.M. and Sherrell, D.L., 1989. Extending the concept of shopping: An investigation of browsing activity. *Journal of the Academy of Marketing Science*, 17(1), 13–21. https://doi.org/10.1007/BF02726349.

Breen, P., 2009. *Shaping Retail: The Use of Virtual Store Simulations in Marketing Research and Beyond*. Industry Insights. Chicago, IL: In-Store Marketing Institute, January.

Bruce, N.D.B. and Tsotos, J.K., 2009. Saliency, attention, and visual search: An information theoretic approach. *Journal of Vision*, 9(5), 1–24. https://doi.org/10.1167/9.3.5.

Bucklin, R.E. and Sismeiro, C., 2003. A model of web site browsing behavior estimated on clickstream data. *Journal of Marketing Research*, 40(3), 249–267. https://doi.org/10.1509/jmkr.40.3.249.19241.

Burke, R.R., 1993. Marsh Supermarkets Inc. (A): The Marsh Super Study, case #594–042. *Harvard Business School* (Rev. 3/95), 1–21.

Burke, R.R., 1996. Virtual shopping: Breakthrough in marketing research. *Harvard Business Review*, 74(March–April), 120–131.

Burke, R.R., 2005. Retail shoppability: A measure of the world's best stores. In *Future Retail Now: 40 of the World's Best Stores*. Washington, DC: The Retail Industry Leaders Association, 206–219.

Burke, R.R., 2006. The third wave of marketing intelligence. In M. Krafft and M. Mantrala, eds. *Retailing in the 21st Century: Current and Future Trends*. New York: Springer, 113–125.

Burke, R.R., 2009. Behavioral effects of digital signage. *Journal of Advertising Research*, 49(2), 180–185. https://doi.org/10.2501/S0021849909090254.

Burke, R.R., 2018. Virtual reality for marketing research. In L. Moutinho and M. Sokele, eds. *Innovative Research Methodologies in Management: Volume II: Futures, Biometrics and Neuroscience Research*. London: Palgrave Macmillan, 63–82. https://doi.org/10.1007/978-3-319-64400-4_3.

Burke, R.R., Harlam, B., Kahn, B. and Lodish, L., 1992. Comparing dynamic consumer choice in real and computer-simulated environments. *Journal of Consumer Research*, 19(1), 71–82. https://doi.org/10.1086/209287.

Cerf, M., Frady, P.E. and Koch, C., 2009. Faces and text attract gaze independent of the task: Experimental data and computer model. *Journal of Vision*, 9(12), 10–10. https://doi.org/10.1167/9.12.10.

Chaiken, S., 1980. Heuristic versus systematic information processing and the use of source versus message cues in persuasion. *Journal of Personality and Social Psychology*, 39, 752–766. https://doi.org/10.1037/0022-3514.39.5.752.

Chan, E. and Sengupta, J., 2013. Observing flattery: A social comparison perspective. *Journal of Consumer Research*, 40(4), 740–758. https://doi.org/10.1086/672357.

Chandon, P., Hutchinson, J.W., Bradlow, E.T. and Young, S.H., 2008. Measuring the value of point-of-purchase marketing with commercial eye-tracking data. In M. Wedel and R. Pieters, eds. *Visual Marketing: From Attention to Action*. New York: Lawrence Erlbaum Associates, 225–258. https://doi.org/10.2139/ssrn.1032162.

Chandon, P., Hutchinson, J.W., Bradlow, E.T. and Young, S.H., 2009. Does in-store marketing work? Effects of the number and position of shelf facings on brand attention and evaluation at the point of purchase. *Journal of Marketing*, 73(6), 1–17. https://doi.org/10.1509/jmkg.73.6.1.

Colby, C.L., 1991. The neuroanatomy and neurophysiology of attention. *Journal of Child Neurology*, 6(Suppl.), S90–118. https://doi.org/10.1177/0883073891006001s11.

Czerwinski, M., Lightfoot, N. and Shiffrin, R.M., 1992. Automatization and training in visual search. *The American Journal of Psychology*, 105(2), 271–315. https://doi.org/10.2307/1423030.

Dhar, R. and Nowlis, S.M., 1999. The effect of time pressure on consumer choice deferral. *Journal of Consumer Research*, 25(4), 369–384. https://doi.org/10.1086/209545.

Dickson, P.R. and Sawyer, A.G., 1990. The price knowledge and search of supermarket shoppers. *Journal of Marketing*, 54(July), 42–54. https://doi.org/10.1177%2F002224299005400304.

Duncan, J. and Humphreys, G.W., 1989. Visual search and stimulus similarity. *Psychological Review*, 96(3), 433–458. https://psycnet.apa.org/doi/10.1037/0033-295X.96.3.433.

Eckstein, M.P., 1998. The lower visual search efficiency for conjunctions is due to noise and not serial attentional processing. *Psychological Science*, 9(2), 111–118. https://doi.org/10.1016/j.tins.2011.02.003.

Eckstein, M.P., Drescher, B.A. and Shimozaki, S.S., 2006. Attentional cues in real scenes, saccadic targeting, and Bayesian priors. *Psychological Science*, 17(11), 973–980. https://doi.org/10.1167/5.8.917.

Edwards, S. and Shackley, M., 1992. Measuring the effectiveness of retail window display as an element of the marketing mix. *International Journal of Advertising*, 11, 193–202. https://doi.org/10.1080/02650 487.1992.11104494.

Elazary, L. and Itti, L., 2008. Interesting objects are visually salient. *Journal of Vision*, 8(3:3), 1–15. https://doi.org/10.1167/8.3.3.

Elder, R.S. and Krishna, A., 2012. The 'visual depiction effect' in advertising: Facilitating embodied mental simulation through product orientation. *Journal of Consumer Research*, 3 (April), 988–1003. https://doi.org/10.1086/661531.

Fischer, B. and Ramsperger, E., 1984. Human express saccades: Extremely short reaction times of goal directed eye movements. *Experimental Brain Research*, 57(1), 191–195. https://doi.org/10.1007/BF00231145.

Greene, M.R. and Oliva, A., 2009. Recognition of natural scenes from global properties: Seeing the forest without representing the trees. *Cognitive Psychology*, 58(2), 137–176. https://doi.org/10.1016/j.cogpsych.2008.06.001.

Grewal, D., Noble, S.M., Ahlbom, C.P. and Nordfält, J., 2020. The sales impact of using hand-held scanners: Evidence from the field. *Journal of Marketing Research*, 57(3), 527–547. https://doi.org/10.1177/0022243720911624.

Hartman, K.B. and Spiro, R., 2006. *Sales Associate-Customer Interaction Study. Research Report, Center for Education and Research in Retailing*. Bloomington, IN: Center for Education and Research in Retailing, Kelley School of Business, Indiana University, January.

Henderson, J.M., Malcolm, G.L. and Schandl, C., 2009. Searching in the dark: Cognitive relevance drives attention in real-world scenes. *Psychonomic Bulletin and Review*, 16(5), 850–856. https://doi.org/10.3758/PBR.16.5.850.

Hendrickson, K. and Ailawadi, K., 2014. Shopper marketing: Six lessons for retail from six years of mobile eye-tracking research. In D. Grewal, A. Roggeveen and J. Nordfält, eds. *Review of Marketing Research, Volume 11: Shopper Marketing and the Role of In-Store Marketing*. Bingley, UK: Emerald Group, 57–74. https://doi.org/10.1108/S1548-643520140000011002.

Hollingworth, A., 2006. Scene and position specificity in visual memory for objects. *Journal of Experimental Psychology: Learning, Memory and Cognition*, 32(1), 58–69. https://doi.org/10.1037/0278-7393.32.1.58.

Hoyer, W.D., 1984. An examination of consumer decision making for a common repeat purchase product. *Journal of Consumer Research*, 11(3), 822–829. https://doi.org/10.1086/209017.

Hui, S., Bradlow, E. and Fader, P., 2009. Testing behavioral hypotheses using an integrated model of grocery store shopping path and purchase behavior. *Journal of Consumer Research*, 36(3), 478–493. https://doi.org/10.1086/599046.

Hui, S., Fader, P. and Bradlow, E., 2009a. Path data in marketing: An integrative framework and prospectus for model building. *Marketing Science*, 28(2), 320–335. https://doi.org/10.1287/mksc.1080.0400.

Hui, S., Fader, P. and Bradlow, E., 2009b. The traveling salesman goes shopping: The systematic deviations of grocery paths from TSP-optimality. *Marketing Science*, 28(3), 566–572. https://doi.org/10.1287/mksc.1080.0402.

Hui, S., Huang, Y., Suher, J. and Inman, J., 2013. Deconstructing the "first moment of truth": Understanding unplanned consideration and purchase conversion using in-store video tracking. *Journal of Marketing Research*, 50(4), 445–462. https://doi.org/10.1509/jmr.12.0065.

Inman, J., Winer, R. and Ferraro, R., 2009. The interplay among category characteristics, customer characteristics, and customer activities on in-store decision making. *Journal of Marketing*, 73(5), 19–29. https://doi.org/10.1509/jmkg.73.5.19.

Kanan, C., Tong, M., Zhang, L. and Cottrell, G.W., 2009. SUN: Top-down saliency using natural statistics. *Visual Cognition*, 17, 979–1003. https://doi.org/10.1080/13506280902771138.

Kanwisher, N. and Wojciulik, E., 2000. Visual attention: Insights from brain imaging. *Nature Reviews Neuroscience*, 1(2), 91–100. https://doi.org/10.1038/35039043.

Klingensmith, D., 2013. Eye tracking: Behavioral science in-store. *Shopper Marketing*, Path to Purchase Institute, August 19.

Larson, J.S., Bradlow, E.T. and Fader, P.S., 2005. An exploratory look at supermarket shopping paths. *International Journal of Research in Marketing*, 22(4), 395–414. https://doi.org/10.1016/j.ijresmar.2005.09.005.

Lynch, Jr., J.G. and Srull, T.K., 1982. Memory and attentional factors in consumer choice: Concepts and research methods. *Journal of Consumer Research*, 9(1), 18–37. https://doi.org/10.1086/208893.

Maljkovic, V. and Nakayama, K., 1994. Priming of pop-out: I. Role of features. *Memory & Cognition*, 22(6), 657–672. https://doi.org/10.3758/BF03209251.

Meißner, M., Musalem, A. and Huber, J., 2016. Eye tracking reveals processes that enable conjoint choices to become increasingly efficient with practice. *Journal of Marketing Research*, 53(1), 1–17. https://doi.org/10.1509/jmr.13.0467.

Meißner, M., Pfeiffer, J., Peukert, C., Dietrich, H. and Pfeiffer, T., 2020. How virtual reality affects consumer choice. *Journal of Business Research*, 117(September), 219–231. https://doi.org/10.1016/j.jbusres.2020.06.004.

Mishra, S., Rusetski, A. and Burke, R.R., 2008. *Measuring the Effects of the Retail Environment on the Consumer Shopping Process*. Research Report. Bloomington, IN: Customer Interface Laboratory, Kelley School, Indiana University, 26 November.

Moe, W., 2003. Buying, searching, or browsing: Differentiating between online shoppers using in-store navigational clickstream. *Journal of Consumer Psychology*, 13(1&2), 29–40. https://doi.org/10.1207/S15327663JCP13-1&2_03.

Montgomery, A.L., Li, S., Srinivasan, K. and Liechty, J.C., 2004. Modeling online browsing and path analysis using clickstream data. *Marketing Science*, 23(4), 579–595. https://doi.org/10.1287/mksc.1040.0073.

Most, S.B., Scholl, B.J., Clifford, E.R. and Simons, D.J., 2005. What you see is what you set: Sustained inattentional blindness and the capture of awareness. *Psychological Review*, 112(1), 217–242. https://doi.org/10.1037/0033-295X.112.1.217.

Musalem, A., Olivares, M. and Schilkrut, A., 2020. Retail in high definition: Monitoring customer assistance through video analytics. *Manufacturing & Service Operations Management*. https://doi.org/10.1287/msom.2020.0865.

Nelson-Shulman, Y., 1984. Information and environmental stress: Report of a hospital intervention. *Journal of Environmental Systems*, 13(4), 303–316. https://doi.org/10.3390/ijerph15020332.

Orquin, J.L. and Mueller Loose, S., 2013. Attention and choice: A review of eye movements in decision making. *Acta Psychologica*, 144, 190–206. https://doi.org/10.1016/j.actpsy.2013.06.003.

Park, C.W., Iyer, E.S. and Smith, D.C., 1989. The effects of situational factors on in-store grocery shopping behavior: The role of store environment and time available for shopping. *Journal of Consumer Research*, 15(March), 422–433. https://doi.org/10.1086/209182.

Payne, J.W., Bettman, J.R. and Johnson, E.J., 1988. Adaptive strategy selection in decision making. *Journal of Experimental Psychology: Learning, Memory, and Cognition*, 14(July), 534–552. https://doi.org/10.1037/0278-7393.14.3.534.

Pennington, A.L., 1968. Customer-salesman bargaining behavior in retail transactions. *Journal of Marketing Research*, 5(August), 255–262. https://doi.org/10.1177/002224376800500301.

Pieters, R. and Warlop, L., 1999. Visual attention during brand choice: The impact of time pressure and task motivation. *International Journal of Research in Marketing*, 16, 1–16. https://doi.org/10.1016/S0167-8116(98)00022-6.

Pieters, R. and Wedel, M., 2007. Goal control of attention to advertising: The Yarbus implication. *Journal of Consumer Research*, 34(2), 224–233. https://doi.org/10.1086/519150.

Rosenholtz, R., Li, Y. and Nakano, L., 2007. Measuring visual clutter. *Journal of Vision*, 7(2), 1–22. https://doi.org/10.1167/7.2.17.

Russo, J.E. and LeClerc, F., 1994. An eye-fixation analysis of choice processes for consumer nondurables. *Journal of Consumer Research*, 21(September), 274–290. https://doi.org/10.1086/209397.

Sadalla, E.K. and Montello, D.R., 1989. Remembering changes in direction. *Environment and Behavior*, 21(May), 346–363. https://doi.org/10.1177/0013916589213006.

Simons, D.J. and Chabris, C.F., 1999. Gorillas in our midst: Sustained inattentional blindness for dynamic events. *Perception*, 28, 1059–1074. https://doi.org/10.1068/p281059.

Smythies, J.R., 1996. A note on the concept of the visual field in neurology, psychology, and visual neuroscience. *Perception*, 25(3), 369–371. https://doi.org/10.1068/p250369.

Sorensen, H., 2017. *Inside the Mind of the Shopper: The Science of Retailing*, 2nd ed. Old Tappan, NJ: Pearson Education Inc.

Stilley, K., Inman, J. and Wakefield, K., 2010. Spending on the fly: Mental budgets, promotions, and spending behavior. *Journal of Marketing*, 74(May), 34–47. https://doi.org/10.1509/jmkg.74.3.034.

Tatler, B.W. and Vincent, B.T., 2009. The prominence of behavioural biases in eye guidance. *Visual Cognition*, 17(6–7), 1029–1054. https://doi.org/10.1080/13506280902764539.

Theeuwes, J., 1995. Abrupt luminance change pops out: Abrupt color change does not. *Perception and Psychophysics*, 57(5), 637–644. https://doi.org/10.3758/bf03213269.

Titus, P.A. and Everett, P.B., 1995. The consumer retail search process: A conceptual model and research agenda. *Journal of the Academy of Marketing Science*, 23(2), 106–119. https://doi.org/10.1177/0092070395232003.

Torralba, A., Aude, O., Castelhano, M.S. and Henderson, J.M., 2006. Contextual guidance of eye movements and attention in real-world scenes: The role of global features in object search. *Psychological Review*, 113(4), 766–786. https://doi.org/10.1037/0033-295x.113.4.766.

Treisman, A., 1996. The binding problem. *Current Opinion in Neurobiology*, 6(2), 171–178. https://doi.org/10.1016/s0959-4388(96)80070-5.

Treisman, A. and Gormican, S., 1988. Feature analysis in early vision: Evidence from search asymmetries. *Psychological Review*, 95(1), 15–48. https://doi.org/10.1037/0033-295x.95.1.15.

Underhill, P., 1999. *Why We Buy: The Science of Shopping*. New York: Simon & Schuster.

Underhill, P., 2004. *Call of the Mall*. New York: Simon & Schuster.

Van der Lans, R., Pieters, R. and Wedel, M., 2008a. Competitive brand salience. *Marketing Science*, 27(5), 922–931. https://doi.org/10.1287/mksc.1070.0327.

Van der Lans, R., Pieters, R. and Wedel, M., 2008b. Eye-movement analysis of search effectiveness. *Journal of the American Statistical Association*, 103(482), 452–461. https://doi.org/10.1198/016214507000000437.

Van Herpen, E., van den Broek, E., van Trijp, H.C. and Yu, T., 2016. Can a virtual supermarket bring realism into the lab? Comparing shopping behavior using virtual and pictorial store representations to behavior in a physical store. *Appetite*, 107(December), 196–207. https://doi.org/10.1016/j.appet.2016.07.033.

Van Horen, F. and Pieters, R., 2012. When high-similarity copycats lose and moderate-similarity copycats gain: The impact of comparative evaluation. *Journal of Marketing Research*, 49(1), 83–91. https://doi.org/10.1509/jmr.08.0405.

Verde Group, 2007. *He Buys, She Shops: A Study of Gender Differences in the Retail Experience*. Verde/Wharton Retail Experience Research Series, Baker Retailing Initiative. Philadelphia, PA: Wharton School, University of Pennsylvania.

Walter, M., Hildebrand, C., Häubl, G. and Herrmann, A., 2020. Mixing it up: Unsystematic product arrangements promote the choice of unfamiliar products. *Journal of Marketing Research*, 57(3), 509–526. https://doi.org/10.1177/0022243720901520.

Wedel, M. and Pieters, R., 2007. A review of eye-tracking research in marketing. In N.K. Malhotra, ed. *Review of Marketing Research, Volume 4*. Bingley, UK: Emerald Group, 123–147. https://doi.org/10.1108/S1548-6435(2008)0000004009.

Wedel, M. and Pieters, R., 2008. Eye tracking for visual marketing. *Foundations and Trends in Marketing*, 1(4), 231–320. http://doi.org/10.1561/1700000011.

Weisman, G., 1981. Evaluating architectural legibility: Wayfinding in the built environment. *Environment and Behavior*, 13, 189–204. https://doi.org/10.1177/0013916581132004.

Weitz, B.A., 1981. Effectiveness in sales interactions: A contingency framework. *Journal of Marketing*, 45(1), 85–103. https://doi.org/10.1177/002224298104500109.

Wener, R. and Kaminoff, R., 1982. Improving environmental information: Effects of signs on perceived crowding and behavior. *Environment and Behavior*, 14(6), 671–694. https://doi.org/10.1177/0013916583151001.

Wolfe, J.M. and Horowitz, T.S., 2004. What attributes guide the deployment of visual attention and how do they do it? *Nature Reviews: Neuroscience*, 5(June), 1–7. https://doi.org/10.1038/nrn1411.

Wolfe, J.M., Võ, M.L.-H., Evans, K.K. and Greene, M.R., 2011. Visual search in scenes involves selective and nonselective pathways. *Trends in Cognitive Sciences*, 15(2), 77–84. https://doi.org/10.1016/j.tics.2010.12.001.

Yang, L., Toubia, O. and de Jong, M., 2018. Attention, information processing, and choice in incentive-aligned choice experiments. *Journal of Marketing Research*, 55(6), 783–800. https://doi.org/10.1177/0022243718817004.

Young, S., 2010. *Winning at Retail: Insights from 35 Years of Packaging & Shopper Research*. Skokie, IL: In-Store Marketing Institute.

Zelinsky, G., Zhang, W., Yu, B., Chen, X. and Samaras, D., 2005. The role of top-down and bottom-up processes in guiding eye movements during visual search. *Conference on Neural Information Processing Systems*, 1569–1576.

Zhang, X., Li, S. and Burke, R.R., 2018. Modeling the effects of dynamic group influence on shopper zone choice, purchase conversion and spending. *Journal of the Academy of Marketing Science*, 46(6), 1089–1107. https://doi.org/10.1007/s11747-018-0590-9.

Zhang, X., Li, S., Burke, R.R. and Leykin, A., 2014. An examination of social influence on shopper behavior using video tracking data. *Journal of Marketing*, 78(5), 24–41. https://doi.org/10.1509/jm.12.0106.

PART IV

Applications

19

RESEARCHING OLDER CITIZENS AND THEIR ATTITUDES TOWARDS SMART HOMES

Merlin Stone, Eleni Aravopoulou and Geraint Evans

Summary

This chapter explains an approach to researching the needs and perceptions of older adults regarding the idea of the smart home. It investigates differences in attitudes towards and usage of smart devices between current older adults (average age 75–80) and the next generation of older adults (the baby boomers). Although the sample was small, the research showed that while there is a difference between current (average age 80) and future (average age 60) older adults in attitudes to exchanging personal information and to the use of smart technology, the difference was not enormous. It also showed that the positive attitudes in the latter group augured very well for the smartening of cities in future. It suggests that this kind of research approach should be used more widely to support planning and decision-making in this area.

Who are older adults?

A (reasonably well) accepted definition of the generations is given in Table 19.1.

These descriptions of generations are simplistic but shorthand. In more detail, the UK baby boomer generation is the largest generation of older people the world has seen. In comparison with earlier older generations, it is working the longest number of years (and the longest beyond retirement, often part-time) (Office for National Statistics 2019) and doing the most home-working (often in their own business) (Office for National Statistics 2020).

The United Kingdom has an ageing population (Office for National Statistics 2018c). Statistics compiled by Age UK (2019) show that there are nearly 12 million (11,989,322) people aged 65 and above in the United Kingdom of which 5.4 million people are aged 75 or over 75 1.6 million are aged 85 and over 0.58 million are 90 or over, including 14,430 who are centenarians (Office for National Statistics 2018b, 2018c). By 2030, one in five people in the United Kingdom (21.8%) will be aged 65 or over, 6.8% will be aged 75+ and 3.2% will be aged 85+ (Office for National Statistics 2017). The 85+ age group is the fastest growing and is set to

Table 19.1 The generations

Generation	When born
Matures (Greatest/Silent)	Pre–1945
Baby Boomers	1946–1964
Generation X	1965–1981
Generation Y (Millennials)	1982–2004
Generation Z	2005–present

Source: Authors

double to 3.2 million by mid-2041 and treble by 2066 (5.1 million; 7% of the UK population) (Office for National Statistics 2018a).

However, one of the problems of an ageing population is that a higher proportion of the population suffers from multi-morbidity – having two or more long-term medical conditions [in the case of the United Kingdom, this is true of over half of the older population (Kingston *et al.* 2018)]. A very specific risk facing older adults is that of a fall, with a third of people aged 65 or over and over half of people aged 80 or over falling at least once a year (Public Health England 2018), with falls constituting the largest cause of emergency hospital admissions for older people (National Health Service 2017), leading to injury, distress, pain, loss of confidence or independence and mortality (Public Health England 2018). Other obvious threats to their well-being which affect large proportions of older adults where adaptation or smartening of homes can be particularly helpful include sight loss (RNIB 2018), dementia (Dementia UK 2019), mental illness (Royal College of Psychiatrists 2018) and sheer loneliness (Age UK 2018a).

Older adults are a poorly served demographic. They are rich with disposable income and a wealth of knowledge, yet often (and especially when it comes to marketing), they are treated as second-class citizens. Research bears this out (Thomas 2014), with 82% of retirees saying they felt businesses and brands did not understand their lifestyle and 69% believing advertising aimed at the elderly was patronising. Companies are guilty of overlooking the "silver pound", which is worth £43 billion a year (Hurley 2016). It is also worth noting that a report by McKinsey (2016) suggests that by 2030 the 60-plus age group will account for 60% of consumption growth in Western Europe. However, there is still a significant difference in use of modern information and communications technology between different segments of the older adult group, with 36% of those aged 65 or more being offline, lapsed or never users of the Internet, while at the other extreme, 80% of those aged 65–74 had "used the Internet recently", although use is increasing at all ages (Age UK 2018b). Indeed, the changing nature of the definition and outcomes of ageing is one of the central themes of much research, even changing our thinking about when old age is thought to begin (Office for National Statistics 2019).

Many of the previous statements are averages, concealing differences by location, social class, past and present (healthy or not) lifestyles, ethnicity and genes and other dimensions. However, the conclusion from them is that older adults constitute a big, growing, financially important but problematic market segment for suppliers of housing and digital technologies, amongst others.

Older adults, smart cities and smart housing

Much progress has been made in the development of smart cities and smart housing across the globe While best practice is still emergent, there is much innovation taking place (Stone *et al.* 2018) and much documentation of progress, often through awards, such as those of IDC

(2020). 5G telecommunications infrastructure, smart home and sensor technology permit big improvements in areas such as transport capacity planning, health service delivery and capacity planning to ease travel problems, enhance the delivery of services and use intelligent applications to greatly improve the quality of life. However, this progress usually relates to what suppliers and cities are doing rather than what citizens want or what they are prepared to do in terms of exchanging information, particularly those citizens who form most of the population in Western cities and will experience the smartening of cities primarily though the smartening of their homes. As Marston and Van Hoof (2019) identify, there may be a significant gap in thinking about the contribution technology can make to the development of age-friendly cities, which can be remedied by bringing ideas on user needs and technology capabilities more closely together.

Much of the existing research into older adults' needs in relation to smartening of cities and homes focuses on high-level needs rather than detailed developments. For example, in their review of how attitudes to the ageing process may change due to the use of new media and new technology, Damodaran and Olphert (2015) concluded that strategic planning by government and other bodies, for the required systematic and strategic organisational, ethical, cultural and societal change, lags behind technological advances. Government and EU-backed exploratory research into the use of technology that can monitor people's health, keep them connected to family and friends, keep their homes more secure and help them to stay fit and connected has been explored in various initiatives, including the EU-funded "Service orientated programmable smart environments for older Europeans" (Soprano) project. Research into housing choices and aspirations of older people (Abramsson and Andersson 2016; Appleton 2003; Clough *et al.* 2005; Croucher 2008; Tinker *et al.* 2001; Torrington 2014) shows that most older people prefer to remain in their own homes, and most felt that their homes could be adapted for any future needs.

What about the customer?

The Digital Inclusion Evidence Review conducted by Age UK (2018b) found that, despite barriers such as cost, a lack of user-friendliness of equipment and unfamiliarity/resistance to change, many older people already benefit from new technologies, with the benefits including reduced loneliness, more control over their lives, more independence in living and participating in and contributing to society. Ravishankar *et al.* (2015) found that there was a need for to focus on user-centred customised design to meet the personal needs of ageing users. Research on the future housing aspirations of older people (Ward *et al.* 2013) concluded that of respondents aged between 50 and 70 years old, two-thirds (63%) said they thought their current accommodation would continue to meet their needs as they get older – emphasising the need for this to be future proofed. Research into retirement housing residents' experiences (Lychgate Projects 2016) emphasised the importance of proximity to amenities such as shops, doctors' surgeries, pharmacies and public transport, due to aging residents not wishing to feel isolated.

Effect of home smartening on customers

In the last few years, there has been a flow of serious research, often with a medical basis, on specific applications of home smartening, how they affect older adults and the ethical and practical issues associated with this approach, particularly but not exclusively those with specific medical conditions. Various reviews of the smart home literature relating to older adults have been conducted, such as Marikyan *et al.* (2019) and Turjamaa *et al.* (2019), with the latter finding that research showed that smart homes improved older adults' sense of security, quality of daily life and activities and also provided them with information about care they could receive. However, they identified that research into older people's experiences as end-users and on older people playing an active role in developing smart home technology was lacking, which indicates that there is an opportunity for co-creation and greater involvement. This view is echoed by Mannheim *et al.* (2019), who identify that there seems to be a discrepancy between digital technologies that are developed and what older adults actually want and need. They contend that ageing is stereotypically framed as a problem needing to be fixed, with older adults considered frail and incompetent, which is not the case for at least half of them. They identify that it is therefore not surprising that many of the technologies developed for older adults focus on care. They suggest that designers and researchers should involve older adults in the design and research process. Woodcock *et al.* (2020) identify that there is a specific problem in this regard related to the treatment of younger older adults. These issues form part of the context for the study described in this chapter.

Robots

One recent focus has been on the use of automation, robotics in general and humanoid robots. Wilson *et al.* (2019) describe the use of a robot activity support system combining sensing, object detection and mapping and robot interactions to help older adults stay safe in their homes while engaging in routine activities. The use of passive monitoring was researched by Choi *et al.* (2019), Yu *et al.* (2019) and Galambos *et al.* (2019), with the latter finding that sensors were seen as helpful in maintaining independence, health and physical functioning; that willingness to use sensors was motivated by decline in functional status and a desire to remain independent; and that participants were willing to share their health data with providers and select family members. Forkan *et al.* (2019) investigate the use of sensing in an Internet of Things (IoT) context. The IoT is more thoroughly investigated by Carnemolla (2018), Kowalski *et al.* (2019), Robinson *et al.* (2019) and Stigall *et al.* (2019), focusing on the use of voice-assisted technology, with the latter identifying novelty as one of the barriers to adoption, which suggests that as older adults become more familiar with the approach, adoption will increase. Tun *et al.* (2020) focus on the use of wearables using IoT approaches, identifying the range of approaches now available to designers, while Wang *et al.* (2019) study awareness of these and related devices amongst older adults, identifying a big gap between awareness and use, but a positive attitude to sharing data from them. Thakur and Han (2019) describe the development of a system which can not only analyse but also predict the behaviour of elderly people during day-to-day interactions with Internet of Things technology environment, finding the responses to this approach very positive amongst older adults.

In Japan and other parts of the Far East, extensive research has been carried out into how older adults respond to the use of robotics in their home. Particularly in the case of Japan, where a rapidly ageing population has left the country short of care workers, there is strong evidence about the acceptability of robotic company and robotic care, especially but not exclusively companion robots. Studies of the deployment of robots generally confirm feasibility and acceptability, particularly after a period of familiarisation, and the importance of user input into design (Tanabe *et al.* 2019; Chien *et al.* 2019; Miyake *et al.* 2020; Oh and Kim 2019; Shishehgar *et al.* 2019; Obayashi and Masuyama 2020). Elsewhere, the home robotics qualitative study of Deutsch *et al.* (2019) evaluated attitudes and emotional reactions towards different home robotic devices and identified as important factors the need for independence, the need for control, the fear of being replaced and the need for authenticity, with older adults willing to adopt home robotic devices if their concerns are addressed.

A more comprehensive approach

Some studies focus on the adoption of more comprehensive smart home technology by older adults. For example, Arthanat *et al.* (2019) find that gender (being female), with some physical impairment and a fall history and experience in information and communications technology were positively associated with adoption. Pal *et al.* (2019) identify the main barriers to smart-home usage by the elderly people using an online survey in four Asian countries and finding that innovativeness, perceived reliability, perceived interoperability, service cost, privacy concerns, psychological barriers, home administrative policy and government policy were important determinants of adoption. Curumsing *et al.* (2019) identify the failure to focus on older adults' emotions and describe the development and application of emotion-oriented requirement techniques to evaluate the participants' emotional reactions before, during and after trials, showing how a well-designed system leads to older adults developing a strong relation with the system, even feeling frustrated when the system does not respond in the expected or desired ways.

The study

The previous review identified two critically important requirements – the need for holistic research which is not purely focused on technology or products and for research which takes into account the variety of customer segments, in particular the difference between those older adults who have just entered the category and those who have been there for some time. Put simply, we were concerned about the lack of in-depth customer research, particularly concerning the experiences and requirements of the next generation of older adults compared with the current generation.

The best research we had seen came from Ireland, where surveys were carried out on some of the issues covered previously (Cronin *et al.* 2013). So, we decided to carry out comparative research with two groups of older adults, one of baby boomers with an average age of 60 and the other of older adults with an average age of 80. We wanted to examine their views, potential needs and aspirations not in relation to specific technologies but in relation to the benefits these technologies could bring. However, as this was a relatively unexplored area, this study was considered a pilot. Its aim was to identify what kind of information about older adults' attitudes to smartening their homes and cities and the resulting information exchange could feasibly be collected at scale using low-cost web research techniques. This would enable any marketing research of this kind to move quickly beyond the small-scale studies that seem to be normal in this area.

The study received the help of a sheltered/retirement homes provider, who emailed the link to the online questionnaire to their customers, giving the researchers an interesting insight into how to get responses from older adults using web technology. This was therefore skewed to those residents whose interaction with the homes' provider was by email, though it should be noted that this was the older group. The other respondents, broadly the next generation or baby boomers, were from the LinkedIn contacts of one of the authors and were recruited via social media and email (with a stipulation that only those aged over 50 should respond), so skewed towards the marketing community of marketeers, consultant and information technology specialists. The overall bias in this was acknowledged, that is, only those used to digital means of communication could be recruited, but surveys show that these comprise a high proportion of the target users, with many of them having social media profiles, in what Ofcom (2018) referred to as the "rise of the social seniors".

As the aim was more to see what kinds of data could be collected by this method (a Google Forms questionnaire was used) and to see whether we could help people think their way through some of the decisions facing them, the online questionnaire was designed with this aim in mind through the form of the questions, which was very different from normal surveys, as will be seen later.

It was not possible to quantify the response rate from either survey, but as the aim was to test the research instrument, this was not considered a problem. We just wanted enough responses to be able to analyse them in volume. The demography of the two groups of respondents was significantly different, with sheltered/retirement home residents mostly retired and 20 years older on average, less healthy and less well connected digitally than the next generation but not worse off financially. One factor which will affect the results of any future surveys is the rapidly rising number of workers who are beyond state retirement age. Given this, the attitudes to housing, care and health are not as radically different between the two groups as might be expected.

Survey design

The questionnaire was designed using the results of the literature review to identify the topics that were important to older adults and the language they used to describe the ideas to which they were being exposed.

The questionnaire was written in a friendly style, and there was a preamble indicating that the lead researcher was in the target group, in order to build a bond with the respondent. After 18 questions on demography, ownership of home, state of partnership, working status and ownership and use of communications technology, more probing questions were asked in relation to smartening of homes and health and the resulting information exchange. Most of these questions were preceded by a clarificatory statement. Examples of this special wording are given subsequently.

For the question on description of "age friendliness", the preamble text was as follows:

> One of the phrases often used about the area we are researching is "age-friendly housing". By this, we mean housing that is built or adapted to meet people's needs as they grow older, possibly becoming less healthy. Please let us know what you think about the phrase "age-friendly housing", by selecting all that apply, adding a phrase if these don't express what you think.

The options offered were:

- An accurate description;
- Patronising/talks down to me;
- Typical management speak;
- A phrase I could use comfortably;
- An ugly phrase;
- Sounds like a prison to me;
- Other.

For the section on smartening of homes, there was an initial statement about the meaning of smartening, as follows:

> This section includes questions about smart homes, which are homes with systems to connect and operate appliances, thermostats, cameras, televisions, heating and air-conditioning systems, security systems and sensors, to enable you to manage or remotely control or programme them. The benefits of smartening your home include security, energy saving, ease of communication with others and convenience.

This was followed by a request for respondents to indicate their degree of agreement with the following statements:

- I would like my home to welcome me when I come in through the door;
- I would like my home to warn me of any problems in the home;
- I would like my home to update me on particular kinds of news;
- I would like my home to update me of any things I ought to know about in the neighbourhood;
- I love the general idea of smart homes;
- I have already started to make my home smart;
- I look forward to making my home smarter as the costs fall;
- I would like a virtual companion or avatar to help me manage my house and my life;
- I like the idea of a robot to help me manage my house and my life;
- I like the idea of a service on my mobile phone or computer that will help me manage my home and my life;
- I would like all round safety and security monitoring built in;
- I would like all my domestic appliances and furniture connected to the Internet so I can see what is happening with them and so they can manage themselves;
- I would like my home to tell my FAMILY how things are going with me, with my permission;
- I would like my home to tell my FRIENDS how things are going with me, with my permission;
- I would like easy communication with my friends, family and neighbours without having to log on or use a device;
- I like to use home delivery services as much as possible and expect to do it more and more as I get older;
- I would like carers and family to have access to my home, using an access code.

This was then followed by a set of statements (with respondents again being asked to indicate their degree of agreement) on perceptions of their level of health and accountability for it and willingness to use communications technology to communicate with medical services, but these also included questions relating to the role of a smart home in keeping the respondent healthy, as follows:

- I want my home to tell me how healthy I am;
- I would like my home to keep me healthy;
- I would like my home to tell me whether I am having/have had a healthy day.

Finally, attitudes towards accountability for smartening were explored, with respondents being asked to indicate their degree of agreement with these statements, as follows:

- I would not like anyone to create my future home for me – I would like to be left to do it myself;
- I don't care what my future home might be like – it's less important to me than my health;
- As I grow older, I would prefer to adapt my home to my needs (and that of my partner) rather than move home;
- I would expect to take an active role in how I adapt my home as I grow older.

Results

As stated, the demography of the two groups of respondents was different, with retirement home residents mostly retired and 20 years older on average, less healthy and less well connected digitally than the next generation but not worse off financially, as the retirement housing company attracted better-off citizens. The attitudes to housing, care and health are not as radically different as might be expected.

Contrary to the popular perception that the "silver" generation is not technically literate or comfortable, if the findings are representative, it is clear, then, that older adults want their homes to be significantly smarter and to exchange information with them. The results confirmed they want their homes to welcome them, warn them of problems and update them on key events. Some found the idea of an avatar-like robot or assistant welcome. They confirmed that they often use Internet-enabled technology to advise on medical matters. Those who prefer to deal with doctor remotely are moderately correlated with "home smartness". Those who want to be cared for at home also confirm they want to stay in their current home and are open and willing to adapt it to their needs using smart technology such as wearables.

Table 19.2 shows the demographic results. Sample A were those recruited by social media, sample B from the sheltered/retirement home residents. The average age of Sample A was 60, that of Sample B 80. The main item of significance here was the relatively high proportion of Sample B caring for partners (14%).

Table 19.2 Demography of respondents

	A	B
Number of respondents	104	144
Average age	60	80
Male	64%	49%
England (mostly SE)	83%	92%
Scotland	1%	4%
Wales	2%	4%
N America	7%	0%
Not being looked after by any kind of carer	91%	80%
Caring for partner	1%	14%
Caring for someone else	8%	1%
Being looked after by professional carers	0%	3%
Being looked after by family or friends	1%	6%
Married or in permanent partnership	83%	52%

Source: Authors

Note that a relatively low proportion of the respondents were those being looked after by carers.

Table 19.3 gives the answer to questions about work and money. Here, the interesting data relate to the proportion from Sample A running a business from home (21%) and the proportion from that sample considering that they need to be careful about money (48%).

Table 19.4 gives the technology usage data. Here, given that the response was by email, even the older sample (B) showed high levels of Internet use for 5 years or more. The big difference was in smartphones, with many older people not having one (49% having a non-smartphone, 10% having no mobile phone).

Table 19.5 gives the results concerning perception of and attitudes to housing. Perhaps here the most surprising result was the number of adults in segment A who still had a mortgage (35%) and problems associated with the use of the phrase "age friendly".

Table 19.6 gives the results for the question on plans, where the most noteworthy result is the desire not to move, confirming the literature.

Table 19.7 shows the results concerning social and personal development at home. The findings indicate a fair degree of alignment between the two segments in terms of attitudes, with the exception that older people seem to be happier being alone, slightly paradoxically.

Table 19.8 indicates a perhaps surprising degree of acceptance of smart home ideas among the older sample, except that the older segment seems less happy with the idea of avatars and robots, use of mobile phones and connection of appliances.

Table 19.9 shows that, as expected, far fewer adults from the older segment considered themselves healthy.

Table 19.10 shows that younger respondents preferred to use remote technology to deal with doctors – the question is whether they will maintain these preferences as they age!

Table 19.3 Work and money

	A	B
Working full-time	50%	0%
Working part-time	23%	3%
Fully retired	13%	92%
Work as a volunteer	8%	13%
Have partner working	30%	1%
Partner retired	9%	22%
Partner works	30%	1%
Partner works as volunteer	3%	4%
Running own business from home	21%	0%
Working from home	16%	0%
Working and want to continue working as long as possible	53%	5%
Working but want to retire in next year or two	16%	1%
Not working but would like to work	4%	1%
Not working and do not want to work again	13%	88%
Have to work to make ends meet	6%	0%
In quite good situation but needing to be a bit careful about money	48%	45%
With a good savings reserve to enable me to treat myself and my family	30%	28%
With a pension large enough to enable me to allow me to really enjoy life	25%	38%
Budgeting carefully to make ends meet and to avoid having to borrow	17%	8%

Source: Authors

Table 19.4 Technology

	A	B
Use the Internet very often or all the time, every day	88%	46%
Use the Internet every day, but every now and then	12%	35%
Use the Internet once or a few times a week	0%	17%
Don't use Internet at all	0%	3%
Don't use Internet regularly	0%	5%
Regular user of Internet for over 10 years	94%	52%
Regular user of Internet for 5–10 years	6%	33%
Regular user of Internet for less than 5 years	0%	8%
Have had smartphone more than 5 years	72%	13%
Have had smartphone for no more than 5 years	25%	29%
Have mobile phone but not smartphone	3%	49%
Have no mobile phone	0%	10%

Source: Authors

Table 19.5 Housing and attitudes to older adult housing descriptions

	A	B
House with 3 or more bedrooms	75%	1%
House with 2 or fewer bedrooms	7%	1%
Flat with 1 bedroom	3%	23%
Flat with 2+ bedrooms	8%	29%
Live in council housing	4%	0%
Live in sheltered housing	0%	2%
Live in retirement housing	0%	65%
Own with mortgage	35%	1%
Own outright	43%	87%
Rent	11%	1%
My property is owned by my partner	2%	1%
Thought "age friendly" an accurate description	45%	54%
"Age-friendly" is a phrase I could use comfortably	26%	29%
"Age-friendly" is patronising/talks down to me	26%	13%
"Age-friendly" is typical management speak	23%	21%
"Age-friendly" is an ugly phrase	11%	6%
"Age-friendly" sounds like a prison to me	11%	1%
I aim to stay in my current home as long as possible	59%	88%
I aim to move to a smaller property in the next 5 years	14%	0%
I aim to move to a smaller property but in 5–10 years	13%	0%
I aim to move to a smaller property but in over 10 years	9%	0%

Source: Authors

Table 19.11 shows relatively little divergence between the segments on general attitudes, other than on financial matters (the younger group unsurprisingly more likely to want to consider equity release, as the older group had already sorted out their final housing) and the older group more concerned to leave an inheritance.

Table 19.6 Housing and attitudes to older adult descriptions

	A	B
I love my home and don't want to move	52%	62%
I want to live in a warmer home	1%	2%
I am worried about the running costs of my home	11%	3%
My home is too big	12%	1%
I want to live in a home better adapted to my needs or those of my partner	13%	5%

Source: Authors

Table 19.7 Social and personal development

% agreeing or agreeing strongly – 5 scale options	A	B
I want my home to be a centre of social activity for my family	66%	20%
I want my home to be a centre of social activity for my friends	52%	21%
I want my home to support me as I continue to develop myself	67%	56%
I want my home to allow me to carry out my hobbies	81%	66%
If move to a housing development for older people, I would like the housing company I buy from to provide educational and social help	46%	35%
My family and friends are quite enough to keep me happy	65%	53%
There must always be a pet (e.g. a dog or a cat) in my home	44%	13%

Source: Authors

Table 19.8 Home smartening

% agreeing or agreeing strongly – 5 scale options	A	B
I would like my home to welcome me as I come through the door	48%	68%
I would like my home to warn me of any problems in the home	66%	80%
I would like my home to update me on particular kinds of news	29%	44%
I would like my home to update me of any things I ought to know about in the neighbourhood	41%	55%
I love the general idea of smart homes	55%	51%
I have already started to make my home smart	30%	29%
I look forward to making my home smarter as costs fall	48%	34%
I would like a virtual companion or avatar to help me manage my home and my life	18%	6%
I like the idea of a robot to help me manage my home and life	22%	8%
I like the idea of service on my mobile phone/computer that helps me manage my home/my life	53%	23%
I would like all round safety and monitoring built in	64%	76%
I would like all my domestic appliances and furniture connected to the Internet so I can see what is happening with them and so they can manage themselves	32%	13%
I would like my home to tell my FAMILY how things are going with me, with my permission	36%	39%

(Continued)

Table 19.8 (Continued)

% agreeing or agreeing strongly – 5 scale options	A	B
I would like my home to tell my FRIENDS how things are going with me, with my permission	17%	13%
I would like easy communication with my friends, family and neighbours without having to log on or use a device	47%	41%
I like to use home delivery services as much as possible and expect to do it more and more as I get older	54%	44%
I would like carers and family to have access to my home using an access code	49%	52%

Source Authors

Table 19.9 Health – current state

% agreeing or agreeing strongly – 5 scale options	A	B
I consider myself healthy	78%	57%
I have at least one serious illness or condition, but it does not affect my mobility or my lifestyle	18%	24%
I have at least one serious or condition and it makes me much less mobile	2%	15%
My health is good but stable	16%	22%
I have serious problems with hearing	4%	11%
I have serious problems with my eyesight	0%	10%
My health is not good but stable	0%	8%
My health is getting worse slowly	6%	11%

Source: Authors

Table 19.10 Health information and contact preferences

% agreeing or agreeing strongly – 5 scale options	A	B
I would like to deal with my doctor as much as possible remotely, ideally by telephone/email	58%	30%
I like to use the web to research medical matters before I talk to my doctor	62%	29%
I don't want doctors to tell me what technology to put in my home – I want to decide myself	56%	60%
I take full responsibility for my own health	86%	77%
I want my home to tell me how healthy I am	18%	15%
I would like my home to keep me healthy	43%	44%
I would like my home to tell me whether I am having/had had a healthy day	22%	13%

Source: Authors

Table 19.11 General attitudes

% agreeing or agreeing strongly − 5 scale options	A	B
I am/will be proud to be old	51%	59%
I don't/didn't feel less important as I grow/grew older	71%	69%
I would like the home I move to be attractive/exciting	79%	69%
I quite like living by myself/with my partner and do not need lots of interaction with other people	41%	48%
I would not like anyone to create my future home for me − I would like to be left to do it myself	65%	52%
I don't care what my future home might be like − it's less important to me than my health, wealth and happiness	35%	27%
I would like to stay in my current home as long as I can live in it comfortably and healthily	80%	87%
I wouldn't ever want to go into a care home − I would like to be cared for at home	56%	68%
As I grow older, I would prefer to adapt my home to my needs (and that of my partner) rather than move home	80%	78%
I would expect to take an active role in how I adapt my home as I grow older	92%	84%
I would like to hold on to my home as long as possible to provide an inheritance	52%	67%
I expect I will want to release equity in my home (Yes/No − % Yes)	34%	10%
I know how to release equity from my home if I need to	68%	63%
If I save social care costs by staying in my home, I expect the state to subsidise changes I need to make to my home	49%	48%

Source: Authors

Further analysis

The purpose of the survey was to show what information could be collected rather than to find valid results, though the stability of the responses indicated the likelihood of validity. It was therefore considered that more sophisticated analysis (e.g. regression analysis, structured equation modelling) would not be appropriate. Rather, simple correlation analysis was used to identify relationships which seemed to exist and therefore might be worthy of further research. The central finding was that the desire for smartness and information exchange tended to be consistent − respondents who liked one dimension of it tended to like other dimensions and to want smart features in their lives and homes.

The correlation analysis showed broadly that those who like the idea of smart homes want their homes to welcome them, warn of problems and update them on key events and have largely started making their homes smart. They like the idea of connected appliances, are generally in favour of giving access codes and like the idea of a service on their phone or computer to help them manage their lives. Other interesting findings include these:

- Those who like the idea of an avatar like the idea of a robot;
- Those who use the Internet frequently also consult it frequently on medical matters;

- Those who want to be cared for at home want to stay in their current home and adapt it to their needs;
- Those who like home delivery services or prefer to deal with their doctor remotely are moderately correlated with home smartness variables, but preference for home delivery doesn't correlate much with any other items.

Conclusions from the survey

The main aim of this study was to show that data about consumers' preferences for smartness could be collected from older adults using web-based technology and that, provided care was taken – using ideas derived from the literature – to orient the questionnaire to the likely understanding and needs of the respondents, useful results could be achieved. If those in the segment with an average age of 60 maintain their perceptions and preferences as they age, it augurs very well for the prospects of smart homes and smart cities. The implications are that further research needs to be carried out at scale to validate these findings and perhaps deepen the research into specific aspects that are researched in this study.

Implications of this chapter

Most of the technology to deliver what older adults want exists in database systems/platforms, publicly available APIs, 5G networks, wearable devices, sensors, artificial intelligence, apps, messaging devices, Internet of Things and so on that we all use partially. Our study concludes that if the responses are representative of the population, most older adults are very open minded to providing information on their attitudes and also very open to the different ways suggested for smartening homes and cities, particularly if it means they receive more proactive assistance. They confirmed that they would also be happy to see technology and their data used to help them cope with problems in the home and to allow society to help them. However, these conclusions would need to be validated by a much larger survey.

The main implication for marketing researchers is that a more human approach to researching smart homes and their potential for older adults can work, not focused on specific technologies (though these can be usefully researched) but with a focus on "their home". After all, it is the older adults' homes and the relationship between the resident and the home that is the central issue of interest, not particular technologies.

The literature reviewed also indicates another requirement – that marketing researchers need to work very closely with designers to ensure that the latter have a broad understanding of the many different requirements and perceptions of older adults, rather than through the lens of a particular product or technology.

Issues

This chapter was finalised before the full long-term effects of the coronavirus epidemic were apparent. However, if anything, we believe that it will have increased the willingness and ability of older adults to use the smart home approach as well as to use the remote-access approach to shopping, so reinforcing the findings of this survey.

References

Abramsson, M. and Andersson, E., 2016. Changing preferences with ageing: Housing choices and housing plans of older people. *Housing, Theory and Society*, 33(2), 217–241. https://doi.org/10.1080/1403 6096.2015.1104385.

Age UK, 2018a. *The Difference Between Loneliness and Isolation – and Why It Matters* [online]. Available from: www.ageuk.org.uk/our-impact/policy-research/lonelinessresearch-and-resources/loneliness-isolation-understanding-the-difference-why-it-matters/ [Accessed 4 May 2020].

Age UK, 2018b. *Digital Inclusion Evidence Review* [online]. Available from: www.ageuk.org.uk/globalassets/age-uk/documents/reports-and-publications/age_uk_digital_inclusion_evidence_review_2018.pdf [Accessed 4 May 2020].

Age UK, 2019. *Later Life in the United Kingdom 2019*. Available from: www.ageuk.org.uk/globalassets/age-uk/documents/reports-and-publications/later_life_uk_factsheet.pdf [Accessed 4 May 2020].

Appleton, N., 2003. *Ready, Steady . . . but Not Quite Go. Older Home Owners and Equity Release: A Review* [online]. Available from: www.jrf.org.uk/report/ready-steady-not-quite-go-older-home-owners-and-equity-release-review [Accessed 4 May 2020].

Arthanat, S., Wilcox, J. and Macuch, M., 2019. Profiles and predictors of smart home technology adoption by older adults. *OTJR: Occupation, Participation and Health*, 39(4), 247–256. https://doi.org/10.1177/1539449218813906.

Carnemolla, P., 2018. Ageing in place and the Internet of Things – how smart home technologies, the built environment and caregiving intersect. *Visualization in Engineering* (1). https://doi.org/10.1186/s40327-018-0066-5.

Chien, S.E., Chu, L., Lee, H.H., Yang, C.C., Lin, F.H., Yang, P.L., Wang, T.M. and Yeh, S.L., 2019. Age difference in perceived ease of use, curiosity, and implicit negative attitude toward robots. *ACM Transactions on Human-Robot Interaction (THRI)*, 8(2), 1–19. https://doi.org/10.1145/3311788.

Choi, Y.K., Lazar, A., Demiris, G. and Thompson, H.J., 2019. Emerging smart home technologies to facilitate engaging with aging. *Journal of Gerontological Nursing*, 45(12), 41–48. DOI: 10.3928/00989134-20191105-06.

Clough, R., Leamy, M., Miller, V. and Bright, L., 2005. Housing decisions in later life. In R. Clough, M. Leamy, V. Miller and L. Bright, eds. *Housing Decisions in Later Life*. London: Palgrave Macmillan 45–67.

Cronin, H., O'Regan, C., Finucane, C., Kearney, P. and Kenny, R.A., 2013. Health and aging: Development of the Irish longitudinal study on ageing health assessment. *Journal of the American Geriatrics Society*, 61(Suppl. 2), 269–278. https://doi.org/10.1111/jgs.12197.

Croucher, K., 2008. *Housing Choices and Aspirations of Older People: Research from the New Horizons Programme* [online]. Available from: www.york.ac.uk/media/chp/documents/2008/newhorizonsolder-people.pdf [Accessed 4 May 2020].

Curumsing, M., Fernando, N., Abdelrazek, M., Vasa, R., Mouzakis, K. and Grundy, J., 2019. Emotion-oriented requirements engineering: A case study in developing a smart home system for the elderly. *Journal of Systems and Software*, 147, 215–229. DOI: 10.1016/j.jss.2018.06.077.

Damodaran, L. and Olphert, W., 2015. *How Are Attitudes and Behaviours to the Ageing Process Changing in Light of New Media and New Technology? How Might These Continue to Evolve by 2025 and 2040? Future of an Ageing Population: Evidence Review* [online]. Available from: https://assets.publishing.service.gov.uk/government/uploads/system/uploads/attachment_data/file/455176/gs-15-17-future-ageing-attitudes-new-technology-er08.pdf [Accessed 4 May 2020].

Dementia UK, 2019. *What Is Dementia? What Are the Symptoms?* Available from: www.dementiauk.org/understanding-dementia/what-is-dementia/ [Accessed 4 May 2020].

Deutsch, I., Erel, H., Paz, M., Hoffman, G. and Zuckerman, O., 2019. Home robotic devices for older adults: Opportunities and concerns. *Computers in Human Behavior*, 98, 122–133. DOI: 10.1016/j.chb.2019.04.002.

Forkan, A., Branch, P., Jayaraman, P. and Ferretto, A., 2019. Halleyassist: A personalised Internet of Things technology to assist the elderly in daily living. *Proceedings of the 52nd Hawaii International Conference on System Sciences*. DOI: 10.24251/hicss.2019.507.

Galambos, C., Rantz, M., Craver, A., Bongiorno, M., Pelts, M., Holik, A. and Jun, J., 2019. Living with intelligent sensors: Older adult and family member perceptions. *CIN: Computers, Informatics, Nursing*, 37(1), 615–627. DOI: 10.1097/cin.0000000000000555.

Hurley, J., 2016. *Silver Pound Should Be No Grey Area* [online]. Available from: www.thetimes.co.uk/article/silver-pound-should-be-no-grey-area-vqr75qqzn [Accessed 4 May 2020].

IDC, 2020. *Winners Named in IDC Smart Cities North America Awards* [online]. Available from: www.idc.com/getdoc.jsp?containerId=prUS46115120 [Accessed 4 May 2020].

Kingston, A., Robinson, L., Booth, H., Knapp, M. and Jagger, C., 2018. Projections of multi-morbidity in the older population in England to 2035: Estimates from the Population Ageing and Care Simulation (PACSim) model. *Age and Ageing*, 47(3), 374–380. DOI: 10.1093/ageing/afx201.

Kowalski, J., Jaskulska, A., Skorupska, K., Abramczuk, K., Biele, C., Kopeć, W. and Marasek, K., 2019. *Older Adults and Voice Interaction: A Pilot Study with Google Home*. CHI EA'19: Extended Abstracts of the 2019 CHI Conference on Human Factors in Computing Systems, May 2019 Paper No: LBW0187, 1–6. https://doi.org/10.1145/3290607.3312973.

Lychgate Projects Ltd, 2016. *Retirement Housing: Residents' Experiences* [online]. Available from: www.housinglin.org.uk/_assets/Resources/Housing/OtherOrganisation/Retirement_Housing_report.pdf [Accessed 15 February 2019].

Mannheim, I., Schwartz, E., Xi, W., Buttigieg, S.C., McDonnell-Naughton, M., Wouters, E.J. and Van Zaalen, Y., 2019. Inclusion of older adults in the research and design of digital technology. *International Journal of Environmental Research and Public Health*, 16, 3718. DOI: 10.3390/ijerph16193718.

Marikyan, D., Papagiannidis, S. and Alamanos, E., 2019. A systematic review of the smart home literature: A user perspective. *Technological Forecasting and Social Change*, 138, 139–154. https://doi.org/10.1016/j.techfore.2018.08.015.

Marston, H. and van Hoof, J., 2019. Who doesn't think about technology when designing urban environments for older people? A case study approach to a proposed extension of the WHO's age-friendly cities model. *International Journal of Environmental Research and Public Health*, 16(19), 3525. DOI: 10.3390/ijerph16193525.

McKinsey, 2016. *Urban World: The Global Consumer to Watch* [online]. Available from: www.mckinsey.com/~/media/McKinsey/Featured%20Insights/Urbanization/Urban%20world%20The%20global%20consumers%20to%20watch/Urban-World-Global-Consumers-Full-Report.ashx [Accessed 4 May 2020].

Miyake, N., Shibukawa, S., Masaki, H. and Otake-Matsuura, M., 2020. User-oriented design of active monitoring bedside agent for older adults to prevent falls. *Journal of Intelligent & Robotic Systems*, 98(1), 71–84. https://doi.org/10.1007/s10846-019-01050-w.

National Health Service, 2017. *Indicator Facts* [online]. Available from: www.nhs.uk/Scorecard/Pages/IndicatorFacts.aspx?MetricId=8135 [Accessed 4 May 2020].

Obayashi, K. and Masuyama, S., 2020. Pilot and feasibility study on elderly support services using communicative robots and monitoring sensors integrated with cloud robotics. *Clinical Therapeutics*, 2(2), 364–371. DOI: 10.1016/j.clinthera.2020.01.001.

Ofcom, 2018. *Adults' Media Use and Attitudes Report* [online]. Available from: www.ofcom.org.uk/__data/assets/pdf_file/0011/113222/Adults-Media-Use-and-Attitudes-Report-2018.pdf [Accessed 4 May 2020].

Office for National Statistics, 2017. *National Population Projections: 2016-Based* [online]. Available from: www.ons.gov.uk/releases/nationalpopulationprojections2016basedstatisticalbulletin [Accessed 4 May 2020].

Office for National Statistics, 2018a. *Estimates of the Population for the UK, England and Wales, Scotland and Northern Ireland* [online]. Available from: www.ons.gov.uk/peoplepopulationandcommunity/populationandmigration/populationestimates/datasets/populationestimatesforukenglandandwalesscotlandandnorthernireland [Accessed 4 May 2020].

Office for National Statistics, 2018b. *Estimates of the Very Old, Including Centenarians*, UK [online]. Available from: www.ons.gov.uk/peoplepopulationandcommunity/birthsdeathsandmarriages/ageing/bulletins/estimatesoftheveryoldincludingcentenarians/2002to2017 [Accessed 4 May 2020].

Office for National Statistics, 2018c. *Living Longer* [online]. Available from: www.ons.gov.uk/peoplepopulationandcommunity/birthsdeathsandmarriages/ageing/articles/livinglongerhowourpopulationischangingandwhyitmatters/2018-08-13 [Accessed 4 May 2020].

Office for National Statistics, 2019. *Living Longer: Is Age 70 the New Age 65?* Available from: www.ons.gov.uk/peoplepopulationandcommunity/birthsdeathsandmarriages/ageing/articles/livinglongerisage70thenewage65/2019-11-19 [Accessed 4 May 2020].

Office for National Statistics, 2020. *Homeworking in the UK Labour Market* [online]. Available from: www.ons.gov.uk/employmentandlabourmarket/peopleinwork/employmentandemployeetypes/datasets/homeworkingintheuklabourmarket [Accessed 4 May 2020].

Oh, Y. and Kim, J., 2019. Investigating the preferences of older adults concerning the design elements of a companion robot: Analysis on type, weight and material of companion robot. *Interaction Studies*, 2(3), 426–454. https://doi.org/10.1075/is.18070.oh.

Pal, D., Papasratorn, B., Chutimaskul, W. and Funilkul, S., 2019. Embracing the smart-home revolution in Asia by the elderly: An end-user negative perception modelling. *IEEE Access*, 7, 38535–38549. DOI: 10.1109/ACCESS.2019.2906346.

Public Health England, 2018. *Falls: Applying All Our Health* [online]. Available from: www.gov.uk/government/publications/falls-applying-all-our-health [Accessed 4 May 2020].

Ravishankar, V.K., Burleson, W. and Mahoney, D., 2015. Smart home strategies for user-centered functional assessment of older adults. *International Journal of Automation and Smart Technology*, 5(4), 233–242. https://doi.org/10.5875/ausmt.v5i4.952.

RNIB, 2018. *Key Information and Statistics on Sight Loss in the UK* [online]. Available from: www.rnib. org.uk/professionals/knowledge-and-research-hub/key-information-and-statistics [Accessed 4 May 2020].

Robinson, E., Park, G., Shalini, S., Levins, T., Lane, K., Skubic, M. and Markway, B., 2019. Harnessing voice-assisted technology and in-home sensors to manage older adult health: A user preference study, *Innovation in Aging*, 3 (Suppl. 1), S926–S927. https://doi.org/10.1093/geroni/igz038.3374.

Royal College of Psychiatrists, 2018. *Suffering in Silence: Age Inequality in Older People's Mental Health Care* [online]. Available from: www.rcpsych.ac.uk/improving-care/campaigning-for-better-mental-health-policy/college-reports/2018-college-reports/cr221 [Accessed 4 May 2020].

Shishehgar, M., Kerr, D. and Blake, J., 2019. The effectiveness of various robotic technologies in assisting older adults. *Health Informatics Journal*, 25(3), 892–918. https://doi.org/10.1177/1460458217729729.

Stigall, B., Waycott, J., Baker, S. and Caine, K., 2019. Older adults' perception and use of voice user interfaces: A preliminary review of the computing literature. *Proceedings of the 31st Australian Conference on Human-Computer-Interaction*, 423–427. https://doi.org/10.1145/3369457.3369506.

Stone, M., Knapper, J., Evans, G. and Aravopoulou, E., 2018. Information management in the smart city. *The Bottom Line*, 31(3/4), 234–249. https://doi.org/10.1108/BL-07-2018-0033.

Tanabe, S., Saitoh, E., Koyama, S., Kiyono, K., Tatemoto, T., Kumazawa, N., Kagaya, H., Otaka, Y., Mukaino, M., Tsuzuki, A. and Ota, H., 2019. Designing a robotic smart home for everyone, especially the elderly and people with disabilities. *Fujita Medical Journal*, 5(2), 31–35. https://doi.org/10.20407/fmj.2018-009.

Thakur, N. and Han, C., 2019. Framework for an intelligent affect aware smart home environment for elderly people. *International Journal of Recent Trends in Human Computer Interaction (IJHCI)*, 9(1), 23–43.

Thomas, D., 2014. *The Silver Economy: Tech Sector Taps Surge of Connected Boomers* [online]. Available from: www.ft.com/content/a376c950-26c4-11e4-8df5-00144feabdc0 [Accessed 4 May 2020].

Tinker, A., Askham, J., Hancock, R., Mueller, G. and Stuchbury, R., 2001. *85 Not Out: A Study of People Aged 85 and Over at Home* [online]. Available from: https://kclpure.kcl.ac.uk/portal/en/publications/eightyfive-not-out-a-study-of-people-aged-85-and-over-at-home(b2e4ab1f-ad5b-4df0-b33d-97bc29230994)/export.html [Accessed 4 May 2020].

Torrington, J., 2014. *What Developments in the Built Environment Will Support the Adaptation and 'Future Proofing' of Homes and Local Neighbourhoods So That People Can Age Well in Place over the Life Course, Stay Safe and Maintain Independent Lives?* Available from: https://assets.publishing.service.gov.uk/government/uploads/system/uploads/attachment_data/file/445583/gs-15-11-future-ageing-homes-neighbourhoods-er21.pdf [Accessed 4 May 2020].

Tun, S., Madanian, S. and Mirza, F., 2020. Internet of Things (IoT) applications for elderly care: A reflective review. *Aging Clinical and Experimental Research*. https://doi.org/10.1007/s40520-020-01545-9.

Turjamaa, R., Pehkonen, A. and Kangasniemi, M., 2019. How smart homes are used to support older people: An integrative review. *International Journal of Older People Nursing*, 14(4). https://doi.org/10.1111/opn.12260.

Wang, J., Du, Y., Coleman, D., Peck, M., Myneni, S., Kang, H. and Gong, Y., 2019. Mobile and connected health technology needs for older adults aging in place: Cross-sectional survey study. *JMIR Ageing*, 2(1). DOI: 10.2196/13864.

Ward, L., Barnes, M. and Beatrice Gahagan, B., 2013. *Well-Being in Old Age: Findings from Participatory Research: Research on the Future Housing Aspirations of Older People* [online]. Available from: www.nihe. gov.uk/getmedia/c343c58c-f0af-4762-bd25-b6777e547ea9/research_on_the_future_housing_aspirations_of_older_people.pdf.aspx?ext=.pdf [Accessed 4 May 2020].

Wilson, G., Pereyda, C., Raghunath, N., de la Cruz, G., Goel, S., Nesaei, S., Minor, B., Schmitter-Edge-combe, M., Taylor, M. and Cook, D.J., 2019. Robot-enabled support of daily activities in smart home environments. *Cognitive Systems Research*, 54, 258–272. https://doi.org/10.1016/j.cogsys.2018.10.032.

Woodcock, A., Osmond, J. and Holliday, N., 2020. The development of a feature matrix for the design of assistive technology products for young older people. In A. Woodcock, L. Moody, D. McDonagh, A. Jain and L. Jain, eds. *Design of Assistive Technology for Ageing Populations*. New York: Springer, 81–103. DOI: 10.1007/978-3-030-26292-1.

Yu, J., An, N., Hassan, T. and Kong, Q., 2019. A pilot study on a smart home for elders based on continuous in-home unobtrusive monitoring technology. *HERD: Health Environments Research & Design Journal*, 12(3), 206–219. DOI: 10.1177/1937586719826059.

20

MARKETING RESEARCH AND CUSTOMER LOYALTY IN AN ISLAMIC BANKING CULTURE IN THE MIDDLE EAST

A case study of Jordan

Ala' Omar Dandis and Len Tiu Wright

Summary

This chapter focuses on how service quality and customer satisfaction affect customers' behavioural loyalty in Islamic banks and the service quality policies required for banks to succeed in managing their customers well. The results show that compliance, tangibility, responsiveness, assurance and empathy significantly and positively impact behavioural loyalty, with compliance and assurance appearing the most influential factors leading to customer behavioural loyalty. The study's recommendations to Islamic banks include a focus on continuous improvement of service quality due to the direct effect on customer behavioural loyalty. It is essential for Islamic banks to review and endorse all policies and procedures to ensure that their documents and investments are undertaken in line with Islamic law requirements.

Introduction

Customers can choose more freely between suppliers due to the proliferation of information via the Internet. In more politically stable Islamic countries, they are increasingly exposed to information and, along with rising standards of living, this increases consumer power. Due to better education and easy access to financial services offered by international banking channels, customers can be more demanding of products and services. For example, in their study of customer attitudes towards banks, Baron *et al.* (2009) found that 13% of customers closed their accounts because of an encounter with a rude or unhelpful employee, and 11% closed their accounts because they felt that their bank was emotionless and impersonal, while 16% closed their accounts because of a general perception of poor service. Achieving exclusive customer loyalty is a challenging prospect. A more attainable objective is to strive towards customer loyalty as efficiently as possible, to maximise market share and acceptable overall profitability (Keiningham *et al.* 2005). Casaló *et al.* (2008) found that customer loyalty was a main factor in banks' success over time. Banks offer relatively similar products and services, so the best way for a bank to create competitive advantage is by quality of service (Royne Stafford 1996).

Every financial service business, large or small, is looking today for innovative marketing ways to achieve a competitive advantage, to increase customer satisfaction and enhance loyalty (Astuti and Nagase 2014; Buracom 2002). Marketing research has a role to play in providing collection and analyses of data from samples of individuals and organisations and in making recommendations to suppliers about the significance of their relationships with customers in their markets. Establishing, building and maintaining such relationships has become the basis for profitable growth (Astuti and Nagase 2014; Angelova and Zekiri 2011). The different dimensions of service quality, customer satisfaction and customer loyalty are concerns for service businesses since increased emphasis on these issues will improve a business's performance and profits (Angelova and Zekiri 2011; Shaon and Rahman 2015).

Customer loyalty is an under-investigated subject in Jordanian industries (Dandis and Wright 2020). Very few empirical studies (e.g. Dandis and Wright 2020; Jamal and Anastasiadou 2009) focus on service quality, customer satisfaction and customer loyalty in the Islamic context of banking institutions in Jordan. This chapter examines how service quality and customer satisfaction affects Islamic banks. The case study addresses the following questions:

1 What are the service quality dimensions that can be used to measure Islamic banks' performance and influence on behavioural loyalty?
2 What is the nature of the relationship between service quality and behavioural loyalty taking into consideration the mediating role of customer satisfaction?
3 What recommendations can be implemented on the executive level to increase customer loyalty towards Islamic banks?

Literature review

Islamic banking background

The Institute of Islamic Banking defines Islamic banking as "A system of banking or banking activity that is consistent with the principles of the *Shari'ah* (Islamic rulings) and its practical application through the development of Islamic economics" (Belwal and Al Maqbali 2019). A unique feature of Islamic financial institutions is their profit-and-loss sharing (PLS) paradigm (Chong and Liu 2009; Lewis and Algaoud 2001). It means both the clients (debtors) and the Islamic bank (provider of the funds) share the risks, and both prosper when earnings are positive and suffer together when earnings are negative (Masood and Bellalah 2013; Lewis and Algaoud 2001; Al-Sultan 1999).

The Islamic banking industry has experienced steady and continued growth since the 1980s. Islamic banking in the 21st century is practised in over 75 Muslim and non-Muslim countries (Souiden and Rani 2015). Mostly concentrated in the Middle East and Southeast Asia, Islamic banks are gaining popularity in the United States and Europe. According to the International Monetary Fund (IMF), Islamic banking is one of the fastest-growing sectors in the financial industry, with 10–15% annual growth over the past decade. Islamic banking annual asset growth is about 15%. Islamic banks in Pakistan are capturing a large market share compared with traditional banks, with an annual growth rate of 114%. Altwijry and Abduh (2013) show that one reason for the growing popularity of Islamic banks is their flexibility during the financial crisis of 2008–2009, which led to the bankruptcy and financial suffering of several traditional banks. So, the growing support for Islamic banking in both Muslim-majority and western states is not a coincidence. The growth of Islamic banks is evidence of their success.

Objectives of Islamic banks

To understand Islamic banking requires comprehension of its objectives and philosophy. As a *Shari'ah*-oriented business entity, an Islamic bank is expected to be guided by the philosophy of Islamic business. According to Dusuki (2008), there are two reasons for establishing the right philosophies for any Islamic bank. First, the philosophies will be used by the management or policy makers of the banks in formulating corporate objectives and policies. Second, these philosophies indicate whether a given Islamic bank is upholding true Islamic principles. In general, the key objects of any Islamic bank are the following:

1   The Muslim socioeconomic system implements the value system of the *Holy Qur'an* and the *Sunnah* (tradition or practice of Prophet Muhammad). For instance, Islam forbids financing in items which the *Shari'a* deems *haram* (unlawful), such as alcohol, assassination, pork, prostitution, liquor and gambling, as well as forbidding dealing in interest (Masood and Bellalah 2013);
2   Promotion and acceleration of the economic development of the society are fostered through restructuring the financial system to accord with Islamic principles such as in Iran, Pakistan and Sudan (Lewis and Algaoud 2001; Al-Sultan 1999). Hence, business is undertaken and trade activities complement gaining fair and legitimate profits and cooperating with other Islamic banks to foster the economic development and social progress of the Muslim community through Islamic banks (Lewis and Algaoud 2001; Al-Sultan 1999). Al-Omar and Abdel-Haq (1996, p. 27) indicate the duty of Islamic banks towards the society in which they operate by providing a clear expression outlined in the public statement of the International Association of Islamic Banks.

Profitability – despite its importance and priority – is therefore not the sole criterion or the prime element in evaluating the performance of Islamic banks, as they have to balance material and social objectives that serve the interests of the community as a whole and help achieve their role in the sphere of social mutual guarantee. Social goals are understood to form an inseparable element of the Islamic banking system that cannot be dispensed with or neglected.

Strategic performance: Islamic banks versus conventional banks

One of the main features of the Islamic financial system is prohibition of the payment and receipt of *Riba* (interest), which refers to any conditional increase in the principal of a loan or a debt in return for a deferred payment (Masood and Bellalah 2013). The rationale behind the ban of the interest is mentioned in the Holy Quran and the traditions of Prophet Muhammad (sunnah). Interest is similarly forbidden in Christianity and Judaism, which request their followers to avoid interest transactions to protect themselves from burning in hell fire (Lewis and Algaoud 2001; Zaman and Movassaghi 2002).

The Islamic financial system is built on the principle of cooperation and brotherhood between the provider of funds (investor) and the user of funds (entrepreneur), based on fairness sharing, risk sharing and stake taking (Dusuki and Abdullah 2007). The ban on *Riba* (interest), the obligation to pay *Zakah* and the provision of *Quard Hassan* (interest-free loans) are clear illustrations of the Islamic stress on community fairness. Most importantly, all Muslims must pay 2.5 % of total income annually to the poor. They are also encouraged in the *Holy Qur'an* and the traditions of Prophet Muhammad *(sunnah)* to make voluntary contributions called *Sadaqah* (charity) to help the needy and poor and for other social welfare purposes.

God does not deny human beings something without reason. For example, interest means the creditor is guaranteed money without making any effort (Dar and Presley 1999). It violates the value of community justice, in that it remunerates creditors who neither try nor contribute to the risks or losses associated with the projects financed (Amin and Isa 2008; Maali *et al.* 2006). Gambling and Karim (1991, p. 34) refer to this as "unfair trading". As a result, it is also considered exploitative and unproductive. These reasons are thought to lead to unemployment and inflation and to a decline in the social and infrastructural improvement of a country (Shanmugam and Zahari 2009). Hence, the ban on interest protects people from getting excessively indebted and overwhelmed by interest instalments or paying for receipt or extension of credit (Masood and Bellalah 2013).

Fairness requires that the supplier of cash capital ought to share the risk with the entrepreneur (Maali *et al.* 2006). So, it is just for both lender and borrower that they share profits or losses (Dar and Presley 1999). Islam also stresses that persons ought to be dealt with fairly: "God commands justice, the doing of good" *(Qur'an 16:90)*. Table 20.1 summarises the difference between Islamic banks and conventional banks, the latter being non-Islamic and based on Western notions of profit.

Table 20.1 Strategic performance: Islamic banks versus conventional banks

Islamic banking	Conventional banking
"An advance step toward achievement of Islamic economics".	Part of the capitalistic interest-based financial system.
"Try to ensure social justice/welfare or the objectives of Shari'a".	Not concerned.
"Flow of financial resources is in favour of the poor and disadvantaged sections of society".	Not concerned.
"Prepare and implement investment plans to reduce the income inequality and wealth disparity between the rich and poor".	Increase the gap.
"Observe the legitimate and illegitimate criteria fixed by the Shari'a in the case of production and investment".	No such rules and regulations.
"Implement investment plans on Mudaraba and Musharaka to stimulate the income of the people below the poverty line".	No such programme.

(Continued)

Islamic banking	Conventional banking
"Interest and usury is avoided at all levels of financial transactions".	"The basis of all financial transactions is interest and high-level usury".
"Depositors bear the risk, no need for deposit insurance".	"Depositors do not bear any risk; moreover the bank is inclined to pay back principal with a guaranteed interest amount".
"The relationship between depositors and entrepreneurs is friendly and cooperative".	"Creditor–debtor relationship".
"Socially needed investment projects are considered".	"Projects below the fixed interest level are not considered".
"Elimination of the exploitation of interest and its hegemony".	"Helps to increase capital of the capitalists".
"Islamic banks become partner in the business of the client after sanctioning the credit and bear loss".	"Do not bear any loss of client".
"Islamic banking is committed to implementing welfare-oriented principles of financing".	"No such commitment; extend oppression and exploitation".
"Inter-bank transactions are on a profit and loss sharing basis".	"On interest basis and create unusual bubble in the market, i.e. exorbitant increase in the call money rate".
"Islamic banks work under the surveillance of the Shari'a Supervisory Boards".	"No such surveillance"
"Lower rate of moral hazard problem because of the brotherhood relationship between the bank and customers".	"High moral hazard problem because relation is based only on monetary transactions".
"Avoids speculation-related financial activities"	Main functions are speculation-related.
"Bank pays zakat on income and inspires clients to pay zakat, which ensures redistribution of income in favour of the poor".	"No zakat system for the benefit of the poor".
"The basis of business policy is socioeconomic uplifting of the disadvantaged groups of the society".	"Profit is the main target of business, or the prime duty is to maximize the shareholders' value".
"Dual target: implementation of the objectives of *Shari'a* and profit".	"Profit making is the sole objective".

Source: Adapted from Hassan and Lewis (2009, p. 98)

The Islamic alternative to Riba (interest)

The forbidding of interest in an Islamic economy does not mean that capital has no value. Islam is aware of the capital role in the production and consequently its right to a reward. Islamic banks are forbidden from charging pure interest, a key driver of commercial finance systems, and they need to utilise an alternative functioning system more in line with Islamic principles to make profits. This alternative system uses the principles of *Mudharabah, Musharaka, Murabahah* and *Qard Hasan*.

Mudarabah (investment with no participation in administration). Contracts are profit-sharing agreements in which a bank (beneficial owner) provides the full capital needed to fund a business or project and the entrepreneur or customer (*mudarib*) provides the knowledge, administration and labour (Ariff 2014; Nihar and Subramanyam 2011). Business profits are shared by both parties on a pre-agreed (prefixed proportion) basis, but in the event of negative return, financial loss is borne totally by the bank, and the customer loses only his effort and time unless negligence or mismanagement can be proven (Ariff 2014; Al-Ajmi *et al.* 2009; Rashid *et al.* 2009).

Musharaka (partnership) is like a joint venture, involving two or more parties (e.g. Islamic banks and an entrepreneur), where all partners contribute capital and participate in the costs of administration and other necessary services at agreed-upon percentages (Ariff 2014; Metwally 1997; Nihar and Subramanyam 2011; Zaher and Kabir Hassan 2001; Rashid *et al.* 2009). In this respect, profits are shared in proportion to their capital or as pre-agreed ratios, but financial losses are afforded in percentage to equity contribution (Al-Ajmi *et al.* 2009).

Murabaha (cost-plus profit/mark-up). The transaction is principally a cost-plus profit financing transaction in which a good or physical asset is purchased by an Islamic bank per order or specification of a customer from a supplier. The Islamic bank resells the good to its customer in cash or on a deferred payment basis, adding an agreed-upon mark-up that reflects the bank's profit. The mark-up, once fixed, cannot be changed during the life of the contract (Ariff 2014; Nihar and Subramanyam 2011; Zaher and Kabir Hassan 2001; Rashid *et al.* 2009). With *murabaha*, Islamic banks do not share in profits and losses but instead assume the role of a classic financial intermediary (Lewis and Algaoud 2001).

Qard al-Hasanah (benevolent loans). This refers to an interest-free loan provided by the creditor to the debtor. The debtor (customer) is obliged to repay only the principal (Ariff 2014; Metwally 1997; Nihar and Subramanyam 2011; Zaher and Kabir Hassan 2001; Rashid *et al.* 2009; Al-Ajmi *et al.* 2009). The main goal of this loan is to help charity institutions finance their activities or to aid needy persons, make them self-sufficient and increase their income and standard of living (Al-Ajmi *et al.* 2009).

Islamic banking in Jordan: brief background

The number of licensed banks operating in Jordan rose from 21 banks in 2003 to 26 banks at the end of 2018. Of the total, 16 banks are Jordanian (3 of them are Islamic banks), and 10 banks are foreign. The population of Jordan is estimated at 6.5 million. Muslims constitute 92% of the total population in Jordan. The opportunity to benefit from an Islamic bank system is seen as alluring (Mahadin and Akroush 2019). Banks in Jordan are listed on Google websites.

The total assets of banks operating in Jordan increased by 5.18% at the end of 2019 compared with 2018, reaching to JD 51.09 billion, distributed as follows: JD 39.16 billion for Jordanian commercial banks (76.7% of the total assets of banks operating in Jordan), JD 8.86 billion for the Islamic banks (17.3% of total assets) and JD 3.07 billion for foreign banks (6% of total assets) (Association of Banks in Jordan 2020). This indicates that Islamic banks are able to compete against commercial banks. In other words, Islamic banks in Jordan should develop service quality, banking operations, efficiency and experience by the banks' employees to enhance customer loyalty (Mahadin and Akroush 2019).

Service quality, satisfaction and behavioural loyalty in Islamic banking sector

Service quality, customer satisfaction and behavioural loyalty are necessary for the survival of bankers (Amirzadeh and Shoorvarzy 2013). The need for service quality for Islamic banks is not very different from that in conventional banks. Several researchers argue that the concept of quality has its roots in Islamic sources, which defines quality as *Itqan*, meaning to arrange and dispose of things in an artistic manner to obtain the perfect result or higher quality

(Mohd-Shariff and Aniza 2013). Adapting service quality in Islamic banks has become imperative because of its apparent relationship with costs (Yavas *et al.* 2004; Cui *et al.* 2003), profitability (Zeithaml 2000), customer satisfaction (Caruana 2002; Naeem *et al.* 2011), customer loyalty (Maritz 2008), positive word of mouth (Maxham 2001; File and Prince 1992; Caruana 2002) and gaining competitive advantage (Parasuraman *et al.* 1985; Bolton and Drew 1994; Cronin and Taylor 1992; Gounaris *et al.* 2003). Islamic banks must therefore be aware of what and how they will offer the products and services and how their customers perceive them.

Operationally, quality of service is represented by answers to the following question: Is the service received or delivered to clients approximately what they expected, or better or worse than they expected? Islamic banks recognise the importance of service quality in keeping existing clients and attracting new ones (Abdul Rehman 2012). An increase in service quality and professional behaviour increases customer satisfaction and reduces client attrition (Ahmad and Saif 2010). Service quality is an essential determinant of customer satisfaction, relating to complaint behaviour and commitment in the banking industry (Yavas *et al.* 1997 cited Ahmad and Safwan 2011). Haron *et al.* (1994) found that provision of fast and efficient service, speed of transaction and friendliness of bank personnel were the most significant factors in bank patronage by Muslims. Erol and El-Bdour (1989) observed criteria used by Jordanian clients to determine whether to use an Islamic bank or a conventional bank. They found that clients who only banked with the Islamic banks did so due to provision of fast and efficient service, the bank's reputation and image and confidentiality of the bank. Ashraf *et al.* (2015) mentioned that prior studies of Islamic banking suggest that it is not only confidence in the provider as a bank that is relevant but also confidence in terms of compliance and that the bank adheres to Islamic law principles. Haron *et al.* (1994) found that the Islamic bank ought to not focus on the religion element as a strategy in its effort to attract more clients. The Islamic bank ought to also be aware that only 40% of Muslims believe that religion is the key influence in why clients maintain an account with an Islamic bank.

Customer satisfaction in Islamic banking is related to an individual's experience of banking transactions (Hassan *et al.* 2012). Oliver (1997, p. 13) defined satisfaction as "the customer's fulfilment response". It is a judgement that a product or service feature, or the product or service itself, provides (or is providing) a pleasurable level of consumption-related fulfilment, including levels of under- or overfulfilment. The environment of the bank plays a role in building customer satisfaction in Islamic banking (Hassan *et al.* 2012). Masood *et al.* (2009) examined customer satisfaction and Islamic banking preferences in Jordan. They found that most participants showed a high level of satisfaction towards different factors and features of Islamic banking, for instance, an Islamic bank's name and image; client interaction; customer confidentiality; and physical features such as internal layout, suitability of furniture and architectural design of the bank (cited Abdul Rehman 2012). Erol and El-Bdour (1989) and Naser *et al.* (1999) found that customers of Islamic banks were satisfied with the Islamic bank's name and image, customer confidentiality, the wide range of facilities offered and the proficiency of bank personnel.

Hassan *et al.* (2012) reported that a shorter time taken in performing any transaction or function in the bank also enhances the customer's satisfaction. The excellence of communication between the clients and the bank personnel is also significant. If communication is easy and a friendly environment is provided to the client, it supports customer satisfaction. Customer satisfaction plays a great role in the long-term commitment and loyalty of clients to Islamic banks (Hassan *et al.* 2012).

A loyal customer to a bank can be described as the one that will stay with the same bank, probably buy new services and recommend the bank to other people (Ehigie 2006). From a behavioural viewpoint, loyalty is defined as repeated transactions over a defined period of time and is sometimes measured by repeat buying of product and services, buying more or another product from the same company (cross-buying) and recommending the brand/company to other consumers (Day 1969; Gronholdt *et al.* 2000; Ball *et al.* 2004). A loyal client is a satisfied client who cares about the services provided by banks (Ambarwati *et al.* 2015). However, one of the main benefits of having loyal customers is that it helps a business save numerous costs, as acquiring new customers is more expensive than nurturing existing customers (Dick and Basu 1994). Loyalty makes customers less sensitive to price (Rundle-Thiele and Mackay 2001; Mao 2010), less likely to complain (Taap *et al.* 2011) and less inclined to switch to competitors (Buchanan and Gillies 1990). Estiri *et al.* (2011) reported that the two dimensions, customer satisfaction and service quality, have become significant for marketing theory and practice. So, through better service quality, Islamic banks in Jordan will be able to attract new clients while maintaining the loyalty of existing clients. All these lead to more profit, and more profit leads to maintainable growth.

Service quality dimensions

Parasuraman *et al.* (1988) developed the SERVQUAL model to evaluate service quality. It comprises five elements: responsiveness, reliability, tangibility, empathy and assurance. The SERVQUAL model is based on 22 items focusing on variation between the customer's expectations and perceptions. Pakurár *et al.* (2019) reported that the modified SERVQUAL model is useful for addressing customer satisfaction in the Jordanian banking sector. Buttle (1996) claimed that SERVQUAL's five service quality elements have not been fully endorsed. Investigators included further elements in the original model, as the five elements of the model do not fully measure service quality. Othman and Owen (2001) developed a tool to evaluate service quality in Islamic banking with six elements, the CARTER model. CARTER uses the five SERVQUAL elements as well as a new element, "compliance with Islamic law", which is appropriate for Islamic banks.

Distinction between service quality and customer satisfaction

Despite the debates regarding the similarities and differences between service quality and satisfaction, marketing researchers have agreed that both constructs are separate and unique but have a close relationship (e.g. Bloemer *et al.* 1998; Boulding *et al.* 1993; Taylor and Baker 1994; Cronin and Taylor 1992). In the case of the difference between service quality and satisfaction, expectations were originally based on an ideal standard, whereas the disconfirmation paradigm uses predictive (would be) expectations as the norm (Rust and Oliver 1994; Oliver 1993). Cronin and Taylor (1992) and Reeves and Bednar (1994) explain that expectancy in the case of service quality reflects what customers feel a service "should" offer or "something that should be offered by the company", and in the case of satisfaction, expectation reflects predictions of what "would" happen during future transactions or "something that will happen". Boulding *et al.* (1993) remind researchers that the term "expectations" should be treated differently in satisfaction and service quality studies, as the term "expectations" can be a source of confusion.

Another dominant view in distinguishing between satisfaction and service quality issues is that service quality is considered mostly a cognitive judgement, whereas satisfaction includes a number of cognitive and affective judgements such as equity, attributions and cost/benefit analyses that influence satisfaction (Rust and Oliver 1994; Oliver 1993). The cognitive status of service quality is strongly implied in the SERVQUAL scale, which assumes that consumers apply a mental calculus to reach an evaluation (Choi *et al.* 2004). Although early service quality researchers (e.g. Parasuraman *et al.* 1985, 1988; Carman 1990) defined satisfaction as an antecedent of service quality, it has now generally been accepted that satisfaction is a consequence of service quality (e.g. Han *et al.* 2008; McDougall and Levesque 2000; Spreng and Mackoy 1996; Rust and Oliver 1994; Oliver 1993; Cronin and Taylor 1992). Oliver (1993) claims that quality exists ahead of satisfaction. Cronin and Taylor (1992) found that service quality is an antecedent of consumer satisfaction, which in turn influences purchase intentions, and service quality had less impact on purchase intentions than customer satisfaction. The conclusion that satisfaction and service quality are unique concepts obviously poses the question: "What then is specifically the nature of the relationship between these concepts?" Bitner and Hubbert (1994) recommend that these two concepts depend on each other. For example, Iacobucci *et al.* (1995) found that satisfaction will not be developed unless service quality is based on customers desires.

The case study

Research model

This research study adopted the CARTER model to measure service quality in Islamic banks. The research model and hypotheses are shown in Figure 20.1.

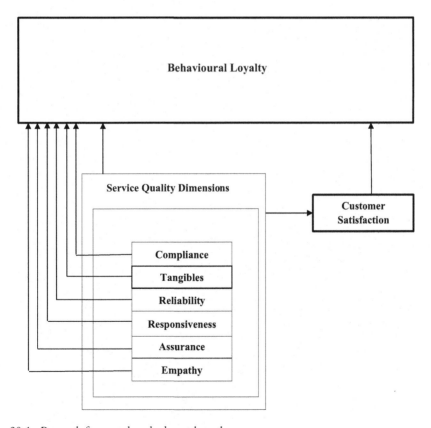

Figure 20.1 Research framework and relevant hypotheses
Source: The authors

Hypothesis development

The relationship between compliance and behavioural loyalty

Compliance describes the ability of the bank to consistently adhere to principles of Islam in any exchange or transaction; that is, the bank operates in accordance with the principles of Islamic law (Misbach and Hadiwidjojo 2013; Othman and Owen 2001). In one of the earliest patronage studies on Islamic banking, Erol and El-Bdour (1989) reported that religious motivation is not a primary criterion or plays little role in the selection of interest-free bank services in Jordan. Haron *et al.* (1994) reported similar results concerning attitudes of Malaysian customers towards interest-free banks. Their findings are disputed by later researchers (e.g. Othman and Owen 2001; Naser *et al.* 1999), who confirm that compliance to Islamic principles is the most significant contributing dimension for the customer satisfaction for Islamic banks in Kuwait, Jordan and Bahrain. Dandis and Wright (2020) confirmed that compliance is one of the main dimensions of service quality leading to attitudinal loyalty in Islamic banks in Jordan. Asnawi *et al.* (2018) found that perceived behavioural control and religiosity are significant predictors of the intention to consume Halal products in international chain restaurants. So, the following hypothesis is offered:

H1: Compliance has a positive effect on behavioural loyalty.

The relationship between tangibles and behavioural loyalty

Tangible qualities of service refer to the appearance of the physical surroundings of the service, consisting of physical facilities, building designs, personnel, tools or equipment, way of communication of the service and other customers in the service facility (Parasuraman *et al.* 1994). In this context, physical clues can play an important role in helping customers form an impression of the service they are getting (Zeithaml *et al.* 2018). Cui *et al.* (2003) recommended that the tangible features of services be viewed as a distinct element of service quality by customers. Similarly, Chang (2000) found that physical environments have a strong effect on customer satisfaction and customer satisfaction has a strong effect on their return intention. So, the following hypothesis is offered:

H2: Tangibles have a positive effect on behavioural loyalty.

The relationship between reliability and behavioural loyalty

Reliability refers to the ability to perform the promised service dependably and accurately (Parasuraman *et al.* 1994). Kandampully (1998) emphasises that fulfilment of the service promise may inspire a long-term relationship, positively affecting long-term customer retention and sustainment and subsequently reduce the likelihood of customer defection. McDougall and Levesqu (1994) claimed that the major strategic focus should be "getting it right the first time". Although some studies found that reliability had an insignificant influence on customer satisfaction and customer loyalty (e.g. Kashif *et al.* 2015; Rehman 2012), other empirical research (e.g. Shaikh and Siddiqui 2018; Kheng *et al.* 2010) has reported a positive relationship between reliability and customer loyalty. So, the following hypothesis is offered:

H3: Reliability has a positive effect on behavioural loyalty.

The relationship between responsiveness and behavioural loyalty

Responsiveness service refers to the willingness of the banks to provide fast service to their customers (Parasuraman *et al.* 1988). Shao Yeh and Li (2009) found that responsiveness is essential as a measure of quality, as well as a diagnostic tool to reveal service quality. Oly Ndubisi and Wah (2005) recommend that personnel commitment to provide quality services, skilful handling of complaints and efficient delivery of services result in satisfied customers for long-term benefits, although Rehman (2012) found an insignificant relationship between the responsiveness dimension and customer satisfaction in Islamic banks in UAE. Other empirical research (e.g. Shaikh and Siddiqui 2018; Badara *et al.* 2013) reports a positive relationship between responsiveness and customer loyalty. So, the following hypothesis is offered:

H4: Responsiveness has a positive effect on behavioural loyalty.

The relationship between assurance and behavioural loyalty

Assurance refers to the knowledge and courtesy of employees and their ability to convey trust and confidence (Parasuraman *et al.* 1988, 1994). According to Abbas *et al.* (2003), sufficient knowledge in various Islamic banking instruments, compounded with other relevant aspects such as ethics, professionalism, duties and responsibilities towards customers and organisations, will enhance efficiency and smooth running of Islamic banking. Arasli *et al.* (2005) report that if the bank can instil feelings of confidence in its customers regarding how they handle customers' affairs and the safety of bank transactions and if it deals with customers in a professional and competent way, then customers will be satisfied with their bank and recommend the bank to others. Pakurár *et al.* (2019) found a significant relationship between empathy and customer satisfaction in Islamic banks in the United Kingdom and Pakistan and a positive relationship between assurance and customer satisfaction, and customer satisfaction has a strong effect on their intention to return (Chang 2000). So, the following hypothesis is offered:

H5: Assurance has a positive effect on behavioural loyalty.

The relationship between empathy and behavioural loyalty

Empathy refers to the level of caring and personalised attention the bank provides for its customers to make them feel valued and special (Parasuraman *et al.* 1988, 1994). Sin *et al.* (2002) described empathy as dealing with a business relationship in a way that enables two parties to see the situation from each other's perspective, that is, seeking to understand somebody else's desires and goals. For example, if customers feel they get individualised and quality attention, there is a big chance that they will return to the company and do business there again (Parasuraman *et al.* 1994). Dandis and Wright (2020) found that empathy is the most influential factor leading to attitudinal loyalty. Similarly, Shaikh and Siddiqui (2018), Taleghani *et al.* (2011) and Butcher *et al.* (2001) have reported a positive relationship between empathy and customer loyalty. So, the following hypothesis is offered:

H6: Empathy has a positive effect on behavioural loyalty.

The relationship between overall service quality, satisfaction and behavioural loyalty

Overall quality of service dimensions is the most important aspect for generating customer satisfaction and loyalty in the banking sector (Eskildsen *et al.* 2004). Jones *et al.* (2002) indicated that there is a positive relationship between service quality and resistance to better alternatives, recommendation and repurchase intention. Deng *et al.* (2010) found that perceived service quality has the strongest effect on customer satisfaction, and customer satisfaction has the greatest effect on customer loyalty. Zafar *et al.* (2012) concluded that customer satisfaction and customer loyalty have a strong positive relationship with each other, and a change in one point of customer satisfaction contributes almost 87% to customer loyalty. Therefore, satisfaction is a necessary precondition for building long-term customer relationships and is likely to increase loyalty (Boonlertvanich 2019; Bloemer and Ruyter 1998). Customer satisfaction is also considered a mediating variable between service quality and customer loyalty (Boonlertvanich 2019; Iqbal *et al.* 2018; Makanyeza and Chikazhe 2017; Kaura *et al.* 2015; Caruana 2002; Cronin *et al.* 2000; Cronin and Taylor 1992). So, the following hypothesis is offered:

H7: Satisfaction mediates the relationship between service quality and attitudinal loyalty.

Methodology

Sampling and data collection

A self-administered survey has been found to be the best method to obtain data, for the following reasons: First, it is designed to deal specifically and directly with the respondents' opinions, beliefs, attitudes and motives (Wright and Crimp 2000). Second, it proves an effective tool, especially when a researcher has little or no control over behavioural activities (Yin 2014). The target population of the current study comprises all customers with an account in Islamic banks operating in the Jordanian market, (Jordan Islamic Bank [JIB], Islamic International Arab Bank PLC [IIAB] and Safwa Bank [formerly known as Jordan Dubai Islamic Bank]). Non-probability convenience sampling was employed in this study, as the population size is unknown and it was deemed impossible to make a randomisation. In fact, there may be no other way to gather data in some cases than to sample a group of individuals who are available as well as providing a captive audience for achieving a response. The final version of the questionnaire was sent to the headquarters of the Islamic banks. From there, it was sent to individual branches and employees of those branches, where the questionnaire was distributed to the customers. A total of 900 questionnaires were distributed to customers who visited the banks, of which 655 were usable and provide sufficient power for the statistical analyses.

Questionnaire and measurements

The scales used to measure tangibles, reliability, responsiveness, assurance and empathy were operationalised with 22 items adopted from Parasuraman *et al.* (1988, 1994). The scale used to measure compliance was adapted from Othman and Owen (2001). The customer satisfaction scale was operationalised with six items. One item expressing interaction satisfaction of bank customers was taken from the study by Leverin and Liljander (2006). Items representing pleasure and reselecting the bank were adapted from the work of Ndubisi and Wah (2005) and Rust and Oliver (1994). The remaining items seeking responses to the customers' satisfaction with their experience and their perception of the selected bank as the right choice were taken from Gremler and Gwinner (2000) and Rust and Oliver (1994). Finally, seven items expressing the behavioural response of bank customers were taken from the study by Zeithaml *et al.* (1996). A total of 40 items were adjusted to the Islamic bank's context.

Results

Descriptive statistics

Table 20.2 shows the research sample characteristics. As shown, 78.6% of the sample populations were males and 21.4% were females. The disparity between males and females can be attributed to the smaller percentage of females in the workforce and the conservative approach in Jordan, where males are more responsible for family finances. The sampling method is a convenience sample and not a random sample for the reasons mentioned previously. Table 2 shows that 63.5% of the sample were young customers aged 26–45 years. This is consistent with Jordanian demographics. As shown in Table 20.1, the highest percentage of the sample customers' monthly income was between 500 and 1000 (40.5%) Jordanian dinars (equivalent to 465–930 GBP). Table 20.2 shows that the great majority of the sample population were well educated: 56.5% of respondents had completed a university degree, and another 18.5% of respondents had received a college degree. Table 20.2 also indicated that highest percentage of occupation was for customers employed in the managerial and professional areas, representing a ratio of 34.7% and 32.5% of the sample, respectively.

Table 20.2 Sample characteristics

Factor	Item	Number of respondents	Percentage
Gender	Male	515	78.6
	Female	140	21.4
	Total	655	100.0
Education	High school or less	99	15.1
	College	123	18.8
	Undergraduate	370	56.5
	Postgraduate	63	9.6
	Total	655	100.0
Age	25 or less	121	18.5
	26–35	257	39.2
	36–45	159	24.3
	46–59	102	15.6
	60 or more	16	2.4
	Total	655	100.0

(Continued)

Table 20.2 (Continued)

Factor	Item	Number of respondents	Percentage
Occupation	Managerial	227	34.7
	Professional	213	32.5
	Business person	79	12.1
	Retired	23	3.5
	Housewife	21	3.2
	Student	13	2.0
	Others	79	12.1
	Total	655	100.0
Income (month)	Less than 500	220	33.6
	500–1000	265	40.5
	1001–1500	64	9.8
	1501–2000	36	5.5
	2001–2500	9	1.4
	2501–3000	12	1.8
	More than 3000	49	7.5
	Total	655	100.0

Source: The authors

Factor analysis

Principal component analysis was used with VARIMAX rotation on 48 items. This resulted in the elimination of one item (depicted low communality, i.e. 0.5), and remaining scale items were again subjected to factor analysis. Factor loadings close to −1 or 1 indicate that the factor strongly affects the variable. Loadings close to zero indicate that the factor has a weak effect on the variable. In this research, loading of ±0.40 or more was considered acceptable. A summary of the factor analysis and reliability test results is presented in Table 20.3.

As can be seen in Table 20.3, item 40, "I will not switch to another bank if I experience a problem with this bank", was removed to increase the reliability and content validity, as the factor loading was below 0.40. The range for factor loadings was 0.617–0.911 for all items. The final factor solution is represented in Table 20.3 along with the items, factor loadings, explained variance and Cronbach's alpha value. The range for the value of the KMO statistic was .792–.883, indicating the appropriateness of factor analysis. Cronbach's alpha for all measures exceeded the recommended threshold value of 0.70 (Schmidt and Hollensen 2006). Therefore, all measures were robust in terms of their reliability.

Data analysis

Table 20.4 shows the mean and standard deviation for the summated scales. The mean scores of the variables were between 3.79 to 4.01, indicating that respondents were inclined towards a favourable direction, that is, towards agreement. Table 20.4 is also informative of the correlations between the investigated constructs, which in turn provides a preliminary way to test the hypotheses. CARTER dimensions have high positive correlations with customer satisfaction and behaviour loyalty, with empathy appearing as the highest positive with satisfaction (0.755) and behaviour loyalty (0.658). A strong positive correlation was also found between overall satisfaction and behaviour loyalty (0.810).

Table 20.3 Factor analysis and reliability analysis test

Variable	No. of items	Factor loadings	Eigenvalue	% of variance explained	KMO	Cronbach's alpha
Compliance			2.909	58.174	.811	0.813
	1	.786				
	2	.780				
	3	.811				
	4	.691				
	5	.739				
Tangibles			2.844	71.104	.792	0.863
	6	.817				
	7	.876				
	8	.860				
	9	.819				
Reliability			3.582	71.641	.876	0.900
	10	.810				
	11	.857				
	12	.871				
	13	.879				
	14	.813				
Responsiveness			2.985	74.635	.811	0.883
	15	.808				
	16	.888				
	17	.881				
	18	.876				
Assurance			2.921	73.015	.821	0.877
	19	.839				
	20	.841				
	21	.905				
	22	.831				
Empathy			3.466	69.322	.827	0.887
	23	.873				
	24	.876				
	25	.851				
	26	.717				
	27	.837				
Satisfaction			4.491	74.856	.883	0.932
	28	.825				
	29	.847				
	30	.895				
	31	.891				
	32	.859				
	33	.873				
Behavioural			4.367	62.376	.882	0.914
	34	.855				
	35	.911				
	36	.885				
	37	.901				
	38	.887				
	39	.617				
	40	.204 Deleted				

Source: The authors

Table 20.4 Correlation matrix

	Mean	S.D.	(1)	(2)	(3)	(4)	(5)	(6)	(7)	(8)
(1) Compliance	3.904	.745	1	.445**	.504**	.463**	.444**	.546**	.528**	.562**
(2) Tangibles	3.974	.764	445**	1	.688**	.579**	.631**	.618**	.630**	.566**
(3) Reliability	3.866	.787	.504**	.688**	1	.679**	.681**	.721**	.681**	.629**
(4) Responsiveness	3.836	.827	.463**	.579**	.697**	1	.734**	.768**	.715**	.612**
(5) Assurance	4.013	.770	.444**	.631**	.681**	.734**	1	.732**	.731**	.629**
(6) Empathy	3.797	.822	.546**	.618**	.721**	.768**	.732**	1	.755**	.658**
(7) Satisfaction	3.859	.818	.528**	.630**	.681**	.715**	.731**	.755**	1	.810**
(8) Behaviour loyalty	3.800	.762	.562**	.566**	.692**	.612**	.629**	.658*	.810**	1

*(**) Indicates correlation is significant at the 0.05 (0.01) level (two-tailed, person).

Table 20.5 Summary of the results of hypothesis testing

Hypothesis	Beta	Sig. value	Results
H1: Compliance positively influences behaviour loyalty	.245	0.000	Supported
H2: Tangibles positively influence behaviour loyalty	.120	0.001	Supported
H3: Reliability positively influences behaviour loyalty	.128	0.003	Supported
H4: Responsiveness positively influences behaviour loyalty	.111	0.011	Supported
H5: Assurance positively influences behaviour loyalty	.171	0.000	Supported
H6: Empathy positively influences behaviour loyalty	.168	0.000	Supported
H7: Overall quality and loyalty: a mediating role of satisfaction	.633	0.000	Supported

Source: The authors

Hypotheses testing

Since the measurement model evaluation provided evidence of reliability and validity, the structural model was examined to evaluate the hypothesised relationships among the constructs in the research model (Agag and El-Masry 2017). The multiple regression tests and hierarchical multiple regressions were conducted by running two steps of analysis separately, as follows:

1   CARTER dimensions as independent variables and loyalty as dependent variable;
2   The indirect relationships with customer satisfaction as a mediating variable between overall CARTER dimensions and behavioural loyalty.

The results show that all hypothesised relationships are supported. Compliance, assurance and empathy are the most influential factors leading to behavioural loyalty. Table 20.5 summarises the research findings in terms of the relationships between CARTER dimensions, customer satisfaction and behavioural loyalty.

Discussion

The aim of this chapter is to contribute to a gap in the academic literature on Islamic banking in Jordan. Research questions are posed in the introduction, with answers from the results achieved shown in the case study. Where there is relevant academic literature, though not on Jordanian banks, the examples from prior literature sources are used to show what findings from our case study could be supported empirically.

A key finding shown in the case study reveals that compliance with *Shari'ah* is the most significant predictor of loyalty compared to other service quality dimensions in the Islamic banking context. This result is supported by previous studies (e.g. Anouze *et al.* 2019; Souiden and Rani 2015; Lee and Ullah 2011) that identified compliance as a valuable predictor of consumer behaviour and consumer purchasing decisions with Islamic banks because their customers believe that Islamic banks are *Shari'ah* compliant. Kaakeh *et al.* (2019) reported that compliance affects attitude directly, and intention is indirectly mediated by attitude. Mbawuni and Nimako (2017) also reported that consumer attitude, readiness to comply with Islamic law, knowledge, perceived innovativeness and perceived benefits were critical determinants of customers' intention to adopt Islamic banking in both Muslim and non-Muslim sub-groups.

A key finding shown in the case study is that assurance has a significant impact on behavioural loyalty. This result is consistent with Kheng *et al.* (2010), who reported that assurance positively influences customer loyalty. From the findings of our case study, it is clear that customers are satisfied by Islamic banks, and their loyalty to Islamic banks can make the customers more confident in transactions depending on *Shari'ah* (Islamic law). From the managerial perspective of Islamic banks, treating customers courteously and ensuring knowledge and training of employees to answer questions from customers are essential attributes to increase customer satisfaction and loyalty.

Another key finding shows that empathy has a positive significant effect on behaviour loyalty; this result is consistent with previous literature (Kheng *et al.* 2010; Butcher 2001). In this regard, it is clear from the case study data analyses that employees who make greater effort to understand the specific needs of the customers and banks giving convenient operating hours score higher.

Given the significant effects of reliability, the case study findings reveal that customers' perceptions of their bank's ability to perform a service dependably and accurately tend to become positive once they perceive that the bank keeps its promises, provides services at the promised time and gives them individual attention. This is in line with prior researchers (e.g. Kheng *et al.* 2010; Zafar *et al.* 2012), who pointed out that reliability plays a critical role for behavioural loyalty. Similarly, Osman *et al.* (2009) found that reliability was perceived as an essential attribute in choosing Islamic financial institutions. This indicates that where customers perceive where Islamic banks can be depended upon, for example, regarding accuracy of service with attention to detail, there follows increasing customer satisfaction, which thereby enhances customer loyalty to an Islamic bank.

A finding of this study reveals that tangibility has a significant impact on customer behavioural loyalty, which is in line with previous literature sources (e.g. Kashif *et al.* 2015; Choudhury 2014). Islamic banks need to provide high standards of physical evidence such as modern equipment, professional appearance of staff and good-looking brochures to improve first impressions of new and existing wealthier customers. The significance of a relaxed and comfortable Islamic banking atmosphere is now perceived to be the theme of "a branch as comfortable as your living room" (Yavas *et al.* 1997).

Responsiveness is a significant predictor of behavioural loyalty, and our finding is consistent with Badara *et al.* (2013), who reported that responsiveness positively influences customer loyalty. From the data analyses in the case study, customers being satisfied helps the loyalty dimension when Islamic banks have able employees to help provide prompt services and readiness in compliance with queries and requests from customers.

Higher dimensions of service quality from various sources (e.g. Boonlertvanich 2019; Makanyeza and Chikazhe 2017; Kaura *et al.* 2015; Caruana 2002) demonstrated higher customer satisfaction and eventually, establishing long-term customer loyalty. We find that customer satisfaction is a mediating variable between service quality and behavioural loyalty. Overall, the marketing research with customers of Jordanian banks in Jordan supports the idea that customer satisfaction mediates the relationship between quality of service and behavioural loyalty. They are highly interrelated in the Jordanian case.

Managerial implications

Based on the findings of the study, the following recommendations are provided for developing the marketing of the Jordan Islamic Bank.

First, compliance, empathy and assurance are the top three influential factors on customer satisfaction and behavioural loyalty. It is important for Islamic banks to review and endorse all policies and procedures of Islamic banks to ensure that their documents and investments are undertaken in line with *Shari'a* requirements. They should be closely involved with the actual practice and implementation of financial transactions from employees or practitioners to obtain a more comprehensive and deeper understanding of the issues. In addition, it is important for Islamic banks to give individual attention to their customers and understand their specific needs, to make them feel further valued and unique. It is important for Islamic banks to pay more attention to their employees' knowledge and use their professional knowledge towards making recommendations and reducing risk for customers as well as helping them to more confident towards future transactions.

Second, although responsiveness, tangibles and reliability are the least influential compared to the other variables, they are still crucial factors. Given the nature of tangibility, managing the evidence and the use of environmental psychology can be treated as powerful marketing tools for managers. Therefore, it is important for Islamic banks to allocate part of their annual budget to renovating and refreshing their physical places to keep their customers fulfilled and to improve customer loyalty. To improve the reliability dimension, managers are encouraged to include reliability concerns in their mission statements, set reliability standards, teach the significance of reliability in training programs, appoint reliability teams to study specific services, recommend ways to improve reliability, measure error rates and reward error-free service. For improving the responsiveness dimension, managers should pay more attention to customers' contact with personnel and telephone calls and messages when issues happen, as speedy responses enhance customers' fulfilment and support, hence continuing loyalty. Furthermore, responsiveness requires that the Islamic bank's personnel appear well informed and empowered in answering customers' requests for information and dealing with their complaints.

Limitations and future research directions

One limitation of this study is that the field research was conducted in one market (Jordan) and focused on one type of service (banking). It was tested in Jordanian Islamic banks, and the results of the study are based on customers' perceptions of their Islamic banks. However, the banking system in Jordan is a dual banking system, with conventional non-Islamic and Islamic banks operating side by side. This is an important issue for future research to compare Islamic with conventional banks in the Jordanian market. Satisfaction and loyalty could be different in other countries (Narteh 2013), so academics should exercise caution when citing the results in other settings. It would be interesting for future research to replicate the study in other countries, knowing that customers do not necessarily behave the same way there, while the methods of operation of the Islamic banks are usually similar in different economic environments and countries. Such replication could advance the understanding of different cultural features affecting customer satisfaction and customer loyalty. Applying the current research model to the business-to-business context would also be useful.

References

Abbas, S.Z.M., Hamid, M.A.A., Joher, H. and Ismail, S., 2003. *Factors That Determine Consumers' Choice in Selecting Islamic Financing Products*. Paper Presented at the International Islamic Banking Conference, Prato, 9–10 September.

Abdul Rehman, A., 2012. Customer satisfaction and service quality in Islamic banking: A comparative study in Pakistan, United Arab Emirates and United Kingdom. *Qualitative Research in Financial Markets*, 4(2/3), 165–175. DOI: 10.1108/17554171211252501.

Agag, G.M. and El-Masry, A.A., 2017. Why do consumers trust online travel websites? Drivers and outcomes of consumer trust toward online travel websites. *Journal of Travel Research*, 56(3), 347–369. DOI: 10.1177/0047287516643185.

Ahmad, A. and Safwan, N., 2011. Testing a model of Islamic banking based on service quality, customer satisfaction and bank performance. *African Journal of Business Management*, 5(5), 1880–1885. https://doi.org/10.5897/AJBM10.982.

Ahmad, A. and Saif, M.I., 2010. Islamic banking experience of Pakistan: Comparison between Islamic and conventional banks. *International Journal of Business and management*, 5(2), 137–143.

Al-Ajmi, J., Hussain, H.A. and Al-Saleh, N., 2009. Clients of conventional and Islamic banks in Bahrain: How they choose which bank to patronize. *International Journal of Social Economics*, 36(11), 1086–1112. DOI: 10.1108/03068290910992642.

Al-Omar, F. and Abdel-Haq, M., 1996. *Islamic Banking: Theory, Practice, and Challenges*. Atlantic Highlands, NJ: Zed Books.

Al-Sultan, W., 1999. *Financial Characteristics of Interest-Free Banks and Conventional Banks*. PhD Thesis, University of Wollongong.

Altwijry, O.I. and Abduh, M., 2013. Customer satisfaction and switching behavior in Saudi Islamic banks: An exploratory study. *Journal of Islamic Finance*, 2(2), 17–25.

Ambarwati, A., Hadiwidjojo, D.Z., Sudiro, A. and Rohman, F., 2015. The role of multichannel marketing in customer retention and loyalty: Study in emerald bank customer in Indonesia. *Asia-Pacific Management and Business Application*, 2(3), 184–200. DOI: 10.21776/ub.apmba.2014.002.03.4.

Amin, M. and Isa, Z., 2008. An examination of the relationship between service quality perception and customer satisfaction: A SEM approach towards Malaysian Islamic banking. *International Journal of Islamic and Middle Eastern Finance and Management*, 1(3), 191–209. DOI: 10.1108/17538390810901131.

Amirzadeh, R. and Shoorvarzy, M.R., 2013. Prioritizing service quality factors in Iranian Islamic banking using a fuzzy approach. *International Journal of Islamic and Middle Eastern Finance and Management*, 6(1), 64–78. DOI: 10.1108/17538391311310752.

Angelova, B. and Zekiri, J., 2011. Measuring customer satisfaction with service quality using American customer satisfaction model (ACSI Model). *International Journal of Academic Research in Business and Social Sciences*, 1(3), 232–258. DOI: 10.6007/ijarbss.v1i2.35.

Anouze, A.L.M., Alamro, A.S. and Awwad, A.S., 2019. Customer satisfaction and its measurement in Islamic banking sector: A revisit and update. *Journal of Islamic Marketing*, 10(2), 565–588. DOI: 10.1108/JIMA-07-2017-0080.

Arasli, H., Mehtap-Smadi, S. and Turan Katircioglu, S., 2005. Customer service quality in the Greek Cypriot banking industry. *Managing Service Quality*, 15(1), 41–56. DOI: 10.1108/09604520510575254.

Ariff, M., 2014. Whither Islamic banking? *The World Economy*, 37(6), 733–746. https://doi.org/10.1111/twec.12171.

Ashraf, S., Robson, J. and Sekhon, Y., 2015. Consumer trust and confidence in the compliance of Islamic banks. *Journal of Financial Services Marketing*, 20(2), 133–144. DOI: 10.1057/fsm.2015.8.

Asnawi, N., Sukoco, B.M. and Fanani, M.A., 2018. Halal products consumption in international chain restaurants among global Moslem consumers. *International Journal of Emerging Markets*, 13(5), 1273–1290. DOI: 10.1108/ijoem-11-2017-0495.

Association of Banks in Jordan, 2020. *Development of the Jordanian Banking Sector*. Amman, Jordan: Association of Banks in Jordan.

Astuti, H.J. and Nagase, K., 2014. Patient loyalty to healthcare organizations: Relationship marketing and satisfaction. *International Journal of Management and Marketing Research*, 7(2), 39–56.

Badara, M.A.S., Mat, N.K.N., Mujtaba, A.M., Al-Refai, A.N., Badara, A.M. and Abubakar, F.M., 2013. Direct effect of service quality dimensions on customer satisfaction and customer loyalty in Nigerian Islamic bank. *Management*, 3(1), 6–11.

Ball, D., Coelho, P.S. and Machas, A., 2004. The role of communication and trust in explaining customer loyalty: An extension to the ECSI model. *European Journal of Marketing*, 38(9/10), 1272–1293. DOI: 10.1108/03090560410548979.

Baron, S., Harris, K. and Hilton, T., 2009. *Services Marketing: Text and Cases*, 3rd ed. Basingstoke: Palgrave Macmillan.

Belwal, R. and Al Maqbali, A., 2019. A study of customers' perception of Islamic banking in Oman. *Journal of Islamic Marketing*, 10(1), 150–167. DOI: 10.1108/JIMA-02-2016-0008.

Bitner, M.J. and Hubbert, A.R., 1994. Encounter satisfaction versus overall satisfaction versus quality. *Service Quality: New Directions in Theory and Practice*, 34(2), 72–94. http://dx.doi.org/10.4135/9781452229102.n3.

Bloemer, J. and De Ruyter, K., 1998. On the relationship between store image, store satisfaction and store loyalty. *European Journal of Marketing*, 32(5/6), 499–513. DOI: 10.1108/03090569810216118.

Bloemer, J., De Ruyter, K. and Peeters, P., 1998. Investigating drivers of bank loyalty: The complex relationship between image, service quality and satisfaction. *International Journal of Bank Marketing*, 16(7), 276–286. DOI: 10.1108/02652329810245984.

Bolton, R.N. and Drew, J.H., 1994. Linking customer satisfaction to service operations and outcomes. *Service Quality: New Directions in Theory and Practice*, 3(2), 173–200. DOI: 10.4135/9781452229102.N8.

Boonlertvanich, K., 2019. Service quality, satisfaction, trust and loyalty: The moderating role of mainbank and wealth status. *International Journal of Bank Marketing*, 37(1), 278–302. DOI: 10.1108/IJBM-02-2018-0021.

Boulding, W., Kalra, A., Staelin, R. and Zeithaml, V.A., 1993 A dynamic process model of service quality: From expectations to behavioral intentions. *Journal of Marketing Research*, 30(1), 7–27. DOI: 10.2307/3172510.

Buchanan, R.W. and Gillies, C.S., 1990. Value managed relationships: The key to customer retention and profitability. *European Management Journal*, 8(4), 523–526. DOI: 10.1016/0263-2373(90)90115-M.

Buracom, K., 2002. *The Relationship Between Service Quality and Customer Satisfaction in the Formation of Customer Loyalty*. Thesis (PhD), University of South Australia, Australia.

Butcher, K., Sparks, B. and O'Callaghan, F., 2001. Evaluative and relational influences on service loyalty. *International Journal of Service Industry Management*, 12(4), 310–327. DOI: 10.1108/09564230110405253.

Buttle, F., 1996. SERVQUAL: Review, critique, research agenda. *European Journal of Marketing*, 30(1), 8–32. DOI: 10.1108/03090569610105762.

Carman, J.M., 1990. Consumer perceptions of service quality: An assessment of the SERVQUAL dimensions. *Journal of Retailing*, 66(1), 33–55.

Caruana, A., 2002. Service loyalty: The effects of service quality and the mediating role of customer satisfaction. *European Journal of Marketing*, 36(7/8), 811–828. DOI: 10.1108/03090560210430818.

Casaló, L.V., Flavián, C. and Guinalíu, M., 2008. The role of satisfaction and website usability in developing customer loyalty and positive word-of-mouth in the e-banking services. *International Journal of Bank Marketing*, 26(6), 399–417. DOI: 10.1108/02652320810902433.

Chang, K., 2000. The impact of perceived physical environments on customers' satisfaction and return intentions. *Journal of Professional Services Marketing*, 21(2), 75–85. DOI: 10.1300/J090v21n02_06.

Choi, K.S., Cho, W.H., Lee, S., Lee, H. and Kim, C., 2004. The relationships among quality, value, satisfaction and behavioral intention in health care provider choice: A South Korean study. *Journal of Business Research*, 57(8), 913–921. DOI: 10.1016/S0148-2963(02)00293-X.

Chong, B.S. and Liu, M.H., 2009. Islamic banking: Interest-free or interest-based? *Pacific-Basin Finance Journal*, 17(1), 125–144. DOI: 10.1016/j.pacfin.2007.12.003.

Choudhury, K., 2014. Service quality and word of mouth: A study of the banking sector. *International Journal of Bank Marketing*, 32(7), 612–627. DOI: 10.1108/IJBM-12-2012-0122.

Cronin Jr, J.J., Brady, M.K. and Hult, G.T.M., 2000. Assessing the effects of quality, value and customer satisfaction on consumer behavioral intentions in service environments. *Journal of Retailing*, 76(2), 193–218. DOI: 10.1016/s0022-4359(00)00028-2.

Cronin, J.J. and Taylor, S.A., 1992. Measuring service quality: A re-examination and extension. *The Journal of Marketing*, 56(3), 55–68. DOI: 10.2307/1252296.

Cui, C.C., Lewis, B.R. and Park, W., 2003. Service quality measurement in the banking sector in South Korea. *International Journal of Bank Marketing*, 21(4), 191–201. DOI: 10.1108/02652320310479187.

Dandis, A.O. and Wright, L.T., 2020. The effects of CARTER model on attitudinal loyalty in Islamic banks. *International Journal of Quality and Service Sciences*, 12(2), 149–171. DOI: 10.1108/IJQSS-03-2019-0050.

Dar, H.A. and Presley, J.R., 1999. Islamic finance: A western perspective. *International Journal of Islamic Financial Services*, 1(1), 3–11.

Day, G.S., 1969. A two-dimensional concept of brand loyalty. *Journal of Advertising Research*, 9(3), 29–31. https://doi.org/10.1007/978-3-642-51565-1_26.

Deng, Z., Lu, Y., Wei, K.K. and Zhang, J., 2010. Understanding customer satisfaction and loyalty: An empirical study of mobile instant messages in China. *International Journal of Information Management*, 30(4), 289–300. DOI: 10.1016/j.ijinfomgt.2009.10.001.

Dick, A.S. and Basu, K., 1994. Customer loyalty: Toward an integrated conceptual framework. *Journal of The Academy of Marketing Science*, 22(2), 99–113. DOI: 10.1177/0092070394222001.

Dusuki, A.W., 2008. Understanding the objectives of Islamic banking: A survey of stakeholders' perspectives. *International Journal of Islamic and Middle Eastern Finance and Management*, 1(2), 132–148. DOI: 10.1108/17538390810880982.

Dusuki, A.W. and Abdullah, N.I., 2007. Why do Malaysian customers patronise Islamic banks? *International Journal of Bank Marketing*, 25(3), 142–160. DOI: 10.1108/02652320710739850.

Ehigie, B.O., 2006. Correlates of customer loyalty to their bank: A case study in Nigeria. *International Journal of Bank Marketing*, 24(7), 494–508. DOI: 10.1108/02652320610712102.

Erol, C. and El-Bdour, R., 1989. Attitudes, behaviour and patronage factors of bank customers towards Islamic banks. *International Journal of Bank Marketing*, 7(6), 31–37. DOI: 10.1108/02652328910132060.

Eskildsen, J., Kristensen, K., Jørn Juhl, H. and Østergaard, P., 2004. The drivers of customer satisfaction and loyalty. The case of Denmark 2000–2002. *Total Quality Management and Business Excellence*, 15(5–6), 859–868. DOI: 10.1080/14783360410001680297.

Estiri, M., Hosseini, F., Yazdani, H. and Nejad, H.J., 2011. Determinants of customer satisfaction in Islamic banking: Evidence from Iran. *International Journal of Islamic and Middle Eastern Finance and Management*, 4(4), 295–307. DOI: 10.1108/17538391111186546.

File, K.M. and Prince, R.A., 1992. Positive word-of-mouth: Customer satisfaction and buyer behaviour. *International Journal of Bank Marketing*, 10(1), 25–29. DOI: 10.1108/02652329210007867.

Gambling, T. and Abdel Karim, R.A., 1991. *Business and Accounting Ethics in Islam*. London: Mansell.

Gounaris, S.P., Stathakopoulos, V. and Athanassopoulos, A.D., 2003. Antecedents to perceived service quality: An exploratory study in the banking industry. *International Journal of Bank Marketing*, 21(4), 168–190. DOI: 10.1108/02652320310479178.

Gremler, D.D. and Gwinner, K.P., 2000. Customer-employee rapport in service relationships. *Journal of Service Research*, 3(1), 82–104. DOI: 10.1177/109467050031006.

Gronholdt, L., Martensen, A. and Kristensen, K., 2000. The relationship between customer satisfaction and loyalty: Cross-industry differences. *Total Quality Management*, 11(4–6), 509–514. DOI: 10.1080/09544120050007823.

Han, X., Kwortnik, R.J. and Wang, C., 2008. Service loyalty: An integrative model and examination across service contexts. *Journal of Service Research*, 11(1), 22–42. DOI: 10.1177/1094670508319094.

Haron, S., Ahmad, N. and Planisek, S.L., 1994. Bank patronage factors of Muslim and non-Muslim customers. *International Journal of Bank Marketing*, 12(1), 32–40. DOI: 10.1108/02652329410049599.

Hassan, K. and Lewis, M., 2009. *Handbook of Islamic Banking*. Cheltenham: Edward Elgar Publishing.

Hassan, M.T., Ahmed, B., Ahmed, S., Habib, U., Riaz, S., Maqbool, N. and Anwar, A., 2012. Measuring customers loyalty of Islamic banking in Bahawalpur region. *International Journal of Learning and Development*, 2(2), 101–111. DOI: 10.5296/ijld.v2i2.1593.

Iacobucci, D., Ostrom, A. and Grayson, K., 1995. Distinguishing service quality and customer satisfaction: The voice of the consumer. *Journal of Consumer Psychology*, 4(3), 277–303. DOI: 10.1207/s15327663jcp0403_04.

Iqbal, M.S., Hassan, M.U. and Habibah, U., 2018. Impact of self-service technology (SST) service quality on customer loyalty and behavioral intention: The mediating role of customer satisfaction. *Cogent Business and Management*, 5(1), 1–23. DOI: 10.1080/23311975.2018.1423770.

Jamal, A. and Anastasiadou, K., 2009. Investigating the effects of service quality dimensions and expertise on loyalty. *European Journal of Marketing*, 43(3/4), 398–420. https://doi.org/10.1108/03090560910935497.

Jones, M.A., Mothersbaugh, D.L. and Beatty, S.E., 2002. Why customers stay: Measuring the underlying dimensions of services switching costs and managing their differential strategic outcomes. *Journal of Business Research*, 55(6), 441–450. DOI: 10.1016/s0148-2963(00)00168-5.

Kaakeh, A., Hassan, M.K. and Van Hemmen Almazor, S.F., 2019. Factors affecting customers' attitude towards Islamic banking in UAE. *International Journal of Emerging Markets*, 14(4), 668–688. DOI: 10.1108/ijoem-11-2017-0502.

Kandampully, J., 1998. Service quality to service loyalty: A relationship which goes beyond customer services. *Total Quality Management*, 9(6), 431–443. DOI: 10.1080/0954412988370.

Kashif, M., Wan Shukran, S.S., Rehman, M.A. and Sarifuddin, S., 2015. Customer satisfaction and loyalty in Malaysian Islamic banks: A PAKSERV investigation. *International Journal of Bank Marketing*, 33(1), 23–40. DOI: 10.1108/ijbm-08-2013-0084.

Kaura, V., Durga Prasad, C.S. and Sharma, S., 2015. Service quality, service convenience, price and fairness, customer loyalty and the mediating role of customer satisfaction. *International Journal of Bank Marketing*, 33(4), 404–422. DOI: 10.1108/ijbm-04-2014-0048.

Keiningham, T.L., Vavra, T.G., Aksoy, L. and Wallard, H., 2005. *Loyalty Myths: Hyped Strategies That Will Put You Out of Business – And Proven Tactics That Really Work*. Hoboken, NJ: John Wiley and Sons.

Kheng, L.L., Mahamad, O., Ramayah, T. and Mosahab, R., 2010. The impact of service quality on customer loyalty: A study of banks in Penang, Malaysia. *International Journal of Marketing Studies*, 2(2), 57–66. DOI: 10.5539/ijms.v2n2p57.

Lee, K.H. and Ullah, S., 2011. Customers' attitude toward Islamic banking in Pakistan. *International Journal of Islamic and Middle Eastern Finance and Management*, 4(2), 131–145. DOI: 10.1108/17538391111144524.

Leverin, A. and Liljander, V., 2006. Does relationship marketing improve customer relationship satisfaction and loyalty? *International Journal of Bank Marketing*, 24(4), 232–251. DOI: 10.1108/02652320610671333.

Lewis, M.K. and Algaoud, L.M., 2001. *Islamic Banking*. Cheltenham, UK: Edward Elgar.

Maali, B., Casson, P. and Napier, C., 2006. Social reporting by Islamic banks. *Abacus*, 42(2), 266–289. DOI: 10.1108/02652320610671333.

Mahadin, B.K. and Akroush, M.N., 2019. A study of factors affecting word of mouth (WOM) towards Islamic banking (IB) in Jordan. *International Journal of Emerging Markets*, 14(4), 639–667. DOI: 10.1108/IJOEM-10-2017-0414.

Makanyeza, C. and Chikazhe, L., 2017. Mediators of the relationship between service quality and customer loyalty: Evidence from the banking sector in Zimbabwe. *International Journal of Bank Marketing*, 35(3), 540–556. DOI: 10.1108/IJBM-11-2016-0164.

Mao, J., 2010. Customer brand loyalty. *International Journal of Business and Management*, 5(7), 213–217. DOI: 10.5539/ijbm.v5n7p213.

Maritz, A., 2008. Entrepreneurial services marketing initiatives facilitating small business growth. *Journal of Small Business and Entrepreneurship*, 21(4), 493–503. DOI: 10.1080/08276331.2008.10593437.

Masood, O. and Bellalah, M., 2013. *Islamic Banking and Finance*. Newcastle upon Tyne, England: Cambridge Scholars Publishing.

Masood, O., Aktan, B. and Amin, Q.A., 2009. Islamic banking: A study of customer satisfaction and preferences in non-Islamic countries. *International Journal of Monetary Economics and Finance*, 2(3–4), 261–285. DOI: 10.1504/IJMEF.2009.029063.

Maxham III, J.G., 2001. Service recovery's influence on consumer satisfaction, positive word-of-mouth and purchase intentions. *Journal of Business Research*, 54(1), 11–24. DOI: 10.1016/s0148-2963(00)00114-4.

Mbawuni, J. and Nimako, S.G., 2017. Determinants of Islamic banking adoption in Ghana. *International Journal of Islamic and Middle Eastern Finance and Management*, 10(2), 264–288. DOI: 10.1108/IMEFM-04-2016-0056.

McDougall, G.H.G. and Levesqu, T.J., 1994. Benefit segmentation using service quality dimensions: An investigation in retail banking. *International Journal of Bank Marketing*, 12(2), 15–23. DOI: 10.1108/02652329410052946.

McDougall, G.H.G. and Levesque, T.J., 2000. Customer satisfaction with services: Putting perceived value into the equation. *The Journal of Services Marketing*, 14(5), 392–410. DOI: 10.1108/08876040010340937.

Metwally, M.M., 1997. Differences between the financial characteristics of interest-free banks and conventional banks. *European Business Review*, 97(2), 92–98. DOI: 10.1108/09555349710162607.

Misbach, I. and Hadiwidjojo, D., 2013. Islamic bank service quality and trust: Study on Islamic Bank in Makassar Indonesia. *International Journal of Business and Management*. 8(5), 48–61. DOI: 10.5539/ijbm.v8n5p48.

Mohd-Shariff, R.O.S. and Aniza, B., 2013. *Service Quality in Islamic and Conventional Banks in Malaysia: An Explorative and Comparative Analysis.* Thesis (PhD), Durham University, Durham.

Naeem, H., Akram, A. and Saif, M.I., 2011. Service quality and its impact on customer satisfaction: An empirical evidence from the Pakistani banking sector. *International Business and Economics Research Journal (IBER)*, 8(12), 99–104. DOI: 10.19030/iber.v8i12.3201.

Narteh, B., 2013. Determinants of students' loyalty in the Ghanaian banking industry. *The TQM Journal*, 25(2), 153–169. DOI: 10.1108/17542731311299591.

Naser, K., Jamal, A. and Al-Khatib, K., 1999. Islamic banking: A study of customer satisfaction and preferences in Jordan. *International Journal of Bank Marketing*, 17(3), 135–151. DOI: 10.1108/02652329910269275.

Ndubisi, N.O. and Wah, C.K., 2005. Factorial and discriminant analyses of the underpinnings of relationship marketing and customer satisfaction. *International Journal of Bank Marketing*, 23(7), 542–557. DOI: 10.1108/02652320510629908.

Nihar, K.L. and Subramanyam, M., 2011. Shari'ah based banking and profit or loss paradigm. *International Journal of Management*, 2(1), 30–40.

Oliver, R.L., 1993. A conceptual model of service quality and service satisfaction: Compatible goals, different concepts. *Advances in Services Marketing and Management*, 2(4), 65–85.

Oliver, R.L., 1997. *Satisfaction: A Behavioral Perspective on the Consumer.* New York: McGraw Hill.

Osman, I., Ali, H., Zainuddin, A., Rashid, W.E.W. and Jusoff, K., 2009. Customer satisfaction in Malaysian Islamic banking. *International Journal of Economics and Finance*, 1(1), 197–202.

Othman, A. and Owen, L., 2001. Adopting and measuring customer service quality (SQ) in Islamic banks: A case study in Kuwait finance house. *International Journal of Islamic Financial Services*, 3(1), 1–26.

Pakurár, M., Haddad, H., Nagy, J., Popp, J. and Oláh, J., 2019. The service quality dimensions that affect customer satisfaction in the Jordanian banking sector. *Sustainability*, 11(4), 1113. DOI: 10.3390/su11041113.

Parasuraman, A.A., 1985. A conceptual model of service quality and its implications for future research. *Journal of Marketing*, 49(4), 41–50. DOI: 10.1177/002224298504900403.

Parasuraman, A.A., Zeithaml, V.A. and Berry, L.L., 1988. SERVQUAL: A multiple-item scale for measuring consumer perceptions of service quality. *Journal of Retailing*, 64(1), 12–40.

Parasuraman, A.A., Zeithaml, V.A. and Berry, L.L., 1994. Alternative scales for measuring service quality: A comparative assessment based on psychometric and diagnostic criteria. *Journal of Retailing*, 70(3), 201–230. DOI: 10.1016/0022-4359(94)90033-7.

Rashid, M., Hassan, M.K. and Ahmad, A.U.F., 2009. Quality perception of the customers towards domestic Islamic banks in Bangladesh. *Journal of Islamic Economics, Banking and Finance*, 5(1), 109–128.

Reeves, C.A. and Bednar, D.A., 1994. Defining quality: Alternatives and implications. *Academy of Management Review*, 19(3), 419–445. DOI: 10.2307/258934.

Rehman, A.A., 2012. Customer satisfaction and service quality in Islamic banking. *Qualitative Research in Financial Markets*, 4(2/3), 165–175. DOI: 10.1108/JIMA-07-2015-0049.

Rundle-Thiele, S. and Mackay, M.M., 2001. Assessing the performance of brand loyalty measures. *Journal of Services Marketing*, 15(7), 529–546. DOI: 10.1108/EUM0000000006210.

Rust, R.T. and Oliver, R.L., 1994. *Service Quality: New Directions in Theory and Practice.* Thousand Oaks, CA: Sage Publications.

Shaikh, R. and Siddiqui, D.A., 2018. Bank service quality on customer satisfaction, loyalty: A study based on Islamic banks in Pakistan. *International Journal of Management and Commerce Innovations*, 6(2), 830–839.

Shanmugam, B. and Zahari, Z.R., 2009. *A Primer on Islamic Finance.* Charlottesville: Research Foundation Publications of CFA Institute.

Shaon, S.K.I. and Rahman, M.H., 2015. A theoretical review of CRM effects on customer satisfaction and loyalty. *Central European Business Review*, 4(1), 23–36. DOI: 10.18267/j.cebr.108.

Sin, L.Y., Alan, C.B., Yau, O.H., Lee, J.S. and Chow, R., 2002. The effect of relationship marketing orientation on business performance in a service-oriented economy. *Journal of Services Marketing*, 16(7), 656–676. DOI: 10.1108/08876040210447360.

Souiden, N. and Rani, M., 2015. Consumer attitudes and purchase intentions toward Islamic banks: The influence of religiosity. *International Journal of Bank Marketing*, 33(2), 143–161. DOI: 10.1108/ijbm-10-2013-0115.

Spreng, R.A. and Mackoy, R.D., 1996. An empirical examination of a model of perceived service quality and satisfaction. *Journal of Retailing*, 72(2), 201–214. DOI: 10.1016/s0022-4359(96)90014-7.

Stafford, M.R., 1996. Demographic discriminators of service quality in the banking industry. *Journal of Services Marketing*, 10(4), 6–22. DOI: 10.1108/08876049610124554.

Taap, A.A., Chong, S.C., Kumar, M. and Fong, T.K., 2011. Measuring service quality of conventional and Islamic banks: A comparative analysis. *International Journal of Quality and Reliability Management*, 28(8), 822–840. DOI: 10.1108/02656711111162505.

Taleghani, M., Gilaninia, S. and Mousavian, S.J., 2011. The role of relationship marketing in customer orientation process in the banking industry with focus on loyalty. *International Journal of Business and Social Science*, 2(19), 155–166.

Taylor, S.A. and Baker, T.L., 1994. An assessment of the relationship between service quality and customer satisfaction in the formation of consumers' purchase intentions. *Journal of Retailing*, 70(2), 163–178. DOI: 10.1016/0022-4359(94)90013-2.

Wright, L.T. and Crimp, M., 2000. *The Marketing Research Process*. London: Financial Times/Prentice Hall.

Yavas, U., Benkenstein, M. and Stuhldreier, U., 2004. Relationships between service quality and behavioral outcomes: A study of private bank customers in Germany. *International Journal of Bank Marketing*, 22(2), 144–157. DOI: 10.1108/02652320410521737.

Yavas, U., Bilgin, Z. and Shemwell, D.J., 1997. Service quality in the banking sector in an emerging economy: A consumer survey. *International Journal of Bank Marketing*, 15(6), 217–223. DOI: 10.1108/02652329710184442.

Yeh, Y.S. and Li, Y.M., 2009. Building trust in m-commerce: Contributions from quality and satisfaction. *Online Information Review*, 33(6), 1066–1086. DOI: 10.1108/14684520911011016.

Yin, R.K., 2014. *Case Study Research: Design and Methods*, 5th ed. Los Angeles, CA: Sage Publications.

Zafar, M., Zafar, S., Asif, A., Hunjra, A.I. and Ahmad, M., 2012. Service quality, customer satisfaction and loyalty: An empirical analysis of banking sector in Pakistan. *Information Management and Business Review*, 4(3), 159–167.

Zaher, T.S. and Kabir Hassan, M., 2001. A comparative literature survey of Islamic finance and banking. *Financial Markets, Institutions and Instruments*, 10(4), 155–199. DOI: 10.1111/1468-0416.00044.

Zaman, M. and Movassaghi, H., 2002. Interest-free Islamic banking: Ideals and reality. *International Journal of Finance*, 14(4), 2428–2442. DOI: 10.1016/j.pacfin.2007.12.003.

Zeithaml, V.A., 2000. Service quality, profitability and the economic worth of customers: What we know and what we need to learn. *Journal of the Academy of Marketing Science*, 28(1), 67–85. DOI: 10.1177/0092070300281007.

Zeithaml, V.A., Berry, L.L. and Parasuraman, A., 1996. The behavioral consequences of service quality. *Journal of Marketing*, 60(2), 31–46. DOI: 10.2307/1251929.

Zeithaml, V.A., Bitner, M.J. and Gremler, D.D., 2018. *Services Marketing: Integrating Customer Focus Across the Firm*. New York: McGraw-Hill Education.

21

SMART CITIES AND SMART TRANSPORT

The role of data and insight

*Merlin Stone, Eleni Aravopoulou, Jonathan Knapper
and Geraint Evans*

Summary

In this chapter, we investigate information management and marketing research in the smart city. It identifies the main trends in progress and how innovation in information technology is helping all those in the smart city ecosystem in terms of generating new sources of data and connecting them. It investigates how information management in the smart city may go through several phases but contests the notion that the co-ordinated information management that is the dream of many city managers is an appropriate vision, given the tendency in the private sector for competing information platforms to develop, giving value in different ways. The Transport for London (TfL) case study (Stone and Aravopoulou 2018) describes how one of the world's largest public transport operations transformed the real-time availability of information for its customers and staff through the open data approach, and what the results of this transformation were. Its purpose is therefore to show what is required for an open data approach to work.

The concept of the smart city

The concept of the "smart city" is frequently referenced in academic research, grey literature and government reports but often interpreted inconsistently (Stone *et al.* 2018). While developments in information management are central to the smartening of cities, there is no agreed-upon framework by which to assess the progress of smartening of a city in relation to information management, and in particular no agreed-upon framework for obtaining customer feedback on the changes that are made to smarten cities or indeed for the role of marketing research in so doing. In this chapter, we review how information management contributes to smartening of cities and suggest a framework for managers and city planners to use in planning and implementing city smartening and measuring progress and for researchers to use in building their conceptual frameworks. We also consider the choices facing those responsible for or involved in city-smartening in terms of business models and centralisation or decentralisation of information management initiatives.

Most city smartening projects involve transforming an existing ecosystem, namely a city, its transport and various other city attributes, mainly by deployment of information management in as pervasive and real time a form as possible rather than by radical change, in which the activities and players change. As experience with city smartening evolves, and as technology evolves, the prospect of more fundamental transformation opens up, with new players emerging, existing players changing what they do and when they do it and new relationships developing between players. These developments will all have significant information management implications.

Definition of smart city

Due to the rapid evolution of thinking about smart cities, there is no consensus on the definition of "smart city". Deakin and Al Waer (2011) suggest that a city is defined by its applications of many kinds of electronic and digital technologies to transform life and working environments in a city, including via embedding the technologies in public systems, combined with a consciousness of all players in the city that they live and work in a smart city and that its "smartness" benefits them. Other definitions, such as that of Caragliu *et al.* (2009), highlight the focus on quality of life, sustainability and engagement of the population and organisations. Most writers agree is that smartening of a city involves changes to energy management, building design and management, mobility services and practices, infrastructure development and use, healthcare design and management, technology implementation and governance and citizen knowledge and behaviour. Given the rate of evolution of relevant technologies, the smart city is best considered not as an endpoint but an unending process.

The analyst firm IDC (2018a) proposes that the concept of "smart cities" is a construct for framing local government transformation so as to meet citizens' rising expectations; to develop sustainably; to improve resilience; and to attract investment, talent and new businesses. In other words, the focus is on what public authorities must do to smarten their cities. IDC (2018b) identifies that most spending for the near future will focus on intelligent transportation, data-driven public safety, resilient energy and infrastructure, visual surveillance, smart outdoor lighting and environmental monitoring.

While the IDC definition captures the direction of most smart city initiatives, it does not include the efforts made by the other players – whether organisations or individuals – involved. As we shall see, it is the co-operation between local (and central government) and a wide variety of organisations and individuals that may hold the key to smartening cities. We agree with IDC that a critical element is the effecting of behaviour change amongst all players, which in turn requires the extensive use of marketing research to identify current and likely future behaviours. However, the focus of IDC's work, which includes a smart city competition, is on identifying tens of use cases for smart city projects (and so implicitly for local government initiatives) and the information technologies that will support them. IDC (2018a) suggests that these use cases will support five strategic priorities: economic development and civic engagement, sustainable urban planning and administration, data-driven public safety, intelligent transportation and resilient energy and infrastructure.

The smart city and information technology

Much smart city research focuses on the information technologies that transform a city from *dumb* to *smart*. The technologies include big data (Wright *et al.* 2018), artificial intelligence and analytics, as well as new ways of collecting and transmitting data – the latter particularly important for enabling smart city participants to keep in touch with the smart city and the smart city to keep in touch with them, their activities and needs. They include sensors and mobile and wireless devices, including innovative use of voice and displays. A key aspect of smart city thinking is the requirement for openness of data, usually through an open data platform, such as London's Open Data Store, to support planning, operational management and citizen engagement. This is the topic of the case study presented at the end of this chapter.

One characteristic of a smart city is that it is a digital city, defined by Yovanof and Hazapis (2009) as a connected community using open digital standards and innovative services to meet the needs of governments, their employees, citizens and businesses, and where citizens are interconnected and share information easily. Smartening a city can help citizens carry out existing activities better, with less stress, but some researchers, such as Komninos and Sefertzi (2009), focus on how city smartening can transform the daily life of those in it.

Planning for smartening cities

Many city leaders have announced smartening plans to cut congestion, remove environmental threats, shift demand to off-peak periods, encourage sharing, make journeys easier for users and more effective or profitable for transport suppliers and encourage employers to ease congestion by being flexible about hours of work or working from home (IDC 2018a). Government support for making cities smarter, easier to live in and more environmental is strong. However, ambitions may clash with the realities of demographic change, regulatory complexity, business demands and budgetary constraints. While some forward-thinking employers are offering flexible hours and work locations, many companies and public-sector organisations are committed to fixed hours of work/operations, creating high peak loads and congestion (Korosec 2018). This is partly because when income rises, the demand for mobility rises faster, and when the price of mobility rises, most are prepared to pay (Dunkerley *et al.* 2014). Although as work in big cities become increasingly services work, with fewer workers and managers sealed up in factories and offices all day, allowing increased flexibility in travel-to-work times, workers may not travel less overall but may drive more – to local hotels for meetings, on the school run, to shops or to evening meetings. So, when regulators try to penalise mobility, demand stays.

Nonetheless, much progress has been made, best demonstrated by the winners of the IDC Smart City Awards for the United States (IDC 2018c). Cities such as London, Singapore, Barcelona and Bristol are cited as being the most advanced (Lofthouse 2018; The Institute of Engineering and Technology 2018). However, progress usually relates to what suppliers and cities are doing to handle the demand from the mass of travellers – see, for example, the US winner in the civic engagement category, Kansas City (AWS 2018). There is little evidence of approaches where individual travellers are an integral part of the optimisation.

Smart city innovation, platforms and ecosystems

Many innovations involving final consumers are enabled by transformative innovations higher up the value chain. Recent examples of this involve new information platforms, where one or more organisations create a platform with which other companies and organisations engage to change how they deliver benefits to the ecosystem in which they work. For such transformations to be successful, several conditions must hold, as follows:

- A supporting ecosystem must arise to facilitate the new approach (Stone 2014a). This often involves the creation of new business models (Stott *et al.* 2016) and, in some cases, moves by companies engaged in related activities into the area;
- Ecosystem firms must invest in systems and skills so that they can deliver (Stone 2014b);

- The transformation must offer an effective way of achieving objectives for different stakeholders;
- Customers for the ecosystem must not only learn how to use and then respond to the approach in sufficient volumes, generating sufficient value for stakeholders, but also to innovate themselves and become smarter in how they approach use of smart information to manage their lives as workers, consumers and travellers.

The transport industry has a strong appetite for embracing innovation, in areas such as automation, self-service and journey planning support. The airline industry has been among the leaders in all parts of the value chain, from airliner scheduling to sales. Some airlines use "dynamic pricing" on their websites and even "surge" pricing according to short-term demand (like the model Uber uses to charge more for rides in the rain or at rush hour). Technological progress has opened up a world of optimised journeys, of cars running on batteries and fuel cells, of driverless vehicles and trains, of sharing of vehicles (with or without drivers) and shared scooters and bikes and of digitally driven transport management.

On more advanced city public transport networks, users access transport information mainly via their mobile phones. Cloud platforms and open data approaches have allowed travellers to find ways to optimise any journey on a wide range of dimensions (time, cost, comfort, accessibility etc.). Transport providers, whether of mobility services or of the infrastructure to support them, are improving operational efficiency and profitability through collection, analysis and sharing of transport-related data, hosted in the cloud and available to app developers. Sensors such as GPS, gyroscopes, microphones, cameras and accelerometers are commonplace, whether in smartphones or transport assets. Their ubiquitous deployment is accompanied by software programmes for management, control, analytics and data collection (Bhoraskar *et al.* 2012; Nemati *et al.* 2017; Pires *et al.* 2016).

The change in consumer culture and its effect

A factor supporting city smartening is a change in consumer culture towards digital living (Ashman *et al.* 2015). Combined with and partly caused by the rise of many large (e.g. Amazon) and small online suppliers, and the switch to online selling by many established retailers and other product and service suppliers, this has transformed or is transforming marketing and indeed whole industries. These include financial services (Stone and Laughlin 2016), utilities (Stone and Ozimek 2010), media and telecommunications (Stone 2015) and many others, as well as leading to the demise or drastic down-sizing of many existing players or their absorption into other firms. The use of the customer data arising from this marketing transformation has changed the way customer information is used to drive marketing strategy (Stone and Woodcock 2014; Woodcock and Stone 2013). This transformation is a critical enabler of the smart city. Without it, many aspirations of local authorities to smarten their cities would be unrealistic. Citizens are generally used to giving high volumes of data, and using data provided by others, in their daily lives and understand the importance of acquiring and learning how to use the many technologies that enable them to do this, particularly smartphones and broadband. For example, Smart Cities World (2018) reported from a survey of 1000 US households that 6 in 10 American citizens are hoping to be a "smart city resident".

In an era where more comprehensive data protection provisions (e.g. General Data Protection Regulation, or GDPR) are being established, one limitation to city smartening relates to citizens' willingness to give the data needed (Finch and Tene 2018; Kitchin 2015; Taylor *et al.* 2016). If a customer does not wish to provide data (e.g. about their location or travel plans), the smartness of the city will be limited, as will the citizen's own quality of service from the smart city. For example, if a citizen is not happy giving data on travel plans, then they cannot be warned of when their plans are likely to be infeasible. Of course, they will – as with any innovation – need to go through a learning curve, and while early adopters may lead the way, being prepared to give data in exchange for improved planning information, others may take time to follow. Because the smart city is not a single innovation, and in many cases not presented to consumers as such, it is not easy to carry out studies on the acceptability of such innovations, although Transport for London's study of the value of open travel data, the results of which are presented subsequently, is a good example of what can be achieved.

Demographic factors may also have an influence. For example, Anderson (2018) indicated that lower-income Americans typically lag in technology adoption. A smart city ecosystem relies partly on the ownership of personal devices, whose diffusion is partly affected by affordability of the device.

For a smart city to work, providers of products, media content, infrastructure and transport equipment need to create more open applications which can interact with the many other smart products and services that are used in the day-to-day life of citizens. Citizens cannot be expected to stick to a single ecosystem. Open application programming interface (API) protocols that allow applications and systems to link to each other will make it more likely that a given information source will be incorporated into the citizen's personal ecosystem.

However, the previous changes have had some negative effects, for example, the rise in congestion caused by home delivery (Visser *et al.* 2014; Goodchild and Toy 2017; Pålsson *et al.* 2017). Bouton *et al.* (2018) estimate that this can account for up to 2–4% of a city's GDP. However, delivery to private addresses might be at an early stage of evolution. For example, the delivery of goods to cars is a recent phenomenon where parcels are placed in the car trunk of a connected (smart) car and remotely unlocked/locked by the driver via a pre-authenticated digital key provided by the parcel's owner (Arthur 2016). This allows delivery organisations to deliver outside usual operating hours (night-time deliveries) or ensure that repeat routing is not required, with more parcels being securely delivered each time. Amazon's experiments with drone delivery fit into the same category of attempts to smart the e-commerce delivery system.

Platforms, big data and the cloud

Platforms rely on the ability of users (whether business or individuals) to create, access and analyse very large amounts of data (or "big data") on a variety of devices, including ones which form part of the Internet of Things, such as sensors. The rise of cloud computing (use of a network of remote servers hosted on the Internet to store, manage and process data, rather than a local computer) has stimulated platform development, allowing data-intense platforms to support the delivery of better customer experience and service (Stone *et al.* 2017). The rise of platforms is driven by several transformative digital technologies. Social networks connect people globally and allow them to maintain their identity online (Woodcock and Stone 2013). Mobile technology allows connection to this global infrastructure anytime, anywhere. "Big data" allows collection, storage and use of massive volumes of data (Wright *et al.* 2018). Rapid progress in analytics and artificial intelligence has increased our ability to analyse these much greater data volumes.

The availability of third-party cloud capacity has facilitated the use of platforms where usage fluctuates greatly. This accounts for the rise of new cloud computing suppliers such as Amazon Web Services (2018), as well as cloud storage provision by existing suppliers such as IBM and Microsoft (Wright *et al.* 2018). This is a critical requirement for a smart city, where information processing loads fluctuate dramatically. Peak hour travel generates high volumes of data, whether in movements of citizens or transport assets or in enquiries about the performance of the assets (e.g. whether trains or buses are on time). Energy usage peaks in the morning and evening, while leisure and entertainment use peaks in the evening.

The discovery that platforms can transform an industry and create new profit opportunities has led to:

- Emergence of firms whose main business aim is the creation and commercial exploitation of a platform (Stone *et al.* 2017);
- Development of platform services by existing players, such as those cited previously.

Many smart city innovations are based on platforms, whether they are used to support interactions between organisations and citizens or between the many organisations involved in smartening cities.

The real-time city and big data

Hashem *et al.* (2016) overview the expansion of big data and the evolution of Internet of Things technologies that play a crucial role in smart city initiatives, allowing valuable insights to be derived from data from a variety of sources, sensors and devices. Townsend (2013) proposed that the emergence of "big urban data" produced by smart cities could offer significant opportunity for real-time analysis of city life that can offer insights that can enhance everyday living and transport decision-making and empower an alternative vision for city development, creating a new mode of urban governance, as well as potentially providing the "raw material" for delivery of more panoptic view of a city – one that is more "efficient, sustainable, competitive, productive, open and transparent". Townsend also warns of the politics and possible corporatisation of smart city governance and the use of technological lock-ins, plus the risk of creating more hackable cities. Al Nuaimi *et al.* (2015) note that various application domains for the smart city can be realised, provided that challenges around security are resolved and rigorous design and development models and methodologies are used. They also link this to the need for highly trained human resources and the need for support by the governing entities. Cheng *et al.* (2015) present an architectural overview of a working big data platform which has been deployed and integrated with SmartSantander (SmartSantander 2018). This is one of the largest smart city testbeds in Europe. It collects city data and then serves the results to a few real-time applications. They conclude that while many of its components can assist in offering timely and valuable inputs for smart city data platform designers to consider, it highlights the need to enhance the support of semantic data to develop better sharing of knowledge between different applications and improved data and system security.

The changing nature of mobility

The growth of high-speed, low-cost delivery services and low-cost, on-demand ride-hailing services has a significant impact, sometimes negative, sometimes positive, on city congestion and mobility (Qi *et al.* 2018). However, the data associated with these and other technologies can provide insights that enable regulators and operators to manage mobility services better and create transportation or logistics networks that serve users' needs better and in a more integrated way. They also allow customers/travellers to reduce time spent travelling or to avoid unnecessary travel altogether. This is important in cities such as London, where the population is growing faster than the additional capacity being provided in public transport systems.

Supplier or customer orientation in smart city development

In much mobility and smart city thinking, the main focus is the perspectives of city managers, public and private transport providers and technology suppliers to maximise the efficiency of the urban transport system by discouraging unnecessary private vehicle use and promoting more effective, healthy and environmental modes of transport, combining "push" mechanisms to reduce use of cars (e.g. parking space restrictions, congestion charging) with the "pull" of improved public transport service (more passenger-friendly stops, bike and ride, better walking routes). However, some initiatives, using the label "active travel management or active travel demand management", are starting to focus on the customer – the travellers and citizens themselves (Hu *et al.* 2015; Ferguson 2018; Petrunoff *et al.* 2016).

According to Merugu *et al.* (2009) the concept of incentivising behaviour through offering prizes has generally shown to be more effective if a small number of large awards are offered frequently rather than small prize awards. A trial was conducted by INFOSYS Technologies in Bangalore, India, in which commuters who took a bus during less congested periods (where there was more bus capacity) received credits, with commuters grouped based on their credit amount. The travellers changing their behaviour most significantly were entered into a prize draw for the highest amount of money, with other groups tied into four sets of rewards of declining value based on their evidence of behaviour change. The Bangalore trial led to a doubling of travel from staff during less congested periods and a 24% decrease in overall average travel time for all bus commuters within the firm, a change so significant that INFOSYS could remove several buses from service, with the cost savings of doing so more than covering the cost of providing the incentives (Merugu *et al.* 2009).

Barlow (2017) confirms that smart city initiatives tend to focus on the tangible benefits of lowering the high public costs of running a city, improving efficiency and reducing expenditures, while technology firms focus on combining advanced computer technologies, sensors, high-speed data networks, predictive analytics, big data and the Internet of Things. The result is solving one problem at a time, so services are vertically integrated but not horizontally integrated, provided more intelligently but not making the city a better place to live. Part of the problem is focusing on technology enablement rather than involving the citizen as an equal partner – especially when the citizen is also a key creator of data. However, there may be a consensus emerging among technology providers on this point. For example, IDC, in conjunction with Microsoft (Clarke 2013), confirmed that connecting systems and siloes is key to delivering an "outcome"-based digital transformation to address the challenges of the competition for talent, business investment, rapidly growing and aging populations, climate change and economic inequality and the digital divide. Clarke suggests starting with smaller, focused, department-level projects and growing, step by step, to a unified city ecosystem with a clear set of priorities having been defined.

Partnership

Partnership is key to solving the challenge of delivering an integrated smart city, as no single vendor offers a true end-to-end solution that can effectively cover devices, connectivity, data, apps and app development (Clarke 2013). Clarke proposes that cities should instead look to vendors who can help provide users with flexibility and customisation through their ecosystem.

McKinsey (2018) notes that while good management is central to smart cities, governments cannot manage all aspects of the ecosystem themselves, as private companies and residents play an active role in shaping a city's performance, while many smart city innovations are revenue-producing ventures from private-sector companies.

Mobility as a service

Mobility as a service aims to manage transport demand in a society that increasingly consumes products and services on an on-demand basis rather than "committed acquisition" basis (European Platform of Mobility Management 2017). For example, instead of buying a bicycle, one can be hired by the hour or shared. Instead of buying or leasing a van, one can also be rented by the hour. Pooling or sharing becomes viable. This applies in many service areas. For example, instead of subscribing to a TV channel for a long period, a subscription can be bought for a day. In transport, travellers become fertile data producers, as knowledge of their patterns of requests and actual use can be used to develop new services. For the approach to work in transport, bookings and payments need to be managed collectively, combining services from public and private transport providers in a unified gateway that creates and manages the trip, which users can pay for with a single account, with a fully integrated ticketing or charging system across all transport modes, requiring management of levels of service, financing of infrastructure and coordination across all provider organisations. However, there is a "trade-off" between maximising individuals' freedom to "travel" and the efficient operation of the transport system. For example, if a typical busload of passengers transfers to driverless cars or even shared bicycles, congestion may rise significantly.

The ecosystem

The smart city transport ecosystem can be depicted as in Figure 21.1.

The result of smartening a city is to create information flows *between* most of the players in the ecosystem and to increase the focus on the quality (e.g. comprehensiveness, reliability, speed of update, ease of access) of information *within* each player. The most important flows are between the three groups at the bottom of the diagram, supported by the activities in the top right of the diagram.

The other change which takes place with smartening is the introduction of platforms which host data arising from the different participants. At the top right-hand side, providers of information systems, services and data may develop from hosting for individual organisations to a situation where data is opened and shared between several organisations, such as in London's Open Data store. However, these platforms may also be created by independent aggregators, such as CityMapper (CityMapper 2018), who may in turn integrate forward into the provision of service, for example, the CityMapper bus service.

Flows of data in the smart city

A key characteristic of smart city evolution is the rapid growth in the depth, breadth, frequency, volume, quality, reliability and accuracy of data flows not just between public authorities and others but between all the players. Just as important is the integration of data from many different sources so that players making decisions can see all the data they need. A good example of this is the Santander smart city initiative in Barcelona involving combining many data sources on one platform on which individuals can access and analyse the data (Barcelona Ciutat Digital

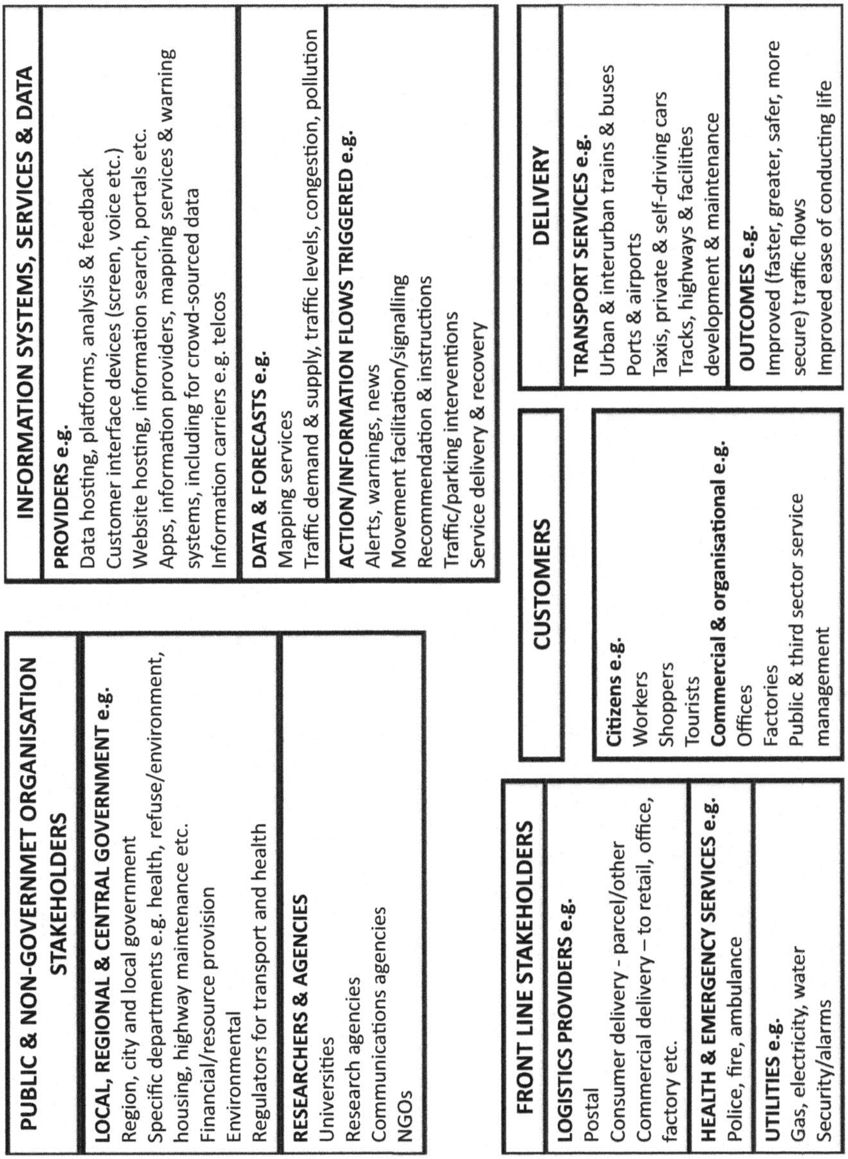

PUBLIC & NON-GOVERNMET ORGANISATION STAKEHOLDERS

LOCAL, REGIONAL & CENTRAL GOVERNMENT e.g.
Region, city and local government
Specific departments e.g. health, refuse/environment, housing, highway maintenance etc.
Financial/resource provision
Environmental
Regulators for transport and health

RESEARCHERS & AGENCIES
Universities
Research agencies
Communications agencies
NGOs

INFORMATION SYSTEMS, SERVICES & DATA

PROVIDERS e.g.
Data hosting, platforms, analysis & feedback
Customer interface devices (screen, voice etc.)
Website hosting, information search, portals etc.
Apps, information providers, mapping services & warning systems, including for crowd-sourced data
Information carriers e.g. telcos

DATA & FORECASTS e.g.
Mapping services
Traffic demand & supply, traffic levels, congestion, pollution

ACTION/INFORMATION FLOWS TRIGGERED e.g.
Alerts, warnings, news
Movement facilitation/signalling
Recommendation & instructions
Traffic/parking interventions
Service delivery & recovery

FRONT LINE STAKEHOLDERS

LOGISTICS PROVIDERS e.g.
Postal
Consumer delivery - parcel/other
Commercial delivery – to retail, office, factory etc.

HEALTH & EMERGENCY SERVICES e.g.
Police, fire, ambulance

UTILITIES e.g.
Gas, electricity, water
Security/alarms

CUSTOMERS

Citizens e.g.
Workers
Shoppers
Tourists

Commercial & organisational e.g.
Offices
Factories
Public & third sector service management

DELIVERY

TRANSPORT SERVICES e.g.
Urban & interurban trains & buses
Ports & airports
Taxis, private & self-driving cars
Tracks, highways & facilities development & maintenance

OUTCOMES e.g.
Improved (faster, greater, safer, more secure) traffic flows
Improved ease of conducting life

Figure 21.1 Smart city ecosystem

Source: The authors

2018). The SmartSantander augmented reality application uses open municipal data to provide information on mobility (traffic and public transport) and weather to users at many points, such as beaches, parks, gardens, points of interest and shops. The London City Dashboard provides similar information, including public transport status, weather, air pollution, news updates and traffic cameras (City Dashboard 2018). The Centro De Operacoes Prefeitura Do Rio in Rio de Janeiro in Brazil brings together data from surveillance and analytics, including data from 30 different agencies, from traffic to crowdsourced user data where algorithms and analysts process this in real time (COR 2018).

Such systems encourage data providers to make their data available and encourage citizens and others to use them. As the smartness of a city increases, more analysis can be carried out on the use of data, allowing data providers to identify which information is most useful and what gaps there are. Much of the information is provided by sensors distributed around the city, and as their number increases, more data becomes available on, for example, traffic status, parking availability or queues. If these sensors are primed to collect data frequently, or even constantly, the accuracy and reliability of the information improves. In the case of mobility, a sensor on each connected car, giving data on location, speed and local traffic conditions, can allow traffic planners to monitor congestion and as a result update information to other drivers in order to ease that congestion. However, as applications like Waze (Amin-Naseri *et al.* 2018) and the example from Rio de Janeiro show, this information may be provided on a crowd-sourced basis without public authority involvement (Batty *et al.* 2012; Jin *et al.* 2014; Farkas *et al.* 2015; Zook 2017).

Smart city grading

As cities become smarter, city planners and governments need planning tools to help them define their strategy and map their progress and to assess their project progress, while private-sector participants need to be able to assess commercial opportunities. We therefore propose a smart city information management model (Table 21.1), adapting the smart product and service model of Porter and Hepplemann (2014). It suggests how smartening of a city progresses through improved information management. As with all such models, there is simplification, with characteristics at each stage being suggestions rather than absolute criteria, but experience in other areas demonstrates the value of such an approach (Parnell *et al.* 2018) in terms of giving a sense of current progress and remaining targets.

The model examines individual assets and ecosystem members, showing the stage that a particular city has reached. It can be used to identify which information management changes are needed to smarten the city further and identify where new datasets are needed and perhaps how the data should be collected, stored and used.

One contentious point is whether the final outcome will be developed, sponsored and/or controlled by the city or by third parties, perhaps commercial members of the ecosystem. Here, a lesson can be drawn from the business model literature (Stott *et al.* 2016), by asking if the business model is of the city or of the city's public transport authority. For example, as shown later, Transport for London runs several different business models, as provider (underground rail services), contract manager (buses), regulator (taxis), road network maintainer (for some roads) and road quality auditor (for other roads maintained by the central government). In an age when much platform innovation is undertaken by the private sector, to the benefit of many private users, whether consumers or businesses (Wright *et al.* 2018), there is no reason smartening of a city should involve monopolisation of the information management aspects by city authorities, given well-documented problems with public-sector innovation and the relative success of

Table 21.1 Smart city information management model

	Suggested characteristics
Dumb	Several information networks exist, but they are not interconnected.
	Many stand-alone sensing and information access devices are in use, feeding into or taking data from individual networks.
	Assets (e.g. cars, buses, trains, highways, tracks) may have basic sensing devices, but these are used only by their own drivers/users or within their own networks, with no connection between these relatively "dumb" assets.
Awakening	Most important devices and assets are connected to a system, but systems are disparate and not connected with each other.
	Ecosystems (including app development) are evolving around the databases/platforms that support individual uses/applications, for example, rail transport, taxis, buses, parking, but they are not connected or at most connected to a subset of other ecosystems.
	Some data is being communicated between certain devices.
Smart connected assets	Assets and individuals are connected with each other over one or more networks and can be accessed from a wide range of devices, but connections are not always automated and may fail, and usability is an issue.
	Platforms and aggregators have emerged and are competing with each other to secure connection of individuals, organisations and assets by providing appropriate incentives, whether financial or service related.
Connected systems	All relevant assets and individuals are connected with each other through a variety of different systems, which members of the ecosystem can choose between.
System of systems	Aggregators now connect all systems at a meta-system level, but there may be more than one of these meta-systems.
	Apps have emerged to allow use of these meta-systems.
	The meta-systems may not be owned and/or managed by the city authorities.
	AI is used not only to optimise individual applications and situations but also to identify meta-level issues such as problems, gaps and so on.

Source: The authors

collaborative, participative and bottom-up approaches (De Vries *et al.* 2016; Arundel *et al.* 2015; Balfour *et al.* 2017; Torfing 2018).

As the experience of Transport for London discussed in the following shows, an open, sharing approach, with competition amongst providers of a wide range of information management services, may be the best approach, with the key role of the city authority being a regulator and standards-setter. In particular, it seems important to establish open application programming interfaces (functions and procedures that permit creation of applications that access the features or data of an operating system, application or other service), as in London and Barcelona (Namiot and Sneps-Sneppe 2014).

Transport for London case study

This case study describes how one of the world's largest public transport operations, Transport for London (TfL), transformed the real-time availability of information for its customers and staff through the open data approach and what the results of this transformation were. This study is based mainly on interviews at TfL and data supplied by TfL directly to the researchers. It describes how TfL makes data available through APIs, static data files and different feeds. This data includes live arrivals, timetables, air quality, network performance and accessibility, available under a version of the Open Government Licence, so it can be used for commercial and non-commercial purposes. TfL does not release personal or commercially sensitive data. Businesses such as Waze, Twitter, Google, Apple, Citymapper, Bus Checker, Bus Times and Mapway, as well as academics and professional developers, partner with TfL and use the data to create commercial and non-commercial customer-facing products and services, which passengers and other road users use to gain a better travel experience. Insights from the data can stimulate new ways of thinking at TfL, increase network demand and improve customer satisfaction.

The context

Urban public transport is part of a wider system that helps hundreds of millions or more people travel every day, whether as workers, tourists or shoppers. It attracts billions of dollars of investment by national and local governments annually. Innovation by urban public transport authorities is a key contributor to industrial progress and to the happiness and well-being of those who live in cities. In London, one of the capitals of the world's digital industries, hosting as it does the European headquarters of some of the world's top digital companies, there is an expectation that public transport management will take advantage of the latest in digital technology. It is TfL's task to ensure that it does so, particularly in the capital of a country where most citizens are comfortable with digital access to information. In this, it is helped, as are some other large city public transport authorities, by the fact that it reports to a single point of authority, the Office of the Mayor, which has few other direct responsibilities, so London's transport quality is a key indicator of the success of the elected mayor. This is against a background of questionable progress in public services innovation, not just in the United Kingdom but also in other developed countries (Kelly *et al.* 2014) and of a realisation that public service transformation requires a new approach to the use of public data (Peel 2017). In the United Kingdom, digital innovation tends to succeed more in public agencies that are relatively compact and very focused on delivering public services efficiently, for example, the Passport Office and the Driver and Vehicle Licensing Agency.

TfL's scale

Public transport services are dominated by TfL, the executive agency for transport in London. TfL controls most public transport, including the Underground, London Buses, Tramlink, the Docklands Light Railway, London River Services and the London Overground train network. It also controls most major roads in London but not minor roads. There are several independent airports in London, including the United Kingdom's busiest airport, Heathrow, the expansion of which will (if it happens) place greater demand upon London's public transport network. TfL is engaged in several major development projects, including the much-delayed Cross-Rail, which will link Heathrow to the centre and East of London, and possibly in the future CrossRail2.

London's public transport network is well developed due to continued investment, leading to a rise in underground and bus service capacity of 29% and 35%, respectively, in 2000–2017, and improved reliability of 47% and 46% for underground and bus. Network improvements have allowed London to rise above other large European cities in the public mode share, from being one of the lowest (24%) in 1995 to the highest (47%) in 2012. Satisfaction with the public transport network exceeds 86% across all modes – an increase of around 7% since 2009/10. The network also includes several national and suburban rail companies not controlled by Transport for London, whose major termini include Victoria, Charing Cross, Waterloo, Paddington, St Pancras International, Euston, Liverpool Street, Fenchurch Street and London Bridge. Bus services are provided under contract by several specialist public transport operators, such as Abellio, Go-Ahead, First Group, RATP, Stagecoach and others.

Opening of data in public transport

The opening of public transport data has attracted increasing interest from academics (Jäppinen *et al.* 2013; Hillsman and Barbeau 2011). One angle is analysis of ticket purchasing data or smart card use (Pelletier *et al.* 2011; Briand *et al.* 2017). Some research is in the wider context of the idea of smart cities, monitored and managed by pervasive computing, with benefits of reduced congestion; more cost-effective travel to and from work and leisure; and wider benefits such as improved lifestyle, innovation, creativity and entrepreneurship (Kitchin 2014; Bakici *et al.* 2013). However, until now, little has been published about how a city moves to opening its public transport data and the consequent benefits to stakeholders, from the passengers (whether leisure or travelling on or to work), to organisations and to the city overall. This is a case study of how London, more specifically TfL, opened its transport data to achieve a range of benefits.

TfL as information platform manager

TfL operates through several different business models, which include the following:

- Direct provider, in the case of the underground rail network;
- Customer, in the case of the bus contracts;
- Regulator, in the case of taxicabs;
- Infrastructure manager, in the case of most of the main roads and their signage and signalling.

Consciousness of the business model and the need to manage business model innovation is an important theme of strategic management thinking (Stott *et al* 2016). This Transport for London case demonstrates the emergence of a further business model, that of information platform manager. Here, TfL is part of a significant trend in which "real" businesses identify that one of their assets is information that arises from their activities, usually their day-to-day operations but in some cases their marketing activities, and that it must be managed as an asset (Stone *et al.* 2017), becoming a platform that unites the activities of an ecosystem.

The digital drive in London

The opening of London's transport data is part of a wider digital drive by TfL. This includes:

- A TfL website offering a full range of services (interactive travel and customer information, email messaging and ticketing services), optimised for mobile access and with on-system travel information provision via electronic information displays providing real-time, multi-modal travel information;

- Data openly syndicated to third parties, where this is commercially, technically and legally feasible;
- Digital marketing channels integrated with traditional media, wherever relevant to the target audience;
- Social media used on the TfL website, and engagement with relevant "off-site" communities;
- TfL digital collateral used to generate secondary revenue and to build strategic partnerships that allow cost-effective service delivery.

The syndication model is via the TfL website, using common licensing, processes and agreed-upon standards for electronic data, with self-service, plus bespoke support for key partners. Core information will be on the TfL website and on-system digital information. Additional TfL services are the mobile version of tfl.gov.uk, syndication of data and digital marketing messages. Third-party services are mobile applications, web services and live travel information on digital signage at venues.

TfL's digital strategy is as follows:

- Providing consistently high-quality user experiences in all channels and touch points, allowing fast and efficient interaction;
- Creating user interfaces that are consistent across services and channels and centred on the user;
- Quality of experience that matches customer expectations in the world outside TfL;
- Integration of customer experience across multiple services and channels, so the same task can be performed on different devices by customers or by staff in a seamless way.

Specific customer-related aspects of this include:

- Experiences can be continued seamlessly from channel to channel;
- Unified customer account for all services with a TfL ID;
- Shared information across all channels and services to serve customers faster and better;
- Each interaction always builds upon the last to save customers time;
- Staff empowered to assist customers with the right details at the right time;
- All customers registered where possible so that they can receive the best service and be notified of things they need to know;
- Push messaging in customers' channels of choice, tailored by customer preferences;
- Using TfL information to get the right message to the right customer at the right time, not overloading the customer.

The importance of innovation

The innovations visible to most TfL customers include the Oyster contactless payment card (and now the use of contactless payment cards of all kinds), the use of data arising from social media to provide information to customers and the use of data on the state of the network to make journey planning easier for travellers. The latter has been shown to be one of the top priorities of travellers (Beck *et al.* 2016). London is not alone in innovating this way – indeed, public transport authorities are known for their sharing of information on innovations.

The role of data

TFL aims to deliver its digital strategy by producing, acquiring, analysing, linking, sharing and using data to improve services, to keep customers and staff better informed and to focus commercial propositions by:

- Investing in storing, linking, analysing and sharing data to improve performance, reduce cost and improve service;
- Using the "Internet of Things" to supply data to power operations and customer services;
- Developing methods and systems to enable a single view of the customer;
- Using interfaces to make existing and new data available to improve service for customers and staff;
- Giving staff access to customer data needed to deliver better service;
- Continuously improving reference and real-time data;
- Providing data to a community of third parties to help address London's challenges, create new and innovative services, link information from different sectors and make things better for customers.

To preserve privacy, TfL explains to customers what data it has and how it will use it, while customers can control how TfL uses their data by giving them a choice of levels of data usage, tracking and control through a TfL privacy centre of information. Customers (and staff) receive information and can interact with TfL in their locations, devices and channels of choice, with universal access to an integrated suite of tools and services through popular web browsers, using native mobile apps for core TfL services on the key mobile platforms, a social media presence to deliver information, engagement and customer service and push notifications through the key messaging platforms.

The shift to customer focus and its information implications

TfL's customer promise, "Every Journey Matters", represented a big shift for TfL, from being a transport operator, focused on operational performance and efficiency, to a customer-focused operation whose main measures of performance relate to whether its customers get to where they want to go when they want to be there. It is, of course, an aspiration. London is one of the world's busiest cities, with – it seems – everyone trying to get to and from the centre in a few hours every day, many of them wanting to do it "their way", whether or not it would make sense to a "rational" transport planner – driving cars into congested areas, travelling when everyone else is travelling. It is the same in most cities, so transport networks come under pressure not just in the morning and evening rush hours but for most of the day. This can be exacerbated by policies with other clear benefits, such as encouraging particular customers (e.g. the young and the old) to use public transport for health and other social reasons (Jones *et al.* 2012, 2013).

The slightest glitch multiplies pressure on transport systems, so customers need not only to know when and where to travel and by what means (or "mode"), if all is going well, but also which Plan B to use when their preferred mode is not operating as they would like or as planned. They therefore need a full and free supply of information, perhaps when they are in a hurry or when moving between different modes or between two parts of the same journey by a given mode – changing trains or buses. The idea of a perfectly integrated transport system has long been in the sights of TfL but is hard to achieve, although customers appreciate the benefits of integration (Chowdhury *et al.* 2015).

A large urban public transport system is very different from an airline, which may have a relatively small number of aircraft arriving and then departing from the same airport. TfL's main focus is to keep the frequency and routes right and avoid delays. The need for this is particularly acute, as London's population keeps growing. If this growth persists with no change in transport habits, particularly use of cars, then London will become more congested, so the Mayor of London's Transport Strategy (2017) aims to increase public transport and foot journeys, that is, excluding car, private hire or taxi services, from 64% to 80% of all journeys by 2041, with the total number of journeys rising from 26.7 million to 32 million. This will be helped by digital technology reducing the number of journeys made to shops and increased ease of working from home. Digital platforms – smartphone apps or websites – help peer-to-peer transactions between those seeking information on or access to transport and transport service providers, including journey planners, car clubs and on-demand private hire, and, when operating in a network, may help travellers to move from ownership of vehicles to their use as a service. A critical step on the path to greater efficiency was to open data on the travel system.

Initial concerns

The journey to opening the data was not smooth. Many at TfL, an operation concerned with the safety and well-being of its customers, saw all the risks. What would happen if the information was not presented accurately or was presented late? What if it was plain wrong? Who would be liable? If there was serious misinformation and this led to overcrowding, who would have to manage the problem? What about the security risks? What about customers who were not connected? What about more vulnerable and younger customers? However, app developers were already downloading PDFs of timetables and "scraping" them to re-digitise the information, but timetables told only a static story of what was meant to be. In other cities and transport sectors such as airlines, opening data was the preferred option (e.g. flight location, planned and actual and forecast arrivals and departures). For TfL, it meant providing the location of every bus and train.

The first steps

The decision to open the information was taken in 2007. The team focused on how to do this in innovative ways, which is a central aspect of management at TfL. TfL first opened the data and then engaged fully with the high-tech industry, particularly app developers. A crucial part of this was the recognition that TfL was effectively a very large information platform, which "happened" to run a transport operation. This advanced view of managing operations is taking hold in many sectors, leading to probing customers' needs for information (including the many organisations that depend on making travel work – including other transport operators – and/or make money out of providing travel information in ways that customers want). Network Rail, responsible for data on national rail services, has followed a similar course in opening its data. Network Rail and TfL work closely together to provide information for journeys combining rail and TfL travel. The contracting bus companies also needed to be included.

TfL faced two choices – to provide all the information itself to customers or to open its information, which is used by at least 42% of Londoners, to any app developer who could provide the information to customers in better ways, on a variety of devices – computers, mobile phones, intelligent agents and so on. TfL chose the latter route, accepting that the public, who funded it, owned the data, and announced that it would be made widely available, as providing free open data was part of TfL's commitment to transparency and offering better products and services for customers. It would help developers use the data to produce innovative and valuable travel information and other apps for the customers. TfL would continue to develop its own resources, such as the Journey Planner and the live bus timetables, complemented by the emerging digital economy or third-party developers creating smartphone apps using TfL data. Some legal issues needed to be dealt with. For example, the terms and conditions for the use of the data were formally for personal use only, and this clearly had to be changed.

In 2010, the Greater London Authority (GLA) set up its London Datastore, the data in which can be used, re-used and redistributed by anyone. It can support operational service improvements and development of new customer-facing products and services, increase transparency and innovation and challenge existing ways of working. It now includes not only TfL data but many other data sets, including planning and employment data. TfL made over 80 data sets, including real-time travel feeds, available to developers via the TfL website and the GLA London Datastore. TfL engaged developers of apps and worked with them on the design of the API, allowing access to early versions and working in partnership to exploit the possibilities that the data provided. TfL's own apps are also important; TfL is particularly strong at apps which deliver accessibility for the 14% of Londoners who have an accessibility need.

Platform requirements

The platform had to be provided:

- Securely – so that it could not be tampered with and so that the running of transport operations could not be affected by unauthorised people;
- Equitably – so that every user had the same excellent quality of access;
- Reliably – so that the data represented the reality;
- In real time – so that the reality was the reality of the second, not that of a few seconds ago;
- Openly – so that anyone who wanted the data could get it unless there was a clear, undisputable legal, commercial or technical reason it could not be provided.

The data includes timetables and real-time tracking of buses and trains, congestion information and fares. The information is accessed about 10 million times per day and is updated at least every 30 seconds.

The timeline

Over the last ten years, TfL has become a leader in publishing Open Data through APIs, the cloud, the web and across its physical network, available to use by registered developers. The timeline for these developments is shown in Table 21.2.

Progress

By 2013, TfL had a new web site, hosted by Amazon Web Services (AWS), guaranteeing that high volumes of usage could be sustained. Amazon's strength lay in its own experience of extraordinarily high data volumes, including of logistics. AWS also hosts data for another UK public service agency cited for its digital innovation, the Driver and Vehicle Standards Agency (Illsley 2016). Other cloud providers are also used.

Migrating TfL's digital projects to the cloud has enabled TfL to become much more agile as it iterates new website and service designs in response to changing customer requirements

Table 21.2 Timeline for opening TfL data

Year	Milestone	Number of registered developers
2007	Embeddable "widgets" for live travel news, map and Journey Planner	
2009	Special area for developers launched on TfL website	
2010	London Datastore launched; additional TfL real-time feeds	100
2011	London Underground train location and Journey Planner APIs launched	1,000+
2012	Live bus arrivals API launched, full Olympic/ Paralympic Games transport data	4,000+
2013	30 data feeds, hundreds of apps on the market. Review finds TfL data saves up to £58m annually for passengers	5,000+
2017	80+ TfL data feeds covering operational and corporate information across all transport modes. Around 75% of data available via APIs	12,000+
	42% of Londoners use an app powered by TfL data; 83% use TfL website	
	TfL has data partnerships with app developers and digital partners, making its data available and receiving data back	
	Data is also made available via the GLA and data. gov.uk	
	Several hackathons held to engage with the community and receive feedback	

Source: Deloitte (2017)

(e.g. a rise in mobile and geolocation-based queries for journey planning) (Wentworth 2015). The migration has made it easier for development teams to access real-time streams of travel and transport data, bringing much more immediacy and higher granularity to its services. TfL has been able to deliver its high volume of interactive services by using AWS services as a buffer between its back-office services and customers.

Peak loads on the website can occur due to bad weather or rail strikes, which can lead to a 20-fold surge in site visitors (most in a single hour at the start of the working day). In the past, TfL would have had to over-provision, but now it can auto-scale on AWS, scaling usage down later, to get more efficiency. Prior to TfL moving to a cloud-based infrastructure, TfL was mainly limited to supply of flat files of data. There were few real-time feeds, and it was difficult to cope with releasing travel data to multiple parties at web scale.

TfL's move to the cloud has unified all its transport data (compared to before, where it was all on different systems, in different formats, in different parts of TfL). This has simplified developers' access to data and facilitated access to real-time streams in consistent formats they can work on. Data is supplied by TfL's own teams (those responsible for managing the services that collect or generate the data). They also become internal data consumers themselves (for TfL's projects based on this data) alongside external developer/researcher consumers in TfL's ecosystem. In some cases, vendors also become involved, where an API is needed to connect with back office systems.

TfL has found AWS's cloud platform very flexible. It can rapidly prototype ideas on its 20 development environments (where it previously only had 4) and replicate the production environment for parallel work to meet the dynamic demands of the business. This has much reduced time to market for new services (for example, being able to move to an entirely new cloud infrastructure for its Journey Planner engine in under two months). TfL has also experienced lower costs because AWS's services are paid for by the hour.

From its growing ecosystem of mobile app developers helping today's travellers get from A to B, to academic research teams helping TfL improve London's transport network in the longer term, TfL's open data policy has enabled third-party organisations to benefit from real-time, highly granular, high-quality transport data. The interest these parties have shown has created a quality feedback loop that has encouraged all data contributors within TfL to improve their data. The success of TfL's third-party app ecosystem has encouraged TfL to make a strategic decision to work more closely with developers.

Apps are the key

Over 600 apps have been developed, reaching millions of active users, although most usage is from a surprisingly small number of apps – just over 40. Live bus travel data accessed via these apps saves as much as £58 million a year by helping Londoners and the city's many visitors plan better routes and avoid long waits at bus stops.

How much does TfL know about journeys and customers?

Despite ticketing innovations (Oyster and other cards), TfL does not have perfect information on all the journeys its customers take. Many bus journeys are not tracked (e.g. for customers with paper Travelcards or where the ticketing machine fails but the bus journey continues). With bus journeys, information is only logged on entry, not leaving. Many journeys from stations with no barriers are missed – for example, by those entitled to free travel. So, the information must be supplemented by classic marketing research-based origin and destination surveys for TfL to meet its objectives of providing travel people want. This approach conforms with that of many public transport authorities, for whom marketing research is a central part of customer-focused innovation (Camacho *et al.* 2016).

An additional information source for TfL is social media. This was valuable during the Olympic Games, when 6 million people used Twitter to talk about TfL. Customers often message about the state of transport, and this ensures that TfL receives notification from customers very quickly.

Passenger flow information is important for another area, TfL's advertising revenue, which funds improvements in the service, as TfL is not a profit-making body. TfL has one of the largest advertising estates in the world, and it is increasingly electronic. On the TfL website, if a customer is investigating a journey to Oxford Circus, then relevant advertising can be displayed, using a programmatic approach to show relevant offers from retailers, for example. Of course, the individual's own data is not revealed, in observance of data protection regulations.

The role of marketing research at TfL

Marketing research is a critical element of customer insight at TfL. The following example shows how it has been used to identify cost-savings, but it covers everything from identifying travel patterns (not just by travel modes managed by TfL) and satisfaction with and attitudes towards the services provided by TfL, safety, information requirements and payment systems. The research is an important input into planning, for as an infrastructure provider, TfL must develop a view of likely travel patterns for a decade or so ahead, working closely with London's government.

The savings

The savings to individual passengers and businesses from opening TfL's data were assessed at £130 million per year (Deloitte 2017), increasing the estimate published earlier (Hogge 2016). The main savings are shown in Table 21.3.

Encouraging its own competition?

TfL understands that by opening data, it may create opportunities for competitors. For example, Citymapper launched a central London bus service using data on bus journey enquiries which users might think relates only to TfL. However, TfL's role is to improve every journey of its

Table 21.3 Savings from opening data

Savings for	Category of saving	Estimated annual savings
TfL passengers and other road users.	Saved time for network passengers on existing journeys due to better journey planning. More journeys taken. Unquantified – improved customer satisfaction from having accurate, instant information available.	£70–90m on existing journeys. Up to £20m on new journeys.
	Savings made from moving from SMS alerts – passengers can use free apps or free web services – a cost saving for those who used to use fee-based SMS alerts.	Up to £2m. Real-time alert services – up to £3m.
London employment, companies and other organisations.	London-based companies generate revenue from TfL data commercially. Job creation.	Gross value added directly and across the supply chain and wider economy – £12–15m. Around 500 jobs in London that would not have existed, 230 indirect jobs in the supply chain and wider economy.

Other savings for TfL include savings from not producing apps in-house, not having to invest in campaign systems, larger contact centres and publishing data and through partnerships with data and software organisations, receiving back significant data where TfL does not itself collect data (e.g. crowdsourced traffic data) and allowing new analyses to be undertaken. In the long term, improved transport products will be facilitated, including transport as a service.

Savings for citizens include improved lifestyle through increased likelihood of taking public transport because data is available, leading to a healthier lifestyle (more walking), with reduced congestion leading to increased cycling. Since 2007, the number of people walking as their main mode of transport has increased by 13%.

Source: Deloitte (2017)

customers and not to make a profit. If a third-party provider, whether Citymapper or Uber, adds to customers' choices, this might be regarded as good. On the other hand, having different bus companies compete can lead to excess capacity and more congestion and pollution, while taxi firms with poor quality processes can threaten customer safety.

Continuing improvements

Information continues to be used to make improvements for travellers. Following trial at 23 Tube stations in February 2016, achieving a 3–5% shift in the times at which people travelled, localised station demand information showing busiest times at each station and on the lines serving it was released for all London Underground stations. The data was launched as part of new functionality on Tube station pages on Transport for London's website. This was complemented with a social media campaign highlighting the busiest times at the 94 most heavily used stations, encouraging travel outside these periods if possible and suggesting alternative travel options, including walking and cycling. Passengers told TfL that they found this useful. Sixty-four percent of those who saw the campaign changed their travel. The busiest times for the River Thames Blackwall Tunnel and for key Dockland Light Railway routes were also released in 2017.

The near future

The future will be interesting, as TfL's status as a massive open data platform meant that the giants of the digital world, such as Facebook, Twitter, Google, Apple and Microsoft, take TfL very seriously. TfL met with these players in its digital partnership accessibility summit in June 2017 to identify how they could cooperate to improve the lives of their shared customers using TfL's open data. Building on several apps already using TfL's open data, major technology organisations, app developers and representatives from disability groups worked on the challenges together.

Trials are being carried out with Facebook on the use of bots. The area of voicebots is under wider exploration, given the success of voice personal assistants such as Siri, Cortana and Alexa. One focus area is disabled people. For example, Moovit, used by more than 60 million users in 1200 cities, has implemented features to help disabled people, including comprehensive VoiceOver/TalkBack support for visually impaired people and larger buttons strategically placed on the app's bottom bar. Moovit announced the most comprehensive route-planning service for London travellers with restricted mobility, such as step-free routes from street level to the train and lift availability. TfL is also working with partners and app developers to standardise features for users through consistent guidelines, irrespective of the app. In late 2015, TfL also began to hold "hackathons" with several London universities to see how TfL data could be used to manage the road network more efficiently.

TfL's open data API has been updated to include London's new cycle superhighways and the first Quietway. This data can be accessed by all app developers and mapping websites, allowing them to incorporate TfL's new cycle routes into their online mapping and journey planning information.

The long-term future – mobility as a service

TfL is examining the idea of mobility as a service (Jittrapirom *et al*. 2017). This involves moving from personal-owned transport towards transport consumed as a service, with public and private transport accessed via a unified gateway that creates and manages trips, which users can pay for with a single account, either pay as you go or on subscription. Services may include sharing of rides, cars and bikes and on-demand "pop-up" buses. Cars may be self-driving. This move involves combining different transport modes into trip chains using unified supply and demand data that allow users and providers to work together more effectively, focusing on mobility between destinations through all transport modes instead of forcing choice between competing modes. Without this integration, higher efficiency within modes can increase congestion, as has the rise of private hire vehicle use in London. Travel planning for customers begins with a travel planner not unlike today's, except that it shows options based on cost, time and convenience and allows combined booking.

Implications of the case study

This case study shows the closeness of the relationship between success in achieving strategic objectives (in this case for customer service) and innovating in information management. It also demonstrates how far the opening of data can be taken, benefitting both supplier and customer. It also shows the benefits when an organisation creates and manages a data platform which it opens it up to end-users and intermediaries, using a partner's high-capacity data hosting for where processing loads are subject to extreme fluctuations.

In teaching strategy, it is conventional (though becoming less common) to separate market-focused elements of strategy (products, target markets etc.) from information management aspects. This case study demonstrates the importance of an integrated approach.

The conclusion from this case study is that TfL's open data policy has significant benefits for London's travellers and the organisations that employ them or receive them as tourists or shoppers and for many others. The opening of the information has been key to these benefits, and as more data becomes available, for example, for the deployment of the Internet of Things, new application areas will be explored, such as improvements in ways of looking after London's growing and ageing population. The open data approach works particularly well in public transport in situations of high user smartphone adoption, increasing ease of access to data and savings from app development as well as trust. Until the approach was adopted, it was hard to estimate the benefits, so public transport authorities might want to take TfL as an example of what is possible in terms of outcomes and benefits and also as an example of how the benefits of opening data may be as large as those from major transport infrastructure development projects (Hogge 2016). Put simply, having a great leap forward in infrastructure may deliver no more benefit than allowing users to use data to optimise their use of existing infrastructure.

However, providers of open data must also be wary of how the market for the information that they are providing freely and openly may develop, to ensure that companies that derive an economic benefit from exploiting data do not try to capture the market for the information.

Conclusions

This chapter identifies that developments at the leading edge of information management as applied to smart cities and their public and private stakeholders may lead to developments which are either convergent, on publicly specified and possibly publicly owned data platforms, or divergent – with the emergence of different platforms, whether public or private, whether complementary or competitive (Schaffers *et al.* 2011). In this respect, the evolution of smart city information platforms may mirror those of information platforms in other digital areas, such as home shopping, insurance or media.

Issues

For those involved with promotion, development or delivery of smart cities, the implications are clear – do not presume that the centralising, controlling approach often adopted by governments for information management approaches involving many ecosystem players will work better than a more liberal, enabling but regulating approach. Providers of possible ecosystem platforms should focus on the benefits of all ecosystem players, particularly those who stand to benefit most from the smartening of a city, whether they be organisations or individuals. They should ensure that collaboration between all members of the ecosystem is established on a firm basis, with recognition that many players will need to forego prioritisation of their own interests in order to focus on the needs of the smart end-user, whether they be citizens or organisations. Those involved in the smartening of cities should use marketing research more widely and deeply to identify the requirements of citizens, travellers and others and to assess their perceptions of and satisfaction with changes made in smartening cities.

Acknowledgements

This chapter draws on the following articles:

Stone, M., Knapper, J., Evans, G. and Aravopoulou, E., 2018. Information management in the smart city. *The Bottom Line*, 31(3/4), 234–249.

Stone, M. and Aravopoulou, E., 2018. Improving journeys by opening data: The case of Transport for London (TfL). *The Bottom Line*, 31(1), 2–15.

References

Al Nuaimi, E., Al Neyadi, H., Mohamed, N. and Al-Jaroodi, J., 2015. Applications of big data to smart cities. *Journal of Internet Services and Applications*, 6(1), 1–15. https://doi.org/10.1186/s13174-015-0041-5.

Amazon Web Services, 2018. *AWS for Smart, Connected and Sustainable Cities* [online]. Available from: https://aws.amazon.com/smart-cities/ [Accessed 26 June 2018].

Amin-Naseri, M., Chakraborty, P., Sharma, A., Gilbert, S.B. and Hong, M., 2018. Evaluating the reliability, coverage, and added value of crowdsourced traffic incident reports from Waze. *Transportation Research Record: Journal of the Transportation Research Board*, 2672(43), 34–43. https://doi.org/10.1177%2F0361198118790619.

Anderson, M., 2018. *Digital Divide Persists Even as Lower-Income Americans Make Gains in Tech Adoption* [online]. Available from: www.pewresearch.org/fact-tank/2017/03/22/digital-divide-persists-even-as-lower-income-americans-make-gains-in-tech-adoption/ [Accessed 26 June 2018].

Arthur, R., 2016. *John Lewis and Jaguar Land Rover Are Trialing Shopping Deliveries Straight to Your Car* [online]. Available from: www.forbes.com/sites/rachelarthur/2017/02/03/john-lewis-and-jaguar-land-rover-are-trialing-shopping-deliveries-straight-to-your-car/#61a95f327f82 [Accessed 26 June 2018].

Arundel, A., Casali, L. and Hollanders, H., 2015. How European public-sector agencies innovate: The use of bottom-up, policy-dependent and knowledge-scanning innovation methods. *Research Policy*, 44(7), 1271–1282. https://doi.org/10.1016/j.respol.2015.04.007.

Ashman, R., Solomon, M. and Wolny, J., 2015. An old model for a new age: Consumer decision making in participatory digital culture. *Journal of Customer Behaviour*, 14(2), 127–146. DOI: 10.1362/147539215X14373846805743.

AWS, 2018. *Kansas City, Missouri, Spurs Growth with Smart City Analytics on AWS* [online]. Available from: https://aws.amazon.com/solutions/case-studies/kansas-city/ [Accessed 20 June 2018].

Bakici, T., Almirall, E. and Wareham, J., 2013. A smart city initiative: The case of Barcelona. *Journal of the Knowledge Economy*, 4(2), 135–148. DOI: 10.1007/s13132-012-0084-4.

Balfour, D. and Demircioglu, M., 2017. Reinventing the wheel? Public sector innovation in the age of governance. *Public Administration Review*, 77(5), 800–805. DOI: 10.1111/puar.12821.

Barcelona Ciutat Digital, 2018. *Barcelona Ciutat Digital* [online]. Available from: https://ajuntament.barcelona.cat/digital/ca [Accessed 26 June 2018].

Barlow, M., 2017. *Smart Cities, Smarter Citizens*. Sebastopol, CA: O'Reilly Media, Inc.

Batty, M., Axhausen, K., Giannotti, F., Pozdnoukhov, A., Bazzani, A., Wachowicz, M., Ouzounis, G. and Portugali, Y., 2012. Smart cities of the future. *The European Physical Journal Special Topics*, 214(1), 481–518. https://doi.org/10.1140/epjst/e2012-01703-3.

Beck, M. and Rose, J., 2016. The best of times and the worst of times: A new best–worst measure of attitudes toward public transport experiences. *Transportation Research Part A: Policy and Practice*, 86, 108–123. https://doi.org/10.1016/j.tra.2016.02.002.

Bhoraskar, R., Vankadhara, N., Raman, B. and Kulkarni, P., 2012. *Wolverine: Traffic and Road Condition Estimation Using Smartphone Sensors*. Communication Systems and Networks (COMSNETS), Fourth International Conference, IEEE, Las Vegas, 1–6.

Bouton, S., Hannon, E. and Knupfer, S., 2018. The congestion penalty from urban success. *McKinsey Quarterly* [online]. Available from: www.mckinsey.com/featured-insights/future-of-cities/booming-cities-unintended-consequences [Accessed 20 June 2020].

Briand, A., Côme, E., Trépanier, M. and Oukhellou, L., 2017. Analyzing year-to-year changes in public transport passenger behaviour using smart card data. *Transportation Research Part C: Emerging Technologies*, 79, 274–289. DOI: 10.1016/j.trc.2017.03.021.

Camacho, T., Foth, M., Rakotonirainy, A., Rittenbruch, M. and Bunker, J., 2016. The role of passenger-centric innovation in the future of public transport. *Public Transport*, 8(3), 453–475. https://doi.org/10.1007/s12469-016-0148-5.

Caragliu, A., Del Bo, C. and Nijkamp, P., 2009. *Smart Cities in Europe*. Series Research Memoranda 0048, VU University Amsterdam, Faculty of Economics, Business Administration and Econometrics [online]. Available from: https://inta-aivn.org/images/cc/Urbanism/background%20documents/01_03_Nijkamp.pdf [Accessed 20 June 2020].

Cheng, B., Longo, S., Cirillo, F., Bauer, M. and Kovacs, E., 2015. *Building a Big Data Platform for Smart Cities: Experience and Lessons from Santander in Big Data* (Big Data Congress). IEEE International Congress, 592–599. DOI: 10.1109/BigDataCongress.2015.91.

Chowdhury, S., Ceder, A. and Schwalger, B., 2015. The effects of travel time and cost savings on commuters' decision to travel on public transport routes involving transfers. *Journal of Transport Geography*, 43, 151–159. DOI: 10.1016/j.jtrangeo.2015.01.009.

City Dashboard, 2018. *Citydashboardorg* [online]. Available from: http://citydashboard.org/london/ [Accessed 26 June 2018].

Citymapper.com, 2018. *Introducing the Citymapper Smartbus* [online]. Available from: https://citymapper.com/news/1800/introducing-the-citymapper-smartbus [Accessed 26 June 2018].

Clarke, R., 2013. *Smart Cities and the Internet of Everything: The Foundation for Delivering Next-Generation Citizen Services* [online]. Available from: www.cisco.com/c/dam/en_us/solutions/industries/docs/scc/ioe_citizen_svcs_white_paper_idc_2013.pdf [Accessed 20 June 2020].

COR, 2018. *Centro de operações Rio* [online]. Available from: http://cor.talentstecnologia.cloud/ [Accessed 26 June 2018].

De Vries, H., Bekkers, V. and Tummers, L., 2016. Innovation in the public sector: A systematic review and future research agenda. *Public Administration*, 94(1), 146–166. https://doi.org/10.1111/padm.12209.

Deakin, M. and Al Waer, H., 2011. From intelligent to smart cities. *Intelligent Buildings International*, 3(3), 140–152.

Deloitte, 2017. *Assessing the Value of TfL's Open Data and Digital Partnerships*. London: Deloitte [online]. Available from: http://content.tfl.gov.uk/deloitte-report-tfl-open-data.pdf [Accessed 23 December 2017].

Dunkerley, F., Rohr, C. and Daly, A., 2014. *Road Traffic Demand Elasticities: A Rapid Evidence Assessment* [online]. Available from: www.rand.org/pubs/research_reports/RR888.html [Accessed 21 June 2018].

European Platform of Mobility Management, 2017. *The Role of Mobility as a Service in Mobility Management* [online]. Available from: www.epomm.eu/newsletter/v2/content/2017/1217_2/doc/eupdate_en.pdf [Accessed 20 June 2020].

Farkas, K., Feher, G., Benczur, A. and Sidlo, C., 2015. Crowdsensing-based public transport information service in smart cities. *IEEE Communications Magazine*, 53(8), 158–165 [online]. Available from: www.infocommunications.hu/documents/169298/1025723/InfocomJ_2014_4_3_Farkas.pdf [Accessed 20 June 2020].

Ferguson, E., 2018. *Travel Demand Management and Public Policy*. New York: Routledge. https://doi.org/10.4324/9781315204611.

Finch, K, and Tene, O., 2018. Smart cities: Privacy, transparency, and community. In E. Selinger, J. Polonetsky and O. Tene, eds. *The Cambridge Handbook of Consumer Privacy*. Cambridge: Cambridge University Press, 125–148. https://doi.org/10.1017/9781316831960.

Goodchild, A. and Toy, J., 2017. Delivery by drone: An evaluation of unmanned aerial vehicle technology in reducing CO_2 emissions in the delivery service industry. *Transportation Research Part D: Transport and Environment*, 61), 58–67. DOI: 10.1016/j.trd.2017.02.017.

Hashem, I., Chang, V., Anuar, N., Adewole, K., Yaqoob, I., Gani, A., Ahmed, E. and Chiroma, H., 2016. The role of big data in smart city. *International Journal of Information Management*, 36(5), 748–758. https://doi.org/10.1016/j.ijinfomgt.2016.05.002.

Hillsman, E. and Barbeau, S., 2011. *Enabling Cost-Effective Multimodal Trip Planners Through Open Transit Data*. (No. USF 21177926) [online]. Available from: www.nctr.usf.edu/wp-content/uploads/2011/06/77926.pdf [Accessed 20 June 2020].

Hogge, B., 2016. *Open Data's Impact: Transport for London, Get Set, Go!* London: ODIMpact. [online]. Available from: http://odimpact.org/files/case-studies-transport-for-london.pdf [Accessed 28 December 2017].

Hu, X., Chiu, Y. and Zhu, L., 2015. Behavior insights for an incentive-based active demand management platform. *International Journal of Transportation Science and Technology*, 4(2), 119–133. https://doi.org/10.1260/2046-0430.4.2.119.

IDC, 2018a. IDC *Government Insights: Smart Cities Strategies* [online]. Available from: www.idc.com/getdoc.jsp?containerId=IDC_P23432 [Accessed 20 June 2018].

IDC, 2018b. *Investments in Technologies Enabling Smart Cities Initiatives Are Forecast to Reach $80 Billion in 2018, According to a New IDC Spending Guide*. Farmington, MA: IDC.

IDC, 2018c. *Winners Named in IDC Smart Cities North America Awards* [online]. Available from: www.idc.com/getdoc.jsp?containerId=prUS43731718 [Accessed 20 June 2018].

Illsley, R., 2016. *Enterprise Case Study: UK's Vehicle Agency Becomes More Customer-Centric by Turning to the AWS Cloud*. London: Ovum Consulting [online]. Available from: https://d0.awsstatic.com/analyst-reports/Ovum%20Enterprise%20Case%20Study%20UK%27s%20vehicle%20agency%20using%20AWS.pdf [Accessed 23 December 2017].

The Institute of Engineering and Technology, 2018. *London and Bristol Crowned UK's Leading Smart Cities* [online]. Available from: www.theiet.org/ [Accessed 20 June 2018].

Jäppinen, S., Toivonen, T. and Salonen, M., 2013. Modelling the potential effect of shared bicycles on public transport travel times in Greater Helsinki: An open data approach. *Applied Geography*, 43, 13–24. https://doi.org/10.1016/j.apgeog.2013.05.010.

Jin, J., Gubbi, J., Marusic, S. and Palaniswami, M., 2014. An information framework for creating a smart city through Internet of Things. *IEEE Internet of Things Journal*, 1(2), 112–121. https://doi.org/10.1109/JIOT.2013.2296516.

Jittrapirom, P., Caiati, V., Feneri, A., Ebrahimigharehbaghi, S., González, M.J.A. and Narayan, J., 2017. Mobility as a service: A critical review of definitions, assessments of schemes, and key challenges. *Urban Planning*, 2(2), 13–25. DOI: 10.17645/up.v2i2.931.

Jones, A., Goodman, A., Roberts, H., Steinbach, R. and Green, J., 2013. Entitlement to concessionary public transport and wellbeing: A qualitative study of young people and older citizens in London, UK. *Social Science & Medicine*, 91, 202–209. https://doi.org/10.1016/j.socscimed.2012.11.040.

Jones, A., Steinbach, R., Roberts, H., Goodman, A. and Green, J., 2012. Rethinking passive transport: Bus fare exemptions and young people's wellbeing. *Health & Place*, 18(3), 605–612. https://doi.org/10.1016/j.healthplace.2012.01.003.

Kelly, S., Zahawi, N. and Kelsey, T., 2014. *Disruptive Innovation in Public Service Reform*. London: Reform [online]. Available from: www.reform.uk/wp-content/uploads/2014/10/Final_Disruptive_innovation_in_public_service_reform.pdf [Accessed 25 December 2017].

Kitchin, R., 2014. The real-time city? Big data and smart urbanism. *GeoJournal*, 79(1), 1–14. DOI: 10.1007/s10708-013-9516-8.

Kitchin, R., 2015. The promise and peril of smart cities. *Computers and Law: The Journal of the Society for Computers and Law* [online]. Available from: www.scl.org/site.aspx?i=ed42789 [Accessed 23 June 2018].

Komninos, N. and Sefertzi, E., 2009. *Intelligent Cities: R&D Offshoring, Web 2.0 Product Development and Globalization of Innovation Systems*. Second Knowledge Cities Summit [online]. Available from: www.urenio.org/wp-content/uploads/2008/11/Intelligent-Cities-Shenzhen-2009-Komninos-Sefertzi.pdf [Accessed 23 June 2018].

Korosec, K., 2018. *The 10 Most Congested Cities in the World* [online]. Available from: http://fortune.com/2018/02/06/most-congested-cities-worst-traffic/ [Accessed 20 June 2018].

Lofthouse, K., 2018. *London Named Among Top Global Smart Cities* [online]. Available from: www.business-cloud.co.uk/news/london-named-among-top-global-smart-cities [Accessed 20 June 2018].

Mayor of London, 2017. *Draft Transport Strategy* [online]. Available from: https://tfl.gov.uk/corporate/about-tfl/how-we-work/planning-for-the-future/the-mayors-transport-strategy [Accessed 21 December 2017].

McKinsey, 2018. *Smart Cities: Digital Solutions for a More Livable Future* [online]. Available from: www.mckinsey.com/~/media/mckinsey/industries/capital%20projects%20and%20infrastructure/our%20insights/smart%20cities%20digital%20solutions%20for%20a%20more%20livable%20future/mgi-smart-cities-full-report.ashx [Accessed 21 June 2018].

Merugu, D., Prabhakar, B. and Rama, N., 2009. *An Incentive Mechanism for Decongesting the Roads: A Pilot Program in Bangalore.* Proceedings of ACM NetEcon Workshop.

Namiot, D. and Sneps-Sneppe, M., 2014. *On Software Standards for Smart Cities: API or DPI.* Proceedings of ITU Kaleidoscope Academic Conference: Living in a converged world-Impossible without standards?), 169–174. DOI: 10.1109/Kaleidoscope.2014.6858494.

Nemati, E., Batteate, C. and Jerrett, M., 2017. Opportunistic environmental sensing with smartphones: A critical review of current literature and applications. *Current Environmental Health Reports*, 4(3), 306–318. https://doi.org/10.1007/s40572-017-0158-8.

Pålsson, H., Pettersson, F. and Hiselius, L., 2017. Energy consumption in e-commerce versus conventional trade channels – Insights into packaging, the last mile, unsold products and product returns. *Journal of Cleaner Production*, 164, 765–778. http://dx.doi.org/10.1016/j.jclepro.2017.06.242.

Parnell, B., Stone, M. and Aravopoulou, E., 2018. How leaders manage their business models using information. *The Bottom Line*, 31(2), 150–167. DOI: 10.1108/BL-04-2018-0017.

Peel, J., 2017. *Apps, Platforms and Government. Citizen 2020.* Jeffrey Peel [online]. Available from: https://jeffreypeel.com/apps-platforms-and-government/ [Accessed 20 June 2020].

Pelletier, M., Trépanier, M. and Morency, C., 2011. Smart card data use in public transit: A literature review. *Transportation Research Part C: Emerging Technologies*, 19(4), 557–568.

Petrunoff, N., Rissel, C. and Wen, L., 2016. The effect of active travel interventions conducted in work settings on driving to work: A systematic review. *Journal of Transport & Health*, 3(1), 61–76. DOI: 10.1016/j.jth.2015.12.001.

Pires, I., Garcia, N., Pombo, N. and Flórez-Revuelta, F., 2016. From data acquisition to data fusion: A comprehensive review and a roadmap for the identification of activities of daily living using mobile devices. *Sensors*, 16(2), 184. DOI: 10.3390/s16020184.

Porter, M. and Hepplemann, J., 2014. How smart, connected products are transforming competition. *Harvard Business Review*, 92(11), 64–88.

Qi, W., Li, L., Liu, S. and Shen, Z., 2018. Shared mobility for last-mile delivery: Design, operational prescriptions, and environmental impact. *Manufacturing & Service Operations Management*, 20(4), 737–751. https://doi.org/10.1287/msom.2017.0683.

Schaffers, H., Komninos, N., Pallot, M., Trousse, B., Nilsson, M. and Oliveira, A., 2011. Smart cities and the future Internet: Towards cooperation frameworks for open innovation. In J. Domingue, et al., eds. *The Future Internet.* FIA 2011. Lecture Notes in Computer Science, 6656. Berlin, Heidelberg: Springer. https://doi.org/10.1007/978-3-642-20898-0_31.

Smart Cities World, 2018. *Six in 10 'Interested' in Being a Smart City Resident* [online]. Available from: www.smartcitiesworld.net/news/news/six-in-10-interested-in-being-a-smart-city-resident-2180 [Accessed 26 June 2018].

SmartSantander, 2018. *SmartSantanderRA: Santander Augmented Reality Application* [online]. Available from: www.smartsantander.eu/index.php/blog/item/174-smartsantanderra-santander-augmented-reality-application [Accessed 26 June 2018].

Stone, M., 2014a. The new (and ever-evolving) direct and digital marketing ecosystem. *Journal of Direct, Data and Digital Marketing Practice*, 16(2), 71–74. DOI: 10.1057/dddmp.2014.58.

Stone, M., 2014b. Building digital skills through training. *Journal of Direct, Data and Digital Marketing Practice*, 16(1), 3–14. DOI: 10.1057/dddmp.2014.44.

Stone, M., 2015. The evolution of the telecommunications industry – What can we learn from it? *Journal of Direct, Data and Digital Marketing Practice*, 16(3), 157–165.

Stone, M. and Aravopoulou, E., 2018. Improving journeys by opening data: The case of Transport for London (TfL). *The Bottom Line*, 31(1), 2–15.

Stone, M., Aravopoulou, E., Gerardi, G., Todeva, E., Weinzierl, L., Laughlin, P. and Stott, R., 2017. How platforms are transforming customer information management. *The Bottom Line*, 30(3), 216–235. DOI: 10.1108/BL-08-2017-0024.

Stone, M., Knapper, J., Evans, G. and Aravopoulou, E., 2018. Information management in the smart city. *The Bottom Line*, 31(3/4), 234–249.

Stone, M. and Laughlin, P., 2016. How interactive marketing is changing in consumer financial services. *Journal of Research in Interactive Marketing*, 10(4), 338–356. https://doi.org/10.1108/JRIM-01-2016-0001.

Stone, M. and Ozimek, J., 2010. The challenge of new marketing issues in utilities. *Journal of Database Marketing and Customer Strategy Management*, 17(3–4), 188–200. DOI: 10.1057/dbm.2010.20.

Stone, M. and Woodcock, N., 2014. Interactive, direct and digital marketing – a future that depends on better use of business intelligence. *Journal of Research in Interactive Marketing*, 8(1), 4–17. DOI: 10.1108/JRIM-07-2013-0046.

Stott, R., Stone, M. and Fae, J., 2016. Business models in the business to business and business to consumer worlds – what can each world learn from the other. *Journal of Business and Industrial Marketing*, 31(8), 943–954. DOI: 10.1108/JBIM-10-2016-267.

Taylor, L., Richter, C., Jameson, S. and Perez de Pulgar, C., 2016. *Customers, Users or Citizens? Inclusion, Spatial Data and Governance in the Smart City* [online]. Available from: https://research.utwente.nl/en/publications/customers-users-or-citizens-inclusion-spatial-data-and-governance [Accessed 20 June 2018].

Torfing, J., 2018. Collaborative innovation in the public sector: The argument. *Public Management Review*, 21(1), 1–11. https://doi.org/10.1080/14719037.2018.1430248.

Townsend, A.M., 2013. *Smart Cities: Big Data, Civic Hackers, and the Quest for a New Utopia*. New York: WW Norton & Company. ASIN: B00CF2M9AA.

Visser, J., Nemoto, T. and Browne, M., 2014. Home delivery and the impacts on urban freight transport: A review. *Procedia-Social and Behavioral Sciences*, 125, 15–27. https://doi.org/10.1016/j.sbspro.2014.01.1452.

Wentworth, C., 2015. *Transport for London Creates an Open Data Ecosystem with Amazon Web Services*. Horsham: MWD Advisors [online]. Available from: https://d0.awsstatic.com/analyst-reports/MWD_AWS_TFL_Case_Study_Sept_2015.pdf [Accessed 21 December 2017].

Woodcock, N. and Stone, M., 2013. Social intelligence in customer engagement. *Journal of Strategic Marketing*, 21(5), 394–401. https://doi.org/10.1080/0965254X.2013.801613.

Wright, L.-T., Robin, R., Stone, M. and Aravopoulou, E., 2018. Adoption of big data technology for innovation in B2B marketing. *Journal of Business to Business Marketing*, 26(3–4), 281–293. https://doi.org/10.1080/1051712X.2019.1611082.

Yovanof, G. and Hazapis, G., 2009. An architectural framework and enabling wireless technologies for digital cities & intelligent urban environments. *Wireless Personal Communications*, 49(3), 445–463. https://doi.org/10.1007/s11277-009-9693-4.

Zook, M., 2017. Crowd-sourcing the smart city: Using big geosocial media metrics in urban governance. *Big Data & Society*, 4(1), 1–13. https://doi.org/10.1007/s11277-009-9693-4.

22

DESIGN, INNOVATION AND MARKETING RESEARCH

James Woudhuysen, Emmanuel Kosack and Merlin Stone

Summary

This chapter provides a critical overview of current theory and practice in design and innovation in area relevant to marketing research. It offers contemporary definitions of innovation and design and outlines three major challenges now facing the latter. It clarifies how information can best be shared between marketing researchers and designers. Focusing on the flows of information between marketing research and design, the chapter assesses the role of each in different phases of the process of new product and service development, as well as the changing role of marketing research during the maturation of an organisation's use of design. After looking at the credibility problems that now accompany marketing researchers' deployment of surveillance technologies and designers' fondness for their own version of ethnography, the chapter concludes by reviewing the role of the two professions in business-to-business IT and in public services.

Introduction: the expansion of design and getting the balance right about it

If Mark Twain were still with us and somehow represented the everyday practice, in studios, of mainstream design, he might very well repeat, in his immortal words, that the report of his death was an exaggeration.

What the general public understands as 'design' remains very much alive and of considerable moment. Take defective products in the United Kingdom. In just a few months, recalls of such products included a Philips baby monitors whose batteries presented a fire risk (Marcus 2020), as well as baby car seats, made by Norway's HTS BeSafe AS, that had faulty securing brackets (Fox, H. 2020). No fewer than 55,000 Hotpoint and Indesit washing machines assembled by Whirlpool were also recalled, because they could have caught fire. That was in addition to a previous total of half a million Whirlpool machines (Stevens 2020). Finally, many masks and gowns ordered for UK health workers as personal protective equipment during the coronavirus crisis of 2020 turned out to fit poorly.

It is all too easy to overlook such chastening facts – to ignore the dangerous mistakes still being made in basic electrical, mechanical and user interface design. Indeed other, less mundane, more ephemeral and ethereal conceptions of design are today preferred not just by many high-flying design academics but by a growing minority of practising designers. Marketing researchers, then, are not wrong when they suspect that some contemporary interpretations of design can be obscure, if not evasive.

Even before Covid-19, after all, specialist commentators on design attacked it for what one influential writer dismissed as "solution-ism" (Manzini 2016, p. 52). Design was held to be "moving beyond its entanglement with consumer culture and technological innovation towards actively reconstituting ways of living and being in ways that aim to be participatory, ethical and political" (Kimbell 2018, p. 145). Then, when the Covid-19 crisis arrived, others saw the turmoil as an opportunity to "embed design mindsets – empathy, co-design, engagement – within your workforce" (Drew 2020); for graphic designers to become artists, eschew "polished artefacts" and instead engage, once again, in "a practice beyond solutionism" (Gharib 2020); and for designers of urban signage to design street signs that delivered "sustainable wellbeing" (Sign Design Society 2020).

In the modish international design community, the litany continues of "going beyond" a fuddy-duddy past of products, solutions or "heroic, hubristic optimism". For many, that past now deserves ridicule or, at the very least, an "anti-heroic" approach (Kimbell 2018). Indeed, the renowned Dutch fashion designer and forecaster Li Edelkoort, confirming her view that Covid-19 was something to be grateful for, has seemed to call for *less* work for designers: speaking of garments and, no doubt, other consumer items, she wants "draconian changes", adding that there is "no way we can continue to produce as many goods" (Fairs 2020).

In an environmentalist spirit, the consensus among many leading communicators about and more than a few practitioners of design is profoundly hostile to companies using it to build business-to-consumer consumption. On the other hand, this highly dominant school is largely uninterested in the design of business-to-business products and services. It is a significant omission and one likely to become more significant. We return to design in business-to-business markets toward the end of this chapter, concluding with a look at design's new role in government-to-citizen relationships.

In design, grandiose pretensions are of course nothing new; designers have always had them. However, it is just here that we need to be careful, for the orbit of design *has* expanded greatly in recent decades. Circling first, for the most part, around products, graphics and the built environment, designers long ago moved out to encompass user interfaces and service processes as well. Going still further, many now believe that design should be applied to behaviour, obesity, humanitarian challenges in and the economic development of developing countries and the "socio-material policy objects" of governments (Kimbell 2018). Prestigious design consultancies, along with higher-level university degrees, have for some years enthused about "social design". By that, they mean design to aid the building of community coalitions (Brown 2012); design for participation and empowerment in a "new networking" of the individual, civil society, government and the economy (Museum für Gestaltung Zürich and Sachs 2018); and design for good, responsible design and design to change society (Jain and Vy 2019).

One need neither uphold these ideas nor imagine that design has really annexed artificial intelligence (Benton *et al.* 2018, p. 11). But one can agree that design has for some years played an important role in most, if by no means all, sectors in the economy. That is one thing. A rather different phenomenon is the claim, not always originating with designers, that "design" can be applied to business models, organisations and business ecosystems. This, surely, can only be true in a semantic sense. Nevertheless, it is argued that design can assist innovation in business models, permeated as these are with issues around the design of organisations (Foss and Saebi 2015).

At the top of the design of business models and organisational design lies the design of what one management consultant described, long ago but influentially, as business ecosystems (Moore 1993). It is certain that the metaphors James Moore used – "capturing territory" in a "new ecology" of Darwinian competition between "predators and prey" – were unconscionably naturalistic. Yet stripped of its many irrational elements, Moore's schema did anticipate one aspect of what has changed in business these past 30 years. Today's high-tech entrepreneurial venture, in particular, typically depends for its success on liaising with a clutch of external parties, whose knowledge it needs to absorb internally. Therefore, its organisational design may also need to include the design of smooth relations with its surrounding business ecosystem (Colombo *et al.* 2015).

Again, the issues can and should be debated. Some may fairly object that design stretches itself too far when it tries to include business models, the structure of organisations and business ecosystems. To take the design of organisations as an example: an organisation's employees are *not* simply "users" of its design. An organisation's customers *don't* really need its corporate bonds department to be well designed.

Nevertheless, the fact that design claims to have bagged something of these three targets does give an inkling of how its role has expanded – and how, in future, this expansion is likely to proceed further. With varying results, design continues to try to conquer more domains for itself. That fact alone reinforces how marketing research, for its part, may need to work harder to grasp the full importance of design. After all, despite the massive amounts of marketing research done over the years, it has plausibly been argued that corporations "still don't really know their consumers – or how best to connect with them" (Nussbaum 2004, p. 1).

Such a caustic judgement still applies not just to many companies and their relations with consumers but also to the public sector: to central and local government bodies and their relationships with citizens, businesses and each other. It can also apply to non-governmental organisations and the people who give them money or receive their help. Last, ignorance of consumers can permeate whole sectors. In their battle with live streaming media, for example, broadcast media have been widely charged with being out of touch with changing customer preferences.

An ingeniously designed business model *may*, however, be able to bring an organisation or a whole sector "close to the customer" (Peters and Waterman 1982, pp. 156–199). Accompanied, significantly, by adroit interaction design – keyboard-and-screen routines that make user trials, purchasing, logging in and refunds pretty convenient – the subscription "model" of Netflix has swiftly built the $20 billion company a large and loyal audience. Indeed, Netflix may even have designed, almost, reasonable relations with some of its actors, directors and business-to-business suppliers.

What comes out of all this is simple enough. Marketing research needs both to acknowledge the widening dominion of design and to take a critical but constructive attitude to the claims made for it – whether they relate to its outcomes or to its scope.

Innovation, design and how they relate

What, though, is innovation; what is design – and how does design figure in innovation?

Beyond the enormous literature that exists about innovation, there is also a sizable body of writing and research about how design can benefit it (Design Council 2018, p. 26–32). Design can be understood as an "integral part of the development and implementation of product or process innovations" (OECD/Eurostat 2005, p. 96), and as playing a key role "in the development and implementation of innovations" (OECD 2015, pp. 63–64). Others see it as "a human-centred approach to innovation that puts observation and discovery of often highly nuanced, even tacit human needs right at the forefront of the innovation process" (Gruber *et al.* 2015, p. 2).

Quarrels over how to define design have gone on for decades. The reasons are simple: though neither vague nor abstract, the practice of design is always an eclectic and movable feast. Being a social activity, design is, too, always a historical product: its goals, habits, cadre and required training are, at least as much as other professions, if not more, always in flux and always influenced by the prevailing context. With these facts in mind, Table 22.1 offers, for pragmatic purposes, some distinguishing characteristics of innovation and design.

Clearly these distinguishing characteristics can, should and will change again in future. To get a glimpse of how, marketing researchers need to resist the remarkably durable impulse just to *celebrate* the commercial merits of design. Coined in 1973 when he was chief of IBM, Thomas Watson Jr's adage, "Good design is good business" (IBM 2011) is still widely harped upon: an annual prize has been held around it for more than two decades (Architectural Record 2019). But if marketing researchers are to arrive at a less static, more practical conception of design, it makes sense to examine the *difficulties* that envelop the discipline now – difficulties that are likely to grow.

A trinity of challenges for design in the 21st century

There are three challenges designers now face: ways of making, complexity and credibility. The first two are intrinsic to design but now have a new twist; the last has only really emerged in the 21st century. The good news is that marketing researchers can help designers meet all three challenges.

Ways of making

Whatever the future course of inflation, firms and consumers will likely put a premium on radical and measurable cuts in the time and money bound up in getting things done. For the future of design, that has two implications.

First: new ways of making will have a profound influence on design for both goods and services. More than ever, customers and users will demand both low costs and great convenience;

Table 22.1 Some distinguishing characteristics of innovation and design (always provisional)

Innovation	Design
Exploits new ideas, carrying them through to	*Ensures that innovations become practical and attractive*
• New products and new services;	*propositions for customers and users.*
• New processes. With these, companies may be able to engage with customers and users better before, during and after the purchase or use of a product or service and at different stages in the evolution of customers and users, for example, those new to the category or to the provider;	*Deploys creativity to mould physical or virtual systems – including processes – in a human-centred way, despite and because of the fact that design processes, designed systems and their operational contexts are nowadays more and more automated.*
• New ways and structures of working, and – perhaps – whole new business models.	Recognises that customers and users adapt new products and services in use and can also assign new meanings to them.

Source: Based on Cox (2005)

at the same time, since Covid-19, the state is set to insist on "a higher base level of stringency" in the standards of hygiene that surround the making of products and the delivery of services (McCuillagh 2020). Altogether, designers will have to intensify their focus on ease of production and use – and, especially since Covid-19, on the culture, science and identity wars that now attend the production and use of everyday products and services. Designers will certainly be forced to answer more clearly: will the final outcome of your design be marked by maximum process efficiency and flexibility – including finesse in delivery, support, upgrades, maintenance, repair, disposal and so on? But designers will also be asked to clarify something else. They will be asked to account for *the reasons* they have adopted the ways of making that they have.

Second: different ways of making mean that marketing research will have a stronger role than in the past in identifying for designers which features of a product or service are likely to bring the most benefit to customers and consumers in general and to particular segments. In this light, both marketing researchers and designers would do well to acquaint themselves more fully with the history and price/performance issues covered by the long-established methodologies of value engineering (Kiran 2017).

Complexity

Profoundly linked to ways of making is the complexity of what is being made. Today, many design projects are intricate: they are about interconnected systems that are surrounded by rich and varied contexts of use. Bound up with this complexity are multiple interest groups, each of whose interests may not at all be the same, groups which, far from being "stakeholders" with the same stake in the same endeavour, typically have objectives that conflict (Woudhuysen 2012). Adding to all this complexity is the fact that different interest groups often work with different technologies which themselves require integration, both technically and, more importantly, socially. The example of mobile apps to help deal with the Covid-19 pandemic, and their implications for privacy (Chouwdhury *et al.* 2020), as well as for cross-border travel and for those people who do not own smartphones, is emblematic in this regard.

Today's system issues often extend beyond the direct competence of this or that design team. They often require new and clever methods of trying to satisfy not just customers and users, but also employees, suppliers and – especially after Covid-19 – state regulators. Of course, in their efforts, designers can build upon old systems, but these will have their defects. Alternatively, they can start afresh, though that can be a risky, dear and eventually unpopular course. Either way, design now operates on tough terrain.

Yet marketing researchers can help designers with each of these complex problems. The surveys made by marketing researchers of the current attitudes, behaviour and circumstances of different interest groups, of their beliefs, associations, passions and longer-term shifts in values, can furnish designers with insights that go beyond the trawling of different customer or user interactions.

Credibility

In the late 1980s, the CEO of Scandinavian Airlines System focused the attention of international management on particular "moments of truth" for customers (Carlzon 1987), especially on such moments during the delivery of services. Then, in the United States, around the Malcolm Baldrige Award for quality and an article by the CEO of Eastman Kodak (Chandler 1989), managers whose concerns related more to manufacturing came to be exercised by the concept of "customer delight" (Oliver *et al.* 1997; Barnes and Krallman 2019). Since those heady years, both moments of truth and customer delight have been an integral part of marketing and design discourse. In an IT-based multichannel world, complete with omnichannel retailing (Mason and Knights 2019), design has a key role to play with more and different examples of our old friend, customer touchpoints (Schmitt 2003).

In fact, though, the customer experience, encountered through a series of touchpoints, has rarely been "seamless" (Woudhuysen 2007) – let alone delightful. In the Covid-19 crisis, major IT companies, banks and government departments all kept users waiting, sometimes for hours. Since 2016, which saw the election of Donald Trump in America and the UK Referendum on membership of the EU, the narrative of customer delight has looked somewhat vulnerable. Pre-existing personal, tribal, lifestyle and political dispositions and identities, fiercely held by millions, have exposed corporations, media and governments to popular feeling, and in particular the feeling, that, in pursuit of "Wow" (Peters 1994) among their audiences, these institutions often fail, or at the very least fall lamentably short. The controversies in every country over the measures needed and taken in relation to Covid-19 confirm the point. Inevitably, these controversies find their way into design. In a commendably balanced report, one science correspondent wrote, in relation to guarding the public from Covid-19, the following:

> Are paper surgical single-use masks better or is a cloth mask OK?
>
> The evidence on any mask use, outside of surgical masks, is still emerging: there appears to be some benefit, but the exact parameters of which masks are the best and the extent to which they protect the wearer or those around them are still being figured out. A tighter fitting around the face is probably better, but the CDC suggests any covering, including a bandana, is better than none.
>
> One US study investigated which household materials best removed particles of 0.3–1.0 microns in diameter, the typical size of viruses and bacteria, and concluded that good options include vacuum cleaner bags, heavyweight "quilter's cotton" or multiple layers of material. Scarves and bandana material were less effective, but still captured a fraction of particles.
>
> (Devlin 2020)

In masks, as elsewhere, any design solution must now pass the test of credibility.

To some extent, we have been here before. On 2 April 1993, when Philip Morris was forced to make major price cuts in its premium product, a brief but quite impactful dethroning of brands took place after what became known as 'Marlboro Friday' (Blakemore 2018; Denton 2019). Yet if the rise of the sceptical consumer is quite a longstanding phenomenon (Eden *et al.* 2008), that kind of person is now a force to be reckoned with. He or she notices when organisations cut corners, deliver poor value for money, drop the ball in their service processes or, more generally, neglect to deliver on the promises they have made. Moreover, while the promises broken still concern practical matters, they also revolve, nowadays, around matters of ethics. Either way, and very often in both ways, these broken promises can create problems of credibility with the public.

Tomorrow's designers, then, need to help create innovations and experiences that do not over-promise, do not patronise and do not invade privacy. The challenge is to design systems that are inexpensive, unpretentiously simple, speedily and genuinely accessible, fun, and, if possible, transformative – whether for customer, user, company or public-sector body. The challenge is also to design systems that are credible.

This means that marketing research will more and more need to support design by analysing how *really* to delight customers and users. Fielding data on what customers and users have more-or-less recently claimed to need or want, after a limited number of them have struggled through a perfectly unbiased online questionnaire, will not by itself ensure the social credibility of a design. Designers will want marketing research to check every angle.

In the United Kingdom's Covid-19 crisis, some tubes containing blood samples for coronavirus testing often had barcode labels wrapped round them, rather than longitudinally. That meant they could not be analysed by automated means. Worse, because the lids on the tubes could be screwed on poorly, samples tended to leak (Davies 2020). These are the real and hard moments of truth for design, the ones with which the 2020s have opened. To help designers with them, marketing research will have to widen and deepen its enquiries.

The sharing of information between marketing researchers and designers

Over the decades, some major innovation projects have failed because of marketing research – most notoriously the Ford Edsel in 1958 (Hartley 1992) and New Coke in 1985 (Hartley 2013, pp. 77, 392). Nevertheless, marketing research has played a historic role in new product development, the development of new services and aiding designers engaged in these tasks. It is well known that, in the design process, research about a new product's likely markets is essential at an early stage if costly and time-consuming modifications are not to follow later (Cooper and Evans 2006, p. 68).

Traditionally, designers received valuable contextual information from marketing research people about market sizes and customer profiles. In the consumer domain, quantitative data – demographic, geographical, socioeconomic – allowed designers to turn marketing research intelligence into tangible product and service offerings (Cooper and Evans 2006, p. 69). The same was true in business-to-business markets.

Nevertheless, in business-to-consumer markets, the individualism of modern consumers limits the usefulness of traditional marketing research techniques, for though consumers look like they are the most qualified to discuss their current wants and needs, they are rarely as good at telling researchers what they are likely to want or purchase in the future – or to know what they want "on an abstract level" (Cooper and Evans 2006, p. 69).

Given the humanistic and future-oriented sensibilities that characterise the best designers, Calabretta and Kleinsmann (2017) are therefore right to suggest that, working closely and in a complementary manner with marketing research, design can do much to help organisations address these elusive but important wants. But there is more. In the world of IT, for instance, users typically both *adapt to and adapt new interfaces*. Users also *learn new talents*: thus, since the founding of Google in 1998, billions of people have found and continued to refine a talent for "search".

Developments like these confirm that, whether consumers, distributors, business clients, government units or non-governmental organisations, people are not just "customers" or "users" who can be researched from on high. People are also active human subjects, with aptitudes, skills, talents and improvisations all their own (Woudhuysen 2002).

That people are or can be autonomous agents, exerting a degree of free will, holds not just in business-to-consumer but also in business-to-business and government-to-citizen relationships. When, for instance, managers buy in aircraft components, or the expertise of design consultants, they will of course make decisions in light of corporate procurement budgets and practices. Especially after the supply-chain crises that attended Covid-19, we can also expect growth in the discipline of *design for procurement* (Brewer and Arnette 2016): still more design projects will bring in procurement teams, standardisation, suppliers and "supply base maintenance", as well as environmental considerations, early on in the new product development process. However, we can be sure that the managers engaged in all this procurement of goods and services are made of flesh and blood and not just of spreadsheets. They can be moved by the integrity of the designs put before them as much as they can be moved by the integrity of the supplying firm, its salesmen and its designers.

All this makes the sharing of information between marketing researchers and designers more important than ever – a sharing that must go one better than looking down on "target markets" together. And it would be as well to recognise that such sharing rarely runs smoothly. Marketing research may be unaware of or fail to understand the complexity of the design process and the kinds of information and knowledge that are useful to designers (Cooper and Evans 2006, p. 69).

Obviously, companies use Big Data to inform strategic marketing decisions (Tan *et al.* 2013; Fan *et al.* 2015; Kopanakis *et al.* 2016; Harkness 2016, pp. 111–115), including decisions about design. However, Big Data has complicated the flow of information from marketing research to designers. Because it describes today's multiplying and complex interactions between suppliers and customers and across business ecosystems, Big Data now offers such volumes of information that marketing research can have difficulty understanding and applying it – and especially applying it to design (Calabretta and Kleinsmann 2017).

What new kinds of information do designers now need from marketing research?

Technological and social change, together with burgeoning legislation, have created new markets and profoundly altered old ones. Alongside this have come new and sometimes intractable problems, fresh threats, but also fantastic opportunities. Such developments deserve innovative solutions. In particular, an organisation's business agility has for some years been seen as a critical imperative for management, and, with the usual disputes about it, as a significant part of management theory (da Silva *et al.* 2011). For example: Chinese scholars have recently underlined the role of business intelligence, a close cousin of marketing research, to business agility, finding it to have a significant influence on the speed of internationalisation of some 250 small and medium enterprises in the Yangtze River Delta area in China (Cheng *et al.* 2020).

To help fulfil the modern imperative of business agility, designers already use techniques such as computer simulations, rapid prototyping and 3D printing (Redwood *et al.* 2017). However, their newer requirement may be for something broader: for information which can allow systems and designs to gracefully undergo conversion to new tasks.

In this sense, a fourth challenge for designers may emerge out of the three we have outlined: that of making business agility real and credible, not just a matter of soundbites, in tomorrow's production of products and services and in tomorrow's processes of new product and service development.

In the Covid-19 crisis, new face masks, hospital gowns and ventilators were not just turned out by established suppliers of medical equipment but also and, it should be said, not without difficulty, by household producers based at home, by handbag manufacturers and by carmakers. Marketing research, therefore, looks like it will be asked to provide more and better information about why converting and systems and design to new tasks might be necessary and about how and where to flex – and to flex back.

The role of marketing research in three different phases of the new product development process

In a significant article, Wheelwright and Clark (1994) divided the new product development process into three phases – design, build and test.

In the design phase, a team responsible for new product development needs to frame problems as clearly and in as much detail as possible. For example, there might be a dilemma around the sound of the winding mechanism of a new, if conventional, camera, one caused by the type of material used for that mechanism (Wheelwright and Clark 1994, p. 34). In this phase, marketing research must really know what customers – in this case, photographers – think about a problem: do they want the noise of the winding mechanism cut out, so as not to alert the human or animal subjects of their shots, or would they rather prefer the mechanism's sound to be a satisfying whir?

In the cameras that come with today's smartphones, of course, one can turn off the artificial click that accompanies the typical shot. But what the example confirms is that designers need, from marketing research, plenty of high-quality information about how products are used and what users feel about them. The next step, before moving to the second phase, is to make – in sketches, drawings or cardboard mock-ups – several design options based on analysis of the relationship "between design parameters and customer attributes" (Wheelwright and Clark 1994, p. 35). In principle and very often in practice, these options allow designers and other team members to explore those parameters and attributes still further.

In the build phase, options are more fully created and scrutinised. To do that, they're translated into a physical prototype (Wheelwright and Clark 1994) and/or computer simulations that tend toward virtual reality. Using these, marketing research will typically obtain further data about human responses to different options.

In the final test phase, scrutiny becomes still more intense, turning to particular aspects of the design or to full-scale evaluations of it as a whole system (Wheelwright and Clark 1994, p. 36). The involvement of potential or existing customers and users becomes still more direct, since they can be asked to interact with more or less realistic prototypes and simulations and give their reactions; nowadays, they are often filmed while doing this. The results of this test phase will generally give even deeper insights into the mutual relations between different design parameters. Repeating tests is wise here so as to lower random results caused by fluctuations in the environment.

In all stages, Wheelwright and Clark acknowledged, the regular exchange of knowledge between marketing research and design, through rich and tight communications, plays an important role. Yet things have changed since they wrote. The imperatives of business agility, and the early involvement of customers, users and regulators, press hard. Much more than in the early 1990s, enquiries are typically pursued fast, in parallel, digitally and with varied interest groups watching and trying to have their say. Finally, in the future, we can expect more and hopefully less troublesome attempts at system and design conversion to new tasks than emerged in response to Covid-19.

Marketing research now marches, therefore, to a more compressed timetable in which there are more commanders making tougher demands. Throughout, it must plan for, acquire, analyse, apply and revisit data as that data arises in each phase of new product development. And yet in all the rush, marketing research should, at the start of each new each project, join with design to debate, in a realistic spirit, exactly what the benefits sought are likely to be.

The role of design in four different phases of the new product development process

Wheelwright and Clark's three phases of new product development highlight the information that marketing research should furnish for designers. At the same time, marketing researchers need to know that what designers do during the process of new product and service development changes, depending on just how far any particular project has progressed.

Throughout the process of new product development, the work designers do is typically multidisciplinary and iterative. It is important that, however much a cross-functional new product and service development team evolves, designers participate from the earliest possible moment and do so continually, from the beginning right through to end of the project (Micheli 2013, p. 16). Throughout, designers need not just to speak the language of the different professional disciplines gathered round the new product development table but also deepen their understanding of those disciplines.

On top of this continuity of approach, however, in the literature and more importantly the practical conduct of design, the processes of new product and service development are widely felt to fall into four broad phases. In Table 22.2, we use these phases to fill out our own, always provisional synthesis of some of the main tasks that fall to designers within each of the four.

By themselves, and broadly interpreted though they can be, the headlines for the four phases that detain designers in new product and service development – discover, define, develop, deliver – need prompt no dissent. Still, the contents of heuristic devices such as Table 22.2 can only be very malleable. Like definitions of design and the practical design process itself, the tasks of design are always be subject to revision, because they are essentially open-ended.

That is a key point. The methods deployed in a practical design process, like its priorities and allocation of people's time, are contingent on the apparent and real problem at hand. They are not formal or immutable.

For example, Design Council, a British charity, claims that its "double diamond" depiction of the design process is "universally accepted" (Ball 2020). This is an extraordinary claim. Such a scale of acceptance that does not exist even in Britain, let alone worldwide. In fact, that kind of acceptance *cannot* be the case among practising designers, who are renowned for the varied and idiosyncratic approaches they bring to their work.

To illustrate one important matter raised by Table 22.2: the *uses and meanings* that people attach to products can change over the years. As human subjects, users don't just adapt to and adapt many of the technologies that big companies introduce, as we have argued. Their views of *what a product represents* tend to evolve. Americans are no different. Over the decades, they have actively assigned several different, if often overlapping, meanings to the automobile.

At the outset, and even today, the car was a symbol of freedom and, in some ways, an emblem of citizenship. After 1945, for American teenage men, learning how to drive and going on to use cars formed an important rite of passage. But with a new century, President Donald Trump has attached a new meaning to cars, declaring that some were being imported "in such quantities and under such circumstances as to threaten to impair the national security of the United States" (Trump 2019).

In a speech to real estate agents in Washington, Trump named as villains Mercedes-Benz and BMW. Now, whether car designers at these firms can do anything about this is anybody's guess: perhaps they can make the grilles on their sedans and SUVs look less German, less aggressive. But in the light of the changing social connotations that attach to the car, Verganti was right to flag the issue of meaning in design (2009). Marketing researchers will need to redouble their efforts to get hold of design-related information around changed meanings, conflicting interest groups and fluid customer or user talents.

Table 22.2 How the tasks of designers change over four broad phases in new product and service development

Phase 1: discover	Phase 2: define	Phase 3: develop	Phase 4: deliver
Perform desk, market and field research into and collaboration with customers and users: know them, their contexts and the changing uses and meanings they assign to products and services.	Use insights gained in Phase 1 to redefine the new product or service development challenge.	Explore varied solution options through visualisations and prototypes.	Test and refine prototypes for technical robustness, effectiveness and how they align to or create current and future customer and user needs, contexts, meanings, trends and talents.
Liaise with R&D, marketing research and forecasters to register current and future:	Check for prejudices that the designer can easily introduce to the 'problem as taken'.	Estimate and assess how different interest groups respond to these options.	
• Internal, organisational capabilities;		Search out, accept and also develop or modify the creative inputs available from different interest groups.	
• External market rivals;			
• External trends and countertendencies in society, science, technology, costs and regulation (including environmental regulation).			
Question and re-interpret the brief or the 'problem as given'. Prepare for problems, solutions and interest groups to co-evolve through all phases of the design process.			

Source: Based on Verganti (2009), Harfield (2007), Halstrøm and Galle (2014), Woudhuysen (1996, 2002, 2012)

The role of marketing research in a four-step ladder of design maturity

An unstated premise of the narrative so far is that an organisation using design is conscious of the fact and knowledgeable about how to match the discipline to various opportunities and constraints. This, however, isn't necessarily the case. More than 20 years ago, it was recognised that, in many organisations, employees were often engaged in work that could accurately be described as design but were unaware of the fact; they were practising "silent design" (Gorb and Dumas 1987; Heap and Coles 2020).

In 2001, home truths like these led the Danish Design Centre, Copenhagen, to develop what it called the Design Ladder. The Ladder's merit was to highlight the evolution of companies' use of design over time – from the most primitive, unconscious, silent" application of it to its most sophisticated deployment. The higher up the Ladder a company climbs, the more deeply design is embedded in its culture and processes and the more benefits a company's use of design can bring. The Ladder, though, was based on a dubious hypothesis: that the more a company emphasised design in the early stages of new product and service development, and the more central it made design to its overall business strategy, the higher the *earnings* it would accrue (Danish Design Centre 2015, p. 2).

In a new century, many authorities drew a more or less direct connection between design inputs to a company and its outputs – earnings, turnover, profitability, the attraction of new customers or stock market performance (Design Council 2020; Candi 2009). The approach, too, still lives on today in the McKinsey Design Index, which claims to measure the "business value" of design (McKinsey 2018). It is a mistaken approach, given all the many and varied factors determine company performance: these efforts to quantify the financial effects of design maturity are reductionist and have been widely criticised for that (Heartfield 2005). Nevertheless, the qualitative insights of the Design Ladder are not to be sneered at.

After field research in Australia lasting nearly a year, conducted at a multisite 160-employee manufacturer of window frames, Doherty *et al.* acknowledged the Ladder's limitations yet allowed that it enabled different companies to be compared on a simple but on the whole undisputed scale in terms of their perspective on and application of design (Doherty *et al.* 2014). Figure 21.1 therefore depicts the four stages of maturity in a company's handling of design.

The following discussion of the Design Ladder summarises and builds on the work of Doherty *et al.* (2014) and also that of Kretzschmar (2003, p. 28). It should be noted that, as originally developed, the Ladder applied mainly to products and manufacturers. However, in

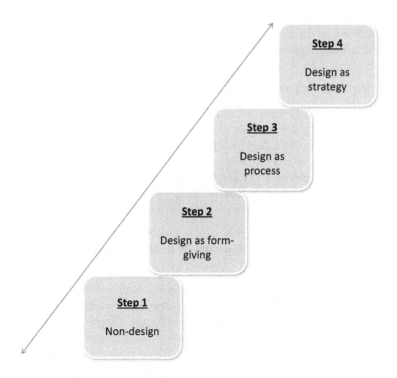

Figure 22.1 The Design Ladder: four steps up in the ladder of design maturity

Source: Based on Danish Design Centre 2015, p. 1

broad terms, it is easy enough to think through the Ladder's special and different implications for the way services are thought about and delivered. We should not forget that manufactured products have, anyway, for many years been strongly accompanied by services (Baines and Lightfoot 2013; Society of Serviceology 2018). For national economies, too, it has long been difficult clearly to distinguish between manufacturing and services.

Step 1: non-design – no systematic application

Here design's role is inconspicuous and not done by professional designers. It plays a marginal role in the company. Customers, users and others influence new product development in neither functionality nor aesthetics.

On this Ground Zero step of the Design Ladder, the skills of marketing researchers will usually play a purely negligible role in assisting such design as is going on in their company. Marketing research will bend its data on markets, prices and competitors to other tasks – not least, buttressing marketing communications. It will not be preoccupied with supplying the kind of information which might benefit design in new product and service development.

Step 2: design as form-giving, or style

Here the company does recognise that better product aesthetics can lead to greater acceptance by the market. However, work on aesthetics is still not conducted by professional designers but mainly by professionals in other disciplines. More encouragingly, at this step, marketing research does furnish information about target markets and audiences to help steer the professionals charged with working on product aesthetics. Marketing research may also be used to check just how acceptable the final design is to its potential customers. Nevertheless, marketing research at this level is still tactical in nature and pretty much entirely focused on the product.

Step 3: design as a process – part of the development process

A company moves up a further step when professional designers perform its design work and do so using design not just as a tool but also as a methodology. Here both design process and solution can and, as we argued earlier, must be equal to the task in hand. There is now a focus on the end-user and other interested parties, and a mix of disciplines is fielded alongside designers: process technicians, materials technologists, marketing specialists, organisational people and so on. By this time, marketing research deepens and extends its influence across the design of products and services and is brought into the design process at an early stage.

Step 4: design as strategy

On this, the final step of the ladder, professional designers collaborate with management in adopting an innovative approach to several of the foundations upon which the business is built. Design plays a decisive part in the strategic development of the company, tending to inform management's vision of the future and to try to improve the company's position in the value chain.

On this final step, marketing research is indispensable to both the designers and the senior managers involved in the design process. There is an urgent need for continual customer and competitor insights and also for specific insights before the design of a new product or service begins. On this step, marketing research works to ensure that the company's design processes and business model are fit for purpose.

In general, companies on Steps 3 and 4 perform better than those on the bottom two steps. Through many other and mediated causes, there is some correlation between a systematic approach to design and commercial results. That correlation may also apply to businesses which employ external design consultancies, instead of or more usually alongside an in-house design team.

The Design Ladder does not describe exactly how to integrate design into a company or how design should work with marketing research. The Ladder is not a framework for integrating design, as it only measures integration outcomes at an operational level (Doherty *et al.* 2014). Nevertheless, the European Union adapted the Design Ladder for its Innobarometer surveys for 2015 and 2016, which quantified the number of EU, Swiss and American firms at each of several levels that are quite similar to the Ladder's four (European Commission 2015; European Commission 2016; Abbasi *et al.* 2019).

Many other variations of the ladder exist (Melioranski 2015; Pettigrew *et al.* 2016). But once more, it is wise to be frank. A heuristic is only that – a heuristic. In practice, it can be hard to work out which stage a given company is really at: once Step 3 in the Ladder is reached, internal and often confidential measures, such as budgets for design, become relevant, not just external ones such as turnover (Björklund *et al.* 2018). Despite the limitations of the Design Ladder, marketing researchers would do well to have something like it in mind when they assess what kind of information it is appropriate and possible for them to put at the disposal of designers.

Two "technologies" of marketing research and design: credibility problems

In what it offers by way of scale, scope, detail and speed of access to information, IT has helped improve the insights marketing research has to offer designers. While the smartphone and the tablet have by no means eliminated the paper-based questionnaire, digital methods have increased the agility of designers in the processes of new product and service development – from conception and testing, through market launch and finally to the inevitable adjustments as customers and users take up, actively adapt and give new meanings to new products and services. Thus, Liu *et al.* (2013) show how designers value consumer opinions gathered online. In such surveys, the product features that inspire positive or negative consumer feelings can be identified so as to help designers evaluate the value of each from the user's point of view (Jin *et al.* 2016, p. 15).

The new IT has given impetus to some old technologies. Retailers, for instance, have long engaged in eye-tracking exercises to find out more about what catches shoppers' attention than what those shoppers say they are looking at (Nyukorong 2017, p. 5). In the living room, the technologies of TV audience research have grown more sophisticated. Outside the home, with automatic face recognition and the recognition of gaits, gestures and facial expressions, we can expect marketing research to offer still more and better information to designers about what people are like.

At the same time, with these marketing research techniques now comes the issue of credibility. How legitimate are they? How much will they continue to command the assent of an overwhelming proportion of the population? If we now take a second "technology", this time not of marketing research but of design, we can see some problems. Let's take design's use of contextual observation and ethnography.

It was partly the "pursuit of customer insights, specifically unaddressed and latent needs" (Luchs *et al.* 2015, p. 326) that powered the rise of contextual observation and ethnography in design. In particular, from the 1980s onward, designers' resorting to ethnography – in their hands, the use of personal observation, interviews and camerawork in the homes, workplaces and elsewhere – grew out of the considerable amount of research in the United States then going into computer-supported collaborative work (CSCW). This was research which pioneered much of the substance of what has become IT in the 21st century. Ethnography also grew out of the venerable Palo Alto Research Center (PARC) run by Xerox Corporation (Wasson 2000, pp. 380–381). However, as Wasson showed as early as 2000, some professionals working in the "hotly contested ethical terrain" of anthropology felt that getting hired for their skills by design consultants was "questionable, arguing that the field of design primarily exists to promote consumption". Wasson felt that there was a tendency for design consultants "to skimp on analysis" (Wasson 2000, pp. 378, 385).

To make a tiny contribution to the death of skimping, some of the factors that designers need to have information about for successful new product and service development are evoked in Figure 22.2.

Now, of course, like design itself, the ethnographic dimensions of design research should be investigated and brought to bear at the front end of the product development process if they are to have maximum effect (Rosenthal and Capper 2006, p. 233). In this light, data must also be communicated to designers in ways that allow them to transform it into consequences for the human senses: to be of any use, it mustn't be "too quantitative and sterile" (Cooper and Evans 2006, p. 69). Understanding, categorising and assessing the quality of the data collected in the

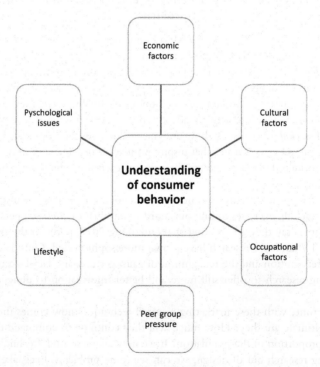

Figure 22.2 Some of the different kinds of information that designers need from marketing research

Source: Based on Cooper and Evans 2006, p. 69

cause of customer insight will be vital to marketing research. Likewise, for designers the important but difficult job will be to translate analyses of data into improvements to the value of their designs (Calabretta and Kleinsmann 2017).

Yet there is a change in the weather. Especially since the outbreak of Covid-19, society's concerns about privacy may ensure that ethnographic techniques, when wielded by designers, prompt nervousness on the part of those observed. Many people, after all, have already been "consulted". In the Covid-19 lockdown, quite a few neighbours were spied upon. At the time of writing, Ikea's French subsidiary and 15 individuals, including former executives and police officials, face trial on charges of spying on employees and customers (Agence France-Presse 2020). These developments augur badly both for surveillance by electronic marketing research and for ethnographic prodding by designers.

In saying this, we don't agree with overblown accounts of surveillance, any more than we would attribute bad intentions to design ethnographers. Over the years, under the influence of Bentham and Foucault, Western writers obsessed with surveillance have discovered *The Naked Society* (Packard 1964), rhetorics of surveillance (Levin 2002), *The Age of Surveillance Capitalism* (Zuboff 2019) and Britain's population passively "slouching toward dystopia" in its attitude to surveillance (Naughton 2020, pp. 25–29). There is little need for such familiar, rather paranoid visions. But precisely because these visions are quite popular, it is as well not to note that, with surveillance and probably with ethnography too, marketing researchers will, like designers, have some serious decisions to square up to in years to come.

The old ethical dilemma posed of designers, ever since the hallowed 1970s of Schumacher, Papanek, Illich and Commoner, was always whether to boost consumption, given that consumption was held, more or less, to be laying waste to the planet. But from the 2020s onward, there will also be two new dilemmas bearing down on designers. Hotly contested will be:

- The *ethic of progress* in products and services, for all the past's distortions of economic growth;
- What designers should do in terms of their *attitude toward democracy and the state*.

In their research and in their professional desire to assist, marketing researchers will need to know the lay of the land among their designer colleagues. Some designers will still be gung-ho for progress, however one defines it and despite all its excesses. Others will not. Some designers will be suspicious of the regulation of behaviour and design; others will not. And, as never before, designers will find themselves wrestling with the balance between supply-side technologies on the one hand and the culture, texture and power of customer and user demand on the other.

Technology push and demand pull: marketing research and design in business-to-business IT

How has that balance evolved, historically? From the late 1950s onwards, the propulsive powers of technological innovation were widely lauded in the West. European companies, for instance, fretted about a "technology gap" with America. However, in just two decades, the tide had turned (Woudhuysen 1977). From the 1960s onward, in the cause of measurable cost effectiveness in the procurement of weapons systems, the US military had pioneered a series of studies showing that demand-side factors, not just the results of basic scientific research, were important to technological innovation (Godin and Lane 2013).

Brief history of a debate

In the wake of the energy crisis of 1973/4, disenchantment with the bills, social consequences and environmental impact of high-technology projects, together with the uncertainties inherent in planning for continual scientific discovery or measuring a return on it, dampened down earlier enthusiasm for "invention push". Anyway, what was at issue was not inventions or patents but the much larger enterprise of innovation – of corporate and government budgets for R&D and competitive performance on world markets.

Gradually, sentiment shifted. A fertile British study found that the close involvement of users was a key to successful technological innovation (Rothwell and Teubal 1977). Theorists of innovation then slugged it out between push, pull and back again (Freeman 1974; von Hippel 1976; Rosenberg 1982).

Today the dynamics of technology push and demand pull are still subject to strong debate: they are complicated and vary by sector and country. Yet, though it is important not to be cynical about invention or blue-sky research, it remains famously the case that it was not Steve Jobs of Apple who invented "Gorilla glass", the very thin and strong glass on the screens of iPhones. That glass was in fact developed and made by Corning, but it was Jobs who spotted it and applied it to iPhones. His gift was to take an invention, use it to help in technological and design innovation, then bring the whole package to market (Isaacson 2012).

Over the decades, the balance of opinion about technology push and demand pull has gravitated toward the latter. Except for writers such as the late Clayton Christensen, a less ambitious capitalism has tended to put the accent on demand pull. One change for the better, though, is that, as mentioned, IT in principle allows designers to acquire fine-grained market information quickly. That enables demand pull to be geared to technology push more directly, and perhaps more productively, than in the past.

In the IT sector, tight feedback loops between suppliers and clients give marketing research its moment

The tight, new, IT-enabled feedback loop between push and pull is not as prevalent in business as some believe. Nevertheless, the business-to-business parts of the IT sector itself have always evolved through close synchronisations between suppliers and clients. In IT hardware and software, feedback loops between technology push and demand pull really have been tight.

In general, in new product development, the kick-off event in any new project might be an idea in a supplier's development lab or design studio, or it might be a client's expression of a need. But in the information technology sector, subsequent steps of development, testing and modification normally draw supplier and client closely together. In the German software sector, for example, the spread of stakeholder management and design thinking (Simon, 1969) among suppliers may have shortened feedback loops (Brem and Voigt 2009).

The tighter the loop between supplier and client, the more marketing research is likely to be in demand. But there is another fact to consider. It is typical of the information technology sector that, for example, both Intel (processors) and Microsoft (software) are suppliers to Dell (Kraemer *et al.* 2000). Each of these companies also has a range of other relationships. In the case of Intel, these are with all the other computer hardware companies which use its processors – as well as with companies supplying software products that depend for their functioning on Intel's processors. In the case of Microsoft, the software giant has relationships with many end-users, as well as with other software companies whose products run on Windows. In the case of Dell, relationships exist with all the companies that supply components and software for use on its computers, as well as with clients that range widely: from very large organisations, through distribution channels, to individual consumers who go customising their PCs for assembly by Dell.

These complex and often overlapping business ecosystems, if we are forced to return to the term, give marketing research a still more pivotal position to play – not just in quantifying potential markets but also in providing information on the big picture. To take an example: if one big business-to-business client in information technology is interested in an innovation, which others might be? Marketing research ought to and does answer questions like this.

Or, to take another example in the shape of Dell's Embedded Box PC 5000, launched in 2016, a "ruggedized" workhorse computer for industrial environments: Dell claims that it can operate 24/7, at temperatures anywhere between 0° and 50°. The machine comes complete with Intel memories and more than 30 ports, slots and LEDs. It also exemplifies silent design in the literal sense. To increase longevity, cut maintenance and reduce dust coming into it, the machine is fanless – so that it is also noiseless, something that recommends it for use in medical environments on top of industrial ones.

So far, so technology push. Yet as early as 2018, Dell gave evidence of where the big picture in client demand was pulling it – over to the domain of Chinese traditional medicine. In that year, Dell reported that Beijing Physicare Science and Technology, a high-tech specialist developer of appliances for traditional Chinese medicine, had come up with what that company calls a palm-shaped meridian detector – a device, built on Dell's machine, which applies 12 sensors to each of a patient's hands, measuring electrical currents and producing reports on "meridian status and internal-organ function" (Dell EMC and Intel 2018).

Whatever position one takes on Chinese traditional medicine and the diagnostic equipment that goes with it, Beijing Physicare Science and Technology's upgrading of Dell's IT hardware is a textbook example of modern demand pull and its influence on technological innovation. It also shows how the ecosystem of Dell's clients, and the designs into which the Embedded Box PC 5000 is itself incorporated, has expanded into a vast field of medical doctrine and practice largely unknown in the West.

When clients turn into suppliers

Marketing research has helped very advanced business-to-business clients push the frontiers of software and platform development (Cuatrecasas 2019). Indeed, one of Netflix's major systems suppliers, Amazon, was initially a client of Netflix but eventually became, through its software arm Amazon Web Services, a supplier to Netflix. There is also historical precedent for this: once just a buyer of ticketing and booking systems, American Airlines became a supplier of them through its Sabre Global Distribution System. This same process, often starting with modification of supplier systems at the hands of a client, is also extant in much smaller firms – hence the spread of user-entrepreneurs (Chatterji *et al.* 2008; Chandra and Coviello 2010).

The idea of users as innovators is not, as some claim, equivalent to demand-side innovation (Baldwin and von Hippel 2010; Priem *et al.* 2012) but more akin to demand-side clients for IT moving to become suppliers as they change their business model. One interesting study shows that shifting priorities, new market information or new partners can all make technology-push start-ups switch to a market-pull orientation. Conversely, however, other start-ups can just as easily swerve from a market-pull orientation into a technology-push one, especially when their experiences on the market side make them identify a need – whether that need is to improve processes and productivity, upgrade product specifications or meet a demand for complementary products (Lubik *et al.* 2013).

Despite, then, Silicon Valley's reputation as a kind of autonomous dynamo or Catherine wheel, relentlessly and "exponentially" spinning out innovations, the IT sector isn't all technology push. Although breakthroughs in electronics have made new products and services feasible, pressure from clients has also egged suppliers on. To repeat: clients for IT don't just have to choose between competing IT paradigms or platforms, for such paradigms "may also find their origin in demand conditions" (Van den Ende and Dolfsma 2005, p. 96). It is the same with RAM suppliers and computer manufacturer clients for random access memories (Kim and Lee 2009).

Perhaps unsurprisingly, flows of knowledge turn out to be critical in processes like these, and not just in the information technology sector (Antonelli and Gehringer 2019). Critical, too, are marketing researchers. Yet there is also a special role for designers here. We argued early on in this chapter that the decisions which characterise business-to-business demand-side purchasing and procurement are bounded by business context but that they remain human decisions all the same. Therefore, marketing researchers need to agree that the skills, sensibilities and research conclusions of designers in relation purchasers and users will be as useful to business-to-consumer projects as they are to business-to-consumer ones.

At any moment, the rapid diffusion of business-to-business IT may or may not be an indicator of pent-up or latent demand. However, in IT, as in other sectors, it may be more sensible to distinguish different historical periods in which first one side of the push/pull equation has the upper hand, then the other. From its inception, for example, IT enjoyed a long period in which the demand pull tended to dominate (1900–1960). After that, technology push came to the fore (1960–1990) and then, since 1990, a mixture of the two (Van den Ende and Dolfsma 2005). Thus, although the IT sector will always generate fine examples of pure demand-side or supply-side innovation, neither extreme forms the main route through which it has developed and will develops. Rather, symbiotic arrangements between leading-edge suppliers and leading-edge customers seem to be the norm. Around autonomous vehicles and advanced robots, for instance, what may count most are feedback loops of collaboration and information between technologists, those in charge of business models, customers and users, regulators and the leading client (Yun *et al.* 2016).

Complexity makes innovation and design hard work and conflictual

As a final caution against simplistic models of technology push and demand pull, it is as well to recall that the typical process of new product and service development has a "fuzzy front end" (FFE) in the sense that, at the start of a project, requirements and information are somewhat blurred (Smith and Reinertsen 1991; Ford and Woudhuysen 2012). In a longitudinal study of SNCF, the French railway company, and 52 different FFE workshops that it held between June 2011 and 2018 in the cause of radical innovation projects, Hooge *et al.* (2019) have more recently provided a useful typology of goals and simple-to-developed conceptual maps and trees with which to clarify the FFE. They also introduce a nice innovation in themselves, demanding that radical innovation projects search also for "the desirable unknown".

Their approach underlines how innovation is not, as much opinion has it, simply a combination of previous developments; it is also a way of exploring and testing out whole new ideas. Even the much-trumpeted advance of information technology is, in fact, like progress in any sector, typically has fuzzy beginnings and false starts. Innovation is a goatish mountain climb, full of uncertainty, hesitation and retreat. That's the fun and the progress in it. Yes, marketing researchers and designers should be fully involved in the innovation process, from soup to nuts.

But, if only because of the complexity of modern problems, that process is often accompanied by a fair amount of failure and chaos. Both innovation and design are hard work and conflictual.

It is well that marketing researchers grasp the nettle. In the best case, the one that is so much preferred by the literature, designers can prove to be good mediators between clients and suppliers, orchestrators and conductors of different disciplines, editors, ambassadors and cult heroes. They can be anti-heroes clad in black, even, working in a cooperative manner to improve value and meet all the challenges identified throughout this chapter.

That is in the best case. However, the attentive reader will have noticed that this chapter, in line with others, has designated the following disciplines and skills as factors that must, on top of design, be brought in early to the process of new product and new service development:

- Marketing research;
- Procurement teams, standardisation, suppliers, supply base maintenance, environmental considerations;
- Customers, users and regulators;
- R&D, forecasters.

This is many constituencies to have around the table. In such a sobering context, marketing researchers need to know that tomorrow's good designers may be "passionate" not about their or anyone else's brand but about wanting to disturb cosy client-supplier or client-regulator relationships – especially if they suspect that clients are hiring them more as a feelgood bauble than as part of a genuine commitment to innovation. In both their own discipline and that of design, marketing researchers can fully expect yet more passionate debates about safety, risk, uncertainty, rationality, fake news, the environment, medicine, statistics and information design from here on in. It will be less possible for innovation and design projects to have the occasional cosmetic component to them.

The expansion of design into public services and policy

So far, we have focused more on private-sector companies than on public-sector services. We now consider design in public, government-to-citizen services – first returning, though, to the opening theme of this chapter: the expansion of design, its merits and its demerits.

Back in the 1980s, what was known as user-centred design, much of it originating around the US IT sector, became an important cause for a liberal design community that sometimes felt harassed by the top-down style of Ronald Reagan, Margaret Thatcher, the stock market and the corporation. Widespread exasperation with clunky user interfaces in IT helped give designers the feeling that, in consumer markets, technology needed humanising – and that, in some ways, the skills of designers were superior to those of technologists.

Since the publication of *Change by Design* by the head of the prestigious design consultants IDEO (Brown 2019), what was once user-centred design became "design thinking", a collection of more or less articulated, design-focused tools for getting close to the customer and user and other interest groups: tools which managers in pretty much any sector could easily assimilate. Here we need not go into any detail about these tools, if only because, in formulaic ways, they are widely written about. They are also, and more recently, widely and severely critiqued (Woudhuysen 2011); after one foolhardy advocate on a *Fortune* magazine newsletter declared that design thinking could, applied to China's healthcare system and the country's wet markets, beat Covid-19 (Chandler 2020), he was subjected to ridicule (Levitt 2020).

Imperial overstretch and new targets for public services designers

For the purposes of marketing researchers, two issues deserve attention here.

First, in design thinking, we meet again what, in a geopolitical context, the British historian Paul Kennedy famously used to describe as imperial overstretch (2017). Thus, we find that the Youth Leadership Programme of the United Nations Development Programme (UNDP) has design thinking as its "foundational methodology". Funded by Denmark's Ministry of Foreign Affairs, its Innovation Facility has promoted design thinking as a way of bringing peace, no less, to the long war-torn country of Sudan (UNDP Innovation Facility 2017). More recently, in the Covid-19 crisis, the UNDP is proud to have worked with Nudge Lebanon and 70 other partners to design "nudges" to get young people over the "behavioural barriers" that prevent "hand washing, physical distancing, and self-isolation". Moreover, the UNDP has done this with only a passing reference to what most people might imagine is a more convincing province for design in the Middle East: namely several non-behavioural barriers, such as limited availability of water and soap (UNDP 2020).

Second, the UNDP's application of design thinking in developing countries is only a single international instance of what a distinguished university professor at London's Victoria and Albert Museum describes as new objects of design for public-sector innovation. Thus, while the old world of reified design objects has not disappeared, for Julier there has been a shift from design as output to the design as process – particularly in the public sector. Instead of being about outputs such as chairs, logos, posters or packaging, this design as process is about

> Walls of Post-it notes . . . matchboxes, Play-Doh and string, annotated with marker-pens, model neighbourhoods; sketch-notes on A1 sheets [that] expose the networks of issues; breakout groups of concerned citizens discussing their concerns . . . role-plays with civil servants and service users. Welcome to the new world of service design jams, policy prototyping days and design sprints.
>
> (Julier 2017, p. 145)

According to Julier, it is in the public sector that, defined as process, design "looks beyond the singularised object of design to map the user journey through a service that is made up of a series of encounters". Maps of that journey made of Post-its and Play-Doh pay attention to the "human, material, spatial and temporal relationships of the system or service . . . to the *situated* realities of everyday life whether these actually exist or are speculations" (Julier 2017, p. 145). This is an excellent description of the public sector's wholesale embrace of "the field of 'design thinking'. . . service design processes, co-creation, participatory design, design for community, design activism, design for social innovation and design for policy" (Julier 2017, p. 146). However, the idea that design must conceive of users by situating them in the varied contexts of use is no 21st-century breakthrough. Influenced by John Seely Brown – later director of Xerox Palo Alto Research Centre and subsequently the Xerox Corporation's chief scientist – American designers first began to absorb that idea more than 30 years ago.

Situated users and the location of value

Seely Brown published and still publishes widely. In the 1980s, he co-wrote articles, such as "Situated Cognition and the Culture of Learning" (Seely Brown *et al.* 1989), which had a profound influence on American designers – not just among those orienting to the classroom or to photocopying machines and general office equipment but also and especially, as we have seen, among those engaged in projects. Significantly, too, that seminal article was about teaching, a service very often delivered by the public sector.

Julier's is a somewhat breathless account of 21st-century design and public-sector innovation. After all, marketing researchers have long taken seriously the customer journey and the decisions customers make at points along it. However, marketing researchers should also recognise how much further expansionist conceptions of design still have to run – particularly in the public sector, and particularly with regard to . . . marketing research. For, according to Julier:

> there is a shift in the location of value here. Traditional and, if you like, twentieth-century conceptions of design regarded as putting added value into the object (by making it more attractive, more utilitarian or both). Instead, here, an evidence-base is used to understand 'value-in-use' . . .
>
> This shift in understanding value has a rich theoretical background . . . value is not inscribed in the objects themselves; rather it is mobile and contextual . . . the outcome of social processes such as its imbrication in everyday routines . . . [value] surfaces through its enacting in ways that are also configured by design itself . . . [value] comes into being in the right place at the right time.
>
> (Julier 2017, p. 146)

Just what this "evidence-base" consists of is, like the meaning of the second paragraph, none too clear. More important, the author's hip suggestion that there has been a contemporary shift in the location of value from production to consumption has everything wrong. In economic theory, that took place with the demise of classical political economy in the late 19th century, not with the rise of user-centred public service design in the early 21st.

With the fall of Adam Smith, David Ricardo and Karl Marx came the rise of neo-classical economics, and in particular the "marginal utility" school, whose starting point was accurately if quaintly described as "not the socio-economic relations between men [sic] as producers, but the psychological relation between men and finished goods" (Meek 1977). As espoused by Carl Menger and the better known – if widely reviled – figure of Friedrich von Hayek, this heavily Austrian school held that the value of things was determined not by the work put into them but rather was subjective, being determined by the degree of their users' appreciation of them – almost, perhaps, by the degree to which things prompted customer delight.

It is a beguiling gambit – this conviction not just that it is just the market, the consumer, that establishes the value of a product but also that this doctrine represents a new, if long overdue, 21st-century rebalancing of the theory of design and innovation. After all, the late, great historian of design, John Heskett himself, lamented what he saw as the delusions of those involved in the world of production and in the challenge represented by ways of making, complaining that today there are still many designers and managers who seem to believe that what they do and supply is the determinant of value" (Heskett 2017, pp. 80–81). Heskett too joined the consensus that the design, management, science, R&D, labour and technology push behind an innovation was of no significance to its value, which could be determined only in and by the judgement of the market.

The previous discussion should serve as a warning to marketing researchers seeking to help design for the public sector. It is true that public service users, like users generally, are always situated in particular contexts and that the use of a public service is not the same as its delivery. But it is also true that the discoveries made by design theorists betray a striking historical amnesia on these points. They forget, too, that users of public services are citizens, taxpayers, patients, recipients of benefits and more or less political animals, in ways that they are not when they are in conventional consumer roles.

Avoiding employees, annexing marketing research

The shift in the location of value that the neophytes unearth for designers largely absolves marketing researchers of the task of learning about the public service employees actually delivering those services. Instead, marketing researchers would need for the most part only to orient to the users of public services. Alternatively, insofar as workplace design in general and its delivery of "government services" is considered, the task for marketing research, as for design, is to orient to "employee *experiences, not just workflows and tools*" (Gruber *et al.* 2015, pp. 4, 5).

No Smithian division of labour need bother the workplace designer much here! In fact, the public-sector design that many commentators propose is a beast that marketing researchers may not recognise. With healthcare, for instance, it sets out to design not so much hospital environments and medical equipment for doctors and nurses to deliver the best possible care for victims of Covid-19 as to design the feelings of these professionals and, even more, the feelings of recipients of the care they deliver. It is a world where marketing researchers collaborate with designers but primarily around the "emotional labour" of service workers, especially around interpersonal moments of truth (Groth *et al.* 2019), the dignity of patients (Design Council 2015) and the psychological trauma involved for both (BBC News 2020). It is a world where, like a Deliveroo employee knocking at a comfortable home, Julier's value magically "comes into being in the right place at the right time".

Such a subjective and emotional reading of design for the public sector would, for marketing researchers, be a seriously skewed agenda to follow. It is one which public consultations and low-cost, low-scale, low-risk prototypes effortlessly overcome the silos between different public-sector agencies (McNabola *et al.* 2013) – even though, when endlessly repeated, such consultations have often strained the credibility of design. It is an agenda which is alive much more to the privatisation of public services through outsourcing or third-party provision (Julier 2017, pp. 144, 148–153) than it is to the subordination of private-sector services to the state or to the blurring of private and state sectors in the public mind. It is, finally, an agenda which can row back from the idiocies of Play-Doh design processes, recognise their "performative" or primarily theatrical function and yet at the same time hope that social designers can be made "accountable to their publics" and made, too, to adopt "a political agenda" for design that enables "transitions to sustainable futures" (Julier and Kimbell 2019).

On the other hand, and despite the fashion for Green Deals (Mazzucato 2019) and Green New Deals, this agenda for public-sector design rarely imagines that it might consider artefactual products, industrial policy, high-speed trains, ports, meals on wheels, the design of care-homes or that bound up with what are dismissed as "megaprojects" – vanity projects – in civil engineering (Woudhuysen 2016).

Conclusion: what design's conquest of the public sector tells us about the future of marketing research

Marketing researchers need to know that the public sector has not so much adopted design and design thinking as has a generation of youngish graduates in social design, design thinking and behavioural science invaded senior management in the public sector, only to be shaken by the hand – if only because this latter group feels its own crisis of credibility with the public and, not least, with its employees.

In its winner-takes-all conquest of the public sector, design's concerns have become public policy, nudging and mass observation. Perhaps all this is proper; yet, previously, marketing researchers probably imagined that such domains formed a province of their own kingdom not that of designers. Already it is clear, too, that several of the capabilities that designers need to do their job well, such as a focus on customers and experience of ethnography, relate closely to the world of marketing research (Hernandez *et al.* 2017).

Marketing researchers, on your guard! Already, today's theorists of public-sector design have made the "service-dominant logic" of Vargo and Lusch their own territory to have and to hold. They enthuse, in a one-sided manner, about the shift away from tangibles toward intangibles (Vargo and Lusch 2004a, p. 15). They are troubled neither by their two heroes' hatred of manufacturing (Vargo and Lusch 2004b), nor by the people who inspire Vargo and Lusch – the Reverend Thomas Malthus, Hayek (again), the deep Green author Paul Hawken, the Green consultants Amory and L Hunter Lovins of the Rocky Mountain Institute and the Green Democratic party guru Jeremy Rifkin.

No. The visionaries of design and design thinking will plunge on still further, insisting that Vargo and Lusch's obscure category of "operant resources" – workers – is vital after all (Klaus *et al.* 2013). But in practice it is the micromanagement of the minute-to-minute everyday life of "consumers", for the unassailable reasons of sustainability and disease control, that will preoccupy designers for a few years to come.

The Covid-19 crisis has confirmed that much government-to-citizen work is based upon documentation and information, the communication of policy and detailed, multi-page and constantly changing requirements for compliance – how to obtain a benefit, how to stay within the law. This kind of information design requires a strong focus on research into how citizens obtain, use, adapt to and also alter information: for instance, particularly in relation to health-related anxiety, reassuring the public may not actually reassure (particularly once a quantifiable danger has passed) but rather promote distress (Wessely and Daniels 2020).

Still, the better kind of public documents today are no longer static, uncreative and unengaging. When form triumphs over content, of course, public information design still remains unclear. Nevertheless, storytelling can be a powerful technique here (Stone *et al.* 2015), even if, in the wrong hands, it can carry a whiff of a "Jack and Jill" approach to explanation.

Marketing researchers should be under no illusions. Many design theorists would like to turn government-to-citizen, public-sector design and every avenue of design into one big instruction manual for how to meet, greet, walk, run, drive, use transport systems, shop, cook, eat, pursue leisure and work and indeed think (Fox, C. 2020). These theorists will always struggle to put altruism, safety and victims first, with the personal freedoms of citizens, the taking of risks, technological innovation and the active human subject coming a weak second. There is a place for altruism, safety and victims. However, should today's design theorists meet with complete success, it would be a bad day not just for innovation and design but also for marketing research.

References

Abbasi, M., Cullen, J., Li, C., Molinari, F., Morelli, N., Rausell, P., Simeone, L., Stergioulas, L., Tosoni, L. and Van Dam, K., 2019. A triplet under focus: Innovation, design and the city. In G. Concilio and I. Tosoni, eds. *Innovation Capacity and the City*. New York: Springer Briefs in Applied Sciences and Technology, 15–41. https://doi.org/10.1007/978-3-030-00123-0_2.

Agence France-Presse, 2020. Ikea France to face trial over claims it spied on staff and customers. *The Guardian*, 14 May [online]. Available from: www.theguardian.com/world/2020/may/14/ikea-france-to-face-trial-over-claims-it-spied-on-staff-and-customers [Accessed 1 June 2020].

Antonelli, C. and Gehringer, A., 2019. Competent demand-pull and technological flows within sectoral systems: The evidence on differences within Europe. *Cambridge Journal of Economics*, 43(6), 1525–1547. https://doi.org/10.1093/cje/bez002.

Architectural Record, 2019. Good design is good business. *Architectural Record*, 3 June [online]. Available from: www.architecturalrecord.com/articles/14109-good-design-is-good-business-2019 [Accessed 19 May 2020].

Baines, T. and Lightfoot, H., 2013. *Made to Serve: How Manufacturers Can Compete Through Servitization and Product Service Systems*. Chichester: Wiley.

Baldwin, C. and von Hippel, E., 2010. *Modeling a Paradigm Shift: From Producer Innovation to User and Open Collaborative Innovation*. Working Paper 4764–09, MIT Sloan School of Management, Cambridge, MA. https://dx.doi.org/10.2139/ssrn.1502864.

Ball, J., 2020. The double diamond: A universally accepted depiction of the design process. *Design Council* [online]. Available from: www.designcouncil.org.uk/news-opinion/double-diamond-universally-accepted-depiction-design-process [Accessed 19 May 2020].

Barnes, D. and Krallman, A., 2019. Customer delight: A review and agenda for research. *Journal of Marketing Theory and Practice*, 27(2), 174–195. https://doi.org/10.1080/10696679.2019.1577686.

BBC News, 2020. Coronavirus: NHS staff being offered trauma therapy. *BBC News*, 12 May [online]. Available from: www.bbc.co.uk/news/uk-england-birmingham-52630208 [Accessed 19 May 2020].

Benton, S., Miller, S. and Reid, S., 2018. The design economy 2018. *Design Council*. Enterprise Research Centre, BMG Research, BOP Consulting [online]. Available from: www.designcouncil.org.uk/resources/report/design-economy-2018 [Accessed 19 May 2020].

Björklund, T., Hannukainen, P. and Manninen, T., 2018. *Measuring the Impact of Design, Service Design and Design Thinking in Organizations on Different Maturity Levels*. Service Design Proof of Concept, Proceedings of the ServDes, 2018 Conference, Linköping University Electronic Press, Milano, 500–511 [online]. Available from: www.ep.liu.se/ecp/150/040/ecp18150040.pdf [Accessed 27 November 2019].

Blakemore, E., 2018. Marlboro Friday: The stock market shock that nearly tanked an iconic brand. *History*, 22 August [online]. Available from: www.history.com/news/marlboro-friday-stock-market-brand [Accessed 1 June 2020].

Brem, A. and Voigt, K., 2009. Integration of market pull and technology push in the corporate front end and innovation management: Insights from the German software industry. *Technovation*, 29(5), 351–367. DOI: 10.1016/j.technovation.2008.06.003.

Brewer, B. and Arnette, A., 2017. Design for procurement: What procurement driven design initiatives result in environmental and economic performance improvement? *Journal of Purchasing and Supply Management*, 23(1), 28–39. DOI: 10.1016/j.pursup.2016.06.003.

Brown, J., Collins, A. and Duguid, P., 1989. Situated cognition and the culture of learning. *Educational Researcher*, 18(1), 32–42. https://doi.org/10.3102%2F0013189X018001032.

Brown, T., 2012. 5 inspiring social design pioneers. *IDEO Design Thinking* [online]. https://designthinking.ideo.com/blog/5-inspiring-social-design-pioneers [Accessed 19 May 2020].

Brown, T., 2019. *Change by Design: How Design Thinking Transforms Organizations and Inspires Innovation*, revised and updated ed. New York: HarperCollins. ASIN: B002PEP4EG.

Calabretta, G. and Kleinsmann, M., 2017. Technology-driven evolution of design practices: Envisioning the role of design in the digital era. *Journal of Marketing Management*, 33(3–4), 292–304. https://doi.org/10.1080/0267257X.2017.1284436.

Candi, M., 2010. The sound of silence: Re-visiting silent design in the Internet age. *Design Studies*, 31(2), 187–202. DOI: 10.1016/j.destud.2009.05.003.

Carlzon, J., 1987. *Moments of Truth*. New York: Harper Business.

Chandler, C., 1989. Beyond customer satisfaction. *Quality Progress*, 22(2), 30–32.

Chandler, C., 2020. The coronavirus problem could be solved with design thinking. *Fortune: Business x Design*, 28 January [online]. Available from: https://fortune.com/2020/01/28/the-coronavirus-problem-could-be-solved-by-design-thinking/ [Accessed 19 May 2020].

Chandra, Y. and Coviello, N., 2010. Broadening the concept of international entrepreneurship: Consumers as international entrepreneurs. *Journal of World Business*, 45, 228–236. DOI: 10.1016/j.jwb.2009.09.006.

Chatterji, A., Fabrizio, K., Mitchell, W. and Schulman, K., 2008. Physician-industry cooperation in the medical device industry. *Health Affairs*, 27, 1532–1543. https://doi.org/10.1377/hlthaff.27.6.1532.

Cheng, C., Zhong, H. and Cao, L., 2020. Facilitating speed of internationalization: The roles of business intelligence and organizational agility. *Journal of Business Research*, 110, 95–103. DOI: 10.1016/j. jbusres.2020.01.003.

Chowdhury, H., Field, M. and Murphy, M., 2020. NHS track and trace app: How will it work and when can you download it? *The Daily Telegraph*, 28 May [online]. Available from: www.telegraph.co.uk/ technology/2020/05/28/nhs-app-track-trace-uk-coronavirus/ [Accessed 1 June 2020].

Colombo, M., Mohammadi, A. and Lamastra, C., 2015. Innovative business models for high-tech entrepreneurial ventures: The organizational design challenges. In N. Foss and T. Saebi, eds. *Business Model Innovation: The Organisational Dimension*. Oxford: Oxford University Press.

Cooper, R. and Evans, M., 2006. Breaking from tradition: Market research. Consumer needs, and design futures. *Design Management Review*, 17(1), 68–74. https://doi.org/10.1111/j.1948-7169.2006. tb00032.x.

Cox, G., 2005. *Cox Review of Creativity in Business: Building on the UK's Strengths*. Department of Trade and Industry. London: HM Government [online]. Available from: https://webarchive.nationalarchives. gov.uk/20120704143146/www.hm-treasury.gov.uk/d/Cox_review-foreword-definition-terms-exec-summary.pdf [Accessed 19 May 2020].

Cuatrecasas, P., 2019. *Go Tech or Go Extinct*. London: Berkeley Street Press.

Da Silva, T., Martin, A., Maurer, F. and Silveira, M., 2011. *User-Centered Design and Agile Methods: A Systematic Review*. 2011 AGILE Conference, IEEE, 77–86 [online]. Available from: http://citeseerx.ist.psu. edu/viewdoc/download?doi=10.1.1.224.4925&rep=rep1&type=pdf [Accessed 19 May 2020].

Danish Design Center, 2015. *The Design Ladder: Four Steps of Design Use* [online]. Available from: https:// danskdesigncenter.dk/en/design-ladder-four-steps-design-use?ref=publicdesignvault [Accessed 19 May 2020].

Davies, G., 2020. Lab technician reveals 'hiccups' holding up UK's coronavirus testing programme. *The Daily Telegraph*, 20 May [online]. Available from: www.telegraph.co.uk/news/2020/05/20/barcodes-wrongly-attached-unscrewed-swab-tubes-lab-technician/ [Accessed 1 June 2020].

Dell EMC and Intel, 2018. *Digital Transformation in Traditional Chinese Medicine* [online]. Available from: www.dellemc.com/en-ca/collaterals/unauth/customer-profiles-case-studies/dellemc-customer-pro-file-beijing-physicare-science-technology-for-publication.pdf [Accessed 19 May 2020].

Denton, J., 2019. What is with all the bad corporate tweets? *Pacific Standard*, 18 June [online]. Available from: https://psmag.com/social-justice/what-is-with-all-the-bad-corporate-tweets [Accessed 1 June 2020].

Design Council, 2015. *Design for Patient Dignity*. London: Design Council, 3 February [online]. Available from: www.designcouncil.org.uk/resources/case-study/design-patient-dignity [Accessed 19 May 2020].

Design Council, 2018. *Understanding Design-Intensive Innovation*. London: Design Council [online]. Available from: www.designcouncil.org.uk/sites/default/files/asset/document/Understanding_design-intensive_innovation.pdf [Accessed 19 May 2020].

Design Council, 2020. *What Is the Framework for Innovation? Design Council's Evolved Double Diamond*. London: Design Council [online]. Available from: www.designcouncil.org.uk/news-opinion/what-framework-innovation-design-councils-evolved-double-diamond [Accessed 19 May 2020].

Devlin, H., 2020. Which kind of face mask will best protect you against coronavirus? *The Guardian*, 27 May [online]. Available from: www.theguardian.com/world/2020/may/27/which-kind-of-face-mask-will-best-protect-you-against-coronavirus [Accessed 1 June 2020].

Doherty, R., Wrigley, C., Matthews, J. and Bucolo, S., 2014. Climbing the design ladder: Step by step. In A. Rieple, R. Cooper, E. Bohemia and J. Liedtka, eds. *Proceedings of the 19th DMI: Academic Design Management Conference*. London: Design Management Institute, 2578–2599.

Drew, C., 2020. What businesses and brands can learn from design during the pandemic. *Medium*, 22 April [online]. Available from: https://medium.com/design-council/what-businesses-and-brands-can-learn-from-design-during-the-pandemic-7d7d355b6b36 [Accessed 19 May 2020].

Eden, S., Bear, C. and Walker, G., 2008. The sceptical consumer? Exploring views about food assurance. *Food Policy*, 33(6), 624–630. DOI: 10.1016/j.foodpol.2008.02.003.

European Commission, 2015. *Innobarometer 2015 – The Innovation Trends at EU Enterprises* [online]. Available from: https://ec.europa.eu/commfrontoffice/publicopinion/index.cfm/Survey/getSurveyDetail/ instruments/FLASH/yearFrom/1974/yearTo/2015/surveyKy/2054 [Accessed 15 September 2019].

European Commission, 2016. *Innobarometer 2016 – EU Business Innovation Trends* [online]. Available from: https://ec.europa.eu/commfrontoffice/publicopinion/index.cfm/Survey/getSurveyDetail/instruments/FLASH/yearFrom/1974/yearTo/2016/surveyKy/2064 [Accessed 15 September 2019].

Fairs, M., 2020. Coronavirus offers "blank page for a new beginning' says Li Edelkoort. *Dezeen*, 9 March [online]. Available from: www.dezeen.com/2020/03/09/li-edelkoort-coronavirus-reset/ [Accessed 19 May 2020].

Fan, S., Lau, R. and Zhao, J., 2015. Demystifying big data analytics for business intelligence through the lens of marketing mix. *Big Data Research*, 2(1), 28–32. https://doi.org/10.1016/j.bdr.2015.02.006.

Ford, P. and Woudhuysen, J., 2012. *The Fuzzy Front End of Product Design Projects: How Universities Can Manage Knowledge Transfer and Creation*. Leading Innovation Through Design Proceedings of the Design Management Institute International Research Conference August 8th-9th, Boston, MA, 595–612.

Foss, N. and Saebi, T., eds., 2015. *Business Model Innovation: The Organisational Dimension*. Oxford: Oxford University Press. DOI: 10.1093/acprof:oso/9780198701873.001.0001.

Fox, C., 2020. My fears about the "new normal". *The Spectator*, 18 May [online]. Available from: www.spectator.co.uk/article/my-fears-about-the-new-normal-/amp?__twitter_impression=true [Accessed 19 May 2020].

Fox, H., 2020. Car seat recall: BeSafe warns against using the iZi Go X1 with Isofix base. *Which?* 26 March [online]. Available from: www.which.co.uk/news/2020/03/car-seat-recall-besafe-warns-against-using-the-izi-go-x1-with-isofix-base [Accessed 19 May 2020].

Freeman, C., 1974. *The Economics of Industrial Innovation*. Harmondsworth, UK: Penguin.

Gharib, L., 2020. Disrupting time and space. *Design Observer*, 11 February [online]. Available from: https://designobserver.com/feature/disrupting-time-and-space/40174/ [Accessed 19 May 2020].

Godin, B. and Lane, J., 2013. Pushes and pulls: Hi(S)tory of the demand-pull model of innovation. *Science, Technology and Human Values*, 38(5), 621–654.

Gorb, P. and Dumas, A., 1987. Silent design. *Design Studies* (3), 150–156.

Groth, M., Wu, Y., Nguyen, H. and Johnson, A., 2019. The moment of truth: A review, synthesis, and research agenda for the customer service experience. *Annual Review of Organizational Psychology and Organizational Behavior*, 6, 89–113. https://doi.org/10.1146/annurev-orgpsych-012218-015056.

Gruber, M., De Leon, N., George, G. and Thompson, P., 2015. Managing by design. *Academy of Management Journal*, 58(1), 1–7. https://doi.org/10.5465/amj.2015.4001.

Halstrøm, P.L. and Per Galle, P., 2014. Design as co-evolution of problem, solution, and audience. *Artifact*, III(4), 3.1–3.13. https://doi.org/10.14434/artifact.v3i4.12815.

Harfield, S., 2007. On design 'problematization': Theorising differences in designed outcomes. *Design Studies*, 28(2), 159–173. DOI: 10.1016/j.destud.2006.11.005.

Harkness, T., 2016. *Big Data: Does Size Matter?* London: Bloomsbury Sigma. ASIN: B01AS2XZ2Y.

Hartley, R.F., 1992. *Coca-Cola's Classic Blunder. Marketing Mistakes*. New York: Wiley & Sons.

Hartley, R.F., 2013. *Marketing, Mistakes and Successes*, 12th ed. Hoboken, NJ: Wiley.

Heap, D. and Coles, C., 2020. Silent design and the business value of creative ideas. Ch., 10 In R. Granger, ed. *Value Construction in the Creative Economy*. New York: Springer. DOI 10.1007/978-3-030-37035-0.

Heartfield, J., 2005. *The Creativity Gap*. Blueprint Broadside [online]. Available from: www.heartfield.org/Creativity_Gap.pdf [Accessed 19 May 2020].

Hernandez, R.J., Cooper, R. and Jung, J., 2017. The understanding and use of design in the UK Industry: Reflecting on the future of design and designing in industry and beyond. *The Design Journal*, 20(Suppl 1), S2823–S2836.

Heskett, J., 2017. *Design and the Creation of Value*. London: Bloomsbury. ASIN: B01N45ZNY1.

Hooge, S., Milena Chen, M. and Laousse, D., 2019. *Managing the Emergence of Concepts in Fuzzy Front End: A Framework of Strategic Performance and Emerging Process of Innovation Briefs*. Lisbon, Portugal: European Academy of Management, June [online]. Available from: https://hal.archives-ouvertes.fr/hal-02167857/document [Accessed 1 June 2020].

IBM, 2011. *Good Design Is Good Business*. IBM100 [online]. Available from: www.ibm.com/ibm/history/ibm100/us/en/icons/gooddesign/ [Accessed 19 May 2020].

Isaacson, W., 2012. The real leadership lessons of Steve Jobs. *Harvard Business Review*, 90(4), 92–102.

Jain, I. and Vy, H., 2019. Is design just for products, buildings and services: An introduction to social design. *Your Story*, 24 April [online]. Available from: https://yourstory.com/2019/04/an-introduction-to-social-design [Accessed 19 May 2020].

Jin, J., Liu, Y., Ji, P. and Liu, H., 2016. Understanding big consumer opinion data for market-driven product design. *International Journal of Production Research*, 54(10), 3019–3041. https://doi.org/10.1080/00 207543.2016.1154208.

Julier, G., 2017. *Economies of Design*. London: Sage Publications.

Julier, G. and Kimbell, L., 2019. Keeping the system going: Social design and the reproduction of inequalities in neoliberal times. *Design Issues*, 35(4), 12–22. https://doi.org/10.1162/desi_a_00560.

Kennedy, P., 2017. *The Rise and Fall of the Great Powers: Economic Change and Military Conflict from 1500–2000*. New York: Random House. ASIN: B074DP83C3.

Kim, W. and Lee, J.D., 2009. Measuring the role of technology-push and demand-pull in the dynamic development of the semiconductor industry: The case of the global DRAM market. *Journal of Applied Economics*, 12(1), 83–108. https://doi.org/10.1016/S1514-0326(09)60007-6.

Kimbell, L., 2018. Designing policy objects: Anti-heroic design. In T. Fisher and L. Gamman, eds. *Tricky Design: The Ethics of Things*. London: Bloomsbury, 145–157.

Kiran, D., 2017. Value engineering. Ch. 33 In D.J. Kiran, ed. *Total Quality Management: Key Concepts and Case Studies*. Oxford: Butterworth-Heinemann.

Klaus, P. and Edvardsson, B., 2013. *A Critical Examination of Service System's Role in Implementing Customer Experience Strategies*. Cambridge Academic Design Conference, 4–5 September, Cambridge, England [online]. Available from: www.ifm.eng.cam.ac.uk/uploads/Resources/Conference/CADMC_2013_Proceedings__web.pdf [Accessed 19 May 2020].

Kopanakis, I., Vassakis, K. and Mastorakis, G., 2016. *Big Data in Data-Driven Innovation: Applications, Prospects and Limitations in Marketing*. Conference: 4th International Conference on Contemporary Marketing Issues, ICCMI 2016, Heraklion, 22–24 June [online]. Available from: www.research gate.net/profile/Lambros_Sdrolias/publication/311714563_Exploring_charterers%27_buying_crite ria_for_ship_transportation_services_Empirical_evidence_from_Greek_tanker_management_firms/ links/5b0db87b0f7e9b1ed7011fe5/Exploring-charterers-buying-criteria-for-ship-transportation-services-Empirical-evidence-from-Greek-tanker-management-firms.pdf [Accessed 16 April 2020].

Kraemer, K., Dedrick, J. and Yamashiro, S., 2000. Refining and extending the business model with information technology: Dell computer corporation. *The Information Society*, 16(1), 5–21. https://doi.org/10.1080/019722400128293.

Kretzschmar, A., 2003. *The Economic Effects of Design*. National Agency for Enterprise and Housing [online]. Available from: https://pdfs.semanticscholar.org/754f/a0095d0c7ec4cb1c0c0b4cd1a95c c5b1050b.pdf [Accessed 16 April 2020].

Levin, T., 2002. *CTRL. Space: Rhetorics of Surveillance from Bentham to Big Brother*. London; Cambridge, MA: MIT Press.

Levitt, D., 2020. Design thinking jumps shark; declares it can solve coronavirus. *Medium*, 3, 4 March [online]. Available from: https://medium.com/delta-cx/design-thinking-jumps-shark-declares-it-can-solve-coronavirus-1ae1ccaebecc [Accessed 19 May 2020].

Liu, Y., Jin, J., Ji, P., Harding, J. and Fung, R., 2013. Identifying helpful online reviews: A product designer's perspective. *Computer-Aided Design*, 45(2), 180–194. https://doi.org/10.1016/j.cad.2012.07.008.

Lubik, S., Lim, S., Platts, K. and Minshall, T., 2013. Market-pull and technology-push in manufacturing start-ups in emerging industries. *Journal of Manufacturing Technology Management*, 21(1), 10–27. DOI: 10.1108/17410381311287463.

Luchs, M., Swan, K. and Creusen, M., 2015. Perspective: A review of marketing research on product design with directions for future research. *The Journal of Product Innovation Management*, 33(3), 320–341. https://doi.org/10.1111/jpim.12276.

Manzini, E., 2016. Design culture and dialogic design. *Design Issues*, 32(1), 52–59. DOI: 10.1162/DESI_a_00364.

Marcus, R., 2020. Philips Avent digital video baby monitors recalled over fire risk. *Which?* 13 January [online]. Available from: www.which.co.uk/news/2020/01/philips-avent-digital-video-baby-moni tors-recalled-over-fire-risk/ [Accessed 19 May 2020].

Mason, T. and Knights, M., 2019. *Omnichannel Retail: How to Build Winning Stores in a Digital World*. New York: Kogan Page.

Mazzucato, M., 2019. *Governing Missions in the European Union. European Commission Directorate-General for Research and Innovation* [online]. Available from: www.kowi.de/Portaldata/2/Resources/Horizon2020/mazzucato_report_2019.pdf [Accessed 19 May 2020].

McCuillagh, K., 2020. Innovation after corona: This does not change everything. *LinkedIn*, 16 April [online]. Available from: www.linkedin.com/pulse/innovation-after-corona-does-change-everything-kevin-mccullagh/ [Accessed 19 May 2020].

McKinsey. 2018., *The Business Value of Design* [online]. Available from: The business value of design | McKinsey, Available from https://www.mckinsey.com/business-functions/mckinsey-design/our-insights/the-business-value-of-design [Accessed 3 February 2021].

McNabola, A., Moseley, J., Reed, B., Bisgaard, T., Jossiasen, A.D., Melander, C., Whicher, A., Hytönen, J. and Schultz, O., 2013. *Design for Public Good*. London: Design Council, supported by the European Commission [online]. Available from: www.designcouncil.org.uk/sites/default/files/asset/document/Design%20for%20Public%20Good.pdf [Accessed 16 April 2020].

Meek, R., 1977. Marginalism and Marxism. In *Smith, Marx and After*. Boston: Springer, 165–175.

Melioranski, R.H., 2015. *Tackling Societal Challenges Requires Improved Design Methodology* [online]. Available from: https://wiki.aalto.fi/download/attachments/108252896/Synnyt_Humancentredness_Melioranski.pdf?version=2&modificationDate=1441796896665&api=v2 [Accessed 5 September 2019].

Micheli, P., 2013. *Leading Business by Design: Why and How Business Leaders Invest in Design* [online]. Available from: www.designcouncil.org.uk/sites/default/files/asset/document/dc_lbbd_report_08.11.13_FA_LORES.pdf [Accessed 19 May 2020].

Moore, J., 1993. Predators and prey: A new ecology of competition. *Harvard Business Review*.

Museum für Gestaltung Zürich and Sachs, A., 2018. *Social design: Participation and empowerment*. Zurich: Lars Müller Publishers [online]. Available from: www.lars-mueller-publishers.com/social-design-0 [Accessed 19 May 2020].

Naughton, J., 2020. Slouching toward dystopia. *New Statesman*, 28 February [online]. Available from: www.newstatesman.com/2020/02/slouching-towards-dystopia-rise-surveillance-capitalism-and-death-privacy [Accessed 19 May 2020].

Nussbaum, B., 2004. The power of design. *Business Week*, 17(5), 1–9 [online]. Available from: www.bloomberg.com/news/articles/2004-05-16/the-power-of-design [Accessed 19 May 2020].

Nyukorong, R., 2017. Conducting market research: An aid to organisational decision making. *European Scientific Journal*, 13(10), 1–17. http://dx.doi.org/10.19044/esj.2017.v13n10p1.

OECD, 2015. *Frascati Manual 2015: Guidelines for Collecting and Reporting Data on Research and Experimental Development. The Measurement of Scientific, Technological and Innovation Activities*. Paris: OECD Publishing [online]. Available from: www.oecd.org/publications/frascati-manual-2015-9789264239012-en.htm [Accessed 20 June 2020].

OECD/Eurostat, 2005. *Oslo Manual: Guidelines for Collecting and Interpreting Innovation Data*, 3rd ed. The measurement of scientific and technological activities. Paris: OECD Publishing.

Oliver, R., Rust, R. and Varki, S., 1997. Customer delight: Foundations, findings, and managerial insight. *Journal of Retailing*, 73(3), 311–336. https://doi.org/10.1016/S0022-4359(97)90021-X.

Packard, V., 1964. *The Naked Society*. London: Longmans.

Peters, T., 1994. *The Pursuit of Wow! Every Person's Guide to Topsy-Turvy Times*. New York: Vintage.

Peters, T. and Waterman, R., 1982. *In Search of Excellence: Lessons from America's Best-Run Companies*. New York: Harper and Row. ASIN: B009YM9VOQ.

Pettigrew, D., Thurgood, C. and Bucolo, S., 2016. A design innovation adoption tool for SMEs. In *20th DMI: Academic Design Management Conference*. Boston: Design Management Institute), 14–38 [online]. Available from: https://opus.lib.uts.edu.au/bitstream/10453/47175/1/David%20Pettigrew.pdf [Accessed 10 November 2019].

Priem, R., Li, S. and Carr, J., 2012. Insights and new directions from demand-side approaches to technology innovation, entrepreneurship, and strategic management research. *Journal of Management*, 38(1), 346–374. https://doi.org/10.1177%2F0149206311429614.

Redwood, B., Schöffer, F. and Garret, B., 2017. *The 3D Printing Handbook: Technologies, Design and Applications*. Amsterdam: 3D Hubs. ASIN: B077T39X6C.

Rosenberg, N., 1982. *Inside the Black Box: Technology and Economics*. Cambridge, UK: Cambridge University Press. https://doi.org/10.2307/3324062.

Rosenthal, S.R. and Capper, M., 2006. Ethnographies in the front end: Designing for enhanced customer experiences. *The Journal of Product Innovation Management*, 23(3), 215–237. https://doi.org/10.1111/j.1540-5885.2006.00195.x.

Rothwell, R. and Teubal, M., 1977. SAPPHO revisited: A re-appraisal of the SAPPHO Data. In *Innovation, Economic Change and Technology Policies*. Basel: Birkhäuser, 39–59.

Schmitt, B., 2003. *Customer Experience Management: A Revolutionary Approach to Connecting with Your Customers*. Hoboken, NJ: Wiley.

Sign Design Society, 2020. Walk this way to sustainable wayfinding and wellbeing in 2020 whilst maintaining social distancing. *Sign Design Society*, 5 May [online]. Available from: www.signdesignsociety. co.uk/steers-innovative-board-walk-injects-playfulness-into-the-urban-realm-at-bankside/ [Accessed 19 May 2020].

Simon, H., 1969. *The Sciences of the Artificial*. Cambridge, MA: MIT Press.

Smith, P. and Reinertsen, D., 1991. *Developing Products in Half the Time*. New York: Van Nostrand Reinhold.

Society of Serviceology, 2018. Joint international conference on service science and innovation and serviceology. *Proceedings* (November), 13–15.

Stevens, M., 2020. 55,000 additional fire-risk washing machines revealed by Whirlpool. *Which?* 29 April [online]. Available from: www.which.co.uk/news/2020/04/55000-more-dangerous-fire-risk-washing-machines-revealed-by-whirlpool/ [Accessed 19 May 2020].

Stone, M., Machtynger, L. and Machtynger, J., 2015. Managing customer insight creatively through storytelling. *Journal of Direct, Data and Digital Marketing Practice*, 17(2), 77–83. https://doi.org/10.1057/dddmp.2015.45.

Tan, W., Blake, M.B., Saleh, I. and Dustdar, S., 2013. Social-network-sourced big data analytics. *IEEE Internet Computing*, 17(5), 62–69. https://doi.org/10.1109/MIC.2013.100.

Trump, D., 2019. Adjusting imports of automobiles and automobile parts into the United States. *White House*, 17 May [online]. Available from: www.whitehouse.gov/presidential-actions/adjusting-imports-automobiles-automobile-parts-united-states/ [Accessed 19 May 2020].

UNDP Innovation Facility, 2017. *Spark, Scale Sustain: 2016 Year in Review*. New York: UNDP [online]. Available from: www.undp.org/content/dam/undp/library/innovation/Version%2024%20web%20friendly%20-%20August%202%20-%20Annual%20Report%202016%20V17.pdf [Accessed 19 May 2020].

UNDP Innovation and Youth Teams at the UNDP Regional Hub for the Arab States, Nudge Lebanon and B4Development, 2020. Using behavioural insights to respond to COVID-19. *United Nations Development Programme*, 7 May [online]. Available from: www.undp.org/content/undp/en/home/stories/using-behavioural-insights-to-respond-to-covid-19-.html [Accessed 19 May 2020].

Van den Ende, J. and Dolfsma, W., 2005. Technology-push, demand-pull and the shaping of technological paradigms – Patterns in the development of computing technology. *Journal of Evolutionary Economics*, 15(1), 83–99. https://doi.org/10.1007/s00191-004-0220-1.

Vargo, S.L. and Lusch, R.F., 2004a. Evolving to a new dominant logic for marketing. *Journal of Marketing*, 68(1), 1–17. https://doi.org/10.1509/jmkg.68.1.1.24036.

Vargo, S.L. and Lusch, R.F., 2004b. The four service marketing myths: Remnants of a goods-based, manufacturing model. *Journal of Service Research*, 6(4), 324–335. https://doi.org/10.1177%2F1094670503262946.

Verganti, R., 2009. *Design-Driven Innovation. Changing the Rules of Competition by Radically Innovating What Things Mean*. Boston, MA: Harvard Business School Publishing. ASIN: B004OC078A.

von Hippel, E., 1976. The dominant role of users in the scientific instrument innovation process. *Research Policy*, 5, 212–239.

Wasson, C., 2000. Ethnography in the field of design. *Human Organisation*, 59(4), 377–388. https://doi.org/10.17730/humo.59.4.h13326628n127516.

Wessely, S. and Daniels, J., 2020. Why reassuring the public may not be the best way to end lockdown. *Kings College London News Centre*, 9 May [online]. Available from: www.kcl.ac.uk/news/why-reassuring-the-public-may-not-be-the-best-way-to-end-lockdown [Accessed 19 May 2020].

Wheelwright, S.C. and Clark, K., 1994. Accelerating the design-build-test cycle for effective product development. *International Marketing Review*, 11(1), 32–46.

Woudhuysen, J., 1977. Information bridges the invention/demand gap. *Design*, 343 (July).

Woudhuysen, J., 1996. The battle for the living room. *Design Management Journal* (Fall) [online]. Available from: https://onlinelibrary.wiley.com/doi/abs/10.1111/j.1948-7169.1996.tb00623.x.

Woudhuysen, J., 2002. Usability cult sacrifices innovation. *Computing*. 31 May [online]. Available from: www.computing.co.uk/analysis/1815618/comment-usability-cult-sacrifices-innovation [Accessed 20 June 2020].

Woudhuysen, J., 2007. Farewell to 'seamless': How CIOs can make enterprises agile. In *Open Minds*. Munich: Siemens [online]. Available from: www.woudhuysen.com/farewell-to-seamless-how-cios-can-make-enterprises-agile/ [Accessed 19 May 2020].

Woudhuysen, J., 2011. The craze for design thinking: Roots, a critique, and toward an alternative. *Design Principles and Practices: An International Journal*, 5(6), 235–248.

Woudhuysen, J., 2012. The next trend in design. *Design Management Journal*, 27–39. Available from: https://onlinelibrary.wiley.com/doi/abs/10.1111/j.1948-7177.2011.00021.x [Accessed 19 May 2020].

Woudhuysen, J., 2016. Innovation in megaprojects. *Blueprint*, July [online]. Available from: www.woudhuysen.com/innovation-in-megaprojects/ [Accessed 19 May 2020].

Yun, J.J., Won, D., Jeong, E., Park, K., Yang, J. and Park, J., 2016. The relationship between technology, business model, and market in autonomous car and intelligent robot industries. *Technological Forecasting and Social Change*, 103, 142–155. DOI: 10.1016/j.techfore.2015.11.016.

Zuboff, S., 2019. *The Age of Surveillance Capitalism: The Fight for a Human Future at the New Frontier of Power*. London: Profile Books. ASIN: B01N7UERGX.

23

RESEARCHING THE ADVANTAGE OF LOW QUALITY IN SHORT LIFE CYCLE PRODUCTS

Yang Sun, Helen Huifen Cai, Rui Su, Qianhui Shen and Merlin Stone

Summary

This chapter discusses how the configurations of low quality, design factors, and price influence customer purchase intention on products with short lifecycles. The main proposition is that consumers may purchase a new product to replace the old one before it has problems or fails completely. The fashion and technology industries are excellent representations of industries for fast product updating (Zhou *et al.* 2015). Fast product updating refers to the idea that the product or technique is in a constant state of updating, which may mean that the design of the product and the product itself has a short lifecycle. Currently, fast-fashion items and electronic products are more popular among younger generations. The strategic view of fast-fashion retailers is often "here today, gone tomorrow", leading consumers to visit a store many times to keep up with trends. Customers therefore purchase clothes more frequently, which increases company incomes (Bhardwaj and Fairhurst 2010). Newly designed clothes are only on the market for a short time, and this stimulates consumer purchase impulses (Foroohar 2005). This means that customers will have a variety of idle fast-fashion products at home. As newer ones on the market quickly replace these products, their lifecycles remain short. This chapter provides further insights into the link between customers' purchase intention and product quality (Sun *et al.* 2019). It identifies that a product's price and design both play an important role in a customer's acceptance of low-quality products, so enterprises can still convince customers to buy low-quality products by setting an appropriate price and design. For this reason, this chapter has significance for fast-fashion enterprises and electronic industries, and any others that rely on frequent product updates and replacements.

Introduction

The trade-off between quality and price is a matter of particular interest in scholarly literature. From a consumer's perspective, the best outcome would be a product of high quality purchased at a low price. (Dodds *et al.* 1991; Alfred 2013; Shirai 2015,). However, high-quality products are a costly endeavour for companies. Furthermore, price is not the only factor that drives consumer-purchasing behaviour. Homburg *et al.* (2015) note that product design, corporate culture, and brand can induce consumers to pay a higher price for a lower-quality product. Though this notion is an interesting phenomenon, there is a lack of research on the advantage of low-quality products (Schubert 2017).

The lifecycle for most electronic products is 1–2 years or less; as developing technology has accelerated the reduction of the electronic product lifecycle, so fast-fashion products and electronic products have a rapid product update speed. As a means of cutting costs on the constant updating and replacement of products, lower-quality products are made to keep up with demand and to save money.

Literature review

Short life cycle products

Gan *et al.* (2015) identify that rapid innovation and development in technology is the main driver of short lifecycle products. Good examples of this are smartphones and fast-fashion products: their lifecycles are short, and their prices change over time. Companies are constantly innovating and updating products in order to keep up with competition, the latest technologies, and the popular styles. However, the launch of new products has great influence on the price of the old ones (Zhou *et al.* 2015). Helo (2004) states that the product lifecycle is significantly shortened by rapid technological improvement and fashionable design, which attract more frequent purchases of new products. Hsueh (2011) demonstrates that the product life cycle in technology-based industries is shorter than ever before, due to rapid technological innovation, so a technologically "archaic" product can be abandoned even if it is still in good and workable condition. Short lifecycle products make sense in fast fashion too, because design and fashion change rapidly and products may not continue to be stylish. This may lead a consumer to abandon an old product in purchasing a new one, even if there is nothing physically wrong with it.

Low-quality products

The product itself is the element that brings the most value to the customer. While products mainly offer the consumer their function, they also offer service, design, brand name, and packaging. These are all intangible values that augment customers' perceptions of product quality. Product quality is also essential for marketing teams to position products in increasingly competitive markets.

Product quality is the most vital factor in the electronics industry, particularly for smartphones and computers, simply because industry competition is focused on price (Alfred 2013). However, it is hard to meet customers' expectations on quality because of their varied and inconsistent understanding of what quality means. Some customers believe that high-quality products merit a high price and that a low price means low quality. Others are more likely to buy high-quality products at low prices. The influences of economic, technologic, social, and cultural factors are major reasons for different quality perspectives among customers (Dabade and Wankhade 2006). To give a better product quality image to customers, a company must learn about quality perceptions and understand quality from the customer's viewpoint. This requires the company to help customers differentiate between what Alfred (2013) notes as "how things ought to be" and "how things are". This can be used to compare "actual performance" with "perceived requirements" in products to find differences that can be improved.

The low-quality advantage is an attractive point for companies to reset their strategies using quality-price-based targets. The low-quality advantage is where the low-quality firm achieves a larger market share and earns higher profits than its top-quality competitor (Schubert 2017). Many companies achieve success in serving low-quality products to most consumers (Schubert 2017).

Product design

Product design is a key interface between users and a product and consequently the company's brand (Mishra 2016). A few studies connect product design with consumption experiences (Luchs and Swan 2011). A well-designed product creates meaning and experiences for customers as users translate some specific attributes of products into their intrinsic perceptions (Gutman 1982; Hekkert and Leder 2008). A special or meaningful design provides more reasons for customers to purchase and keep a product. The means–end theory suggests that a customer's subjective interpretation of a product helps them attain value, thus offering a positive experience or an enhanced attachment to the brand (Graeff 1997). Studies of consumer-based brand equity clarify benefits achieved via product attributes and resultant user experiences, which are antecedents of brand image and brand associations (Keller 1993). So there is strong theoretical background support for exploring the connection between product design and a customer's perception of it. This chapter focuses on how product design can influence customers' purchase intention towards low-quality products.

Product design is a source of significant competitive advantage for companies (Gemser and Leenders 2001; Noble and Kumar 2010). Product design can increase the customer base and company profit (Hertenstein *et al.* 2005; Candi 2010), particularly relevant in today's marketplace because product design has become an iconic sign of product differentiation (Homburg *et al.* 2015). The theoretical framework of product design developed by Homburg *et al.* (2015) is based on four elements: aesthetics, functionality, symbolism, and high fashionability (Kim *et al.* 2013). As some of these are visual and some non-visual, product design is measured from both perspectives.

Aesthetics

This refers specifically to the appearance and beauty that customers perceive in a product (Desmet and Hekkert 2007; Bloch 2011). Aesthetics is also defined as either an attribute of the product itself or as created in the eye of the beholder but can also be a combination of these two (Reber *et al.* 2004). The aesthetics dimension is subjective, judged by customers themselves. In this chapter, aesthetics in product design refers to a combination of the attributes of the product itself and the customer's subjective experience as a means to correspond to the multilevel definition of product design. This multilevel definition notes that product design is the property a product has that leads to a perception of beauty for the beholder (Leder *et al.* 2004). Thus, the following propositions are offered:

Proposition 1: Product aesthetics affects consumer purchase intention on low-quality products.

Functionality

This indicates the consumer's perceptions of a product's ability to achieve its purpose (Boztepe 2007; Bloch 2011). A car's function, for instance, can only be properly evaluated when it is consumed or used. However, in many cases, consumers can only evaluate the functionality of a product through observation (Hoegg and Alba 2011; Radford and Bloch 2011). This

461

perception is particularly important for online stores, as consumers do not have the opportunity to fully experience the product (Spears and Yazdanparast 2014). Thus, the second proposition is as follows:

Proposition 2: Product function affects consumer purchase intention on low-quality products.

Symbolism

This refers to a consumers' perception relating to how a product conveys the consumer's image to others based on visual elements (Belk 1988; Bloch 2011). Symbolism can evoke different connotations, including associations with a place or time (Creusen and Schoormans 2005). It can also be used to express personal values and tendencies or to inform the customer's sense of identity (McCracken 1986). Symbolism is an important dimension because aesthetics and functions do not fully capture product design (Rindova and Petkova 2007; Bloch 2011). For example, the aesthetic and symbolic dimensions may be in conflict, for example, where a consumer likes a colourful design (aesthetic dimension) but does not buy it because it looks naive (Creusen and Schoormans 2005). Verganti (2008) notes that the symbolic dimension is "as important as the utilitarian view" because products often reflect the consumer's desire to express their self-extension (Belk 1988; Holt 1997; Kleine *et al.* 1993). Based on these notions, a further proposition is as follows.

Proposition 3: Product symbolism affects consumer purchase intention on low-quality products.

High fashionability

This refers to the idea that some products cannot be used for more than one or two seasons (Kim *et al.* 2013). This may be because the product style is too trendy to be used for a long time, or the product style is too sensitive to adapt to changing trends. Consequently, the final proposition on product design elements is as follows.

Proposition 4: Product fashionability affects consumer purchase intention on low-quality products.

Price

For customers, price is a critical cue in the evaluation of the quality of a product (Zeithaml 1988; Panzone 2012). Previous studies focus on the relationship between price and perceived quality (Monroe 1973; Rao and Monroe 1989; Kirmani and Rao 2000; Rao 2005), assuming a positive correlation between price and supply cost and hence quality. Consumers use prices to rank products when quality is difficult to assess in advance. Specifically, consumers tend to use price to rank products by quality (Rao 2005).

Price is an important determinant in a customer's expected utility of a product. Sometimes, consumers cannot pay more than a certain price. Others may be able to afford a price but believe that spending money in another way will satisfy them more (Alfred 2013). However, for a product to be simple and inexpensive is not enough. Products must achieve a certain performance for the customer. McConnell (1968) argues that price can determine how brands or quality are perceived without other cues, though for some big brand products, quality is not as high as the customer expects, despite the belief that the higher price ensures quality.

Price is a major influence factor on a consumer's choice in buying a product (Stafford and Enis 1969). As long as a product performs well and the price is not higher than expected, customers are generally willing to accept prices. Price awareness also varies by customer. Given that price plays an important role in decision-making, the proposition on price is as follows:

Proposition 5: Price affects consumer purchase intention on low-quality products.

Demographics

Many studies include demographic variables representing different consumer attributes (e.g. Wu *et al.* 2014; Woodside 2015; Woodside 2017). This chapter explores the effects of consumers' features such as gender, age, and income. The demographic proposition is as follows.

Proposition 6: Complex demographic configurations affect purchase intention on low-quality products.

Purchase intention

During the product evaluation stage, consumers develop purchase intentions towards products, Usually, consumers make decisions based on purchase intention, but the final decision will be affected by other factors. This study focuses on purchase intentions rather than consumer behaviour, as intentions have broader implications and tend to have positive effects on individual behaviour (Ajzen and Driver 1992; Pierre *et al.* 2005; Schlosser *et al.* 2006). Purchase intention relates to the consumer planning or being willing to buy a certain product or service (Wu *et al.* 2011; Martins *et al.* 2019). Shen (2015) notes that smart shopping has affected determinants such as attitudes, subjective norms, and perceived behavioural control in a customer's willingness to buy.

Research method

Data and measurement

The full-scale primary data collection method was an online survey. The sample comprised 100 valid questionnaires from an online survey in July 2017. The target industries were fast-fashion and smartphones. The measurements of prices were based on Huang *et al.* (2004) and Lichtenstein *et al.* (1993), with instruments adopted from Homburg *et al.* (2015) and Kim *et al.* (2013) to measure design. Purchase intention was measured using well-tested scales (Lee and Lee 2009; Wang *et al.* 2012). Constructs were measured using a 5-point Likert scale. One hundred cases were analysed (Marx 2006). Data on gender, age, and household income were also used in the analysis shown in Table 23.1.

Case-based modelling

Woodside (2015) notes the tendency of studies to use symmetry tests to confirm or reject variables. However, given that the use of a single variable or the condition of variables may not accurately predict outcomes, such tests are limited in empirical behavioural science and business

Table 23.1 Demographics of sample

Category		Frequency	Percent
Gender	Men	28	28
	Women	72	72
Age	Less than 20	25	25
	20~30	72	72
	31~40	1	1
	More than 40	2	2
Household income	Less than 100,000	37	37
(yearly/RMB)	100,000~150,000	34	34
	150,000~200,000	14	14
	200,000~250,000	5	5
	More than 250,0000	10	10

Source: The authors

research (Woodside 2016). Qualitative comparative analysis (QCA) is where an outcome may follow from several different combinations of causal conditions or "recipes". For example, a researcher may to suspect that there are several different recipes that determine whether customers stay loyal. By examining the outcome for of customers with different configurations of causally relevant conditions, it is possible, using QCA, to identify the decisive recipes and so unravel causal complexity (Ragin 2008), unlike a regression analysis (Ragin 2000; Ragin and Fiss 2008; Woodside *et al.* 2011).

As opposed to using structural equation modelling to identify positive or negative influences, fuzzy set QCA can indicate condition contribution to the observation outcomes (Woodside 2015). This is most suitable for small samples (Ragin 2009). To overcome the limitations of regression analysis, complexity theory, which refers to the fact that the relationship among variables can be non-linear, occurs in different situations with different effects and is often used in commercial research and behavioural science (Wu *et al.* 2014). These methods include the causal asymmetry principle, Boolean algebra, and fuzzy set qualitative comparative analysis (fsQCA) to determine Y levels (Woodside 2015; Xie *et al.* 2016). fsQCA is a configuration method that indicates whether an observation result is associated with a particular causal combination (i.e. configuration) or only a single condition (Woodside *et al.* 2013; McNamara 2015). (e.g. low price [single condition] may lead to purchase intention; low price with good quality [configuration with one identical variable] may also lead to purchase intention, or good design, high brand image but high price [configuration with different variables] may also lead to consumer purchase intention [i.e. the same result]). Therefore, fsQCA can be used to find different combinations that lead to the same result or different combinations that lead to diverse results. In this study, the statistical packages SPSS 21.0 and fsQCA 2.5 were used for analysis (Ragin and Davey 2014). Figure 23.1 shows the configuration model of this study.

Reliability analysis and calibration

This study used Cronbach's α reliability test measures, shown in Table 23.2. For the fast-fashion industry, Cronbach's alpha values are between .715 and .942 and .711 and .945 for further research on the smartphone industry, from .711 to .94, indicating good reliability (Kim 1998).

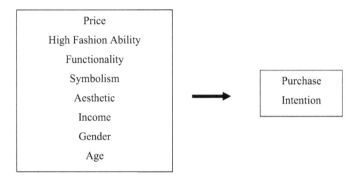

Figure 23.1 Configuration model

Source: The authors

Table 23.2 Summary of Cronbach's α reliability test

Variables	Items	Fast fashion	Smartphone	References
Aesthetics (ae)	Visually striking Good looking Looks appealing	.893	.868	Homburg *et al.* 2015 Kim *et al.* 2013
Functionality (fu)	Likely fit (perform) well Capable doing its job To be functional	.942	.869	
Symbolism (sy)	Establish distinctive image Distinguish from mass Symbolise or express achievement	.897	.945	
Overly Trendy (ot)	Too trendy to use for long Too sensitive to changing trends	.828	.894	
Price (pr)	Low quality means low price Price shows quality Consumers can accept the low price	.715	.722	Huang *et al.* (2004); Lichtenstein *et al.* (1993)
Purchase Intention (pi)	Probably purchase poor design Probably purchase low price Probably purchase low quality Search information with purchase intention The product importance to me	.752	.711	Lee and Lee (2009); Wang *et al.* (2012)

Source: The authors

Before the data sets are analysed by fuzzy sets software, the fsQCA can be used to analyse the data from 0.00 to 1.00. The survey data used a 5-point Likert scale, which means it must be calibrated, unlike conventional variables (Ragin 2008; Sun *et al.* 2020). This study uses the fsQCA 2.5 calibration function to calibrate the data. "The membership scores run from 0.00 to 1.00. The less than or equal sign ('≤') signifies that the cases for complex antecedent conditions that the model specifies should have scores less than or equal to the scores of the outcome condition" (Woodside 2015, p. 252). The calibrations have three breakpoints: 0 for full non-membership, 1 for full membership, and 0.5 for the crossover point of maximum membership ambiguity (Ragin 2008; Sun *et al.* 2020). A score of 5 was the threshold for full membership; 1 indicated full non-membership, and 3 was the crossover point, indicating the maximum point of ambiguity.

This study calibrates demographic features such as gender using crisp sets. These differ from fuzzy sets, where the measure is from 0.00 to 1.00, while crisp sets only have 0 and 1 (e.g. 0 represents man, 1 represents woman). The threshold for income was from very low to very high (0, 0.25, 0.5, 0.75, 1), and the threshold for age groups is represented as 0.25, 0.5, 0.75, and 1.

Research results

In comparison to regression models, QCA uses set theory for logical statements about causal conditions (Ragin 2000). The consistency index indicates whether the model is reliable for simple or complex antecedents. The score should be equal to or less than the member score of the case outcome condition. The software can provide three solutions that emerge from this process, categorised as either complex solution, intermediate solution, or parsimonious solution. These are defined as follows. Complex solutions can be very intricate, as little or no simplification occurs, and parsimonious solutions can be unrealistically simple, due to incorporation of many (easy and difficult) counterfactual combinations, while intermediate solutions are a balance between parsimony and complexity (Ragin 2017). In following Ragin (2000), this study focuses on intermediate solutions. The consistency index should exceed 0.85, while a minimum value of 0.05 is criterial for the coverage index (Woodside 2015). Based on the consistency and coverage rates, this chapter employs major models to analyse data and lists additional models for each data set. The landscape character "~" represents a negative, while the asterisk "*" represents a logical "and" condition (Woodside 2015). In the result, some variables are not present in the configurations, indicating that they are not the key factors that lead to a configuration result. However, these variables may be present in other configurations.

Research 1

Research 1 was an effort to explore the different kinds of variable configurations that can lead a consumer to intend to purchase low-quality fast-fashion products, shown in Table 23.3. There are three configurations that can lead consumers to be willing to purchase low-quality fast-fashion products:

1   price*overly trendy*~symbolism*~functionality*~aesthetic*~income*gender*~age
2   price*overly trendy*symbolism*functionality*aesthetic*income*gender*~age
3   price*overly trendy*symbolism*functionality*aesthetic*~income*gender*age.

The three major factors in these configurations include the consumer's gender (female), the price of the product (low), and the perceived trendiness of the product (overly trendy). These were the key findings of the analysis:

*   Female customers consider low price and high trendiness the main factors in accepting low-quality fast-fashion products;

Table 23.3 Consumers purchase low-quality products in fast fashion context (intermediate solution)

Causal configuration	Raw coverage	Unique coverage	Consistency
Model:			
price*overly trendy*symbolism*functionality*aesthetic*~income*gender*age	0.391938	0.121175	0.910321
Additional models:			
price*overly trendy*~symbolism*~functionality*~aesthetic*~income*gender*~age	0.228023	0.035454	0.888363
price*overly trendy*symbolism*functionality*aesthetic*income*gender*~age	0.248907	0.061680	0.855593
Solution coverage: 0.489072			
Solution consistency: 0.845508			

Source: The authors

- Young women (under the age of 30) with low household income only consider low price and overly trendy; thus, they may tolerate bad design (~aesthetics, ~functionality, ~symbolism);
- Young women (under the age of 30) with higher household incomes not only consider low price but also the design elements of products (symbolism, functionality, aesthetics, overly trendy). Under these circumstances, these consumers will accept low-quality fast-fashion products;
- Older women (over the age of 30) with low household income also have a comprehensive consideration of variables in the purchase of low-quality fast-fashion products, which is almost the same young women with high household income (price, overly trendy, symbolism, functionality, aesthetics).

This result indicates that companies can produce low-quality fast-fashion products targeted specifically at young women with low household income. There should be more profit from this target group, as they will have fewer requirements of low-quality products than other cohorts.

Given the high raw coverage and consistency, the major model of Research 1 was chosen as price*overly trendy*symbolism*functionality*aesthetic*~income*gender*age.

The model demonstrates that low prices are key in encouraging older women with lower income to purchase low-quality fast-fashion products. Most consumers are also attracted by this attribute. However, older women with low household income require that the low-quality fast-fashion products also have good product design qualities. A customer will not be satisfied with a low price unless the product has good attributes. Older women pay more attention to the practical value of fast-fashion products. A low-price but useless fast-fashion product would be a waste for this cohort. Older women with low household incomes will not buy a fast-fashion product if it cannot fulfil all the factors of design. This cohort has high expectation of products they buy, but these expectations are not always met. However, this group can be targeted with special discounts (e.g. last season's products, inventory sell-outs etc.).

In this and the following tables, the headings are as defined by Ragin and Fiss (2008), where raw coverage measures the proportion of outcome memberships explained by each solution term, unique coverage measures the proportion of outcome memberships explained by each solution term (memberships not covered by other terms), while solution consistency measures how far solution membership is a subset of membership in the outcome.

Research 2

Research 2 was an effort to test conditions that influence the purchase intention of low-quality products in the smartphone industry. Table 23.4 denotes six configurations that can lead consumers to be willing to purchase a low-quality smartphone:

1   price*~overly trendy*functionality*aesthetic*~income*gender*~age
2   price*~overly trendy*~symbolism*~functionality*~aesthetic*~income*~gender*~age
3   price*overly trendy*symbolism*~functionality*~aesthetic*~income*gender*~age
4   price*~overly trendy*~symbolism*functionality*~aesthetic*income*gender*~age
5   price*overly trendy*symbolism*functionality*aesthetic*income*gender*~age
6   price*overly trendy*symbolism*functionality*aesthetic*~income*gender*age.

Based on these configurations, it is evident that a low price is the most important factor. This is present in all configurations, including influencing the intent to purchase a low-quality smartphone. So, no matter how the design, income, gender, and age change, a low price is always the driving factor in a customer purchasing a low-quality smartphone. These were the findings:

- Regardless of income, young women (ages 30 and under) only consider low price and can tolerate some elements of bad design in a smartphone (~aesthetics, ~functionality, ~symbolism, or ~overly trendy);
- Some young women (ages 30 and under) who have a higher household income will accept a low-quality smartphone only when it has low price as well as good design (aesthetics, functionality, symbolism, and overly trendy);
- Older women (ages 30 and over) with low household income think similarly;
- Young male customers (ages 30 and under) with low household income only consider low price and can tolerate bad design (~aesthetics ~functionality, ~symbolism, and ~overly trendy).

The research implies that companies can produce low-quality smartphones for target customers that include young males and young females with low household income. These groups mainly consider price and can tolerate some bad design elements.

The most representative model is the one used as the major model in our analysis of the fast-fashion industry (Table 23.4)

price*overly trendy*symbolism*functionality*aesthetic*~income*gender*age.

It demonstrates that older women with low household income also prefer low-quality smartphones with good design; that is, this means that the practical approach of this cohort is reflected in their buying of both fast fashion and smartphones. Practical value is their main reason for purchasing a product. The suggestion for marketing to this group is similar to that mentioned in the fast-fashion research.

Table 23.4 Consumers want to purchase low-quality products in smartphone context (intermediate solution)

Causal configuration	Raw coverage	Unique coverage	Consistency
Model:			
price*overly trendy*symbolism*functionality *aesthetic*~income*gender*age	0.292885	0.056324	0.906977
Additional models:			
price*~overly trendy*functionality*aesthetic* ~income*gender*~age	0.380237	0.100988	0.854352
price*~overly trendy*~symbolism*~function ality*~aesthetic*~income*~gender*~age	0.112846	0.112846	0.982788
price*overly trendy*symbolism*~functionalit y*~aesthetic*~income*gender*~age	0.207115	0.008498	0.863974
price*~overly trendy*~symbolism*functional ity*~aesthetic*income*gender*~age	0.162846	0.008696	0.890811
price*overly trendy*symbolism*functionality *aesthetic*income*gender*~age	0.190909	0.039328	0.939689
Solution coverage: 0.629644			
Solution consistency: 0.859455			

Source: The authors

Research 3

Research 3 tests the reasons consumers want to purchase low-quality products in a fast-fashion context regardless of price. There are four configurations in Table 23.5:

1 ~age*~income*gender*overly trendy*~symbolism*~functionality*~aesthetic;
2 ~age*~income*gender*~overly trendy*symbolism*functionality*~aesthetic;
3 age*~income*gender*overly trendy*symbolism*functionality*aesthetic;
4 ~age*income*gender*overly trendy*symbolism*functionality*aesthetic.

The main reason for customers to choose low-quality products is design. These were the findings:

- Only two kinds of customers will accept low-quality products: young and older women;
- Young women (ages 30 and under) with low household income would accept low fast-fashion products with good design or at least one good element of design (overly trendy, symbolism, or functionality);
- For older women (ages 30 and over) with low household income and young women (ages 30 and under) with high household income, good design is the determining factor for purchasing low-quality fast-fashion products (overly trendy, symbolism, functionality, and aesthetics).

So, product design is another key influencing factor, in addition to price, in encouraging consumers to purchase low-quality fast-fashion products.

Table 23.5 Consumers want to purchase low-quality products in fast-fashion context regardless of price (intermediate solution)

causal configuration	raw coverage	unique coverage	consistency
Model:			
age*~income*gender*overly tren dy*symbolism*functionality*ae sthetic	0.394852	0.083293	0.904841
Additional models:			
~age*~income*gender*overly tren dy*~symbolism*~functionality* ~aesthetic	0.228023	0.022827	0.888363
~age*~income*gender*~overly tre ndy*symbolism*functionality*~ aesthetic	0.318844	0.041525	0.886563
~age*income*gender*overly tren dy*symbolism*functionality*ae sthetic	0.256678	0.068965	0.859350
Solution coverage: 0.541282			
Solution consistency: 0.827394			

Source: the authors

The main model for Research 3 is

age*~income*gender*overly trendy*symbolism*functionality*aesthetic.

Regardless of price, older women (ages 30 and over) still consider good design in their consideration to purchase fast-fashion products. This notion can be taken as the reason that elder women have high expectations for fast-fashion products, whether or not they have low prices.

Research 4

Research 4 tested why consumers want to purchase low-quality products in a smartphone context, regardless of prices shown in Table 23.6. There are six configurations that demonstrate the possible reasons:

1   ~income*~age*~overly trendy*~symbolism*~functionality*~aesthetic;
2   ~income*gender*~age*~overly trendy*functionality*aesthetic;
3   ~income*gender*~age*overly trendy*symbolism*~functionality*~aesthetic;
4   income*gender*~age*~overly trendy*~symbolism*functionality*~aesthetic;
5   income*gender*~age*overly trendy*symbolism*functionality*aesthetic;
6   ~income*gender*age*overly trendy*symbolism*functionality*aesthetic.

The results were the following:

• For the most part, younger generations with low household income will buy low-quality smartphones even if they do not have any elements of good product design (~overly trendy, ~symbolism, ~functionality, or ~aesthetics);

470

Table 23.6 Consumers want to purchase low-quality products in smartphone context regardless of price (intermediate solution)

Causal configuration	Raw coverage	Unique coverage	Consistency
Model:			
~income*~age*~overly trendy*~symbolism*~functionality*~aesthetic	0.362648	0.132016	0.901720
Additional models:			
~income*gender*~age*~overly trendy*functionality*aesthetic	0.419763	0.117984	0.838531
~income*gender*~age*overly trendy*symbolism*~functionality*~aesthetic	0.211660	0.004941	0.866505
income*gender*~age*~overly trendy*~symbolism*functionality*~aesthetic	0.165415	0.008696	0.883844
income*gender*~age*overly trendy*symbolism*functionality*aesthetic	0.192688	0.041107	0.908667
~income*gender*age*overly trendy*symbolism*functionality*aesthetic	0.299802	0.056324	0.897633
Solution coverage: 0.691304			
Solution consistency: 0.831076			

Source: The authors

- Sometimes, young women (ages 30 and under) with low household income will buy a low-quality smartphone that has some or even all elements of good design (overly trendy, symbolism, functionality, and aesthetics);
- Young women (ages 30 and under) with high household incomes consider functionality an important element of product design but also consider all elements of good design in their purchase (overly trendy, symbolism, functionality, and aesthetics).

Combining these results with those of Research 3, it is apparent that good design is an important factor to female customers. This may indicate to companies that female customers are more willing to spend money on smartphones with good design. Some big brand companies could therefore target female customers and focus on the design of smartphone as a means to enhance profits.

The most representative model for Research 4 is

income*~age*~overly trendy*~symbolism*~functionality*~aesthetic.

Groups with low income will not consider smartphone design regardless of price. For them, a low price is almost the only factor in buying low-quality products. It can be concluded that groups with low household incomes have a kind of saving psychology, as they consider price the most important factor in purchasing products. Because of the limitations of disposable personal income, product expectations are reduced in these groups. Companies would do well to group to clear inventory or sell off the last generation of smartphone.

Discussion and conclusions

Main findings and discussion

This study aims to examine under which conditions customers will accept low-quality products. Price was discovered to be a factor, if not the most important one, in influencing intended purchases. This may be because price is the consumer's most determinable cost and so plays an important role in decision-making (Alfred 2013). Having a low product price is a strong competitive factor. Low prices on low-quality products can be achieved more easily than with high-quality products due to the lower cost of raw materials or configurations. The connection between quality and price may indicate that customers will accept low-quality products with low prices. The data dictates that different generations are equally affected by the low price condition, regardless of customer gender and household income.

According to Schubert (2017), lower income households will be affected more by the low-quality advantage than higher income households. In the case of fast-fashion products and electronic products, sales volume is the key factor for high profit. To attract the most customers, lower household incomes should not be ignored. They represent a large segment and sizable purchasing power. Low-quality products can still have a relatively high-quality product design, meeting at least some of the customer's needs. Moreover, according to Zhou *et al.* (2015), change in demand for fast-fashion and electronic products can be extremely rapid, creating internal competition between generations. This may result in extra costs to companies. Consequently, faster sales of products help companies reduce inventories.

Design affects female customers for the most part. Younger and older females will consider both low prices and good design in low-quality products. So, the key points for companies are low price and good design. Having a product with a low price is easily achievable through cost reduction. It is important for companies to try to deliver innovative designs at a low cost.

There are many similarities and differences in the influencing factors in both fast-fashion and smartphone industries. The configuration in both fast-fashion and smartphone industries is similar regarding high expectations of products. Low price plays quite an important role in both contexts, proving that price is one of the most important factors in this study. To most consumers, low quality should mean low price. Women are more likely to accept low-quality products compared to men, but most women only accept low price products if they have good designs. Age is an influencing factor, with younger generations more likely to accept low-quality products than older generations in both markets.

The differences in the fast-fashion and smartphone industries are due to difference in choices. The determining variable in the fast-fashion industry is gender; only women accept low-quality products. Low-quality fast-fashion products are less attractive to men. In comparison to the smartphone industry, however, a low price is one of the most important factors. Household income has a great influence on fast-fashion, while it has less effect on the purchasing of low-quality smartphones.

The similarly high consistency and raw coverage in Tables 23.3 and 23.4 demonstrates that older Chinese women (ages 30 and over) tend to accept both fast-fashion products and smartphones if they have both good design and a low price. However, the fast-fashion and smartphone industries face the dilemma of cutting costs as well as improving all attributes of product design. Most young people require low prices and few attributes of product design, which means designers can cut costs in this area.

Contributions and managerial implications

This study is one of the first to measure clearly the advantages of low-quality short-life products and apply fsQCA to exploring customer purchase intentions for low-quality products. It expands on prior knowledge of low-quality products, especially in China. Rather than using a structural equation model to identify positive or negative influences, fsQCA can reveal particular configurations of factors.

This study offers several managerial implications. With the rapid changes in consumers' aesthetic senses and developing technologies, it is imperative that companies consider how to attract more customers and earn higher profits. Most customers follow a practical approach in buying products and pay more attention to price. Selling low-quality products at a low price may get a good response from these groups, thereby allowing companies to achieve greater successes.

Companies may consider establishing subordinate brands to avoid reducing the image of the main brand. Regardless of price, product design is a driving factor in customer choice, even with low quality. Low-quality products can accelerate the replacement cycle. A customer may be more willing to accept low-quality products with lower prices if they have good design, so quality may not be the determining factor in a customer's choice. If companies set a low price or produce a novel design, customers may be more willing to accept the low-quality product. Companies and customers can achieve a win-win situation. However, the satisfaction of customers who have bought low-quality products can be researched to find ways to improve product quality or other attributes. Low-quality products can be good ways to research potential high-quality products.

Future studies

There are some limitations in this research. First, due to concern about business ethics, hidden low-quality products (where companies sell low-quality products to customers without informing them) were not tested, as it was important that product quality be perceived as accurately as possible. Second, this chapter tests limited diversity in the low-quality area – some potentially relevant variables ware not tested. Future research can explore more variables such as country of origin, product involvement, and so on. This chapter focused solely on Chinese customers. Wider studies might reveal cultural differences between countries in buying behaviour. Other industries could be covered. This chapter focuses only on fast-fashion and smartphones. Also, the company perspective rather than consumer perspectives could be studied.

Acknowledgements

This chapter is based on Sun, Y., Cai, H.H., Su, R. and Shen, Q., 2019. Advantage of low quality in short life cycle products. *Asia Pacific Journal of Marketing and Logistics*, 32(5), 1038–1054.

References

Ajzen, I. and Driver, B.L., 1992. application of the theory of planned behavior to leisure choice. *Journal of Leisure Research*, 24(3), 207–224. https://doi.org/10.1080/00222216.1992.11969889.

Alfred, O., 2013. Influences of price and quality on consumer purchase of smart phone in the Kumasi metropolis in Ghana: A comparative study. *European Journal of Business and Management*, 5(1), 179–198. ISSN 2222-1905.

Belk, R.W., 1988. Possessions and the extended self. *Journal of Consumer Research*, 15(2), 139–168. https://doi.org/10.1086/209154.

Bhardwaj, V. and Fairhurst, A., 2010. Fast-fashion: Response to changes in the fashion industry. *The International Review of Retail Distribution and Consumer Research*, 20, 165–173. https://doi.org/10.1080/09593960903498300.

Bloch, P.H., 2011. Product design and marketing: Reflections after fifteen years. *Journal of Product Innovation Management*, 28(3), 378–380. https://doi.org/10.1111/j.1540-5885.2011.00805.x.

Boztepe, S., 2007. User value: Competing theories and models. *International Journal of Design*, 1(2), 55–63. www.ijdesign.org/index.php/IJDesign/article/view/61/29.

Candi, M., 2010. Benefits of aesthetic design as an element of new service development. *Journal of Product Innovation Management*, 27(7), 1047–1064. https://doi.org/10.1111/j.1540-5885.2010.00770.x.

Creusen, M.E. and Schoormans, J.P., 2005. The different roles of product appearance in consumer choice. *Journal of Product Innovation Management*, 22(1), 63–81.

Dabade, B.M. and Wankhade, L., 2006. TQM with quality perception: A system dynamics approach. *TQM Magazine*, 18(4), 341–357. https://doi.org/10.1108/09544780610671020.

Desmet, P. and Hekkert, P., 2007. Framework of product experience. *National Science Council Taipei*, 1(1), 56–66. www.ijdesign.org/index.php/IJDesign/article/view/66/15.

Dodds, W.B., Monroe, K.B. and Grewal, D., 1991. Effects of price, brand and store information on buyers' product evaluations. *Journal of Marketing Research*, 28(3), 307–319. DOI: 10.2307/3172866.

Foroohar, R., 2005. Fabulous fashion. *Newsweek* [online]. Available from: www.newsweek.com/fabulous-fashion-121093 [Accessed 15 Oct 2020].

Gan, S.S., Pujawan, I.N., Suparno, A. and Widodo, B., 2015. Pricing decision model for new and remanufactured short-life cycle products with time-dependent demand. *Operations Research Perspectives*, 2(C), 1–12. https://doi.org/10.1016/j.orp.2014.11.001.

Gemser, G. and Leenders, M., 2001. How integrating industrial design in the product development process impacts on company performance. *Journal of Product Innovation Management*, 18(1), 28–38. https://doi.org/10.1016/S0737-6782(00)00069-2.

Graeff, T.R., 1997. Comprehending product attributes and benefits: The role of product knowledge and means-end chain inferences. *Psychology and Marketing*, 14(14), 163–183. https://doi.org/10.1002/(SICI)1520-6793(199703)14:2<163::AID-MAR4>3.0.CO;2-B.

Gutman, J., 1982. A means–end chain model based on consumer categorization processes. *Journal of Marketing*, 46(2), 60–72. DOI: 10.2307/3203341.

Hekkert, P. and Leder, H., 2008. Product aesthetics. In H.N.J. Schifferstein and P. Hekkert, eds. *Product Experience*. New York: Elsevier Science Publishers, 259–285. https://doi.org/10.1016/B978-008045089-6.50013-7.

Helo, P., 2004. Managing agility and productivity in the electronics industry. *Industrial Management and Data Systems*, 104(7), 567–577. DOI: 10.1108/02635570410550232.

Hertenstein, J.H., Platt, M.B. and Veryzer, R.W., 2005. The impact of industrial design effectiveness on corporate financial performance. *Journal of Product Innovation Management*, 22(1), 3–21. https://doi.org/10.1111/j.0737-6782.2005.00100.x.

Kleine, R.E., Kleine, S.S. and Kernan, J.B., 1993. Mundane consumption and the self: A social-identity perspective. *Journal of Consumer Psychology*, 2(3), 209–235. https://doi.org/10.1016/S1057-7408(08)80015-0.

Hoegg, J.A. and Alba, J.W., 2011. Seeing is believing (too much): The influence of product form on perceptions of functional performance. *Journal of Product Innovation Management*, 28(3), 346–359. DOI: 10.1111/j.1540-5885.2011.00802.x.

Holt, D.B., 1997. Poststructuralist lifestyle analysis: Conceptualizing the social patterning of consumption in postmodernity. *Journal of Consumer Research*, 23(4), 326–350 [online]. Available from: www.jstor.org/stable/2489569.

Homburg, C., Schwemmle, M. and Kuehnl, C., 2015. New product design: Concept, measurement and consequences. *Journal of Marketing*, 79(3), 41–56. https://doi.org/10.1509/jm.14.0199.

Hsueh, C.F., 2011. An inventory control model with consideration of remanufacturing and product life cycle. *International Journal of Production Economics*, 133(2), 645–652. https://doi.org/10.1016/j.ijpe.2011.05.007.

Huang, J., Lee, B.C.Y. and Shu, H.H., 2004. Consumer attitude toward gray market goods. *International Marketing Review*, 21(6), 598–614. DOI 10.1108/02651330410568033.

Keller, K.L., 1993. Conceptualizing, measuring and managing customer-based brand equity. *Journal of Marketing*, 57(1), 1–22. DOI: 10.2307/1252054.

Kim, H., Choo, H.J. and Yoon, N., 2013. The motivational drivers of fast-fashion avoidance. *Journal of Fashion Marketing and Management*, 17(2), 243–260. https://doi.org/10.1108/JFMM-10-2011-0070.

Kim, K.H., 1998. An analysis of optimum number of response categories for Korean consumers. *Journal of Global Scholars of Marketing Science*, 1(1), 61–86. DOI: 10.1080/12297119.1998.9707386.

Kirmani, A. and Rao, A.R., 2000. No pain, no gain: A critical review of the literature on signaling unobservable product quality. *Journal of Marketing*, 64(2), 66–79. www.jstor.org/stable/3203443?seq=1.

Lee, J.K. and Lee, W.N., 2009. Country-of-origin effects on consumer product evaluation and purchase intention: The role of objective versus subjective knowledge. *Journal of International Consumer Marketing*, 21(2), 137–151. https://doi.org/10.1080/08961530802153722.

Leder, H., Belke, B., Oeberst, A. and Augustin, D., 2004. A model of aesthetic appreciation and aesthetic judgments. *British Journal of Psychology*, 95(4), 489–508. DOI: 10.1348/0007126042369811.

Lichtenstein, D.R., Ridgway, N.M. and Netemeyer, R.G., 1993. Price perceptions and consumer shopping behavior: A field study. *Journal of Marketing Research*, 30(2), 234–245. https://doi.org/10.1177/002224379303000208.

Luchs, M. and Swan, K.S., 2011. The emergence of product design as a field of marketing inquiry. *Journal of Product Innovation Management*, 28(3), 327–345. DOI: 10.2139/ssrn.1645313.

Martins, J., Costa, C., Oliveira, T., Gonçalves, R. and Branco, F., 2019. How smartphone advertising influences consumers' purchase intention. *Journal of Business Research*, 94, 378–387. https://doi.org/10.1016/j.jbusres.2017.12.047.

Marx, A., 2006. *Towards More Robust Model Specification in QCA Results from a Methodological Experiment. COMPASSS WP Series 2006–43*. Antwerp, Belgium: Hogeschool Antwerp [online]. Available from: http:\\www. compasss. org\wpseries\Marx2006.pdf [Accessed 15 December 2015].

McConnell, J.D., 1968. The price-quality relationship in an experimental setting. *Journal of Marketing Research*, 5(3), 300–303. DOI: 10.2307/3150348.

McCracken, G., 1986. Culture and consumption: A theoretical account of the structure and movement of the cultural meaning of consumer goods. *Journal of Consumer Research*, 13(1), 71–84. https://doi.org/10.1086/209048.

McNamara, C., 2015. Trade liberalization, social policies and health: An empirical case study. *Globalization and Health*, 11(1), 1–19. https://doi.org/10.1186/s12992-015-0126-8.

Mishra, A., 2016. Attribute-based design perceptions and consumer-brand relationship: Role of user expertise. *Journal of Business Research*, 69(12), 5983–5992. https://doi.org/10.1016/j.jbusres.2016.05.012.

Monroe, K.B., 1973. Buyers' subjective perceptions of price. *Journal of Marketing Research*, 10(1), 70–80. DOI: 10.2307/3149411.

Noble, C.H. and Kumar, M., 2010. Exploring the appeal of product design: A grounded, value-based model of key design elements and relationships. *Journal of Product Innovation Management*, 27(5), 640–657. https://doi.org/10.1111/j.1540-5885.2010.00742.x.

Panzone, L.A., 2012. Alcohol tax, price–quality proxy and discounting: A reason why alcohol taxes may rebound. *Journal of Agricultural Economics*, 63(3), 715–736. DOI: 10.1111/j.1477-9552.2012.00351.x.

Pierre, C., Morwitz, V.G. and Reinartz, W.J., 2005. Do intentions really predict behavior? Self-generated validity effects in survey research. *Journal of Marketing*, 69(2), 1–14. https://doi.org/10.1509/jmkg.69.2.1.60755.

Radford, S.K. and Bloch, P.H., 2011. Linking innovation to design: Consumer responses to visual product newness. *Journal of Product Innovation Management*, 28(1), 208–220. DOI: 10.1111/j.1540-5885.2011.00871.x.

Ragin, C.C., 2000. *Fuzzy Set Social Science*. Chicago: University of Chicago Press.

Ragin, C.C., 2008. *Redesigning Social Inquiry: Fuzzy Sets and Beyond*. Chicago: The University of Chicago Press.

Ragin, C.C., 2009. Qualitative comparative analysis using fuzzy sets (fsQCA). In B. Rihoux and C.C. Ragin, eds. *Configurational Comparative Methods: Qualitative Comparative Analysis (QCA) and Related Techniques (Applied Social Research Methods)*. Thousand Oaks, CA; London: Sage Publications, 87–121. https://dx.doi.org/10.4135/9781452226569.n5.

Ragin, C.C. and Davey, S., 2014. *Fuzzy-Set/Qualitative Comparative Analysis 2.5*. Irvine, CA: Department of Sociology, University of California. www.socsci.uci.edu/~cragin/fsQCA/.

Ragin, C.C. and Fiss, P.C., 2008. Net effects versus configurational analysis: An empirical demonstration. In C.C. Ragin, ed. *Redesigning Social Inquiry: Fuzzy sets and Beyond*. Chicago: University of Chicago Press, 190–212. www.researchgate.net/publication/285868778_Net_effects_analysis_versus_configurational_analysis_An_empirical_demonstration.

Ragin, C.C., Strand, S.I. and Rubinson, C., 2017 *User's Guide to Fuzzy-Set/Qualitative Comparative Analysis*. University of Arizona, 87 [online]. Available from: www.socsci.uci.edu/~cragin/fsQCA/download/fsQCAManual.pdf [Accessed 14 October 2020].

Rao, A.R., 2005. The quality of price as a quality cue. *Journal of Marketing Research*, 42(4), 401–405. www.jstor.org/stable/30162389?seq=1.

Rao, A.R. and Monroe, K.B., 1989. The effect of price, brand name and store name on buyers' perceptions of product quality: An integrative review. *Journal of Marketing Research*, 26(3), 351–357. DOI: 10.2307/3172907.

Reber, R., Schwarz, N. and Winkielman, P., 2004. Processing fluency and aesthetic pleasure: Is beauty in the perceiver's processing experience? *Personality and Social Psychology Review*, 8(4), 364–382. https://doi.org/10.1207/s15327957pspr0804_3.

Rindova, V.P. and Petkova, A.P., 2007. When is a new thing a good thing? Technological change, product form design and perceptions of value for product innovations. *Organization Science*, 18(2), 217–232. https://doi.org/10.1287/orsc.1060.0233.

Schlosser, A.E., White, T.B. and Lloyd, S.M., 2006. Converting website visitors into buyers: How website investment increases consumer trusting beliefs and online purchase intentions. *Journal of Marketing*, 70, 133–148. https://doi.org/10.1509/jmkg.70.2.133.

Schubert, S., 2017. The low-quality advantage in vertical product differentiation. *Managerial and Decision Economics*, 38(7), 923–928. https://doi.org/10.1002/mde.2825.

Shen, G.C.-C., 2015. Users' adoption of mobile applications: Product type and message framing's moderating effect. *Journal of Business Research*, 68(11), 2317–2321. DOI: 10.1016/j.jbusres.2015.06.018.

Shirai, M., 2015. Impact of "high quality, low price" appeal on consumer evaluations. *Journal of Promotion Management*, 21(6), 776–797. DOI: 10.1080/10496491.2015.1088922.

Spears, N. and Yazdanparast, A., 2014. Revealing obstacles to the consumer imagination. *Journal of Consumer Psychology*, 24(3), 363–372. https://doi.org/10.1016/j.jcps.2014.01.003.

Stafford, J.E. and Enis, B.M., 1969. The price-quality relationship: An extension. *Journal of Marketing Research*, 7(4), 456–458. DOI: 10.2307/3150082.

Sun, Y., Cai, H.H., Su, R. and Shen, Q., 2019. Advantage of low quality in short life cycle products. *Asia Pacific Journal of Marketing and Logistics*, 32(5), 1038–1054. https://doi.org/10.1108/APJML-03-2019-0148.

Sun, Y., Garrett, C.T., Phau, I. and Zheng, B., 2020. Case-based models of customer-perceived sustainable marketing and its effect on perceived customer equity. *Journal of Business Research*, 117, 615–622. DOI: 10.1016/j.jbusres.2018.09.007.

Verganti, R., 2008. Design, meanings and radical innovation: A metamodel and a research agenda. *Journal of Product Innovation Management*, 25(5), 436–456. https://doi.org/10.1111/j.1540-5885.2008.00313.x.

Wang, C.L., Li, D., Barnes, B.R. and Ahn, J., 2012. Country image, product image and consumer purchase intention: Evidence from an emerging economy. *International Business Review*, 21(6), 1041–1051. https://doi.org/10.1016/j.ibusrev.2011.11.010.

Woodside, A.G., 2015. Visualizing matching generalizing: Case identification hypotheses and case-level data analysis. *Australasian Marketing Journal*, 23, 246–258. DOI: 10.1108/978-1-78560-461-420152002.

Woodside, A.G., 2016. The good practices manifesto: Overcoming bad practices pervasive in current research in business. *Journal of Business Research*, 69(2), 365–381. https://doi.org/10.1016/j.jbusres.2015.09.008.

Woodside, A.G., ed., 2017. *The Complexity Turn: Cultural, Management and Marketing Applications*. New York: Springer. DOI: 10.1007/978-3-319-47028-3.

Woodside, A.G., Hsu, S.Y. and Marshall, R., 2011. General theory of cultures' consequences on international tourism behavior. *Journal of Business Research*, 64(8), 785–799. https://doi.org/10.1016/j.jbusres.2010.10.008.

Woodside, A.G., Schpektor, A. and Xia, X., 2013. Triple sense-making of findings from marketing experiments using the dominant variable based-logic, case-based logic and isomorphic modeling. *International Journal of Business and Economics*, 12(2), 131–153. http://hdl.handle.net/20.500.11937/18244.

Wu, P.L., Yeh, G. and Hsiao, C., 2011. The effect of store image and service quality on brand image and purchase intention for private label brands. *Australasian Marketing Journal*, 19(1), 30–39. https://doi.org/10.1016/j.ausmj.2010.11.001.

Wu, P.L., Yeh, S.S., Huan, T.C. and Woodside, A.G., 2014. Applying complexity theory to deepen service dominant logic: Configural analysis of customer experience-and-outcome assessments of professional services for personal transformations. *Journal of Business Research*, 67(8), 1647–1670. https://doi.org/10.1016/j.jbusres.2014.03.012.

Xie, X., Fang, L., Zeng, S., 2016. Collaborative innovation network and knowledge transfer performance: A fsQCA approach. *Journal of Business Research*, 69, 5210–5215. https://doi.org/10.1016/j.jbusres.2016.04.114.

Zeithaml, V.A., 1988. Consumer perceptions of price, quality and value: A means-end model and synthesis of evidence. *Journal of Marketing*, 52(3), 2–22. DOI: 10.2307/1251446.

Zhou, E., Zhang, J., Gou, Q. and Liang, L., 2015. A two period pricing model for new fashion style launching strategy. *International Journal of Production Economics*, 160, 144–156. https://doi.org/10.1016/j.ijpe.2014.10.008.

PART V

Reflections and futures

24

FORESIGHT IN MARKETING AND MARKETING RESEARCH

Sérgio Brodsky

Summary

This chapter explores both the endogenous and exogenous appropriateness, challenges, and benefits of employing strategic foresight and futures thinking as an overall practice in marketing research and, more broadly, marketing as a discipline and the marketing communications industry. This is in accordance with foresight's seven usability dimensions, namely 1. learning focused; 2. continuous, adaptive, and narrative-based; 3. challenges a used future; 4. offers alternative futures; 5. inclusive and cognitively diverse; 6. supported by worldview and underlying narrative or metaphor; and 7. a vision, neither too far nor too near, and one that enables and ennobles. The author draws from his experience in the above mentioned fields to allow for a more pragmatic and nuanced appreciation of foresight in marketing practice.

Introduction

People buy into ideas, shop on trends, and consume philosophies through similar mental processes to those they apply when purchasing their next holiday, car or pair of shoes (Brodsky 2015) Thus, understanding human behaviour, culture, and the impact of technology and having the ability to anticipate demand is marketing's ultimate source of value.

Marketing, as the most encompassing of all social sciences, has greatly benefited from knowledge domains as distinct as anthropology, psychology, evolutionary biology, statistical modelling, and many others. Research methods deriving from the disciplines of strategic foresight and futures thinking (SFFT) represent yet another niche able to deliver unique value for practitioners, their organisations, and the many stakeholders they serve or relate to. Differences between traditional market research and foresight are many. Time horizons in foresight will often range between 10 and 20 years and beyond, and market research will often focus on much shorter timespans (usually 5–10 years). Last, while foresight orients decision-making (for policy and also business) in a general way and only in specific cases does it lead to concrete strategy building, traditional market research can be used for concrete short- to medium-term company business and strategy planning (Zweck and Zweck 2007). This is particularly important considering the data-led short-termism dominating business practices and its negative impact, having led to an overall crisis in effective marketing.

Short-term marketing activities are often enabled with immediate feedback in the form of responses, clicks, or promotional sales. For marketers, the ability to see the direct impact of their short-term efforts provides great reassurance. But the sum total of combined, sequential short-term effects does not lead to long-term growth. Moreover, that is a fake sentiment, as it is narrowly manufactured and at the expense of brand building – the most valuable business tool ever invented (Roach 2018) – and often positively impacting short-term effects as well. All that despite the seminal work from Field and Binet, which fundamentally proves – through empirical data – that orchestrating long-term brand-building with short-term direct response campaigns is best practice (Binet 2011). Supporting that is the work from Professor Byron Sharp and his colleagues at the Ehrenberg-Bass Institute, where successful marketing is distilled to two simple principles, mental availability and physical availability. While the latter is a matter of distribution and supply-chain effectiveness, the former is a lengthy, continuous journey of creating memories in consumers' minds with strong, positive associations about a given brand. And because of short-termism pressures, investment in creativity also has dropped for over a decade now, compromising the effectiveness of campaigns.

Figure 24.1 shows the ongoing decline of marketing effectiveness, which coincides with the growing adoption of digital marketing technologies and their real-time metrics. Figure 24.2 shows the decline in the effectiveness of campaigns that won creative awards.

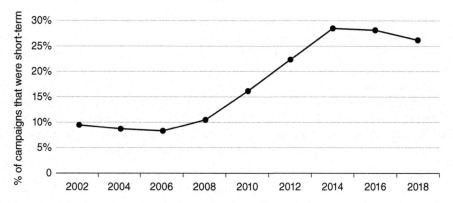

Figure 24.1 Short-termism in marketing creating an illusion of success for marketers

Source: Institute of Practitioners of Advertising (IPA) Databank 1998–2018 UK

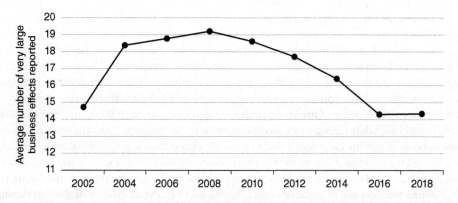

Figure 24.2 Short-termism responsible for decreasing the effectiveness of creativity in advertising

Source: Institute of Practitioners of Advertising (IPA) Databank 1998–2018 UK

In the context of the unprecedented COVID-19 pandemic, the acceleration of e-commerce and digital transformation is distracting organisations' marketing departments – even more – from focusing on long-term growth with short-term metrics. For companies to grow for the long term, they do not need big data: they need long data. They need to track things over long periods of time and not just the right here, right now and their myriad correlations. For that to be possible, setting up a vision that transcends finite financial calendars and, most importantly, committing to it is of fundamental importance.

When looking at the bigger picture, marketing is, arguably, one of the most dominant forces in our civilisation. Marketing has been a key driver of technological adoption, scientific advancements, and the creation of brands able to influence and actualise people's desired life-styles. On the other hand, the marketing communications (marcomms) industry polluted cities, annoyed consumers, and is gradually commoditising itself. Beyond a mass-media cacophony, the marcomms industry has also contributed to a significant carbon footprint and runaway consumption, leading towards severe environmental threats.

In the United Kingdom, for instance, advertising is responsible for two million tons of carbon dioxide emissions annually, equivalent to heating 50% of London's social housing, according to *CarbonTrack* (Ward 2010). Researchers also found that only around 20% of emissions for which we are individually responsible come from direct usage, such as driving a car or having a shower. The rest is all hidden in the supply chains of what we buy (Ivanova 2016). And between production and purchase lies promotion – powered by media advertising – the last frontier in terms of redesigning our economy's supply chain from linear to circular.

Because of that, considering SFFT as more than a tool within the marketing function but a lens to reassessing its role in commerce and society is of equal, if not greater, importance. Yet, for foresight to be meaningful, it needs to be integrated fundamentally into the ways of working, which is why we need to look at how foresight can be managed and implemented (Inayatullah 2015). Rather than examining the validity of foresight and marketing frameworks, the focus will be on the practicalities of enhancing the latter with the former. In this chapter, we will explore both the endogenous as well as exogenous appropriateness of employing SFFT as an overall practice in the marketing discipline, in accordance with its seven usability dimensions (Inayatullah 2015), which are explained in Table 24.1.

The internal context of marketers and foresight

Futurists and marketers have more in common than one might think. Whilst the former focuses on projecting unimaginable scenarios across the most varied contexts, the latter focuses on communicating a business promise that is expected to be kept. Despite having different lines of work, both projections and promises exist as bridges between the present and the future. The use of strategic narratives is what unites both practitioners. In the case of marketers, strategic narratives can be deployed to communicate the very essence of a brand via visual and verbal identities or articulate a moment in time via advertising campaigns. Yet, such narratives are often limited by their brevity. Brand narratives, composed of marketing's 4Ps – price, product, place, and promotion – are usually sustained for periods of three to ten years prior to a brand refresh, repositioning, or even a total rebrand. Advertising campaigns will not exceed a few weeks on air, ideally leveraging a cultural moment, trend, or conversation. While many brands do surpass a ten-year lifespan, their narratives are cyclically refreshed to avoid becoming "wall-paper" in market, with their management often organised annually.

Still, while a brand must plan in 12-month increments, it should not avoid the long-term view and plan a longer course. So, while the long-term aspiration might be to increase consideration by pushing the perceptions of fairness, speed, and friendliness, marketers set all

Table 24.1 The seven usability dimensions of futures marketing

Dimension	Explanation	Example
1 Learning focused	Rather than predictions and extrapolations, the future needs to be used through a learning trajectory, involving object and subjects, where scenarios guide assumptions and knowledge is malleable enough to evolve and transform as it improves.	Nation-branding programs, given their scope and dimensions, tend to employ more flexible approaches so emerging issues, shocks or novelties become information that is learnt and able to course-correct the trajectory towards a desired future.
2 Continuous, adaptive, and narrative-based	Foresight cannot be a set-and-forget exercise. It is ongoing, ensuring the trajectory is aligned with the desired destination, making participants accountable by involving them as key actors of their futures narrative.	Brand China's current strategy encompasses an annual Chinese Brands Day every May 10th and a nationwide China Council for Brand Development, sustaining the learning journey and coordinating the many efforts contributing towards the nation's perceived narrative.
3 Challenges a used future	Every organisation has particular practices that it engages in that do not reflect its preferred future. Indeed, it often lives strategies that move counter to its vision. This conformity creates situations where the future becomes used, since its veracity is not one held by reality but by earlier worldviews.	Zero-based budgeting, the practice of predefining an organisation's marketing investment, not based on past year's extrapolations from the finance department but on future projections guided by clear objectives and led by a marketer, is one of the most effective ways to challenge an organisation's used future.
4 Offers alternative futures	Using alternative futures is a crucial principle in practicing foresight to negotiate such uncertainty. Alternative futures or scenarios can help an organisation become more flexible and adaptable. They also help develop a range of alternative visions and strategies.	These scenarios can be developed through many techniques, and what has appeared to be most useful is to challenge one's core assumptions about the way the world is and the way the world is developing. CLA game and the Sarkar game ensure that participants actually feel their way into alternative futures.
5 Inclusive and cognitively diverse	As the future is uncertain, bringing in alternative voices from varied fields can help reduce uncertainty and find new solutions. In foresight projects, bringing in the full range of stakeholders, while messy, enhances the robustness of the scenarios and the strategies developed.	Exploratory workshops will usually aim at bringing together a balanced mix of stakeholders to create scenarios. To ensure cognitive diversity is applied, subsequent validation workshops and/or surveys can help bring new voices to the fore.

Dimension	Explanation	Example
6 Supported by worldview and underlying narrative or metaphor	Context is everything; it shapes and frames our beliefs and behaviours. Hence, to change the worldview, one needs to first understand the dominant one to propose a new construct to emerge. Without understanding deeper perspectives, strategies often fail, as they reinforce the worldview of the dominant. Thus, learning from those who are challenging the system, who see reality differently and, based on that, find the worldview and develop new cognitive patterns that support the new story is key to affecting change.	Urban brand-utility is an approach that challenges the worldview of marketing communications from being "a driver of conspicuous consumption that hijacks culture" to becoming a regenerative force for sustainable cities that advances culture. The underlying metaphor of "soul of capitalism" was also repurposed as "turbine for the circular economy".
7 A vision, neither too far nor too near, and one that enables and ennobles	Visioning involves citizens, experts (collecting the data, testing the data, searching for disruptors), and leaders (who can champion particular projects or resist change). And it is personal. Each person must ask themselves questions like these: • Where do they want to be in 20 or 30 years? • Who is with them? • What does nature look like? • What technologies do they wish to use? • What is the built environment like?	It is not by chance Apple has consistently been one of the strongest brands in the world. Steve Jobs's vision of "making a dent in the world" wasn't only a journey without a clear destination but one where every new beginning – in the form of new innovations – could lead to that.

Source: The author

these objectives with the next 12 months as the target, even though it is a five-year mission. Because of these dynamics, attempts at future-proofing an organisation on the long-term future (+10 years) challenges the marketer as change agent in organisations and institutions. As the brand and customer champion, the marketer will find her/himself in a constant tension between the short and the long, from technical lists of things to do, often immediately relevant, adaptive strategies, through to the more transformative journey of rewiring the brands they work for, beyond financial cycles. A brand's strategy at its best can and should be a key source for foresight narratives.

Figure 24.3 shows the evolution of brand from being a subset of marketing to becoming an organisation's guiding principle and a gateway into the future.

Strong brands like Nike, Apple, or Chanel are strong because their core narratives can easily unfold into multiple futures. For example, it is not hard to imagine what each of those three brands would be like as an airline, hotel, or restaurant. But, when taking a company like, for instance, Marriot, it becomes quite hard to imagine what it could be in sectors such as apparel, electronics, or fashion. That is because Marriot is mainly a logo, not a brand. Its narrative is

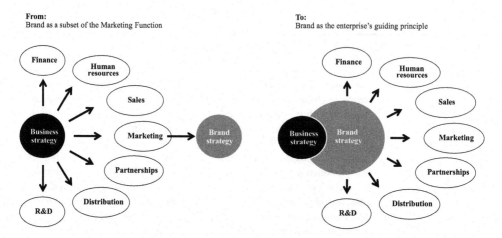

From:
Brand as a subset of the Marketing Function

To:
Brand as the enterprise's guiding principle

Figure 24.3 Brand as purpose, belief system, and business direction

Source: The author

contrived, uninspiring, and lacks meaning consumers can relate to – not conducive for more expansive futures to being imagined.

Short-term marketing, while also requiring the capacity to foresee alternatives, will often return to business as usual once tactics have been deployed. The allure towards quick fixes with immediate returns can blind marketers from greater gains and numb deeper professional ambitions. However, the mechanistic, heavily specialised, and action-oriented short term can easily fail as individuals in the organisation are not prepared to confront what they do not know. As a result, anxiety overwhelms and, as Peter Drucker is purported to have said, "culture eats strategy for breakfast" (2013).

Transformative journeys – learning spirals – require a champion, institutional support, a willingness to engage with emerging issues and use scenarios wisely, and the capacity to move beyond a simple fix-it solution to embrace the long run (Inayatullah 2015). The readiness to learn from this longer journey as much as learning from learning is *sine qua non* for its fruition. This is needed since identifying emerging issues and weak signals and exploring alternative futures are but a means to re-imagining the core narrative of the business, creating new equity for the brand and enabling new futures to unfold. Using causal layered analysis, the new brand recasts, reframes what is counted, what systemic interventions are required, and how stakeholders see the organisation (Milojević and Milojević 2015).

It is this deeper level of foresight that moves organisations to make the transition from technical fixes to adaptive responses and even to transformative journeys, where they change as they create new futures. Foresight at its best does that (Inayatullah 2015).

The external context of the marketing industry and foresight

Traditional foresight models focused on forecasting the future (Armstrong 1970). They assumed that the good futurist was focused on accurate forecasts. He needed to follow, as much as possible, the scientific method, to control for worldview bias by ensuring that the data was solid and the forecasts were based on quantitative models. However, the interpretive turn in the social sciences brought in questions of meaning: what does the future mean to the person making and using the forecast? The parallel here is to question what does the future of the marketing communications industry mean to the marketer (Inayatullah 2015)? This is not only a paradigm shift in SFFT but also in marketing, economics, and, ideally, the entire planet to moving away from a mechanistic view of the world to a more humane one. While efficiency (i.e. short-term) versus effectiveness (i.e. long-term) is the most visible tension in marketing today, beneath the surface an epistemological shift – championed by the idea of brand purpose – is in full swing. Brand purpose, the idea of using your brand communications to raise awareness about (and seldom address) social issues still needs to prove how it makes marketing better.

On the other hand, just as Kate Raeworth's doughnut economics theory (2018) is re-teaching the discipline through a more holistic lens, considering human wellbeing and planetary resources, the goal posts for marketers could also be repurposed. And within the economy are the markets that marketers design. The "marketing concept", originated in Adam Smith's book *The Wealth of Nations*, proposes that its role is to anticipate the needs and wants of potential consumers and satisfy them more effectively than an organisation's competitors. The concept evolved at a similar pace of the neoliberal views of economics, where marketing becomes the oil in the maximisation of profits machine, gaining a public understanding of it as "the art of telling stories so enthralling that people lose track of their wallets" (Duhigg 2017). That said, corporations were originally established with clear public purposes. It is only over the last half century that corporate purpose has come to be equated solely with profit. This has been damaging for corporations' role in society, trust in business, and the impact that business has had on the environment, inequality, and social cohesion. In addition, globalisation and technological advances are exacerbating problems of regulatory lag (The British Academy 2018). Hence, redefining the future(s) of the corporation is paramount to ensure long-term prosperity, not only short-term financial returns. At the helm of it is Colin Mayer, professor of management at the Saïd Business School at the University of Oxford, who along with the British Academy has been leading an ongoing research project aiming at understanding how business might be able to solve the problems it created. In Mayer's view, it begins at redefining the very purpose of business as "to produce profitable solutions to the problems of people and planet, and in the process, it produces profits" (2017).

If structural change is the destination, individual change needs to be means. This same degree of foresight was what also enabled the creation of the Marketing Academy (TMA), a non-profit and voluntary organisation established in 2010 in the United Kingdom and for a few years now present in the United States and Australia. TMA develops leadership capability in talented marketers from the marketing, advertising and communications industries through mentoring, coaching, and experiential learning. A free, highly selective 15-day learning programme is delivered over nine months for 30 carefully selected delegates. The Marketing Academy is concerned about technical skills – still part of the problem – but the emphasis is on leadership. To that end, the organisation converted marketing's traditional 4Ps (price, product, place, promotion) into (The Marketing Academy n.d.):

- Personal: Become an extraordinary human being;
- People: Become an inspirational leader;
- Professional: Become an exceptional marketer;
- Purpose: Become a change maker.

Positive change is happening, yet, clearly, the marketing communications industry was never so challenged, beginning with the fact that most people dislike ads (Ritson 2019); do not really care about brands (Rogers 2019; Albarda 2015); have become cynical about goods and services due to planned obsolescence; and are increasingly engaging with pre-programmed, seamless, and automated services where the human experience is replaced by frictionless interactions. Using an AI deep-learning algorithm developed at CERN to manage its stock, German retailer Otto has been able to predict what customers will order with 90% accuracy. Otto buys products from suppliers without human intervention by looking at 30 billion transactions and 200 variables (i.e. weather). This reduced 2 million stock returns and surplus stock by 20%. Wheelys Moby Store is a 24-hour, unmanned mobile shop that captures biometric data to avoid theft and ensure greater personalisation. The start-up's founders have plans for a cloud-based system that will store and analyse information about customers' behaviours and preferences, helping shop owners predict what products to sell and where. They even see a time when the wheeled shop will be able to autonomously restock by driving itself back to warehouses when supplies run low and increase sales by moving to different locations according to predictions of demand.

Hence, if the act of shopping turns from proactive to reactive, meaning a deselection of what your ecommerce platform of choice decides you need, why would any stimuli be required when choice is no longer a part of the purchase equation? This commoditisation of the marketing function and consequently industry has lowered the barriers for new entrants as well as agencies' and media owners' bargain power. Also, the rise of "grey literature", meaning non-academic, thought-leadership content produced to influence more than enlighten and written by consultants, researchers, and analysts – not necessarily trained marketers, since many companies abolished the need for certifications for marketing department candidates – emphasises the commoditisation challenge (Tzempelikos *et al.* 2020).

The fact that IBM is now the largest design firm on the planet (Fabricant 2014); Accenture the largest digital marketing agency; the Alexa Superbowl ad was produced by an agency acquired by Amazon; and almost 70% of every digital marketing dollar invested is pocketed by Google, Amazon, and Facebook is quite telling (Sterling 2019). Management consultancy and advisory firms have been driving an acquisition spree of several marketing communications agencies with no sign of slowing down (Gianatasio 2017), despite the famous 50/50 merger and acquisition success rate, which shows how the communications function has been moving from the centre to the periphery of bigger corporate ecosystems.

The business of agencies will likely grow a meagre 1% over the long term, according to a report by Credit Suisse (Pash 2020). Further, the tenure of chief marketing officers (CMOs) has for some time been the shortest amongst C-suites and keeps falling (Ives 2020). Consequently, marketing budgets have also, in recent years, been consistently reduced to fund lower prices, new product developments, or convenience. Additionally, automation advancements fuelled by sophisticated machine learning algorithms and supported by long-tail ecommerce platforms may, in the middle-term future, challenge the need to communicate your brand.

As an industry, marketing communications cannot afford to simply evolve; it must leapfrog its trajectory. Data (big or small) has already given us enough insight. It's time to embrace ambiguity and apply genuine foresight to avoid posing for a notorious "Kodak moment". This happens when worldview bias is not a factor to be controlled for but a variable that leads to the richness of foresight and moreover ensures that the policies and strategies that are ensued can be implemented, since there is now ownership. Just as marketers are exemplary in leveraging culture to enhance their organisation's brand-relevance, the opportunity is then to step up and leverage the organisation as an open system where the forecast is situated in multiple perspectives, which in turn gets nested in multiple worldviews, not just describing the organisation but creating its future trajectory (Rabinow 1984).

In this sense, the role of the marketer-futurist is not just to write trend reports, listen to the worldviews of others, and critically (Boulding 1995) bring truth to power but to make a difference in the organisation and the world out there (Dator 2002) through the entire marketing mix of product, promotion, people, place, and other interventions. And, this is crucial, to be aware of his or her own narrative (Inayatullah 2015). The marketer-futurist needs to be positioned as part of the problem and part of the possible solution, not the external observer. For this, the notion of double loop reflection and narrative foresight has been doubly important. First, the marketer-futurist explores his or her own narrative in the field, becomes epistemologically clean, as it were, and second, understands that these stories are based on meanings, worldviews, and practices. That is, the objective and subjective interpenetrate and learn from each other (Inayatullah 2015).

This is the context of the marketing communications industry, which should sharpen the marketer-futurist's proficiency of how he/she uses the future and likewise how the future uses him or her. This means a requirement for data about today and emerging issues, to be filtered by how different stakeholders construct their life stories and their futures. Using critical theory – in the causal layered analysis framework – foresight needs to challenge assumptions and assist – governments, citizen groups, nongovernmental organisations, friends, governments, small business, corporations – in the creation of alternative and preferred futures (Inayatullah 2015). Foresight that works will deliver a new strategy and metaphor that can help create, all the while mindful of the marketer-futurist's own strategy and metaphor in the process.

Principle 1: the learning journey dimension

The first principle, as mentioned earlier, is to frame the foresight journey as learning based. Short-term financial and political output pressures are thus reduced, and with calm minds, experiments can be conducted that optimise productivity and enhance innovation. If this is not done, then at the first failed forecast or the first sign of difficulty – politics at the board level or loss of heart from stakeholders – the foresight process is abandoned. We are back at square one. Worse, since the process was derailed by the incorrect forecast – the common "what happened to paperless offices?" quip to avoid engaging in the future – the entire foresight process is abandoned, and the organisation reverts to being reactive until there is another external shock (Inayatullah 2015).

For instance, back in 2012, Mexico's President Felipe Calderon hired nation-branding expert Simon Anholt for strategic advice to improve the nation's image. In 2018, consultancy firm Brand Finance ranked brand Mexico the most valuable in Latin America. By 2019, Mexico became America's top trading partner (Kopf 2019). Brand Mexico clearly achieved positive outcomes, but that cannot be considered transformative. The international trade and investment agency ProMéxico and the Tourism Promotion Council both made extensive use of the "México" trademark. However, as part of wider austerity measures, the current federal government disbanded both agencies, effectively killing off the "México" brand. In other words, once financial objectives were reached, the 15-year effort died without leaving hints about possible new futures. In fact, if anything, confusion is an outcome that can be verified from a weekend plebiscite in the city of Mexicali, where 76.1% of voters cast ballots against a $1.4 billion brewery, proposed by Constellation Brands to brew beer for export – including Corona, Modelo, and Pacifico. Mexico is the world's biggest beer exporter, but the industry has become the focus for resentment in the arid north, where breweries are perceived as using scarce water resources to quench America's thirst at a time when climate change is exacerbating droughts in the region. Mexican President Andrés Manuel López Obrador said the consultation was necessary because the company and local authorities "didn't take the people into account". Had people and the role of brand Mexico been considered, other than its commodified objectives towards increased tourism, foreign direct investments, and attracting talent, the plebiscite would most likely not have been necessary.

Above and beyond, a brand cannot be built in one administration, be it in the public or private sectors, just as much as a foresight narrative that unfolds into new possibilities.

Brand Japan, on the other hand, offers a rather enlightening learning journey that changed the course of its future. Until the Meiji Restoration (1868–1912) Japan would have been defined by words like samurai, kimono, geisha, and others associated with its folklore. Japan's industrial revolution opened space for a new word and world: modern. However, Japanese modernity only became memorable and globally resonant after the Meiji period when associated with brands like Hitachi (1910), Panasonic (1918), Fujifilm (1934), Toyota (1937), and of course Sony (1946) and the Walkman (1979), among many others.

The "Charter Oath" of April 1868 that formally ended feudal rule decreed that "knowledge shall be sought throughout the world". Some 50 officials set off on a tour of America and Europe to learn about administration, trade, industry, and military affairs. On their return, and with foreign help, they threw their country into a race to catch up with the West, building railways and roads, pursuing land reform that redistributed the old feudal estates, establishing a Western-based system of education, and building a modern army (D.Z. 2018). By 1871, all the feudal class privileges were abolished and replaced by a prefecture system that remains in place even to the present day. In the following year, Japan introduced the Universal Education System. By the end of 1912, Japan had a highly educated population. At present, Japan has a more than 99% literacy rate. The new government also took a major step in 1880 when it sold most of its industries to private investors. A constitution was introduced, leading to the creation of an elected parliament. Japan's new identity emerged alongside the new identity of the Japanese citizen. Further, in 2015, the Japanese government – in an effort to promote the restoration's 150th anniversary – pursued UNESCO's "world heritage" status for various spots important in the ensuing industrial revolution, another way to reinforce the learning journey and bridge the gap between those in the past and those continuously designing Japan's futures. Understanding that change takes time and a critical mass is required, brand Japan has been able to build capacity and capability to execute a narrative that overcomes attempts of propaganda. Regarding the then-emerging new Japanese, it is not only the depth of methodological approach which is important but also the depth within the practitioner. This means that foresight practitioners need to continue to be self-reflective in their own inner thoughts and consciousness and how that influences their use of methodology (Slaughter 1990).

Although key stakeholders would not be aware, they were engaging in a foresight narrative journey; the longitudinal view of the period allows a deconstruction of factors in hindsight. For the foresight practitioner and the marketer, post-analysis is of tremendous value and, indeed, part of the learning journey. That said, one must be careful not to fall in the narrative fallacy trap. The narrative fallacy addresses our limited ability to look at sequences of facts without weaving an explanation into them, or, equivalently, forcing a logical link upon them, binding facts together. Where this propensity can go wrong is when it increases our impression of understanding (Taleb 2010).

While "ingenuity" was a marked feature of Britain's industrial revolution, resourcefulness was Japan's most defining trait. It is not an accident that all medals for the 2021 Tokyo Olympic Games will be made from recycled parts from cellular phones and other electronic devices; it's their brand. Tokyo could've become "the city of lights" but instead became a city of tech. In this sense, as Dator has argued, futures studies need to be seen as a hypothesis, not as ideology (Inayatullah 2013). The brand, therefore, enabled different hypotheses where the most commercially fit thrived, mutually reinforcing Japan's desired industrialised future.

In the marketing industry, predictions abound. New products, new and dying channels, shifting behaviours, and more. Yet the future is ours to create and not to predict. Thus, for marketing practitioners, it becomes a matter of deliberately designing holistic learning trajectories where their organisations' transformation is also their own – the double loop spiral.

Principle 2: challenge the used future

The second principle is to challenge the "used future". Every organisation has particular practices that it engages in that do not reflect its preferred future. Indeed, it often lives strategies that move counter to its vision (Inayatullah 2015). This conformity creates situations where the future becomes used, since its veracity is not one held by reality but by earlier worldviews. In the foresight process, participants are asked: what might be these routinised practices, their used futures?

In marketing communications, this has been the worldview of "interrupt for attention", a multisensory show of disrupting people's moments to manufacturing a brand interaction and changing behaviour. To illustrate this, let us focus on a behaviour that – for the social good – has been greatly encouraged to change but quite unsuccessfully.

Many different messaging angles are used: the first encouraging altruism, then inciting fear, which is followed by a punishment warning and finally some humour. Despite all that, dog waste remains a huge issue in many cities worldwide. Dogs can harbour lots of viruses, bacteria, and parasites – including harmful pathogens like *E. coli*, giardia, and salmonella – a single gram contains an estimated 23 million bacteria (Freinkel 2014). Studies have traced 20 to 30% of the bacteria in water samples from urban watersheds to dog waste (Watson 2002). Just two to three days of waste from 100 dogs can contribute enough bacteria, nitrogen, and phosphorous to close 20 miles of a bay-watershed to swimming and shell fishing, according to the US Environmental Protection Agency. It also can get into the air we breathe: a study of air samples in Cleveland, Ohio, and Detroit, Michigan, found that 10 to 50% of the bacteria came from dog poop.

The problem is particularly bad in cities, where green spaces are few and lonely souls seeking "puppy love" plentiful. New York boasts over 600,000 hounds – one for every 14 people – generating over 100,000 tons of poo a year. Some of it smudges unlucky stilettoes, but 60% (average of collections) is dutifully tossed into rubbish bins and hauled to landfills, at *a cost of over $100 per ton.*

And so, cities are devoting precious brainstorming hours to inventing ever-more-novel ways to combat the issue. Madrid, in 2016, announced a "shock plan" to force dog owners in two districts to clean up after their pets (Brulliard 2016a, 2016b). Those caught not doing so must either spend a few days as substitute street cleaners or face a $1700 fine. The Spanish capital's city hall said "there is still excrement in the streets, parks and other places" despite "repeated public awareness campaigns" and the distribution of millions of free poo bags.

But if anti-dog poop campaigns are any guide, Spain has an epic battle on its hands. In 2015, the city of Tarragona announced a plan to use DNA testing to match droppings to dogs. Before that, the town of Colmenar Viejo dispatched a private detective to record videos of offending dog owners, who were then fined by police. In 2013, Brunete, a suburb of Madrid, boxed up dog faeces and mailed them to the careless dog owners (Europa Press 2013). For two weeks, volunteers spied on dog walkers, sidled up to those who didn't scoop, and asked the name of the pooch – which, because most were registered with the city, was usually enough information to determine the owner's address. Brunete's mayor stated that dog waste was the number-one constituent complaint, and that the mail-bombs had improved things by 70%

(Dale 2013). However, without changing the context or meaning underneath such actions, the desired behaviour and indeed a desired poo-free future cannot actualise.

A case in point was the deployment of smart bins by Internet provider Portal Terra across ten parks in Mexico City, during the Poo Wi-Fi campaign (Almeida 2012). By rewarding dog owners when throwing their doggy bags in the bins with free Wi-Fi connectivity, this micro waste-management infrastructure helped counter the 10,000 tons of dog poo randomly dropped every year and the city's incurred cleaning costs.

The Mexican campaign shows an alternative where advertising can enhance, instead of interrupt, people's moments and, by creating a new context (via smart bins) and new meaning (dog poo moving from rubbish to a connectivity currency), effectively change behaviour and drive brand preference. Paraphrasing visionary R. Buckminster Fuller, change rarely happens by fighting the existing reality; instead we should aim at creating a new model that makes the existing one obsolete.

Principle 3: search for emerging issues

The third principle is to search for emerging issues or disruptors. This is especially important during periods of rapid change – technological, demographic, and geo-political, for example. These emerging issues can be forthcoming problems or possible opportunities. The challenge is to identify them before they become easy-to-spot trends, through the methodology of the s-curve, as developed by Molitor (2004).

A decade or more ago, one health insurer noted the move toward prevention and wellness. They understood, that as the 4P model of health (Inayatullah 2009) – prediction via big data; prevention via behavioural changes such as meditation, better diet, and exercise; patient participation via peer-to-peer networks; and personalisation via genomics and bio-monitoring devices – grew in importance, they needed to make a strategic shift from downstream to upstream. This meant proactive measures to keep their customers healthy – providing dietary advice, for example, and developing apps that customers could use to monitor their health. Working with a health insurance company during its transition from a health insurer to a healthcare company, the author was directly involved in helping them create a newsroom where online content replaced, to a degree, the role of doctors. Content is organised under verticals labelled "Caring", "Families", "Healthier", and "Manage & Recover". These are not just relevant topics but distinct aspects of a business being digitised to ensure its relevance in the long run.

In the marketing communications industry, having a "big idea" has for a long time been a source of competitive advantage. In fact, it still is. Creativity has been proven to amplify the commercial impact of marketing investment by a factor of 11 (Field 2011). Yet, the big idea has been, by and large, intertwined with the interruption predicative, to capture attention and change behaviour. In practical terms, this translates as: louder, brighter, and more frequent. Additionally, the big idea has also been a big driver of awards – reinforcing the cycle. However, being wacky, different, and crazier will not necessarily result in being more effective, certainly an emerging issue that some have been branding as "tactification of marketing" (Ritson 2019). Last, the difficulty and cost of coming up with these new, big ideas – not just across marketing communications but also other industries – has dramatically increased (Relihan 2018).

Since its launch in July 2016, Meet Graham has been one of the most talked-about brand campaigns worldwide, branded a "new weapon in the fight against death on the road". The commissioning of a deformed humanoid by Australia's Transport Accident Commission (TAC) to celebrated Australian sculptor Patricia Piccinini was an interesting approach to promoting safer driving and reducing death and trauma on roads. The already award-winning campaign became a social media phenomenon, making headlines worldwide from the *New York Times* to London's *Daily Mail*, the *Washington Post*, BBC, CNN, India Today, and Al Jazeera. Despite all the fanfare and a brand-funded art piece, what is the true value of Meet Graham? Has it delivered on its promise? As of December 2016, 270 people had lost their lives on Victorian roads, 36 more than the 2015 toll. And this was the number that client and agency did not promote. Moreover, the reason a hyper-elaborated, expensive and convoluted way of telling people something they already know has become so unanimously praised is the "big idea" worldview.

Other scenarios are possible. The big idea could become a big utility and, rather than interrupt, enhance people's moments and the role played by the brand then and there. In other words, the deployment of marketing communications that goes beyond communicating an issue in an interesting way to actually solving it. Domino's Pizza looked beyond the traditional path to purchase to permeate people's life-journeys. Aware that potholes, cracks, and bumps in the road can cause irreversible damage to people's pizzas during the drive home, Domino's decided to pave towns across the United States to save its customers' pizzas from the bad roads. Obviously, not only Domino's customers benefited from this effort but every single driver going through the few selected roads. In the United States, the annual investment required by all levels of government to simply maintain the nation's highways, roads, and bridges is estimated to be $185 billion per year for the next 50 years. Today, the nation annually invests about $68 billion (National Surface Transportation Policy and Revenue Study Commission of the US Congress 2016). Mayors and city managers from the municipalities where the "paving for pizza" effort has taken place have acknowledged the creation of shared value (Domino's Pizza 2019). According to Bill Scherer, mayor of Bartonville, Texas:

> This unique, innovative partnership allowed the Town of Bartonville to accomplish more potholes repairs.

The city manager of Milford, DE, Eric Norenberg, stated:

> We appreciated the extra Paving for Pizza funds to stretch our street repair budget as we addressed more potholes than usual.
>
> (Smart Cities World 2018)

Principle 4: create scenarios

Even if one can accurately or usefully discern new innovations, not only is the trajectory of the emerging issue not easy to forecast, but organisational culture is challenging to change. Using alternative futures is a crucial principle in practicing foresight to negotiate such uncertainty (Inayatullah 2015). Alternative futures or scenarios can help an organisation become more flexible and adaptable. They also help develop a range of alternative visions and strategies. These scenarios can be developed through many techniques, and what has appeared to be most useful is to be based on challenging one's core assumptions about the way the world is and the way the world is developing (Inayatullah 2015). While the futurist may offer examples and guiding questions, it is crucial that the workshop participants develop the actual scenarios. Scenarios need to be lived alternatives, embedded in the culture and embodied in the person. As much as possible, utilising games like the CLA game and the Sarkar game ensures that participants actually feel their way into alternative futures (Inayatullah 2015).

While there are hundreds of examples to draw on, a recent, relevant case comes from an energy company exploring temporal horizons of transformation.

The author of this article was commissioned to define the enterprise-wide purpose of an incumbent company in the energy sector. From "keeping the lights on" to . . . something else able to ensure the company's long-term relevance and alignment with its evolving corporate and product strategies. It is not exaggerated to say the energy sector is in the eye of a storm: price wars, poor infrastructure, antiquate market regulations, climate change pressures, de-centralisation, and the emergence of *produmers – consumers who produce*. On the other hand, opportunities abound. The brand landscape is homogenous, big aspirational messages do not translate into actions, and few realised we have entered the age of the electron, where selling energy is just the beginning and not the end of customer relationships and transactions. The process was heavily consultative, allowing us to gather the most disparate points of view to pro-viding a few hypothetical scenarios.

However, before elaborating scenarios, their "perimeters of meaning" were also defined (see Figure 24.4). It was important not to alienate employees and the market about the company's heritage in trading energy commodities. It was also important to create an innovative edge through product innovations but without becoming a product-led company at the expense of brand. Third, parallel market acquisitions also meant that from one or a few services, the new default offering had to be a multiservice one. Last, internal stakeholders agreed that the biggest competitive advantage would come from the deployment of experiences, not just the conveni-ence of aggregated services. Once defined, each "narrative quadrant" (i.e. commodity, prod-uct, multiservice, experience) was stretched (Figure 24.5), helping envisage implications and possibilities within domains of meaning and required support to turning those into a desired future. This visualisation allowed participants to understand how to pull "meaning levers" able to inform and communicate the company's unfolding new futures.

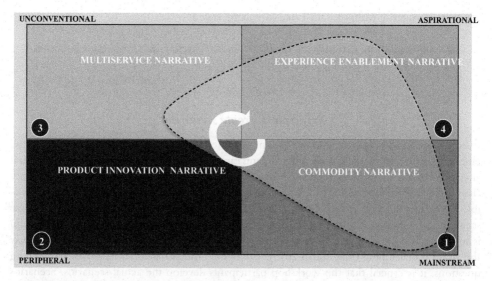

Figure 24.4 Four possible foresight narratives, blending in accordance to a constructed perimeter of meaning

Source: The author

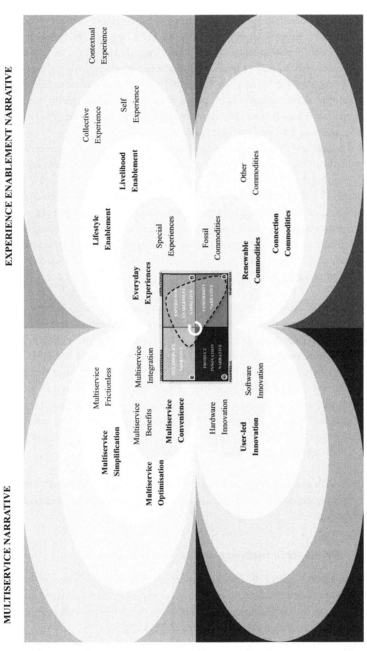

Figure 24.5 Stretched narrative quadrants

Source: The author

From a total of eight scenarios, three were further refined. Moodboards were utilised to express the abstraction of energy, decommoditising it and creating new meaning able to point the organisation to distinctively different directions or, as we like saying, possible futures. Each image was purposefully chosen to express desirable factors within scenarios. Choice of images was informed by previous consultations and the analysis of the energy category. Moodboards were also paired with short purpose statements, two to three words able to encapsulate the meaning each scenario could potentially convey. The value of the approach lies in creating boundaries without necessarily imposing business limitations; they are all about meaning. This way, participants are encouraged to bring their individual and collective responsibilities in a way that expands the development of scenarios, as opposed to contriving those due to specific mergers, divestments, corporate agendas, product innovation horizons, and more. These factors are also considered and repurposed within each scenario.

By converting the scenarios into value propositions – for customers, government, and employees – those in the room realised they were just as essential as their ideas to make that alternative future a possibility.

This intervention had a direct application, which was to define a guiding purpose able to orchestrate the unfolding of the company's foresight narrative. Indirectly, however, the contribution could have been even greater by helping an internal market foresight capability, which proved to positively influence three important dimensions of new product development – creativity, speed to market, and market-entry timing. The head of brand of the energy company made an insightful point towards the conclusion of the project:

> I think something to consider, is that the conversation we have been having about the future of the business is a massive strategic business conversation. One of the challenges you and I face is that these decisions are relegated to brand and marketing, but are actually quite senior competitive decisions, so with the demise of the CMO and CMOs increasingly being pushed to be short term focused and with high turnovers, who then leads that conversation? The CEO? That's been my challenge in my last two Head of Brand positions both here and in health insurance. It is like the modern corporate structure no longer supports brand management as strategic enterprise marketing – where should brand leadership sit? Food for thought – no easy answers, just one of the challenges for those of us on the inside!

Moreover, companies with a strong corporate culture are resilient to changes due to the support of trust and corporate communities, team spirit, and high employee commitment to a long-term vision (Verdenhofa 2018).

Principle 5: inclusive and cognitively diverse

The fifth principle asserts essentially "the more the merrier." As the future is uncertain, bringing in alternative voices from varied fields can help reduce uncertainty and find new solutions. In foresight projects, bringing in the full range of stakeholders, while messy, enhances the robustness of the scenarios and the strategies developed (Inayatullah 2015).

If marketing had commandments, "know thy audience" would be the first. This implies both the consumer market as well as peers in the organisation and other relevant stakeholders. Understanding that the marketer is not the market is, therefore, the first step to ensuring an inclusive and cognitively diverse process will be carried on. In fact, one of the overall objectives of prediction and foresight marketing is indeed to construct new networks and relations

---

State of Escape new narrative, which immediately inspired alternative futures for all staff

State of Escape Brand Manifesto

We are State of Escape, an international design brand created to enable the discerning, contemporary Flâneuse to escape back to their true selves. We are driven by a strong, purposeful sense of wanderlust, making us gravitate towards original artistry that breaks away from the monotonous rhythm of society.

We exist to equip and entice with pragmatism, style and flâneuserie. Through our creative genius, we have crafted a bag that audaciously invites you to reroute the paths you were expected to take and disrupt the life you were expected to live.

This freedom is fruit of our ESCAPE PLAN™, a system designed to encourage spontaneity and elevate the everyday with wondrous escapes. For that, we had to push simplicity to the extreme, so the timeless elegance of classics could be reimagined through our edgy spirit.

From worldly women to worldly women, this our journey . . .

Escape to the unexpected. Escape into solitude. Escape to the childhood lost along the way to adulthood. For not all those who wander are lost, they are venturing into their State of Escape . . . and may just find it.

---

between clusters, sectors, and markets or around problem members for the discussion of strategic issues and the innovative marketing policy of the enterprise (UNIDO 2005). It is through this participatory integration, analysing the alternative perspectives of the future and prioritising them, through intensive negotiations among system participants and stakeholders, that an agreed-upon model of the future can be created (Verdenhofa 2018).

Principle 6: find the worldview and narrative

The sixth principle is finding the worldview informing the used future and developing a new cognitive pattern that supports the new story. With such inclusion, a change of conversation and strategy remains possible. This is especially critical in futures thinking, where uncertainty is higher the further into the future one projects (Inayatullah 2015). Without understanding deeper perspectives, strategies often fail, as they reinforce the dominant worldview.

Narratives are not right or wrong. The critical question is whether they serve or hinder where the organisation wishes to go. Working with international up-and-coming fashion brand State of Escape, I was tasked with reclaiming a richer narrative that was diluted in favour of more descriptive product articulations but at the expense of brand. Product descriptions were favoured due to the innovative employment of neoprene on high-end tote bags to help educate the market about the innovation. Yet, after a few years employing the same communications strategy, the company felt stuck. While the "escape" idea originated from the founders' desire to create a business that enabled them to escape back to their true selves and live desired lifestyles, the main message was a lot more transactional, referring to the product as versatile due to material and style. With such a narrow narrative, the brand got suppressed in favour of a logo. The tangibility of the product became a limiting factor for staff to use as a springboard for new product developments.

The approach was to compare State of Escape with luxury watchmaker Hublot due to its characteristic "rubber band". The tale of Hublot's fascination with rubber is one of audacity and vision. It is the very foundation of Hublot's "Art of Fusion" positioning that still resonates today. As a result, art of fusion came to mean a lot more than just adding a rubber band where it previously was metal or leather. It became the guiding principle for new product developments within and beyond the timepiece category. For State of Escape, we utilised the metaphor of the Flâneuse. Contrary to its male counterpart – the Flaneur character – the Flâneuse is not aimlessly wondering through life. The Flâneuse has an element of transgression: she goes where she is not supposed to. This flânerie inspiring women to reroute the paths they were expected to take and disrupt the lives they were expected to live deeply resonated with the entire staff. Now, rather than ideating around new neoprene products, they are considering what the State of Escape art gallery, resort, or fragrance may be like as well as launching a program employing female inmates to enable them to escape back to their true selves.

The text box shows the new narrative of State of Escape, subtly informing its possible futures. Foresight methodologies and tools were not explicitly deployed but "baked in" to the strategic process utilised to reposition the brand. As a practicing "brand-futurist", the author enjoys the benefit of stealthily combining different aspects from SFFT with brand marketing. This has often proved to be an easier "sell" than separately itemising tools and approaches within the brand strategy process. That is possibly due to clients' lack of familiarity and limited appreciation of SFFT as a whole, since these will often come from a marketing department as opposed to the executive or board levels of the organisation, where futures are often contextualised in the corporate strategy and not always infused across the brand strategy. In this sense, asking clients to consider their brand beyond the category they exist in is a way to provoke their imaginations and stretch the narrative into less predictable futures.

To animate the narrative, a moodboard (see Figure 24.6) was created. Another function of it is to aid the creation of a new visual language that translates the new positioning. Importantly,

Figure 24.6 Visual representation of State of Escape's new narrative

Source: The author

the worldview of the Flâneuse is expressed but also equipped with blazes, encouraging the brand to chart new paths. In other words, as much as the moodboard guides the evolution of the brand's visual identity, it also primes those working behind it, planting a "futures seed" through images able to stick with meaning.

A noteworthy example on how to best understand and eventually repurpose an individual's or a collective's narrative is Facebook's experimental new immersive digital universe, Horizon. Horizon is a virtual reality sandbox universe where users can build their own environments to play and socialise with friends or just explore the user-generated landscapes (Constine 2019). In this immersive environment with reduced social inhibitors, users become Horizon's citizens, initially oriented around a town square and able to choose how they look and what they wear from an expansive and inclusive set of avatar tools. From inside VR, users will be able to use the Horizon World Builder to create gaming arenas, vacation chill-spots, and activities to fill them without the need to know how to code. In other words, inner beliefs and worldviews are not only expressed but also manifested by every choice or move played in the game.

Principle 7: create the vision

In turbulent times, it is critical to have a clear vision of where one wishes to go. This cannot be too near nor too far. Too near leads to being trapped by the present. Too far becomes science fiction. The vision must also enable – enhance the capacity to deliver – and ennoble, bring out the best in people so that they can create systemic structures to deliver the best. Visioning involves citizens, experts (collecting the data, testing the data, searching for disruptors), and leaders (who can champion particular projects or resist change). And it is personal. Each person must ask themselves where they want to be in 20 or 30 years. Who is with them? What does nature look like? What technologies do they wish to use? What is the built environment like? Once the link between the external and the inner is made, the value of foresight become obvious and legacy becomes critical (Inayatullah 2015).

At this juncture, it feels appropriate to share the author's vision, coined urban brand-utility (UBU) and aiming at rewriting the marcomms playbook. Since the publication of Marshall McLuhan's *Understanding Media: The Extensions of Man* in 1964, the dominant view of marketing communications has been that "the medium is the message", meaning that the nature of a medium (the channel through which a message is transmitted) is more important than the meaning or content of the message. To prove his point, McLuhan then published a book entitled *The Medium Is the Massage*. By replacing the word "message" with "massage" the author demonstrates that a medium is not something neutral – it does something to people. It takes hold of them. It rubs them, it massages them and bumps them around, chiropractically, as it were, and the general roughing up that any new society gets from a medium, especially a new medium, is what is intended in that title (McLuhan 1967).

In fact, in media studies, mediatisation is a theory that argues that the media shapes and frames the processes and discourse of political communication as well as the society in which that communication takes place. As a consequence of this process, institutions and whole societies are shaped by and dependent on mass media. In this sense, reframing advertising from the promotion of conspicuous consumption into a regenerative force accelerating sustainable development can prove quite instrumental to influencing the generations having to design the promise that will redefine our social contract. This is less about sharing messages of sustainability and more about deploying media in a circular, sustainable way, minimising waste as well as delivering new utilities, where consumption has been making its biggest impact (good and bad) – in cities.

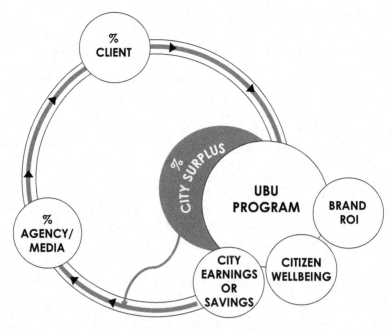

Figure 24.7   The UBU model and its three core objectives
Source: Brodsky (2017, p. 88)

UBU is a radically innovative model (see Figure 24.7) which can transform the marketing communications industry with a new vision where the medium becomes a useful urban action. It has three main objectives:

1   Enabling savings or new earnings for cities;
2   Creating urban shared value to the cities' inhabitants;
3   Delivering superior return on media investment.

It shows a vision that needs to materialise by creating a network of creative urban resilience turning potential liabilities into new assets for the city, its residents, and those in the marketing communications industry, as well as helping address some of the growing pains of our rapidly urbanising planet. The model demonstrates how media communications integrate with the urban environment to supplement the provision of public utility services, enhancing a city's resilience and creating new income streams.

For example, the Indian energy company Halonix communicated its brand through LED billboards that lit up at night, making streets safer. This campaign had three main impacts: it supplemented Delhi's energy grid, it alleviated the police force, and it is now helping remove the city's stigma around sexual harassment. The success has been amplified by the citizens who have explicitly requested that the campaign be rolled out nationally. By creating new meaning in an unprecedented way, Halonix achieved the feat of de-commoditising energy and bypassing enduring price wars. The medium, not the message, delivered a useful urban action. A key insight from this campaign is the fact that behaviour effectively changed as a result of changing the context (brightening dark streets), as opposed to asking criminals to stop committing crimes. Considering we live in a participatory culture, a term coined by MIT media scholar

Henry Jenkins, this represents a massive opportunity for advertisers to reinvent their rules of engagement and turn consumers into civic or creative collaborators.

An interesting civic engagement campaign was New York City's Participatory Budgeting, through which New Yorkers had to decide how to spend $1,000,000 of the public budget. This means that the same touchpoint used to communicate was also used to enable the action it asks audiences to undertake, a paradigm shift where advertising can finally walk its talk. The company behind the "voting outdoor panels", Intersection, started up by repurposing New York City's now obsolete pay phones as totems offering free broadband Wi-Fi connectivity to residents and visitors and media space for advertisers. Besides supplementing New York's broadband network and now enhancing civic life, by unlocking new value from underutilised assets, the City of New York has projected an incremental US$500 million in ad revenue as part of a 12-year contract.

Importantly, to develop the vision, the author had to engage in a learning spiral where he also had to evolve his own self-narrative, from an Abrahamic figure acting as an iconoclast in a lonely journey to becoming the Avenger able to assemble heroic individuals willing to bring about meaningful change. Hence, this resulted in a double-loop causal layered analysis where the first focused on reframing the marketer and the second his – not just "the" – industry. Following (see Tables 24.2 and 24.3) are the summaries of the applied CLA exercises:

Here is a hypothetical situation. Let us assume that Domino's Paving for Pizza program is taken to its full potential, generating a large surplus to the city of Bartonville by minimising the costs from dealing with potholes. Rather than treating this as a one-off campaign, smart mayors would try to create a virtuous cycle, where 50% of the surplus is retained by the city, 25% is returned to the advertiser, and 25% to the agency and media owner – a value only unlocked by repeating the approach. The more advertisers communicate their messages in a way that benefits brand, people, and city, the cheaper it becomes to do more of it. And, the more cities encourage such an approach, the faster societal problems would be addressed. As with the idea of a circular economy where products and services go beyond an end user's finite life cycle, UBU looks at brand communications as closed loops by designing a system bigger than fixed campaign periods, target audiences, and business-as-usual key performance indicators. This

Table 24.2 CLA exercise applied to the author as the *auteur* in his industry

Causal layers	From	To
Litany	Rebel agency-strategist	Cross-industry aggregator
Systemic approaches	Application of data-led insights to developing commercially successful communications campaigns	Application of data-inspired foresight to redesigning communication campaigns to include people, planet, and prosperity, not just profit as key outcome
Worldviews	Agency-strategists pigeonholed in their marketing communications discipline	Transdisciplinary strategists liberated to redefine industries' boundaries
Narrative and metaphors	Abraham, the iconoclast against the money-worshipping masses	Avenger, assembling fluid partnerships with like-minded peers

Source: The author

Table 24.3 CLA exercise applied to urban brand-utility to redefining the role of the marketing communications industry

Causal layers	From	To
Litany	Ad-avoidance behaviour	Ad-enabled resilience
Systemic approaches	Interrupting people's attention to drive sales	Enhancing people's moments to create shared value
Worldviews	Marketing as a driver of conspicuous consumption that hijacks culture	Marketing as a regenerative force for sustainable development and the advancement of culture
Narrative and metaphors	Soul of capitalism	Turbine for the circular economy

Source: The author

way, marketing budgets are effectively turned into investment funds with returns in the form of brand cut-through, happier customers, social impact, and more effective city management. In the case of Domino's, considering that the paving for pizza program has already positively impacted 50 states in the United States (Domino's Pizza 2019), the approach could also be scaled from local to federal government.

To challenge marcomms' used future, I was able to gather several case studies where a commercial communications program can supplement public utility services as diverse as education, leisure, air, water, safety, housing, and many others. These cases have been presented in the form of articles and keynotes worldwide to help generate momentum for the vision. Dr. Savvas Verdis, founder of the Executive Masters in Cities from the London School of Economics, is confident about the vision:

> I am sure that Urban Brand-Utility will provide some much needed expertise and transformation [in the marketing communications industry] and particularly in generating new business opportunities for infrastructure, development, tech companies and others tendering with cities through an innovative use of media.
>
> (Brodsky 2016)

To animate the narrative, a moodboard was created. Another function of it is to aid the creation of a new visual language that translates the new positioning. Importantly, the worldview of the Flâneuse is expressed but also equipped with blazes (see Figure 24.8), encouraging the brand to create new paths. In other words, as much as the moodboard guides the evolution of the brand's visual identity, it also primes those working behind it, planting a "futures seed" through images able to stick with meaning.

The UBU conceptual framework flips the current advertising model by enhancing, instead of interrupting, moments of brand interaction with the deployment of public utility services. Such logic can turn brand communications into a regenerative force for cities, where the promotion of goods and services is not only more profitable but also environmentally enriching and socially virtuous.

This can be done by following six strategic imperatives:

1 Translate the big idea that defines your brand into a big utility that can operationalise its impact;
2 Replace interruptive interactions with enhancing ones by delivering a public utility service;

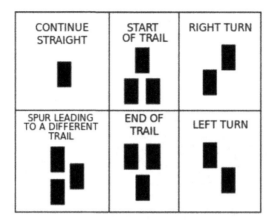

Figure 24.8 Symbols commonly used in trail blazing in the United States

Source: https://en.wikipedia.org/wiki/Trail_blazing

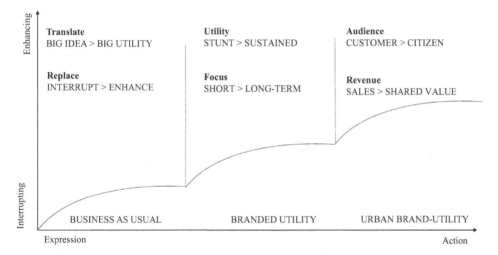

Figure 24.9 Visual representation of urban brand-utility's learning journey, from business-as-usual to branded utilities to UBU programmes

Source: The author

3   Turn any existing utility of a communications effort from a stunt into a sustained practice;
4   Shift your business focus from short-term sales results to longer-term profitability;
5   Broaden your audiences from customers to citizens, expanding paths-to-purchase onto life journeys;
6   Diversify revenue from sales to the creation of shared value.

These are shown graphically in Figure 24.9.

The operationalisation of UBU would then be a matter of matching of brands that align with specific urban challenges. This way, instead of top-down public-private contracts, issues

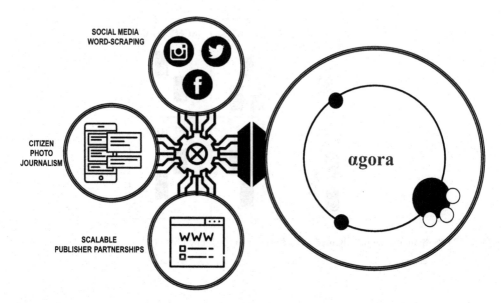

Figure 24.10 Visualisation of Agora, the future interface empowering citizens to guide brands towards social problem-solving initiatives

Source: The author

are identified by local constituents informing future UBU programs, as wanted by the people and enabled by advertising media. This would happen through a digital platform playing the role of Agora, where geo-tagged and time-stamped citizens' voices are clustered to inform the type of actions wanted and the brands becoming the vehicles for that (Figure 24.10). The Agora would also replace the brief, commonly used between client and agency to define a marketing effort. This would happen via passive data inputs from social media commentary and reputable publications and by encouraging citizens to proactively voice their views of change, potentially augmenting our notions of democracy whereby every dollar spent or attention unit invested would also count as a vote.

Ultimately, the UBU vision is one where advertisers become key players in public-private partnerships, with marketing funds deployed for their brands' commercial success and society's prosperity. For the sake of perspective, Magna Global estimated that in 2018, global media spending in brand communications will reach US$551 billion, but, according to the Pike Institute, by 2020, investment in Smart City infrastructure will not surpass US$108 billion, an approximate 5:1 ratio. Through the UBU approach, the current US$551 billion could merge into the much larger pie of global welfare and security spend of US$40.5 trillion, a figure obtained by dividing gross world product by the 30% global average spent on welfare and security per the International Monetary Fund.

Finally, visioning also moves from the desired future back to the present – it is transformational. To that end, aside from the development of the Agora platform, the UBU vision is one that opened the doors of mayors' cabinets, prominent conferences, investors, and new colleagues. In this sense, treating the desired future as a "long now" being gradually trailed allows for continuity and execution of the vision.

Conclusion

Justifying marketing investment on long-term brand building for which the company cannot see immediate results is a hard battle. But doing the opposite keeps companies stuck in short-term reactiveness and chasing cash flow. As a result of organisations' ability to measure performance and demonstrate results almost immediately, marketing has, too, become short term, tactified, and often heavily focused on digital channels. If marketing is disconnected from the rest of the business and society-at-large, then how can it aspire to develop relevant value propositions (i.e. promises) that are delightfully delivered? If the business cannot deliver against the brand promise, then changes need to be made to either the promise and/or its delivery until it becomes viable. But that is business as usual, a pendulum between past performance and present gains, an approach that will suffer when operating conditions change. To hold a brand's promise accountable and make it relevant, anticipating market changes and dynamically producing scenarios that enhance the organisation's and the marketer's preparedness is, ultimately, the unique contribution SFFT can bring to the discipline, the professional, and the industry – and one that needs to be considered more often and more seriously.

Issues

There is no greater fear than the fear of the unknown. SFFT faces a great lack of awareness and understanding. In the marketing industry, the most vivid memories – about SFFT – will resonate with trends reports, "future of" types of analyses, or keynotes from self-anointed gurus, ninjas, and hackers or salespeople without any proper training in foresight. The issue is twofold. First, the futurist brand is a bit of a blur. Those outside the community do not understand what futurists are, and futurists themselves have a hard time explaining what they do and how value is added from their craft. Second, marketers have been discredited from failing to speak the language of the boardroom – the language of money. Marketing's new developments can indeed be quite distracting given their high frequency and volume. In trying to make sense of the new, marketers end up losing touch with their business realities and priorities, having even been mocked as belonging to the "colouring-in department". In fact, in an experiment that involved interviewing 30 board members from Fortune 1000 companies, Google accumulated more than 1300 minutes of audio and over 100,000 words about the role of the CMO (Think with Google 2020), which was then summarised in one long, important paragraph:

> The 21st century CMO is expected to be a marketing miracle worker, an alchemist who combines classic art of branding with the latest advances in data and measurement. All this while you serve as the connective tissue of the C-suite and stay a step ahead of the rapidly changing landscape of digital technology, cultural trends, and shifting consumer expectations – things becoming ever more important to the stock price. Customers matter more than ever, and since you're responsible for them, your role should matter more than ever too. But board members do not seem to have one cohesive definition of the role. So, what are you to do? Internally, steer expectations for your role by defining growth, you have some control over. And recognize that the talent of your team is half the battle to achieving that growth. Hire the best measurement people because marketing will be held to some metric that is currently beyond reach, and you'll need them to invent it. There are many ways you can impact revenue – but be prepared to show the "I'm indispensable" math. And do not forget

the most visible CMOs also take big risks. Only 3% of board members interviewed were marketers. Likely, they do not hear you. Listen closely and find the overlap between what the board is interested in and your responsibilities. And instead of building slides about everything you do, build one slide that puts you in a position to start a conversation around those common interests and goals.

What is interesting to note is that SFFT is all over the paragraph and yet nowhere in it. As haiku-esque as a statement, this is the closest to the truth. Strategic foresight or futures thinking is not explicitly mentioned but implicitly dominates the subtext. To continue to "dumb it down" may help with selling the odd project but will not create the gravitas required for marketers and their peers to normalise the allocation of foresight investment. If education is key to opening more doors for foresight, appropriate use of language is the red carpet welcoming the long-awaited guests who can help reshape the future for the better.

References

Albarda, M., 2015. *Most Consumers Do Not Care About Brands* [online]. Available from: www.media-post.com/publications/article/254859/most-consumers-do-not-care-about-brands.html [Accessed 10 September 2020].

Almeida, B., 2012. *Bruno Almeida YouTube Channel* [online]. Available from: www.youtube.com/watch?v=d8_KNPKWmsA [Accessed 27 July 2020].

Armstrong, J.S., 1970. *Long-Range Forecasting: From Crystal Ball to Computer*. New York: John Wiley and Sons.

Binet, P.F. and Field, P., 2011. *The Long and the Short of It: Balancing Short and Long-Term Marketing Strategies*. London: Institute of Practitioners in Advertising (IPA).

Boulding, E.B. and Boulding, K., 1995. *The Future: Images and Processes*. London: Sage Publications.

The British Academy, 2018. *Reforming Business for the 21st Century: A Framework for the Future of the Corporation*. London: The British Academy.

Brodsky, S., 2015. What da Vinci can teach you about unlocking big data. *Marketing Magazine*, 23 September, 78–79.

Brodsky, S., 2016. *Sergio-brodsky.com* [online]. Available from: www.sergio-brodsky.com/urban-brand-utility [Accessed 27 July 2020].

Brodsky, S., 2017 Urban brand-utility. *Berlin Marketing Journal*, 3(2), 88–93.

Brulliard, K., 2016a. Cities go to extreme lengths to tackle a dog poop epidemic. *The Washington Post*, 28 April.

Brulliard, K., 2016b. *Madrid Dog Owners Who Don't Pick Up Poo Will Have to Clean Streets* [online]. Available from: www.washingtonpost.com/news/animalia/wp/2016/04/27/madrid-is-the-latest-city-to-fight-a-dog-poop-epidemic-that-just-wont-go-away/ [Accessed 10 September 2020].

Constine, J., 2019. *Facebook Announces Horizon, a VR Massive-Multiplayer World* [online]. Available from: https://techcrunch.com/2019/09/25/facebook-horizon/ [Accessed 11 September 2020].

Daley, S., 2013. *The New York Times* [online]. Available from: www.nytimes.com/2013/08/07/world/europe/a-special-delivery-of-sorts-to-warn-dog-owners-in-spain.html [Accessed 27 July 2020].

Dator, J., 2002. Introduction: The Future lies Behind. In J. Dator, ed. *Thirty Years of Teaching Futures Studies*. Westport, CT: Praeger, 1–33.

Domino's Pizza, 2019. *Paving for Pizza* [online]. Available from: www.pavingforpizza.com/ [Accessed 27 July 2020].

Drucker, P., 2013. Culture eats your structure for lunch. *Thoughts on management*, 10 July.

Duhigg, C., 2017. *The New York Times* [online]. Available from: www.nytimes.com/2017/06/14/business/media/marketing-charity-water-syria.html [Accessed 27 July 2020].

D.Z., 2018. *After 150 Years, Why Does the Meiji Restoration Matter?* [online]. Available from: www.economist.com/the-economist-explains/2018/02/05/after-150-years-why-does-the-meiji-restoration-matter [Accessed 11 September 2020].

Europa Press, 2013. *Europa Press YouTube Channel* [online]. Available from: www.youtube.com/watch?v=uph204r5BZI [Accessed 27 July 2020].

Fabricant, R., 2014. *The Rapidly Disappearing Business of Design* [online]. Available from: www.wired. com/2014/12/disappearing-business-of-design/ [Accessed 9 September 2020].

Field, P., 2011. *The Link Between Creativity and Effectiveness*. London: The Institute of Practitioners in Advertising (IPA).

Freinkel, S., 2014. *The Poop Problem: What to Do With 10 Million Tons of Dog Waste* [online]. Available from: www.livescience.com/44732-eliminating-pet-poop-pollution.html [Accessed 10 September 2020].

Gianatasio, D., 2017. *Global Consultancies Are Buying Up Agencies and Reshaping the Brand Marketing World* [online]. Available from: www.adweek.com/brand-marketing/global-consultancies-are-buying-up-agencies-and-reshaping-the-brand-marketing-world/ [Accessed 7 September 2020].

Inayatullah, S., 2009. From 'she'll be right' to the prevention culture: The futures of the Australian health system. *The Australian Hospital and Healthcare Bulletin*, 44–48. Record ID 99449658502621.

Inayatullah, S., 2013. Learnings from futures studies: Learnings from Dator. *Journal of Futures Studies*, 18(2), 1–12. Corpus ID: 56119393.

Inayatullah, S., 2015. *What Work*, 1st ed. Taiwan: Tamsui Tamkang Press. Corpus ID: 157259632.

Ivanova, D., 2016. Environmental impact assessment of household consumption. *Journal of Industrial Ecology*, 20(3), 526–536. DOI: 10.1111/jiec.12371.

Ives, N., 2020. Average tenure of CMOs falls again. *The Wall Street Journal*, 27 May [online]. Available from: www.wsj.com/articles/average-tenure-of-cmos-falls-again-11590573600 [Accessed 5 September 2020].

Kopf, D., 2019. *Mexico Is Finally the US's Number-One Trading Partner* [online]. Available from: https:// qz.com/1682861/mexico-is-now-americas-number-one-trading-partner/?utm_source=dlvr.it&utm_ medium=twitter [Accessed 20 September 2020].

The Marketing Academy, n.d. *The Marketing Academy* [online]. Available from: https://themarketingacademy.org/au/wp-content/uploads/2019/07/TMA-AUS-2020-Scholarship-Guide.pdf [Accessed 21 July 2020].

Mayer, C., 2017. *The British Academy* [online]. Available from: www.thebritishacademy.ac.uk/programmes/ future-of-the-corporation/ [Accessed 27 July 2020].

McLuhan, M., 1967. *Now the Medium Is the Massage* [online]. Available from: https://timesmachine. nytimes.com/timesmachine/1967/03/19/107185353.html?action=click&contentCollection=Arch ives&module=LedeAsset&region=ArchiveBody&pgtype=article&pageNumber=179 [Accessed 22 July 2020].

Milojević, S.I. and Milojević, I., 2015. *CLA 2.0. Transformative Research in Theory and Practice*, 1st ed. Taiwan: Tamsui Tamkang University. Corpus ID: 129006863.

Molitor, G., 2004. *The Power to Change the World – the art of forecasting*. Potomac, MD: Public Policy Forecasting.

National Surface Transportation Policy and Revenue Study Commission of the US Congress, 2016. *PotholeInfo.com* [online]. Available from: www.pothole.info/the-facts/ [Accessed 27 July 2020].

Pash, C., 2020. *ANALYSIS: A Tough Gig for Advertising Agencies Beyond the Pandemic* [online]. Available from: www.adnews.com.au/news/analysis-a-tough-gig-for-advertising-agencies-beyond-the-pandemic [Accessed 3 October 2020].

Rabinow, P., 1984. *The Foucault Reader*. New York: Pantheon Books.

Raeworth, K., 2018. *Doughnut Economics: Seven Ways to Think Like a 21st-Century Economist*, 1st ed. London: Random House.

Relihan, T., 2018. *MIT Management Sloan School* [online]. Available from: https://mitsloan.mit. edu/ideas-made-to-matter/new-ideas-are-getting-harder-to-find-and-more-expensive?utm_ source=mitsloanlinkedin&utm_medium=social&utm_campaign=ideas [Accessed 27 July 2020].

Ritson, M., 2019. *Accept It, People Hate Ads – Yes, All of Them* [online]. Available from: www.marketingweek.com/mark-ritson-people-hate-ads/ [Accessed 14 September 2020].

Roach, T., 2018. *Fwd to CEO: The Most Valuable Business Tool Ever Invented* [online]. Available from: http://bbh-labs.com/fwd-to-ceo-the-most-valuable-business-tool-ever-invented/ [Accessed 11 September 2020].

Rogers, C., 2019. *81% of Brands Could Disappear and European Consumers Wouldn't Care* [online]. Available from: www.marketingweek.com/brands-disappear/ [Accessed 6 September 2020].

Slaughter, R., 1990. The foresight principles. *Futures*, 22(8), 801–809. DOI: 10.1016/0016-3287(90)90017-C.

Smart Cities World, 2018. *Public-Private Pizza* [online]. Available from: https://www.smartcitiesworld.net/ editors-blog/editors-blog/public-privatepizza-3011 [Accessed 3 February 2021].

Sterling, G., 2019. *Almost 70% of Digital Ad Spending Going to Google, Facebook, Amazon, Says Analyst Firm* [online]. Available from: https://marketingland.com/almost-70-of-digital-ad-spending-going-to-google-facebook-amazon-says-analyst-firm-262565 [Accessed 5 September 2020].

Taleb, N.N., 2010. *The Black Swan*, 2nd ed. s.l.: Random House Trade Paperbacks.

Think with Google, 2020. *What Board Members Say About the CMO – Off the Record* [online]. Available from: www.thinkwithgoogle.com/feature/cmo-insights [Accessed 3 September 2020].

Tzempelikos, N., Kooli, K., Stone, M., Aravopoulou, E., Birn, R. and Kosack, E., 2020. Distribution of marketing research material to universities: The case of archive of market and social research (AMSR). *Journal of Business-to-Business Marketing*, 27(2), 187–202.

UNIDO, 2005. *Technology Foresight Manual*, 1st ed. Vienna: United Nations Industrial Development Organization.

Verdenhofa, O., 2018. The conceptual bases of introduction of foresight marketing into business. *Problems and Perspectives in Management*, 16(3), 163–173. DOI: 10.21511/ppm.16(3).2018.13.

Ward, M., 2010. *Businesses Can Now Measure the Carbon Impact of Advertising* [online]. Available from: www.theguardian.com/sustainable-business/business-measure-carbon-impact-advertising#:~:text=CarbonTrack%2C%20a%20measurement%20tool%20designed,measuring%20carbon%20emissions%20from%20advertising [Accessed 7 September 2020].

Watson, T., 2002. *Dog Waste Poses Threat to Water* [online]. Available from: https://usatoday30.usatoday.com/news/science/2002-06-07-dog-usat.htm [Accessed 8 September 2020].

Zweck, N.M. and Zweck, A., 2007. Bridging the gap between foresight and market research: Integrating methods to assess the economic potential of nanotechnology. *Technological Forecasting & Social Change*, 74(2007), 1805–1822. DOI: 10.1016/j.techfore.2007.05.010.

25

FAKES AND FUTURES

*Merlin Stone, Eleni Aravopoulou, Geraint Evans, Esra AlDhaen
and Brett Parnell*

Summary

This chapter reviews developments at the frontiers of marketing research through two different prisms – fakes and futures. It starts with an examination of problems caused by marketers - disingenuity in decision-making. This is an area where marketing research may be complicit, with research designed, consciously or not, to reinforce a decision already taken or one which is favoured by managers, in decisions, for example, about sampling frames, form of questions or interpretation of results. This issue is not confined to marketing or marketing research but is particularly dangerous for marketing, because it usually concerns information which is sourced, developed, managed and interpreted in ways that cannot just be "objective". that is, external information. The discussion then turns to one application of marketing research where interpretation become even more important, forecasting, particularly for new products and high technology and science-based areas, where data from existing customers is relatively weak, so big data cannot be used so powerfully, as most big data is mainly about current and past behaviour of customers. In marketing forecasting – from market size to the prospects for new products and services – the marketing research industry is joined by several other types of suppliers, such as analysts, marketing communications agencies and consultancies (and sometimes joined within firms as the border between marketing research agencies and these other parties has become very fuzzy in the last two decades), all of whom have particular interests which can affect what they forecast.

Introduction

In an article marking his assumption of the editorship of the *International Journal of Marketing Research*, Nunan (2020) identified several research priorities to guide future authors, including several themes that are the focus of this chapter, especially:

- Data and technologies, especially measuring behaviour rather than asking people about it;
- Getting beyond the hype of artificial intelligence;
- Research automation;
- More effective use by policymakers of evidence;

- Restoring/building public trust in research practice;
- "Fake news" and using rhetoric of research evidence to spread misinformation.

This chapter explores these and related themes as they occur in marketing research, linking them with wider managerial issues but also with the professional issues concerning marketing researchers. Nunan (2020) emphasised that one of the problems marketing researchers face is that although new technologies allow the generation of insight more easily and faster, the social, cultural and political contexts in which they are used tend to overshadow the insights themselves. This is investigated particularly in the first part of this chapter. The need for tougher scrutiny and for a strong ethical position in marketing research is greater than ever.

The dark side: fake news and misinformation

There have been many recent examples of what we call "dark side information behaviour" (DSIB) but no reliable studies of its frequency or severity of impact, partly because there is no accepted definition or taxonomy of DSIB or a way of measuring it and its impact.

A simple listing of DSIB behaviours is given in Table 25.1.

Table 25.1 Types of DSIB

DSIB type	Examples
Deliberate falsification	Deliberate denial.
	Concealment.
	Deliberate individual falsification of source information.
	Conspiracy with others to falsify source information.
	Deliberate individual misinterpretation.
	Conspiracy with others to misinterpret.
Sins of omission	Ignorance.
	Unconscious denial.
	Avoidance of information search.
	Unconscious misinterpretation.
	Omission from data gathering or analysis of important stakeholders or audiences.
Sins of commission	Poor prioritisation/weak focus on essentials (risks, benefits).
	Overconfidence.
	Over-reliance on intuition.
	Over-reliance on existing systems and processes
	Optimistic interpretation of information that might be regarded as negative or not supporting a particular decision.
	Business case flawed (e.g. benefits exaggerated, costs minimised).
	Information changed to fit the business case rather than reality.
	Choice of analytical tools and data sources based on incentives from suppliers rather than choice of correct tools and sources.
	Deliberate supply of false or biased information because of benefits accruing to the providers of the information.
	Biased governance – stakeholders with interests that conflict with those of the organisation influencing decisions in favour of their own interests.
System or process problems	Information incompetence – systems and processes do not deliver required information and situation is tolerated.
	Unconscious or deliberate creation/sustaining of a process/system known to support a particular type of DSIB.

Source: The authors

However, the increasing focus on the incentives operating on managers, stimulated partly by the rise of organisational and behavioural economics and finance (e.g. Kahneman *et al.* 1991) and related aspects such as agency theory (e.g. Eisenhardt 1989), has led to the creation of many tools to identify and analyse DSIB. Environmental factors, such as the deregulation of financial markets, the globalisation of trade, the collapse of communism and the increasing incidence of outsourcing, have increased incentives to engage in DSIB and the ease of doing so. Meanwhile, the insistence of regulators on stronger disclosure has led to many revelations that would not otherwise have taken place. In recent years, there has been much more awareness of how to capitalise on cognitive biases, and indeed the use of technology allows much of this to be operationalised and scaled to tens/hundreds of millions of target customers or decision-makers. The data sources that allow this to occur are often voluntarily surrendered through social media but also exploited, in many cases illegally, through breaches of data protection, use of hidden third parties (e.g. Cambridge Analytica) and shadow profiles (e.g. Facebook). The ready availability of data science tools, inexpensive computing power and simple techniques for deriving targets' influencers, motivators and preferences can also be applied to multiple digital channels at very low costs.

Marketing research has always been a possible antidote to many of the sins of DSIB, able to bring truth to bear. If managers are uncertain about the likely demand for a product or service, the requirement for particular features, the price that could be charged or how to communicate the virtues of the product or to whom, the two normal responses are "let's test it" or "let's research it". However, as this chapter shows, that is just the beginning of the story. Knowing what might be done with the information, how it will be used and how it might be distorted or denied is now an essential part of the armoury of the customer insight manager. Moving from the unknown to the known is not necessarily a smooth path!

Known unknowns and the world of Rumsfeld

To provide a framework for analysing dark side information behaviour, we need to consider what protagonists (those inside organisations involved in making decisions) and other stakeholders knew – or did not before, during and after the initiative (plan or project where the DSIB is alleged to have taken place, and what analysts (those viewing the situation from the outside) know or knew. These include:

- What was knowable at the time;
- Analysts' wisdom in retrospect (what analysts later found out about the situation);
- Protagonists' wisdom in retrospect (what protagonists later admitted or denied about the situation, perhaps in response to others' wisdom in retrospect – their response might range from denial or reengineering of the facts to honesty);
- The balance/contrast between analyst and protagonist wisdom (one's word against another's).

Donald Rumsfeld, then US Secretary of Defense, stated at a 2002 press conference that "we know there are known unknowns, that is to say we know there are some things we do not know. However, there are also unknown unknowns – the ones we don't know we don't know" (U.S. Department of Defence 2018). Although he was mocked by some at the time, he was making a serious statement reflecting common issues in risk and project management. In fact, it is more complicated than Rumsfeld suggested. If we take the first "unknown" as referring to protagonists' knowledge of whether there is something to be known, that is, whether there is an area, situation and so on that protagonists need to know about, and the second "unknown" as referring to what there is to be known about that situation, that is, the details of the knowledge, then there is a third possibility (apart from the obvious fourth, the known known, that is, protagonists know that there is an area or situation that exists and know the details of it). This is the "unknown known", an area or situation of which the protagonists do not know the existence or the importance of which they do not understand, but its details and/or importance are known to others – but not to protagonists. They may be known to third parties – analysts, competitors, governments, the people within the situation – but not by protagonists or decision-makers.

This four-way classification is best represented by Table 25.2.

"We didn't know"

The "unknown known" is often the refuge of perpetrators of DSIB, in forms such as "but we had no idea at the time that this was even a problem", "this was a completely unintended consequence, which we did not even consider a risk" or "I was never told about this area, although I discovered later that my people knew about it". In these areas, data mining and artificial intelligence and machine learning may be helpful. For example, if a health service manager wants to find areas of risk while not knowing what these are, systems can be used to identify and learn about possible problem areas, such as high death rates in particular areas or hospitals (e.g. to know them), overcoming the problems caused by health services being assessed using quality standards based on "known knowns" (Beaussier *et al.* 2016). When this information is communicated to the manager, it then becomes a "known known".

"We didn't expect it"

Using the idea of unanticipated consequences as an excuse has been legitimised by writing about unexpected events, or "black swans" (Taleb 2007). However, in some cases, a supposed "black swan" is really an example of poor risk analytics or risk management (Paté-Cornell 2012; Aven 2015). However, whilst a black swan phenomenon, according to Taleb (2007) signifies an event that occurs as a surprise, often associated with characteristics such as rarity, extreme impact and retrospective predictability, a black elephant signifies a known event that was ignored. In other words, a black swan is completely unpredictable except in hindsight, whereas a black elephant relates to a case where many know about it based on existing evidence but is often ignored because everyone is reluctant to deal with it. So, a black swan is concerns unknown-unknowns or beyond hypothetical assumptions, whereas a black elephant is about known-unknowns.

Table 25.2 A typology of misinformation

| | | *Whether known to the protagonist* | |
		Known	*Unknown*
What there is to be known	**Unknown**	Protagonist knows about the area but does not know the data that describes the area or arises from it.	Protagonist does not know about the area, nor do third parties.
	Known	Protagonist knows about the area and knows the data about it.	Protagonist does not know the area exists, but third parties do.

Source: The authors

It's even more complicated

However, the situation is more complicated than shown in Tables 25.1 and 25.2, for several reasons:

- In practice, the known/unknown distinction is rarely binary but a continuum from completely unknown, to suspected but not known, to part known, to known but not in detail, to known in detail. Some risks may be emerging, perhaps deriving from a new phenomenon, for example, a pattern of behaviour and so perhaps unknown, partly known or even just suspected by different parties (Renn 2014; O'Rourke 2016). Emergent risk is particularly important in the insurance industry, where failure to spot and mitigate emerging risk can threaten profit via an unanticipated claims level;
- Saying that "an organisation knows" commits the sin of personification. An organisation does not know, but its people do. So, some may know well, some partly and some not at all;
- Protagonists and analysts may not be clearly separated. They may be in the same organisation, or the analysts may be in the pay of the protagonists, such as in the case of auditors, when their independence and desired scepticism may be compromised by the nature of the commercial relationship, as we explain later in this chapter. In the case of external organisations in the formal position of analysts, this relationship can be very complex (Stone *et al.* 2017b; Stone *et al.* 2003);
- Techniques for analysing complex sets of information are advancing rapidly, transforming how humans relate to data (Slowik and Spinoni 2018). For example, as we note later, artificial intelligence is becoming essential in analysis of large data sets;
- There may be information asymmetry between protagonists and analysts and between different categories of protagonists and analysts, so one group may carry out an analysis for which another group has not got the resources to carry out, and depending on the results of the analysis, DSIB may occur. This issue is particularly important in relation to governance (Brennan *et al.* 2016);
- There may be a culture of DSIB in an organisation, coming from middle or senior management, usually from leaders (Pfeffer 2016), conspired in by many members of the organisation, so from an independent analyst's point of view, nothing said by protagonists to be known or unknown can reliably be classified as such. This culture may be related to the organisation's strategic situation. For example, market incumbents may construct a view of the world that confirms their dominance (Stone 1984, 2015). One example is mainstream media, where there may be an overt recognised political bias in a newspaper or a television channel. The content is clearly one sided, aligned to an obvious agenda, and the target audience prone to accepting the content, because it confirms their existing biases and because readers or viewers love information that confirms bias, minimises cognitive dissonance and delivers "supporting evidence" to support the agenda. The target reader or viewer considers it "truth-telling", but a different view would be taken by those of different political views;
- Protagonists may change their description of what is known or unknown because of errors made by their leaders or because of pressure from their leaders. Leaders may engage in deliberate DSIB, with middle management being forced to comply with it for fear of dismissal, while middle management may engage in deliberate DSIB because otherwise information would reveal their incompetence, and top management may unconsciously fall in line with the DSIB because they do not know of its existence;
- Some DSIB behaviours engaged in by those who are in positions of power or who want customers to respond in a certain way assume that the target audience is ignorant and open

to "ludicrous" influence. This may well be true, as some would argue that the results of recent referenda or presidential elections show!

- There are many ways of gaining understanding of a situation. In a simple situation, the truest results may come from marketing research with clear and specific objectives, clear target audiences, questions and categorised answers. In more complicated, chaotic or/and emergent situations, while marketing research techniques may be helpful – the marketing research itself needs to be more emergent and may need to be combined with actions, sensing, testing and responding (Mark and Snowden 2006). This ties in with the idea that it is not just what is known that is important but also what is done about it and whether it achieves the desires objectives – this is all more difficult in complex, chaotic and emergent situations.

Lying and behavioural bias

Amongst the first researchers to signal the general risk of DSIB were Cyert and March (1963), who suggested that members of an organisation may have incentives to manipulate information, from lying to presenting data in a biased way, so as to influence decisions. DSIB is systematic and widespread in business. The combination of overconfidence and biased governance is particularly toxic! Grover (2005) found that lying is part of every manager's life and that people may lie purely for their own benefit, but many lies are associated with competitive and social pressures. People vary in their propensity to lie, with nearly everyone lying in bargaining situations, but only some people lie when faced with conflicting expectations.

People need to rationalise their lies (e.g. Ariely 2012), and organisational cultures emphasising honesty do not seem to reduce lying but rather drive lying underground. Lovallo and Kahneman (2003) found that many business initiatives fail due to "delusional optimism", which includes emphasising projects' potential benefits, underestimating their likely costs and creating and promoting success scenarios while ignoring the possibility of errors. This is due to cognitive biases and organisational pressures to accentuate the positive. Aggressive goals can motivate teams and improve the chances of success, but external forecasts should be used to decide whether to commit. However, this implies that the managers concerned have an interest in realism, although they may not, particularly if the pay-off is distant and the returns are near term.

DSIB in the strategic decision-making process (SDMP)

Although the rapidly growing literature on the strategic decision-making process (SDMP) has not focused on DSIB, it gives much insight into the nature of the SDMP and hence its vulnerability to DSIB. Here are some examples. Thomas and McDaniel (1990) found that strategy and information-processing structures are partly determined by how business leaders define and analyse strategic situations, so the bias of the SDMP towards the leader's interpretation of strategic situations must be recognised and challenged. Hough and White (2004), in their research into scanning and information gathering for strategic decision-making in situations of environmental dynamism, found that scanning behaviour may be unrelated to the need for information and is vulnerable to bias by those scanning or managing scanning, concluding that scanning and information gathering are critical activities and require stronger governance, particularly in situations of environmental dynamism, where it may not be clear which information is most needed for decisions.

Aravopoulou (2015) and Aravopoulou et al. (2018) showed that during the SDMP, decision-makers also rely on their intuition – based on their experience. Frishammar (2003) found that the SDMP starts with soft information (visions, ideas, intuition, cognitive structures, etc.) used to decide which hard information is relevant, moving to hard/numerical information, then back to soft information for the final decision. Internal/close information sources (e.g. staff, customers) seem to be preferred over external ones, while solicited information tends to be preferred to unsolicited information. Managers may not be sufficiently active in seeking more of the important information they need and may be biased in their solicitation of information. Tough questions should therefore always be asked about the information gathering and interpretation process that supports SDMP. Papadakis *et al.* (1998) showed that managers may manipulate meaning or categorisation of strategic issues to influence organisational responses, for example, manipulating information from external to internal systems, such as "environmental scanning", "strategic issue management" or "boundary spanning" systems, to serve their own goals. Strong governance is required to control this tendency. Miller and Ireland (2005) showed that intuition is particularly vulnerable to DSIB, so strong governance is required.

Behavioural and managerial factors

There are various behavioural and managerial ways to avoid DSIB. They include avoidance of politics, improved governance, trust, honesty – including awareness of pressures to engage in DSIB and balancing intuition and rationality. Several relate specifically to information, such as learning from experience via detailed analysis of past similar situations, admission and investigation of the known/ unknown situation and frequent recalibration in line with new information. In situations where DSIB occurs, it makes sense to evaluate these factors to see where improvements are required.

Another issue at play here is the question of who is exposed to or sees the results of marketing research, particularly when it has strategic implications, how broadly it is shared and the timescales in which actions take place as a result of the research. In some cases, research which should be presented more widely in an organisation and acted upon more broadly is presented only to a few people (often top management) and then either suppressed or subjected to a limited range of actions which do not address all the issues raised in the research.

Use of information technology

The advent of big data should have made mismanagement based on any kind of information error (including DSIB) less common, particularly given the emergence of the insight discipline (particularly customer insight, which emerged as a discipline well before the term "big data" became popular), the increased ease of managing and accessing information (Stone *et al.* 2017a) and analysis of how to make insight more effective by ensuring that senior managers understand the story told by the data (Stone *et al.* 2015). However, big data without intelligence and analysis merely leads to a situation of overload, which is why big data and analytics should go hand in hand (Wright *et al.* 2019).

In "soft" situations (Petkov *et al.* 2007; Hicks 2004), one problem is knowing where to focus analysis. A report from Tata Communications (2018) suggests that artificial intelligence may help by offering a counter-opinion, avoiding the problem of false consensus and groupthink. This builds on research on the importance of cognitive diversity, which so far has focused mainly on the importance of having different points of views, often from the perspective of different players, particularly serious in the area of forecasting.

Another idea worthy of exploration is that of "thick data", which focuses on the "why" of data rather than the "what" and how the two should be blended to support decision-making (Bornakke and Due 2018).

Artificial intelligence may in the future provide the answer to the question of how human bias (deliberate or not) can be removed from the interpretation of data, including that arising from marketing research. However, it should be emphasised that companies do not face a choice between traditional marketing research as used by marketing departments and the use of artificial intelligence to automate marketing decision-making and possibly strategy. The rise of marketing analytics, customer behavioural analysis, econometrics and other more sophisticated statistical models for marketing mix attribution or return on marketing investment calculations are all important developments. The options for combining these or altering the mix going forward is more nuanced than a choice between two approaches, with many possible interim levels of improvement and sophistication (Boobier 2018).

Forecasting

Marketing research has several advantages over big data when it comes to forecasting. It can ask:

- Customers what they are thinking about doing or planning to do, although this has the disadvantage that users' views can be myopic, as users of products or ones similar to products envisaged, in the case of new product forecasting (Tauber 1974);
- Experts about what they think is going to happen (broadly, the Delphi technique, where the contribution of research depends crucially on who the experts are, how well they understand the market and how well they can make allowance for what customers do not know). There is some scepticism about the value of expertise, of course;
- Competitors what they are planning to do – although this might be called competitive intelligence.

The outputs of such research may be a central forecast, a range or even work as inputs into scenario planning (Postma *et al.* 2007; Postma and Liebl 2005).

For new products, forecasting is not a one-time event, because in many areas, particularly in services, testing is possible, so customers' acceptance of a new concept can be assessed without a long and complex design and manufacture cycle (though the work involved in developing new service concepts should not be underestimated). However, for products which do require such initial investments, test marketing and forecasting may be a well-rehearsed process for some types of products, such as grocery foods (Fader *et al.* 2003; Ali *et al.* 2009), while for more revolutionary products, such as electric vehicles, new approaches, based on consumer attitudes and preferences, may be needed (e.g. Brase 2019). However, just because a forecasting process is routine and repeated does not make it better (Fildes *et al.* 2019). Just as important is the need to build forecasting (and artificial intelligence) into the marketing automation systems that are now widely in use, to ensure that the forecasts are actually used in managing marketing resources.

The risk of the self-fulfilling prophecy

With all these methods, there is one risk, which is that the results of such research can motivate suppliers to act in a certain way, creating a market that might not have existed without the research. However, from the point of view of the individual supplier, this is not necessarily a bad thing. If the intent was to find out which customers would or should be wanting it, at what price, with what ease of use and so on, and then suppliers as a group end up creating the demand, then the forecast proves to be accurate. There is of course no such thing as objectivity in marketing! The power of emulation and imitation is very important, with followers following leaders, whether as suppliers or customers. There is a further power, that once committed to making a market successful, suppliers will do a lot to create the success, even if it means changing initial plans for market targeting, pricing, marketing communications and product specification (which products are to be sold, with what features). In other words, the product life cycle becomes a target rather than a prediction (McBurney *et al.* 2002).

The importance of combining forecasting methods for discontinuous innovation

Where the forecast is for a very new concept, then it can be argued that triangulation of the outcomes of several different methods is the best approach (Mackay and Metcalfe 2002). It can be argued that the Delphi approach is particularly consistent with scenario planning – lack of consensus among experts can lead to the generation of different scenarios, which can each be triangulated by using other forecasting approaches, such as:

- Forecasts of broader market categories based on econometrics, time series, data mining or neural network techniques;
- Product lifecycle-based forecasts (Hu *et al.* 2017);
- Market diffusion of innovation-based forecasts (Meade and Islam 2006) for individual products or markets, including learning curves and pricing (Rowe and Wright 2001; Gregory and Duran 2001);
- Forecasts based on likely developments in industrial structure, based on industrial economic analysis of certain industries, market shares or competitive analysis (Pilinkienė 2008);
- Techniques suited to certain categories, such as origin and destination modelling in transport and tourism forecasting (Song and Li 2008), or technology acceptance modelling for telecommunication, computing and other technological markets (Singh *et al.* 2010).

Given the options listed previously and the much stronger sets of data and analytical technologies available, it can be argued that the Delphi method is best used in combination with such techniques rather than as a substitute, even for forecasting more remote periods.

A new source – search by customers

The Internet has created new sources for forecasters, the search patterns of consumers, social media discourse and online product reviews. These can claim to be an indicator of what customers would like, a particularly valuable source for near-term forecasting whether of product markets or of more general factors such as consumer confidence (where the dominant form of forecast was a questionnaire-based survey) but also for new product development (Vosen and Schmidt 2011; van den Brakel *et al.* 2017; Schneider and Gupta 2016; Fan *et al.* 2017). This may be most valuable for services, whose specifications, targeting and pricing can sometimes be changed more easily than for physical products.

The problem of bias in interpreting forecasts

The issues discussed earlier in this chapter have been shown to apply to forecasting (Bolton 2003). However, the interpretation of forecasts can be misleading, and thus attention is required. This is because "judgement" is a dangerous concept, involving such aspects as (sometimes inappropriate) analogies, persistence of prior beliefs or attractive, smooth-flowing scenarios which are full of biases and which may lead to preferences for best-case scenarios and the like – or non-analytic thinking.

The problem of understanding

One problem with using complex statistical methods, whether in forecasting or in marketing research more generally, is lack of understanding by managers of what procedures are involved and how they achieve their results (Fader and Hardie 2005). For example, simple customer base analysis using spreadsheets of purchase patterns and counts of customers, with simple assumptions about changes in purchasing ratios and rates of growth, may or may not be more accurate than complex statistical methods, but at least they will be understood and be communicable to other managers in the organisation. Marketing researchers and forecasters always need to balance the sophistication of their work with its presentability, although advances in visualisation technology and the growing experience of marketing researchers in using it have greatly reduced the seriousness of this problem. Still, the problem of understanding can be particularly acute when artificial intelligence or machine learning methods are used (ul Haq *et al.* 2020), because they tend to be "black box" in nature.

Conclusions

As stated at the beginning of this chapter, marketing research should be one of the sources of "truth" for an organisation. However, it can also be part of DSIB. To avoid this problem, marketing researchers should consider questions such as these not just at the beginning of a research project but throughout it:

- Does the information that is to be used have the right quality – completeness, currency, integrity, accuracy, accessibility, consistency, objectivity, transparency, relevance?
- Is the interdependence between different elements of information understood – in relation to both quality and value of data items?
- Is there diversity in the sources and interpretation of information?
- Is the brief designed to confirm the bias of a senior manager or sponsors?
- Is the budget allocated to the research likely to be able to fund the research required to answer the brief?
- Are any target respondents suggested by the organisation appropriate for answering the research questions?
- Are the target respondents likely to be able to answer the likely questions without resort to fantasy, because they have no experience of the subject of the research (e.g. a radical new product)?
- Is any suggested sampling frame designed to produce certain predetermined conclusions?
- Are the results of the research likely to be presented in a biased or selective way?
- Is any forecasting based on the research output likely to be subject to DSIB issues?

Issues for marketing researchers

One question that lies behind the developments discussed in this chapter is whether marketing researchers and research agencies are being forced to choose between traditional approaches and an approach dominated by futuristic technologies such as artificial intelligence. The good news for those wishing to pursue a career in marketing research is that it is not the case. Many agencies have been evolving for years, engaged in areas such as mobile research, sentiment analysis, measurement of emotions, eye tracking, user testing, semi-automated research, implicit research methods and a growing convergence with behavioural analytics. Intellectually, in some ways, marketing research is more stimulating than it has ever been.

Acknowledgements

This chapters draws on the following article:
Stone, M., Aravopoulou, E., Evans, G., AlDhaen, E. and Parnell, B.D., 2019. From information misman-agement to misinformation – the dark side of information management. *The Bottom Line*, 32(1), 47–70.

References

Ali, Ö., Sayın, S., Van Woensel, T. and Fransoo, J., 2009. SKU demand forecasting in the presence of promotions. *Expert Systems with Applications*, 36(10), 12340–12348. DOI: 10.1016/j.eswa.2009.04.052.

Aravopoulou, E., 2015. *The Development of an Integrated Model of the Relationship Among Strategic Decision-Making Process, Organisational Change and Employees' EVLN Behavioural Responses*. Doctoral Thesis, University of Abertay Dundee, UK [online]. Available from: https://rke.abertay.ac.uk/ws/portalfiles/portal/8473385/Aravopoulou_TheDevelopmentsofanIntegratedModel_PhD_2015.pdf [Accessed 20 June 2020].

Aravopoulou, E., Branine, M., Stone, M., Mitsakis, F. and Paul, G., 2018. Strategic decision-making process (SDMP) in times of crisis: Evidence from Greek banks. *Journal of Business & Retail Management Research*, 12(4), 26–36. http://doi.org/10.24052/jbrmr/v12is04/art-03.

Ariely, D., 2012. *The (Honest) Truth About Dishonesty*. New York: Harper Collins.

Aven, T., 2015. Implications of black swans to the foundations and practice of risk assessment and management. *Reliability Engineering & System Safety*, 134, 83–91. DOI: 10.1016/j.ress.2014.10.004.

Beaussier, A., Demeritt, D., Griffiths, A. and Rothstein, H., 2016. Accounting for failure: Risk-based regulation and the problems of ensuring healthcare quality in the NHS. *Health, Risk & Society*, 18(3/4), 205–224.

Bolton, L., 2003. Stickier priors: The effects of nonanalytic versus analytic thinking in new product forecasting. *Journal of Marketing Research*, 40(1), 65–79.

Boobier, T., 2018. Advanced Analytics and AI: Impact, implementation, and the future of work. Chichester, UK: John Wiley & Sons.

Bornakke, T. and Due, B.L., 2018. Big–thick blending: A method for mixing analytical insights from big and thick data sources. *Big Data & Society*, 5(1), 1–16. https://doi.org/10.1177%2F2053951718765026.

Brase, G., 2019. What would it take to get you into an electric car? Consumer perceptions and decision making about electric vehicles. *The Journal of Psychology*, 153(2), 214–236.

Brennan, N., Kirwan, C.E. and Redmond, J., 2016. Should non-executive directors know as much as managers? *Accountancy Ireland*, 48(2), 66–67.

Cyert, R. and March, J., 1963. *A Behavioral Theory of the Firm*, ed. J. Miner. Englewood Cliffs, NJ: Prentice-Hall, 169–187.

Eisenhardt, K., 1989. Agency theory: An assessment and review. *Academy of Management Review*, 14(1), 57–74.

Fader, P. and Hardie, B., 2005. The value of simple models in new product forecasting and customer-base analysis. *Applied Stochastic Models in Business and Industry*, 21(4/5), 461–473.

Fader, P., Hardie, B. and Zeithammer, R., 2003. Forecasting new product trial in a controlled test market environment. *Journal of Forecasting*, 22(5), 391–410.

Fan, Z., Che, Y. and Chen, Z., 2017. Product sales forecasting using online reviews and historical sales data: A method combining the Bass model and sentiment analysis. *Journal of Business Research*, 74, 90–100.

Fildes, R., Ma, S. and Kolassa, S., 2019. Retail forecasting: Research and practice. *International Journal of Forecasting*. https://doi.org/10.1016/j.ijforecast.2019.06.004.

Frishammar, J., 2003. Information use in strategic decision making. *Management Decision*, 41(4), 318–326.

Gregory, W. and Duran, A., 2001. *Scenarios and Acceptance of Forecasts, in Principles of Forecasting*. Boston, MA: Springer, 519–540.

Grover, S., 2005. The truth, the whole truth, and nothing but the truth: The causes and management of workplace lying. *Academy of Management Perspectives*, 19(2), 148–157.

Hicks, M., 2004. Problem solving and decision-making: Hard, soft and creative approaches. London: Cengage Learning EMEA.

Hough, J. and White, M.A., 2004. Scanning actions and environmental dynamism: Gathering information for strategic decision making. *Management Decision*, 42(6), 781–793.

Hu, K., Acimovic, J., Erize, F., Thomas, D. and Van Mieghem, J.A., 2017. Forecasting new product life cycle curves: Practical approach and empirical analysis. *Manufacturing & Service Operations Management*, 21(1), 66–85.

Kahneman, D., Knetsch, J. and Thaler, R., 1991. Anomalies: The endowment effect, loss aversion, and status quo bias. *Journal of Economic Perspectives*, 5(1), 193–206.

Lovallo, D. and Kahneman, D., 2003. Delusions of success: How optimism undermines executives' decisions. *Harvard Business Review*, 81(7), 56–63.

Mackay, M. and Metcalfe, M., 2002. Multiple method forecasts for discontinuous innovations. *Technological Forecasting and Social Change*, 69(3), 221–232. https://doi.org/10.1016/S0040-1625(01)00143-3.

Mark, A. and Snowden, D., 2006. Researching practice or practicing research: Innovating methods in healthcare – the contribution of Cynefin. In A. Casebeer, A. Harrison. and A. Mark, eds. *Innovations in Health Care*. Basingstoke: Palgrave McMillan.

McBurney, P., Parsons, S. and Green, J., 2002. Forecasting market demand for new telecommunications services: An introduction. *Telematics and Informatics*, 19(3), 225–249. DOI: 10.1016/S0736-5853(01)00004-1.

Meade, N. and Islam, T., 2006. Modelling and forecasting the diffusion of innovation – A 25-year review. *International Journal of Forecasting*, 22(3), 519–545. http://dx.doi.org/10.1016/j.ijforecast.

Miller, C. and Ireland, R., 2005. Intuition in strategic decision making: Friend or foe in the fast-paced 21st century? *Academy of Management Perspectives*, 19(1), 19–30. https://doi.org/10.5465/ame.2005.15841948.

Nunan, D., 2020. Research priorities for data, marketing research, and insights. *International Journal of Marketing Research*, 62(2), 121–123. DOI: 10.1177/1470785320908161.

O'Rourke, M., 2016. Emerging risks for the insurance industry. *Risk Management*, 63(6), 44.

Papadakis, V., Lioukas, S. and Chambers, D., 1998. Strategic decision-making processes: The role of management and context. *Strategic Management Journal*, 19(2), 115–147. https://doi.org/10.1002/(SICI)1097-0266(199802)19:2<115::AID-SMJ941>3.0.CO;2-5.

Paté-Cornell, E., 2012. On "black swans" and "perfect storms": Risk analysis and management when statistics are not enough. *Risk Analysis: An International Journal*, 32(11), 1823–1833. https://doi.org/10.1111/j.1539-6924.2011.01787.x.

Petkov, D., Petkov, O., Andrew, T. and Nepal, T., 2007. Mixing multiple criteria decision making with soft systems thinking techniques for decision support in complex situations. *Decision Support Systems*, 43(4), 1615–1629. https://doi.org/10.1016/j.dss.2006.03.006.

Pfeffer, J., 2016. *Why Deception Is Probably the Single Most Important Leadership Skill* [online]. Available from: https://fortune.com/2016/06/02/lying-leadership-skills-expectations-communication/ [Accessed 20 June 2020].

Pilinkienė, V., 2008. Market demand forecasting models and their elements in the context of competitive market. *Engineering Economics*, 5(60), 24–31.

Postma, T., Alers, J.C., Terpstra, S. and Zuurbier, A., 2007. Medical technology decisions in The Netherlands: How to solve the dilemma of technology foresight versus marketing research? *Technological Forecasting and Social Change*, 74(9), 1823–1833.

Postma, T. and Liebl, F., 2005. How to improve scenario analysis as a strategic management tool? *Technological Forecasting and Social Change*, 72(2), 161–173. DOI: 10.1016/j.techfore.2003.11.005.

Renn, O., 2014. Emerging risks: Methodology, classification and policy implications. *Journal of Risk Analysis and Crisis Response*, 4(3), 114–132. DOI: 10.2991/jrarc.2014.4.3.1.

Rowe, G. and Wright, G., 2001. Expert opinions in forecasting: The role of the Delphi technique. In J. Armstrong, ed. *Principles of Forecasting*. Boston, MA: Springer, 125–144.

Schneider, M. and Gupta, S., 2016. Forecasting sales of new and existing products using consumer reviews: A random projections approach. *International Journal of Forecasting*, 32(2), 243–256. DOI: 10.1016/j.ijforecast.2015.08.005.

Singh, S., Singh, D., Singh, M. and Singh, S., 2010. The forecasting of 3G market in India based on revised technology acceptance model. *International Journal of Next-Generation Networks*, 2(2), 61–68. DOI: 10.5121/ijngn.2010.2206.

Slowik, M. and Spinoni, E., 2018. *Augmenting or Substituting? How the Workforce Should Tackle the Fear of AI* [online]. Available from: http://blog-idcuk.com/category/artificial-intelligence/ [Accessed 26 September 2018].

Song, H. and Li, G., 2008. Tourism demand modelling and forecasting – A review of recent research. *Tourism Management*, 29(2), 203–220. DOI: 10.1016/j.tourman.2007.07.016.

Stone, M., 1984. Competing with Japan – the rules of the game. *Long Range Planning*, 17(2), 33–47.

Stone, M., 2015. Competitive marketing intelligence in a digital, data-based world. *Journal of Direct, Data & Digital Marketing Practice*, 17(1), 20–29. DOI: 10.1057/dddmp.2015.42.

Stone, M., Laughlin, P., Aravopoulou, E., Gerardi, G., Todeva, E. and Weinzierl, L., 2017a. How platforms are transforming customer information management. *The Bottom Line*, 30(3), 216–235. DOI: 10.1108/BL-08-2017-0024.

Stone, M., Machtynger, L. and Machtynger, J., 2015. Managing customer insight creatively through storytelling. *Journal of Direct, Data & Digital Marketing*, 17(2), 77–83. DOI: 10.1057/dddmp.2015.45.

Stone, M., Parnell, B., Stott, R., Aravopoulou, E. and Timms, L., 2017b. Business model innovation, strategic information & the role of analyst firms. *The Bottom Line*, 30(2), 151–162. https://doi.org/10.1108/BL-06-2017-0012.

Stone, M., Woodcock, N. and Starkey, M., 2003. The role of academics & analysts in misleading businesses – the case of CRM, *Journal of Database Marketing & Customer Strategy Management* 11(2), 121–132. https://doi.org/10.1057/palgrave.dbm.3240213.

Taleb, N., 2007. *The Black Swan: The Impact of the Highly Improbable*. New York: Random House.

Tata Communications, 2018. *Cognitive Diversity: AI and the Future of Work*. Mumbai: Tata Communications [online]. Available from: www.tatacommunications.com/wp-content/uploads/2018/09/Report_Cognitive-Diversity_AI-and-The-Future-of-Work.pdf [Accessed 20 June 020].

Tauber, E.M., 1974. How marketing research discourages major innovation. *Business Horizons*, 17(3), 22–26. https://doi.org/10.1016/0007-6813(74)90070-6.

Thomas, J. and McDaniel Jr, R., 1990. Interpreting strategic issues: Effects of strategy and the information-processing structure of top management teams. *Academy of Management Journal*, 33(2), 286–306. DOI: 10.2307/256326.

ul Haq, A., Majeed, A., Magoulas, G. and Jamal, A., 2020. *Transformative Power of Smart Technologies Enabled by Advances in AI: Changing Landscape for Digital Marketing*. Handbook of Research on Innovations in Technology and Marketing for the Connected Consumer, IGI Global, 1–17. Https://doi.org/10.4018/978-1-7998-0131-3.ch001.

U.S. Department of Defence, 2018. *DoD News Briefing – Secretary Rumsfeld and Gen. Myers* [online]. Available from: http://archive.defense.gov/Transcripts/Transcript.aspx?TranscriptID=2636 [Accessed 5 September 2018].

van den Brakel, J., Söhler, E., Daas, P. and Buelens, B., 2017. Social media as a data source for official statistics: The Dutch consumer confidence index. *Survey Methodology*, 34(2), 183–210. Available from: www.pietdaas.nl/beta/pubs/pubs/2016_Soc_media_CCI.pdf [Accessed 20 June 2020].

Vosen, S. and Schmidt, T., 2011. Forecasting private consumption: Survey-based indicators vs. Google trends. *Journal of Forecasting*, 30(6), 565–578. https://doi.org/10.1002/for.1213.

Wright, L., Robin, R., Stone, M. and Aravopoulou, E., 2019. Adoption of big data technology for innovation in B2B marketing. *Journal of Business-to-Business Marketing*, 26(3/4), 281–293.

26

FUTURING MARKETING RESEARCH STRATEGY

Luiz Moutinho

Summary

This chapter covers transfiguration of marketing research. This includes developments, such as the shift to insights management, the increasing use of real-time research, the new search for and implementation of expressive research, the role of big data and avoidance of dark data. A particular emphasis is placed on the variety of ethnographic methods becoming available. It also includes the need for permission based predictive modelling and analysis, the era of consumer data, the emergence of the small data/little data phenomenon, the incredible developments in artificial intelligence and machine learning and the clear movement towards data transparency. Finally, it covers new formats, such as in-the-moment research.

Marketing research versus insights management

The term "marketing research" has been incredibly detrimental to the industry, as it focuses on the process and not the value of data-driven strategy. The term "marketing research" has minimised the industry's influence in the corporate decision-making structure by reinforcing the notion that marketing research is all process and data and that marketing researchers manage the process and date delivery but not the insights or strategy that flows from this process. Time and again we see institutional blindness, compounded by dangerously misleading survey results. Consumers change their minds, faster than market research can predict them! What we need is insight, not just data! Actually, "insights" is a much better term, because it concentrates the mind on the value derived from the data. However, "insights" as a term is still sub-optimal in that it completely omits (a) what will be done with these insights and (b) the strategy that will flow from them.

The line between data and insight will diminish

Integrated data-mining tools that will integrate data from social media data, sales and retail with customer profiles will be used in predictive models to forecast behaviours and trends. The impact of each data-based decision will be assessed through financial value, that is, cost of analysis and revenue generated. Old methodologies are getting new looks. Ethnographies certainly seem to be making a comeback, as do the kind of lengthy in-depth interviews needed for some of the newest collaging exercises. This trend is called "deep qual" or "qualitania".

Insights management

With the geometric expansion in volumes of consumer data, the need for management of this data gas become intense. At a very granular level, the simple fact is that corporations that choose to be data-driven have more consumer data streams (attitudinal, conversational and behavioural) than ever before. Making sense of these data streams and interpreting new data within the context of past research is incredibly important. There is a significant need for "insight management and archiving", and this market niche may prove highly lucrative to the firm that produces the most useable system and interface. While this need will be filled by software, it will ultimately require the spark of human cognition in order to pull macro-level insights from numerous data streams. Without "insight management and archiving", institutions will waste precious resources and time relearning that which has already been discovered.

Democratisation of data and analytics

There was once a time when access to vast piles of market-research data and processing power was contingent on huge budgets. While that is still true in many cases, digital networks have made more data more accessible – even sometimes to the point of open-source or free. An interesting manifestation is the growth of free metrics services like Google Trends and BlogPulse to understand web behaviours. The Internet is not the only aspect of the digital environment that is changing marketing research. Other innovations, such as 3D graphics, kiosks and infrared tracking systems are also increasingly being used to enhance the research process.

A shift toward ongoing, real-time research

There is a cataclysmic shift in the marketplace that is just beginning. We are seeing executives moving away from periodic, big and expensive research projects performed by third parties. Commissioning a once-a-year study just won't cut it anymore. The speed of market learning is a real and sustainable differentiation, and so we are seeing executives starting to move this in-house as a core competency and running their research in an always-on, real-time, agile, iterative fashion. There is a new research tool – real-time experience tracking (RET) – which seeks to capture how people respond to experiences and interactions with a given brand, all in real-time. Examples of companies using it are PepsiCo and Gatorade. Others like Unilever, BskyB, HP, Energizer and Microsoft have all used RET successfully.

Real-time insights

A more accurate picture of consumer opinion is now being created from using real-time insights. This can result in quicker implementation of changes to services and products through better understanding of emotional response to brands at a deep level than by using traditional survey methods. Whilst the neuroscience umbrella covers a whole spectrum of requirements including heart monitors and brain scans, other less intrusive measures can be used to rate the emotional reaction of customers. Online surveys, for example, via webcams, can record subtle movement in the facial expressions of the subject and, once analysed, show their reactions to what they are looking at. The ability to interpret these signs allows brands to adjust much more quickly to the

Table 26.1 Reflexive vs expressive research

Definition	Reflexive research	Expressive research
		Real-time
Main characteristics	Circular relationship of cause and effect	Use of networks by revealing the structure and mechanics of meaning
Typical methods	Survey research	Ethnographic research
Benefits	Quantification	Deeper levels of meaning
Costs	Varies from £5,000 upwards depending on the sample size	Varies from £1,000 upwards depending on the number of observations
Example of users	Most large fast-moving consumer goods (FMCG) and services companies	HP, Dell, Apple, ASUS and ACER

Source: The author

changes required in their creative output. As traditional market research methods increasingly incorporate neuroscience, this practice will continue to improve and grow. To use real-time tracking effectively, the right technology is required, along with internal expertise to optimise the results. Carefully defined parameters must be set by the marketers to ensure the correct data is gathered and is in alignment with the marketing aims required by each individual brand.

Marketing research is experiencing a shift from reflective research to expressive research. In fact, there is a new era of expressive research. Expressive research is based on real-time research. The circular relationship of cause and effect confirmation gives rise to the use of networks by revealing the structure and mechanics of meaning (Table 26.1).

Big data – massive data

Along with analytic techniques, big data has the ability to augment marketing research. Market research combined with "big data" can create a powerful and intense toolkit when used by people who know how to exploit these to their full potential. Big data has the ability to enhance the extent of the range of the survey industry, not supersede it.

Big data can be found in two separate categories:

* Predictive analytics use for data;
* Social network data.

Predictive analytics use for data

The definition of this suggests that corporations will collect and store such data for the purpose of analytics. An insurance company can collect data on possible fraud sources. A mortgage company can keep a list of possible mortgage candidates. Large shopping companies can use the data to predict shifting trends in product interests by using data from past experiences.

Social network data

Social networks such as Twitter, Facebook, Flickr and LinkedIn provide unstructured data. The information and comments flow freely between participants. Control rooms in companies such as Starbucks or Nike have been set up to monitor and track such information with the intention to control brand conversations. Sentiment analysis and social media network analysis fields are appearing. Social media monitoring is being utilised by large advertising firms with the intention to attempt to control the unstructured data universe. There are now very many web analytics companies.

Benefits and limitations of each

Even though big data has limitations, both the previous aspects of big data can further increase the quality of marketing research for companies that store huge amounts of customer information, using predictive analytics to add segmented value to survey data. Survey researchers can also manipulate data mining information from these stores to bring to existence custom segmentations or reports.

CHAID, CART trees, neural networks, regression analysis and other such conventional data mining tools are used by marketing research. Predictive analytics, text analytics, sentiment analytics and social visualisation are all critical tools required to bring meaning to any fully textured marketing research report. This is a beneficial mixture of qualitative and quantitative connection within marketing research, for example, where online chats take place after a quantitative survey. Social media platforms such as Twitter, Facebook and Flickr groups can add their own valuable insight to any branding project but do not have the ability to completely replace the process.

The "big" in big data is only one of the features of new data assets. "Big" refers to the extent, size and capabilities of the data, which is at the forefront of all actions because it is beyond the physical limits of anything we have seen before. However, there are also other significant characteristics to these new data streams. They often appear as unstructured, raw data with little formatting and can be unpredictable. "Entity analytics" is an emerging area of data management, helping manage the information in big data. Entity analytics can analyse data sets and identify the number of relevant components and their individual observations, resulting in complete and useful information and removing any data errors. Creation of context surrounding big data assets is still needed, to take stock of our previous experience, category expertise and analytic strength. Many analysts are concluding that it is a source of competitive advantage to be able to manage the uncertainty that exists in big data, as it results in better decision-making. Here, primary research can contribute creation, content and analysis within big data, in new areas of survey-based exploration, providing further insight into a wide range of strategic issues, helping companies move closer to the end goal of improving brand communications.

Passive data collection

We are about to experience a huge explosion in data volume as everything around us becomes smart and connected. It will become the norm for data to be emitted from everyday items such as clothes, often without us knowing. Every aspect of our life will generate data. The trend today is towards more observations but even more so, to radically larger numbers of variables – voracious, automatic, systematic collection of hyper-informative detail about each observed instance.

Data integration comes of age

With more customer and data touch points comes the need for more data integration and better market modelling. In forecasting, planning, adjusting and evaluating, data integration is where myriad measurements will achieve clarity, dimension and action. Classical methods are simply not designed to cope with this kind of explosive growth of dimensionality of the observation vector. However, as big data increases, we see a parallel growth in the need for "small data" to answer the questions it raises. Big data promises to deliver greater customer insight at a more granular level than ever possible before. Indeed, organisations can now access a wealth of information on their customers – transaction histories, web and search behaviour, location data, social medial activity and more – that can inform their customer experience strategies and tactics. However big data is no silver bullet. Many companies are data rich but insight poor, and not just because they lack analytics tools or expertise. They are not effectively integrating more nuanced "small data" with their big data to produce a full understanding of their customers. Examples of companies using small data/little data include Lowes Foods, United Stated Postal Service, LEGO, Walt Disney, Pepsi and Kellogg's.

Big data uses predictive analysis and machine intelligence to predict the probability of a specific result or consequence. Theoretically, these predictive insights can be applied to support sales opportunities and support lead generation, though for such campaigns to be considered measurable, these insights must be actionable by marketers. Predictive insights can become more practical and actionable when the small data is used, helping translate big data from theory to practice. In the context of predictive analysis, bigger is not necessarily always better. It's a place to start but is often unmanageable and overwhelming.

In the realm of big data, possession means much less than comprehension. You really cannot derive insights of significant value from your big data using solutions from a different data era – at least not within a timeframe appropriate to the speed of business or a budget that suits most companies. So, while your data scientists can analyse some parts of the data, other parts remain hidden behind pre-aggregated tables and views. In fact, data consumers are highly aware of the restrictive modelling problem and are taking matters into their own hands.

Having big data is one thing, but understanding it is a whole other ball game. Deficiencies in today's big data analytics paradigms result in missed opportunities. Companies operate without a comprehensive understanding of the business intelligence available to them and cannot fully identify, understand or react to market and business trends. Organisations that learn to turn data into actionable insights – to comprehend and not just possess – are the ones in true possession of value and business advancing competitive advantage.

Businesses are learning to marry data analytics and qualitative research. Small data is defined as "slices or subsets" of big data, or small chunks of actionable data. It may incorporate neglected customer detail normally found in unstructured data. While definitions of small data vary from case to case, they all conclude that the data must be small enough to be important and actionable, while big data allows marketers to develop a broader, more useful view of their target market or audience.

There is a direct relationship between small data and the "intention economy". Big data is not a well-understood topic amongst many companies today. Its large volumes make it difficult to manage by nature, and finding those actionable insights you can count on is even more difficult. However, businesses can spend a lot of time and resources mining data analytics and still not understand the psychology of their audience without a qualitative research aspect.

Increasingly, the paradigm shift is putting the consumers in charge. Who owns the marketplace? Is it the business or the customer? Customers are on the verge of becoming truly free and independent actors in the marketplace, with the power to tell vendors what they want, how, when and where they want it. This shift in customer power will alter the balance of the market and usher in the "intention economy".

Take, for example, sales managers or business owners from small to medium-sized companies. With considerable analysis, acquired data regarding their potential customers can be very specific, allowing them to mount campaigns to help these customers meet the challenges that they are facing.

A great example of the power of small data is the story of how LEGO went from the tiny bricks to inventing the Lego Movie and today is the number-one company in the world in this children's' market. As big data tries to become smarter, the humans behind small data will become even smarter. Thick data is data brought to light using qualitative, ethnographic research methods that uncover people's emotions, stories and models of their world. Nokia had been offered insights derived from small data/little data, using 100 ethnographic observations; the company rejected this research approach, and just look at what happened to the company – it was bought by Microsoft.

Blending data streams

Data scientists already have access to data on the majority of the population and can focus on the observable data collected by companies or third parties with the aim of being able to predict what might be coming or simply answer questions about present behaviour. The ability that businesses now have, to capture data relating to their customer base, has created a dynamic stream, requiring resources to be shifted from traditional research methods and into the "big data" field. However, to seek a broader view of the data, the information on customer movements must be merged and insight acquired into why they do what they are doing. The blending of data streams allows users to use data science algorithms to present insights from surveys, allowing marketers to understand the behaviour patterns of certain groups of customers and to make decisions or take actions and monitor the results through tracking customer behaviour.

Statistical machine learning

High volumes of data are generated from any marketing campaign and can be used to identify customer behaviour and preferences. Structured data is included in this (e.g. name, locations, information that is provided voluntarily by the respondent), along with many other forms of information making up unstructured and semi-structured data. Emails, photos, text messages and navigation behaviour on a website are a few examples of unstructured data that reveals preferences of any customer who is being studied but may not be connected to any specific conclusions.

Prediction

Machine learning (ML) predicts future behaviour by making use of past patterns. ML algorithms can be set to predict the probability of the customer seeing a purchase through to fruition, or of quitting the process early and without purchase, in response to different marketing actions, by analysing their patterns of behaviour and their responses to marketing mix decisions. Most ML in eCommerce is derived from clustering. Where the algorithm picks up thousands of user instances and navigational patterns, this results in "unsupervised learning". The collected data can then be separated into many categories and channelled into a marketing automation setup, resulting in the algorithm using different conditions to trigger actions according to rules set by the marketer.

Segmentation

Artificial intelligence (AI) and ML can be used in the segmentation process to get the best out of available resources and data and help achieve key business goals. Segments can be as simple as demographic (e.g. gender and age), but for larger consumer customers and business customers, more complex variables such as their past behaviours and buying personas are used. Being able to target groups of people with specific interests allows companies to cross- and up-sell their products. Sending personalised content to a customer not only increases their probability of buying the product but also their brand or business loyalty.

Recommendations

A recommender system refers to a system that can predict a user's preferences within a set of items. These systems come in two classifications:

- User-based systems which measure the similarity between target users and other users, that is, "users who are similar to you also liked product X";
- Item-based systems which measure the similarity between the items that target users interact with and other possible items, that is, "users who liked this item also liked product X".

Rotation estimation

Also known as cross-validation, this is an extremely important aspect of ML, where predictions should come from partial data sets. Cross-validation requires the use of a historic data set for this one-time procedure, with the intention of generalising an independent data set. Cross-validation is a continuous process in ML that continues to add each new data into the original dataset and then recalculates its interpretation of the results based on the updated information. As it would require the analysis of millions of data points to complete such an intricate technique, heavy duty data tools such as Hadoop are considered essential for this.

Cross-validation is a statistical method used to estimate the skill of ML models. It is commonly used in applied ML to compare and select a model for a given predictive modelling problem because it is easy to understand, easy to implement and results in skill estimates that generally have a lower bias than other methods. System analysts can apply the k-fold cross-validation procedure for estimating the skill of machine learning models. The k-fold cross validation is a procedure used to estimate the skill of the model on new data. There are common tactics that can be used to select the value of k for the dataset. There are also commonly used variations on cross-validation such as a stratified and repeated that are available in scikit-learn.

Overfitting

A major flaw with machine learning, when connected to marketing, is overfitting. Machine learning algorithms can become too specific when tracking millions of behavioural data points, and the end result may be that they have been unsuccessful in categorising a specific data point within a general category. The success of such actions can be that as little as 20% of the input data is successfully categorised. This means that ML is not an effective tool in identifying certain behaviours which makes the process ineffective.

Progress to-date

ML is not yet a mainstream technology within marketing. Although overfitting as a factor can reduce the overall effectiveness in the early stages, machine learning is too beneficial to be dismissed. AI has an obvious application helping with data cleaning and serious statistical analysis, but researchers say it also has a role to play reading open-ended responses, determining sample size and to a smaller degree finding insights in data just like a researcher would do. According to research carried out by Qualtrics in 2018, overall, about half of market researchers feel confident they know what AI is, but nearly all predict that AI will have a significant impact on the market-research industry within 10 years. Some of that optimism may be due to high-tech hype, but what used to be hype is starting to look like real life, as we are now have conversations with our phones and climb into cars with no driver. Researchers believe that nearly 1 in 4 surveys will be spoken to a digital assistant within 5 years. Spoken surveys could capture a quarter of the industry's text survey market share with a relatively short period of time. But volume does not mean quality, at least not yet. Thirty-two percent of researchers believe that spoken surveys will be a better experience for respondents than typed surveys, and 26% of researchers believe that spoken surveys will yield higher data quality than typed surveys

The future of AI in marketing research

To understand the impact that artificial intelligence will have on market research, it is first important to be clear about what exactly AI is and what it is not. Artificial intelligence is the intelligence displayed by machines, often characterised by learning and the ability to adapt. It is not the same as automation. Automation is already widely used throughout the insights industry to speed up many processes. From recruitment to data collection and analysis, automation is simply the set of rules that a machine follows to perform a task without human assistance. When complex logic and branching paths are introduced, it can be difficult to distinguish this from AI. However, there is an important difference. Even in it is most complex forms, when a task is automated, software follows the instructions it has been given. The software (or machine) does not make any decisions or learn something new each time the process runs. Learning is what distinguishes artificial intelligence from automation. And it is what offers the greatest opportunities for those that embrace it.

AI is making people better at their jobs in three ways: automation of tasks that can help a person perform their job more effectively, the ability to generate insights from large amounts of data and ability to enable interactions with technology via natural-language conversations. Automation, insight generation and natural language processing enable businesses to survey the market continually rather than dedicating specific time, labour and money to the process. AI solutions are producing insights in seconds that used to take teams of people days or even weeks to produce. Early adopters are seeing financial benefits already. An advantage of using AI in marketing research is that the time involved in creating an overview of consumer needs is cut down enormously. When AI is used to understand the comprehensive picture painted by all the data available via social media people's movements, behaviours that can be observed and the corresponding actions taken, we are seeing firms develop insights which give them a better picture than they have ever been able to generate. Using AI also means data can be digested in real time.

Much contemporary AI is "narrow"; that is, the AI is designed to perform a specific task. Already, there are several ways in which AI can empower researchers with insights and analysis that would not have been previously possible. Most notable is the ability to process large, unstructured datasets.

Big qual

Processing open-ended data has been dubbed "big qual" – the process of applying statistical analysis techniques to huge volumes of written data aims to distil quantitative results. The Google Cloud Natural Language application provides a demonstration of this in action. For example, the program recognises "AI" as the most salient entity in a given paragraph (i.e. the most central to the text). It is also able to recognise the category of text and syntactic structure and offer insights on sentiment. For example, it might find that the first and third sentence had a negative sentiment, while the second was overall more positive. In one highly visible example, using natural language processing, IBM-Watson parsed the vocabulary of social media influencers to pinpoint which ones showed the traits Kia Cars (South Korea) were looking for – openness to change, artistic interest and striving for achievement. The decisions Watson made are ones that would be difficult for a human to make, demonstrating the possibility that AI may be able to understand us better than we can ourselves.

AI in collecting and analysing data

A question still hangs over whether AI could be used to gather conversational qualitative research at scale. Today's research chatbots are limited to pre-programmed questions, presented in a user interface typical of an online conversation. However, as advances in AI continue, so may these online question delivery formats. The ultimate test will be whether such a tool could interpret answers from respondents so as to allow the following questions to be tailored and interesting points to be probed. This will signal the evolution from question delivery format to virtual moderator.

It seems that AI in marketing research is currently able to unearth, read and analyse data far more quickly than human beings. The ability to extract real insights from written comments is a great example of how AI in marketing research can improve insight time. Firms that used to rely on analysts to review consumer feedback can now see key themes people care about in real time. Over 80% of the data produced every day is unstructured – written feedback, photos and so on – and this data is not being used by AI solutions to provide real insights in a way that was not possible without AI. Harnessing this unused data to create a continuous big picture of customer insights can alert marketing teams to patterns and trends sooner than traditional methods, helping firms stay on top of consumer needs.

Combining humans and AI

AI and human beings can work in harmony, each augmenting each other's strengths. AI excels at storing and remembering huge amounts of data and making very complex calculations based on those data sets. People are very skilled at social interactions and complex tasks, critical thinking and creativity. What could a combination of human and AI skills achieve? Trained AI can go beyond what a human can do by finding the connections in the data at a scale that would be impossible for humans, helping us understand not just the known unknowns but the unknown unknowns, the things we did not know we did not know. With such boundless possibilities, the advantages of using AI in marketing research to reduce insight time are clear and very exciting. However, despite the broad scope of AI, much of the debate surrounding AI in marketing research centres on the topic of coding and how AI could speed up analysis of qualitative data. While this is important, the range of applications AI could have in the insights industry is much broader. For insight professionals to make the most of this powerful technology, still very much in its infancy, it is important that this greater range of applications be fully explored, combining these two elements in a holistic process.

- The "why" of survey research (attitudes and intentions explored in samples;
- The "what" of data sciences (descriptions of very large numbers, perhaps complete markets of people/customers and their behaviour), using a holistic approach.

Holism

Holism refers to the theory that parts of a whole that cannot exist independently of each other; that is, "the whole is greater than the sum of its parts". A holistic approach suggests that further explanation is required with each level of detail but with the inclusion of emergent properties this cannot be reduced to the level below. Reduction explanations are considered inappropriate when attached to the study of human subjectivity. Although they may work in some circumstances, it is not acceptable here because the entire person must be taken into consideration. Without this rule, there is no sense in trying to understand the meaning of any human behaviour. Holism implies completeness: where, how, why, when and so on all matter. Participant answers, for instance, may vary according to setting or an interviewer's formality or informality. Considering these elements is critical in any research. Researchers most not only guess possible variables – they must also decide to control them or not.

While sometimes used to describe a study's broadness, holism does not just mean a project's totality. A holistic approach is the understanding of how details affect outcomes. A qualitative study consisting of a few focus groups benefits from holistic planning as much as a large-scale project involving field research. It is important to distinguish between a project's holism and the content of its findings. Thus, a study that uses a holistic design may offer specific, rather than broad, insight.

Types of insight

Contextual insight – an important edge in market research

Contextual insight relates to the idea that consumers are a much broader spectrum than can be addressed in any single focus group or survey. Understanding consumers requires a broad world view, industry knowledge, consumer knowledge, meta-analysis, risk and a powerfully interest-evoking framework. Data transparency, engaging insight reporting and tactful moderation and panel management are worth a mention, but the most important point is that it goes beyond surveys or focus groups. Marketing research is much more than just surveys and focus groups. The first sign of a mature insight strategy is that the research is planned to reflect and produce high-quality data and insights to help achieve research and business goals. This planning approach is crucial, and if it is not used, the rest of the research will not be very effective.

Micro surveys (also known as quick surveys, mini surveys or bit surveys), an abbreviated form of surveying with less than five questions in total and taking take less than a minute to answer, are useful. They are short for the writer and the participant, ensuring a quick turnaround time for fieldwork, as there is less data to process, although there may be more participants. If a higher response rate, higher engagement and quick turnaround are required, then a micro survey is the obvious choice. If the requirement is for more questions to be answered, then a longer survey would be more helpful.

Deeper insight into the whole consumer

While it is true that we have more data on consumer than ever before and more approaches to qualitatively surveying them, we are still starved for a holistic understanding of the whole consumer. The only way to truly develop this full understanding of the whole consumer is via ethnography, and this is why ethnographic tools are coming quickly back into vogue within the market research industry (see Table 26.2). In a world where consumers are less and less likely to respond to a basic survey, ethnographic data may be an important part of the industry's transition. Interestingly, the trends towards ethnography and hosted online communities may squeeze traditional focus groups from both sides, reducing future growth of this qualitative workhorse.

Table 26.2 Ethnographic methods

Approach	*Definition*	*Benefits*	*Costs*	*Example*
Digital anthropology	Digital anthropology is the anthropological study of the relationship between humans and digital-era technology. The field is new and thus has a variety of names with a variety of emphases. These include techno-anthropology, digital ethnography, cyberanthropology and virtual anthropology.	Digital anthropology typically goes beyond demographics to study the wider cultural and social context – contradictions, messiness and all – of human beings in the digital age.	Varies according to the dimension of the study. From £2000 upwards.	Samsung Intel Xerox
Mobile ethnography	Mobile ethnography is an innovative market research technique that combines traditional ethnography with mobile research. Ethnography in market research involves observing consumers in a natural environment, allowing you to gain a reliable understanding of their behaviour, values and beliefs.	Participant engagement. In-the-moment feedback. Cost-effective. Quick turnaround. Enhanced project scope. Engaging insights.	Varies according to the dimension of the study. From £1000 upwards.	HTC Ethos Firefish Kraft Foods

Approach	Definition	Benefits	Costs	Example
Ethnographic mimicry	The combination of ethnographic research with mimicry. Mimicry is the resemblance of one organism to another, usually as the result of evolution in response to a selective advantage. Mimicry can involve physical or behavioural traits, and well-studied examples are Batesian and Mullerian mimicry.	During social interactions, people tend to automatically align with, or mimic their interactor's facial expressions, vocalisations, postures and other bodily states. Automatic mimicry might be implicated in empathy and affiliation and is impaired in several pathologies.	Varies according to the dimension of the study. From £5000 upwards.	Allstate Insurance
Network narratives	Network narrative analysis is a genre of analytic frames whereby researchers interpret stories that are told within the context of research and/or are shared in everyday life gathered from social networks.	Researchers who conduct this type of analysis make diverse – yet equally substantial and meaningful – interpretations and conclusions by focusing on different elements. These elements include, but are not limited to, how the story is structured, what functions the story serves, what the substance of the story is and how the story is performed.	Varies according to the number of social networks and the number of stories to be analysed in the study. From £3,000 upwards.	Mitsubishi car company Starbucks
Mobile ethnography		A new trend – more and more research will be done on mobile devices – not simply because of their proliferation		

(Continued)

Table 26.2 (Continued)

Approach	Definition	Benefits	Costs	Example
	in the market and share of usage vs. desktop computers but because of the ability to intercept respondents while they are in the middle of certain actions or at certain locations, therefore becoming more achievable and accurate.			
Sensory ethnography	Sensory ethnography is a methodology. It is an approach to doing ethnography that takes account of sensory experience, sensory perception and sensory categories that we use when we talk about our experiences and our everyday life.	Provides an important framework for thinking about sensory ethnography, stressing the numerous ways that smell, taste, touch and vision can be interconnected and interrelated within research.	Varies according to the number of acquisitions of sensory inputs and the type of techniques and devices used in the study. From £3000 upwards.	Xerox Starbucks Food companies
Digital ethnography	Digital ethnography, which is sometimes referred to as netnography or virtual ethnography, is the term used to describe carrying out ethnographic market research in an online space. Online spaces are often accessed by researcher to observe the participants in their natural environment.	From video diaries to accompanied shops, digital ethnographic research gives researchers an unbeatable opportunity to peek into respondents' lives more easily than ever before. It's good fun, it fits around peoples' busy lives and it also empowers participants – making a winning methodology.	Varies according to the type of techniques and devices used in the study. From £2000 upwards.	Johnson & Johnson Astra Zeneca

Approach	Definition	Benefits	Costs	Example
Ethnographic episodes	The blending of ethnographic methods based on a research approach where you look at people in their cultural setting, with the goal of producing a narrative account of that particular culture, against a theoretical backdrop, but in this case relying on the dissection of temporal everyday life episodes.	The episodic interview method combines the traditional theme interview with elements of the narrative interview. This method allows the division of the phenomenon under study into different themes. A narrative part of a question is linked to the themes, which makes it possible to get information about everyday life episodes connected to these themes.	Costs varies according to the dimensions of the study and the number of everyday life episodes. From £5000 upwards.	3M TUI (Thomas Cook)

Source: The author

Observational measurements

Observational research techniques, sometimes called digital ethnography, are not a replacement for more overt data-collection methods, like face-to-face surveys, but are an important addition for obtaining natural, unprompted insights into the behaviour of customers and prospects.

In-the-moment research

The human memory is not completely reliable. We had far few feasible options available to us in the past, but with in-the-moment research, we can remedy the failings of human memory, for example, failed recall, clouded judgement and added bias when recalling memories. Many distortions occur when recalling facts, for example, attention bias, hindsight bias, confirmation bias, availability, peak-end and the halo effect. In-the-moment research is very good from an accuracy stance, unless you are trying to prove a point related to verification with long-term memory retention. With regard to communication research, in-the-moment research is a better form for presenting things correctly rather than accepting the respondents' versions. It also reveals details and information regarding influences or events that help the consumer make decisions that would not be reported in a retrospective study. In-the-moment pictures and videos provide reality and context. The research collected provides great insight into real behaviour and live situations. There are several techniques available, with the best approach depending on the respondent profile, the required observation and the considerations of timing and market along with several other factors. Here are a few examples of this approach.

Moodstates and video diaries

Online research has progressed past simplistic text response, which may lead to misunderstandings and misinterpretation of temperament and mood and failure to observe other subtle communications. Emotions change constantly, and so the process of mapping the emotional changes of a person over time can produce insight into how best to engage a target audience. Do we consider which times of the day a person is more approachable? How do we trigger a reaction? What long-lasting emotions can influence brand experience within a customer base?

Online video diaries can involve anywhere from 10–25 people. A contributor is required to record and then upload a series of videos involving their mood-state every day. These can be recorded at certain times of the day or whenever there is a change of mood state, depending on the aim of the research. The contributor or participant is evaluated on their thoughts, tone of comments and facial expressions. The outcome is an intimate insight into the range of emotions portrayed and allows researchers to detect shared commonalities within the participants.

Virtual ethnography

Deeper insights can be gathered through subtle observation when a longer time is spent with the customer with virtual ethnography, using experiential journals or discussion topics over different time periods, days, weeks or even months. This is ideal for studies of product usability, consumption tasks or process mapping. Around 15 to 25 respondents can be asked to provide opinions and insight by reporting any defining moment or incident. This could be a wide range of activities from use of a product to a drink they have consumed. The respondents are asked to use the digital devices provided or video their progress.

Virtual shop-along

This requires respondents to shop from a specific shop for a specific item to help the researcher understand the experience and process better. Watching this experience can disclose the intent behind each purchasing decision, as it takes place and within each aisle, and deliver an abundance of information. What process did the customer follow to conclude about the purchase? Did any aspects of the store appeal to the customer? Was there any missing information that prevented the purchase decision being concluded? Were there any products the consumer failed to notice? Which products were the most popular? Did the store staff have the expertise needed to sell the product? Various of methods can be put into place to ensure that whatever is being used to examine the customer's behaviour, depending on the precise issue being evaluated.

Live screen sharing

This approach links the interviewers with each individual respondent by phone, providing a recording of the respondent's computer screen and simultaneous remote observation, allowing the moderator to observe and question the respondent in real time, asking or viewing how easy or difficult the site is to navigate or guiding through specific tasks. The entire experience is monitored and creates a link allowing analysis of pauses, tripping points and frustrations that may jeopardise the preconceived experience.

In-vehicle video

This is like video diaries and virtual ethnography. Respondents are asked to put video cameras in their cars for a time. Video and audio capture and record all in-car experiences while the vehicle is travelling, including the road in front of the vehicle, speed, force of gravity and GPS information as the car turns corners. This in-vehicle video allows researchers to watch the customers on their daily journeys around town, to and from shops, drive-through experiences and in-car consumption. It highlights any issues during such journeys that could be addressed, shows what products are used or consumed within the car and records conversations and topics.

Voicemail/audio journaling

In-the-moment research takes the collection of videos, texts and images a step further than simply collecting data. Mobile phones have facilitated in-the-moment research, but they are not the only way. The telephone functions on mobile phones appeal to most people, so this is a less expensive option for the inexperienced user. The respondent can be asked to call a number or receive a call. Data collection can be completed by answering survey-style questions or using open-ended questioning. This can be used to capture emotional triggers or decision moments and the overall shopper experience. The process can be kept simple by using voicemail journaling, which customers can do easily. Respondents can organise a convenient time to call in daily to answer a couple of questions, or they can request a call at a time that suits them. Voicemail journaling data collection normally lasts 7 to 10 days.

Experiencing-self of consumers

As brands increase efforts to measure the experiencing-self of consumers along with the remembering-self of consumers that was traditionally measured, integrating the two becomes important. Research methodologies like monitoring and ethnography must be paired with data from survey research to better understand the full picture of what is going on with consumers. Five broad categories of experience have been identified:

* Interaction within a group;
* Discovering something new;
* Contributing to society;
* Affirming identity;
* Becoming transported.

Using these categories, engagement measures can be identified by marketers as distinctly different from existing metrics such as contentment. These categories were chosen by researchers because of their ability to cover a wide variety of experiences.

DIY user research

With the abundance of self-service data collection platforms, their simple scripting and large choice of sample groups, these surveys deliver low-cost quick access to customers and prospects.

It is easy to get an audience of 1000 people from an online DIY survey provider, but you need to know if your target audience is well balanced or relevant. If a company wants the first 1000 responses, then this is what the DIY platform will produce, no matter what the relevance or balance of respondents. The results would be skewed by the unbalanced sample. More advanced selection criteria become more expensive as selection options are added. Once all relevant survey requirements have been added, there may be minimal cost difference between DIY and agency research.

The rise of the bot

A proactive approach to defining the required audience may help address the issues arising from inputting fake information or contamination from bots interfering with research results. Bots significantly contribute to the spread of misinformation online, as well as showing how quickly these messages can spread. Bots amplify a message's volume and visibility until it is more likely to be shared broadly, despite only representing a small fraction of the accounts that spread viral messages.

Ethical research organisations are continuously adopting techniques to confirm the genuineness of survey responses. Is a respondent answering truthfully or simply pressing buttons to get through the survey? Bots and AI are finding a way into the sample creation marketplace, requiring organisations to check the viability of studies and remove up to 20% of responses. This raises major concerns regarding the quality and relevance of the data. Online research is invaluable as an effective component of market research, but good quality control and processes, along with a detailed knowledge of analysis techniques and the understanding of what comprises a statistical sample, are needed for research to be trustworthy. DIY may be cheaper, but how much damage could the wrong decision based on faulty research do? Marketing research experts can ensure the script is coded correctly while checking the project's objectives, the audience and the analysis. Validity and reliability are key.

Validity – how sound the research is – applies to both the design and the methods of research. Validity in data collection means that findings truly represent the phenomenon they claim to measure. Reliability is whether the process of collection and interpretation has done the job properly and whether doing it again would lead to the same result. Sampling is full of traps, even if it from a company's own customers. What if only those who like the company respond or those with a grievance? Did the questionnaire avoid leading the respondent and getting a biased answer? People speak freely of their behaviour in most instances, but if the research is about things that lie outside social norms, respondents may lie. Drinking, smoking, eating, driving and relationships are all open to little white lies, but so are many other things, even if they seem quite straightforward subjects.

So, DIY research is fraught with issues, though that is not to say there is no place for it. A short, simple survey can aid in the design and direction of more detailed research. The greatest challenge is knowing the limitations of DIY capabilities and judging when to pass the job to professional researchers.

Conclusions

This chapter has highlighted the transfiguration of marketing research as we know it, through insights management, real-time research, expressive research, big data, predictive analysis, the era of consumer data, small data, artificial intelligence, machine learning, ethnography, data transparency, in-the-moment research and do-it-yourself. The agenda of change should be kept alive by any company that uses or delivers research, as the agenda itself will continue to change.

Issues

These are the main issues relating to the future of market research, whether for clients or agencies:

- Client organisations and marketing research agencies must adopt a new vision and a future posture that takes as paramount the changing role of human beings and society and the impact of huge and continuing technological developments;
- Companies – agencies and clients – should avoid rear-mirror research, in which research is often weeks or even months old before the results are presented;
- Future research must be done *with* human beings and not *on* them. It is critical to transform data patterns and movements into relevant information and insight;
- Agencies need to anticipate technological advances like affective computing, cognitive computing, deep learning, convoluted neural networks and brain uploading, among many other breakthroughs in knowledge and society trends.

27

FURTHER FUTURING IN MARKETING RESEARCH TECHNIQUES

Luiz Moutinho

Summary

This chapter explains the emergence and role of specific new techniques in marketing research, such as biometrics and neuroscience, intelligent data agents and their role as critical gatekeepers, sensor technologies and virtual reality in marketing research. It also covers the resurgence of futures research methodologies and methods in marketing research.

The age of polymeasures

If marketing research is to survive and continue to add value to marketers, in an age when marketers are awash with data about consumers' browsing, enquiries, ratings or products; use of social media; purchasing; customer satisfaction ratings; complaints – the list is nearly endless – it needs to go well beyond this data and start to use a plethora of new measurements.

The use of neuroscience is increasing and showing significant progress as brands look to garner greater insight from consumer responses. For example, the measurement of reaction times and facial expressions allow marketers to rapidly develop a comprehensive and thorough picture of the marked effect that advertising can have on viewers in real time. There are new bio-physio measures – biological measures and physiological measures, applied through laboratory and mechanical observation. Biometrics and neuroscience – this last one a protoscience – play a critical role here.

Experience-sampling measures (ESMs) deal with self-reporting of mental processes. There is an important concern related to the validity of these type of measures, and one needs to establish a direct correlation between buying behaviour and ESMs. ESMs are associated with physiological measures and psychological tests and can produce behavioural indices. Implicit and indirect measures will also be useful in the future. One needs to analyse the functional properties of these types of measures and specifically the objective property of the measurement itself. These measures are not for self-assessment but are used to record other behaviours. They do not allow registering of stable structures, but they can provide unique insights into the effects of automatic processing on real-life attitudes, feelings and behaviour, for example, moods, emotions, voice prints, facial electromyography and so on.

Traditional self-reporting instruments are also part of the spectrum of polymeasures. Still, researchers should be concerned with several critical issues, such as validity of causal conclusions based on data analysis, systematic response distortions, method variance, mono-method bias and the psychometric properties (reliability and validity) of questionnaire scales. Attention should also be given to the context-design of studies and the statistical analysis methods chosen.

Biometrics and biological measures will have a big impact on marketing research. Many techniques will be increasingly applied. These range from scan brain waves, retinal scan and facial coding to glasses-mounted cameras, voice pitch analysis and utterance analysis, as shown in Table 27.1

Table 27.1 Biological methods

Method	*Definition*
Facial coding	Facial coding involves measuring human emotions through facial expressions. Emotions can be detected by computer algorithms for automatic emotion recognition that record facial expressions via webcam. This can be applied to understand of people's reactions to visual stimuli.
Iris recognition	Iris recognition is an automated method of biometric identification that uses mathematical pattern-recognition techniques on video images of one or both irises of an individual's eyes, whose complex patterns are unique and stable and can be seen from some distance.
Retinal scan	A retinal scan is a biometric technique that uses unique patterns on a person's retina blood vessels. It is not to be confused with other ocular-based technologies: iris recognition, commonly called an "iris scan", and eye-vein verification, which uses scleral veins.
Fingerprint recognition	Fingerprint recognition refers to the automated method of identifying or confirming the identity of an individual based on the comparison of two fingerprints. Fingerprint recognition is one of the most well-known biometrics, and it is by far the most-used biometric solution for authentication on computerised systems.
Handwritten biometric recognition	Handwritten biometric recognition is a process for identifying the author of a given text. It belongs to behavioural biometric systems, as it is based on something that the user has learned to do.
Voice prints	A voiceprint is a set of measurable characteristics of a human voice that uniquely identifies an individual. These characteristics, based on the physical configuration of the mouth and throat, can be expressed as a mathematical formula. The term applies to a vocal sample recorded for that purpose, the derived mathematical formula and its graphical representation.
Voice-pitch analysis (VOPAN)	A research technique of analysing a subject's voice during their responses, to test their feelings and attitudes about a subject of study.
Utterance analysis	With a new multimodal dataset consisting of sentiment annotated utterances extracted from video reviews, multimodal sentiment analysis can be effectively performed, and combined visual, acoustic and linguistic modalities can lead to error rate reductions.
Human-computer interaction	Human-computer interaction studies the design and use of computer technology, focused on the interfaces between people and computers. Researchers in this field observe how humans interact with computers and design technologies that let humans interact with computers in novel ways.
Vein matching	Vein matching, also called vascular technology, is biometric identification via analysis of the patterns of blood vessels visible from the skin's surface.

(Continued)

Table 27.1 (Continued)

Method	Definition
Palm vein recognition	Palm vein recognition examines unique patterns in palm veins using a safe, near-infrared light source (as in a TV remote control) by scanning veins inside the hand and creating a digital template that represents it.
Palm dorsa vein pattern (PDVP)	This is a biometric-based system for human identity recognition for robust identification of humans using far infrared (FIR) thermal PDVP images as a physiological biometric feature.
Scan brain waves	Electroencephalography (EEG) is an electrophysiological monitoring method to record different types of brain waves. It produces analyses of the neural oscillations (popularly called "brain waves") that can be observed in EEG signals in the appropriate frequency domain.
Pupillometrics	Pupillometry is measurement of pupil size and reactivity, measuring cognitive and emotional processes.
Heart rate variability (HRV)	This is the physiological variation in the interval between consecutive heartbeats. A normal, healthy heart does not tick evenly like a metronome, but there is variation in the milliseconds between heartbeats
Diagnosis of degree of sweating	This is an emerging non-invasive technique provide insights into the health of the human body.
Eye-tracking	This involves measuring either the point of gaze (where one is looking) or the motion of an eye relative to the head.
Wearables, for example, glasses mounted cameras	This comes in different forms. Some devices are built into a visor, some into electronic spectacles and some have a clip-on camera that attaches to spectacles or a head strap.
Telemetric measures for electrodermal activity (EDA)	This is a non-invasive peripheral measure of sympathetic nervous system activation commonly used to assess physiological arousal. EDA is typically measured using a recording device containing two small sensors placed on the skin of the fingers, palm, feet or other parts of the body.

Source: The author

Physiological measures (neuroscience)

Other important polymeasures are appearing from the protoscience of neurology. Brain physiology has the advantage that participants cannot change the outcome or lie about their responses). The approaches are summarised in Table 27.2.

Other new measurements are also appearing, for example, in psychophysics – the scientific study of the relationship between stimulus and sensation, that is, analysis of perceptual processes by studying the effect on a subject's experience or behaviour by systematically varying stimulus properties.

Complementarity

Physiological data is unlikely to capture the full experience of emotion. Physiological data is continuous and can be measured without the conscious introspection required for self-reporting. The big problem with conscious introspection about emotion is that it is divorced from how we tend to experience emotion in real life. Physiological data is objective and can be reliably measured. Examples include the utilisation of markers such as oxytocin, heart rate variability, galvanic skin response and dopamine.

Table 27.2 Neuroscience techniques

Technique	Application	Benefits	Drawbacks
Electroencephalography	Records electrical activity along the scalp. Voltage fluctuations from ionic current flows within neurons of the brain. Neural oscillations.	One of the biggest advantages is the ability to see brain activity as it unfolds in real time, in milliseconds (thousandths of a second).	One of the big disadvantages is that it is hard to figure out where in the brain the electrical activity is coming from.
Positron emission tomography (PET) scans	3D image/picture of functional processes in the body. Pairs of gamma rays. Tracer concentration.	In general, a scan has the advantage of short study time (15 to 20 minutes) with high-quality images.	Because the radioactive material is combined with glucose and then injected into the patient, this can be a concern for some diabetic patients. Before having a scan, a diabetic patient's blood sugar level will be evaluated, and a glucose serum blood test might be administered.
Magnetic resonance imaging (MRI) or nuclear (NMRI) or MRT (tomography) – for visualisation of internal structures of the body	Uses magnetic field gradients that allow spatial information.	MRI is non-invasive and does not use radiation. MRI contrasting agent is less likely to produce an allergic reaction that may occur when iodine-based substances are used for x-rays and CT scans.	MRI is expensive ($1000–$1500). Because of the small bore of the magnet, some patients experience claustrophobia and have difficulty in cooperating during the study.
Functional MRI – which measures brain activity by deleting associated changes in blood flow	BOLD/contrasts (hemodynamic response).	It does not use radiation like x-rays, computed tomography (CT) and positron emission tomography (PET) scans.	If done correctly, it has virtually no risks. It can evaluate brain function safely, noninvasively and effectively.
Transcranial magnetic stimulation (TMS) – depolarisation or hyperpolarisation in the neurons of the brain	Uses electromagnetic induction with weak electric currents. Uses a rapidly changing magnetic field.	It is effective, non-invasive and safe and requires no medication. This also greatly cuts down on potential side effects, largely reducing the side effects to infrequent headaches and scalp discomfort.	Facial twitching during the treatment. Skin redness at site of coil placement. Anxiety before and during treatment. Mild discomfort. Headache.

(Continued)

Table 27.2 (Continued)

Technique	Application	Benefits	Drawbacks
Transcranial direct current stimulation (tDCS) – a form of neurostimulation which uses constant low current directly to areas of the brain via small electrodes	Can increase cognitive performance.	Non-invasive brain stimulation technique that provides unique potential to directly improve human capability on a temporary, as-needed basis.	The technique is still relatively new and has been associated with mild and transient discomfort in some people, including reported tingling, itching and burning sensations under the electrodes.
Functional near-infrared spectroscopy (fNIRS) or diffuse optical topography (DOT) (as it is called in Japan) – the use of near-infrared spectroscopy for functional neuroimaging and for assessment of depression (NIRSIT)	Cerebral hemodynamic responses are measured by near-infrared light, which go in line with cerebral activation or deactivation.	Used outside hospital environments, allows interaction with participants, less stringent in selection of participants.	Only reaches the surface cortex, and it is not possible to examine all the brain simultaneously.

Source: The author

Intelligent data agents

The arrival of early-stage intelligent agents (IAs) or bots is gaining momentum amongst consumers. With the newfound love for the proactive and customised utilities that IAs provide, IAs can then gain access to the interactions that customers use practically and effectively to interact with brands. Companies that integrate IAs will develop and flourish, while those that do not will see their customer base dwindle. The International Data Corporation (IDC) has predicted that within three years, up to 40% of e-commerce transactions could be carried out by artificially intelligent or cognitive agent shoppers. These intelligent assistants collect a lot of information about consumers. As people research, they want the information they need as quickly as possible and are increasingly turning to voice search as the technology advances. Many companies are now considering designing their own bots to handle brand-specific knowledge, allowing them to interact directly with their customers alongside the more general "concierge agents" like Alexa, Siri and Cortana. The colonisation of all sorts of devices is already underway by these concierge agents.

It appears that the golden age of advertising might be ending. Advertising via television, websites or search engines may be superseded. Even email inboxes have become cluttered, so buyers have moved to social media to follow the brands they really care about. Consumers now have control – the ability to opt out, block and unfollow any brand that betrays their trust. With the help of messaging apps, bots help consumers find solutions no matter where they are or what device they use – no forms, cluttered inboxes or wasted minutes spent searching and scrolling through content. Communication, service and transactions intertwine. Unlike in the self-serving marketing of the past, bots provide a service. Chatbots are drastically changing the way businesses interact with customers, manage campaigns for lead generation and automate payments. *Chatbots Magazine* found 67% of US millennials said they are likely to purchase products and services from brands using a chatbot.

AI optimisation

This new form of optimisation may need to incorporate bot personas and concierge agents. These concierge agents require the specialist information in order to best serve customers. A reinvention of marketing and adverts may be needed to allow these agents to handle customer requirements.

Marketing-research agents

Without "intelligent data-interpretation agents", useful information and insights may be buried inside vast databases or lost in cyberspace. Intelligent agents can help search the Internet for specific information (e.g. hotbot.com), compile information according to user preferences (e.g. pointcast.com) or correlate information in useful ways (e.g. Firefly, now part of Microsoft).

Foresight-futures research

The next evolution in market research may be in the area of futures research or foresight, in which futures markets and Delphi panels play a leading role. A greater appreciation for the impact of so-called "wild-card events" (low-probability, high-impact events) on attitudes and behaviour may push forward-thinking organisations to create a futures/scenario planning function in order to move swiftly in an inflection point.

Futures research

Futures research involves systematic study of possible future circumstances and events. This is forecasting in a different way, looking ahead with forward orientation, with no mathematical input. However, it has a downside − situations or events cannot be completely or accurately predicted. However, while futures studies cannot produce complete or accurate detail about the future, some details or information is better than nothing for producing a long-term perspective. There are many methodologies, techniques and methods of futures research that can be applied to marketing research, depending on the research objective (Tables 27.3 and 27.4). Apart from Delphi and scenario planning, most companies are unaware of and do not utilise most of the futures research methodologies and methods. Costs vary tremendously by the type of application, dimension and setting.

Table 27.3 Futures research − methodologies

Approach	Definition
Real-time Delphi	Real-time Delphi is an advanced form of the Delphi method. The advanced method "is a consultative process that uses computer technology" to increase efficiency of the Delphi process.
Causal layered analysis (CLA)	Causal layered analysis is used in strategic planning and futurology to more effectively shape the future. The technique was pioneered by Sohail Inayatullah.

Source: The author

Table 27.4 Futures research – detailed methods

Approach	Definition
Cross-impact analysis	Cross-impact analysis is a methodology developed by Theodore Gordon and Olaf Helmer in 1966 to help determine how relationships between events would impact resulting events and reduce uncertainty in the future.
Online mind mapping	A mind map is a diagram used to visually organise information. A mind map is hierarchical and shows relationships among pieces of the whole. Mindmaps is a mind mapping app. It lets you create neat-looking mind maps in the browser.
Morphological analysis	Morphological analysis or general morphological analysis is used for exploring possible solutions to a multi-dimensional, non-quantified complex problem. It was developed by Fritz Zwicky.
Analytic hierarchic process	This is a structured technique for organising and analysing complex decisions, based on mathematics and psychology. It was developed by Thomas L. Saaty in the 1970s. He partnered with Ernest Forman to develop Expert Choice in 1983. This has been extensively studied and refined since then.
Backcasting	This is a planning method that starts with defining a desirable future and then works backwards to identify policies and programs that will connect that specified future to the present. Its fundamentals were outlined by John B. Robinson from the University of Waterloo in 1990.
Visioning/preferred futures	This is a method for determining a compelling vision of a preferred future. Its outcomes include pictures that communicate preferred futures and their benefits powerfully.
Means-end chain	This has been defined as a hierarchy of goals that represents potential identities of the actions necessary for the person to reach his or her goal.
Charrette	This is an intensive, multi-disciplinary workshop with the aim of developing a design or vision for a project or planning activity. Charrettes are often conducted to design such things as parks and buildings or to plan communities or transportation systems.
Futures wheel	This is a method for graphical visualisation of direct and indirect future consequences of a particular change or development. It was invented by Jerome C. Glenn in 1971.

Source: The author

Virtual reality marketing research

Virtual reality (VR) is a 3D simulation of a computer-generated environment. In this environment, sounds and images can be copied to reproduce the user's current environment. This is different from augmented reality, which uses computer generated digital data and places it over real-world environments. Both forms require head-mounted displays such as Google Cardboard for VR, which immerses users in the virtual world, and Microsoft HoloLens, which allows interaction with holograms in mixed reality (virtual and real-world). VR technologies are being used by marketing researchers to measure consumer experience. The customer can be instantly transported to virtual shops where they can interact with products that hold their interest, while the virtual stores garner useful information on how the customer reacts and interacts with the product, discovering if how they navigate their way through the store.

VR 360-degree cameras allows clients to experience exactly what consumers see when navigating a site, allowing them to fully immerse themselves in the shopping experience. This has been described as the "empathy window", and with this newfound understanding, clients can visualise and understand the consumer's decision-making process. Companies can now achieve a more human-centred research approach. Some research companies already offer virtual facilities to focus groups, allowing clients to view live groups. This also allows consumers from all over the world to meet each other through their avatars in a virtual environment where they can share web links, audio and videos, which they can watch on their computer screen. These online sites allow easy connection between people, keep venue costs and recruitment low and allow participants some anonymity.

Augmented reality may be used to grab people's attention and encourage them to participate in surveys through glasses or on mobile phones. Virtual reality simulations allow marketers to test new marketing ideas quickly, inexpensively and confidentially. Today, virtual reality simulations are new to consumers, who spend more time navigating through the aisles and interacting with products in the simulation than they would in the conventional store. To overcome this limitation, researchers often ask consumers to go on many shopping trips through several product categories. By the third or fourth trip, most consumers take about the same time to navigate as a conventional store, and that is when shelf displays are manipulated.

VR in marketing research is a mature technology, in development for decades and used by many large firms for a decade or more. Over ten years ago, paper manufacturer Kimberly-Clark and Wal-Mart built their own studios specifically to conduct VR marketing research. Since then, VR has seen widespread use from a host of other companies with deep market research expertise. VR allows marketers to test new market ideas quickly, inexpensively and confidentially. For example, many car manufacturers use VR to show new models available for a test drive to allow people to customise vehicles to their own liking, including colour and styling, and to test drive the car.

Going from prototype to product is a major step for Cybershoes, but it represents a giant leap for the virtual reality world that was captured by the initial Cybershoes design the company exhibited at a recent show. Following its recent Consumer Technology Association's CES Innovation Award recognition, the company exhibited its finished Cybershoes product at CES with a new feature, enabling users to track their physical activity and determine the distance of their virtual travels. The Cybershoes are strapped directly onto the feet of the consumer, who is then seated in a swivel bar stool, ready for their VR adventure. Cybershoes are compatible with any VR game and function with SteamVR, the HTC Vive, Oculus Rift, the Quest via Oculus Link, Virtual Desktop and Oculus store games, Windows Mixed Reality and Pimax. With Cybershoes, the consumer's virtual movements are controlled by their physical movement, allowing them to walk alongside giants through snow-covered canyons, ramble through battlefields set alight with dragon fire or experience any shopping or store environment. Research showed that those aged 50–69 did not appreciate the concept and felt a certain detachment from their avatars, but millennials thought that VR was as good as real life. Familiarity will play a key role. As the millennials become the older generation, their familiarity with the technology will mean AR and VR will be a common tool for the marketing researcher.

Avatar marketing research

With the ability to integrate users of virtual worlds into new product development processes, companies can use the latest technology available to tap into their customers' innovative capacity to develop the future. By connecting the technology within virtual worlds while keeping the customer as the central feature, companies can focus on open innovation, allowing them to capitalise on the customers' innovativeness in the new product development process. The digital environment is conducive to creative and innovative tasks. Consumers and producers alike can interact in virtual worlds, along with other like-minded individuals, to invent and create new products while finding relevant audiences to use, test and give valuable feedback on their creations. The avatar can play an active role throughout the entire process. Some companies already undertake discoveries and experiment with avatars to innovate. Toyota, Mazda, Steelcase and Osram have found ways to link the abstractness of open innovation with virtual worlds in new product development. To fully exploit the potential of avatar-based innovation, companies must generate captivating open innovation experiences, exploiting the eccentricities of virtual worlds.

Portable place-based research tools and components

A serious focus is now required on location, via the data provided by the mobile phone about the consumer's location or that of groups of consumers, allowing instant targeting through real-time insights, especially valuable on mobile. Place-based research tools can be used to understand all stages of the shopper journey, from planning and gathering information through to purchase, including delivery. Examples include:

- Understanding barriers to purchase and how to eliminate them;
- Identifying shopper navigation, leading to ideal signage placement;
- Unravelling shopper processes and stages for high-involvement purchases;
- Understanding decision points and how to influence decisions.

Companies providing these research services include Explorer Research and Persistence Market Research. Examples of client organisations include J.P. Morgan and General Electric.

A powerful tool in any marketers' arsenal is location-based targeting of marketing communications – targeting audiences at the right moment and in the right location. Location intelligence can be used to solve the personalisation problem. Location data from mobile devices are gathered by Wi-Fi, geofences and beacons. If a combination of sensors is implemented, better accuracy and greater scalability of data can be achieved.

Location-based attribution is the ability to measure advertising effectiveness offline. Location-based advertising is allowing marketers to better understand the total impact their efforts have in the real world. Location-based attribution is the use of accurate mobile device data to fill in the gaps in traditional attribution models. Understanding where and how people move becomes scalable and precise and helps make attribution more accurate. Ad-tech companies offering it include Coconut Water, Epic Signal (Mekanism) and VideoAmp, among others, and have also used the location-based attribution approach. Real-world, out-of-home adverts are big business for marketers, but the main problem is how to measure the results. It is hard to accredit purchases and store visits to this form of advertising or even to prove how many people encounter the advertising. These insights become transparent through location data.

Combining technologies

Behaviour in the real home or workplace setting is hard to simulate in a laboratory. The interaction of people with other people and objects leads to unexpected behaviour that is hard to anticipate with focus groups, surveys and other standard product development and marketing inquiry methods. However, researchers have developed a collection of small, portable and inexpensive wireless sensors, wearable devices and associated algorithms and methodologies enabling mobile information technology researchers and sponsors to conduct research in every-day places of living, work environments and public spaces.

As the motion-control market is continuing to grow, so does the demand for the sensor con-trols that can develop and guide it. Several different markets will see advances in smart motion systems enhance their sales. These markets have massive growth potential due to the growth in smart motion systems, incorporating speed sensors, torque (rotating system) sensors, position and displacement sensors and proximity sensors. A displacement sensor measures the distance between the sensor and an object by detecting the amount of displacement through various ele-ments and converting it into a distance. Depending on what element is used, there are several types of sensors, such as optical displacement sensors, linear proximity sensors and ultrasonic displacement sensors. A displacement sensor (displacement gauge) is used to measure travel range between where an object is and a reference position. Displacement sensors can be used for dimension measurement to determine an object's height, thickness and width in addition to travel range. Sentiance is a data science company turning IOT sensor data into rich insights about people's behaviour and real-time context. These insights enable companies to understand how customers go through their everyday lives, discover and anticipate the moments that matter the most and adapt their engagement to real-world behaviour and real-time context. Sentiance context intelligence enables solutions for lifestyle-based insurance, contextual marketing and commerce, smart mobility, connected health, smart homes, smart cities and connected cars.

Wearable motion sensors are small, comfortable and low-cost accelerometer devices that can be easily worn for days or weeks and used to collect data on what people are doing. Algorithms have been developed to detect specific activities, such as walking, cleaning activities, moderate physical activity, and body posture. In combination with a mobile computing device (e.g. tablet, telephone, watch), sensors can detect specific activities in real time and give context-specific information.

Context-aware experience sampling

Context-aware experience sampling (CAES) is the term used for a certain type of data collec-tion based on the experience sampling method, which uses monitoring devices to evaluate and assess situations in real time as they occur to capture data about people in natural settings. This maximises the validity of the data by avoiding the need for retrospective recall. CAES improves with ESM when merging sensing technology, and computational perception is merged. This can detect certain events which may possibly trigger sampling and, from there, data collec-tion. CAES allows further in-depth and sophisticated event-contingent sampling to take place, requiring the computer to detect a specific event or context that will provide a signalling cue. As algorithms continue to improve, investigators are more likely to identify the potential for specific activities of interest, allowing use of the CAES tool sample, at any point during the activity. This will allow much more extensive sampling regarding the situation than is available now without unduly affecting those using it. Also, the sensors involved in activity and context detection can also collect raw data. For example, location sensors or heart rate monitors can also be used in real time to identify the presence of movement or as a measurement stored for future analysis.

Software has been developed to acquire data- and context-specific feedback from people. Sensors may be used to trigger questions and data capture. For instance, a personal device can monitor heart rate and ask the consumer questions based upon variation in heart rate. Tape-on sensor kits can detect on-off, open-closed and object movement events. Algorithms can then be used to study data and automatically detect certain activities in real time. The tape-on sensors can be used to develop and test technology that automatically presents information based upon a person's activities. Many wearable options available including adhesives that stick to the skin, Velcro bands, wristbands, belt clip-ons, wall-mounts and more. Client organisations using this type of sensing device include technology industry leaders such as Apple, Google, Siemens, Nissan and the US Olympic team. Location beacons are low-cost radio frequency devices that permit approximate position detection within their environments and the tracking of movement over time.

Conclusions

The future of the market research industry is full of challenges and opportunities. New technologies such as artificial intelligence and machine learning will enable faster analytics and report creation. To be successful, researchers should embrace new technologies available for streamlining and automating data collection and analysis, freeing time for higher-level problem solving and storytelling. Over 70% of market researchers believe automation, artificial intelligence and video analysis technology will be very important over the next five years. However, market researchers are most excited about technologies that offer a human touch. New technologies require agencies to master new tools and develop skillsets outside of the traditional researcher's background. The typical market research company/agency will be different, with many more data scientists and those with AI and automation experience. Agencies who do not have the budgets for new technologies and skills will be under threat.

Traditional market research agencies that refuse to change will go out of business. DIY market research will catch on even more and will democratise the sector. Social listening analytics will be a must-have for every marketing and market research manager. Agile research will become mainstream and will be facilitated by online communities. Micro surveys and intercepts will eventually replace long monthly customer tracking studies. Processing behavioural data in motion and delivering real-time micro insights will be a core competence of any expert insight agency. Related marketing services such as customer engagement, enterprise feedback management and customer advocacy will become solutions offered by the market research companies of the future. Data scientists will be the new insight experts, utilising a lot more predictive analytics than rear-view mirror analytics.

More and more companies are investing in better market research technologies. Big data continues to grow, while the insights industry continues to adopt and invest in automation and machine learning. For example, Salesforce acquired Datorama, an AI-powered marketing intelligence platform. These types of acquisitions give companies powerful capabilities for data unification, integration and collection capabilities and the ability to get a more accurate real-time view of consumer behaviour.

Issues

Neuroimaging technologies such as electroencephalogram and magnetic resonance imaging allow use to analyse consumers' brains in real time as they experience emotions. These technologies collect and integrate data on consumers' brains for big data analytics. Do consumers' self-reported choices and their neural representations tell different stories? Definitely! Also, research studies have demonstrated that biometric techniques such as voice emotion response produced much better results than marketing research based on self-reporting. Biometrics and neuroscience are an important part of making the future of digital analytics.

For many consumer neuromarketing researchers, the use of functional magnetic resonance imaging has been the most preferred neuroscience technique. However, electroencephalography, eye tracking and implicit measurements are becoming increasingly popular market research methods due to rapid technological improvements and reduced costs. Throughout the consumer neuroscience and marketing research literature, there is a lack of comprehensive evaluation of the relative merits of all neuroscience research tools. There is no rigorous analysis of the relative appropriateness of all the neuroscience, physiological and biometric research tools currently used in consumer neuroscience market research.

28

A PRACTITIONER'S VIEW OF CUSTOMER INSIGHT

Past, present and future

Tony Mooney

Summary

This chapter gives the author's reflection on 35 years of experience working in customer insight and decision science. He gives his views about the current state of development in these areas, including the way in which marketing research and customer data disciplines are merging and the future of customer insight, which he believes to be increasingly one of automated decisioning.

Introduction

I regard myself as a bit of an unusual phenomenon in customer insight. I have no background in analytics, operational research or technology. My mathematical skills are quite limited. Yet, over the last 25 years, I have built and directed several world-leading data and insight organisations for major corporations in the telecoms and media sector, including Sky, Orange and Centrica. In each case, I designed, created and deployed advanced consumer data and insight capabilities to deliver demonstrable growth, competitive advantage and help achieve business objectives. I have managed over 2000 analysts and researchers in my career and recruited probably three or four times that number. The 600-strong team I developed at Sky was the largest and most integrated insight and decision science function I have seen anywhere on the planet.

Unusually for an insight professional, I have also operated at the board or C-level in large corporates in several business sectors and geographies and consequently been the senior executive accountable for using data and analytics to drive improved business performance. I was always the one the C-Suite held responsible for proving a positive impact on profits from insight and analytics. Or else, why should they employ me and spend money on all that capability? I can tell you that kind of scrutiny from hard-nosed business executives tends to focus the mind and has been a major influence on my approach and attitude to insight.

As well as selling insight internally, I have also been a successful managing director of business-to-business service businesses, selling data and analytics solutions to some of the world's largest consumer brands, including Lloyds Bank, Barclays, HBOS, RBS, Orange, Vodafone, Homeserve, Zurich and Centrica, as well as Microsoft in the United States and financial services companies in the Far East.

After retiring from corporate life a few years ago, I now manage a portfolio of activities. I still have an interest in insight and decision science, running a small advisory and training business to help executives and companies deliver effective and profitable analytics transformation to drive growth in profits. In addition, I am a non-executive director, which gives me a wider perspective on how consumer businesses can succeed.

There are many critical success factors when transforming a business to an intelligent data-driven enterprise, but one of the biggest challenges to overcome is the change in decision culture required. In my experience, many organisations still struggle to extract meaningful and actionable business benefits from insight. This can be as frustrating for the insight producers as it is for the insight consumers. Left unaddressed, it leads to a perception that insight teams are not aligned to business objectives or lack competency. It can also severely restrict or reduce the board's willingness to invest in the people and capabilities required.

My education

I have never regarded my academic capabilities or qualifications as amounting to much. I achieved a very average set of school examinations and had no idea what to study in further education or, indeed, what I might be good at.

I applied to study a BSc honours degree in Business at Brighton University. The course contained an eclectic mix of subjects, including the obvious ones such as accounting, marketing, law and statistics. However, the core of this degree was behavioural science, a topic that I found fascinating and compelling and has been a central life skill in all the jobs I have done in my career.

The thing that attracted me about behavioural science was the study of how we, as human beings, function and interact with the world. I was particularly interested in the psychological interplay between what we think, what we say and what we do. As I shall come to later, I have always believed this is a fundamental challenge in the world of consumer insight.

Behavioural science also helped me gain an understanding of how human beings work (or do not work) together in teams, groups, clubs and organisations. As I moved into the world of work, this knowledge was invaluable. I found that academic studies and business textbooks did not convey the same picture of how an enterprise worked as I found in reality. I must say that I do not think this has changed very much. Real life is a lot messier and more complicated, ambiguous, irrational and uncertain than most books or courses would have you think.

The other point that I would make about the differences between academic study and the real world concerns the sheer pace of change we have seen over the past 20 years, in technology, in society, in business and with globalisation. Driven by the explosion in pervasive computing and a huge amount of data being generated, the world of consumer insight is constantly changing and at a rate which makes it very difficult for the academic world to keep up.

My career, my experiences and my consequent philosophies and approaches to insight

Starting out

I did not begin my career in customer insight. In fact, the first 10 or so years of my career were spent in business-to-business (B2B) in the electronics, computing, environmental services and construction sectors. The common thread of all my roles was marketing and, of course, customer insight was an important component. I worked for both large and small enterprises, which gave me some good experience and understanding of both the pros and cons of marketing and insight in different-sized organisations. My main observations were that, in small organisations, there was less politics and it was easier to get things done. However, access to resources was much more difficult, and just as money follows money, I always found it much easier to get "free stuff", such as advice and insight reports, when I worked in a larger enterprise than a small one.

Customer relationship management and customer insight in financial services – Lloyds Banking Group

My focus on customer insight started when I was fortunate enough to get a role in the Lloyds Banking Group, specifically in its Life Assurance division. The director who recruited me took a big gamble, as I had hitherto only worked in the B2B sector. To this day, I am very grateful that he did not follow the more common prejudice and instead selected me based on the abilities and achievements he saw and not the brands I had worked for previously.

I soon became responsible for all the marketing communications of the company, including above-the-line advertising on TV and in press, as well as direct marketing activity on TV, press and direct mail. I was also responsible for driving lead generation activity for the 2500-strong financial advisors who worked with us. I had a small team with a very basic database and analytical capability. Marketing research was run as a separate function.

Culturally, this business was run on the numbers. Most of the senior executives were exactuaries and strongly focused on cost-to-income ratios. Whilst this would present an enormous challenge for a conventional brand marketer, I found the forensic decision-making culture played very much to my strengths. Although it was tough, I liked the evidence-based and numerate discipline that determined marketing strategy and expenditure. It meant that almost all marketing activity needed to be financially justified and results demonstrated satisfactorily to the executive before approval to spend more. Consequently, I ran several successful and award-winning multimedia campaigns based on a direct marketing model, even on television, where we could analyse results and deploy resources with a high degree of science. This was very good learning for me at this stage of my career and a good foundation for my later roles, especially as they featured so much interaction with the company board.

Centrica and the power utility business

I was then headhunted by Centrica to join their marketing department, shortly after the privatisation of the old British Gas. Although initially employed in product marketing, I convinced the marketing director of the importance and value of customer relationship management to the business. I was given a new role as customer management director, given responsibility for about half the marketing department and charged with building a capability that would drive Centrica's strategy and customer base defence as the deregulation of the gas and electricity markets took place.

This was the first time in my career that I had been given a job with very vague expectations from my employer. The area was so new that it made it very difficult to specify, especially at the start. Whilst it made the job enormously challenging, it also set the pattern for the rest of my career. Ever since, in every role I have done, I have been responsible for writing my own job description, selling vision, strategy, capability and projected outcomes and being held accountable for adding something worthwhile to company profits and creating enterprise value. It has proven an invaluable approach.

In my new role at Centrica, I was responsible for direct marketing, database management, analytics and marketing research. I was accountable for the targeting capabilities to support the acquisition of customers for electricity as well as retaining those customers of British Gas.

We built the single customer view and analytical capability for Centrica to help drive business growth, contribute to the launch of the successful Goldfish credit card, support Centrica's entry into the telecoms market and play a key role in the successful Centrica take-over of the AA Group (the motoring services and financial products company).

I also carried specific sales targets for electricity acquisition. When you carry a target like that, it certainly focuses the mind. You need to get away from PowerPoint presentations and theory and become very practical and outcome focused. This was the first role I had that required me to set a substantial strategy and vision for change. Not only did I have to consider the operating model for this new world of insight-driven customer management, but I had to organise, motivate and train my people, at all levels, to be able to deliver it. This taught me the importance of active leadership.

This was also the first time that I managed the disciplines of marketing research and analytics together, and it was clear that the practitioners of each methodology regarded the other side with deep suspicion. I tried to integrate research and analytics but without much success. It was like oil and water. However, I took this learning with me into later roles, where I did achieve a much better result in integrated insight.

Orange and the mobile telecommunications industry

The mobile telecoms operator, Orange, asked me to join them as director of customer relationship management (CRM). I was charged with creating a CRM directorate for Orange as it transitioned from its high customer growth phase, driven by broad brand marketing and marketing research, to a stage requiring much more scientific capability to be able to grow, optimise and retain customer value.

I discovered I had an already existing team, many of whom did not have the skills required. I was also faced with several separate insight silos around the organisation. They had traditionally competed with each other and created different "versions of the truth" across the business. As in my previous roles, I knew that I had to move rapidly from theory to vision and from strategy to action if we were to achieve success. One of the first and most important things I did was to bring together as many of these disparate insight groups as possible into one function and close the insight "cottage industries" that existed around the business. This is always a highly charged, political process and one that requires good influencing and negotiating skills as well as a great deal of pragmatism and flexibility. To be clear, this is not about centralising everything, just ensuring that the insight ecosystem across an enterprise has appropriate consistency and alignment to deliver effectively to organisational objectives.

I confess that I made many mistakes in my zeal to create the perfect enterprise insight model, specifically in not bringing other stakeholder groups with me well enough and being somewhat over-theoretical in pitching to the company board. It is a difficult balance to achieve; to be strong enough in conviction to drive through necessary change but flexible enough to allow others to not feel steamrollered. That said, over four years, the CRM function achieved significant results both in starting up a new insight capability and using it to bring profit benefits to the business. The new capabilities delivered large-scale, integrated cross-selling and retention programmes worth over £50 million per year.

Amongst the many successful initiatives that we delivered, the most salient and valuable was the operationalisation of insight, deployed using analytics and modelling to improve outcomes from call centre retention interactions and to bring highly personalised cross-sell and up-sell messaging into operational customer billing communications. As an insight team, we achieved far more positive attention and investment for operationalising what we knew about customers than we ever would have done through the provision of "offline" reporting or research, however well executed.

It was an outcome that reinforced my experiences in Lloyds and Centrica and confirmed the mantra that I carry with me to this day: "the only purpose of insight is to deliver a better decision".

Moving to the supplier side – Experian

Following my stint at Orange, I moved to what friends called "the dark side" and spent several years in the data and insight service sector, essentially providing the kinds of capability I had developed whilst inside organisations, but now as an external vendor. As managing director of one of Experian's business units, my role was an interesting admixture of effective provision of data, analytics and insight with the critical additional requirement – to ensure that we were paid for it. I inherited a good database business and then built, on top of it, an insight and decision science team that enabled us to provide a value-based proposition to large corporate clients using the same principles that I had learnt in my previous client-side roles. After all, if we could not demonstrate to clients that we had capability that could deliver superior financial results, why else would they buy from us? We had some turbulent years during the credit crunch, in which I had to undertake significant transformation to bring the business back into profit. This kind of adversity teaches you a lot about the importance of good leadership and resilience.

One of the largest clients we acquired was Sky, and, over two or three years, we essentially became its customer analytics and decisioning engine, providing a single customer view data mart, analytics and campaign management to power its accelerated growth from 7 million to 10 million UK households in less than four years. I also led an insight task force that analysed in depth Sky's serious customer attrition (churn) issues, determined mitigation strategies and put the company back on track to hit its very public customer growth target. Many of the insight techniques and methods I developed during that period became standard templates and training for my teams over subsequent years.

Sky buys us in

As Victor Kiam used to say in the famous Remington Razor adverts: "I liked it so much that I bought the company". In 2010, Sky bought most of my division from Experian, including some third-party clients. Around 120 of my staff and I became employees of Sky.

An assessment of Sky's insight and reporting capability at the time had concluded that:

- Business demand was "just-in-time" and driven by overly autocratic behaviours;
- There was fractured capability and a history of under-investment;
- There was no measurement of benefits and lost learning.

I set about transformation and consolidation, as the Sky board charged me with integrating its many and various reporting, research, analytics and data silos into an efficient and effective whole. Within four years, I had configured an insight and decision science directorate of about 600 people, around 120 of which were offshore, covering 35 different business stakeholder groups across the whole Sky Business.

One of the main aspects I wanted to change was the means by which Sky commissioned and consumed insight to make and deploy its decisions. Around 80% of demand from the business was either for reporting, research and analysis of "what happened" or marketing research into the attractiveness of potential propositions and campaigns. My aim was to change that demand to be more future-facing, customer-centric and actionable within the billions of interactions with customers through the expansion and adoption of capabilities such as optimisation, decisioning and personalisation.

Learnings from my career

It is worth a short diversion here to explain how all the learnings from my career to this point came together to inform my approach to Sky's transformation. It is an approach that I believe will be even more relevant to consumer insight in the future

The only purpose of data is to create better insight, and the only purpose of this is to make better decisions. Data should produce insight to support decision-making. So, it is important to understand what decisions are to be made before determining what insight is required and when and what data best informs this.

Types of decision-making

In the modern enterprise, I believe decision-making can be conveniently divided into big decisions (decision support) and small decisions (automated decision management). The former type comprises the traditional processes and methodologies that deliver insight to human beings, who subsequently make decisions. Techniques include reporting (business intelligence or BI), marketing research, research analytics and econometrics. The growth of digital channels, with the increased complexity and velocity, has meant that this decision model alone is no longer adequate. This has led to the rise of automated decision management – in which computer cognition drives every interaction between an enterprise and its consumers (or machines) without human employee intermediation. Techniques such as machine learning, artificial intelligence (AI) and real-time decisioning are required, while human involvement is re-engineered to sit at the "head-end" of the process, focused on review, evaluation, diagnosis, planning, forecasting and scenario modelling. Decision support still has a vital place in this new decision ecosystem, feeding insight to human employees in this "offline" head-end process, but these big decisions are then often disaggregated, deployed and, importantly, modified in automated systems that manage billions of individual interactions.

At Sky, I ensured an alignment of the insight and decision science team's purpose with the business's objectives and targets. We identified the following key drivers:

- Our customers want products and services configured how they want when they want, where they want and expect more value;
- Mass market take-up of converged media and digital TV has generated massive amounts of data and the demand to analyse it;
- There is a need for "one source of truth" for data, systems and insight to target and measure;
- We must manage and optimise the combination of millions of customers, products, offers, different states across many interfaces to drive greater revenue and profit;
- We need a smarter allocation and management of our customer investments (e.g. offers);
- We need the ability to make and deploy better decisions from our data and insight around the individual customer and consumer segment rather than just product or function.

We also set ourselves both a vision and goals:

1 To ensure that Sky's decision-making is in tune with our consumer knowledge;
2 To have a comprehensive and deep understanding of each consumer such that we can deliver a better customer experience, drive business growth and deliver greater efficiency.

The insight and decision science function I created was designed to be a fully integrated capability with an insight ecosystem that used appropriately centralised and federated components to ensure the best balance between efficiency, agility and effectiveness.

Let's consider the operating model first. Establishing this is by far the biggest challenge.

I cannot emphasise enough that the customer strategy should dictate the decisioning business process (the operating model), and this should then determine capability. Developing centralised decisioning as a technology solution and then thinking about how it will work operationally is definitely the wrong way around and, I believe, will condemn any transformation initiative to failure.

Components of the enterprise decisioning operating model

There are four components to an enterprise decisioning operating model:

1   The customer contact process (or automated decision management process);
2   The decision support process;
3   Integrated insight and decision science;
4   Agile data development and management.

This operating model is depicted graphically in Figure 28.1.

The first of these, the customer contact process, is the kernel of the model and is an iterative, "always-on" process designed to transition from review, evaluate, plan, optimise, deploy and measure and back to review in a cyclical fashion. The second component, decision support, is a necessary process that provides "offline" reporting and insight to support the business in its more macro decisions, such as business strategy, brand development, product development and cost reduction initiatives. The remaining two elements are foundations that enable and power the first two processes. All components must be seamlessly integrated.

The customer contact process is the centrepiece of the operating model and an integrated, agile process incorporating all key business actors in the review, plan and optimise stages. This is required to ensure common understanding of performance drivers, that you capture new business requirements and constraints and that you are able to arbitrate our various and competing business objectives and to agree which of the optimised customer scenarios created by the analytics capability should be deployed.

The starting point is to get all customer contacts across all (participating) business units, functions and channels mapped onto a single program pro-forma.

The enterprise decisioning process

The process then follows the following ten steps:

1   Gathering business objectives and inputs;
2   Customer intelligence delivering descriptive and diagnostics (what happened and why);
3   Next-cycle programme optimisation – working out what the "best" scenario looks like from all the business inputs;
4   Holding a planning meeting to agree a unitary, omnichannel plan;
5   Building the customer contact plan and enabling the data;

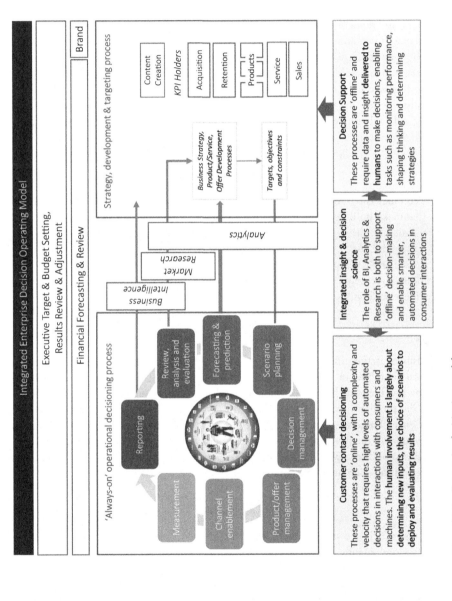

Figure 28.1 Enterprise decisioning model

Source: The author

6   Developing creative and proposition;
7   Customer selections and contact assignment;
8   Channel deployment;
9   Response management;
10 Monitoring and outcome evaluation (which feeds back into 1).

The decision support process ensures that business users are properly supplied with performance reporting (sales, upgrades, churn, customers, products, customer contacts and much more), research analytics (including modelling, data science and econometrics – advanced statistical tools that help understand and predict consumer behaviour), marketing research (using a variety of powerful techniques and capabilities and integrating what consumers say [research data] with what they do [behavioural data]) and forecasting and scenario planning.

Importantly, the decision support capability must allow any decisions made by the business to be quickly and easily implemented in campaigns or contacts to individual customers or prospects through the customer contact process.

The integrated capability

Now let us consider the integrated insight and decision science capability. Whilst the various disciplines that make up insight and decision science do not necessarily have to sit within one organisation structure, they must be part of a single, integrated process in order to make centralised decisioning work. At Sky, I had brought all the disciplines into one function, which made life easier, particularly to eliminate overlap and entropy.

The skill categories required to be integrated (and therefore were the elements of my division at Sky) are as follows.

Insight specialists

These are business partner roles that provide an interface between business stakeholders and the more technical disciplines in decision science. These roles should contain a mixture of experience and expertise, blending business, marketing, analysis, research and technical skills so that an organisation can profitably exploit its capability to deliver better business performance and customer experience. These specialists can also help determine business requirements and insight roadmaps that inform the development of new capability for particular stakeholder groups. The role holder acts as both receiver of business commissions, requests and requirements and as the embedded expert, offering help with "the art of the possible".

Data managers

Even when core data is in a system, much work is required to transform and shape the data for it to be useful. Consequently, there is a need to have data experts with specialisms across all types of data: transactions, risk, digital, data that is externally acquired. This team must have a deep knowledge of business data and understand what each data item means. If data is like oil, then these skills are like a refinery, transforming the raw material into something that can be turned into useful products. There is also a need to manage and protect customer data and have data quality and governance specialists who ensure that data is secure and used in accordance with company policy and data protection law.

Business analysts and project managers

Almost every activity will involve something to do with data, from a minor change to a product or service to a major new proposition launch. Much data development and many change projects are required, and these need skilled management, analysis and prioritisation.

Report developers

Every business has a huge demand for reporting and requires a team of skilled developers who know the data intimately and can build reports and (much better) create and manage automated, distributed business intelligence systems to support reporting needs.

Analysts, data scientists and econometricians

Analytics is an essential capability that manifests in several different types of skills. Data analysts will have data manipulation and statistical skills that enable them to solve complex business questions involving many data variables. Modellers use sophisticated techniques and tools to develop highly predictive models that can be used to understand individual consumer propensity and ensure business targets the right thing to the right consumer. Data scientists have the qualifications and skills to explore huge new data sets (e.g. big data) to determine patterns of consumer behaviour that may improve understanding. Finally, econometrics can use both internal and external data to forensically understand the factors that impact our business, forecast future trends and recommend how best to deploy marketing investments.

Marketing researchers

Marketing research is another essential capability and usually an area of high demand from the business. Team skills include quantitative as well as qualitative research, data science and user interface research.

Data planners and decision executives

These are the people who plan, target and implement direct, personalised communications to customers and prospects through all channels; there is a need for a team of data planners who help different business areas determine the right consumers to select for their particular objectives and ensure results can be evaluated. Once this is determined, the selection, journey development and implementation of consumers for direct campaigns and next best actions are carried out by decision executives, who are also responsible for ensuring compliance both with customer consent and data protection legislation.

Agile data development and management

The last component, but arguably the one without which nothing else can succeed, is the data. There are many myths about data; its importance is routinely emphasised, but, regrettably, the reality of data management and development is usually far removed from the promise. It sits firmly in the "dull but important" category. Whilst many functions of a business will eagerly squabble and fight over the ownership of insight commissioning, production and distribution, very few have much interest, let alone focus, on ensuring that data is of the right quality and recency to be useful.

Data capabilities required

At the highest level, data can be divided into two categories; behavioural and stated. Behavioural data is collected as the result of people or machines doing things. Examples include transactions, interactions, browsing and viewing. Stated data is gathered from processes that collect or monitor humans expressing attitudes, views and opinions. Market and customer surveys, focus groups, recommendation surveys, reviews and blogs are examples of this. Ideally, both types of data are required to provide the most robust insight. A reliance on insight derived just from stated preferences or opinions can be problematic. As David Ogilvy once said, "the problem is that people do not think what they feel, say what they think or do what they say".

Connected pervasive computing has created huge volumes of behavioural data as well as new stated data. Although there remain many situations where stated data is the only source available (new product development, for example), building your research foundation on behavioural data, before embarking on stated data, is desirable whenever possible. This enables the researcher to understand ("what happened") and objectively diagnose the behaviours that caused it ("why it happened") to help focus the collection of stated data, either from primary or secondary sources. This represents the best opportunity to integrate what people say and what they do and avoid cognitive biases.

Collection of data does not by itself lead to competitive advantage. This is created by what you can do with it. Not all data is valuable. Some data is much more valuable than other data. Organisations often do not have the data or do not have it in a format to do what they want.

The effective development of data solutions to enable the reporting, analysis and decisioning about consumers requires specific expertise and experience in a technology function. All data is not the same. This technology skill needs to be closely coupled with the data exploitation teams.

Managing interactions

At its core, for every interaction a person has with a brand, the technical capability is needed to make an evidence-based decision for acquiring, retaining or increasing the value of a person to the business whilst minimising the cost to the business for each individual person. This requires the provision of a gold standard for a person's customer interaction data with the business to operationalise these decisions out to customers and provide self-service tools to make customer insight that is always available to the business.

To deliver these capabilities, a team should be made up of people who are skilled in building data repositories and analytical environments to manage data and developers who take the raw data and make it available in the right place in the right format at the right time.

This requires suitably qualified solution architects, data developers, database builders and software engineers to create the data platforms, data models and applications needed as the foundations for what is needed. Note that the demands of centralised customer decisioning require a particular set of technology skills.

One of the most common features of failure in centralised decisioning is the inability of technology departments to grasp the essential business requirements of operational (always-on) analytics. Capability approaches are either too traditional (waterfall, data warehousing etc.) or, increasingly, blindly over-zealous computer science based (agile, data science, open source, cloud etc). The first approach features extended development times and often creates sclerotic capability that does not meet the needs of high-velocity decision systems. The second approach often wastes money in careless implementation and technical debt. It also creates systems that require too many technical intermediaries, presenting barriers to the rapid business decision change desired from centralised decisioning and often resulting in risky key person dependencies (e.g. "the data scientist that built the algorithm has now left the business").

Techniques and technology are not everything

In this short description of my career and experience in insight, you might be surprised that I have not written about the efficacy or otherwise of any research or analytical techniques. Nor have I examined any database, decisioning or digital technologies. The reason for this is that the aspects I have written about are the ones that matter. The best research, the best model, the greatest database in the world will not enable an enterprise to succeed if it has inadequate decision culture, operating models, skills and organisation. Get these right and you can do great things with some basic techniques and technologies.

The analytical and data capabilities I developed for Sky were critical in helping deliver all its core growth initiatives many years, including targeted acquisition, cross-sell and churn management and launching its Broadband and Talk, Now TV and Sky Mobile, as well as digital channel migration.

The exploitation of analytical capability powered Sky's drive to achieve a 50% increase in customer base in three years. Insight, analytics and segmentation to reduce churn and retention costs and analytics and modelling to expand headroom, improve conversion and cost per sale reduction were critical to the successful realisation of Sky's ambitious business objective.

I was responsible for building the world's largest proportional viewing panel and globally pre-eminent single consumer view. By itself, that is not very useful. However, by enabling this asset with analytics, insight and research, we supported Sky's award-winning AdSmart targeted advertising systems as well as new services, delivering large new revenue streams for the business.

I used a variety of methodologies and technologies to do, this but the key for me was establishing the right skills in the right operating model and ensuring an unrelenting focus on outcomes. Insight is only worthwhile if you enable smarter decisions.

The future

The biggest development in the world of customer insight over the past few years is how operational it has become, and this trend will only accelerate in future. It has profound implications for those that work in the discipline as more insight development is automated and deployed using artificial intelligence methodologies. The questions are whether AI is an existential threat to humanity or a transformational capability that delivers a better world for us all, whether it changes everything you ever believed about how businesses or organisations work or is just a powerful-but-complementary automated insight technology for improving performance and enabling better experiences.

Like most developments in human history, the answer to these questions comes down to how AI is used. We are right at the foothills on AI at present. Whilst it can deliver value for organisations, I think most organisations are tripping up in the implementation of AI.

The context

Connected pervasive computing is driving our next industrial – and social – revolution. Across the world, we face disruption, uncertainty, convergence and complexity. Connected pervasive computing (my definition of the word "digital") is creating winner-takes-all economics.

It makes digital transformation one of the biggest strategic issues for global business, education and government, and analytics is seen as the key enabler, particularly in the form of automated decisioning, or AI. I will be using these terms interchangeably.

It is worth clarifying what AI actually is. AI has been around for decades. I like to define AI by its purpose: to make smarter, timely decisions in complex interactions faster and cheaper than a human being. The word "decisions" is the key one for me, as I will shortly explain.

For humans, making decisions is not just a function of heuristics or empiricism. In making decisions, our brains are also using history and current context to calculate future probabilities. Unfortunately, we all succumb to one or more of the many cognitive biases in making decisions.

My point is that decision-making relies on probabilities. We live in a world not of self-evident truths but probabilities. Because humans prefer clarity to uncertainty, our policymakers, economists and journalists often cast probabilities as facts. Saddam Hussein had weapons of mass destruction, the financial system was crash-proof, diesel cars polluted less. All were probabilistic judgments presented as facts; all were catastrophically wrong. Is climate change a fact? No. A (high) probability? Yes.

And that's what AI is – predictive model management, the automation of mathematical probabilities. However, the huge increments in processing power and interconnectivity have dramatically accelerated the scope and scale of the application of predictive modelling into real-time, operational processes, be that search, recommendations, robotics, driverless cars, piloting aircraft or managing customer service.

Consequently, for all organisations, the effective adoption of AI into the decision-making process and systems across the enterprise will be the *sine qua non* of future survival, let alone success.

For start-ups and new entrants, this upheaval should represent an opportunity. They can design customer propositions and business operating models mindful of the capabilities and advantages of AI to achieve creative disruption. For incumbents, the task is one of business transformation, arguably a much more difficult challenge.

Either way, in my view, most organisations are struggling to land automated decisioning. Consequently, they are not realising either the scale and timeliness of benefits from their investments and efforts. At best, this represents a drag on performance; at worst, an existential threat.

So, what's happening?

Digital has changed the process of decision-making for both consumer-citizens and the entities that serve them. And I do not believe this fact is properly understood by most organisations.

I believe there is still widespread ignorance about the topic, which leads to investment mistakes, poor implementation and disillusionment in what should be a transformative capability.

- Disillusionment: One executive said to me recently: "so far our big data/AI investments have just made our stupidity more scalable";
- Ignorance: A senior colleague once told me (with a straight face): "AI means that 'the machine' will just tell me the answer without me having to ask";

- Evangelical delusion: One does not have to look far to find blind zealotry with little real critical evaluation, such as this quote from a respected consultancy: "operators should learn from Facebook and Google, where data is king and every product decision flows from what the data says about customers and how it can be used".

In my view, there is far too much obsession with acquiring technology and computer scientists and not enough thought and effort going in to transforming decision culture and business operating models.

You cannot just write a cheque for a new decision-culture and operating model, like you can with technology or data scientists. Changing decision-culture in a large organisation is particularly difficult, especially with executive preferences for managing by macro-decisions; heavy reliance on heuristics and hunch; decision-based fact-making; and the financial, functional or product-based command-and-control models of management.

All this runs counter to the effective adoption of automated decisioning.

You may have heard of Conway's law, which was an idea put forward in 1967 by Melvin Conway, a US software engineer, about the impact of an organisation's communication structure has on the design of its software. Transferring his law to this topic, I'd suggest the central problem is that an organisation will organise itself based on the decision capability it has today, not the decision capability it *could* develop.

Besotted by the magical promises of a world of AI and machine learning, many executives seem to have either ignored or downplayed the human factor. But it remains essential. The ultimate target variable of AI is the human being; consumer, citizen, student. Businesses and organisations will continue to be run by humans. Even if a machine decides, that decision needs to be understood and controlled by a human (unless you really do expect the kind of future displayed in sci-fi films such as *The Matrix* and *Terminator*)

US author Andrew Keen believes that the key relationships in the future will not be between people but between people and machines. I think that's right. The advantages will lie with those who have superior abilities to make the tech work for the human. That's called business enablement. Hence, the focus on technology and the blind spot about business enablement is, in my opinion, the biggest single reason why AI implementation fails.

What is the answer?

Tom Siebel nailed it for me when he said that "It [digital] changes everything . . . it forces CEOs to rethink how companies execute, with new business processes, management practices and information systems, as well as everything about the nature of customer relationships".

For the boards and executives of consumer businesses, this means a focus on:

- Creating enormous value for customers;
- Redefining the company's role in an ecosystem;
- Offering new (disruptive) business-value propositions or models;
- Whilst driving significant improvement in existing business.

This requires a transformation in operating model to enable the enterprise to be suitably:

1 Agile – rapidly changeable to cope with new regulations or business conditions;
2 Analytical – putting data to work improving the quality and effectiveness of decisions;

3   Adaptable – learning from what works and what does not work to continuously improve over time.

This is where automated decisioning (AI) should greatly assist:

- Agility – advanced automated analytical ecosystems can manage complexity, velocity and change with far greater effectiveness than human employees can;
- Analytical – deploying advanced analytics to not just manage but optimise interactions throughout the enterprise model with an ability to calculate and trade-off billions of micro-decisions in a way that is beyond human staff. I think the enormous benefits from the optimisation of the allocation of business resources are missed completely by most providers and users of AI;
- Adaptable – AI also offers the benefits of micro-to-macro objectivity, which is a valuable component of understanding what works, what does not work and what would probably work better in the future.

However, the most important consideration is *how* AI is implemented. Any organisation seeking to do so successfully needs transform and enable three critical, interdependent factors:

- Executive decision culture – how an organisation determines decisions on resource allocation to achieve maximum returns. It's the opposite of top-down, fewer, bigger, better. If executives believe they can maintain the same decision culture whilst adding AI, they will be very disappointed with results. Executives must extract themselves from the detailed process and focus on what outputs they require and what inputs they are willing to make. The critical capability needed is to optimise the billions of interactions. If you are familiar with the marginal gains approach of Dave Brailsford (GB Olympic cycling team and Team Sky), you will know how many small improvements can lead to a big result;
- Operating model and organisation – the way an organisation designs and manages the accountabilities, roles and flows in its decision ecosystem for maximum effectiveness and efficiency. The existing financial, functional or product-based model and structures may not be the most suitable, and shoe-horning new technology and algorithms into a traditional operating structure usually fails. Both the operating model and organisation need to be designed around the opportunities for AI to drive benefits;
- Business adoption – the way an organisation enables its human capital to effectively use its AI capability to drive performance improvements and business objectives. In my view, there is not enough upskilling and development of employees to ensure this new capability can be exploited to the maximum. It requires different approaches and techniques. It requires different thinking (and we do not adequately teach people thinking skills). You cannot just dump new technologies or analytics methodologies on staff and expect a different result. An 18-year-old uses a smartphone quite differently from a pensioner, despite it being the same device.

I have already mentioned the agility and adaptive advantages that AI offers in winner-takes-all economics. But much writing about AI benefits appears to concentrate on cost reduction by replacing expensive human beings with machines. I understand the attraction of operating expense (and margin) benefits, especially for large incumbents in banking, retail and telecoms. Significant savings are achievable. However, no one achieves growth through cost-cutting. The real prize is in the deployment of AI to winkle out micro-improvements in every decision, in every interaction that, taken together, provide significant gains to growth.

From my experience, deploying AI for decision optimisation can increase end value by up to 30% over standard targeting. If your organisation is not even using standard targeting, it would be more like 60%. I have personally seen uplifts of +200% when moving from the sort of faux-decisioning one finds in digital platforms to proper real-time, dynamic decisioning (AI).

Conclusions

- Automated decisioning or AI is coming of age and has powered a few businesses from start-up to the biggest companies in the world in less than a decade;
- Much of it does not yet work very well, and many of the current applications that deliver high financial benefits are in specific areas – advertising, online retail, fraud and security, investment;
- Many future applications suggested for AI may, in fact, not be either desirable or viable;
- Do not be blind-sided by the snake oil. Vendors, consultancies, journalists and academics may tell you it's all about the algorithm or black box or 300-strong data science team you need to recruit. It is not;
- You may need AI to be agile, analytic and adaptive, but you will also need to pay close attention to the human factors, in both customers/citizens and your employees;
- You need to get enterprise decision culture, operating model and business adoption right to take advantage of the opportunities in the time you have available to grasp them;
- The prizes for the winners are significant, and the penalties for the losers could be lethal.

My advice is not to believe all you are told or expend your energies finding that apocalyptic bolthole for when it all goes wrong. Instead, diligently kick the tyres yourself and actively engage to ensure the potential of AI delivers a better outcome for consumers, employees, citizens and shareholders.

29

A PRACTITIONER'S VIEW OF CUSTOMER INSIGHT

Past, present and future

Paul Laughlin

Summary

This chapter gives the authors reflections on over 25 years of working in the field of customer insight. It gives his views about the current state of customer insight in commercial practice. He focuses on how the disciplines of marketing research and customer data analytics have merged and on the future of customer insight.

Academic study

Appropriately for the current emphasis on data science, my journey into the world of work began with a science degree. More unusually, I studied for a BSc in meteorology, oceanography and astronomy. The latter gave me a good grounding in mathematics and statistics. Of equal relevance to my later career, all elements of that degree developed in me a focus on observation, the rigour of the scientific method and consideration of impact on people's lives. Each of these three is important for customer insight.

Later in my career, I chose to study an MSc in computing for commerce and industry with the UK's Open University. That helped inform both my career in information technology (IT) roles and an understanding of IT infrastructure, databases, projects and programming. Although the technologies have changed, the principles I learnt have continued to aid my understanding of the potential of each new wave of technology.

Jobs before my focus on customer insight

At first, after I left university, like many science graduates, I had dreams of a research career. I applied to the British Antarctic Survey and was offered a place to study a PhD on ice formation in the Baltic. However, family circumstances meant that I needed a higher income than the very low amount paid to researchers. That is why I chose a career in IT.

So, I learnt my trade as a programmer within the civil service. After mastering several technical roles, I left to work for the UK's Trustee Savings Bank. There, I continued to explore different roles in IT, including programming, project management, operations, technical support and R&D. This broad experience has served me well since – especially in collaborating with IT colleagues.

Eventually the appeal of IT roles waned. They all seemed to involve simply responding to requests from the business or adding bureaucracy in order to defend against possible future blame.

So, I was delighted when I was headhunted by a company's chief actuary in an insurance company's actuarial team to create a data warehouse and lead its building. It was involvement in and completion of this project that first opened my eyes to how poorly the potential of data was being realised.

Jobs creating and leading customer insight teams

My first venture into customer insight (although we did not call it that then) was when I inherited a statistician in my team. Holders of every other role in the department was involved in studying for actuarial or underwriting exams, but we had opportunity to do something different. Our first foray in customer insight involved just some basic descriptive and behavioural analytics into customer retention. In the late 20th century, this was a green field area for insurers and promised big financial rewards. By identifying those customers most likely to leave, we could both retain more customers through preventative action and stop marketing to those who were unlikely to stay.

Such an approach resulted in millions of pounds of savings for the large UK insurer for which I worked and so not surprisingly attracted the interest and sponsorship of our CEO. The following years developed as an evolutionary journey of further investment in the team, resulting in greater benefits but insufficient capacity to meet the growing demand for our services across the business. This approach of proving value, one use case at a time, led to further investment in our team and its growth. The result was that my team grew to 44 members and we delivered a measurable benefit of more than £11 million additional profit per annum.

To achieve the capability that we needed in order to meet the demand for our services, we needed an expansion in both our skills and application areas. After growing a team of statisticians and analysts working on behavioural analytics and predictive models, I merged other teams into ours to achieve synergies. Over ten years, this included adding data management, database marketing and market research teams into one integrated department. However, this did not just achieve economies of scale. By working as one team, we learned the benefits of sharing knowledge, skills and best practice. This resulted in my expanded view of what I now call "holistic customer insight".

A growing understanding of the meaning of customer insight

During this period, we agreed a definition of customer insight as:

> A non-obvious understanding about your customers, which if acted upon, has the potential to change their behaviour for mutual benefit.

Four elements of that definition that are worth highlighting:

- "Non-obvious": Real insights into your customers rarely come from one source (one piece of analytics or one research report). They almost always require digging further;
- "Acted upon": Customer insight is of no value if it is not acted upon. This is for two reasons – because to generate commercial or customer value from insight requires acting on recommendations but also because insights are hypotheses until they are tested in the real world with real customers;
- "Change their behaviour": Too much of what passes for insight is just predictions based on assuming that people are creatures of habit and that similar people will continue to act as they have in the past. However, real insights involve identifying motivations that are deep enough to provoke a change in behaviour, rather than continue behaving as before;

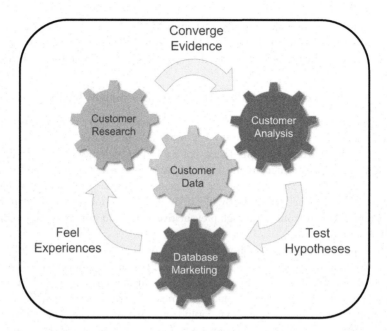

Figure 29.1 A model of holistic customer insight

Source: The author

- "Mutual benefit": In today's trust economy, where social media are critical, it is foolish short-termism to seek to take advantage of your customers in order to make a quick profit. Sustainable profit growth comes from mutual value sharing enabled by insights that help you really understand customer needs and the jobs they want to get done.

During this time, I also learnt that to achieve a rich and deep understanding of customers and to act upon that understanding required the capabilities of the different technical teams that we had integrated. This resulted in the identification of what became termed the Customer Insight Engine. Figure 29.1 summarises a model for combining different technical skills to generate and test potential customer insights.

This model of how to combine the strengths of four distinct but related technical disciplines emerged through experience. Over the years of incremental delivery, specific projects or challenges helped us to identify what was missing or where collective action could improve quality. After a decade of managing such teams, I was leading a function that includes the technical skills of data, analytics, database marketing and market research teams. The insight I had into what enabled us to generate the quality of customer insights outlined in my previous definition was that it came through the collaboration of these four technical skills. As illustrated in the figure, each had an important part to play.

How the Customer Insight Engine works

Here is how the Customer Insight Engine is intended to operate.

Customer data management

No significant progress can be made on identifying or acting on customer insights without good quality customer data. Although data quality and data management may be the least glamorous team in this technical world, it is vital. All the successful data science, analytics and customer insight leaders I know have learnt not to neglect it.

So, the key for this team to play its part in the Customer Insight Engine is first to implement a robust programme of data quality management. This needs to include regular reporting and resolution of data quality issues at source. It should also involve achieving data ownership within business teams (not within the IT function) and a serious focus on metadata/data dictionaries. For the purposes of the Customer Insight Engine, this team needs to deliver a "single version of the truth" for all other teams.

I learnt over many setbacks that this does not need to be a perfect or even complete data warehouse. Virtual/logical "single customer views" that organise more disparate data sources can also work. In these days of non-relational databases (NoSQL), Hadoop and other solutions, this is viable. For many organisations with some data "in the cloud", it may be essential. What matters more for customer insight is that all the other teams are working from a common source that enables reconciliation and transfer of data between teams.

Customer analysis

This work can vary hugely in complexity. It includes what would now be described as business intelligence (descriptive analytics, profiling and reporting), as well as behavioural, predictive and even prescriptive analytics. So, far from being an outdated concept, analysis is a super category that includes more technical data science coding and modelling.

Leading such a team for decades also teaches you that technology is not the most important consideration. It can help to have a wide repertoire of algorithmic responses to difference business needs and customer data. However, if your goal is actionable insights about your customers, relevance trumps sophistication. Leaders need to ensure analysts or data scientists develop enough domain knowledge and commercial awareness to recognise what level of sophistication is needed.

For the purpose of our Customer Insight Engine, the output of this team is a stream of hypotheses to be tested. I deliberately use the term "hypotheses" rather than "insights "or even "interpretations" as the goal of our definition is an understanding that can change behaviour. Validation that has been achieved requires testing. The rigour of the scientific method requires differentiated action and accurate capture of data on the outcomes of the different actions. But, before moving to this, let me explore the need for such hypotheses to be grounded in converging analytics and research.

Customer research

Marketing research teams still have a vital role to play in generating customer insights. Whether marketing (or consumer) researchers are working in distinct roles or as sub-teams, I learnt that a leader needs to protect some of their focus for understanding customers. The competing (and equally important) demands of market and competitor intelligence must not be allowed to consume team resources. Equally, marketing researchers benefit from having their eyes opened by working alongside analysts and even data scientists.

Years of experience focusing on self-reporting by customers (stating what they have done or intend to do), even with the protection of a well-designed research programme (with appropriate selection, qualitative research and quantitative testing), can create a mindset. On the positive side, marketing researchers with that mindset focus on awareness of personality types, customer segments, sentiment and motivations. On the negative side, it can lead to researchers asking customers, when a better solution is to experiment and measure actual behaviour. The popularity of research on behavioural economics, which demonstrates amongst other things the extent of bias in how consumers report their perceptions and actions, has also cast a shadow over a discipline too often perceived as blind to unconscious biases.

However, in a well-functioning customer insight department, I found the opposite. Due to a high proportion of marketing researchers coming from psychology or humanities backgrounds, they are well equipped to deal with behavioural biases. For that reason, once receptive to the idea of bringing together evidence from both behavioural analytics and consumer research, they can be very productive. They also recognise that perception matters as well as reality, that it is not enough to predict what customers will do, but you also need to understand what they perceive and how to talk with them. In other words, research + analytics = deeper customer insights.

To produce this combination of expertise, I developed the idea of running customer insight generation workshops. Members of both the customer analysis and customer research teams have a vital role to play in curating the material for such workshops. In the workshop, representatives from functions across the business bring together evidence and use root cause analysis techniques to generate hypotheses. These are the raw materials provided to the fourth team.

Database marketing

Most businesses have had for many years a direct marketing or marketing communications team that generates leads and executes campaigns. They should also develop ever improved targeting for their communications, based on measurement of results. The duties of these teams can vary hugely and include roles focused on customer experience (CX) or customer relationship management (CRM) and marketing operations roles but also data and analytics capabilities. Having provided such a team with the marketing measurement and targeting models needed for many years, I came to realise the benefits of also including these technical roles in a customer insight department.

One of the advantages of including such roles in a customer insight department is the ability to demonstrate short-term return on investment. Having an execution capability in the team enables improvements to be measured in terms of reduced cost or increased income within a financial year. This can demonstrate the benefit of this department to the business as a whole and help to protect and fund longer-term work, such as strategic analysis or proposition development based on customer insight.

Another benefit is the execution capability itself. A skilled database marketing team is well versed in experimental design. So, when given hypotheses from customer insight generation workshops, the team can work with other teams to design a test to confirm or reject hypotheses. Vital considerations like control groups or the measures to demonstrate uplift (e.g. gains analysis) can be considered early. Practical data capture requirements can also be agreed with the data management team.

However, the virtuous cycle of the Customer Insight Engine does not stop with a successful hypothesis test. Because the goal is an ever-deepening understanding of your customers and sustainable value exchange, it is also vital to understand "how was it for you?" This is a vital role for marketing researchers. New experiments (e.g. improved targeting, new products or new communications) need to be measured not just in terms of behaviour (e.g. take-up, click-through) but also perception. Researchers need to design surveys or built-in research to capture the customer experience. Once this is completed, we have the raw material to go around the cycle once more, with analytics and research results converging to produce a comprehensive picture.

Applications for commercial businesses

All that sounds fine in theory, but my working life has not been made up of theoretical lectures or attractive models. All business leaders need to achieve a pragmatic balance between developing a strong capability for the future of the business, delivering commercial returns and satisfying (or delighting) both customers and employees. So, what have I learnt about that in 25 years of practice?

Use cases that have proved valuable

The range of application areas for holistic customer insight are broad. So, before I discuss delivering against the triple challenge of building future capability, delighting customers and delivering commercial returns – let me highlight a few application areas. The model outlined previously has proved effective when working to deliver each of these use cases:

- **Consumer segmentation** – the holistic customer insight model made it possible to go beyond the restrictions of more traditional siloed approaches. A leading UK general insurer developed an attitudinal segmentation approach based on qualitative and quantitative research and then appended that data to existing comprehensive behavioural data and used it (via factor analysis) to develop a suite of logistic regression models to predict membership of each attitudinal segment. The attribution algorithm was a key element to success, as it weighted the difficulties of predicting each segment. However, the result was an ability to operationalise and deploy an attitudinal segmentation that could be used to differentiate communications and treatments to customers and some prospects;
- **Insight generation for proposition development** – the holistic customer insight model helped here, too. Building on the industry-standard insight generation approach used in packaged consumer goods firms, a cross-functional team in a UK bank brought together curated evidence from research, behavioural analytics, operational marketing information and market intelligence to generate insights. This was further strengthened through interaction with actual customers (voting and giving feedback). This approach led to the development of successful new propositions with more robust evidence of demand and recommended targeting, prior to the launch of campaigns;
- **Marketing measurement** – this involves broad triangulation of evidence when measuring the effectiveness of total marketing spend. Rather than separate assessments, using control-group based testing for direct marketing, econometrics for broadcast media and regional testing for other channels, combining analytics and research delivers clearer insight. Brand tracking surveys are conducted more often and at a more granular level. A broad range of stakeholders are included in econometric modelling workshops (including results from direct marketing A/B testing). Combining all that evidence with sentiment tracking and brand satisfaction and recommendation surveys makes it possible to identify aggregate impact and develop more robust multi-touch attribution modelling.

The task for customer insight leaders

Now let us consider what else customer insight leaders need to consider in the real world of delivering in today's businesses. My top list is:

- A capability for the future;
- Satisfying, even delighting, customers and employees;
- Delivering commercial returns.

A capability for the future

One of the lessons you learn early on as a leader of a customer insight a function is that demand will outstrip supply. If you have done an effective job of communicating the capability and potential benefits of your team, you will be inundated with requests. However, if you leave the market to determine your demand, it is likely to "dumb down" your delivery, leading to most of your analysts working on business intelligence reporting, descriptive analytics or data wrangling – transforming and mapping data from one "raw" form into another, to make it suit other purposes.

To avoid this, leaders learn to ruthlessly prioritise and to protect resources for other important long-term work. Prioritisation means clearly identifying the business need for a given request (Socratic questioning skills can help there) and then force ranking the request against other requests. Scoring should use both the traditional Eisenhower matrix (urgency versus importance) and factors like do-ability or potential value, together with how well it aligns with strategic priorities for the organisation. Business partnerships and active account management can also help in decision-making and resource allocation when discussing choices with directors of client functions. It helps to visualise the demand and what has been requested (in order of importance) from each directors' function. It requires the company to choose what matters most immediately. It is important to ring-fence teams to ensure appropriate staffing to support different business divisions.

A benefit of combining the different technical teams identified in the holistic customer insight model into one centre of excellence can be the opportunity for ensuring longer-term capability investments are made by delivering short-term profits. Database marketing teams can provide evidence to the wider business of tangible delivery contributing to current financial year targets. Analytics teams can also protect a portion of their time for delivering short-term focused delivery that enables visible value added (especially for other teams to achieve their targets) this year. The benefit of the ensuing positive reputation should be used to protect work that is of longer-term benefit. Strategic analytics, segmentation, research and analysis for new product and service development, together with a significant portion of market research work, usually only deliver results beyond the current financial year, so they need to be protected by a wise leader who can argue that it is also needed in the mix of technical skills that deliver the valued within-year profit.

Such an approach should also be used to protect time for continuous professional development by all team members. Staff in all the technical areas should perceive that they are developing their skills and should see a range of possible career paths ahead if they continue. Many surveys have confirmed that analysts and data scientists see this as vital to their choosing to stay with an employer. In the current climate of scarce technical talent, focusing on what will help you retain talented staff is vital.

Satisfying (or delighting) customers and employees

It has been wisely said that customer experience has evolved into a good practice of thinking about human-to-human interactions with (and within) your business. This means that you cannot separate the impact of customer experience from employee engagement. Likewise, customer insight leaders cannot afford to focus just on how to deliver improved marketing or customer experience but also how they support and motivate their team members.

Where customers are concerned, the importance of developing a culture of empathy cannot be overstated. Here customer insight leaders can often benefit from initiatives that customer experience leaders will also be keen to undertake. In many data, analytics and research teams (both those I have led and those of my clients), I have seen the benefit of ensuring that analysts and researchers have opportunity to meet customers and build an emotional connection. Remembering that the data relates to real people and feeling an empathy for their needs, challenges and frustrations can improve everything from the briefs defining the work, data selection to analysis, interpretation and communication of recommendations.

Beyond that necessary customer-centric focus, customer insight leaders also need to provide tangible evidence to their teams that they care about their development. One of the best tools to help make this more than fine words is a competency framework. Today, too often, such a tool is the province of human resources teams and so unsurprisingly is too generic to be useful to a specialist technical team. However, it does not have to be so. I have seen the benefit of developing bespoke competency frameworks for data, analytics and customer insight teams, ones that capture the set of both the technical and the softer capabilities needed for each role. This can be a useful tool, which can help leaders design the roles needed in a team. It can identify a team's skills gaps and be used as a more objective assessment for personal development conversations. It can also enable mapping their career paths mentioned earlier.

Delivering commercial returns

The previously mentioned capabilities can be particularly effective at bringing together many sources of evidence to provide deeper insights into the contexts, perspectives and sometimes motivations for behaviour. However, if customer insight, analytics and data teams are not to suffer because they are not seen to contribute to the business, they need to be seen to make money. Through my experience of leading customer insight teams, I have learnt a few principles to help guide leaders and such teams toward financial returns. I recommend that leaders establish metrics (via a series of assumptions that would seem familiar to an economist) to track their return on investment. A concise presentation summarising results is central to dialogue with CEOs.

The following recommendations are based on my experience over a decade in which I focused on return on investment:

- Understanding of your organisation's profit levers will help identify where the smallest improvements will deliver the largest profits. For instance, general insurers should always focus first on improving customer retention. Single percentage point improvements can be worth millions of pounds of incremental profit;
- Remember that relevance trumps sophistication. A focus on effective stakeholder management so you understand the pain points of your organisation will help guide your focus. It is important to be involved in business, not just technical, conversations. Then focus on what would improve or fix the current problem, even if it is a simplistic data or business intelligence solution. Prioritising making a difference first will buy time for you and your and allies to return and transform parts of your business later;
- Think about execution from the start. One of the encouraging developments in the fields of data science and data engineering has been realisation of the need for a data operations team. After the time taken to bring data into a suitable format, the biggest barrier to adding value that leaders mention to me is problems deploying models or analytics recommendations. For that reason, it pays to filter out early on work that will be too hard to operationalise. Greater value can also be realised in some cases by starting the conversations with IT and operations teams early.

The state of customer insight in business today

Much has changed since I first created a customer insight team in 2002. That was before anyone was using the terms data science or big data and few talked about customer insight or analytics (as we now use those terms). Data warehouses were in fashion, and the long journey to master data management and single customer views had begun. Since then, much technical progress has been made in the fields of data, analytics and data science. Technological progress has transformed the types and volumes of data that can be processed. More applications have been pioneered and more organisations aspire to use all this intelligence in order to become customer centric.

However, as the old saying goes "the more things change, the more they stay the same". I have participated in two revolutions in artificial intelligence (AI), but still most organisations do not deliver intelligent interactions with their customers and staff. Much more data is being used by many organisations, and yet most still lack the organisation, quality management and metadata needed to curate and use that data well. A wider range of technical skills in this function are now employed by most large organisations, and yet most in those roles still lack a professional body or clear view of best practice.

In many ways, this feels strangely like the progress made with data warehouses, CRM and AI applications (then mainly called expert systems) in the late 1990s. I hope we can avoid the backlash that followed. Perhaps rightly what happened next was the AI Winter (setting back widespread adoption for nearly 20 years) and boardrooms across the world swearing to never waste money on over-hyper CRM systems or "data graveyards" again.

So, as I contemplate the exciting progress being made today, I am both encouraged and fearful. I am encouraged that data and analytics capabilities have become fashionable and are receiving more investment than ever, but fearful that unless they deliver on their promise, we have another "winter" coming. To avoid that I recommend a focus on holistic customer insight, rather than technical modelling for the sake of it. Together with a focus on delivering a measured return on investment and not neglecting the still important (even if unfashionable) role of marketing research teams.

What might be the future for customer insight leaders

Over six years ago I launched the Customer Insight Leader blog (now accompanied by a podcast of the same name). Now, many posts and interviews later, it has been interesting to observe how other leaders experience has mirrored and differed from my own. Having also had the privilege of tutoring postgraduate data science students, I have had the chance to watch as an over-hyped field matures into a better understood discipline. But what does all that have to do with the future for customer insight?

I have sometimes been tempted to change my brand, "Customer Insight Leader". However, the need for a better understanding of customers and acting on that understanding in marketing, products and service continues. I believe that these will be even more important in an economy which is majority-online sales and service.

I hope organisations will recognise the need to use their technical teams in a more coordinated way to deliver holistic customer insights and execute actions to test recommended responses. One encouraging sign I see from my own training and mentoring service is a growing focus on softer skills development. Leaders are recognising that if their analysts and researchers are to work more effectively as a team and make an impact on the wider organisation, they need softer skills too.

To support that need, I developed a nine-step model to provide a framework for training and other support services. Data, analytics and customer insight teams will need to focus increasingly on developing capability in these areas:

1   Questioning skills – to identify real need, not just delivering what is requested;
2   Planning skills – to use best practice from agile working methods to improve efficiency;
3   Securing buy-in skills – stakeholder mapping, segmentation and changing personal style to engage them;
4   Data curation skills – understanding the provenance of data, its meaning, permissioning and its organisational impact;
5   Analytical thinking skills – curiosity beyond algorithms, time for exploratory data analysis and taking context into account;
6   Insight generation skills – bringing together evidence, as described in holistic customer insight model;
7   Negotiating sign-off skills – political awareness and negotiation skills, to navigate implications with internal and external clients and partners;
8   Visual storytelling skills – combining best of storytelling and data visualisation skills;
9   Solution delivery skills – influencing the real world solution beyond technical work and creating feedback loops.

In response to rising automation and use of AI in our work (and home) lives, I predict an increasing focus on the human aspects. This is a tremendous opportunity for market researchers, if they learn to understand and collaborate with their technical peers. Leaders and teams who can effectively combine data management, advanced analytics, database marketing (and in the future data operations) and research will succeed. As people in all these roles will also need to focus on developing their softer skills, there is opportunity here to further enhance the role of leaders as self-aware coaches. So, I finish this chapter with hope. Precisely because we live in era of renaissance of technology and AI, researchers should grasp the opportunity to focus on the human insight and skills that also distinguished the European Renaissance hundreds of years ago.

30

EPILOGUE

A more strategic look at the future of marketing research

Merlin Stone, Len Tiu Wright and Luiz Moutinho

Summary

This chapter summarises the main themes covered in this book, in particular the relationship between insights derived from "big data" – the high volumes of data arising from digital interactions between firms and customers, between firms (in partnerships, supply chains and distribution relationships) and between customers themselves (in social media and on the websites of companies and others, especially aggregator sites and consumer ratings sites). It concludes that best practice insight is a combination of big data and marketing research, with the latter increasingly taking the role of exploring customers' perceptions, needs and behaviour in depth rather than quantifying them. It suggests that the disciplines of marketing research have a vital role to play in determining some aspects of how the big data is collected, for example, the questions asked of customers who are buying online. The issues of the strategic use of marketing research and its positioning in the enterprise, particularly where increasing numbers of companies are automating their marketing and sales, is explored, taking into account the results of the Market Research Society's initiative, Intelligence Capital.

Introduction

In this book, we have reviewed many aspects of marketing research. A recurring theme of the book is the relationship between insights derived from "big data" – the high volumes of data arising from digital interactions between firms and customers, between firms (in partnerships, supply chains and distribution relationships) and between customers themselves (in social media and on the websites of companies and others, especially aggregator sites and consumer ratings sites).

The broad conclusion of our research into these topics is that best practice insight is a combination of big data and marketing research, with the latter increasingly taking the role of exploring customers' perceptions, needs and behaviour in depth rather than quantifying them, but that the disciplines of marketing research have a vital role to play in determining some aspects of how the big data is collected, for example, the questions asked of customers who are buying online.

However, there are still some important questions to be asked – and answered – relating to the strategic use of marketing research and its positioning in the enterprise, particularly where increasing numbers of companies are automating their marketing and sales. This subject is explored in the Market Research Society's initiative, Intelligence Capital, which we discuss later in this chapter.

Insight in a world of marketing and sales automation

Increasingly, the role of marketing researchers must be understood in the context of the marketing automation that is increasingly common in companies.

Marketing and sales systems underwent extremely rapid evolution in the second decade of the 21st century and continue to evolve. This evolution is due partly to the emergence of giant software companies, using cloud computing to provide advanced marketing and sales automation capabilities and services to their clients. These companies include the giant, such as Google, Amazon Web Services, Microsoft, Salesforce.com and Adobe, as well as social media companies such as Facebook, but also many other companies, large and small. This development has been accompanied by rapid changes in the marketing services world, with most marketing communications agencies providing a wide range of services, using the capabilities supplied by the previously mentioned companies. The boundary between marketing communications agencies and suppliers of consultancy and systems services has been blurred by the systems and software companies packaging their services so that they are ready to be used by end-clients, as well as by mergers and acquisitions amongst suppliers, such as the many acquisitions that transformed the consultancy and services company Accenture into the world's largest digital marketing agency. The role of marketing researchers, whether agencies, in-house staff or consultancies, is changing to become the role of provider of insight to support the automation of marketing and sales.

The services provided by these companies allow clients of all sizes to benefit from them. Even the smallest companies can open accounts with some of these companies, allowing them to advertise, manage content, track sales and measure the results of their marketing and sales efforts. In other words, marketing and sales automation, which may once have been the preserve of large clients, is now available to all. Cloud computing approaches allow clients to scale their activities up or down much more easily and cost-effectively, according to the number and volume of marketing and sales activities.

In an area of systems deployment where technological progress is so fast, there is naturally a gap between the practices of leading-edge users and those at different stages of following – a classic diffusion of innovation cycle. However, in this area, as in many other areas of information and communications technology (ICT), the shift to the hosting of software in "the cloud" has made a very big difference to the speed with which users practice is updated, particularly in the most advanced companies. To understand best practice, therefore, we need to focus mainly on companies that are at the frontier.

An additional issue is that many of the main providers of these systems are constantly updating their software, so much so that weekly updates may be published by third parties to ensure that customers know what new features and facilities are available. This has the paradoxical result that the most advanced users may become even more advanced because they incorporate these new features and facilities in their approach, while users who are struggling to come to grips with the complexity of systems available have their hands full with just coping with basic systems.

What is marketing and sales automation?

Before we outline what is available to companies, we need to define marketing and sales automation (MSA). We define it as follows, but note that we do not force a division between marketing automation and sales automation, as the very nature of MSA is that it bridges the gap between what marketers and salespeople do, ensuring that marketing analysis, planning and decision-making are translated automatically into sales actions and results,

In its most advanced form, MSA is technology that automates the management (planning, delivery, measurement) of marketing and sales processes, analysis, decisions, communication campaigns and other customer-facing activities and measurement across all the channels of communication and distribution that a company uses – digital and physical, combining the many different data sets involved (e.g. data on customers and their behaviour, product and advertising content, advertising and channel costs, social commentary) to ensure optimal decision-making, and allow marketing and sales management to measure the performance of any aspect of marketing and sales. The aim of using MSA is to improve effectiveness, minimise costs, reduce the errors and delays caused by human intervention and allow marketers and salespeople to focus on activities which cannot be automated.

What MSA allows clients to do

MSA allows businesses to target customers, automating messaging to them across all digital channels, using workflows or sets of instructions which are developed as a result of planning, increasingly using artificial intelligence to identify optimum workflows, strategies and tactics and with widespread use of testing to find what works best. In selling, MSA supports segmentation of customers, identification of individual target customers, serving them the right content for the appropriate products at the right time (for the supplier and the customer, using information from their customer profiles), enquiry and lead management (e.g. generation, prioritization – using scoring – conversion and measurement) and customizing the contact, content, pricing, customer experience and customer journey over many contacts and sales cycles and in some cases over the lifetime of the customer and over different levels of customer engagement, from first acquaintance and becoming a customer through to loyalty, advocacy and recommendation.

In its most advanced form, it handles groups of customers, too (families in B2C, whole companies in B2B). It removes the need for manual intervention, for example, in deciding to send a given customer a certain message, which may itself by personalized using customer profile data. To build customer profiles, MSA uses data on customers collected from many sources – directly from customers through their digital and real interaction with the supplier, through social media and from third party sources. In some cases, it will integrate with the logistics, supply chain, resource management and risk management systems of the company, so that, for example, only products or services which are available are promoted or orderable and so that pricing can be customized (as in yield management systems used by transport and logistics operations, or quotation management systems used by insurance companies).

Degrees of automation

Marketing automation is not binary. There are many different degrees of automation, while some marketing activities are more amenable to automation than others. Automation does not mean being completely free of human intervention. The extent to which this is possible depends not just on the capabilities of information and communications technology but also on how far self-service is possible and also whether the situation is a first-time buy for the customer, or a modified or a routine rebuy (Robinson *et al.* 1967). A very complicated product or service might require a very human-intensive process on both supplier and client-side for a first-time purchase. Straight rebuys might be left to online buying through self-service, and even modified rebuys might also be automatable if the product is modular. However, many of the interactions during even a complicated sales/buying process might be automatable, for example, the delivery of content. The deployment of artificial intelligence may turn situations where human intervention was necessary into ones where it is not. However, although self-service has been greatly facilitated by the Web, with buyers having the options of viewing reviews by similar clients and checking references more easily (including conflict of interest if the purchase is really important and the buyer needs to check the credentials of reference givers), there is still a tendency for buyers of complex products and services, both consumer and business, to make wrong decisions because they believe they have the needed expertise and so avoid using intermediaries or advisors (Stone 2009).

The components of MSA

The main channel components of MSA include:

- Email – particularly for lead generation and management;
- Social media messaging and management;
- Mobile messaging and management;
- Own website management – content display and customization, lead capture;
- Advertising management via the Internet, television and streaming media, often using real-time bidding, and including dealing with difficult issues such as privacy (this applies to most of MSA) and ad-blocking, but also the opportunities offered by the big platform providers mentioned earlier.

An overview of MSA systems is given in Figure 30.1.
At the frontiers of development of MSA systems are areas such as:

- The use of artificial intelligence and machine learning in every area, from analysis to lead management and provision of bots to answer customer queries and manage sales cycles;
- Advanced content management, including using AI to customise images and text;
- Working with advertising demand and supply side platforms to optimise advertising.

The main activities that are supported by MSA systems include:

- Identify target market and optimum contact method – including integration with sales force activity;
- Use outputs of own- and third-party data systems to build profiles;
- Development or identification of content need to support marketing and selling;
- Use predictive analytics to predict customer value;
- Build targeted lists (including retargeting of customers who have been in contact but not bought);
- Arrange personalization of content and messaging;
- Use customer and industry data to create personalized communication;
- Prospect identification;
- Opportunity identification;
- Plan campaigns/events/contact cycles;
- Execute campaigns;
- Media buying;
- Lead generation;
- Measure responses – email, website and so on;

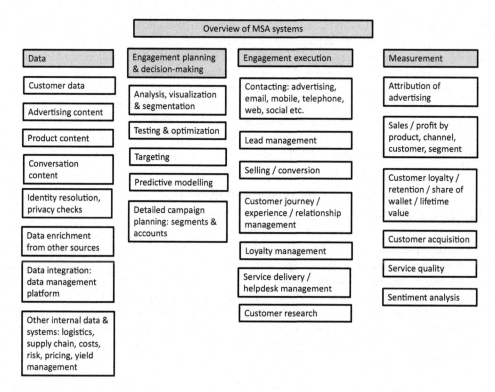

Figure 30.1 Overview of MSA systems

Source: The authors

- Route qualified leads to CRM process/system;
- Lead management – scoring, prioritization (qualify for response management/contact), allocation of contact strategies, move warm leads to nurturing cycle and so on;
- Lead conversion;
- Sales enablement provision;
- Prospect enquiry management;
- Online activity tracking;
- Conversion of prospect to sale;
- Solution selling and delivery;
- Payment processing and management and other financial transfers, including fraud and risk management;
- Early stage account management;
- Mature account management;
- Customer service – routine and problems, and contacting during resolution process;
- Voice of customer program, which integrates all information coming from the customer – sources: all data feeds, surveys, login/my account pages, error pages, support/FAQ use, purchasing, logistics, chat, surveys, customer service, emails, customer sat, NPS, customer effort score, first contact resolution and so on;
- Analyse results of whole process;
- Communication to all stakeholders at all stages.

The main flows of data around MSA systems are depicted in Figure 30.2.

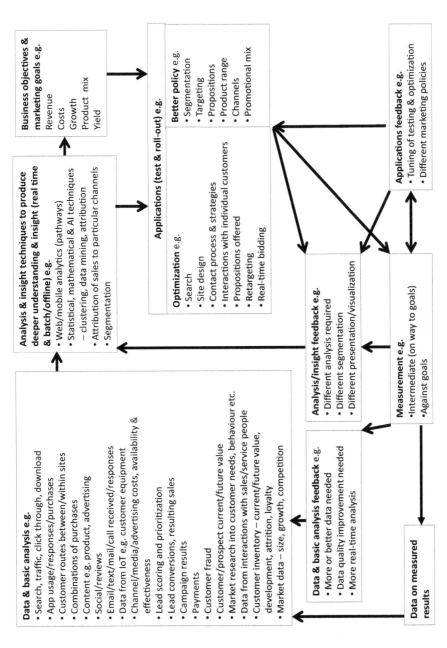

Figure 30.2 Main flows of data around MSA systems

Source: The authors

The ecosystem

The marketing and sales automation ecosystem has evolved considerably since it was documented by Stone (2014). Systems suppliers now play a much more central role in the ecosystem, integrating data flows and activities. The ecosystem can be considered – from the point of view of each company – as having two parts, the internal ecosystem and the external ecosystem, as in the following. The internal ecosystem, in larger companies, tends to merge the capabilities of different departments or units, some of which used to work separately.

The boundary between internal and external ecosystems is constantly shifting, as companies decide on the relative merits and costs of outsourcing to companies which have assets, data or capabilities that a client company needs, and of insourcing, to keep capabilities away from competitors

The main members of the internal marketing and sales automation ecosystem are shown in Table 30.1.

The main external marketing and sales ecosystem automation members are listed in Table 30.2.

An important component of MSA is the multichannel marketing hub. This may be within a more general MSA system or be a "best of breed" separate system which interfaces with all the other systems required. The hub enables collation of all data about individual customers into a single identity, segmentation and targeting, campaign timing, response management for all channels used, attribution of results to channels, predictive analytics (including using AI), personalization and consent/privacy management.

Another important component of MSA for some suppliers is digital commerce advertising management. This automates processes for advertising on e-commerce sites, marketplaces (Amazon is the leader) and platforms such as Google Shopping, Facebook/Instagram and others. It includes bid optimization, channel attribution and reporting. Some systems allow campaigns to be managed across other channels, for example, paid search, paid social and display advertising.

The adoption of MSA systems

This varies by a whole range of factors, such as company type and size, maturity, range of products/services, competitive structure of industry, size and complexity of customer base, channels used, culture, budget available and systems skills/understanding. Interestingly, the more complex the company, the harder it is to achieve full marketing automation, but generally the greater the benefit. The main enablers are skills, technological competence, resources, top management support, (big) data strategies and whether interlocking business processes are being automated or are already automated. Skills shortages have been shown to be an important barrier to implementation of marketing and sales automation, but systems skills become less of a problem with MSA based on cloud computing. However, as we showed in our work on AI, it is clear that human failures in decision-making are still an issue.

As new approaches emerge, the companies supplying them are as likely to be acquired as to progress as independent companies. As we move away from an on-premise software model (Stone *et al.* 2020), mergers and acquisitions become less disruptive, as the acquirer takes over the company without disturbing existing relationships and then integrates the functionality of the acquired software with that of its existing software. This may be technically complex but does not require reinstallation by the client. This facilitates adoption by clients.

Impact of use of marketing automation

MSA requires not only smart systems and good data. In a large company, with many markets, products and channels, it requires changes to conventional modes of marketing. In particular, it

Table 30.1 Internal marketing and sales automation ecosystem members

Internal ecosystem members	Role
Internal clients (e.g. brand, product and sector managers, programme managers, marketing communications specialists, pricing managers)	Responsible for delivering the client company's profit through marketing and sales
Direct and digital marketing specialists	Manage digital marketing and selling on behalf of the client – here there has been a big increase in their importance because of the complexity of digital marketing and selling and the need to specialise in different aspects of it
Account-based marketers	Manage individual clients or groups of clients, working closely with sales management and salespeople
Sales management and field salespeople	Manage the details of the sales cycle with clients
Systems, database and business intelligence professionals	Play an important role in supporting marketing by managing marketing, sales and service information and liaising with external suppliers (Stone and Woodcock 2014)
Insight managers	Develop objectives, strategies and tactics to help their company understand their customers, partners, distributors and competitors better, including identifying the need for particular analyses (digital and offline), and then carry them out and present conclusions for action
Contact centres	Covering web, email and telephone-based interactions
Customer service staff	Manage customers after the sales
Distribution channel management	Manage and implement choice of distribution channel
Human resources professionals	Ensure that the client has the skills required by all the previous

Source: The authors

requires a move to a team approach, where conventional divisions within and between different marketing and sales specialisms disappear. It generally requires a commitment to a culture and to decision-making processes that are characterized by collaboration, quantification of every step – from market targeting and goal setting to measurement of results, agility, data and insight orientation and curiosity about what works (Netflix references to way of working) and how to establish it through testing, which can be on content, targeting, timing, creative, devices, segments, lifecycle management or any of the other aspects of the marketing and sales mix. Testing of targeting was traditionally focused on demographics, psychographics, firmographics and basic propensity models (recency, frequency, amount bought) but today focuses much more on contextual issues such as view time, habits, last action, purchase intent, geo-location, device and external factors (i.e. weather), using the company's own real-time data on customers,

Because of the complexity of MSA, success generally requires a move to a culture in which the value of visualization is to the fore, from process visualizations to identify optimum workflows to understanding of customers and market segments. It also requires a commitment to a

Table 30.2 External marketing and sales automation ecosystem members

External ecosystem members	Role
Marketing and sales automation systems suppliers	Provide systems to automate most aspects of marketing and sales.
Marketing agencies	Help clients develop and implement marketing and communications strategies and targeted campaigns – these are increasingly digital, that is, web-based, and a whole new generation of small agencies has arisen to serve the needs of particular customers or to provide specialized services.
Market research companies.	Help clients understand their customers and prospects.
Telecommunications network companies	Help client companies to be in touch with their customers anywhere, any time.
Telecommunications services suppliers, such as contact centres and associated software suppliers	Help companies establish and maintain contact with customers and meet their customer service needs.
Database management companies	Manage client companies' customer data (in whole or in part).
Data brokers	Provide data to enhance these databases, for example, individual and household/company characteristics sourced from lifestyle surveys, other companies' customer files, the electoral roll, and credit referencing.
Database software suppliers	Help companies hold and access data (for processing, analysis and use at point of contact with customers) and, in some cases, visualize the outcomes of analysis so decisions can be made better and faster.
Analysis software suppliers	Enable analytics to be undertaken.
Analytics consultants	Specializing in advanced analytical methods.
Application providers that are specialists in their sector for example, mobile banking	Help clients manage the needs of particular types of customers.
Web software providers (browser, search engine, social media etc).	Provide online ways of finding and managing customers and, in some cases, provide the analytics to help clients understand effectiveness.
Affiliates	"Grab" customers from the web and "sell" them to client companies or their agencies.
Marketing/management consultants	Help companies strategize and manage their developments in this area.
Training organizations	Help all the previous maintain and develop the skills they need.

Source: The authors

more methodical approach to the digital generation, storage and use of communications content and messaging.

The impact on management is summarised in Table 30.3.

The future

The main future developments in MSA are likely to be:

- Continued growth of giant platform providers, with the giants buying best technology and often buying from each other, (e.g. Salesforce.com, Amazon, Adobe), making life more difficult for smaller ones and conventional advertising agencies;
- Integration of consultancy, systems and agency (e.g. Accenture acquisition of Yesler);
- Emergence/deepening of marketing and selling as a service – costs and benefits;
- Total integration of customer insight with marketing and sales action.

General theories of management relating to insight

It is important to place the debate about the role of marketing research in this rapidly changing world in its theoretical context. Unsurprisingly, much of the academic writing in this area today relates to the use of big data and how it improves firm performance,

For example, Mikalef *et al.* (2020), using Norwegian data, focus on the use of big data in creating competitive advantage, drawing on the resource-based, dynamic capabilities view. This view focuses on the idea that competitive advantage comes from resources that may be special to the firm, hard to assemble and imitate, possibly intangible and may result from partnerships and other relationships as much as from resources that the firm owns or controls (Barney 1991). Mikalef *et al.* (2020) conclude that appropriately managed, big data can generate insight that strengthens firm's dynamic capabilities, which include a firm's capacity to sense, shape and seize opportunities, innovate, develop new products, manage threats and reconfigure or transform its intangible and tangible assets and resources and develop new business models to serve the evolving needs of customers using its knowledge, skills and resources that relate to market needs (Pisano and Teece 2007; Teece 2019). A particularly important dynamic capability is sensing, which includes identification and assessment of customer needs.

Dynamic capabilities arise in part from learning, and some of them are resident primarily with the top management team, The way that enterprises build capabilities that are hard to imitate, grow and create competitive advantage is the key to how they rise above the crowd of other firms and, indeed, to how nations prosper, too. These dynamic capabilities are built through investment in discovery, knowledge generation and learning. Closing gaps in marketing insight capabilities requires a deep understanding of customer needs, which comes mainly from interreacting with them in many market segments (Teece 2019). It seems clear that as big data from interactions with customers has allowed companies to develop a much finer picture of customer needs, this has threatened the role of market research as part of the sensing capability. This applies particularly in markets characterised by high uncertainty and volatility, caused for example by rapid technological progress and/or social change, where the firm's ability to create rather than just respond to markets becomes critical (Teece 2019).

A closely related area of research focuses on absorptive capacity, which can be defined as the capacity of an organisation to recognize the value of, assimilate, integrate and commercially apply new information, combining internal and external sources. Organizations with high

Table 30.3 Impact of MSA on different parts of the marketing and sales organisation

Who	Type of impact
General management	Vision, culture, structure, process, people
	Managing expectation, metrics
	Prioritization of development
Marketing management	Changes in decision-making processes
	Targeting, conversion and other performance metrics
	Workflow management – efficiency, quality
Marketing communications people	Content management, especially content personalization; message governance
	Availability of different testing approaches, for example, A/B testing and more sophisticated approaches such as econometric analysis of tests
	Targeting – product, content, dialogue
	Metrics
	Online community management (also for customer service)
	Relationship with agencies
	Exhibitions and roadshows
	Channel information
Marketing research and customer insight	Impact of AI/ML
	Customer knowledge management
	Forecasting
	Relationship with agencies
Sales management and salespeople	Availability of content (and whether pushed to them or self-service)
	Involvement in design and implementation of strategies
	Use of automated and contacting technology
	Incentives and rewards
	Customer management – over whole sales/ relationship cycle, including pricing, negotiation
	Online vs salesforce channel competition
	Relationship with field-marketing and similar agencies
Customer service	Quality of delivery
	Customer education
Customers	Change in nature of dialogue and experience – speed, efficiency, accuracy, customization of experience/journey and so on
	Increased ease of customization of products and services
	Facilitating product/service research
	Reference checking
	Privacy risks
Marketing communications agencies	Continued displacement of role by platform giants
	Possible acquisition by consultancy companies

Source: The authors

absorptive capacity proactively exploit technologies and market opportunities, independent of their current performance, by combining these sources, particularly in real time or close to real time (Božič and Dimovski 2019). This is a dynamic capability and involves the continuous acquisition, search and management of knowledge (Pavlou and El Sawy 2010).

The central characteristics of absorptive capacity, in situations of high market volatility and uncertainty, are agility, flexibility and resilience. For existing rather than new firms, these need to be combined with the ability to continue operations in a high-quality, efficient manner – the characteristic of ambidexterity, which is a dynamic capability (O'Reilly and Tushman 2008; Prange and Schlegelmilch, B. 2009). It is particularly required in hypercompetitive markets, defined as ones demonstrating extreme volatility and fast-paced competition, turbulence, demand fluctuation, easy market entry and intensified product life cycles (Kriz *et al.* 2014). Ambidexterity allows reconfiguration of capabilities for game-changing exploration while improving existing operations (O'Reilly and Tushman 2008).

More specific studies of analytics capability

Using one or other of the previous frameworks or ideas, many studies have focused on the role of insights and analytics. For example, Cao *et al.* (2019a) identify a link between the value, rarity and inimitability of information processing capability and competitive advantage, with decision-making effectiveness being an important mediating factor. Cao *et al.* (2019b) demonstrated the impact of marketing analytics capability, combined with that of data availability, on marketing decision-making and thence on sustained competitive advantage and the importance of managerial support on marketing decision-making (Cao *et al.* 2019b). Côrte-Real *et al.* (2017) identified that to use analytics to create and then exploit knowledge resources from business analytics, firms must sense, acquire, process, store and analyse the data and convert it into knowledge. Sharma *et al.* (2014), identify that insights arise from engagement between analysts and business managers, using data and analytic tools to produce new knowledge. Chen *et al.* (2012) identified how business intelligence and analytics applied to big data can improve intelligence about customer needs and opinions, leading to new business opportunities.

Erevelles *et al.* (2016) identify the importance of using consumer insight to enhance dynamic capabilities and identify that the impact of big data use on the marketing mix is game changing in some cases, a view echoed by Fan *et al.* (2015). Chen *et al.* (2015) showed that big data analytics leads to a greater dynamic information processing capability, allowing uncertainty reduction by creating insights and knowledge and enhancing strategic decision-making capability, and that competitors' use of marketing analytics is likely to stimulate increased use of analytics. However, that very capability may itself be unstable, as new approaches replace older ones (Eisenhardt and Martin 2000). Further the marketing advantages that firms seek to create through better use of insight might themselves be temporary, a portfolio of temporary advantages (Chen *et al.* 2010). Knowledge management – defined as the process of capturing, distributing, and effectively using knowledge (Davenport 1994) – is one of the most important aspects of the use of marketing insight. Ferraris *et al.* (2019) demonstrate the importance of knowledge management orientation in the exploitation of big data analytics for competitive advantage. A closely related area is that of business intelligence (Stone and Woodcock 2014), where a critical discussion relates to the extent of centralization as compared with self-service.

Marketing research is to some extent bound to have problems coping with a highly complex reality – indeed, it could be argued that one of the roles of marketing research is to try to simplify reality and translate it into actionable insights. The advent of big data combined with the digital marketing techniques which give rise to much of the data allows companies to implement quite complex and variegated marketing strategies. Complexity theory suggests that reality is a complex system, made up of many parts with countless interactions between them, which in turn change the nature of the system. For example, customers are an integral part of the customer journey system, and their involvement in managing the customer journey changes its nature (Varnali 2018). Acknowledging this leads to the thought that marketing research, capturing data in a specific period, is at a disadvantage unless its analytical contents from the data are fed to key personnel to act upon speedily compared with properly sourced and computer-analysed big data arising from current transactions that supply upfront regular updates.

Control of marketing activities is needed at all levels in organisations, from senior management to frontline staff dealing with customers in face-to-face interactions. Similarly, analyses from marketing research need to be directed to relevant key personnel with responsibilities for managing strategic programmes and resources. The corporate mission of "how and what should be accomplished to achieve long and short term goals" should lead to questions such as "how are we doing now?", in particular examining "where are we being reactive or proactive in our markets?", "what elements of our strategic plans have worked?" and "where should we be taking corrective actions and new steps now?"

Management information systems and business intelligence

Managers need information to:

- Control annual, medium and long-range planning functions to assess whether the planned results have been achieved;
- Control costs to determine the impact of marketing expenditures;
- Control profitability of products, sales territories, order sizes, distribution channels and market segments;
- Assess whether the organisation in its strategy is making the best use of its human, financial and technological assets to achieve best opportunities with reference to the marketplace and competition (Wright and Crimp 2000) Typically, marketing analysis covers the classic six items of the PESTLE analysis – political, economic, socio-demographic technological, legal and environmental – and more detailed market forces – customers, competitors, intermediaries, suppliers, partners and the relevant business ecosystems. Marketing research has a key role to play in all of these, although, as we identified in Chapter 1, today secondary data and data directly from customers and other companies plays a more important role than it used to.

Further, the general openness of organisations and customers created by the Internet and by social media means that information about a wide range of factors – not just market needs and demands but, for example, costs, supply chain issues and quality problems – is available as secondary data. This is not bad news for marketing research, as it means that many gaps in the information organisations need to take decisions which cannot be filled by marketing research can now be filled by other means, with the marketing research or insight function now playing a key role in integrating a much wider data set. However, this does mean the professional marketing researchers must cultivate a strong awareness of all the secondary sources available, whether the research is being carried out to support the most aggregated level of planning, such as recalibrating organisational mission and strategy, or the most detailed level, to support marketing mix decisions on products, pricing, channels and marketing communication or individual marketing campaigns. The role of marketing research in building and developing a computerised marketing information or business intelligence system, covering information gathering, storage, update and retrieval in is therefore critical (Stone and Woodcock 2013, 2014).

Will market research analysts be replaced by robots?

For most of its history, marketing research was done by humans, but this is now being questioned, partly due to the issue of bias. Will robotic interviewers really catch on? They might! For this, we must thank Furhat Robotics, creators of Tengai. This AI and social robotics company has spent the past four years building a human-like computer interface that can replicate speech and subtle facial expressions. The idea is that a human-like robot is much less frightening than a machine-like one. The Swedish recruitment firm TNG is trialing Tenga for early interviews, while many other companies, including those involved in marketing research, already use some form of AI in their selection process. Avatars are becoming common as interfaces between companies and human subjects, so perhaps this is just the beginning.

Wearables in marketing research of the future

Though nobody knows exactly what new applications of wearables and neurotech are going to be hits, people have plenty of ideas (Perry 2019). Here are some of possibilities.

Mind-reading smart glasses

Julia Brown, CEO of MindX, said that her company plans to produce glasses that let you "access information with a single thought." The company is using technology licensed from the Johns Hopkins Applied Physics lab to pick up signals from eye movement and from brain waves to know where you are looking and what you are thinking when you look there. Brown is excited about the possibilities of visual search, for example. The company is still in the development stage and at the time of writing was looking to hire a brain computer interface software engineer who is a "full stack neuro nerd" and a neural data scientist who is "expert in extracting meaning from bio signals," along with more traditional software engineers.

Sweat-sensing glasses that can measure consumer emotions

Google Glass may have gone down in consumer electronics history as a fail, but developers have not given up. Joseph Wang, director of the Center for Wearable Sensors at the University of California, San Diego, says that for health-centric wearables, it is important to monitor chemical changes in the body, not just activity levels and vital signs. His ideas include chemical-sensing smart glasses, with disposable nose-piece pads that collect and analyse sweat. Wang also pointed to the possibilities of slightly invasive – but painless – wearables, like flexible stickers full of microneedle sensor arrays that can track chemical changes just under the skin.

A gadget that lets you listen to your body

Startup Data Garden started out building devices that let people listen to their plants. The company's newest project, in beta testing at the time of writing, involves an algorithm that translates someone's heartbeat, as tracked by the user's wearable of choice, into music. To create the musical track, each heartbeat triggers the choice of a note, while other algorithms choose the appropriate instruments. This is not just a party trick, said Jon Shapiro, Data Garden chief product officer. For example, it could provide useful information to people using apps that guide meditation or pace running without requiring them to look at a screen. In the future, Shapiro said, the software will be able to scrape a user's Spotify history to personalize the timbre of the music.

Messages from your future self

Walter Greenleaf, a behavioural neuroscientist at Stanford, has been working on software that uses information from wearables and other sources about how you are treating your body to age an image of your future self. In testing on Stanford students, he discovered that seeing an image of themselves age as few as five years can make them highly motivated to take better care of themselves in the present.

Consumer neuroscience research

This applies tools and theories from neuroscience to improve understanding of decision-making and related processes. Is it really possible to upload a mind to a computer? The short answer is, yes, theoretically. The 2045 Initiative is a non-profit organization that develops a network and community of researchers in the field of life extension, focusing on combining brain emulation and robotics to create forms of cyborgs. It was founded by Russian entrepreneur Dmitry Itskov in February 2011 with the participation of Russian specialists in the field of neural interfaces, robotics, artificial organs and systems. The main goal of the 2045 Initiative, as stated on its website, is "to create technologies enabling the transfer of an individual's personality to a more advanced non-biological carrier, and extending life, including to the point of immortality."

How would whole brain emulation (WBE) work? It requires scanning a brain, interpreting the brain data and building a software model and running the model so that it will behave in the same way as the original brain. This is closely tied to the concepts of "mind uploading" and "brain downloading."

Are brain implants the future of thinking? Beyond typing, no one is too specific. Brain commands to smart speakers? Brain-to-brain communication? Enhanced memory? The most obvious application may be brain-controlled typing. Some imagine a scenario where people who have grown up texting and typing – and are wholly dependent on their fingers for that – lose functionality as they age. Frustrated that they cannot maintain their speed, they may seek other ways to preserve their technological capability. Eventually, a tipping point will occur as people see brain-computer interfaces working better than the human body. If the technology becomes safe, it will be easy to use, and it gives consumers better technology control, and there will be people who will want to pay for that.

However, while brain-computer interfaces may be portrayed as being able to "mind read" and "decode thoughts" – stoking fears that they will unearth innermost secrets – they are recording from very small areas of the brain, mostly related to movement, and require the user's mental effort to make them work. So, some ethical issues concerning privacy may not apply.

While the idea of a network of brains directly communicating via brain-to-brain interfaces may sound like science fiction to some, it is not. They allow technology-mediated direct communication between two brains without involving the peripheral nervous system. They consist of two components: a brain-computer interface that detects neural signals from one brain and translates them into computer commands, and a computer-brain interface that delivers computer commands to another brain. One research approach can encompass more than three individuals and thus provides the basis for direct brain-to-brain communication involving networks.

The authors state (Jiang *et al.* 2019, p. 1): "Our results raise the possibility of future brain-to-brain interfaces that enable cooperative problem solving by humans using a 'social network' of connected brains." When talking about connected brains, the authors allude to social networks and similarities between multi-person BCIs and social networks.

The Intelligence Capital project

The previous developments are exciting, but they may not be in common use for some time, Meanwhile, given the findings about the importance of insight, analytics and research, particularly in the context of organisational competitiveness and evolution, how does the actual situation compare with a theoretical reality of insight-driven organisations, from the perspective of marketing research?

Partly to answer this question, in 2019, the UK's Market Research Society issued a report called "The Responsive Business: Creating Growth and Value Through Intelligence Capital" (Kantar 2019). It was produced by the leading market research agency, Kantar. In 2020, it issued a similar report, produced by Savanta (2020), called "Capital 2020: A Practitioner's Guide – Building Competitive Advantage Through Research." Both reports focused on a central topic for market researchers, the building and deployment of an insight capability.

In this chapter, we analyse both reports in the context of the content of this book. The main aim of this chapter, therefore, is to compare the perceptions, attitudes and practices of leading marketing research clients in touch with the issues that are raised in this book rather than to focus on recommendations relating to how to achieve the nirvana of intelligence capital. In the background to this chapter is the counter-hypothesis, that businesses that disrupt markets and dominate other companies pursue a very different approach, in which big data is already at the heart of everything they do, and marketing research and its associated insight are an extremely valuable addition to understanding in depth the phenomena and markets which these disruptive companies create.

The difference between these two perspectives is made clear in the 2019 report (Kantar 2019, p. 10), which gives the example of Nokia's failure to adapt to the changes in the mobile telephone market, despite having the patents and technology needed to make smartphones, comparing it with Apple's strategy of spotting the next big technology shift and shaping the company to match it. The alternative hypothesis interpretation is that Apple was partly responsible for creating the technology shift, working with several other leading high-tech companies. The 2019 report (Kantar 2019, p. 10) suggest that sometimes companies are lucky when the market realigns with their business model, quoting Lidl and Aldi as companies whose business models were "better fit with changing consumer attitudes to choice, not just because they were discounting at a time of financial stress." In fact, we would argue they were not discounting, merely providing good value for money merchandise across a deliberately tight range, allowing them to achieve massive economies of scale through Europe-wide buying. They made the market rather than responding to it.

Definitions

Both reports define intelligence capital as:

> A comprehensive knowledge asset coupled with the capability to use that asset to identify and activate growth opportunities.
>
> (Kantar 2019, p. 6)

It consists of:

- Structural intelligence, that is, what the business knows about its markets, performance, customers and wider business context. It includes trends and foresight; marketplace, environmental and regulatory monitoring; needs assessments, usage and attitude research; demand space mapping; cultural values, social trends; social media and behaviour monitoring; brand performance monitoring (perceptions, equity, sales); customer experience and behaviour monitoring; competitive intelligence; and intelligence supporting the identification of market opportunities;
- Activation intelligence, that is, the knowledge used to design market initiatives designed to capture opportunities for innovation and growth and to acquire new knowledge. It includes communications development and validation, innovation development and validation, media planning insights, retail strategy and activation development, marketing and sales effectiveness measurement, business model pilots, new market trials and intelligence used to optimise and validate actions to capture growth;
- Human intelligence, which connects structural and activation intelligence through assessing data and information, identifying new insights from it and applying them to markets to create value. It requires support from the senior team, the right mix of specialist multi-disciplinary skills, a reward and development system that attracts and retains the best-quality people, permission to raise questions and make business recommendations, measures that enable it to quantify its business impact, decision processes that embed the use of intelligence and leadership that models the application of intelligence.

It combines information, processes and people to "scan the wider environment, the marketplace, and the business' own performance to understand how each of these is changing, and to act on this understanding" (Kantar 2019, p. 6).

Its benefits are classic. It allows a business to improve brand value, speed to market and efficiency and generate revenue streams. Uniting them all is said to be an intelligence culture, involving commitment to knowledge, sharing learning, curiosity and embedding intelligence in decision-making.

The 2019 report gives a clue as to its target market, because it refers to the problem of how to find growth in a world of slowing growth, with the remedy being to be responsive and:

- Ensure the business is pulled by existing and potential markets rather than pushed by the existing patterns and capabilities of the business;
- Learn faster than markets are changing;
- Translate learning into market-facing action, fast;
- Be alert to new and emerging external risks.

The 2019 report (Kantar 2019, p. 15) also draws on the results of the Kantar Insight 2020 project, involving interviews with over 350 business leaders and surveys of over 10,000 practitioners in 60 countries, showing the relationship between the following factors and over-performance:

- Capability to synthesise disparate data sources;
- Engagement/participation by the insight unit in strategic decisions at all levels;
- Encouraging testing, trial and error and experimentation.

What intelligence capital respondents say

The respondents to the research for both reports were leading users of marketing research. Let us see what they said. Readers of this chapter are of course encouraged to read the original reports, as what follows summarises the results at a high level.

- Between a fifth and a third are less involved than they should be;
- There is great weakness use of state-of-the-art analytical techniques, while use of insight to create foresight is not as strong as it should be;
- The performance-intention gap is a problem for many firms;
- Their companies provide weak information to investors on the value of their assets and brands;
- Finance does not respect the contribution of research as much as it should.

We would argue that many of the problems identified previously relate to treating insights as something which are in some sense separate from the operations of the business rather than being an integral part of how it operates and of how it transforms itself to maintain competitiveness, including via marketing and sales automation, and that capitalist intelligence, the alternative, is one in which intelligence arises naturally from how the business works as a competitive, capitalist entity and where the key capabilities of the firm not only include insight but also the ability of the firm to transform itself using insight and to use insight better, in an ambidextrous manner.

The 2020 report, produced by Savanta, reviewed Market Research Award winners and interviewed many senior MRS members on the client side (2020, p. 38). The report identifies the importance of activating intelligence, liberalizing access and making intelligence accessible and activating it. Once again, it conveys the image of intelligence being produced by one group and being accessed and activated by another rather than intelligence arising from the capitalist and competitive operation of the business. However, the difference in the 2020 report is that it emphasises the importance of involvement of a broad group of stakeholders, such that the dividing line between researchers and users fades.

The report identifies several specific weaknesses, many of which are related to the problem of separation of insight from business operations. For example, the report confirms weaknesses relating to

- The review of external literature (often in our experience read by practitioners rather than marketing researchers);
- Market reporting and dashboarding tools (making it harder for users to self-serve);
- Social listening;
- Sharing of insights with value chain partners (a contrast with the practice of many platform businesses, some of whom share at a cost; that is, they sell insight, but at least they share it);
- Conflict between departments concerning the outcomes of projects;
- Lack of perceived importance of research findings;
- Weak feeding of research into strategic decisions;
- Lack of digestible and engaging formats;
- Failure to identify benefit to the organisation;
- Lack of an evidence culture.

However, some excellent practice which counters some of these weaknesses is cited, for example, the development of an insight platform which is used as an integral part of decision-making.

Conclusions

Our conclusion from the surveys is that marketing research as a discipline would benefit greatly from an effort to take into account not only the theories reviewed in this chapter but also the contents of all the chapters in this book. As we read material such as those in the Intelligence Capital survey, we cannot but suggest that in many companies, marketing research has been pushed into a corner where it focuses on operational intelligence, neglecting the transformational intelligence required to achieve the ambidexterity required for survival and prosperity in a turbulent age and the role of insight as integrated with marketing and sales action, often automated, rather than as a discrete element. Practitioner readers who see this as applying to their company should consider suggesting a review of the role of marketing research in strategic insight generation and in strategy itself.

References

Barney, J., 1991. Firm resources and sustained competitive advantage. *Journal of Management*, 17(1), 99–120. DOI: 10.1177/014920639101700108.

Božič, K. and Dimovski, V., 2019. Business intelligence and analytics for value creation: The role of absorptive capacity. *International Journal of Information Management*, 46, 93–103. https://doi.org/10.1016/j.ijinfomgt.2018.11.020.

Cao, G., Duan, Y. and Cadden, T., 2019a. The link between information processing capability and competitive advantage mediated through decision-making effectiveness. *International Journal of Information Management*, 44, 121–131. https://doi.org/10.1016/j.ijinfomgt.2018.10.003.

Cao, G., Duan, Y. and El Banna, A., 2019b. A dynamic capability view of marketing analytics: Evidence from UK firms. *Industrial Marketing Management*, 76, 72–83. https://doi.org/10.1016/j.indmarman.2018.08.002.

Chen, D., Preston, D. and Swink, M., 2015. How the use of big data analytics affects value creation in supply chain management. *Journal of Management Information Systems*, 32(4), 4–39. DOI: 10.1080/07421222.2015.1138364.

Chen, E., Katila, R., McDonald, R. and Eisenhardt, K., 2010. Life in the fast lane: Origins of competitive interaction in new vs. established markets. *Strategic Management Journal*, 31, 1527–1547. DOI: 10.1002/smj.894.

Chen, H., Chiang, R. and Storey, V., 2012. Business intelligence and analytics: From big data to big impact. *MIS Quarterly*, 36(4), 1165–1188. DOI: 10.2307/41703503.

Côrte-Real, N., Oliveira, T. and Ruivo, P., 2017. Assessing business value of big data analytics in European firms. *Journal of Business Research*, 70, 379–390. DOI: 10.1016/j.jbusres.2016.08.011.

Davenport, T., 1994. Saving IT's soul: Human centered information management. *Harvard Business Review*, 72(2), 119–131.

Eisenhardt, K. and Martin, J., 2000. Dynamic capabilities: What are they?" *Strategic Management Journal*, 21, 1105–1121. DOI: 10.1002/1097-0266(200010/11)21:10/11,1105:aidsmj133.3.0.co;2-e.

Erevelles, N., Fukawa, N. and Swayne, L., 2016. Big data consumer analytics and the transformation of marketing. *Journal of Business Research*, 69(2) 897–904. DOI: 10.1016/j.jbusres.2015.07.001.

Fan, S., Lau, R. and Zhao, J., 2015. Demystifying big data analytics for business intelligence through the lens of marketing mix. *Big Data Research*, 2(1), 28–32. https://doi.org/10.1016/j.bdr.2015.02.006.

Ferraris, A., Mazzoleni, A., Devalle, A. and Couturier, J., 2019. Big data analytics capabilities and knowledge management: Impact on firm performance. *Management Decision*, 57(8), 1923–1936. https://doi.org/10.1108/MD-07-2018-0825.

Jiang, L., Stocco, A., Losey, D.M., Abernethy, J.A., Prat, C.S. and Rao, R.P.N., 2019. BrainNet: A multiperson brain-to-brain interface for direct collaboration between brains. *Scientific Reports*, 9, 6115. DOI: 10.1038/s41598-019-41895-7.

Kantar, 2019. *The Responsive Business: Creating Growth and Value Through Intelligence Capital*. London: Kantar [online]. Available from: https://uk.kantar.com/business/brands/2019/responsive-businesses-create-growth-and-value-through-intelligence-capital/ [Accessed 9 June 2020].

Kriz, A., Voola, R. and Yuksel, U., 2014. The dynamic capability of ambidexterity in hypercompetition: Qualitative insights. *Journal of Strategic Marketing*, 22(4), 287–299. https://doi.org/10.1080/0965254X.2013.876075.

Mikalef, P., Krogstie, J., Pappas, I.O. and Pavlou, P., 2020. Exploring the relationship between big data analytics capability and competitive performance: The mediating roles of dynamic and operational capabilities". *Information & Management*, 57(2), 103169. https://doi.org/10.1016/j.im.2019.05.004.

O'Reilly, C. and Tushman, M., 2008. Ambidexterity as a dynamic capability: Resolving the innovator's dilemma. *Research in Organizational Behavior*, 28, 185–206. DOI: 10.1016/j.riob.2008.06.002.

Pavlou, P. and El Sawy, O., 2010. The "Third hand": IT-Enabled competitive advantage in turbulence through improvisational capabilities. *Information Systems Research*, 21(3), 443–471. https://doi.org/10.1287/isre.1100.0280.

Perry, T., 2019. A peek into the future of wearables. *IEEE Spectrum*, 14 March [online]. Available from: https://spectrum.ieee.org/view-from-the-valley/consumer-electronics/gadgets/a-peek-into-the-future-of-wearables.

Pisano, G. and Teece, D.J., 2007. How to capture value from innovation: Shaping intellectual property and industry architecture. *California Management Review*, 50(1), 278–296. https://doi.org/10.2307%2F41166428.

Prange, C. and Schlegelmilch, B., 2009. The role of ambidexterity in marketing strategy implementation: Resolving the exploration-exploitation dilemma. *Business Research*, 2(2), 215–240. https://doi.org/10.1007/BF03342712.

Robinson, P.J., Faris, C.W. and Wind, Y., 1967. *Industrial Buying and Creative Marketing*. New York: Allyn & Bacon and the Marketing Science Institute.

Savanta, 2020. *Intelligence Capital 2020: A Practitioners Guide*. London: Savanta ComRes [online]. Available from: www.mrs.org.uk/resources/intelligence-capital-2020?MKTG=IC2020 [Accessed 9 June 2020].

Sharma, R., Mithas, S. and Kankanhalli, A., 2014. Transforming decision-making processes: A research agenda for understanding the impact of business analytics on organisations. *European Journal of Information Systems*, 23(4), 433–441. https://doi.org/10.1057/ejis.2014.17.

Stone, M., 2009. Staying customer-focused and trusted: Web 2.0 and Customer 2.0 in financial services. *Journal of Database Marketing & Customer Strategy Management*, 16(2), 101–131.

Stone, M., 2014. The new (and ever-evolving) direct and digital marketing ecosystem. *Journal of Direct, Data and Digital Marketing Practice*, 16(2), 71–74.

Stone, M., Kosack, E. and Aravopoulou, E., 2020. Relevance of academic research in information technology and information management. *The Bottom Line*. https://doi.org/10.1108/BL-05-2020-0034.

Stone, M. and Woodcock, N., 2013. Social intelligence in customer engagement. *Journal of Strategic Marketing*, 21(5), 394–401. https://doi.org/10.1080/0965254X.2013.801613.

Stone, M. and Woodcock, N., 2014. Interactive, direct & digital marketing – a future that depends on better use of business intelligence. *Journal of Research in Interactive Marketing*, 8(1) 4–17. DOI: 10.1108/JRIM-07-2013-0046.

Teece, D., 2019. A capability theory of the firm: An economics and (strategic) management perspective. *New Zealand Economic Papers*, 53(1), 1–43. https://doi.org/10.1080/00779954.2017.1371208.

Varnali, K., 2019. Understanding customer journey from the lenses of complexity theory. *The Service Industries Journal*, 39(11–12), 820–835. https://doi.org/10.1080/02642069.2018.1445725.

Wright, L. and Crimp, M., 2000. *The Marketing Research Process*. London: FT Prentice Hall.

INDEX

Note: Page numbers in *italics* indicate figures; page numbers in **bold** indicate tables.

598

Piccinini, Patricia 492
Pike Institute 504
pilot study *80*, 89
Pindrop 49
Pinterest 133
place-based research tools 548
platforms: case studies of 48–50; definition of 47; development and survival of 47–48; future issues for 51; rise of customer information 46–47; term 47
Play-Doh 448, 450
polymeasures 540, 542; biological methods **541–542**
Poo Wi-Fi campaign 492
population: appropriate number of participants 90–91; target, and sampling 89–90
positivism 74, 76
positron emission tomography (PET) 259, **543**; indirect measure of neural activity **267**
Post-its 448
power spectral density (PSD) 276
practitioner's view of customer insight (Laughlin): academic study 568; applications for commercial businesses 573; capability for future 574; customer analysis 571; customer data management 571; customer research 571–572; database marketing 572; delivering commercial returns 575; future of customer insight leaders 576–577; growing understanding of meaning of 569–570; jobs before focus on 568–569; jobs creating and leading insight teams 569–576; model of holistic customer insight *570*; satisfying customers and employees 574–575; state of business today 576; task for leaders 573
practitioner's view of customer insight (Mooney): career and experiences 553–556; data capabilities 562; education 553; enterprise decisioning process 558, 560; enterprise decisioning model 558, *559*; future 563–567; integrated capability 560–562; learnings from career 557–563; managing interactions 562–563; techniques and technology 563; types of decision-making 557–558
price: literature review of 462–463; product quality and 462–463
primary data: secondary or 186–187; term 186
privacy: control and 140–141; Covid-19 lockdowns 443; customers and 184; data management 183; information disclosure and 140; protecting customers 141–142; terms and conditions 141
product: trade-off between quality and price 459–460, 472–473; *see also* low-quality products; short lifecycle products
product as a service 56
product design: aesthetics 461; functionality 461–462; high fashionability 462; literature review 461–462; symbolism 462

product development process: marketing research for 435–436; role of design in 436–437, **438**
produmers, consumers who produce 494
professional briefing process 238
profiling, data protection 183
project delivery 14
project managers 561
proposal process, briefing and 238
proximity sensors 549
public services and policy: design expansion into 447–450; future of marketing research 450–451; imperial overstretch and new targets 448; situated users and location of value 448–450
published research 235–236
pupillometrics **542**
purchase intention (PI) 297; on brand interest **299**; literature review 463; mixture amount model *291*; prediction profiler 298, **299**, *300*, *301*; significance tests *297*; *see also* advertising

QSR NVivo software 83
qualitania 523
qualitative comparative analysis (QCA), fuzzy set (fsQCA) 464–466
qualitative journals 212
qualitative methods *79*; combining quantitative and **78–79**; focus groups *81*, 86; in-depth interviews *81*, 85–86; planning management and data interpretation 82–84; stages of coding process **82**
Qualtrics 529
quantitative methods *79*; combining qualitative and **78–79**; pilot study 88–89

Raeworth, Kate 487
RBS 552
Reagan, Ronald 234, 447
real-time experience tracking (RET) 242, 523
Reddit 133
Red Nose Day 139
reliability 119; case study 122; qualitative research 84, **85**; test for determining case study 125, **127–128**, 129
report developers 561
research database, building 193
research design: application of in-depth interviews and focus groups **81**; benefits and limitations of content analysis **88**; criteria of trustworthiness **85**; domain constructs 87; exploratory fieldwork (phase one) *80*, 81–86; focus groups 86; generation of measurement items 87; instrument and scale development (phase two) *80*, 86–88; interviews 85–86; main survey (third phase) *80*, 89–91; measurement scale development 79, *80*; purifying measurement scales 87–88; qualitative stage 82–84; quantitative assessment (pilot study) *80*, 88–89;

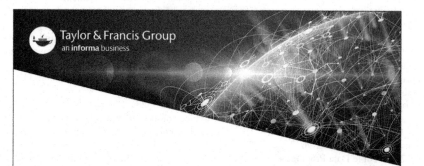